Contents

PERSONNEL MANAGEMENT

A Comprehensive Guide to Theory and Practice in Britain

Edited by

KEITH SISSON

First published as Personnel Management in Britain 1989
Second edition 1994
Reprinted 1995 (twice), 1996

Blackwell Publishers Ltd
108 Cowley Road
Oxford OX4 1JF, UK

Blackwell Publishers Inc.
238 Main Street
Cambridge, Massachusetts 02142, USA

British Library Cataloguing in Publication Data
A CIP catalogue record for this book is available from the British Library

Library of Congress Cataloging in Publication Data
Library of Congress data has been applied for.

ISBN   0–631–18821–5 (pbk)

Typeset in 11 on 13pt Plantin
by Best-set Typesetter Ltd., Hong Kong
Printed and bound in Great Britain by T. J. Press Ltd, Padstow, Cornwall

This book is printed on acid-free paper

List of Figures and Tables

Figures

Tables

viii *List of Figures and Tables*

Contributors

Stephen Bach, Lecturer in Industrial Relations, School of Industrial & Business Studies, University of Warwick

Paul Blyton, Senior Lecturer in Industrial Relations, Cardiff Business School, University of Wales

William Brown, Professor of Industrial Relations, University of Cambridge

David A. Buchanan, Professor of Human Resource Management, Loughborough University Business School, Loughborough University

Jon Clark, Professor of Industrial Relations, Department of Sociology and Social Policy, University of Southampton

Linda Dickens, Professor of Industrial Relations, School of Industrial & Business Studies, University of Warwick

Paul Edwards, Professor of Industrial Relations and Deputy Director, Industrial Relations Research Unit, University of Warwick

Arthur Francis, Professor of Business Policy, Glasgow Business School, University of Glasgow

John F. Geary, Lecturer in Industrial Relations, Graduate School of Business, University College, Dublin

Ewart Keep, Senior Research Fellow, Industrial Relations Research Unit, University of Warwick

Ian Kessler, Research Fellow, Templeton College, Oxford

Karen Legge, Professor of Organisation Behaviour, Department of Behaviour in Organisation, University of Lancaster

Mick Marchington, Senior Lecturer in Industrial Relations, Manchester School of Management, UMIST

Liz Price, Senior Lecturer in Human Resource Management, Department of Hotel and Catering, Oxford Brookes University

Robert Price, Personnel Director, Agriculture and Food Research Council

Helen Rainbird, Reader in Social Sciences, Nene College, Northampton

Gerry Randell, Professor of Organisational Behaviour, Management Centre, University of Bradford

Keith Sisson, Professor of Industrial Relations and Director, Industrial Relations Research Unit, University of Warwick

John Storey, Senior Lecturer, Human Resource Management, Loughborough University Business School, Loughborough University

Stuart Timperley, Professor of Management Development, London Business School

Barbara Townley, Associate Professor, Department of Organizational Analysis, Faculty of Business, University of Alberta

Janet Walsh, Lecturer in Industrial Relations, School of Business and Economic Studies, University of Leeds

Thom Watson, Senior Lecturer in Organisational Behaviour, School of Industrial & Business Studies, University of Warwick

David Winchester, Senior Lecturer in Industrial Relations, School of Industrial & Business Studies, University of Warwick

Foreword

The 'Industrial Relations in Context' series of books was launched by George Bain in 1983 to complement the established research monographs, 'Warwick Studies in Industrial Relations'. The volumes in the series provide comprehensive, authoritative and up-to-date analyses of current issues and trends in the entire field of employment relations. They are informed by empirical research and scholarship, and by an awareness of recent trends and developments and the wider social, economic, and political contexts.

The series is intended for students doing diploma, undergraduate or postgraduate courses in human resource management and industrial relations at colleges and universities, as well as those studying industrial sociology, labour economics, labour law and business studies. It is also addressed to those in adult education, to those seeking membership of professional bodies like the Institute of Personnel Management, to practitioners in both unions and management, and to the general reader who wants to find out more about employment relations today.

Each volume is composed of original essays that bring together theoretical and empirical knowledge and understanding. Each chapter is stamped with the views of the authors, who are experts in their fields. Each emphasizes analysis and explanation as well as description. Each focuses on trends over recent decades and says something about likely future developments. And in each volume the text is welded into a coherent whole by editors who combine a distinguished research record with a proven ability to communicate to a wider audience.

The series began with *Industrial Relations in Britain*, edited by George Bain. Subsequent volumes were *Labour Law in Britain*, edited by Roy Lewis, *Employment in Britain*, edited by Duncan

Gallie, and *Personnel Management in Britain*, edited by Keith Sisson. More recently, the growing importance of the European context for British industrial relations is reflected in the seventeen-country text, *Industrial Relations in the New Europe*, edited by Anthony Ferner and Richard Hyman. A companion volume, *New Frontiers of European Industrial Relations*, is in the final stages of preparation as is a second edition of *Industrial Relations in Britain* under the editorship of Paul Edwards.

The present volume, *Personnel Management*, edited by Keith Sisson, is a completely revised version of the highly successful *Personnel Management in Britain*, which has sold some 10,000 copies since it was published in 1989. Not only has the coverage of the topics which appeared in *Personnel Management in Britain* been revised and updated, but half a dozen new topics have also been added in response to suggestions from readers. True to the tradition of the series, each has been written by an acknowledged expert in the field. In the foreword to the 1989 edition, George Bain suggested that the result was the most up-to-date, comprehensive and authoritative account of personnel management in Britain. The present volume has an even stronger claim to this accolade.

Paul Edwards
Anthony Ferner
Richard Hyman

Preface

Like its predecessor, *Personnel Management in Britain*, this volume is very much in the industrial relations tradition. Its treatment of the subject is, therefore, substantially different from the standard personnel management texts in two major respects. First, whereas most of these regard personnel management as being more or less synonymous with the techniques and activities associated with, if not necessarily performed by, specialist personnel managers, this collection is primarily concerned with personnel management as a system of employment regulation: the ways in which people in work organizations are selected, appraised, trained, paid, disciplined, and so on. Second, and perhaps even more importantly, although it raises and throws considerable light on a great many policy issues – in particular, the significance for personnel management of the wider economic, political and social context – the book is not directly prescriptive as most textbooks in the area tend to be: the objective is to understand the ways in which people in work organizations in Britain are actually selected, appraised, trained, paid, and disciplined, rather than offering seemingly 'universal' solutions to the problem of managing the employment relationship. The aim, as well as contributing to the growing debate about the significance of the management of human resources, is to meet the demands of teachers and students, at every level, for the breadth and depth of description, explanation and analysis they have come to expect in other areas of industrial relations.

The case for such an approach has been considerably strengthened in recent years. One reason is the growing recognition of the importance of line managers in personnel management. Personnel specialists, as the Workplace Industrial Relations Surveys have confirmed, are very much the exception rather than the rule in most workplaces. Also, even where personnel specialists are present, line managers are becoming more involved in the taking of initiatives as well as in the day-to-day activities of personnel management.

A second reason involves a major theme running through many of the chapters which follow, namely the gap between the rhetoric and reality of personnel management in Britain. Such a gap, it can be argued, has always existed and always will. It has taken on a particular significance in recent years, however. There is growing evidence to suggest that the rhetoric is being used in a manipulative way – in an attempt to persuade people that the situation is very different to what it is in reality. In these circumstances, an approach which deals in evidence is especially valuable.

A third reason, which is closely related, is to do with policy. Although not overtly prescriptive, the approach adopted here can make a significant contribution to improving the quality of analysis and data available to policy-makers. A major problem with the prescriptive tradition that has dominated the study of personnel management is that it restricts itself to the immediate workplace; it sees policy issues largely in terms of the choices made by managers, and, if managers do not make the 'right' choices, there is little that can be done apart from exhortation. The analytical approach, in seeing the workplace within the wider context, emphasizes that managers' choices are not made in a vacuum, and that they reflect the impact of such structural features as the status of the personnel function, the arrangements for corporate governance and government policy. Changes in these areas may be the key to improving the quality of human resources. Policy-makers may find the implications extremely uncomfortable and may prefer, as suggested above, to take refuge in rhetoric rather than confront the issues. This does not make the approach any less valid, however. On the contrary, it makes it even more important that social scientists continue to tell things how they see them.

In terms of major themes, the outline of the present volume is very similar to that of *Personnel Management in Britain*. The introduction in Part I offers an overview of trends and developments in the theory and practice of personnel management, and is as much a conclusion as an introduction. The chapters in Part II are concerned with the design of organizations and deal with issues which are too often neglected in personnel management textbooks, largely because they are usually outside the control of personnel managers. The chapters in the other four parts deal with themes which, although dealt with differently from the standard texts, will be readily recognizable: planning and resourcing, employee development, the wage–work bargain, and participation and involvement.

In each case the treatment of the topics that appeared in *Personnel Management in Britain* has been thoroughly revised. In some cases, such as training, it has been expanded; in others there is a different author, reflecting retirement or the need to have a more wide-ranging contribution. Every effort has also been made to meet the comments on and criticisms of the previous edition. Thus, extra chapters have been included on health and safety, equal opportunities, managing culture, performance pay, working time, and management–trade union relations.

As well as the authors, and their colleagues who commented on the chapters, many people helped to make this book possible. Special thanks are due to Norma Griffiths for undertaking the substantial amount of secretarial work associated with such a project; to Paul Stringer for doing the bulk of the copy-editing and preparing the final version of the manuscript for printing; and to Geraldine Beare for producing the index. Last, but certainly by no means least, I have to thank Jan for helping me to live through yet more anxious months as the book moved through its many stages.

Keith Sisson

PART I

Introduction

1

Personnel Management: Paradigms, Practice and Prospects

Keith Sisson

At first sight, a revolution seems to be taking place in personnel management in most developed economies. Not only are there major changes in practice which go far beyond the choice of this or that technique, there is also said to be a paradigm shift occurring in thinking about personnel management which shows a new theoretical sophistication. The new paradigm seems capable both of describing and explaining the changes in practice and of providing the rationale for elevating personnel management or, to use the increasingly preferred title, human resource management (HRM) to strategic importance in the running of organizations. Essentially, it sees management, faced with ever intensifying competition in an increasingly global economy, obliged to rethink the sources of competitive advantage and to make strategic choices about future directions. The developed economies, it is argued, cannot compete head-on solely in terms of cost with their competitors in Eastern Europe and the Far East, let alone the third world: they would have to lower wages and living standards to socially and politically unacceptable levels in what, in any event, would be a vain attempt. They must put the emphasis instead on the quality of goods and services. Quality goods and services, however, require a quality workforce. From this it follows that people, and the way they are managed, become the major source of competitive advantage.

Closer inspection, however, suggests that the reality of personnel management is very different from the rhetoric. This is above all true of Britain. Not only is there very little evidence of the implementation of HRM associated with the new paradigm outside of a relatively few, mostly 'greenfield' and foreign-owned, workplaces. It remains a moot point whether British managements are developing a more strategic approach to managing human resources or whether they are essentially muddling through. It also seems, much more significantly, that a very different approach from that recommended is emerging in many organizations. This is not the people-centred approach of HRM, but its very antithesis.

In seeking to make sense of what is going on, this chapter doubles as an introduction and a conclusion to the collection as a whole. The chapter's starting point is the analysis and prescription of the new paradigm increasingly being referred to in explaining and justifying what organizations are doing or should be doing. The first section tries to set out the ideals as clearly and fully as possible, without any reservations, before going on to show that many of the key assumptions are suspect and, even more importantly, that their ambiguity and rhetoric can camouflage any number of very different positions. The emphasis in the second section moves from theory to practice. This section discusses some of the key distinguishing features of personnel management in Britain, considers the directions in which the changes that are actually taking place are leading us and compares the outcomes with some of the regimes of Britain's main competitors. The third and final section offers a view of future prospects for personnel management in Britain.

People: The Key to Success?

As will become apparent, there are many formulations of the new paradigm – the devil is in the detail. For present purposes, however, it is the essentials that are important. At the risk of over-simplification, these are set out as clearly as possible before going on to draw attention to some of the major flaws in the new thinking which are important in helping to explain the gap between the rhetoric and reality.

The analysis

The starting point is the recognition that people are not simply one of the factors of production, along with money and machinery, but the major source of competitive advantage (see, for example, National Economic Development Office/Manpower Services Commission, 1987). How organizations recruit, train, reward, motivate and discipline their employees is of central importance to business success. Firms' choices of specific practices, and the extent to which these practices are integrated in a policy linked to business strategies, are especially important for competitiveness. The same is true, at the level of nation states and of supra-national entities, such as the European Community, of decisions about social and employment policies in general and labour law in particular. The talk is of competition between different types of industrial relations or personnel management 'regimes' (see, for example, Streeck, 1991).

An important corollary is that there has to be a fundamental change or transformation in the traditional methods of managing people. Many of our policies and practices, it is argued, are associated with the mass-production methods which have their origins in the system developed most fully by the Ford Motor Company in the period immediately before the First World War (for a review of the many sources, see Pollert, 1991; Nolan and O'Donnell, 1991; Kochan and Dyer, 1992). This system is characterized by the production of standard goods for mass markets using dedicated machinery and work methods associated with such industrial engineers as Taylor (1911). Three main features of these traditional so-called 'Fordist' or 'Taylorist' methods are the targets. One is hierarchy, in which there is a separation of decision making from doing and in which the few at the top give orders to the many below. A second is bureaucracy, i.e. a system of explicit rules and procedures which are designed to achieve the control and compliance of subordinates to the orders of those who 'command' organizations. The third is specialization, in which functions, jobs and tasks are broken down and defined as narrowly as possible in the belief that this brings the greatest efficiency.

The reasons why these traditional methods are increasingly said to be dysfunctional relate to the changing context of business. Some attention has focused on what might be described as the supply side. People, it is argued, are better educated and have greater expectations of their work, which is leading to increased social awareness and responsibility on the part of those running major organizations. A major concern is the impact of the 'demographic timebomb', that is, the substantial reduction in the number of young people coming onto the labour market over the next decade in most developed economies. This, coupled with concerns about skill shortages, has led to the suggestion that there may be a seller's rather than a buyer's labour market with employees even being in a position to choose their 'preferred' employer rather than the other way round.

Important though these considerations may be, they pale into insignificance when compared to the pressures which are generated in the product market. The context is set by the ever intensifying competition in an increasingly international or global economy. Technology – leading, in particular, to considerably improved information flows – has played a part in bringing about this global economy: improved communications, for example, have drastically reduced the time and expense involved in trading between continents. So too has the development of wider markets such as the European Economic Community: trade barriers have come down and inward investment is encouraged to take advantage of the larger market. The major factor, however, has been the emergence of a large number of international companies which operate on a worldwide basis. Operations in these companies are organized increasingly around international product or service divisions rather than national companies. In so far as the product market allows, operations are sited where it is most cost-effective. Significantly, too, multiple sourcing is used to create an internal market for investment in order to drive down costs and to improve quality and performance. Increasingly, in other words, a significant engine of competition is not just comparisons between different international companies but also competition within these companies.

Within this global market-place, two developments are deemed to be especially important. One is the rise of manufacturers in low labour-cost countries who are able to take advantage of modern technology and challenge the established producer countries. Their presence has been especially important in such industries as clothing, footwear and textiles and is increasingly becoming so in industries such as steel, chemicals and aircraft manufacture – it means that companies in the traditional producer countries cannot compete without taking radical measures. A second is Japanese companies' growing dominance of markets in such manufacturing industries as automobiles and electronics. In this case it is not cheap labour which has been critical, but the successful use of 'lean production' systems involving new working methods such as 'just-in-time', *kaizen* or continuous improvement, and the direct participation of the workforce. The latter, in particular, it is agreed, has made it possible for Japanese companies to improve quality and reduce costs simultaneously and continuously by cutting out the layers of management and control systems deemed to be necessary under traditional 'Fordist' or 'Taylorist' methods.

The prescription

The simple message is to copy the Japanese. In more elaborate language, it means switching from mass production to 'flexible specialization' (i.e. the provision of high quality semi-customized goods and services tailored for niche markets). This, in turn, means getting much closer to the customer to establish his or her desires and introducing 'total quality management' (TQM) designed to achieve continuous improvement, as well as reductions in cost, in product and service.

In terms of managing people, the prescription, which is very often contrasted, sometimes unfairly, with traditional personnel management, takes various formulations and titles – the 'flexible organization', the 'empowered organization', the 'learning organization', the 'open company', as well as 'human resource management' – some of the different nuances of which will be picked up in later chapters. Most of the key features are common, however, and have as their principal aim the development of a highly committed and adaptable workforce willing and able to learn new skills and take on new tasks. They include the elevation of the management of people to the very highest levels of decision making in the organization and its integration into the strategic planning process; an emphasis on trust and respect rather than rules and procedures; and a new role for managers – they become leaders whose job it is to facilitate cultural change by harnessing the co-operation and commitment of others. Instead of the hierarchical organization with a number of tiers of management, separate functions and tightly defined job descriptions, organizations should be much 'flatter' and more 'federal' (i.e. greater decentralization and devolution to quasi-independent business units). Flexibility of function, task, time and reward are also keystones as is team-working. Finally, there should be an appropriate set of personnel policies, built on single status and equal opportunities, to back up the other changes. Figure 1.1 tries to summarize the key features in a single model labelled the 'HRM organization'.

As a footnote, many personnel practitioners, especially in the UK (e.g. Armstrong, M., 1987; Fowler, 1987), have found it difficult to understand what the fuss is about – HRM looks very much like the

---

Beliefs and Assumptions
Business and customer (internal and external) needs are main referent. Search for excellence and quality and continuous improvement are dominant values. Aim to go 'beyond contract'; emphasis on 'can-do' outlook and high energy. Widespread use of team analogy and metaphors. High levels of trust. HRM central to business strategy.

Managerial Role
Top managers are highly visible and provide a vision for the future that employees can share. They also offer transformational 'leadership', setting the mission and values of the organization. Middle managers inspire, encourage, enable and facilitate change by harnessing commitment and co-operation of employees; they also see the development of employees as a primary role.

Organization Design
'Federal', highly decentralized, 'flat' organization structures. Job design congruent with organization structure, technology and personnel policies. 'Cross-functional' project teams and informal groups responsible for particular products or services or customers; they 'contract' contribution to organization with jobs defined in terms of team role. Teams enjoy large measure of autonomy and there is great deal of 'task' flexibility, if not interchangeability, between members.

Personnel Policies
Numerical flexibility, i.e. core and periphery workforce. Time flexibility, e.g. annual hours etc. Single status, i.e. reward etc. of core employees reflects contribution. Selection – emphasis on attitudes as well as skills. Appraisal – open and participative with emphasis on two-way feedback. Training – learning, growth and development of core employees are fundamental values; lateral as well as upward career advancement with emphasis on 'general' as well as 'specific' 'employability'. Equal opportunities. Reward systems – individual and group performance pay; skill-based pay; profit and gain sharing; share ownership; flexible benefits package, e.g. 'cafeteria' principle. Participation and involvement – extensive use of two-way communication and problem-solving groups.

Main sources: Jones, 1991; Kinsley Lord, 1992; Storey, 1992

Figure 1.1 A model of the 'HRM organization'

personnel management that they thought they were practising. Not only that, the rationale also seems hardly different from the thinking of the neo-human relations school associated with Maslow (1943), Hertzberg (1966) and McGregor (1960). For example, the conclusion which McGregor came to in contrasting his famous theory X and theory Y styles or approaches to managing people quite clearly anticipates many of the ideas discussed above.

There are three related aspects which, arguably, are 'new'. One is the link between managing human resources and business strategy: it is the state of competition which, in effect, is requiring management to make changes. A second is the key role which senior line managers are expected to play: managing human resources becomes their major activity. A third is the emphasis on the integration of policies and practices with each other as well as with business strategy.

Crucially, too, above all in the USA, the approach has become institutionalized in business schools – HRM, Guest (1987) reminds us, was one of the first optional courses to be made compulsory on the MBA at Harvard in many years. Personnel management, rightly or wrongly, has been seen largely as low level administrative routine and so has been ignored in the curricula of key management programmes such as the MBA. Human resource management, with its emphasis on 'strategy', 'strategic choice' and 'competitive advantage', has proved to be much more acceptable. Indeed, if people are the key to success, it offers those who teach HRM an opportunity to argue that their subject is as important, if not more important, than marketing and finance, which have hitherto reigned supreme.

Major flaws?

There has been a vast outpouring of books and articles dealing with the new paradigm. One stream has been concerned with the nature of HRM – whether, in particular, HRM is different from personnel management; whether it is an advance on neo-human relations thinking of Maslow (1943), Hertzberg (1966) and McGregor (1960); and so on (e.g. Storey, 1989; Blyton and Turnbull, 1992; Boxall, 1992). A second, above all in the UK, has addressed the take-up and the impact of the practices and policies associated with HRM (e.g. Storey, 1992).

A major and growing concern, which has developed out of this second stream, is that there is a major discrepancy between the rhetoric of HRM and the reality of practice. As the next section argues in more detail, there is very little evidence that British managements are developing a more strategic approach to managing human resources, let alone that they are implementing the HRM associated with the new paradigm. Much more significantly, the approach emerging in many organizations seems to be the very antithesis of that of the HRM organization.

Further reflection suggests that there are two fundamental flaws in the thinking associated with the new paradigm which help to account for this state of affairs. One is that it makes a number of unrealistic assumptions – notably about the ability of managers to exercise strategic choice – which ignore the importance of the structures within which this choice is exercised. The other is that it is extremely ambiguous – its rhetoric makes it possible to camouflage any number of positions.

False assumptions? The new paradigm assumes that business planning is a rational and ordered process. All the evidence, as chapter 5 argues in more detail, points to the contrary. At best, strategies emerge as a result of a series of decisions made by people at many levels in the organization; they involve continual reassessments and readjustments of position. Depending on the particular ways in which the organization is run, a strategy, in the sense of a set of medium- and long-term plans, may not emerge at all – there may simply be a series of vague statements or even financial ratios. In the circumstances, managing in the sense of 'coping' or 'muddling through' is the best that can be expected. Certainly it is hardly feasible to expect the detailed integration of personnel policies and practices implied in the paradigm shift, let alone the fundamental shift in attitudes and behaviours that managing culture or task participation discussed in chapters 12 and 19 involve.

A second assumption which must be queried, especially given the nature of the planning process, is that senior managers will necessarily accept that the policies and practices associated with the model of the 'HRM organization' are as strategically important as it is suggested. Two aspects are involved. One is the issue of leadership. Those who run organizations could be forgiven for thinking that leadership is the critical factor in the 'HRM organization' and that the project is really about the management of managers rather than the workforce as a whole (see also, on this point, Legge, 1989: 27). The other is the relative effectiveness of the proposed methods of working in comparison with the traditional 'Fordist' or 'Taylorist' methods. Intuitively, faced with intensifying international competition, it might be expected that managers – and politicians, judging from the significance British government ministers attach to social costs in declining European competitiveness – would opt for a cost reduction approach. In most cases, as chapter 3 points out for changes in methods of working, this is usually the easier and less risky option to take. This is especially so as there is little hard evidence to demonstrate that the 'HRM organization', like neo-human relations thinking before it, will necessarily bring the promised return on the investment. Even when they are able to point to apparently successful examples of the prescription, those espousing the 'HRM organization' run into a major problem: it is extremely difficult to disentangle the many factors involved.

A third, and in many ways the most critical, assumption which has come under scrutiny (e.g. Storey and Sisson, 1989; Guest, 1991) is that senior managers have sufficient strategic choice to respond to their environment by moving up market into quality products and by bringing about the changes that are being put forward. At first sight, to question this assumption might appear perverse since managers, especially those who run large private sector companies, have enormous resources at their disposal and a significant measure of control over large numbers of employees (see, for example, the arguments on strategic choice of Child, 1972; 1973). Yet this is what the evidence of practice forces us to do. For example, faced with the relatively poor take-up in the USA of the HRM ideas discussed in the previous section, one of the key figures in their propagation has had to recognize that the

> 'strategic' human resource management models of the 1980s were too limited . . . because they depended so heavily on the values, strategies and support of top executives . . . While we see [these] as necessary conditions, we do not see them as sufficient to support the transformational process. A model capable of achieving sustained and transformational change will, therefore, need to incorporate more active roles of other stakeholders in the employment relationship, including government, employees and union representatives as well as line managers. (Kochan and Dyer, 1992: 1)

The key point most commentators have missed is that strategic choices are not made in a vacuum. Far from it. The notion of strategic choice implies, at the very least, circumstances over which even chief executives do not have total control. It is not simply a matter of the prevailing economic climate either. The structures within which this choice is exercised – for example, the legal framework, the patterns of association among employers and the relationship between employers and institutional investors – are profoundly important: they can support or hinder the approach. Such structures are deeply rooted and they are not easily changed. Decision makers may even fight shy of trying to do so, preferring instead to argue that there is no alternative to reducing costs.

There is no simple model of the factors that support the development of HRM. One thing is clear, however. Paradoxical as it may seem, the evidence suggests that, in Streeck's (1992: 10) words, a 'regime of free markets and private hierarchies is not enough to generate and support a pattern of . . . quality production'. It is those countries, such as Germany and Japan, with regimes characterized by interlocking and mutually reinforcing institutional arrangements and processes which seem to offer the most favourable environment. By contrast, it is those countries with regimes characterized by *laissez-faire* and a 'market' approach, such as the UK and the USA, which seem to provide the least fertile ground. Hence Kochan's plea for a coalition of stakeholders to bring about change. The next section, which includes a review of some of the distinctive features of personnel management in Britain, develops the argument in more detail.

It is important to note that, even if national regimes are favourable, this does not necessarily mean that managements in every company will be able to take advantage. Given different exposures to intensifying international competition, a range of positions is much more likely. One, which links with the discussion of feasibility above, is that managers may recognize the logic of the 'HRM organization' and may genuinely wish to introduce it. Yet they may not be able, because of circumstances beyond their control, to afford the investment in human capital that is entailed. A second is that they may believe that they have no choice but to implement what, for most commentators, is the unmentionable alternative – that is to say, to compete on the basis of low cost; this may even be the price that many managements have to pay, especially in small and medium-size supply firms, for some larger companies to be able to follow the quality route. A third position is that they may be under too much pressure to develop a strategic response of any kind – they may simply seek to muddle through.

Hard and soft HRM   Explaining why there are so few examples of the 'HRM organization' is only part of the problem. It is also important to understand why the practice which is emerging in many organizations, even though it hardly resembles the model, is nonetheless often cloaked in the language of HRM. Here the paradigm's ambiguity is important. Take, for example, trade unions and collective bargaining in particular and proceduralism more generally. Although there are formulations which give an important place to trade unions (e.g. Kochan, Katz and McKersie, 1986; Jones, 1991), most are silent on the issues or assume a non-union environment. This is why no mention of them is made in figure 1.1. The implication is that unions are at best unnecessary and at worst to be avoided. Similarly, although it is a moot point whether the 'HRM organization' can do without a firm basis in procedures to ensure consistency of behaviour (see, for example, the debate between Clark and Storey

(Clark, 1993; Storey, 1994)), the impression firmly given is that flexibility is everything and the desired state is that management can do and should be able to do anything it likes. This is hardly compatible with the notions of rights and obligations set out in legislation or collective agreements.

Critically, too, there has also been a widespread failure, especially among prescriptive commentators, to recognize that there is a Jekyll and Hyde quality about HRM. As chapter 5 outlines, there are many varieties of the approach, including 'best practice' and 'contingency' models, but it is also conveniently forgotten in most formulations that there are so-called 'hard' and 'soft' versions.

> The one [the 'hard' version] emphasises the quantitative, calculative and business-strategic aspects of managing the headcounts resource in as 'rational' a way as for any other economic factor'. By contrast, the 'soft' version traces its roots to the human-relations school: it emphasises communication, motivation and leadership'. (Storey, 1989: 8)

Both versions share key elements of the analysis and the prescription of the new paradigm: that organizations are under pressure to re-think their approach to managing people; that they are and should be seeking a better fit between their human resource strategies and business strategies; and that they are and should be transforming their practice. The two versions differ fundamentally, however, in their views on the direction that this transformation should take. The 'soft' version, which is involved in the model in figure 1.1, entails a range of specific policies and practices which are essentially people-centred. The 'hard' version admits anything that fits the business strategy. In certain circumstances, the response could be very low pay or substantial employment insecurity.

One of the clearest statements of the 'hard' version, along with the underlying rationale for managements' behaviour, comes from Burawoy (1985) writing in the labour process tradition. Contrary to the impression sometimes given, to paraphrase his argument, HRM does not involve replacing the simple, technical and bureaucratic controls under Taylorist organizations (for further details, see Edwards, 1979) with which they are contrasted. These controls are just as much in evidence as ever they were. Indeed, it can be argued, that there is evidence of their more intensive use – for example, in the form of the demands of new manufacturing methods such as 'just-in-time' or individual appraisal and pay systems or the 'surveillance' associated with some information systems (e.g. Sewell and Wilkinson, 1992). The problem is that many of the bureaucratic controls which developed in the wake of 'Fordist' and 'Taylorist' methods, says Burawoy (1985: 263), have 'established constraints on the deployment of capital, whether by tying wages to profits or by creating internal labour markets, collective bargaining and grievance machinery which hamstrung management's domination of the workplace'. From this perspective, HRM is seen as a fundamental attack on established rights. It differs from previous management attempts to push back the frontier of control only in its subtlety.

It may be unfair of Burawoy to dismiss all versions of HRM as nothing more than a confidence trick. It is the case, however, that the dividing line between the 'soft' and 'hard' versions is very fine, even where there are the best of intentions. Faced with ever increasing demands of competition, senior managers have to engage in the delicate exercise of simultaneously cutting costs and fostering greater consent.

Surely, it might be asserted, it is easy to distinguish between the 'hard' and 'soft' versions of HRM. It is here that the language, metaphors and symbols that have come to be associated with the 'HRM organization' take on such critical importance. They can be used, as Keenoy and Anthony (1992: 233) have powerfully argued, to 'reconstruct our images of "reality"' – to make us think, no less, that things are different from what they really are. Certainly they can be used to camouflage the 'hard' version. Figure 1.2, for example, shows how a number of the words and phrases which have come to be associated with the 'HRM organization' – and which are increasingly finding their way into the everyday vocabulary of managers – can be used to give a very different impression of what is going on. A range of possible positions was discussed in the previous section. In each case there must be the danger that managers will be tempted to use the language of the 'HRM organization' to cover the reality of what they are doing. They may even delude themselves into believing that they are introducing the 'HRM organization'.

Conclusion

It is not surprising that the new paradigm has received so much attention. Not only does it seem to offer a guide to best practice which is far better grounded and integrated than ever before, but it is also extremely optimistic. Here is a model that appears to be able

Rhetoric	Reality
Customer first	Market forces supreme
Total quality management	Doing more with less
Lean production	Mean production
Flexibility	Management 'can do' what it wants
Core and periphery	Reducing the organizations' commitments
Devolution/delayering	Reducing the number of middle managers
Down-sizing/right-sizing	Redundancy
New working patterns	Part-time instead of full-time jobs
Empowerment	Making someone else take the risk and responsibility
Training and development	Manipulation
Employability	No employment security
Recognizing contribution of the individual	Undermining the trade union and collective bargaining
Team-working	Reducing the individual's discretion

Figure 1.2 The 'HRM organization' – rhetoric and reality?

to satisfy everyone: it meets the demand for economic efficiency and makes a significant contribution to improving the quality of working life. No less important, the stress on the significance of the management of human resources to the competitive advantage of the organization would appear to give the personnel function, if not necessarily personnel managers, the status which so many commentators, above all in Britain, have been seeking. Similarly, it has provided an opportunity for those who teach in business schools to develop new courses and to demand space on MBA programmes hitherto denied them.

Closer inspection suggests that the HRM paradigm must be treated with the greatest caution. It is at best a very partial model. The assumptions on which it depends mean that only a minority of companies will find it a feasible option, and even they will require a supporting set of structures. Much more worrying is the deception to which it can give rise. There is a growing body of evidence discussed in the next section to suggest that a transformation may be taking place in personnel management. It is a very different transformation from the one intended by the proponents of HRM, however. The rhetoric may be the people-centred approach of the 'soft' version: the reality is the cost reduction approach of the 'hard' version.

Personnel Management in Practice

The focus in this section shifts from the theory to the practice of personnel management. The section begins by outlining some of the distinctive features of personnel management in Britain relevant to what has been happening in recent years. It then moves on to consider the directions that personnel management in Britain is taking. It discusses the evidence on the practice of HRM, the changing balance between individualism and collectivism in management's approach, and the model unfolding in the non-union workplaces, which account for the majority of employees. The section then goes on to review some of the outcomes of personnel management in Britain, i.e. pay and productivity, patterns of employment, and training and skills. A discussion of these issues not only provides further valuable information on the directions of personnel management, but also tells us how UK practice has been performing in comparison with other major competitor countries.

Distinctive features of personnel management in Britain

There are three closely related features of Britain's personnel management or industrial relations regime which are important in helping to explain the practice discussed later. They are voluntarism, the structure of collective bargaining, and the status of the personnel function. Although the first two have been significantly influenced by recent government policy, each is deeply rooted in Britain's early and protracted industrialization.

Voluntarism   In the publicity material produced for potential inward investors, the Department of Trade and Industry draws attention to the most distinguishing characteristic of Britain's industrial relations or personnel management system:

> Unlike most continental European countries, employment regulations are largely on a voluntary basis with no requirements for works councils and no mandatory union agreements, while single-union agreements are relatively easy to negotiate (quoted in *The Guardian*, 9 April 1992).

The voluntary or *laissez-faire* approach of the state in the sphere of employment is virtually unique (Kahn-Freund, 1983; Wedderburn, 1991). There has never been much direct regulation of the employment relationship by the state. Labour codes to pressurize employers into adopting framework of rights and obligations, together with statutory provisions for participation and involvement, are noticeable by their absence. In most countries, a series of positive rights established the status of trade unions – for example, the right to belong to a trade union, the right to strike and so on – whereas, in Britain, legislation took the form of immunities for trade unions from common law liabilities. Uniquely, too, the relationship between management and trade unions was allowed to develop its own informal logic. Thus, collective bargaining is built on procedural rules, whereas in most other countries it rests on a code of substantive rules in force for a specified period. Also these procedural rules, along with the substantive rules to which they give rise, are deemed to be 'gentlemen's agreements', binding in honour only, rather than legally enforceable contracts. Britain is also generally regarded as having a voluntary system of training: responsibility for education, until recently, has been in the hands of local authorities and independent examination boards, and the assumption was that vocational training was a matter for employers and employees.

The four Conservative governments which have been in power since 1979 have given their own particular twist to the tradition of voluntarism. Anxious to avoid what they see as the failures of the past, they have sought to introduce an 'enterprise culture' in which individuals and organizations, rather than governments, are held responsible for economic performance. Thus, the maintenance of full employment has been rejected as a major policy objective: the level of employment is to find its own 'natural' level through the operation of the forces of supply and demand in the labour market. The government has effectively abandoned the commitment of its predecessors to voluntary collective bargaining as the most effective method of determining pay and conditions: trade unions – and the collective bargaining for which they are responsible – are seen as major factors in the stickiness of the response of wages to changes in demand and supply, and the government has introduced a series of Employment Acts to limit the powers of trade unions (for further details, see Lewis, 1986; McCarthy, 1992). The following quotation from the 1992 White Paper dealing with industrial relations, *People, Jobs and Opportunity*, gives a very strong flavour of the government's ideal state.

> There is new recognition of the role and importance of the individual employee. Traditional patterns of industrial relations, based on collective bargaining and collective agreements, seem increasingly inappropriate and are in decline . . .

Many employers are replacing outdated personnel practice with new policies for human resource management, which put the emphasis on developing the talents and capacities of each individual employee. Many are also looking to communicate directly with their employees rather than through the medium of a trade union or a formal works council. There is a growing trend to individually negotiated reward packages which reflect the individual's personal skills, experience, efforts and performance. Employees in turn have higher expectations of their employer. They are increasingly aware of the contribution they are making – as individuals – to the business for which they work. They want to know how it is performing and to contribute to its development. They increasingly expect to influence their own development and to be rewarded for their achievement and initiative . . .

They also want the opportunity to influence, in some cases to negotiate, their own terms and conditions of employment, rather than leaving them to the outcome of some distant negotiations between employers and trade unions . . . (Employment Department, 1992)

The government has also extended voluntarism to employer–employee relations. Thus, it has sought to reduce the limited floor of individual employment rights which had grown up since the mid-1960s. It has also vigorously opposed the European Commission's 'Social Charter' which provides for a series of employment rights. Indeed, such has been its opposition that it successfully fought to secure an opt-out of the Maastricht treaty in December 1991 in respect of social policy.

The structure of collective bargaining   A second distinguishing feature is a highly complex and diverse structure of collective bargaining. Superficially, the multi-employer bargaining which developed at national level in the private sector after 1918 was very similar to that in other European countries: the Donovan Royal Commission of 1968 described it as the 'formal' system of industrial relations. Multi-employer bargaining in the UK private sector never achieved the status it did in other countries, however, and has been in decline for several decades (for further details, see Sisson, 1987). In many industries, multi-employer agreements set minimum terms directly affecting only a minority of employees. In others, including engineering, multi-employer agreements have been terminated altogether. Significantly, too, many of the large international companies, which are members of employers' organizations in other countries, including the large car manufacturers (Ford, Peugeot-Talbot, and Vauxhall (General Motors)), are not members of their industry employers' organization in the UK. Many large chemical companies, such as BP, ICI and Shell, are 'non-conforming' members: they belong to the employers' organization, but do not follow the terms of the multi-employer agreement. Only in industries such as clothing, where there is a large number of small and highly competitive companies, is multi-employer bargaining significant – even here the statutory wages council is an important consideration.

Britain neither possesses the detailed multi-employer agreements, which supplement and extend the legislative framework, nor the 'dual' system found in countries such as France and Germany. That is to say, there is no clear-cut distinction between collective bargaining, defining the role which trade unions play outside the workplace, and the joint consultation and employee-based systems of representation, such as works councils, which take place inside the workplace. Most important of all, however, the decentralization of collective bargaining, together with the absence of a comprehensive legal framework, has encouraged yet further fragmentation in what was already a highly diversified set of arrangements. The key policy implication is that, unlike other European countries, there is no longer the means to influence the strategic direction of developments – everything depends on local circumstances.

In the public sector, the major programmes of privatization and commercialization implemented by successive Conservative governments are likewise bringing about the break-up of the once-dominant Whitley system of national collective bargaining and consultation. In the case of the nationalized industries, the government has pursued a vigorous policy of privatization. In both the public services and the remaining public enterprises where privatization has not yet been implemented – notably, coal, railways and the Post Office – external financial limits and cash limits have been used to ensure substantial reorganization, cost-cutting and improvements in efficiency. In the public services, the civil service, local government and the National Health Service, the government has required managements to tender and, where appropriate, to subcontract to the private sector such activities as refuse collection, catering or cleaning, previously performed by their direct employees. It has also introduced 'internal markets', market testing and decentralization (executive agencies, NHS trusts and opting out of schools) more generally. Last but not least, the government has sponsored a number of specific initiatives, such as the introduction of appraisal and merit pay, in an attempt to move away from standardized terms and conditions. A key implication of these changes is that the traditional role of the public sector as the 'good' or 'model' employer, setting standards for others to follow, has effectively been abandoned.

A Cinderella function? A third distinguishing characteristic, the relative low status of the personnel function, is much less tangible than others, but is a common theme in many reviews. In a famous article, appropriately entitled 'Personnel Management in the UK – A Case for Urgent Treatment?', Thurley (1981) listed a number of comments and criticisms made over the years about personnel management as a specialist activity, including: Flanders' (1970) strictures about the lack of planning; the lack of credibility of personnel specialist managers in many organizations cited in the works of Legge (1978), Watson (1977) and Marsh (subsequently published in 1983); and the contradictory nature of personnel policies to which Batstone (1980) had drawn attention. Thurley also talked in terms of personnel policy having developed in an '*ad hoc* way'; of UK manufacturing organizations being 'inefficient in using human resources'; of 'poor labour and machine utilization'; of the growth of non-productive personnel due largely to the problems of maintaining control. He even suggested that personnel management in Britain was a victim of 'stunted growth' and queried whether personnel managers were 'working against the grain of British culture and values'. All this, he suggested, appeared to be in strong contrast with other countries, notably Japan and the US, where there was a closer relationship between personnel management and business strategy.

Although not enough is known about the detailed practice in other countries to make a definitive judgement, there is little reason to quarrel with the general thrust of Thurley's conclusions. It remains the case, for example, that the personnel function is represented at board level only in a minority of British companies. In this, and many other aspects, surveys have attested to the differences between UK and foreign-owned companies on a range of issues from individual practices to a philosophy or approach (Millward and Stevens, 1986; Millward et al., 1992; Purcell et al., 1987; Marginson et al., 1993).

In the search for explanations, a common thread is the ambiguity which arises from the very particular development of the function in

Britain. No less than four different traditions can be identified. The oldest is the 'welfare' tradition, which grew out of the industrial betterment movement associated with many of the Quaker companies at the turn of the century and which gave rise to the notion of the personnel manager being a member of the 'loyal opposition' or 'the corporate conscience' representing the interests of workers to management. The second, the 'manpower control tradition', reflected the growth of large bureaucratic organizations in the 1920s and 1930s and the need for policies and procedures covering both management–employee and management–trade union relations. The third, the 'professional tradition', grew out of the quest for status on the part of personnel managers themselves in the post-Second World War period and emphasizes the possession of specialist knowledge and expertise. The fourth, the 'industrial relations tradition', reflected the rise in workplace bargaining in the 1960s and 1970s, especially in manufacturing, and emphasized the importance of managing the relationship with trade unions (for further details, see Thomason, 1981: 15–23; Tyson and Fell, 1986: 18–21). The result is that the personnel manager has been likened to the general medical practitioner (Torrington, 1989). While this analogy may give some comfort to the professional aspirations of personnel managers, it is also a reminder that the 'jack-of-all-trades' rarely enjoys the same status as the 'specialist' (see also Guest, 1991: 167).

A second theme, which echoes Thurley's comments about personnel managers working against the grain, relates to the structures of corporate governance in Britain. Several features, it can be argued, militate against the introduction of the 'HRM organization' discussed earlier. One is the composition of management. The functional divisions within British management run deep, and the dominance of the finance function, of accountancy logic and accountancy-driven management control systems is overwhelming (Armstrong, P., 1984; 1989). It has not only hindered the development of personnel management, it can be argued, but also that of general management. A second is the pattern of institutional investment and the relationship between industry and the financial markets (the 'City') – the overriding importance of such institutions as investment trusts and pension funds, plus the threat of takeover in the form of the presence of large conglomerates (e.g. BTR, Hanson) anxious to maintain the price/earnings ratio of their shares, has put considerable pressure on maintaining dividends and delivering 'short-term' financial results. A third and fourth are closely related:

the adoption of business strategies which favour domestic markets or defence, and organization structures which have reinforced short-term thinking. The past two decades have seen the widespread adoption of the multi-divisional pattern of organization within major companies which, coupled, with a tradition of corporate head offices emphasizing control rather than development, has reinforced the emphasis on 'numbers driven' rather than 'issue driven' planning (McKinsey and Co. Inc, 1988). The upshot is 'short-termism' in approach.

> ... managerial performance horizons are adjusted to meet annual, half-year and even quarterly reporting schedules. The exigencies of this regime place a premium on behaviours and investments which have a immediate payback. This, up to a point, may act as a useful discipline. But, a consequential effect is to discourage, and even penalise, actions which are geared to a beneficial return over a longer term horizon. Many HRM initiatives would fall into this category – most notably those which relate to training and development and investments of time and resources in winning commitment. (Storey and Sisson, 1993: 73)

The directions of personnel management in Britain

Views about what has been happening to personnel management in Britain in recent years turn on two related judgements which should be made explicit. One is the choice of cases. A focus on the greenfield workplaces which have received so much publicity might lead to a similar conclusion to that of Kochan et al. (1986) in respect of the USA, namely that personnel management is being transformed. A focus on the brownfield workplaces of mainstream organizations in the public and private sector, on the other hand, or on the increasing number of non-union workplaces, leads to very different conclusions. The second judgement involves the balance of emphasis between change and continuity. Especially difficult is distinguishing underlying developments from the impact of the recession which enveloped Britain and much of the rest of the world in the early 1990s. The emphasis here is very much on the former.

The coming of HRM?   In discussions about what has been happening to personnel management in Britain in recent years, a great deal of attention has focused on the policies and practices introduced on greenfield workplaces, notably by Continental Can, Nissan, Sony and others. Indeed, these are the model for many of the developments described in the first section of this chapter. As chapter 21 describes, in the case of the Pirelli operation in South Wales, their packages, which vary from case to case, have typically involved such novel features as: a commitment to an explicit philosophy or style of management; flexibility of working; single status; integrated salary structures; continuous training and the payment for skills acquired; direct communication with the workforce through regular meetings; a joint consultative council, together with (in some cases) the exclusive recognition of a single union; 'no strike' provisions which rule out industrial action even as a last resort; and pendulum arbitration (for further details, see Bassett, 1986; Trevor, 1988; Wickens, 1987).

Such initiatives, although relatively small in numbers – latest estimates suggest that no more than 70–80 are involved (*Industrial Relations Review and Report*, 1992) – have been extremely significant. First, they do seem to represent a fairly radical departure from traditional practices – above all in the approach of management (e.g. Jones, 1991; Newell, 1992; Clark, 1994). Second, they also seem to have been a contributory factor in achieving the competitive advantage that managements have been seeking: output and quality at Nissan on Teeside, for example, are reckoned to be on par with workplaces in Japan (Wickens, 1987). Third, they have been important in encouraging the managements of other organizations to think about the way they manage as well as in formulating hypotheses about possible future directions.

As well as the greenfield workplaces cited above, there is also evidence of major changes in recent years in the long-established or 'brownfield' workplaces of the large private sector companies and public sector organizations which have featured in reviews of personnel practice down through the years. Much of it, at first sight, also appears to be of the type associated with the 'HRM organization' discussed earlier. Thus, as chapter 2 will explain in greater detail, in an attempt to deal with the problems of acceptability and control in the large and complex organizations that continue to dominate the British economy, many managements have abandoned the highly centralized functional structures which, along with the loose 'holding company structure', were the characteristic forms of internal organization of the past. In their place they have introduced arrangements that emphasize the separation of strategic from operating management, the disaggregation of the enterprise into quasi-independent divisions and business units, and the decentralization of responsibility for day-to-day operations.

Similar developments have taken place in the public sector. British Rail and the Post Office, for example, have been divided into a number of profit-responsible sectors or divisions. In the National Health Service, the introduction of 'trust' status has involved a considerable devolution of cost responsibility to individual units such as hospitals. In education, the local management of schools initiative and the provision for the opting out of schools from local authority control have similar implications.

Both the survey and the cast study evidence suggest that there has been very considerable take-up of many of the practices associated with HRM. The third Workplace Industrial Relations Survey (WIRS 3) suggests a growth in the number of employees in receipt of merit pay; in the forms of communications such as team briefing; in task participation; and in financial participation, i.e. profit sharing and share ownership. Another finding which accords with HRM thinking is the growing significance of line management in personnel matters. Not only were a growing number of line managers spending a large part of their time on personnel matters, notably in areas such as recruitment, but they were also getting better qualified in personnel techniques (for further details, see Millward et al., 1992: 27–41; 165–7; 175–80; 260–6).

As for the case study evidence, Storey (1992: 28), after a detailed study of 15 mainstream organizations, talks in terms of the 'remarkable take-up by large British companies of initiatives which are in the style of the "human resource management" model'. At the risk of over-simplification, these initiatives take the form of the three main types of strategies discussed in more detail in chapter 12 and other chapters. One is *reorganization* – new structures and ways of working (chapters 3 and 19), appraisal and reward systems (chapters 7 and 14) and hours of working (chapter 15), as well as the major decentralization touched on above. A second is *re-educative* – improved communication systems such as briefing groups, quality circles, training and management development, and equal opportunities programmes (chapters 8, 10, 11, 12, 18 and 19). A third is *replacement* – including tightening up of the standards and methods of selection, discipline promotion and redundancy (chapters 6 and 17). In many cases these strategies have involved very significant symbolic as well as instrumental expression: examples include the redesign of premises, such as has happened in the case of the clearing banks, the wearing of standardized dress, for example at Rover, and the emphasis on customers and quality in organization language, which appears to be a common feature.

It is important not to get carried away, however. Several notes of caution must be introduced. One is the interpretation which is to be put on some of these developments. It is a moot point for example whether the widespread adoption of the multi-divisional pattern of organization is part of a move towards the 'HRM organization': in most cases it has much more to with the accountancy-driven logic discussed earlier than it does with personnel policy. Similarly, as is discussed below, in some cases the take-up of practices, such as individual performance pay and direct communications, has more to do with an assertion of management control over trade unions and collective bargaining than it does with the adoption of the model of the 'HRM organization'. Even those who have advocated the broad thrust of the government's policy such as Mather (1990) have lamented the failure of British management to take advantage of the deregulation of the labour market to introduce genuinely individual contracts which set out the mutual obligations and expectations of employer and employee. Second, there must also be question marks about the breadth, depth and the permanency of many of the changes. For example, chapter 16 confirms that some practices such as single status and guarantees of employment security are noticeable by their absence in many cases: chapter 8 similarly observes that equal opportunities policies are not as widespread as is popularly believed and, even where they do exist, are often honoured in the breach. Some revised working arrangements turn out to be relatively superficial on close inspection: some practices, such as team briefings, have fallen into disuse. Moreover, closer inspection often reveals that the main target for the new practices is management rather than the workforce as a whole. Third, there is the question of integration. Many of the initiatives associated with HRM, as Storey's (1992) study confirms, where they are practised, rarely seem to add up to an integrated approach. There are also major inconsistencies – an emphasis on team-working, for example, and yet an insistence on having individual performance pay; the different forms of participation and involvement being seen as alternatives rather than complementary; 'human resource' and 'industrial relations' departments being kept separate. Finally, it must be emphasized that the organizations introducing even some of the practices associated with the 'HRM organization' are the exception. Above all, WIRS 3 confirms that these practices are very rare in the non-union workplaces, which now account for the majority of employees.

Individualism versus collectivism? It was suggested earlier that, although there are some formulations of the 'HRM organization' which see a role for trade unions and collective bargaining (e.g. Kochan et al., 1986; Jones, 1991), most are silent on the issue or assume that the organization is non-union. The key issue for many observers, therefore, is whether, under the pretext of moving in the direction of the 'HRM organization', British management is essentially seeking to bring about a fundamental shift in its approach from 'collectivism' (i.e. management–trade union relations) to 'individualism' (i.e. management–employee relations). In recent years, as the previous section indicated, managements seem to have been putting more and more emphasis on relations with individual employees. Less clear, however, is whether it is a question of individualism and collectivism or individualism versus collectivism.

As chapter 21 suggests, there is certainly evidence of a shift away from 'collectivism' generally. Thus, there has not only been a marked drop in the aggregate coverage of collective bargaining – from 71 per cent in 1984 to 54 per cent in 1990 (Millward et al., 1992: 93–6) – but there has also been an increase in derecognition in the second half of the 1980s. The very considerable decentralization of collective bargaining in the UK, especially the shift from multi-employer to single-employer bargaining, also takes on a special significance in this context. This, as chapter 21 argues, can be seen as a form of derecognition. The range of issues that trade union representatives can raise tends to be limited to the workplace. There is also evidence to suggest that, where management continues to recognize trade unions, the nature of the relationship has changed. Although this is very difficult to generalize about because of the massive informality of collective bargaining in the UK, there is some consensus, however, that managers are much tougher – collective bargaining is not so much like the joint regulation of the 1970s but more like joint consultation or straightforward communications. Equally there is some consensus that, except in relatively few cases such as Ford and Rover, there are no obvious signs of managements developing a more positive relationship with trade unions. In Storey's (1992: 258–9) words:

> Across the variety of approaches, one startling fact stood out: while the old-style industrial relations 'firefighting' was disavowed, there

was hardly an instance where anything approaching a 'strategic' stance towards unions and industrial relations could be readily discerned as having taken its place. It would appear that identifying clear managerial policies towards trade unions and collective bargaining is as difficult to do now, if not indeed more difficult, than it was 20–30 years ago when the lack of policy on such matters was frequently berated . . .

The much lauded single union and single table bargaining, for example, remain relatively rare.

It is also interesting that British managers seem no more enthusiastic about joint consultation than they do about collective bargaining. Certainly, as chapter 20 points out, there has been no increase in joint consultation, which might have been expected if British management had been seeking to substitute joint consultation for collective bargaining. In terms of numbers little had changed. There has been an overall reduction in the number of workplaces with joint consultation committees (from 34 per cent in 1984 to 29 per cent in 1990) but this is explained by the changing composition of the workplaces rather than general abandonment.

Not all the evidence points in the same direction, however. Withdrawal of recognition remains rare, especially compared to the situation in the USA. Interestingly, too, a number of managements of greenfield workplaces have agreed to recognize trade unions. Moreover, there is some evidence to suggest that, if anything, the range of subjects in collective bargaining has increased. Admittedly, the WIRS survey found little or no change (Millward et al., 1992: 249–55) but other surveys (e.g. *Industrial Relations Review and Report*, 1993: 7–8) and case studies, however, suggest that a number of new aspects are on the agenda. Agreements on skills-based pay, for example, have emerged from major restructuring exercises and the drive for improved performance. Similarly, many managers at local level find that they need the co-operation of shop stewards and local trade union representatives in handling contracting out or the introduction of team-working, whatever the views of senior managers (see, for example, the findings of Colling and Geary, 1992).

In the circumstances, an uneasy balance of 'individualism' and 'collectivism' is perhaps the best interpretation that can be put on what is developing in many organizations. It is clear that, given a choice, many managers would prefer not to deal with trade unions (see, for example, the discussion of the views of many of his management colleagues by the former chairman of the Post Office (Nicholson, 1992)): few certainly see the need to develop the relationship with trade unions (see, for example, some of the responses to the 'Towards Industrial Partnership' initiative, sponsored by the Involvement and Participation Association, in Stevens, 1992). Even so, the 'traditional' route that many small and medium-size enterprises seem to be taking is not a serious option for the larger traditionally unionized organizations in the public or the private sector. 'Macho' management – as experience in some organizations suggests (for example, Rover and the Post Office in the 1980s) – may bring short-run success, but does not achieve the long-term commitment that is needed. Equally, for the reasons given in an earlier section, there are relatively few organizations that can afford the time and resources that would be involved in a full-scale adoption of the 'HRM organization', which is why single status and guarantees of employment security are so notably absent despite the emphasis put on them by some managers of 'greenfield' workplaces (e.g. Wickens, 1993): they also do not have the managers who can manage individually. For the time being, therefore, even if it looks like 'muddling through', the 'dual' approach identified by Storey (1992: 258–62), in which managements experiment with 'individualism' at the same time as they maintain much of the machinery of 'collectivism', is not perhaps as illogical as it may at first appear.

Whither non-union workplaces? The majority of the workforce are now employed in non-union workplaces and so the model that is unfolding here is especially important. Other things being equal, as the WIRS 3 team itself points out (Millward et al., 1992: 363), one might have expected that these would have been the most likely workplaces in which evidence of HRM would be found. This is where, to develop the point made in the previous section, many of the practices are said to have originated in the USA (Foulkes, 1980; Kochan, Katz and McKersie, 1986). It is also where commentators have suggested HRM might be found in its most developed state in the UK (Sisson, 1989). In the event, the position is the exact opposite. It is the union rather than the non-union workplaces which exhibit the fragments of HRM that are to be found.

Thus, not only did a sizeable minority of non-union workplaces have no procedures for raising grievances or health and safety issues, but they also did little to communicate with or involve their employees. It is worth quoting the WIRS 3 team in full on these points, because they are among the most important findings of the whole investigation.

> On a wide range of matters that could be expected to be of interest to employees our results showed that managers in the non-union sector were much less likely to collect information on a regular basis to review performance or policies. They were also far less likely to disseminate such information to employees or their representatives. Even on a matter of such broad interest as the financial position of their workplace, as many as half of managements gave their employees no regular information at all.

> Methods of communication reflected the greater informality. Managements in non-union workplaces were considerably less likely to use each of the main methods of communications covered by our questioning. A third of them used regular meetings between supervisors and all the employees they supervised. A similar number used an annual or more frequent meeting between senior managers and all sections of the workforce. Only half systematically used the management chain to communicate to all employees. Only a fifth had a consultative committee or similar body for consulting employees on general matters. Yet consultation with employees was one of the most important employee relations issues according to managers in the non-union sector, as important as in the union sector where the formalised methods and structures for consulting and informing employees were so much more common. (Millward et al., 1992: 364–5)

As for pay determination, pay levels were set unilaterally by managements in the great majority of cases, differentials were wider and lower paid employees were more common. There was also a lack of employment security. Workforce reductions were no more common in non-union than in union workplaces, but were much more likely to be achieved by compulsory redundancies. Non-union workplaces also made greater use of freelance and temporary contracts.

It is also interesting to note that, although industrial relations may have been perceived as being 'good' or 'very good' in union-free workplaces and strikes unheard of, forms of 'unorganized conflict' were much in evidence. Turnover was as high as in union workplaces and safety, measured by a higher rate of accidents than in union workplaces, was a major concern (see also chapter 4). Dismissals other than those arising from redundancy were nearly twice as frequent per employee as in the union sector. Claims to industrial tribunals for unfair dismissal and other alleged mistreatment were no less common than in union workplaces.

There are two possible interpretations to be put on this data. One holds that informality is to be expected in small and medium-size enterprises, which account for the great bulk not only of non-union workplaces but also of enterprises more generally (see tables 1.1 and 1.2); that there is little need for formal procedures; and that this is the natural order of things and should be little cause for concern. (For general analyses of personnel management in what is a very diverse category, see Scott et al., 1989; Hendry et al., 1991.) The other, which the WIRS team hints at diplomatically, is that there is a cause for concern because the situation in many of these organizations looks like the 'traditional' model of personnel management, which had been assumed to be a relic of the past (see, for example, Rogaly, 1977; Purcell and Sisson, 1983: Sisson, 1989). In other words, rather than the model of the 'HRM organization' discussed above, the prevailing approach is more one of employees being seen primarily as a commodity to be hired and fired as appropriate.

The weight of evidence from other sources, coupled with what is known about the very difficult experience of many of these busi-

Table 1.1   Number of enterprises by size group in EC Member States

	1–9		10–499		500+	
	Enterprises	*%*	*Enterprises*	*%*	*Enterprises*	*%*
Belgium	409,479	94.35	24,044	5.54	477	0.11
Denmark	—	—	—	—	—	—
France	1,888,700	93.50	12,928	6.40	2,020	0.10
Germany	1,622,412	86.04	260,031	13.79	3,206	0.17
Greece	—	—	—	—	—	—
Ireland	—	—	—	—	—	—
Italy	2,864,496	90.60	295,935	9.36	1,265	0.04
Lux	10,618	88.20	1,407	11.69	14	0.12
Neth	493,853	91.21	45,860	8.47	596	0.11
Portugal	616,834	95.20	31,101	4.80	324	0.05
Spain	1,739,501	94.90	93,482	5.10	733	0.04
UK	1,967,199	90.09	212,682	9.74	3,930	0.18

Source: Commission of the European Communities, 1990. Re-working of Tables 4.6, 5.6, 6.6, 7.6, 8.6, 9.6, 10.6, 13.5, 15.6. For details, see Appendix 1

nesses during the recent recession (i.e. record closures and bank-ruptcies), would seem to support the second conclusion. Thus, both ACAS (1992; 1993) and the Citizens' Advice Bureaux (1993) have reported a significant upsurge in unfair dismissal complaints, and the latter suggests that there is considerable abuse generally of employment rights (see also the discussion of 'status' in chapter 16). There also appear to be few compensating advantages in terms of training and development; small and medium-size employers rank consistently low in the surveys of training activity (see, for example, the review in Keep, 1993).

The outcomes of personnel management in Britain

There are two reasons for considering data on the *outcomes* as well as the *processes* of personnel management in Britain. The first is that these data provide additional information on the debate about the directions that personnel management in Britain is taking and the reasons for them. The second reason is that they make it possible to compare the performance of the UK's industrial relations or personnel management regime with those of other countries.

Table 1.2 Number of employees by size group in EC Member States

	1–9		10–499		500+	
	Employees	*%*	*Employees*	*%*	*Employees*	*%*
Belgium	852,084	31.03	1,111,855	40.49	782,061	28.48
Denmark	—	—	—	—	—	—
France	2,922,415	22.30	5,438,575	41.50	4,744,010	36.20
Germany	4,042,620	18.21	10,212,000	46.00	7,945,380	35.79
Greece	—	—	—	—	—	—
Ireland	—	—	—	—	—	—
Italy	6,489,910	40.31	6,847,330	42.53	2,762,760	17.16
Lux	29,365	26.36	55,020	49.39	27,026	24.26
Neth	694,908	19.40	1,500,858	41.90	1,386,234	38.70
Portugal	767,550	35.70	971,800	45.20	408,500	19.00
Spain	3,255,679	41.30	3,988,798	50.60	638,523	8.10
UK	4,471,810	23.17	9,032,400	46.80	5,795,790	30.03

Source: Commission of the European Communities, 1990. Re-working of Tables 4.6, 5.6, 7.6, 8.6, 9.6, 10.6, 13.5, 15.6. For further details, see Appendix 1

It must be emphasized that our knowledge is not yet sufficient to make definitive judgements about the outcomes of personnel management. It is not just that the data are in short supply. It is a moot point whether some indicators such as training and skills are an input or an output. It is also difficult to distinguish the contribution of a change in personnel management practice from the many other inputs that go into economic performance, such as research and development, capital investment, and so on.

Even so, data from the Organization for Economic Co-operation and Development (OECD) and other sources are available on a broadly comparable basis for a number of the key indicators such as pay and productivity, patterns of employment, and training and skills – all of which are significant for economic performance. Moreover, the findings are consistent with the picture that emerges from the survey and case study evidence discussed above.

Pay and productivity The picture so far as pay is concerned is clear enough. As table 1.3 shows, the UK is very much a low pay economy. The UK not only has one of the lowest levels of pay of the OECD countries, but also has one of the lowest levels of labour costs, i.e. pay plus social charges such as pensions, insurance etc.

Turning to productivity, both labour productivity and total factor productivity increased more than in many other OECD countries throughout the 1980s. There was little or no equivalent improve-

Table 1.3 International labour costs in manufacturing in the mid-1980s (UK = 100)

	USA	Japan	France	Germany	UK
Hourly labour costs in 1986*					
Hourly earnings	170	154	98	135	100
Additional labour costs (holidays, social security, training, welfare etc.) as % of hourly earnings	36	19	87	85	40
Total hourly labour costs	165	131	131	178	100
Productivity and unit costs in 1985**					
Real value added per person working	200	134	162	143	100
Unit labour costs	111	89	69	88	100

Sources: * Ray, 1987; 1990: ** Roy, 1989

ment in unit labour costs, however, as table 1.4 shows. The UK is a low productivity as well as a low pay economy.

Three reasons can be offered for the discrepancy. First, as table 1.4 also shows, despite the very high levels of unemployment discussed below, pay in the UK rose much faster throughout the 1980s than in most other OECD countries – a reflection some have argued (e.g. *Industrial Relations Review and Report*, 1991a) of Britain's increasingly decentralized pay arrangements, which encourage upward pressure on pay settlements. There was no year, for example, in which average earnings in manufacturing did not reach more than 7 per cent ('New Earnings Survey', quoted in *Industrial Relations Review and Report*, 1991b) and the increase in management pay was considerably in excess of even that figure ('Remuneration Economics/British Institute of Management Survey', quoted in *Industrial Relations Review and Report*, 1991a). Second, there was no substantial increase in investment in new technology – capital spending per employee was much less than in other OECD countries (see, for example, the calculation, based on OECD figures, of the CBI, 1991). Third, as the next-but-one section suggests, the UK continued to remain a relatively low skilled economy.

Patterns of employment The UK seems to have enjoyed no obvious offsetting advantages from its relatively low labour costs in terms of the level of employment. This much is clear from table 1.5. Not only was there a doubling (from approximately 5 to 10 per cent) in unemployment in the UK between the 1980s and the 1970s, but also the average level of this unemployment was slightly above that of each of the major groupings ('OECD Europe', 'EEC', and 'Total OECD') throughout the 1980s: it was considerably higher than that in Germany and Japan as well as the USA.

A similar conclusion is inescapable in the case of the structure of employment. Like other countries, there was a shift in the UK from manufacturing to services. A major feature in this shift, as table 1.6 confirms, was the growing significance of part-time employment. Two aspects are worthy of comment. First, the UK had one of the highest levels of part-time employment of OECD countries by the end of the 1980s – part-time employment was significantly higher in the UK than in countries of comparable size such as France, Germany and Italy. Second, despite starting from a high base, the increase in part-time employment throughout the 1980s was relatively high; the UK also saw an increase in *both* male and female

Table 1.4 Labour costs in the OECD area business sector[a] (% changes from previous period)

	Compensation per employee						Unit labour costs					
	1977–87	1988	1989	1990	1991	1992	1977–87	1988	1989	1990	1991	1992
North America	6.3	5.0	3.2	3.7	4.4	4.3	5.7	3.6	3.1	4.4	3.8	2.8
Canada	7.0	6.9	6.9	6.7	5.9	4.1	5.7	5.7	5.7	6.3	5.2	2.2
United States	6.2	4.8	2.8	3.4	4.2	4.3	5.7	3.5	2.9	4.2	3.7	2.9
Japan	4.6	3.2	4.1	4.3	4.0	3.9	1.5	−1.4	1.1	0.5	1.9	1.7
Central and Western Europe	7.6	4.6	4.7	6.1	6.3	5.7	5.3	1.9	2.8	4.9	4.7	3.4
Austria	6.4	3.6	5.4	6.0	5.9	6.1	4.8	−0.7	1.8	2.9	4.0	3.9
Belgium	6.5	2.6	3.8	6.0	5.8	5.5	4.1	−1.0	0.9	3.1	3.6	2.8
France	10.3	4.8	5.1	4.9	4.8	4.8	7.4	0.9	2.0	3.1	3.3	1.8
Germany	4.6	3.2	3.0	4.6	5.8	5.4	2.9	0.1	0.4	2.6	4.7	4.6
Ireland	12.9	6.3	4.9	4.8	5.2	5.4	8.9	1.9	−1.9	3.1	3.3	2.4
Netherlands	3.9	1.9	0.4	4.5	4.9	4.9	2.5	0.4	−2.1	2.7	3.3	3.2
Switzerland	5.3	4.7	5.6	6.6	7.2	6.0	3.9	2.8	3.0	5.0	6.4	4.4
United Kingdom	10.7	8.1	8.1	10.9	9.2	7.5	8.0	7.3	10.1	12.5	6.9	3.5
Southern Europe[b]	14.6	8.0	8.8	9.4	8.7	8.0	12.0	4.7	6.0	8.2	7.1	5.5
Greece	18.5	20.8	16.2	20.6	16.0	11.8	17.2	17.7	13.0	21.0	14.6	9.4
Italy	14.4	8.0	9.1	8.9	8.2	7.8	11.9	4.3	5.8	7.8	6.8	5.4
Portugal	19.3	7.1	12.7	14.3	16.4	15.1	17.0	5.5	8.8	11.6	14.6	12.8
Spain	14.0	6.2	6.1	8.1	7.8	7.0	10.5	3.5	5.2	6.8	5.8	4.5

Nordic countries[b]	9.1	7.1	8.2	7.8	6.4	4.6	6.8	5.4	5.3	7.1	5.0	2.9
Denmark	8.3	1.8	3.9	3.4	3.5	3.5	6.3	−2.3	0	0.5	1.5	1.6
Finland	10.4	10.9	11.5	10.1	6.5	2.2	6.6	4.4	5.3	9.9	4.5	−1.0
Norway	9.3	6.7	5.0	6.2	6.1	6.4	8.4	11.6	3.3	4.6	5.1	5.6
Sweden	8.8	8.6	10.6	10.1	8.3	5.8	6.5	7.6	9.6	11.1	7.6	4.5
Oceania	9.6	6.9	7.7	6.8	5.1	4.5	8.1	6.3	7.1	7.1	3.7	3.5
Australia	9.0	6.6	8.5	7.6	5.4	4.9	7.3	7.1	8.4	8.0	3.9	3.9
New Zealand	12.5	8.5	3.4	2.7	3.4	2.5	12.1	1.7	0	2.2	2.7	1.4
OECD Europe[b]	9.3	5.6	5.9	7.0	6.8	6.1	7.0	2.8	3.8	5.9	5.3	3.9
EEC	9.6	5.5	5.7	6.9	6.8	6.2	7.2	2.6	3.6	5.7	5.2	3.9
Total OECD[b]	7.2	4.9	4.5	5.2	5.3	5.0	5.4	2.4	3.1	4.3	4.0	3.0

[a] Aggregates are computed on the basis of 1987 values expressed in 1987 US dollars
[b] Countries shown

Source: OECD, 1991a

Table 1.5 Unemployment in the OECD area[a]

	000s	% of labour force[b]					Millions				
	1989	1980–88	1989	1990	1991	1992	1980–88	1989	1990	1991	1992
North America	7,540.4	7.7	5.5	5.8	7.0	6.7	9.7	7.5	8.0	9.8	9.4
Canada	1,017.4	9.5	7.5	8.1	10.1	10.1	1.2	1.0	1.1	1.4	1.4
United States	6,523.0	7.5	5.3	5.5	6.7	6.3	8.5	6.5	6.9	8.4	8.0
Japan	1,432.7	2.5	2.3	2.1	2.2	2.3	1.5	1.4	1.3	1.4	1.5
Central and Western Europe	6,812.9	7.9	6.8	6.3	7.1	7.6	7.7	6.8	6.3	7.3	7.8
Austria	109.0	3.1	3.2	3.3	3.5	3.8	0.1	0.1	0.1	0.1	0.1
Belgium	383.9	11.3	9.3	8.8	8.8	8.9	0.5	0.4	0.4	0.4	0.4
France	2,281.2	9.0	9.4	9.0	9.4	9.7	2.2	2.3	2.2	2.3	2.4
Germany	1,651.4	5.6	5.6	5.1	5.0	5.1	1.6	1.7	1.5	1.5	1.6
Ireland	202.0	14.1	15.6	14.0	14.7	15.1	0.2	0.2	0.2	0.2	0.2
Luxembourg	2.6	1.4	1.4	1.3	1.4	1.5	0	0	0	0	0
Netherlands[c]	390.0	8.6	7.4	6.5	6.5	6.4	0.4	0.4	0.3	0.3	0.3
Switzerland	22.6	0.6	0.6	0.6	1.1	1.2	0	0	0	0	0
United Kingdom	1,770.2	10.0	6.2	5.5	8.2	9.6	2.7	1.8	1.6	2.4	2.7
Southern Europe	7,867.2	11.8	12.0	11.3	11.7	11.7	7.3	7.9	7.5	7.8	7.9
Greece	297.0	6.5	7.5	7.7	9.0	10.0	0.3	0.3	0.3	0.4	0.4
Italy	2,865.2	10.1	12.1	11.0	11.3	11.2	2.3	2.9	2.6	2.7	2.7
Portugal	232.0	7.7	5.0	4.6	4.5	4.6	0.3	0.2	0.2	0.2	0.2
Spain	2,559.9	18.1	17.3	16.2	15.9	15.6	2.5	2.6	2.4	2.4	2.4
Turkey	1,913.2	11.2	10.2	10.1	11.1	11.4	1.9	1.9	1.9	2.1	2.2

Nordic countries	523.4	4.4	4.3	4.4	5.4	5.7	0.5	0.5	0.5	0.7	0.7
Denmark	264.9	8.9	9.3	9.6	9.8	9.2	0.2	0.3	0.3	0.3	0.3
Finland	88.8	5.1	3.5	3.4	5.9	6.9	0.1	0.1	0.1	0.1	0.2
Iceland	2.3	0.7	1.7	1.7	2.1	1.8	0	0	0	0	0
Norway	106.0	2.5	4.9	5.2	5.1	4.5	0.1	0.1	0.1	0.1	0.1
Sweden	61.3	2.2	1.4	1.5	2.8	3.6	0.1	0.1	0.1	0.1	0.2
Oceania	620.8	7.0	6.3	7.1	9.8	9.9	0.6	0.6	0.7	1.0	1.0
Australia	508.7	7.7	6.1	6.9	9.9	9.9	0.6	0.5	0.6	0.9	0.9
New Zealand	112.1	4.1	7.1	7.8	9.3	10.0	0.1	0.1	0.1	0.1	0.2
OECD Europe	15,203.5	9.1	8.5	8.0	8.7	9.0	15.6	15.2	14.4	15.8	16.4
EEC	12,900.3	9.6	9.0	8.4	9.0	9.3	13.3	12.9	12.1	13.1	13.6
Total OECD	24,797.4	7.5	6.4	6.2	7.1	7.1	27.4	24.8	24.4	28.0	28.4

[a] For sources and definitions, see OECD, 1991a
[b] The rates are not necessarily comparable between countries
[c] Values for 1987 and 1988 use the new national measurement method

Table 1.6 Size and composition of part-time employment 1979–1990[a] (%)

| | Part-time employment as a proportion of | | | | | | | | | Women's share in part-time employment | | |
| | Total employment | | | Male employment | | | Female employment | | | | | |
	1979	1983	1990	1979	1983	1990	1979	1983	1990	1979	1983	1990
Australia	15.9	17.5	21.3	5.2	6.2	8.0	35.2	36.4	40.1	78.7	78.0	78.1
Austria	7.6	8.4	8.8[b]	1.5	1.5	1.6[b]	18.0	20.0	20.0[b]	87.8	88.4	88.8[b]
Belgium	6.0	8.1	10.2[b]	1.0	2.0	1.7[b]	16.5	19.7	25.0[b]	88.9	84.0	89.6[b]
Canada	12.5	15.4	15.4	5.7	7.6	8.1	23.3	26.1	24.4	72.1	71.3	71.0
Denmark	22.7	23.8	23.7[c]	5.2	6.6	9.0[c]	46.3	44.7	41.5[c]	86.9	84.7	79.4[c]
Finland[c]	6.7	8.3	7.2	3.2	4.5	4.4	10.6	12.5	10.2	74.7	71.7	67.8
France[e]	8.2	9.7	12.0	2.4	2.6	3.5	16.9	20.0	23.8	82.2	84.4	83.1
Germany	11.4	12.6	13.2[c]	1.5	1.7	2.1[c]	27.6	30.0	30.6[c]	91.6	91.9	90.5[c]
Greece	—	6.5	5.5[c]	—	3.7	2.9[c]	—	12.1	10.3[c]	—	61.2	65.7[c]
Ireland	5.1	6.6	8.1[c]	2.1	2.7	3.8[c]	13.1	15.5	17.1[c]	71.2	71.6	68.2[c]
Italy	5.3	4.6	5.7[b]	3.0	2.4	3.1[b]	10.6	9.4	10.9[b]	61.4	64.8	64.7[b]
Japan	15.4	16.2	17.6[b]	7.5	7.3	8.0[b]	27.8	29.8	31.9[b]	70.1	72.9	73.0[b]
Luxembourg	5.8	6.3	6.5[c]	1.0	1.0	2.0[c]	17.1	17.0	15.1[c]	87.5	88.9	80.0[c]
Netherlands[d]	16.6	21.4	33.2	5.5	7.2	15.8	44.0	50.1	61.7	76.4	77.3	70.4

New Zealand	13.9	15.3	20.1	4.9	5.0	8.5	29.1	31.4	35.2	77.7	79.8	76.1
Norway	25.3	29.0	26.6	7.3	7.7	8.8	50.9	63.3	48.2	83.0	83.7	81.8
Portugal	7.8	—	5.9[b]	2.5	—	3.1[b]	16.5	—	10.0[b]	80.4	—	69.8[b]
Spain	—	—	4.8[b]	—	—	1.6[b]	—	—	11.9[b]	—	—	77.2[b]
Sweden	23.6	24.8	23.2	5.4	6.3	7.3	46.0	45.9	40.5	87.5	86.6	83.7
United Kingdom	16.4	19.4	21.8[b]	1.9	3.3	5.0[b]	39.0	42.4	43.8[b]	92.8	89.8	87.0[b]
United States	16.4	18.4	16.9	9.0	10.8	10.0	26.7	28.1	25.2	68.0	66.8	67.6

[a] For sources and definitions, see Annex 1.B OECD Employment Outlook 1989 and Annex 1.C OECD Employment Outlook 1990, except as indicated below
    for the Netherlands
[b] Data are for 1989
[c] Data are for 1988
[d] Break in series in 1985
[e] The 1990 data for male employment include conscripts, contrary to the situation for earlier years

Sources:
Australia: Australian Bureau of Statistics, The Labour Force Australia
Austria: Central Statistical Office, Mikrozensus
Belgium, Denmark, France, Germany, Greece, Ireland, Italy, Luxembourg, and United Kingdom: EUROSTAT, Labour Force Sample Survey
Canada: Statistics Canada, The Labour Force
Finland: Central Statistical Office of Finland, Labour Force Survey
Japan: Bureau of Statistics, Labour Force Survey. Data refer to non-agricultural industries
New Zealand: Labour and Employment Gazette
Netherlands: Data were provided by the Central Bureau of Statistics
Norway: Central Bureau of Statistics, Labour Market Statistics
Sweden: National Central Bureau of Statistics, The Labour Force Survey
United States: US Department of Labor, Bureau of Labor Statistics, Employment and Earnings

part-time working. By contrast, most other countries with relatively high levels of female part-time employment at the beginning of the decade, notably the Scandinavian countries and the USA, saw a slight shift, in proportionate terms, from part-time to full-time female employment by the end of the 1980s.

More detailed analysis (e.g. OECD, 1991b: 46, 48; Keep, 1993; European Network for Small Business Research, 1993) reveals a number of characteristics of these part-time jobs which are important for the earlier discussion about the directions of personnel management in Britain. Many were contributed by small businesses employing less than ten people; they were also concentrated in occupations such as clerical and selling, and catering, cleaning, hairdressing and other personal services; a much higher proportion than in other comparable countries, such as Germany, also worked less than half time (i.e. less than 20 hours per week), which means that their positions were relatively precarious. In other words, in the great majority of cases, these were relatively low paid, low status and low skill jobs – they did not provide qualifications or much training or employment rights.

Skills and training OECD statistics in this area are fraught with difficulties of interpretation (see OECD, 1991b). It is clear from other sources described in more detail in chapters 9, 10 and 11, however, that the UK remains a low skill economy relative to many other OECD countries. First, young people in the UK entering the labour market at 16 were not as well educated as in countries such as France, Germany and Japan, and the proportion staying in higher education was considerably less than other OECD counties (see also recent studies carried out by the National Institute for Economic and Social Research (NIESR), 1993). Second, the levels of education and qualifications, whether acquired before or in work, were considerably less than many other countries. Significantly, too, this was true not only of technical and craft qualifications (see, for example, the collection of studies produced by NIESR in Prais, 1990), but also of managers: despite the widely held view that the UK at least educates its elite, the educational qualifications of British managers were below those in a number of other countries such as France, Germany, Japan and the USA (Handy et al., 1987; Storey et al., 1991). Third, a number of studies suggested that the time and resources that British companies typically put into training and development were less than other OECD countries, while other

NIESR studies (e.g. Daly et al., 1985) and work of the Industrial Relations Research Unit (Storey et al., 1991) have emphasized that the role of first line and middle managers in training and development in the UK was less than that in other countries.

Summary and Conclusion

The discussion of outcomes offers further support for the conclusions emerging from the analysis of the process of personnel management. Significant changes are taking place in personnel management in Britain: it may even be appropriate to talk in terms of a transformation. In only a small number of cases, however, is this transformation in the direction of the 'HRM organization' which so many pundits have proclaimed. Rather it appears to be taking the form of the substitution of individualism for collectivism, a reduction in standards and an assertion of management freedom from constraints. Indeed, the likelihood is that, for the average UK employee, the experience of personnel management in Britain in the mid-1990s is less like the 'HRM organization' that it was a decade ago.

As well as the recession which enveloped the country in the early 1990s, a key part of the explanation lies in the distinctive features of personnel management in Britain: the tradition of voluntarism, the structure of collective bargaining and the relatively low status of the personnel function. There has been little pressure on management to maintain standards either by legislation or collective bargaining, while the arrangements for corporate governance and, in particular, the short-termism which they engender, could hardly be more inimical to investment in human capital.

The findings in respect of pay and productivity, patterns of employment, and skills and training, are also important: they confirm what an increasing number of commentators have recognized, namely that the processes and outcomes of personnel management in Britain are mutually reinforcing (e.g. Finegold and Soskice, 1988; Nolan, 1989; Keep and Mayhew, 1994). That is to say, much of the growth in employment has been in part-time jobs in the service sector. Many of these jobs are low paid and involve little training. Because they are low paid and involve little training, there is little incentive for employers to substitute capital for labour in the form of new technology. There is even a case for suggesting that low pay has become an important consideration in demand. Many British companies are encouraged, in other words, to produce relatively low quality goods and services because low paid consumers cannot afford better. The conclusion, unpalatable though it may be, is that personnel management in many organizations in Britain is locked into a vicious circle of low pay, low skill, and low productivity.

Future Imperfect?

It is difficult to envisage, even when the recession ends, the wide-spread take-up of the 'HRM organization' in Britain. The managements of some 'greenfield' workplaces, especially those of foreign-owned companies, will introduce it. Similarly, the managements of a small number of 'brownfield' workplaces, notably those which are in direct competition with Japanese companies, will have to follow suit if they wish to remain in business. Even together, however, these two groups will account for only a fraction of the total number of employees. Most large British companies, faced with ever intensifying international competition and scarce resources, will most probably seek what they perceive to be the benefits of the model (e.g. co-operation, commitment, flexibility etc.) and yet will be unable to incur the costs involved in implementing it in full. They are likely to exhibit an odd 'hybrid' of HRM practices, further moves away from collectivism, and bouts of macho management. Among the great majority of non-union workplaces, which now employ the bulk of the workforce, the signs are that the 'HRM organization' will simply not be an issue. Here the problem will be survival: personnel management will be characterized by low pay, low skill and low productivity.

If this scenario seems excessively pessimistic, it is important to appreciate what would be required to bring about the widespread implementation of the 'HRM organization'. The prescriptive message is implicit in the analysis. It is not a question of this or that technique. There would have to be a fundamental reappraisal of the way in which British companies are run. At one level, it would mean rethinking the role and status of the personnel function: it is difficult to envisage the introduction of the 'HRM organization' if the function is not represented on the main board by people of the highest calibre. At another, deeper level, it would mean reviewing current approaches to issues such as single status, employment security, training and development budgets, the balance between individualism and collectivism and so on. Such a review would involve substantial ongoing investments in human capital and so would require, in turn, major changes in the relationships between companies and institutional investors.

The reappraisal would have to be particularly fundamental in the large multi-divisional organizations which are so important in setting the terms of debate of personnel management in Britain. The conventional wisdom is that the centre devolves as much responsibility as it can to the individual business units and 'manages' them through the financial control system. A growing body of evidence suggests that, while this may be fine in theory, in practice it is a major barrier to the development of more effective HRM policies in the UK. The organization does not get the synergies of its size if each and every individual unit is pursuing its own policies, while the focus on short-term profitability means that the policies which these individual units are able to develop will be correspondingly limited in scope. In short, a better balance is required between centralization and decentralization similar to that which many foreign-owned companies have achieved (see, for example, the discussion in Goold and Campbell, 1987).

It also has to be recognized that, even if those who run organizations did what they could in these directions, it is unlikely to be sufficient. Chief executives, however powerful they may appear to be, do not enjoy the degree of 'strategic choice' many people credit them with. As has already been pointed out, writing of the USA, which suffers from a very similar set of structural features, one of the authors of the highly influential book *The Transformation of American Industrial Relations* has been forced to recognize that, for serious change to take place in the management of human resources, there will need to be significant changes in the national as well as company framework (Kochan and Dyer, 1992).

The case for a similar approach – and, in particular, for a more active role for the government in developing such a framework – can also be made for the UK. A policy of *laissez-faire* not only sends the wrong signals, above all to small and medium-size businesses, it also fails to take into account that, left to their own devices, many UK managements will find the 'high pay, high skill, high productivity' route simply beyond them.

Clearly, even though there has been an about-turn in economic policy since withdrawal from the Exchange Rate Mechanism in September 1992, the prospects of the government taking the initiatives involved – overhauling the regulatory framework of companies and their relationships with the city; developing an appropriate train-

ing system; and introducing a legal framework of rights and obligations that would help to raise standards – are extremely remote. Not
only would such a programme require the government to abandon
its commitment to unfettered market forces, it would also involve
taking a greater measure of responsibility than any British government, Labour as well as Conservative, has ever been prepared to
undertake. It will no doubt be argued that it also involves the kind of
framework that our partners in Europe are anxious to introduce in
the form of the Social Charter. It will thus be seen to threaten what
has been one of the central planks of the government's *de facto*
industrial strategy, namely the deregulation of the labour market in
the hope that low pay and the absence of legal regulations governing dismissal, participation and involvement will encourage inward
investment by international companies.

For the foreseeable future, two sets of circumstances are likely
to be influential in the debate over the most appropriate personnel management regime for Britain. One is the relative success of
the government in deregulating the labour market. If this produces a significant number of jobs, it may be that the government
will be forgiven for the relatively poor quality that most of these are
likely to involve. If it does not – perhaps because inward investors
are frightened off by doubts about Britain's ability to stay in the
European 'fast lane' or because the low cost approach, given the
increasing availability of cheap labour worldwide, does not offer
any comparative advantage – it could face the wrath of the voter
at future elections. The second is the performance of the regimes
of other countries, notably those of France and Germany, where
there is much greater social and legal regulation of the employment relationship. If governments in these countries prove unable
to resist pressures for substantial reductions in social costs, supporters of deregulation will argue that their approach will have been
vindicated. If, on the other hand, high pay, high skill and high
productivity continue to help to give these countries the competitive
edge that they did throughout the 1980s, especially in manufacturing, the case for a reversal of policy in the UK will be considerably
strengthened.

Bibliography

ACAS. 1992. *Annual Report*. London: Advisory, Conciliation and Arbitration Service.

ACAS. 1993. *Annual Report*. London: Advisory, Conciliation and Arbitration Service.

Armstrong, M. 1987. 'Human Resource Management: A Case of the Emperor's New Clothes'. *Personnel Management*, August, 30–5.

Armstrong, P. 1984. 'Competition Between the Organisational Professions and the Evolution of Management Control Strategies'. In Thompson, K. (ed.) *Work, Employment and Unemployment*. Milton Keynes: Open University Press, 97–120.

Armstrong, P. 1989. 'Limits and Possibilities for HRM in an Age of Management Accounting'. In Storey, J. (ed.) *New Perspectives on Human Resource Management*. London: Routledge & Kegan Paul.

Bassett, P. 1986. *Strike Free*. Oxford: Blackwell.

Batstone, E. V. 1980. 'What have Personnel Managers Done for Industrial Relations?'. *Personnel Management*, June, 36–9.

Blyton, P. and Turnbull, P. (eds) 1992. *Reassessing Human Resource Management*. London: Sage.

Boxhall, P. F. 1992. 'Strategic Human Resource Management: Beginnings of a New Orthodoxy?, *Human Resource Management Journal*, Vol. 2, No. 3, 60–79.

Braverman, H. A. 1974. *Labor and Monopoly Capital: The Degradation of Work in the Twentieth Century*. New York: Monthly Review Press.

Brown, W. A. 1992. 'Bargaining Structure and the Impact of the Law'. In McCarthy, W. E. J. (ed.) *Legal Intervention in Industrial Relations: Gains and Losses*. Oxford: Blackwell.

Burawoy, M. 1985. *The Politics of Production: Factory Regimes Under Capitalism and Socialism*. London: Verso.

CBI. 1991. *Competing with the World's Best – The Report of the CBI Manufacturing Advisory Group*. London: Confederation of British Industry.

Child, J. 1972. 'Organisational Structure, Environment and Performance: The Role of Strategic Choice'. *Sociology*, Vol. 6, No. 1, 1–22.

Child, J. 1973. 'Organisation: The Choice for Man'. In Child, J. (ed.) *Man and Organisation*. London: George Allen & Unwin.

Citizens' Advice Bureaux. 1993. *Job Insecurity*. London: Social Policy Section, Citizens' Advice Bureaux.

Clark, J. 1993. 'Procedures and Consistency versus Flexibility and Commitment in Employee Relations: A Comment on Storey'. *Human Resource Management Journal*, Vol. 3, No. 4.

Clark, J. 1994. *The Management of Change*. London: Sage.

Colling, T. and Geary, J. 1992. 'Trade Unions and the Management of Change in the Workplace'. Paper presented at the IREC Conference, Changing Systems of Workplace Representation in Europe, Dublin, 5–6 November, 1992. Mimeo.

Commission of the European Communities: Eurostat and the Directorate General for Economic Policy. 1990. *Enterprises in the European Community*. Brussels-Luxembourg: ECSC-EEC-EAEC.

Daly, A., Hitchens, D. M. W. N. and Wagner, K. 1985. 'Productivity, Machinery and Skills in a Sample of British and German Manufacturing Plants'. *National Institute for Economic and Social Research Review*, February, 48–61.

Donovan, Lord. 1968. *Report of the Royal Commission on Trades Unions and Employers' Associations*. London: HMSO.

Edwards, P. K. E., Hall, M., Marginson, P., Sisson, K., Waddington, J. and Winchester, D. 1992. 'Great Britain: Still Muddling Through?'. In Ferner, A. and Hyman, R. (eds) *Industrial Relations in the New Europe*. Oxford: Blackwell.

Edwards, R. 1979. *Contested Terrain: The Transformation of the Workplace in the Twentieth Century*. London: Heinemann.

Employment Department. 1992. *People, Jobs and Opportunity*. London: HMSO.

European Network for Small Business Research. 1993. The European Observatory for SMEs. *First Annual Report*. Zoetermeer, Netherlands: EIM Small Business and Research Consultancy.

Finegold, D. and Soskice, D. 1988. 'The Failure of Training in Britain: Analysis and Prescription'. *Oxford Review of Economic Policy*, Vol. 4, No. 3, 21–53.

Flanders, A. 1970. *Management and Trade Unions: The Theory and Reform of Industrial Relations*. London: Faber.

Foulkes, F. 1980. *Personnel Policies in Large Non-Union Companies*. Englewood Cliffs, NJ: Prentice Hall.

Fowler, A. 1987. 'When Chief Executives Discover Human Resource Management'. *Personnel Management*, January, 3.

Goold, M. and Campbell, A. 1987. *Strategies and Styles: The Role of the Centre in Managing Diversified Corporations*. Oxford: Blackwell.

Guest, D. 1987. 'Human Resources Management and Industrial Relations'. *Journal of Management Studies*, 24, September, 503–22.

Guest, D. 1991. 'Personnel Management: The End of Orthodoxy?'. *British Journal of Industrial Relations*, Vol. 29, No. 2, 149–75.

Handy, C. et al., 1987. *The Making of Managers: A Report on Management Education, Training and Development in the United States, West Germany, France, Japan and the UK*. London: National Economic Development Office.

Hendry, C., Jones, A., Arthur, M. and Pettigrew, A. 1991. 'Human Resource Development in Small to Medium Sized Enterprises'. *Department of Employment Research Paper No. 88*. Sheffield: Employment Department.

Hertzberg, F. 1966. *Work and the Nature of Man*. London: Staples Press.

Industrial Relations Review and Report. 1991a. 'Long-Term Earnings Trends 1971–91'. 500, November.

Industrial Relations Review and Report. 1991b. Coordinated Pay Bargaining:

A Conference Report from Industrial Relations Services. London: Industrial Relations Services.

Industrial Relations Review and Report. 1992. 'Single Union Deals in Perspective'. 523, November, 6–15.

Industrial Relations Review and Report. 1993. 'The Changing Role of Trade Union Officers 2: Collective Bargaining and Working Practices'. 527. January, 3–11.

Jones, G. 1991. 'Quality of Working Life and Total Quality Management'. *Work Research Unit Occasional Paper No. 50.* London: ACAS.

Kahn-Freund, O. 1983. In Davies, P. and Freedland, M. (eds) *Labour and the Law*, 3rd edn. London: Steven.

Kanter, R. M. 1989. *When Giants Learn to Dance.* London: Unwin.

Keenoy, T. and Anthony, P. 1992. 'HRM: Metaphor, Meaning and Morality'. In Blyton, P. and Turnbull, P. (eds) *Reassessing Human Resource Management.* London: Sage.

Keep, E. 1993. 'UK Training Policy – Assumptions and Reality'. Mimeo. Coventry: Industrial Relations Research Unit.

Keep, E. and Mayhew, K. 1994. *The British Vocational and Educational Training System: A Critical Analysis.* Oxford: Oxford University Press.

Kinsley Lord. 1992. *Building the Empowered Organisation.* London: Kinsley Lord Ltd.

Kochan, T. A. and Dyer, L. 1992. 'Managing Transformational Change: The Role of Human Resource Professionals'. Proceedings of the Conference of the International Industrial Relations Association, Sydney, 1992. Geneva: International Industrial Relations Association.

Kochan, T. A., Katz, H. C. and McKersie, R. B. 1986. *The Transformation of American Industrial Relations.* New York: Basic Books.

Legge, K. 1978. *Power, Innovation and Problem-Solving in Personnel Management.* London: McGraw-Hill.

Legge, K. 1989. 'Human Resource Management: A Critical Analysis'. In Storey, J. (ed.) *New Perspectives on Human Resource Management.* London: Routledge.

Lewis, R. 1986. 'The Role of Law in Employment Relations'. In Lewis, R. (ed.) *Labour Law in Britain.* Oxford: Blackwell.

Long, P. 1984. 'Would You Put Your Daughter in Personnel?'. *Personnel Management*, April, 16–20.

McCarthy, W. E. J. 1992. 'The Rise and Fall of Collective Laissez-Faire'. In McCarthy, W. E. J. (ed.) *Legal Intervention in Industrial Relations: Gains and Losses.* Oxford: Blackwell.

McGregor, D. C. 1960. *The Human Side of the Enterprise.* New York: McGraw-Hill.

McInness, J. 1987. *Thatcherism at Work.* London: Hutchinson.

McKinsey and Co. Inc, 1988. *Strengthening Competitiveness in UK Electronics.* London: National Economic Development Office.

Marginson, P., Armstrong, P., Edwards, P. K. and Purcell, J. 1993.

Second Company Level Industrial Relations Survey: Executive Summary of Findings. Mimeo. Coventry: Industrial Relations Research Unit.

Marginson, P., Edwards, P. K., Martin, R., Purcell, J. and Sisson, K. 1988. *Beyond the Workplace. The Management of Industrial Relations in Large Enterprises.* Oxford: Blackwell.

Marsh, A. 1983. *Employee Relations Policy and Decision Making.* Aldershot: Gower.

Maslow, A. 1943. 'A Theory of Human Motivation'. *Psychological Development*, 50, 370–96.

Mather, G. 1990. *Promoting Greater Use of Employment Contracts.* London: Institute of Economic Affairs.

Millward, N. and Stevens, M. 1986. *British Workplace Industrial Relations 1980–1984: The DE/PSI/ACAS Surveys.* Aldershot: Gower.

Millward, N., Stevens, M., Smart, D. and Hawes, W. R. 1992. *Workplace Industrial Relations in Transition: The ED/ESRC/PSI/ACAS Surveys.* Aldershot: Gower.

National Economic Development Office/Manpower Services Commission. 1987. *People: The Key to Success.* London: NEDO.

National Institute for Economic and Social Research. 1993. *Educational Provision, Educational Attainment and the Needs of Industry: A Review of Research for Germany, France, Japan, the US and Britain.* London: NIESR.

Newell, H. 1992. 'Exploding the Myth of Greenfield Sites'. *Personnel Management*, January, 20–3.

Nicholson, B. 1992. 'Royal Mail Reshapes its Industrial Relations'. *Involvement and Participation*, No. 615, November, 12–19.

Nolan, P. 1989. 'The Productivity Miracle?'. In Green, F. (ed.) *The Restructuring of the British Economy.* Brighton: Harvester.

Nolan, P. and O'Donnell, K. 1991. 'Restructuring and the Politics of Industrial Renewal: The Limits of Flexible Specialization'. In Pollert, A. (ed.) *Farewell to Flexibility.* Oxford: Blackwell.

OECD. 1991a. 'Labour Markets in the 1980s'. *Employment Outlook*, No. 49, June. Paris: Organization for Economic Co-operation and Development.

OECD. 1991b. 'Training by Firms'. *Employment Outlook*, July. Paris: Organization for Economic Co-operation and Development.

Pollert, A. 1991. 'The Orthodoxy of Flexibility'. In Pollert, A. (ed.) *Farewell to Flexibility.* Oxford: Blackwell.

Prais, S. (ed.) 1990. *Productivity, Education and Training.* London: National Institute for Economic and Social Research.

Purcell, J., Marginson, P., Edwards, P. K. and Sisson, K. 1987. 'The Industrial Relations Practices of Multi-Plant Foreign Owned Firms'. *Industrial Relations Journal*, 18, Summer, 130–7.

Purcell, J. and Sisson, K. 1983. 'Strategies and Practice in the Management of Industrial Relations'. In Bain, G. S. (ed.) *Industrial Relations in Britain.* Oxford: Blackwell, 95–120.

Ray, G. F. 1987. 'Labour Costs in Manufacturing'. *National Institute for Economic and Social Research Review*, Vol. 120, May, 71–4.

Ray, G. F. 1990. 'International Labour Costs in Manufacturing 1960–88'. *National Institute for Economic and Social Research Review*, Vol. 132, May.

Rogaly, J. 1977. *Grunwick*. Harmondsworth: Penguin.

Roy, D. 1989. 'Labour Productivity in 1985: An International Comparison'. Mimeo. International Association for Research in Income and Wealth.

Scott, M., Roberts, I., Holroyd, G. and Sawbridge, D. 1989. *Management and Industrial Relations in Small Firms*. Department of Employment Research Paper No. 70. London: HMSO.

Sewell, G. and Wilkinson, B. 1992. 'Empowerment or Emasculation? Shopfloor Surveillance in a Total Quality Organisation'. In Blyton, P. and Turnbull, P. (eds) *Reassessing Human Resource Management*. London: Sage.

Sisson, K. 1987. *The Management of Collective Bargaining: An International Comparison*. Oxford: Blackwell.

Sisson, K. 1989. 'Personnel Management in Perspective'. In Sisson, K. (ed.) *Personnel Management in Britain*, 1st edn. Oxford: Blackwell.

Stevens, B. 1992. 'IPA Launches Towards Industrial Partnership'. *Involvement and Participation*, No. 615, November, 20–3.

Storey, J. (ed.) 1989. *New Perspectives on Human Resource Management*. London: Routledge & Kegan Paul.

Storey, J. 1992. *Developments in the Management of Human Resources*. Oxford: Blackwell.

Storey, J. 1994. 'Procedures and Consistency versus Flexibility and Commitment in Employee Relations: A Reply to Clark'. *Human Resource Management Journal*, Vol. 4, No. 3.

Storey, J. and Sisson, K. 1989. 'The Limits to Transformation: Human Resource Management in the British Context'. *Industrial Relations Journal*, Vol. 21, Spring, 60–5.

Storey, J. and Sisson, K. 1993. *Managing Human Resources and Industrial Relations*. Milton Keynes: Open University Press.

Storey, J., Okasaki-Ward, L., Gow, I., Edwards, P. K. E. and Sisson, K. 1991. 'Managerial Careers and Management Development: A Comparative Analysis of Britain and Japan'. *Human Resource Management Journal*, Vol. 1, No. 3, 33–57.

Streeck, W. 1985. 'Industrial Relations and Industrial Change in the Motor Industry: An International View'. Public Lecture. University of Warwick: Industrial Relations Research Unit.

Streeck, W. 1991. 'More Uncertainties: German Unions Facing 1992'. *Industrial Relations*, Vol. 30, No. 2, 317–49.

Streeck, W. 1992. *Social Institutions and Economic Performance: Studies of*

Industrial Relations in Advanced Industrial Countries. London: Sage.

Taylor, F. W. 1911. *The Principles of Scientific Management*. New York: Harper.

Thomason, G. 1981. *A Textbook of Personnel Management*. London: Institute of Personnel Management.

Thurley, K. 1981. 'Personnel Management in the UK – A Case for Urgent Treatment?'. *Personnel Management*, August, 24–8.

Torrington, D. 1989. 'Human Resource Management and the Personnel Function'. In Storey, J. (ed.) *New Perspectives on Human Resource Management*. London: Routledge & Kegan Paul.

Trevor, M. 1988. *Toshiba's New British Company: Competitiveness through Innovation in Industry*. London: Policy Studies Institute.

Tyson, S. and Fell, A. 1986. *Evaluating the Personnel Function*. London: Hutchinson.

Walton, R. E. 1985. 'From Control to Commitment in the Workplace'. *Harvard Business Review*, 63, March/April, 76–84.

Watson, T. J. 1977. *The Personnel Managers*. London: Routledge & Kegan Paul.

Wedderburn, K. K. (Lord). 1991. *Employment Rights in Britain and Europe*. London: Lawrence & Wisehart.

Wickens, P. 1987. *The Road to Nissan: Flexibility, Quality, Teamwork*. London: Macmillan.

Wickens, P. 1993. 'Lean Production and Beyond: The System, its Critics and the Future'. *Human Resource Management Journal*, Vol. 3, No. 4, 75–90.

PART II
Work Organizations

2

The Structure of Organizations

Arthur Francis

Work organizations take many forms. Solicitors' practices, worker co-operatives and owner-managed small engineering companies, for example, differ considerably and systematically in their organizational structures: they vary in the way in which tasks are divided, activities co-ordinated and decisions taken, as well as in the amount of power, influence and status enjoyed by each organizational member. There are also differences between the structures of larger scale organizations. Universities are organized on a different basis from the civil service, and civil service organizational structures differ from those in many business concerns. Within the business sector, variations are also considerable. For example, one multinational corporation, the Hanson Trust, operates with a headquarters executive staff of 20 in the UK and 12 in the USA (Goold and Campbell 1987: 114); Imperial Tobacco, on its acquisition by Hanson Trust, employed 800 in its head office operations (*The Guardian*, 8 September 1987). Differences of this magnitude do not result from overmanning. They imply the use of different principles in shaping their organizational arrangements.

The purpose of this chapter is to set out the range of organizational forms adopted by business enterprises, and the circumstances in which each type is likely to be chosen. Though the bulk of material in this chapter concerns business organizations – for it is within these that most people in Britain are employed – many of the principles underlying the arguments and research findings reported here are applicable across a wider range, including public sector and voluntary organizations.

The Dimensions of Organizational Structure

We begin our exploration of how enterprises are organized, and how organizations differ, by picturing the organization as a pyramid-shaped managerial hierarchy. By doing this we can discuss the dimensions of an organization's structure. This approach was first taken by Weber (1947) in his classic study of bureaucracy (literally, rule by office-holders) and developed by Pugh and others in a series of detailed survey-based studies, initially carried out at Aston University in Birmingham and since known throughout the world as the Aston studies. They identified five dimensions of organization structure – specialization, standardization, formalization, configuration and centralization.

Specialization

Organization becomes necessary when a product or service is so large or complex that more than one person's effort and/or skills are required to produce it. One fundamental element, therefore, is the way in which the tasks necessary for the completion of the product are divided up between organizational members. Though this issue will be discussed in the following chapter on job design, it should be noted here that a key dimension of organizational structure, and an important influence on the choices made about other aspects of that structure, is the nature of the division of labour within the enterprise. The Aston studies attempted to measure this by counting the number of different occupational types or functional departments within an enterprise (Pugh et al., 1968). This measure can be misleading, however, as it fails to distinguish between two quite different phenomena. One is where the task to be performed is rather simple, requires little expertise, and hence relatively few occupational types are involved – for example, in routine assembly work. The other is where the task may be complex, but is performed by flexible multi-skilled workers, each person performing a range of operations, and occupational labelling may be deliberately reduced to a minimum – for example, in firms using Japanese-type production systems which emphasize flexible team-working. In each case the firm will score low on the specialization measure though the co-ordination requirements of each type of low specialization are likely to be different.

Standardization and formalization

Two further important organizational dimensions relate to the extent to which organizational relationships and procedures are standardized and formalized, that is, subject to standard procedures and rules for doing things (standardization) some of which may be written down (formalization). Examples of formalization are written policies, procedures, rules, job definitions and standing orders.

Configuration (tall or flat?)

Until relatively recently, it was generally believed that the optimum number of people a manager could supervise was between six and eight. It is now known that there is no such optimum figure. The size of the span of control depends on a variety of factors discussed later in the chapter.

This span also determines, to some extent, the number of levels in the managerial hierarchy. An organization of a given size with a short span of control will, by simple arithmetic, have more managerial levels than one of an equivalent size with a longer span of control. Therefore, the extent to which an organization may be 'tall' or 'flat' is a fourth dimension in which organizational structures vary.

Centralization

Though decisions vary in importance, and therefore some get made at higher levels in the organization than others, organizations do appear to differ systematically in the extent to which they centralize or decentralize their decision making. In one organization, for example, an operator may be allowed, and even encouraged, to decide how a job is done, whereas in another this decision will have been centralized with detailed procedures laid down for the way tasks should be carried out. Capital expenditure and budgeting decisions involving specific amounts of funds will be made higher up the managerial hierarchy in some firms than others.

As Goold and Campbell (1987) have established, difference in the nature and extent of centralization are especially marked in the case of the large multi-establishment enterprise. At one extreme, there were enterprises in their study – such as BOC (industrial gases), Lex (automotive services) and STC (telecommunications) – which saw an essential role for corporate management in developing the strategy of the subsidiary businesses and in co-ordinating their activities. At the other extreme, there were enterprises – such as BTR (services), Tarmac (construction), Hanson Trust and GEC – in which responsibility for strategy was devolved to the subsidiary businesses, though there was close monitoring of performance against budget and strong personal incentives for managers to meet targets. In between were enterprises – such as Courtaulds (textiles), ICI, the Imperial Group (now part of Hanson Trust), Plessey (telecommunications) and Vickers (engineering) – which had established planning processes but left a great deal of initiative to subsidiary managers in drawing up the plans.

Organizational types

So far, five separate dimensions of organization structure have been identified. Are these dimensions independent, in the sense that an organization will take up a position on one dimension independent of the position it takes on any other, or are they linked in some way? For example, does an organization which is highly standardized also have a very formalized structure with centralized decision making? Perhaps surprisingly, research has shown an inverse correlation between centralization and the degree of standardization and formalization (Child, 1973). It appears that managers view these as alternative forms of control. When organizations are standardized and formalized, there is less need for senior managers to be involved in detailed decision-making because junior staff are constrained to carry out senior management's wishes by the rules and procedure surrounding their decision-making process. Hence the formalized organization is decentralized in its decision making.

Other research has indicated that all five dimensions are related. One early and influential study (Burns and Stalker, 1966: 5–6) suggested that there seemed in practice to be just two divergent systems of management and forms of organizational structure. Though subsequent research has shown this view to be rather too simple, leading to the development of a more sophisticated and complex view of organizational types (discussed later), this early idea of two extreme types illuminates a wide variety of possibilities.

The researchers label their two types 'mechanistic' and 'organic' and describe the differences thus:

> In mechanistic systems the problems and tasks facing the concern as a whole are broken down into specialisms. Each individual pursues his

task as something distinct from the real tasks of the concern as a whole, as if it were the subject of a sub-contract. 'Somebody at the top' is responsible for seeing to its relevance. The technical methods, duties, and powers attached to each functional role are precisely defined. Interaction within management tends to be vertical, i.e. between superior and subordinate. Operations and working behaviour are governed by instructions and decisions issued by superiors. This command hierarchy is maintained by the implicit assumption that all knowledge about the situation of the firm and its tasks is, or should be, available only to the head of the firm. Management, often visualized as the complex hierarchy familiar in the organization charts, operates a simple control system, with information flowing up through a succession of filters, and decisions and instructions flowing downwards though a succession of amplifiers.

Organic systems are adapted to unstable conditions, when problems and requirements for action arise which cannot be broken down and distributed among specialist roles within a clearly defined hierarchy. Individuals have to perform their special tasks in the light of their knowledge of the tasks of the firm as a whole. Jobs lose much of their formal definition in terms of methods, duties, and powers, which have to be redefined continually by interaction with others participating in a task. Interaction runs laterally as much as vertically. Communication between people of different ranks tends to resemble lateral consultation rather than vertical command. Omniscience can no longer be imputed to the head of the concern.

Grouping of activities

A second aspect of the configuration dimension is the way activities are grouped. When organizations are involved in the production of two or more products or services, management has to choose whether to group activities around each organizational function, around each product or service, or some combination of the two. In the first of these possibilities, the organization is structured around the main departmental functions of the business: research and development, production, sales and marketing, accounts and finance, etc., with each department handling the complete range of the firm's products or services. The alternative is for each product to have its own range of departments, headed by a product manager. Each arrangement has its costs and benefits, discussed in the next section, and an increasingly popular organizational form is that of the matrix, which attempts to obtain the benefits of both functional and product organization while minimizing the costs. In this organizational form there are both functional department heads and product heads, each providing leadership in their own area, with individuals working on particular products or services being responsible to both managers, to the former for the technical content of their work and to the latter for the progress and co-ordination of the provision of the product or service.

The question of functional, product or matrix form of organization is one which has to be addressed at both plant and enterprise levels. It is at enterprise level, however, that the decisions have greatest impact, because they determine the overall shape of the organization. It is also at this level that the terminology is most developed. Enterprises which are organized around the main departments are known as functional organizations and are sometimes referred to as 'U' form in type, while those which are divided into divisions, defined either by product or geography, are known as 'M'

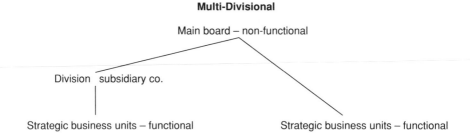

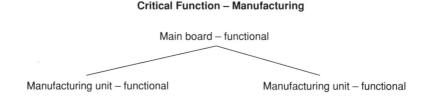

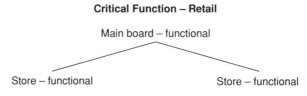

Figure 2.1 Types of organization structure

form organizations (see Williamson, 1975, for further details, see also figure 2.1 for examples).

In terms of practice, although there has been considerable decentralization in recent years, especially in the nationalized industries, such as British Rail and the Post Office which have been divided into sectors or divisions, in the public sector most organizations have been of the functional type. Personnel, for example, has usually been a critical function, and decision making about pay and conditions of employment has been highly centralized. In the private sector, the multi-divisional or 'M' form type is increasingly the dominant pattern and only a few multi-establishment enterprises, usually single business enterprises such as Marks and Spencer or Ford, are functionally organized. Thus, Hill and Pickering (1986: 29) found that, of 144 enterprises surveyed in the early 1980s, all of which were among the 500 largest UK companies, no less than 80 per cent were organized along divisional lines. Overall, some 38 per cent were divided on the basis of product divisions and nearly 10 per cent on the basis of geographical divisions. Furthermore, 20 per cent had a mixture of product and geographical divisions and almost 12 per cent had a mixture of product and international divisions.

Approaches to Organization Theory

Our understanding of organizations has not progressed smoothly nor has knowledge developed in a cumulative fashion. Indeed, the current state of knowledge is still characterized by lively debates about the most fruitful and insightful ways of understanding organizational processes and the development of organizational structures. This is for at least two reasons. One is to do with the *purposes* of organization. The other is to do with its *nature*. In our discussion so far, we have assumed that the primary purpose of an organization is to solve the co-ordination problems caused by the complexity of the tasks needed to produce goods or services. But an enterprise's organization serves at least two other purposes. People at work are social beings who are more or less motivated by, and committed to, their jobs. Organization is therefore not just about co-ordination but also about the generation of motivation and commitment. We discuss below the difficulty experienced by the National Coal Board when it changed its organizational structure to one which demotivated the miners.

Organization structures also embody power relations. Enterprises are likely to contain within them, or be controlled by, particular interest groups with particular objectives. Organization structures may therefore also, to some extent, reflect the desire by particular interest groups to exercise power and control over others. An obvious example is the power exercised by managers on behalf of shareholders over employees in pursuit of maximum profits. We discuss below how organization structures are shaped by this interest. We should not neglect other powerful vested interests, though. Craft occupations have usually tried to ensure that work is organized in such a way that managers' influence is limited and key decisions about work allocation, pace and quality are taken by members of the craft group. Members of the professions operate in the same way. Lawyers and doctors have always fought against managerial 'interference' in the organization of their work and enterprises dominated by professionals tend not to have managerial hierarchies.

There is also lively and contentious debate about the *nature* of organization. Although a business firm or a hospital has both a legal form and a physical manifestation in the form of its buildings and employees, the *organization* of that firm or hospital is less easily observed. It is not a 'thing' in the same way as are books or machine tools. It cannot be directly observed, handled, or manipulated. People try to illustrate it by means of organization charts but we all know that the way things are organized in any enterprise is much more complex than just the formal reporting relationships between people with different job titles. What an organization *is*, and how we can *know* about it, (sometimes referred to as the 'ontological' and 'epistemological' questions) are two of the most important, and contentious issues in organization theory (see, for example, Burrell and Morgan, 1979).

The approaches to organization theory to be discussed in this section owe their origins, in large measure, to differences in the emphasis each approach places on the three organizational purposes identified above and to these different ontological and epistomological assumptions. Contingency theory as well as agency theory and transactions cost analysis emphasize the co-ordination and decision-making functions of the organization to which writers in the 'scientific principles' tradition first drew attention. The sociotechnical systems approach focuses much more on motivational and organizational commitment aspects; while the so-called radical critique explores the extent to which organization structures reflect and, possibly, amplify coercive social relations in wider society. Most of these approaches do not concern themselves with epistemology and ontology. We discuss these approaches first, roughly in the date order in which they were developed, and then look at the debates surrounding the question of what is the nature of organization.

Scientific principles

Until about 25 years ago, any manager who attended a course in business administration would have been instructed in the one best way to organize the business. Several simple principles would have been enunciated, many of which had been borrowed from centuries of practice in the armed forces. In a paper entitled 'Scientific Principles and Organization', published in 1938, Urwick, a famed international management consultant, summarized the current set of beliefs in the form of eight principles. As late as 1957, Brech (1957: 374), a noted British exponent of this classical management school, quoted these eight principles 'because of their importance and long-standing acceptance'.

1 All organizations and each part of any undertaking should be the expression of a purpose, either explicit or implied – the 'principle of the objective'.
2 Formal authority and responsibility must be coterminous and coequal – the 'principle of correspondence'.
3 The responsibility of higher authority for the acts of its subordinates is absolute – the 'principle of responsibility'.
4 There must be a clear line of formal authority running from the top to the bottom of every organization – the 'scalar principle'.
5 No superior can supervise directly the work of more than five or, at the most, six subordinates whose work interlocks – the 'principle of the span of control'.
6 The work of every person in the organization should be confined as far as possible to the performance of a single leading function – the 'principle of specialization'.
7 The final object of all organization is smooth and effective co-ordination – the 'principle of co-ordination'.
8 Every position in every organization should be clearly prescribed in writing – the 'principle of definition'.

Contingency theory

The second approach, contingency theory, grew out of attempts in the late 1950s to test the validity of these 'scientific principles' by empirical research. One group of researchers, led by Woodward (1965), investigated the extent to which a sample of over 100 firms in the south-east of England has organization structures which accorded to these principles. They measured the organization structures and the business performance of all the firms in their sample and, despite over half the firms having organization structures which departed significantly from the eight classical principles of management, found no relationship between organization structure and performance. Had Woodward and her researchers given up at this point, organization theory might well have disappeared off the business school agenda, but persistent analysis of the data led to the discovery that use and non-use of the eight classical principles were not randomly distributed, but were associated with the type of technology used in each firm. The researchers went further. Having established what kind of structure a firm with a particular technology was likely to have, they then measured the extent to which the structure fitted the technology, and how well that firm performed. Their results showed that firms which had adopted a structure appropriate to their production technology performed on average better than those with an inappropriate structure.

We have already referred to Burns and Stalker's study. They were not teachers of management, but were familiar with the precepts of classical management theory. They were unsurprised to discover that one of the plants in their study, a rayon mill, was organized in this manner, but within the second plant surveyed, an engineering concern, they found that positions and functions in the management hierarchy were ill-defined and this was the deliberate policy of the head of the concern. Although there were considerable feelings of insecurity and stress among individuals in the organization, to the extent that cliques and cabals had formed and people squandered much energy in internal politics, the firm was nevertheless a commercial and technical success. The researchers wondered if the firm's success would have been even greater if they had sorted out the organization structure and reduced the level of stress and anxiety, or, conversely, might the insecurity, stress, and anxiety be the mainspring of the management system and the cause of the success? The questions became the focus of a series of further investigations into nearly 20 other firms which led Burns and Stalker to their conclusions about mechanistics and organic types of organizational structure, the former being akin to Urwick's eight principles.

The importance of Burns and Stalker's research findings has been twofold. First, they set out a clear alternative to the classical management theorists' prescription for the structure of an organization. This finding, in conjunction with Woodward's results, put paid to the idea that there was 'one best way' to organize an enterprise, and led to the development of 'contingency' theory, the approach which suggests that the structure of organization most appropriate to a particular enterprise is contingent upon a number of features of that enterprise. Secondly, Burns and Stalker, along with Woodward, suggested that the rate of environmental change – in particular the rate of change in the technological basis of production and in the market situation – was the crucial contingent factor in determining what form of organization is most appropriate.

The most useful outcome of contingency theory has not been a set of measuring instruments and precise predictions about specific structural features for a particular task, its size and environmental attributes, however, but a conceptual and analytical framework which can be used by those involved in organizational design to aid them in their own analyses.

One of the most helpful formulations of the general findings of contingency theory is by Galbraith, who focuses on the information-processing function of organization. To the extent that organization exists to process information, 'uncertainty is the core concept upon which the organization design frameworks are based' (Galbraith, 1977: 36–7). 'Uncertainty' he defines as 'the difference between the amount of information required to perform the task and the amount of information already possessed by the organization'. The strength of the approach is that it captures within this general formulation of uncertainty the various attempts to measure those attributes of technology, task and environment identified by earlier researchers as having a significant influence on organization structure.

Galbraith then goes on to pull together the various findings of the researchers within the contingency theory tradition about the variety of structural forms an organization can take. His general argument is that, as the level of uncertainty facing an organization increases, it must adopt increasingly sophisticated organization structures. The nature of these various options is described below but, before turning to this, it is worth mentioning the factors which, according to

Galbraith, are likely to increase the level of uncertainty faced by an organization because they are found in many enterprises in the early 1990s. He identifies three. One is the diversity of goals the organization is attempting to achieve. Such goals relate to the number of different products, different markets, different clients, etc. with which the organization is concerned. An increase in the number of goals will increase the amount of information which needs to be processed and hence increase the overall level of uncertainty. A second factor is the complexity of the division of labour in the organization: those with a simple division of labour need to process less information, other things being equal, than those with many different categories of personnel. Hence an increase in the division of labour will increase the level of uncertainty. Thirdly, there is the level of performance needed to remain viable in the organization's chosen domain. 'The higher the level of performance', says Galbraith, 'the larger the number of variables that must be considered simultaneously when allocating resources, setting priorities, or determining schedules' (ibid.: 37).

Galbraith's approach becomes particularly interesting and insightful when he describes possible organizational responses to rising uncertainty. He suggests that the organization faces a choice between two competing strategic responses. It can adopt the strategy of reducing the need to process more information, or it can increase the organization's capacity to process information. If management chooses the former strategy, which it may do by default, there are three possible tactical responses which can be made. One, which he labels environmental management, is to attempt to modify the environment rather than the organization's internal structure. If, for example, a new competitive challenge arises, the organization could, instead of improving its own performance, choose to mount an advertising campaign to attempt to convince its environment (i.e. its customers) that its own performance was adequate. Another environmental management technique might be to engage in vertical integration, by buying either the prior or subsequent stage in the production chain, thus containing or reducing the level of uncertainty which the core organization faces.

A second tactic, within the overall strategy of reducing the need for information processing, is to create slack resources. It is this particular tactic that is the one most likely to be adopted by default. If, for example, the demand facing the organization fluctuates fairly widely, one response would be to attempt to predict the fluctuations, or to be responsive to the fluctuations, so that production levels rose and fell in accordance with demand. This may require a great deal of information processing. The 'slack resource' option is to cope with the fluctuations by producing surplus stock in the periods of low demand and allowing a backlog of orders to build up during peak demand. Another way of coping with higher levels of uncertainty by the use of slack resources would be to reduce the level of performance. Galbraith cites the example of the aircraft company engaging in wing design. Under pressure, the company could increase the amount of time or man-hours scheduled to do the design, or increase the weight of the wing. 'In each case more resources would be consumed. These additional resources are called slack resources' (Galbraith, 1977: 50).

Of course, each of these tactics incurs cost. To advertise heavily, or to buy up other companies in the production chain, is expensive, and an even greater expense may be incurred by postponing the day when the relatively poor performance is found out and the competition puts the poorly performing company out of business. Using slack resources costs money too. Goods built for stock incur interest charges. Extra man-hours scheduled to design the wing add to labour costs. Using backlogs of work and waiting lists as a substitute for market intelligence or flexible production schedules may lose orders to competitors, perhaps for ever. The question for the organization designer is whether these costs are greater or smaller than those incurred by creating and maintaining a more sophisticated organization capable of processing the information needed to avoid using these other tactics.

The third tactic within the strategy of reducing the need for information processing is that of creating self-contained task units. This organizational response was adopted recently by a Swedish pump manufacturer. For very many years the company had dominated world markets for a particular type of pump, producing a wide range of specifications and sizes of this one specific product. Recently, however, the Japanese had entered the market and were beginning to gain a considerable share of it. They were competing keenly with the Swedish company on both price and delivery date of the pumps which were usually made to customer order. Up to this time, the company had been organized on traditional functional lines – sales, design, production and accounting, and, within production, a single machine shop, assembly shop and testing shop. This structure made efficient use of both machinery and the specialized skills of the sales force, the designers, the accountants and other specialists but, with very many varieties of pump going through the one system, co-ordination between the functions over one order was cumbersome and the lead time between receipt of an order and delivery to the customer was lengthy. The Swedish company responded to the Japanese challenge by setting up a self-contained task unit, or 'factory within a factory', to make the middle-size range pumps which constituted the bulk of the company's production. Thus, when enquiries came in for pumps of that particular size, their cost, design and production methods could be ascertained more speedily, and production control exercised more tightly. Though more expensive in terms of duplicated production facilities and slack resources in the form of extra staff, this self-contained task unit was quicker in getting the goods delivered to the customer.

The shift from function to product organization is also found at corporate level. Chandler's (1966) thorough historical study of the development of the largest US corporations documents how the majority of them eventually abandoned functional corporate structures in favour of product-divisional arrangements. As Chandler says:

> The inherent weakness in the centralized, functionally departmentalized operating company . . . became critical only when the administrative load on the senior executives increased to such an extent that they were unable to handle their entrepreneurial responsibilities efficiently. This situation arose when the operations of the enterprise became too complex and the problems of coordination, appraisal, and policy formulation too intricate for a small number of top officers to handle both long-run, entrepreneurial and short-run operational administrative activities. (1966: 332–3)

The response was to divisionalize the business, with duties officially split between divisional managers responsible for the short-run, operational activities of each business unit and the head office which would continue to handle the long-run, entrepreneurial responsibilities.

The alternative strategy to that of reducing the need for information processing is to increase the information-processing capacity of the organization. Galbraith (1977) suggests two tactics to achieve this: invest in vertical information systems and create lateral relations. The former tactic maintains the integrity of the managerial hierarchy and the principle of information flowing only through officially defined reporting relationships. It acknowledges that, as uncertainty increases and the flow of information passing along these channels becomes more intense, then the capacity of the individuals in the various authority positions becomes overloaded. One technique to reduce this overload is to appoint assistants to people in key positions to help them cope with the required increase in information processing. A second technique is to increase the number of clerical staff assisting those in the hierarchy. A third is the introduction of computer-based management information systems.

The creation of lateral relations is the most radical organizational change and one which many organizations have been adopting since the late 1970s. It goes wholly against classical management principles and for that reason was often greeted with incredulity when the idea was first introduced to managers or management students. One of the classical principles was that communication should go exclusively up and down the hierarchy, and that if two people in different departments, but at the same hierarchical level, wished to communicate, they should do this only via their superiors who in turn passed the information up the hierarchy. The advantage of maintaining this principle is that all those who might have relevant information about the problem, and in particular the senior managers in the enterprise who are assumed to have the broader picture, are kept informed about problems arising and decisions which are being made. The disadvantage, however, is that it slows down transmission of information and distorts it as it passes through so many stages. To give official sanction to direct communication between two lower level individuals or groups so that they can by-pass the hierarchy increases the speed and accuracy of communication, though it reduces the amount of control the more senior managers have over what is going on, and lessens their ability to contribute their own wider knowledge and possibly greater experience.

There are a variety of mechanisms available to encourage lateral relations. The simplest is to allow direct contact between two people who share a problem. If, however, a large volume of contact is needed between two subtasks, such as, to use the example of the Swedish pump factory, the designers and the production engineers, then a liaison role can be created to handle the inter-departmental contacts. Alternatively, if the volume of liaison work is large and likely to continue for some time, the organizational strategy of creating an integrating role might be used. As Galbraith (1977: 53) puts it, 'the function of the role is to represent the general manager in the inter-departmental decisions for a particular brand, product line,

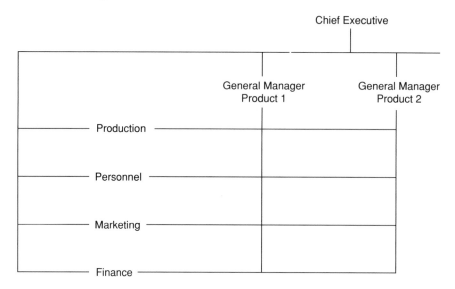

Figure 2.2 Matrix organization

project, country, or geographical unit. These roles are called product managers in commercial firms, project managers in aerospace, and unit managers in hospitals.' Another mechanism, particularly useful if several departments are involved and the need for intense lateral communications is likely to be only short term (for example, when a new product is to be launched), is to set up a task-force or team, comprising members from the departments involved either on a part-time or a full-time basis. Finally, a very common mechanism used to maintain lateral relations is the use of meetings, either on a scheduled and formal, or *ad hoc* and informal, basis. Though such meetings may often be a substitute for action, it may be that, as in Burns and Stalker's 'organic' organizations which created insecurity and anxiety in their members but also had a high performance, the extensive use of 'meetings, bloody meetings' actually increases efficiency.

The ultimate in complexity is the matrix organization which attempts to achieve the advantages of the functional and the product forms without incurring the full disadvantages of either. As figure 2.2 shows, the matrix is made up of two superimposed forms of organization: the functional organization and a system of product or project management.

Every individual in the organization is responsible to a functional manager for the technical aspects of the work and to a product or project manager for the way in which the task in hand is co-ordinated with other tasks relating to the same product or project. To return yet again to the pump factory, had they chosen to adopt a matrix organization, they would have retained their existing functional organization and management, but superimposed product managers for each of the main ranges of pump. A designer would be responsible both to the chief designer for the way in which the design office ran, for overall standards in design and for information and encouragement about developments in pump technology, and, to the product manager for the medium-range pumps, for scheduling the work, for finding out information about particular cost and quality standards to be worked to, and for liaison with the production facilities as the pump went into production.

A rapidly increasing number of companies in the UK are introducing some form of matrix organization. As production technologies have become increasingly complex and automated, as products themselves have become more sophisticated, and as markets have become increasingly competitive in both price and non-price terms, the level of uncertainty facing many enterprises has risen and there is, consequently, a need to process much more information. Moving to a matrix form of organization has been a common response to this, though in many cases the change has needed much preparation, staff training, and careful induction. In the last few years this trend to matrix organization has accelerated as a result of the highly influential MIT and Harvard studies of the world automobile industry (Womack, 1989; Clark and Fujimoto, 1991). These studies demonstrated how very much quicker and more efficient were the Japanese than the Western car producers at bringing out new models. They identified one major cause of this to be the use by the Japanese companies of what they termed 'heavyweight product managers' or 'project execution teams' (Clark and Fujimoto, 1991: 254). These are alternative words for overlay and secondment forms of matrix organization (Knight, 1977). Virtually all the major Western car producers and many of their suppliers have been attempting to shift their organizational arrangements towards this Japanese model and many other firms have been influenced by these studies.

Socio-technical systems theory

Organizations are not only concerned with the processing of information in order to exercise efficient co-ordination, it also serves other functions. People are not just 'canny calculators', they have social and other needs which they may expect the organization to meet. There has been an important strand in the development of organization theory which has been concerned with this particular issue. If the developments sketched out above had their genesis in classical management theory, then the strand to be discussed now has its roots in the work of Mayo and the 'human relations' approach arising from this research. The Hawthorne experiments, to which Mayo was consultant, must be familiar to every management student. In these studies (Roethlisberger and Dickson, 1939), a group of female workers engaged in electrical wiring work was subjected to a series of changes in their environment, such as the level of lighting, length of rest breaks, and length of working day, and the effect on their level of output was carefully monitored. With every environmental change, output went up and, more surprisingly, continued to rise even when all environmental conditions were returned to their original level. Mayo's conclusion was that what was important to the women in the study was not the external conditions of their working environment, but their social relationship with each other, with their supervisor, and with the researchers. Because they had been fully involved in the design and setting up of the research, the women had become committed to its objective – that of working out ways of achieving higher productivity – and had responded by producing that higher productivity. The implication was that organizations should be designed not just to be efficient processors of information, but to enable strong positive social relations to be formed within work groups, and between work groups and management. In this way it was hoped that a strong positive commitment to the firm and norms of high productivity would be established. Eventually, this approach came to be systematized in the form of socio-technical systems theory.

The socio-technical systems approach resulted from the research of a team from the Tavistock Institute in London into the organization of coal-mining (Trist et al., 1963). Concerned that levels of productivity with new mining machinery were much lower than expected, the National Coal Board called in the Tavistock researchers to advise immediately following the nationalization of the mines at the end of the Second World War. As a result of intensive research in several pits, the researchers concluded that the form of work organization adopted when the new technology was introduced had disrupted the previous pattern of social relations. In non-mechanized pits, small groups of miners worked together, each worker having a range of skills, each group sharing a common paynote. The groups were self-selecting and worked out for themselves who did what job. With the introduction of face conveyors and the longwall method of coal abstraction, the size of work groups increased from half a dozen to up to 50. Moreover, an elaborate division of labour was involved, with each worker doing a specialized and fragmented task that required less skill.

There were several problems with this arrangement. The previous small groups required no managerial co-ordination and hence there was no tradition of middle management within the organization to co-ordinate these very large groups of workers with their fragmented jobs. Even if the organization had the structure to provide this co-ordination, it is likely that the miners, having for so many years operated in a highly autonomous way, would have resisted co-ordination and control by a managerial hierarchy. Moreover, underground conditions made managerial control from a distance difficult to exercise. Thirdly, the payment system was now inappropriate for the new method of working. Previously each small group had worked almost on a subcontract basis, being paid for each ton of coal removed. Attempts to manage the new large groups on this subcontract basis ran into difficulty because it involved a great deal of time in haggling over prices for specific tasks, and, with no common denominator for fixing rates, different criteria were used for measuring performance – tonnage, yardage, cubic measures, number of operations completed, and so on – and contradictory interests developed.

It was in response to this that the Tavistock researchers developed their approach. As Trist and his colleagues define it:

> the concept of a socio-technical system arose from the consideration that any production system requires both a technological organization – equipment and process layout – and a work organization relating to each other those who carry out the necessary tasks. The technological demands place limits on the type of work organization possible, but a work organization has social and psychological properties of its own that are independent of technology. (1963: 6)

Using this perspective the research team suggested a different organization structure, known as the composite longwall method of working, which was based on a self-selected group of men who allocated themselves to tasks and shifts and received a comprehensive payment on a common note. This form of work organization attempted to reintroduce an element of responsible autonomy and subcontracting into the organization structure.

The general principle emerging from socio-technical systems theory, therefore, is that organization structure has to meet social and psychological needs of various kinds, in addition to providing efficient channels of communication and authority. These needs, as well as the level of uncertainty posed by the size, technology, and environment of the firm, must be considered by the organizational designer. To put this another way, structures of organization may be required which are not optimal for decision making alone: the needs of the system as a whole must be optimized. Though this is an important insight into the functions of organization structure, it is only a partial view and in a later section of this chapter the limits to this view are challenged.

Agency theory and transaction cost analysis

Organization theory has, until recently, nearly always taken for granted the existence of organization and concerned itself only with the particular structure adopted. It has not been concerned with attempting to explain the circumstances under which organizations might be set up or dismantled. This particular question has become a central issue and is important for two reasons. First, there have been interesting theoretical developments within industrial economics and organization theory which enable intelligent questions to be posed and plausible answers to be given about the determinants of organizational boundaries. Second, the question has become of great practical interest with the growth of a great deal of subcontract work, and large corporations deliberately shrinking by selling off parts of their enterprise and out-sourcing the supply of components, assemblies and services.

It is the economists who have paid most attention to this type of question and the concept that is central to their analysis is that of the transaction. Organizational life is conceptualized as individuals and groups conducting transactions with each other and the question is whether it is more efficient to conduct a transaction by means of making a contract in the market-place (buying and selling) or by internalizing the transaction and handling it by means of a managerial hierarchy. Economists assume that all transactions between any two human beings will be conducted by means of market mechanisms unless there is some good reason for not doing so. The existence of large-scale hierarchical organizations, when apparently many of the transactions conducted within the enterprise could instead have been conducted in the market-place, is a puzzle for the profession.

One attempt to solve this puzzle (Alchian and Demsetz, 1972) is agency theory. In this model, there is a principal–agent relationship, in which the one party (the principal) delegates work to another party (the agent) who performs the work. The principal–agent arrangement may come about when, for a specific task, there is an advantage in co-operative effort or teams. If everyone in the team was happy with an equal share of the compensation, and all team members trusted each other to put in a similar level of effort or were not very concerned about minor degrees of free-riding, there would be no problem for the economist. However, because in many cases these assumptions do not hold, there is a problem about metering effort and rewarding performance fairly. If a group of producers acting as a team was left to its own devices then, suggest the agency theorists, they would either spend a great deal of time attempting to monitor each other's performance and negotiating levels of compensation for each other or, worse still, the stresses caused by the difficulties of metering would either split the group or prevent the team from forming in the first place. Hence, they argue, the principal–agent arrangement comes into being with the principal doing the metering and rewarding. One major question addressed by agency theory has been that of what type of relationship might exist between the principal and agent, and what factors might determine the optimal contract which might govern that relationship. This question covers the employment relationship itself, the vertical integration of relationships within firms between divisions engaged in processes at various points down the chain of production, and relations between organizations.

A fascinating example of work organization which illustrates perfectly the issues identified by agency theory was that adopted in the 1993 British Steel Challenge round-the-world race. The race was between ten identical yachts, each with 13 crew and a skipper. But unlike the conventional command structure of a ship the crew members were the employers and the skipper an employee. The crew members each paid nearly £15,000 to be part of the race, the skippers were selected by a small management company set up to run the race and had their salaries paid out the crew members' subvention. The skippers had no say in choosing their crew and had virtually no possibility of disposing of people they did not take to. Their job was to co-ordinate the activities of the crew, to prevent shirking, and (of course) to bring their particular expertise to bear in seamanship. They, the principals, were paid by their team, the agents, to be controllers, team-builders and motivators (*Financial Times*, 22 May 1993).

Transaction cost analysis, developed primarily by Williamson (1975), takes the economists' perspective on organization a great deal further, and with more sensitivity to social behaviour. At the core of Williamson's analysis are the concepts of complexity, uncertainty, bounded rationality, small numbers, opportunism and 'information impactedness'. This last concept is a term coined by Williamson to describe a situation in which the one party to the transaction has less information relevant to the transaction than the other, and cannot obtain more information without incurring costs. Like the agency theorists, Williamson assumes that markets will be the preferred form of conducting transactions unless there are reasons why they should fail. They do fail, he suggests, when the transactions to be conducted involve high levels of complexity or uncertainty and when there are only small numbers capable of conducting the transaction either as buyers or sellers. His argument is that when there is a high level of complexity or uncertainty then, because of the 'bounded rationality' condition (Simon, 1957), it will be difficult, expensive, or even impossible for each side of the transaction to have full knowledge of all the relevant details of that transaction. If, for example, a car assembler is planning a new car model and is considering buying in, rather than making, the gearboxes, it may attempt to transact with a gearbox manufacturer to set up a contract for supply. But, because of the complexity of the product and the production process, and because of 'bounded rationality', the car assembler may not know whether the supplier has the capability to produce the gearbox in sufficient quantities by the launch date.

The supplier may be tempted to behave opportunistically (defined by Williamson as 'self-interest seeking with guile') and promise delivery by launch date, even if he knows this is impossible. He can do this, however, only if the 'small numbers condition' holds. Although this condition may not hold at the point when the assembler is setting up the contract (as there may be other potential gearbox suppliers), it does by the time delivery of the goods is expected, because at that stage only the contracted supplier is near to being able to supply, and the assembler cannot switch suppliers at this late stage. Thus the supplier will be tempted to win the contract by acting opportunistically and, because of complexity, uncertainty and bounded rationality, the assembler will not know of this. This is information impactedness and leads, suggests Williamson, to market failure. A firm will be unwilling to take this risk and, other things being equal, will therefore make rather than buy-in the product. Of course 'other things' are never equal and in many cases some kind of intermediate arrangement, half-way between managerial hierarchy and a spot-contract in the market-place, is used. One example of this is termed long-term relational contracting. A well-known use of this is by Marks and Spencer in its relation with its suppliers. It is also increasingly used in the car industry between assemblers and their suppliers, for example for the supply of gearboxes in the example above.

We have given examples of vertical integration but transaction cost analysis, and agency theory, is also used to analyse the employment relationship and other inter-organizational relationships. The relevance of the issues dealt with by these theories is illustrated by current practice in many private sector enterprises of out-sourcing (e.g. BP's decision to contract-out its accounting function) and the introduction of market-type arrangements to the public sector (e.g. the use purchaser-provider arrangements in the National Health Service and compulsory competitive tendering in local government). For a more detailed treatment of this economic approach to explaining organization structure, see Douma and Schreuder (1991).

The radical critique of organization theory

Thus far the chapter has dealt with explanations that rest on the assumption that organizational structures reflect, either consciously or unconsciously, the preferences and interests of management whose objectives are to design organizations which optimize decision making, co-ordination, and the commitment of organizational members. This core assumption within both contingency and socio-technical systems theory leaves them open to criticism on at least two counts – on the adequacy of their theoretical basis and on the quality of advice they give to management.

With regard to theoretical adequacy, sociological critiques of conventional organization theory have often drawn attention to one of its most questionable assumptions, namely that there is a common goal to which all organizational members are committed, and that the primary organizational problem is merely that of ensuring that appropriate information gets to individuals so that, as people of goodwill, they can make an appropriate response. Williamson's transaction cost analysis replaces this assumption with the alternative that people behave opportunistically, but even his approach has been criticized for neglecting wider issues of power and social relations (Perrow, 1981; Francis, 1983). The sociological critique of these assumptions points out that organizations are made up of individuals and groups who have their own goals and purposes, and who often attempt to subvert formal organizational goals in order to gain their own ends. Organizational structure is partly the result of an attempt by one powerful group (e.g. management) to impose structures on others (various groups of workers) in order to exercise tight control over them and to ensure that activities are co-ordinated in a way that efficiently meets the goals of the more powerful.

A persuasive example of this radical critique is developed by Marglin (1974) in a paper provocatively titled 'What Do Bosses Do?'. His thesis is that factory production and managerial hierarchies came into being at the time of the Industrial Revolution in Britain, not because of developments in spinning and weaving technology, but because they enabled merchants and capitalists to force employees to work harder than they preferred and thus make more profit for the entrepreneur. Prior to industrialization, most spinning and weaving was done by independent contractors working on a putting-out basis. This arrangement posed several problems for the merchants. They found it difficult to prevent the spinners and weavers from cheating them and they could not use the price mechanisms to raise output because most craftsmen had a strong preference for leisure. Payment was on a piece-work system and, if the price per unit was raised, the craftsmen would work less.

According to Marglin, the merchants set up factories for these and not for technological reasons. His argument is given weight by the historical evidence; many early factories used identical equipment to that found in the cottage-based industry. Factory workers were offered the all-or-nothing choice of a 14-hour day, six-day week and many merchants did not recruit skilled workers to their factories, relying instead on unskilled labour provided by women and children from the workhouses. (For a fuller description see Francis, 1986.)

This line of argument has several implications for discussions about the structure of organization. First, it poses a different explanation from agency theory or transactions cost analysis for the switch from market to hierarchy. If the switch was made because of the power and preferences of the merchants, as Marglin suggests, rather than because hierarchy was more efficient than market, as agency theory or transaction cost analysis would suggest, then the question arises about the extent to which hierarchies today have resulted from the exercise of power in a similar way. The implication of Marglin's analysis is that there is far more opportunity for work to be done by independent contractors than the current situation permits. Second, it poses a different explanation for the complexity of organizational structure. Marglin argues that the merchants and capitalists, in order to provide for themselves a niche in the labour process, deliberately fragmented work and instituted managerial co-ordination rather than direct co-ordination between works in order to safeguard their own role. Again, to the extent that this process still operates, it implies that much work could be organized in a more co-operative rather than managerially directed manner with no loss of efficiency.

Elements of this argument are contained within the more widely known writing of Braverman (1974). His argument is that technology has developed within the kind of process described above, and so the technology itself embodies the interests of capital. Technologies could have been developed which were suitable for use by skilled spinners, weavers, and other home-workers in small-scale production. However, there was no market for this kind of technology, partly because such people did not express a demand for it and partly because they would not have had the capital to buy it. Instead, the demand was for technology suitable for large-scale factory production and this was what was developed. This makes it difficult now to envisage how things could be done in any other way. Moreover, the technology was developed to fit in with the capitalists' need to maintain their niche in the labour process and so, argues Braverman, it was designed deliberately to deskill labour. With labour deskilled by the technology, more extensive managerial hierarchies had to be developed. Indeed, the process goes further. As a result of fragmenting labour and instituting managerial control at the expense of work-group control, informal social controls in the workplace broke down and the hierarchy had to be elaborated still further to exercise control and ensure higher levels of effort.

The radical critique also invites questions about the quality of advice offered to management within conventional theories of organizational structure. Such advice is limited, the critique would suggest, because it neglects consideration of many of the issues posed above and, worse still, encourages management to design structures which build in inherent conflicts. Sophisticated management may already be aware of these deficiencies, but even they may learn something from Marglin and Braverman.

What is organization?

Throughout this chapter we have only used the word organization in the singular. This is to avoid the common confusion of equating organization with the enterprise itself. A large multinational corporation, a university and a hospital are all enterprises concerned with the delivery of various goods and services – for example, oil, knowledge and health. Each possesses an organization which performs the functions we have identified in the preceding sections. But the organization is not the enterprise. So what is the organization? It is an abstraction and not a concrete reality. This is a book about personnel management, and though you might meet a personnel manager in a firm, and the manager has a concrete reality, you will never be introduced to the firm's personnel management. That is an abstraction. It is something that happens in the firm. In the same way, one cannot directly observe a firm's organization, though one may see it operate in practice. The problem with abstractions is how to represent or model them. Moreover, different people prefer different types of representation depending on their own view of the world. For example, some people prefer to take the view that the social world is rather similar to the physical world and that they have a clear objective reality that can be defined, measured, and manipulated on the basis of clear cause-and-effect theories. Classical management theorists in the tradition of Urwick take this view. Organizations are hierarchies and if the span of control is too big one can appoint some more managers. Pugh and the Aston studies are also in this tradition as, to an extent, is all contingency theory. If an enterprise is facing rising uncertainty and turbulence then it can be re-engineered so that it adopts a more organic organizational structure.

Others prefer the view that the social world is to a large extent what we make of it. Between us we construct a set of meanings and our social world comprises these. Within an enterprise, people may, or may not, hold the same view about what it means to be a manager, to exercise authority, to be accountable, to co-operate. It is the meanings that matter. The very concept of authority is socially constructed. It does not exist out there, independent of ourselves, whereas in the physical world a tree exists independently of any definition of what a tree is, or what the notion of a 'tree' might mean. Within this view of the world, students of organization have concentrated much more on the symbolic significance of what goes on within enterprises (e.g. Alvesson and Berg, 1992; Gagliardi, 1990) and written articles with such intriguing titles as 'The Meaning of Management and the Management of Meaning' (Legge and Gowler, 1983). It is this approach which has given rise to the extended use of metaphors to help us understand organizations. Morgan (1986), for example, suggests that we can think of organizations as machines, organisms, brains, cultures, political systems, psychic prisons, flux and transformation, or instruments of domination.

The divide is, in philosophical terms, between those who take a realist view of the world against those who are nominalists and between those who are for or against positivism (Burrell and Morgan, 1979: 3). The nominalism v. realism divide is over the ontological question – is it useful to think of organizations as something out there, or to think of them only as mental constructs? The divide over positivism is the epistemological question – is it useful to try to create operational definitions of organizational features and measure them, or to share insights and experiences, perhaps in the form of metaphors, which help us understand them better? These are divisions arising from major debates within philosophy and science and will never be resolved. It is better to view them as giving rise to different perspectives about organization, each of which is of value and aids our understanding.

Organizational Structures in the Future

We might conclude this chapter by asking whether there is a future for organization structure. All the management 'gurus', and many organization theory scholars, are suggesting that the enterprise of the future will be, if not completely unstructured, very loosely organized. It will be flexible, entrepreneurial, innovative, boundaryless, and a 'learning organization'. Sometimes the phrase 'post-modern' is used to describe such an organization (Clegg, 1990). The days of command-and-control machine bureaucracies are numbered, many claim.

One strong pressure for this development has been the rise in the fixed costs of labour, due to rising labour cost rates and, in some countries, greater employee protection through government legislation. Companies are therefore concerned to minimize the number of direct long-term employees. Ways of doing this include the use of primary and secondary labour markets within the firm; employment of people on short-term contracts; use of agency staff; giving contracts to self-employed individuals (who may perform the work at home); subcontracting work to small firms; and increasing the amount of out-sourcing (Atkinson, 1984). This results in the 'core–periphery' model organization structure, which is discussed in more detail in chapters 5 and 6. Each of these tactics increases the flexibility of the core firm to adjust labour utilization and output in response to market fluctuations.

Another pressure on firms to adopt the 'core–periphery' structure may come from technological developments. For example, in some high-technology industries tasks are so complex that there is much use of self-contained task units. It is possible to co-ordinate such task units by managerial hierarchy, but it may be more efficient to do so through the market-place, for example, by treating its units as subcontractors or independent suppliers from whom the core firm out-sources components or services. Of course, it may not be the core firm which initiates these organizational changes. Technological developments may bring into the market-place independent suppliers who pose so severe a competitive challenge to the core firm's own internal source of supply that it is forced to switch to out-sourcing.

Another technological trigger is the increased availability of information technology. Transaction cost analysis suggests that, if information technology provides all parties to the transaction with adequate information, the chances of 'information impactedness' and 'opportunism' occurring are much reduced, and the market recovers its advantage over hierarchy as the preferred method of handling the transaction. One consequence is a fragmentation (rather than 'peripheralization') of organizations as various units are uncoupled from the managerial hierarchy to trade with each other, and the so-called 'boundaryless' organization (Academy of Management, 1993) begins to emerge.

Not only are there pressures on organizations to become more flexible and boundaryless, they must also be increasingly capable of handling rapid and effective product and process innovations. This pressure is partly stimulated by technological developments and partly by Japanese competition. Peters' two most recent books, *Thriving on Chaos* (1987) and *Liberation Management* (1992), vigorously pursue this theme as does Rosabeth Moss Kanter's work (1984; 1989; 1992). The idea of the entrepreneurial organization has been developed by Pinchot (1985) and that of the learning organization by Senge (1990). Each of these approaches enhances the human resource management approach discussed in chapter 1. They suggest a series of organizational factors which encourage innovation, learning and entrepreneurship, almost all of which have been prefigured in Burns and Stalker's notion of organic organization. Much of the value of these later studies is that they provide case studies of large modern enterprises which have attempted to make the transition from command-and-control bureaucracies to more complex organic forms of organization.

From this, one can forecast that organizations of the future will take many forms. There will doubtless continue to be monolithic organizations, mechanistically structured, producing standard goods for stable markets, in which cost-minimization through economies of scale and strict management control will be the key criteria for success. But there is likely to be a range of other organizational types, linked together in a wide variety of different ways through a combination of contractual and managerial arrangements. Some of these, especially those carrying out core tasks and using specialist staff, will be organized for innovation, using structures based on the Peters, Pinchot, and Kanter models of what is required for intrapreneurship. In these, management will exercise control through encouraging shared values and a participative management style. Other organizations, performing the more mundane 'peripheral' tasks, may be little changed from today.

It remains to be seen how the numerical balance will shift between organizations of different types, and whether flexible, innovation-centred organizations will have as benign a structure as some commentators now predict. In any event, organizational structures do not simply emerge in response to technological and market changes. They are, as has been indicated in this chapter, designed by individuals and groups with particular objectives in mind, and their implementation is a matter of negotiation, formal or informal. Corporate and line management, the personnel function, trade unions and organizational members in general will all play important roles in shaping the organization of the future and their respective influence and preferences will be crucial. The task of the organization theorist is not to predict, but to provide an analytical framework which can assist each of these groups to shape their preferences in an intelligent manner.

Bibliography

Academy of Management. 1993. 'Managing the Boundaryless Organization', theme of the annual conference.

Alchian, A. A. and Demsetz, H. 1972. 'Production, Information Costs, and Economic Organization'. *American Economic Review*, 62, 777–95.

Aldrich, H. E. 1979. *Organizations and Environments*. Englewood Cliffs, NJ: Prentice Hall.

Alvesson, Mats and Berg, Per Olof. 1992. *Corporate Culture and Organizational Symbolism*. Berlin: Walter de Gruyter.

Atkinson, J. 1984. 'Manpower Strategies for Flexible Organizations'. *Personnel Management*, August, 28–31.

Braverman, H. 1974. *Labor and Monopoly Capital: The Degradation of Work in the Twentieth Century*. New York: Monthly Review Press.

Brech, E. F. L. 1957. *Organization: The Framework of Management*. London: Longman.

Burns, T. and Stalker, G. M. 1966. *The Management of Innovation*, 2nd edn. London: Tavistock.

Burrell, Gibson and Morgan, Gareth. 1979. *Sociological Paradigms and Organisational Analysis*. London: Heinemann.

Chandler, A. D. 1966. *Strategy and Structure*. New York: Doubleday.

Child, J. 1973. 'Strategies of Control and Organizational Behavior'. *Administrative Science Quarterly*, 18, March, 1–17.

Clark, Kim B. and Fujimoto, Takahiro. 1991. *Product Development Performance: Strategy, Organization and Management in the World Auto Industry*. Boston, MA: Harvard Business School Press.

Clegg, Stewart R. (1990) *Modern Organizations: Organization Studies in the Postmodern World*. London: Sage.

Douma, Sytse and Schreuder, Hein. 1991. *Economic Approaches to Organizations*. Hemel Hempstead: Prentice Hall.

Francis, A. 1983. 'Markets and Hierarchies: Efficiency or Domination?'. In Francis, A., Turk, J. and Willman, P. (eds) *Power, Efficiency and Institutions*. London: Heinemann, 105–16.

Francis, Arthur. 1986. *New Technology at Work*. Oxford: Clarendon Press.

Financial Times. 1993. 'A Very Polite Middle-Class Mutiny at Sea'. Section II, I, 22 May 1993.

Gagliardi, Pasquale (ed.) 1990. *Symbols and Artifacts: Views of the Corporate Landscape*. Berlin: Walter de Gruyter.

Galbraith, J. 1977. *Organization Design*. Reading, MA: Addison-Wesley.

Goold, M. and Campbell, A. 1987. *Strategies and Styles: The Role of the Centre in Managing Diversified Corporations*. Oxford: Blackwell.

Hill, C. W. L. and Pickering, J. F. 1986. 'Divisionalization, Decentralization and Performance of Large UK Companies'. *Journal of Management Studies*, 23, January, 26–50.

Kanter, R. M. 1984. *The Change Masters: Corporate Entrepreneurs at Work*. London: Allen & Unwin.

Kanter, R. M. 1989. *When Giants Learn to Dance: Mastering the Challenges of Strategy, Management and Careers*. London: Unwin.

Kanter, R. M., Stein, B. A. and Todd, J. D. (1992) *The Challenge of Organizational Change*. New York: The Free Press.

Knight, K. (ed.) 1977. *Matrix Management: A Cross-functional Approach to Organisation*. Farnborough: Gower.

Lawrence, P. R. and Lorsch, J. W. 1967. *Organization and Environment*. Cambridge, MA: Harvard University Press.

Legge, K. and Gowler, D. 1983. 'The Meaning of Management and the Management of Meaning'. In Earl, M. J. (ed.) *New Perspectives on Management*. Oxford: Oxford University Press.

Marglin, S. 1974. 'What Do Bosses Do? The Origins and Functions of Hierarchy in Capitalist Production'. In Gorz, A. (ed.) *The Division of Labour*. Brighton: Harvester Press, 13–54.

Morgan, Gareth, 1986. *Images of Organization*. California: Sage.

Perrow, C. 1970. *Organizational Analysis: A Sociological View*. Belmont, CA: Wadsworth.

Perrow, C. 1981. 'Markets, Hierarchies and Hegemony: A Critique of Chandler and Williamson'. In Van de Van, A. and Joyce, W. (eds), *Perspectives on Organizational Design and Behavior*. New York: John Wiley, 371–86, 403–4.

Peters, T. J. and Waterman, R. H. 1982. *In Search of Excellence*. New York: Harper & Row.

Peters, T. J. 1987. *Thriving on Chaos*. New York: Random House.

Peters, T. J. 1992. *Liberation Management*. London: Macmillan.

Pinchot, G. 1985. *Intrapreneuring: Why You Don't Have to Leave the Corporation to Become an Entrepreneur*. New York: Harper & Row.

Pugh, D., Hickson, D., Hinings, R. and Turner, C. 1968. 'Dimensions of Organizational Structure'. *Administrative Science Quarterly*, 13, June, 65–104.

Roethlisberger, F. J. and Dickson, W. J. 1939. *Management and the Worker*. Cambridge, MA: Harvard University Press.

Senge, P. M. (1990) *The Fifth Discipline: The Art and Practice of the Learning Organization*. New York: Doubleday.

Simon, H. A. 1957. *Administrative Behavior: A Study of Decision-Making Processes in Administrative Organization*. New York: Macmillan.

Thomson, J. 1967. *Organizations in Action*. New York: McGraw-Hill.

Trist, E. L., Higgin, C. W., Murray, H. and Pollock, A. M. 1963. *Organizational Choice*. London: Tavistock.

Weber, Max, 1947. *The Theory of Social and Economic Organization*. Translated by Parsons, T. and Henderson, A. M., with an introduction by T. Parsons. New York: Free Press.

Williamson, O. E. 1970. *Corporate Control and Business Behavior*. Englewood Cliffs, NJ: Prentice Hall.

Williamson, O. E. 1975. *Markets and Hierarchies: Analysis and Antitrust Implications*. New York: Free Press.

Womack, James P., Jones, Daniel T. and Roos, Daniel. 1990. *The Machine that Changed the World*. New York: Rawson Associates.

Woodward, J. 1965. *Industrial Organization: Theory and Practice*. London: Oxford University Press.

Woodward, J. (ed.) 1970. *Industrial Organization: Behaviour and Control*. London: Oxford University Press.

3

Principles and Practice in Work Design

David A. Buchanan

Approaches to the design of work systems have progressed through three broad phases during the twentieth century. The period from 1900 to 1950 was dominated by the 'scientific management' approach to work design, based on techniques of task fragmentation and emphasizing the clear division between manual or clerical work on the one hand and management responsibilities on the other. From 1950 to 1980 the 'quality of working life' (QWL) movement developed with a range of 'job enrichment', 'vertical loading' and 'autonomous group working' techniques as antidotes to scientific management. The QWL movement was particularly popular in the 1960s and 1970s. Since 1980, 'high performance work systems' techniques using team-based approaches to work and organizational design in so-called 'new design plants' have become increasingly popular. These methods extend the concept of the autonomous group, primarily to address competitive pressures by increasing organizational flexibility and responsiveness.

These dates are, of course, approximate. It is instructive to examine past practice, because these approaches are still in use, and because the reasoning behind contemporary thinking in this field lies partly in the known benefits and limitations of earlier approaches. This chapter will, however, argue that current approaches rely on different motives, and that their wider implications are potentially more radical. Early approaches to work design involved tinkering with individual jobs only and these techniques had limited effects. Broad-based organizational strategies are now necessary to develop and sustain the high levels of skill, commitment, performance and responsiveness fundamental to competitiveness and economic growth. The contemporary impact of work design techniques, set in this wider context, extends to organization structures, to employment policies, and to the role of management. It has therefore become increasingly unrealistic to distinguish between work design on the one hand and organizational design on the other. The former now typically implies the latter.

Organization structures are ultimately determined by the ways in which tasks and roles are designed and allocated. The needs of the organization, however, are not necessarily consistent with the needs of the individual job holder. Attempts to discover the elusive common ground for the simultaneous satisfaction of human and organizational goals through the judicious manipulation of job characteristics have been described as the search for 'person–environment fit' (Lawler, 1976: 225). The practice of work design assumes that such a fit can be found. Work design has been defined as 'specification of the contents, methods, and relationships in jobs in order to satisfy technological and organizational requirements as well as the social and personal requirements of the job holder' (Davis, 1966: 21).

The Traditional Approach: Scientific Management

The key figure in the development of traditional approaches to designing work was Taylor (1911). An engineer from Philadelphia who trained as a machinist, Taylor was appalled by the inefficiency of the industrial practices he witnessed and set out to demonstrate how managers and workers could benefit by adopting a more scientific approach. He felt that inefficiency was caused by 'systematic soldiering', the deliberate restriction of output by workers anxious to secure their jobs. Soldiering was easy because management control was weak, and because discretion over work methods was left to individual workers who, in Taylor's view, wasted time and effort with their inefficient working practices. Managers expected their employees to have appropriate skills for the work they were given, or to learn what to do from those around them. Notions of systematic job specifications, clear responsibilities, and training needs analysis were not appreciated. Taylor sought to change this.

Taylor argued that manual and mental work should be separated. Management should specialize in planning and organizing work; workers should specialize in doing it. Taylor saw this as a way of ensuring industrial harmony, as everyone would know exactly what was expected of them. He also saw advantages in making individuals specialize in activities in which they would then become expert.

His technique for designing manual jobs involved the following steps. First, decide the optimum degree of 'task fragmentation', breaking down complex operations into their simple component activities. Second, systematically determine the 'one best way' to perform each activity, designing tools and workplace layout to eliminate unnecessary movements. Finally, select and train employees to carry out the fragmented tasks – one employee being allocated to one task – in precisely the one best way, and reward them for above-average performance. The use of this approach on the high-speed, high-volume assembly line at Ford's Highland Park plant in America led to work cycles of one to two minutes, dictated by the pace of the machinery. This variant has come to be known as 'Fordism'.

Task fragmentation has a number of advantages: the approach made Ford the most productive car manufacturer in the world in the early decades of this century. Workers do not need to be given expensive and time-consuming training. Those who leave or who prove to be unreliable can be replaced quickly. Management is not dependent on potentially scarce skills and knowledge to guarantee the continuity of production. Specialization in one small activity can dramatically increase the speed with which it is carried out. Less skilled work is lower paid work. And it is easier to observe and to control workers carrying out simple fragmented tasks.

However, task fragmentation has clear drawbacks. The work is repetitive and boring. The contribution of the individual to the organization as a whole is comparatively meaningless. Monotony can lead to apathy, dissatisfaction and carelessness. The individual has little or no chance to develop the skills and knowledge that could lead to promotion or to better opportunities in another organization. Taylor's techniques lack any sustained attention to human needs other than those concerning money and rest. His approach to work design appeared to generate efficient ways of working, but instead created fragmented and dissatisfying jobs that were unlikely to contribute to employee skills, commitment or performance.

Despite the disadvantages, Fordism, Taylorism and scientific management have been more widely accepted and applied through the rest of this century than in Taylor's lifetime; he died in 1915. From a survey of 24 American firms around the middle of the century, Davis et al. (1955) found that the work design principles of maximum specialization and repetitiveness were still popular. In his influential critique of scientific management and the dehumanization of work Harry Braverman (1974) demonstrates how Taylor's approach has been extended to clerical and administrative work, creating 'office factories'. Recent analyses of Japanese car assembly methods, sometimes called 'Toyotism', also reveal many similarities with traditional Taylorism (Hammarstrom and Lansbury, 1991).

Modern techniques of work design have been developed and applied in the second half of this century as antidotes to Taylorism. The impact of these alternative techniques has not been as powerful or pervasive as the influence of scientific management on management practice. Why has Taylorism retained its popularity? There are perhaps two reasons. First, it is a plausible, easy and cheap set of techniques which appear to work well in some settings. Managers in Britain have generally preferred common-sense, practical ideas to more complex and sophisticated techniques, particularly those based on 'social science' ideas which are still widely regarded with suspicion and scepticism. Task specialization in assembly work can also reduce work in progress and assembly cycle times, can consume less space, and can simplify production scheduling and control. Such visible and measurable short-term gains may outweigh the uncertain and less quantifiable longer term costs and known disadvantages, which rely on 'soft' arguments about the nature of human attitudes to work.

A second explanation is that Taylor's approach to work design perpetuates the relative status and power of management. Unskilled individuals with no discretion over working methods and with little idea how their fragmented tasks contribute to the organization as a whole do not pose much of a threat to managerial influence and responsibility. Groups of employees who have discretion over the performance of meaningful sections of an organization's operations can be a greater threat to managerial legitimacy and prerogatives.

It is therefore wrong to dismiss scientific management methods as disused and outdated. Many organizations have departed from that approach and adopted the techniques discussed later in this chapter. But Taylor's ideas have become a central feature of the taken-for-granted organizational recipe that many managers still apply to the design and redesign of work without serious question or challenge.

Pressures for Change: The QWL Movement

Why should management have any interest in approaches to the design of work that depart from the simple and practical methods of Taylor's scientific management? Humanitarian considerations contribute to the justification of more sophisticated methods, and most managers would of course deny that they disregard the well-being, physical and psychological, of employees. However, the evidence overwhelmingly shows that managers do not often act to improve working conditions, improve health and safety, or improve quality of working life, unless they are convinced that there will be an adequate return on the time and money invested in these measures, or (in the case of safety at work, for example) they are forced to do so by legislation (Asplund, 1981). The renewed popularity of team-based approaches to work design in the late 1980s, it has been argued, has been stimulated wholly by intensified competitive pressures and not by a revived quality of working life movement (Buchanan, 1989).

Early developments

Management interest in work design is primarily a financial interest. Until the late 1970s, the main considerations were the costs of absenteeism, labour turnover, and low productivity. Those aspects of worker behaviour were attributed to boring, dissatisfying repetitive work. The British Industrial Fatigue Research Board produced the first systematic findings demonstrating that Taylor's methods could adversely affect labour productivity and costs (Vernon et al., 1924). They studied several types of light, 'short cycle', work in the boot and shoe, and tin can industries. The work cycle is simply the time taken to complete one operation. The tasks investigated had cycle times from less than one second to one minute. The Board discovered, not surprisingly, that workers found these tasks boring, and that output could be increased by 20 per cent by job rotation, moving workers from one task to another every half hour. They argued that it should be possible to find the optimum rotation interval for different tasks.

Job rotation, which does not involve changes to job content or methods, was the first work design technique advocated as an antidote to scientific management methods. The work of the British National Institute of Industrial Psychology was partly responsible for developing this simple concept further. In the early 1930s the Institute did some consultancy work for a company that made wireless sets, Kolster-Brandes, which had problems with its repetitive assembly line work (Harding, 1931). This led to the first reported experiment in 'job enlargement'. The experiment lasted for three weeks and involved two operators, one of whom 'had to be dismissed on the [third] Wednesday'. Performance at a 'small' work unit, soldering two or three wires in each set, was compared with that on a 'large' work unit, soldering eight to eleven wires. Harding's aim was to find the optimum size of work unit. The larger task was preferred, and performance was still improving when the experiment was discontinued.

Job enlargement thus involves the recombination of tasks separated by scientific management techniques, with a consequent increase in work cycle. Although British research had demonstrated before the Second World War that Taylor had gone too far with the fragmentation of work and that productivity could be improved by enlarging jobs, these techniques became popular only during the 1950s. In the period of economic growth following the War, management in Western industrialized countries became more aware of the 'hidden' costs of monotonous work and dissatisfied workers. One influential American study of work experience in the early 1950s (Walker and Guest, 1952) took the form of an attitude survey of 180 automobile assembly workers. This study identified six characteristics of mass production: mechanical pacing, repetitiveness, minimum skill requirement, no choice of tools or methods, minute subdivision of product, and surface mental attention. Workers in jobs with high ratings on those characteristics had higher absenteeism. Low absenteeism was related to the absence of those features.

Research has failed to show that unhappy workers are less productive than contented ones. The relationship is more subtle than that. Unhappy workers are more likely to seek employment elsewhere, be absent and turn up late more often, and to create their own variety at work through interesting and creative diversions, games, practical jokes and sabotage. Job rotation and enlargement thus offered simple ways to reduce the costs of turnover, absenteeism and mischief.

The first report of a successful practical application of job enlargement also came from Walker (1950), from the Endicott plant of IBM in 1944. The jobs of machinists were enlarged to include machine set-up and inspection of finished products leading to improved product quality, reduced scrap, less idle time for men and machines, and a 95 per cent reduction in set-up and inspection times. A number of other successful applications, mainly North American, were reported during the 1950s (Buchanan, 1979: 26). The technique was relevant to white-collar office work as well as to manual tasks, and applications continued to be reported sporadically throughout the 1960s and into the 1970s. The technique may not, however, have been as widespread in practice as it appeared to be from the literature. A survey which covered 276 of the 500 largest corporations in America found in 1969 that over 80 per cent of them had never used or considered job enlargement (Schoderbek and Reif, 1969).

One European company which used job enlargement extensively was Philips, which replaced the continuous assembly line in their television plant at Eindhoven in Holland with groups of workers each performing enlarged tasks (van Beek, 1964). Philips also used the approach in one of their Australian plants, with operators completing whole radios instead of performing a fragmented part of the subassembly operation (Pauling, 1968), and in their plant at Hamilton in Scotland where operators moved from a conveyor-paced assembly line to the manufacture of complete fan heaters (Thornely and Valantine, 1968).

Land (1990) reports a recent application of job enlargement, indicating that the technique is still in use, if under the different label of 'single-stage build'. Linn Products has a factory near Glasgow in Scotland where it manufactures high quality hi-fi amplifiers, turntables and speakers. The company was nominated in 1990 by the British Institute of Management as one of Britain's most advanced manufacturers, along with IBM, JCB, Black & Decker, Lucas and Yamazaki. The approach which gained the company this recognition included extensive computerization, automated materials storage and movement, and individual work stations which replaced the conventional assembly line.

The company's managing director explained their methods: 'We have single-stage build. The same person assembles, tests and packages the product. The assembly line approach deskills people and forces them to work at the pace of the slowest. Having one person responsible for the total manufacture of an item makes for efficiency, speed, lower costs and higher satisfaction. When we had just started in business [in 1973], and there were only a few women assembling the product, we thought we were General Motors and we had an assembly line. And a shambles. Customers were told they had to wait up to eight months, and even then Linn failed to meet its delivery targets. We were always having to say sorry to our customers. There were 47 buffer stores feeding the assembly line. All of our attempts to achieve an elegant and sensible solution to balance the line ended in failure. Then one day we asked one of the women on the line to collect all the parts she needed to assemble a turntable and to bring it back when she had put it together. She came back 18 minutes later. The assembly line was taking 27 minutes. Within months, the single-stage build approach had wiped out all the buffer stocks and the goods were being made on the same day that the orders were received' (Tiefenbrun, quoted in Land, 1990).

Each employee on a conventional assembly line must work at the same pace as the others so that the whole line moves continuously in a 'balanced' manner. The first ten minutes of the Charlie Chaplin movie, *Modern Times*, released in 1936, illustrates this concept in a graphic and entertaining manner. The same concept applies to fragmented administrative operations. Single-stage build offers more varied and meaningful work, and it also helps to overcome the line balancing problem.

Autonomous groups

Developments in work design techniques beyond job rotation and enlargement have been influenced by 'humanistic' psychology. Maslow (1943), the most popular and influential figure in this movement, argued that human beings have seven innate needs. 'Physiological' or survival needs concern sunlight, sex, food and water; 'safety' needs concern freedom from threat and the desire for shelter, security, order and predictability; 'love' needs concern relationships, affection, giving and receiving love, and the desire for feelings of belongingness; 'esteem' needs concern strength, achievement, adequacy, confidence, independence, and the desire for reputation, prestige, recognition, attention, importance, appreciation, and for a high self-evaluation based on capability and on respect from others; 'self-actualization' needs concern the development of human capability to the fullest potential; 'freedom of inquiry and expression' needs relate to social conditions that permit free speech, and encourage justice, fairness and honesty; and, finally, 'the need to know and understand' concerns the desire to gain and to systematize knowledge, to satisfy curiosity, to learn, to experiment and to explore. Taylor and Ford appear to have overlooked the possibility that their employees would seek satisfaction of any or all of these needs through work.

Maslow argued that these needs are organized in a loose hierarchy. A person does not normally pay much attention to love and esteem needs, for example, until physical and safety requirements are more or less satisfied. The ultimate goal is self-actualization, the needs for freedom of inquiry and to know and understand being prerequisites for the satisfaction of all the others. The theory is vague, it cannot easily make predictions about human behaviour, it makes some predictions that are inconsistent with the facts, and is more of a social philosophy than a psychological theory. Yet Maslow's influence is clearly stamped across the work design theories and practices of the latter half of the twentieth century and was a key dimension of the 'quality of working life' (QWL) movement that developed through the 1960s and 1970s.

One of the most powerful and enduring approaches to work design, translating Maslow's expression of human needs into work design principles, is based on the experience of management consultants working at the Tavistock Institute of Human Relations in London. The Tavistock consultants were responsible for the concept of the 'composite autonomous work group' or 'self-managing multi-skilled team', first developed in a textile mill in north-west India (Rice, 1953; 1958). The work of a second Tavistock consultant, Trist, in the north-west Durham coal mines in Britain in the early 1950s confirmed the social and economic advantages of self-managing work groups with 'responsible autonomy' (Trist and Bamforth, 1951; Trist et al., 1963). The traditional collier had a 'composite work role'. He was a 'complete collier' who worked unsupervised and was responsible for all face tasks. As each miner could perform all or most aspects of the work, the coal-getting cycle was 'self-regulating'. But what Trist and his colleagues found in Durham was different. Mechanical conveyors increased the length of coal face which could be mined simultaneously. Longwall mining methods displaced the composite autonomous collier by introducing mass production techniques underground. Each shift performed one distinct phase of the mining sequence which involved undercutting and blasting the coal, loading it onto a conveyor, and advancing the roofwork for the next cycle. Each group of miners carried out specific and narrowly defined tasks and were paid on different bases. A lot of productive time was lost in arguments over pay rates for the different groups for 'non-standard' work, such as that made necessary when the previous shift had not finished its part of the cycle. The coal-getting cycle was no longer self-regulating but required constant management co-ordination.

In some pits, however, composite autonomous work groups had developed spontaneously as bad conditions made longwall mining dangerous. These 'composite shortwalls' were worked by multi-skilled groups, on a common pay scheme, responsible for the whole coal-getting cycle on any shift. These were self-selecting and leaderless groups, with over 40 members, and made their own task and shift allocations. The level and continuity of their production were much better than on comparable longwalls and absenteeism was markedly lower. The Tavistock approach to work design has been translated into the psychological requirements that job content should meet (Emery et al., 1965: 5–9). From these considerations, one of Trist's colleagues, Emery (1963) compiled a list of 'hypotheses about the ways in which tasks may be more effectively put together to make jobs' (see also van Beinum, 1966). Seven of these hypotheses concern individual task content and the rest concern the organization of work groups. This approach demonstrates that the design of work is not determined by the technology in use, and is summarized in figure 3.1.

Individual jobs should provide:
- Variety
- A meaningful task
- Optimum work cycle
- Control over work standards and feedback of results
- Preparation and auxiliary tasks
- Use of valued skill and knowledge
- Contribution to end product

The organization of work groups should provide:
- Job rotation or physical proximity where individual tasks:
  (a) are interdependent
  (b) are stressful
  (c) lack perceived contribution to end product
- Grouping of interdependent jobs to provide:
  (a) whole tasks which contribute to end product
  (b) control over work standards and feedback of results
  (c) control over boundary tasks
- Communication opportunities
- Promotion opportunities

Source: Emery, 1963

Figure 3.1 The Tavistock work organization model

Autonomous group working has been used extensively in Scandinavia, notably by the Swedish car manufacturers Saab and Volvo. Gyllenhammar (1977: 15), president of Volvo, explained that, 'we decided to bring people together by replacing the mechanical line with the human work group. In this pattern, employees can act in co-operation, discussing more, deciding among themselves how to organize the work – and, as a result, doing much more. In essence, our approach is based on stimulation rather than restriction. If you view the employees as adults, then you must assume that they will respond to the stimulation: if you view them as children, then the assumption is that they need restriction. The intense emphasis on measurement and control in most factories seems to be a manifestation of the latter viewpoint.'

Valery (1974) estimated that over 1000 experiments had been started in Sweden. Many failed. The Scandinavian quality of working life movement relied on the publicity given to the car manufacturers which became – and remain – management tourist attractions. Volvo's car plant at Kalmar in Sweden was the first factory to be built around the concept of autonomous team-based assembly. The Kalmar plant has twenty assembly areas each with a team of 15 to 20 people, with their own entrance, coffee area, showers and other facilities. Team members rotate jobs, are responsible for their own quality, and can vary their own work pace. Teams have access to all plant information through computer terminals in their work areas. Each team has its own 'buffer' area where work can be 'banked' to enable the group to extend its rest periods. The effectiveness of Kalmar has been challenged by rumours about the plant's inefficiency. Corlett and Sell (1987) argue that this is a myth. Kalmar is Volvo's lowest cost assembly plant and takes 15 per cent fewer hours to make a car than the company average, and the number of man hours per car has been reduced by 60 per cent since 1977. In 1989 Volvo opened a new car plant at Uddevalla in west Sweden, extending the Kalmar approach with small teams building a complete car. In November 1989, Saab opened a new plant at Malmo in Sweden with a modular assembly system in place of the traditional conveyor belt (Lin, 1989). With absenteeism running at 25 per cent in traditional plants, Saab decided to improve the working environment, offering more variety and responsibility in the work. Lin describes how, 'Decorated with greenery and garden ponds, the new factory is more reminiscent of a supermarket than a car plant'. Saab's 'car builders' work in teams of six to ten people, each with its own computer terminal to track stock levels. Each team member has 20 to 60 minutes to complete the production cycle, which could involve building a car door or fitting the transmission system. With a conventional assembly line, the work cycle was around two minutes.

Experience of autonomous group working in the rest of Europe has also been apparently limited to a few well-publicized companies, such as Philips (Philips Report, 1969; den Hertog, 1976) and Fiat (Ruehl, 1974). The approach was not initially popular in North America (see Butteriss and Murdoch, 1976), but gained in prominence considerably in the mid- to late 1980s (Hoerr et al., 1986; Hoerr, 1989; Dumaine, 1990). The well-known American author and management consultant, Peters, has recently endorsed the approach, arguing that, 'the modest-sized, task oriented, semi-autonomous, mainly self-managing team should be the basic organizational building block' (1987: 296). There were until the 1980s few reported applications in Britain (Carby, 1976) although it was used by Shell (Hill, 1971), Scottish and Newcastle Breweries, and a small number of other companies (Butteriss and Murdoch, 1975).

The composite autonomous work group is a powerful tool in the technique of work design and forms the foundation for contemporary developments in 'high performance work systems' and 'new design plants'. Unlike job rotation and enlargement, it relies on a theory of motivation rather than on simplistic notions of monotony and variety. However, it is also based on the concepts of 'sociotechnical system analysis and design', a domain with a rich and complex language which many managers regard as impenetrable. This underpinning, combined with the potential absorption of the responsibilities of supervisory management by self-managing groups, has perhaps served to render the approach less popular than its promise deserves.

Enriched jobs

In 1970, General Motors opened one of the most advanced car assembly plants in the world at that time in Lordstown, Ohio, to make the Chevrolet Vega. The car and the plant were designed for each other. The body had one-third of the components of comparable automobiles and was assembled by automatic welding devices and robots. The plant was designed to produce one hundred vehicles an hour, with single operation cycle times as low as 20 seconds. This was publicized as 'the pattern of vehicle production of the future'. By

January 1972, incomplete and damaged cars were being made faster than they could be repaired. By February 1972 the Union of Auto Workers had lodged over 5000 grievances about work standards, job losses and 'speed up' in the plant. Management complained about sabotage and neglect. Cars were being made with broken windscreens and mirrors, cut upholstery, keys broken in locks and washers in carburettors. Welding machines were mysteriously reprogrammed to weld bodies in the wrong places, and some cars left the line with all their doors locked. The grievances were not resolved, and the result was a strike which lasted a month, affected 7800 employees in the plant and 8800 other workers indirectly, cost the company an estimated $160 million in lost production, and cost the workforce around $11 million in lost wages.

'Blue-collar blues' was the explanation (Gooding, 1970a; 1970b) and Lordstown was a typical example. The workforce had an average age of 24 and their aggression and industrial action indicated their rejection of the monotony of the assembly line. This and subsequent unrest at Lordstown and elsewhere prompted General Motors to change the plant layout and work assignment practices, to appoint a vice-president of personnel development responsible for worker motivation (Wild, 1975), and to develop a programme of employee involvement, suggestion schemes and team problem-solving (Weil, 1981).

The source of the ideas underpinning the General Motors programme was the work of Herzberg whose job enrichment technique was widely publicized through his (1968) article in the *Harvard Business Review* with the desperate title, 'One more time: how do you motivate employees?'. Whatever criticism it may attract today, it is significant to note that the technique was derived from an empirically based theory of work motivation. In the early 1950s, Herzberg and colleagues at the Psychological Service of Pittsburgh had interviewed 203 accountants and engineers and asked them two 'critical incident' questions. They were asked to recall events which had made them feel good about their work and events which had made them feel bad about it. Analysis of these critical incidents suggested that factors which led to satisfaction were different from and not simply the opposite of those which led to dissatisfaction at work. The characteristics of work which led to satisfaction were called 'motivator' or 'content factors' and included achievement, recognition, responsibility, advancement, growth in competence, and the work itself. The events which led to dissatisfaction were called 'hygiene factors' or 'context factors' and included salary, company policy, supervision, status, security, and working conditions. Herzberg called this a 'two factor theory' of motivation. Improvements in 'hygiene', he argued, can overcome dissatisfaction, but do not increase motivation and performance. The enrichment of jobs to this latter purpose must focus on the 'motivators', and Herzberg advocated the use of 'vertical job loading' to achieve this.

The vertical loading factors in Herzberg's job enrichment approach involve removing some controls on employees, increasing individual accountability and discretion, giving employees complete or natural units of work and additional authority, providing direct feedback on performance, introducing new and more difficult tasks, and assigning specialized tasks at which employees can become expert. Herzberg (1966) argued, with Maslow, that humans need 'psychological growth' and that job enrichment was necessary to provide this.

Herzberg's motivation theory has not been able to withstand criticism. The two factors appear to arise through the psychological defence mechanism called 'projection'. We tend to credit ourselves when we are successful and effective, but when things go wrong we tend to 'project' the blame onto people and circumstances beyond our control. Studies of work motivation using different methods do not reveal a split between motivator and hygiene factors. It does, however, appear that the motivator factors have a more powerful effect on motivation and performance than hygiene.

Job enrichment during the 1960s and 1970s remained significantly more popular in practice than autonomous group working on both sides of the Atlantic and there is a vast literature on the background theory and applications (Buchanan, 1979: 52–60). The technique is easy to understand and it readily suggests ways of improving employee motivation and performance without necessarily paying higher wages (a hygiene factor) and without changing organization structures or managerial responsibilities.

In the USA the best publicized applications were in American Telephone and Telegraph which carried out 19 job enrichment projects between 1965 and 1969, affecting over 1000 blue- and white-collar employees (Ford, 1969). The company was concerned about the rising costs of employee dissatisfaction and turnover which were attributed to monotonous jobs. One of the company's personnel staff was reported as saying, 'our company has lost too many people who are still with us!' (Ford, 1969: 16). In Britain, it was ICI which became best known for its reputedly successful job enrichment applications. Paul and Robertson (1970) offer accounts of eight applications between 1967 and 1968, mainly with white-collar employees such as sales representatives, design engineers, foremen and draughtsmen (who, in accordance with Herzberg's advice, were not told that they were experimental subjects).

More recently, job enrichment was used at the enquiry unit at the UK's Driver and Vehicle Licensing Centre in Swansea, when staff complained that they could not deal with the number of public enquiries. The staff were involved in determining the job changes in this application and each staff member was given responsibility for all the case work arising from an enquiry, dealing with problems personally, with back-up only from the manager when requested (Asplund, 1981: 101–2). White (1983) reported a job enrichment application in a continuous process plant where management wanted to reduce labour turnover and improve product quality. New equipment had reduced work variety and increased speed. Management introduced job rotation and breaks which were arranged by the plant operators themselves. Operators were also given increased variety and control in the work and developed a better understanding of the process. Bailey (1980) describes job enrichment at Watney Mann (West) brewery, where management wanted to improve employee participation in decision making and thereby improve efficiency, customer service, and profitability. The distribution department was split into four depots, with rotation and team-work. With clearer goals, employees reported an increased sense of accomplishment, and other benefits included cost savings, flexibility, and better problem-solving and customer satisfaction.

Herzberg's approach has three other notable features. First, he believes that the 'tyranny of the group' suppresses the satisfaction of individual needs: the target of job enrichment is thus the individual job. Second, he argues that employees should not be involved in determining the forms of enrichment to which their jobs are subject because they are unlikely to be sufficiently competent to contribute to the analysis and discussion. Third, Herzberg is a 'psychological universalist' (Lupton, 1971; 1976), claiming that everyone is potentially a motivation-seeker or self-actualizer and that this is evidence of mental health. Herzberg (1987) has more recently claimed not only that the two-factor theory remains valid but also that it applies in many different cultures throughout the world. Hygiene seekers in this view are mentally unhealthy and have been blocked at the hygiene level by some unfortunate past experience. Studies in South Africa appear to discredit the two-factor theory. While managers and skilled workers (black and white) produce the expected pattern, the satisfaction of unskilled workers appears to rely on hygiene factors. Herzberg (1987) concludes that 'the impoverished nature of the unskilled workers' jobs has not provided these workers with motivators – hence the abnormal profile'. He also cites a comparable study of unskilled Indian workers who were 'operating on a dependent hygiene continuum that leads to addiction to hygiene, or strikes and revolution'. Other data on the nature of individual differences in human motivation suggest that Herzberg's position is highly dubious: is it reasonable to question the psychological well-being of everyone who rejects increased work load and responsibility?

The subsequent approach to job enrichment developed by Hackman et al. (1975) overcomes the universalist criticism. Their 'job characteristics model' sets out a causal chain, from implementing concepts, through job dimensions and psychological states, to desirable personal and work outcomes. The key distinction between this and Herzberg's position lies in the claim that the causal chain works only for people with high 'growth need strength', which is not assumed to indicate mental health or psychological well-being, but only to reflect individual differences in motivation. The approach does not work, according to its architects, for those with low growth need strength, low desire for self-actualization, or indeed for those who, in Herzberg's view, are neurotic hygiene seekers.

High Performance Work Systems and New Design Plants

The goals underpinning the QWL movement in the 1960s and 1970s concerned the costs of labour turnover and absenteeism, and other costs arising from boredom and apathy. The objectives of work design in the late 1980s and the 1990s concern the need for quality, flexibility and responsiveness in meeting customer requirements in an increasingly competitive climate. The management motives are therefore strategic rather than operational, concerned with competition and customer satisfaction rather than with employment costs. Peters (1987: 302–3) captures this shift in management thinking in his uncompromising statement: 'There is ample evidence that American economic performance will increasingly depend on quality, service, constant innovation/improvement, and enhanced flexibility/responsiveness. Committed, flexible, multi-skilled, constantly retrained people, joined together in self-managing teams, are the only possible implementers of this strategy.'

The term 'high performance' is used here to refer to systemic, integrated developments in the application of autonomous group working, with multiple and related implications beyond the confines of the original technique, invading the domain of supervisory and management structures, and affecting also training and payment systems as well as other aspects of organizational design and working conditions. Lawler (1986) has described these developments using the label 'new design plants'. These are plants with a common employee entrance and car parking, and with common cafeteria and recreation areas. All employees are salaried and have access to a common fringe benefits package. Payment systems are skills-based and involve profit or gain sharing. Work is allocated in meaningful segments to teams which have their own meeting rooms and personal facilities, and which elect their leaders and are self-managing, and control their own quality and absenteeism. Teams are also multi-skilled and skill-sharing, and conduct their own recruitment and performance reviews. Some support functions are carried out within the teams, with fewer support personnel in specialist engineering, scheduling and quality functions. Remaining support staff serve as consultants and trainers. The process layout is designed to facilitate team-work and communications. The management structure is flat (there are no foremen), the organization culture emphasizes training and personal development, and this 'management philosophy' is clearly expressed and communicated.

Distinguishing these developments from the QWL technique of autonomous group working, which is at the core of the new design plant concept, Lawler argues that: 'Overall, new design plants are clearly different from traditional plants in a number of important ways. Almost no aspect of the organization is left untouched. The reward system, the structure, the physical layout, the personnel management system, and the nature of jobs are all changed in significant ways. Because so many features are altered, *in aggregate they amount to a new kind of organization*' (1986: 178, italics added).

Some examples of current practice will illustrate the trend. The label 'high performance' was used by Digital Equipment Corporation to describe a series of innovations in work organization in their plants in America and Britain (Perry, 1984; Buchanan, 1987; Buchanan and McCalman, 1989; *Industrial Relations Review and Report*, 2 November 1990). Digital's approach illustrates the increased sophistication in contemporary applications of flexible team-working accompanied with organizational redesign. Digital first applied the high performance work systems approach at one of their American plants, at Enfield in Connecticut. This plant made printed circuit boards, and increasing competition and product changes encouraged management to experiment with new approaches. The goal at Enfield was 'flexibility': the capacity to respond quickly and effectively to a highly uncertain environment. Traditional ways to handle uncertainty had included the introduction of new procedures, changing the structure, employing more people, and tightening management controls. These strategies simply increased overheads, increased the complexity of the organization and generated more uncertainty. To deal with these issues, management decided to introduce a more participative style of decision making, multi-skilled operating teams, an innovative rewards system, and systematic career planning and development. The plant manager's review of these changes revealed a 40 per cent reduction in product manufacturing time, a sharp increase in inventory turnover, a reduction of levels of management hierarchy to three, a 38 per cent reduction in standard costs, a 40 per cent reduction in overhead, and equivalent output with half the people and half the space (Perry, 1984).

This and the experience of other American corporations (Procter & Gamble, Zilog, Hewlett Packard) encouraged Digital managers at their plant at Ayr in Scotland to develop a similar approach. This involved the formation in 1984 of 'high performance teams' for the manufacture of small business computer systems. These teams, each with around 12 members, were self-managing and self-organizing, without first line supervision. They had 'front-to-back responsibility' for their part of the production process, from collection of materials from stores to inspection and test and handover to despatch. Team production targets were negotiated with management. Individual team members were expected to be multi-skilled. No job titles were used. Team members were also expected to share their skills, knowledge and experience with each other. A new skills-based payment system was designed with shop-floor participation. Teams operated systems for peer selection and peer performance review. The layout of the shop-floor was open, to facilitate communications, and support staff had desks on the shop floor so that they could be close to the problems with which they were dealing. Front-to-back responsibility for product assembly and test included fault-finding and problem-solving as well as some equipment maintenance. The group members policed their own team discipline and flexitime system. The manufacturing line management hierarchy was reduced to only three levels, with 'displaced' managers moving to other parts of the business or into internal consultancy and development roles.

A review of team performance in 1988 showed that product quality had been high and sustained, that slippage on customer orders had been eliminated, and that response to customer demand was much more flexible. Time to market for new products, a key variable in the competitive equation in the small computer business, was sharply reduced. As part of an integrated package of organizational changes, the high performance teams were clearly seen as fundamental to the plant's competitive strategy, and they were supported by extensive training, a redefinition and eventual elimination of the role of first line supervision, and changes to management structure and style. The semiconductor assembly business at Ayr adopted a similar team-based approach in 1989, with similar commercial benefits (Buchanan and McCalman, 1992).

Kroll (1989) describes the introduction of team-based methods at Smith, Kline & French Laboratories which manufacture 'blister packs' for pharmaceutical products. Due to the convenience and popularity of such packaging, extra manufacturing capacity has been required to meet a steady growth in demand since the mid-1980s. The traditional packaging line required three groups of people. First, supervisors and direct labour, responsible for effective equipment operation, reporting to the blister packaging manager. Second, engineers, responsible for changeovers, equipment settings and fault correction, reporting to the engineering group manager. Third, service operators, responsible for ensuring that there is an adequate supply of materials and for cleaning lines between different runs, reporting to the packaging services manager. The blister packaging manager and packaging services manager reported to the packaging manager. Each of the three groups had its own separate responsibilities, but they were interdependent. When operators identified a minor modification to improve line efficiency, they had to get an engineer to implement it. Additional materials could not be acquired without a service operator. Breakdowns similarly could not be dealt with until an engineer was free. This combination of interdependence and separation of responsibility led to tension and frequent arguments. The managers each had their different objectives and priorities too. The organization structure inhibited efficiency gains, and the company started to look at other approaches.

As the company identified these problems in 1987, a new high-speed blister packaging line was being introduced. The decision was made to run this with a line team – a small group of highly trained operators with all the skills required to carry out the job. The team, with a leader and four members reporting to the packaging manager, became responsible for operating the equipment, carrying out in-process checks, performing equipment changeovers, and for correcting minor faults. The line team was responsible for everything except major breakdowns. The retraining involved a two-month programme which covered machinery, materials, documentation, and team development. The team leader was also put through a leadership skills course. The total cost of the training programme was £17,000. The resultant output was 2.6 times better than previously obtained from equivalent lines. Management felt this was due to a high level of motivation and to integrated team effort. The experiment on this one line was subsequently extended throughout the blister packaging department with similar performance improvements.

A similar, 'integrated working', approach has been developed at the Blue Circle Cement Works at Dunbar in Scotland (Stevens, 1987). Blue Circle management wanted to develop a more flexible and skilled workforce, to remove 'them and us' barriers, and to stabilize income by reducing overtime. Integrated working had six characteristics. First, 23 teams formed the 'basic working unit'. Second, team leaders were given line responsibility; there were no deputies or chargehands, and team leaders have management training in leadership, communications and group skills. Third, 11 per cent of the time of operators and craftsmen was devoted to training. Fourth, a monthly 'watchdog' works committee monitored the progress of the integrated working approach. Fifth, a 'stable income plan' replaced overtime, special payments, bonuses and hourly rates with an annual hours contract, including a 12.5 per cent flexible hours component. Finally, the number of job grades was reduced to four, traditional demarcations were removed, and all personnel were expected to carry out any duty without direct supervision. Some problems remained. For instance, employees complained that the flexible hours component of the annual hours contract was being used for routine work, and not for emergencies as originally intended. And redundancies (which cut the workforce from 480 to 250 in 1987) were felt to have been excessive. Complex clocking procedures were introduced. The speed of change in the company was generating anxiety.

However, there was considerable enthusiasm for the work variety, income stability, increased training, and improved management–employee relationships. The team leaders appreciated the freedom, and the ability to use employee skills more effectively More delegation meant that department heads had more time for planning. With respect to the goal of improved efficiency, the works manager is reported as saying that, 'There is no doubt about that at all. I do not believe that we could have relied on the systems I knew ten years ago to implement the changes we made here. We needed a totally new approach to employee relations. There are still many unresolved difficulties, but our production per employee has risen from 1900 tons per annum in 1983 to potentially over 4000 tons today. Our productivity has increased dramatically, and this has not been due to new equipment and heavy investment alone' (Stevens, 1987: 12).

Looking Back: An Assessment

The concerns which work design techniques address have thus shifted from the elimination of boredom, through variety, to the creation of a quality work experience, and, through increasing responsibility, to the improvement of competitiveness through flexible responsiveness. Traditional job rotation, enlargement and enrichment techniques focus on individual employees and individual jobs. Autonomous team-working and contemporary derivatives focus on organizational groupings. Changes to individual jobs can leave supervisory and management structures intact. Increasing team autonomy leads to changes in management structures and styles, and to revised systems for reward, appraisal and career progression.

The search for new forms of job design has thus been supplanted by a concern to establish more effective 'organizational configurations'. There has also been a shift from task or job oriented techniques to system or organization oriented approaches. While the core techniques may have remained the same since the 1960s, the management motives have changed, the business problems have

QWL in the 1970s	High performance in the 1990s
Aimed to reduce costs of absenteeism and labour turnover and increase productivity	Aims to improve organizational flexibility and product quality for competitive advantage
Based on argument that increased autonomy improves quality of work experience and employee job satisfaction	Based on argument that increased autonomy improves skills decision making, adaptability and use of new technology
Had little impact on the management function beyond first line supervision	Involves change in organization culture and redefinition of management function at all levels
'Quick fix' applied to isolated and problematic work groups	Could take two to three years to change attitudes and behaviour throughout the organization
Personnel administration technique	Human resource management strategy

Figure 3.2 QWL in the 1970s contrasted with the high performance paradigm of the 1990s

intensified, and applications appear to have become more radical in their implications. Figure 3.2 summarizes the main contrasts between the QWL movement during the 1970s and the high performance systems concerns of the 1990s.

The history of work design ideas can also be seen in terms of the evolution of response to the problems of the period. Taylor's problems involved a combination of rapid industrialization with an unskilled immigrant workforce. Ford saw the immense profits to be made from the low-cost mass production of a standard product. Simplified, standardized, repetitive tasks seem appropriate for this context. Management after the Second World War saw employee education, affluence and expectations rising steadily, particularly through the 1960s and 1970s. The Department of Employment commissioned a review of the field (Wilson, 1973) and a Tripartite Steering Group on Job Satisfaction was formed with government, TUC and CBI representation. The operating division of that Steering Group, the Work Research Unit, was charged with disseminating job enrichment techniques and improving quality of working life. Interest then waned in the late 1970s as unemployment rose and concern for working life, regardless of quality, rose accordingly. As domestic and international trading conditions became increasingly turbulent and unpredictable during the 1980s, attention naturally switched to ways of improving flexibility and responsiveness through work and organizational redesign.

Looking back over the century, therefore, it seems that an evolving recognition of the significance of work design techniques has been accompanied by a shift in objectives and by an increasing radicalization of the approaches in use. This move towards the systematic development of new organizational configurations, replacing the cosmetic dickering with individual task specifications, was advocated by a number of commentators in the mid-1970s, when the QWL movement was at its most popular (Wild, 1975; Lupton, 1976; Davis, 1976; Buchanan, 1979). In the first edition of this book, this chapter concluded that, 'if work design techniques are to have a significant impact on the experience of work and organizational performance, then they will have to be more radical than those currently in use, and will need to be more closely integrated with other employment policies'. That trend now seems to have emerged.

Looking Forward: Trends and Prospects

What are the prospects for the further development and application of work design theory and practice? The available evidence appears to be contradictory.

Has there been a genuine, sustained and irreversible shift in management thinking or do contemporary developments reflect simply fashionable cosmetic changes to organization design? The flurry of new labels suggests genuine concern and change: high performance systems, new design plants, integrated working, business teams. Buchanan (1989: 271) argues that 'the climate of acceptability' has changed, and that more significant organizational problems have rendered legitimate the consideration of broader scale approaches to work and organizational redesign. These developments are consistent with the recognition of human resource management as a strategic function linked to corporate goals, not as a personnel activity related to the administration of employment (Storey, 1989).

In support of the 'genuine shift' argument, the search for more efficient manufacturing methods has apparently begun to coalesce in what Drucker (1990) has termed 'a new theory of manufacturing' which will characterize what he calls, 'the post-modern factory of 1999'. Drucker's 'new theory' is founded on four concepts: modular or cellular organizational forms; statistical quality control; strategic manufacturing management accounting; and a 'systems approach to the business of creating value'. A more detailed vision of the properties of Drucker's post-modern factory can be found in the work of Parnaby (1988) on Lucas which has done much to publicize just-in-time and manufacturing systems engineering (MSE) methodologies in Britain during the 1980s.

In contrast with much of the literature on just-in-time and other modern manufacturing techniques, Parnaby – with Drucker – argues for a 'total systems approach' to manufacturing systems engineering. MSE in his view must incorporate a range of related and supportive changes in a number of areas, including factory process control, organization structures, job structures, training programmes, process flow routeing, machine changeover procedures, communications systems, customer and supplier interfaces, project management for continuous improvement, capital expenditure authorization procedures, quality control, materials flow control, scheduling and planning systems, and inter-departmental relationships. Parnaby (1988: 483) thus emphasizes that just-in-time operation is not merely 'the latest gimmick', is not a particular technique, and is not dependent simply on investment in new technology.

Like Drucker, the core of the approach which Parnaby advocates also concerns the formation of a cellular organization structure, 'based upon natural people and machinery groupings around information or material flows' (Parnaby, 1988: 485). This cellular structure should facilitate the simplification of production control, the implementation of just-in-time work flow, the definition of cell and operator accountability for quality, the reduction in layers of organization hierarchy, flexible job structures and multi-skilling, the elimination of traditional work orders and work in progress monitoring, and team-based continuous improvement.

The arguments supporting the development of flexible, team-based manufacturing methods were systematically explored and publicized in the early 1980s (Reich, 1983; Piore and Sabel, 1984). The separate dimensions of the approach are well documented, such as the emulation of Japanese manufacturing methods, the development in particular of just-in-time methodologies, and attempts to introduce flexibility through increased use of out-of-craft and out-of-grade working on the shop floor, and the adoption of multi-skilled teamwork (Schonberger, 1982 and 1986; Oliver and Wilkinson, 1988; Oliver, 1991).

Cellular manufacturing design is not novel – it has its roots in post-war Russian engineering (Mitrofanov, 1955) – and group technology is simply an approach to shop layout in which equipment is located according to product families which have similar processing requirements, and not according to machine function (Gallagher and Knight, 1973). However, MSE has extended this concept of group technology to encompass the notion of 'product autonomous cells'. Autonomy in this context refers to the degree of independence of the production cell from other parts of the organization with respect to manufacturing equipment and services relevant to the manufacture of a particular product or component family.

Considerable caution is necessary before these developments are accepted as confirming the trends noted earlier. Some commentators have noted that, despite the comparatively strong descriptive and speculative literature on novel manufacturing methodologies, organizational analyses of applications in practice are rare (e.g. Grayson, 1990: 12; Oliver, 1991: 26). In addition, much available commentary relies on management accounts; there are few accounts (see, for example, Dawson, 1991) of the shop-floor response to such developments. In useful reviews of the literature and contemporary trends in this area, Turnbull (1988) and Smith (1989) also query the excessive claims in the management literature for the revolutionary implications of new manufacturing methods for work organization and management practice. Smith (1989: 217), for example, speaks of 'continuity within existing structures' in his discussion of flexible specialization. Dawson and Webb (1989: 237) caution against 'gross generalizations' with respect to the impact of just-in-time methods on quality of work life, reversal of division of labour, and increased involvement and autonomy at shop-floor level. Likewise, Elger and Fairbrother (1990) reject the conclusion that manufacturing changes at Lucas Industries represent any simple shift to a new form of participative working.

One study of the application of a manufacturing systems engineering approach in a Midlands engineering company (Buchanan and Preston, 1991) showed that, while it was the management intention to introduce a package of technical, production and organizational changes, only the technical and production changes were introduced. The team-working, the shop-floor autonomy, and the redefined role of the first line supervisor did not take place. Despite such partial implementation, significant commercial benefits were achieved, mainly through equipment moves, reduced materials handling, and improved production scheduling and control. These were relatively straightforward to introduce, and their benefits were immediate and quantifiable. The organizational changes would have been more problematic (involving changes to well-established company-wide job specification and evaluation systems), and time-consuming to introduce, and their benefits were not as visible. Why make the difficult changes if the easy changes bring instant benefit on their own?

Hammarstrom and Lansbury (1991) make a similar point, having compared the experience of the Swedish and Japanese car manufacturers. The Swedish manufacturers were in the forefront of experiments with socio-technical team-based methods. The Japanese manufacturers and, in particular, Toyota, developed fresh approaches involving the ruthless reduction of retooling and equipment adjustment times, the elimination of defects in the production process, and the use of minimum manning, multi-tasking, multi-machine operation, predefined work operations, repetitive short cycle work, powerful first-line supervisors, and a management hierarchy with several levels. Saab was forced to sell its car business to General Motors in 1990; Volvo saw its sales tumble in the late 1980s and early 1990s. The Japanese manufacturers, meanwhile, seemed to go from strength to strength.

Hammarstrom and Lansbury (1991: 87) conclude that, 'For managers in many countries, the Toyota approach appears to be a more "natural" and "safe" method of production. It seems likely that only management faced with shortage of labour, union pressure and reduced wage differentials will be forced to be as imaginative as Volvo has been at Uddevalla.' They raise the painful question, 'will the Volvo model for car production and work organization prevail?' (ibid.: 87). Emulation of Japanese methods became a popular Western management hobby during the 1980s. If systematic comparison of Japanese, Swedish, American and European manufacturing methods points to the relative efficiency of 'Toyotism', the future development of the approaches to work and organizational design outlined in this chapter looks bleak.

Perceptive readers will have noted that the examples cited in this chapter are drawn almost exclusively from manufacturing settings. So, what of the service sector? The number of reported applications of innovative work design has been comparatively small. That trend looks set to be reversed. One of the most publicized non-manufacturing applications of team-based working in America has involved the Shenandoah Life Insurance company (Myers, 1985; Wagner, 1989). They claim to be handling 50 per cent more business with 10 per cent fewer people since the introduction of autonomous teams (Hoerr et al., 1986). One large British insurance company is reorganizing its customer service function (employing 800 people) which has traditionally been organized as a fragmented, clerical production line. A single enquiry, from a customer or from an agent, could be handled by a procession of individuals, and both the company and enquirers have difficulty in tracing requests if they go astray. Proposals and enquiries could thus circulate for weeks or months for the sake of short processing times. The reorganization, introduced in 1992, relied on product-based teams, each with ten members and each concentrating on a single product, such as pensions, ordinary branch life, or industrial life. This reduced processing cycle times, reduced costs, made more flexible use of staff, enriched individual jobs within the teams, and improved customer service – the latter being the main objective in a highly competitive sector.

Another example is the Body Shop, which has a branch in London's Oxford Street run by teams and without managers. The 25 full-time and three part-time staff are split into four teams, and all receive the same rate of salaried pay. The employees, or 'performers' as the company calls them, are responsible for all the day-to-day branch running, including stock, staffing, customer handling and finance. They make their own decisions on type of stock, training, discipline and shift patterns (*Personnel Management Plus*, 3 November 1991).

Bibliography

Asplund, C. 1981. *Redesigning Jobs: Western European Experience*. Brussels: European Trade Union Institute.

Bailey, J. 1980. 'Employee involvement in the brewery industry'. *Industrial and Commercial Training*, September, 360–5.

Beek, H. G. van. 1964. 'The influence of assembly line organization on output, quality and morale'. *Occupational Psychology*, 38, July and October, 161–72.

Beinum, H. van. 1966. *The Morale of the Dublin Busmen*. London: Tavistock Institute.

Braverman, H. 1974. *Labour and Monopoly Capital: The Degradation of Work in the Twentieth Century*. New York: Monthly Review Press.

Buchanan, D. A. 1979. *The Development of Job Design Theories and Tech-*

niques. Aldershot: Saxon House.

Buchanan, D. A. 1987. 'Job enrichment is dead: long live high-performance work design!'. *Personnel Management*, May, 40–3.

Buchanan, D. A. 1989. 'High performance: new boundaries of acceptability in worker control'. In Sauter, S. L., Hurrell, J. J. and Cooper, C. L. (eds) *Job Control and Worker Health*. Chichester: John Wiley, 255–73.

Buchanan, D. A. and Bessant, J. 1985. 'Failure, uncertainty and control: the role of operators in a computer integrated production system'. *Journal of Management Studies*, 22, 3, 292–308.

Buchanan, D. A. and McCalman, J. 1989. *High Performance Work Systems: The Digital Experience*. London: Routledge.

Buchanan, D. A. and McCalman, J. 1992. 'Digital Equipment Scotland: the VLSI story'. In Legge, K., Clegg, C. and Gowler, D. (eds) *Cases in Organizational Behaviour and Human Resource Management*. London: Paul Chapman.

Buchanan, D. A. and Preston, D. 1991. *The floggings will stop when morale improves*. Loughborough University Business School Working Paper Series, September.

Butteriss, M. and Murdoch, R. D. 1975. *Work Restructuring Projects and Experiments in the United Kingdom*. Report 2. London: Work Research Unit.

Butteriss, M. and Murdoch, R. D. 1976. *Work Restructuring Projects and Experiments in the USA*. Report 3. London: Work Research Unit.

Carby, K. 1976. *Job Redesign in Practice*. London: Institute of Personnel Management.

Corlett, N. and Sell, R. 1987. 'Organizational effectiveness and quality of working life: learning from abroad – Sweden'. *Work Research Unit Occasional Paper*, No. 39. London: Work Research Unit.

Davis, L. E. 1966. 'The design of jobs'. *Industrial Relations*, 6, 1, 21–45.

Davis, L. E. 1976. 'Developments in job design'. In Warr, P. (ed.) *Personal Goals and Work Design*. London: Wiley, 67–80.

Davis, L. E., Canter, R. R. and Hoffman, J. 1955. 'Current job design criteria'. *Journal of Industrial Engineering*, 6, 2, 5–11.

Dawson, P. 1991. 'Flexible workcells: teamwork and group technology on the shopfloor'. Paper presented to the Labour Process Conference, Aston/UMIST, April 1991.

Dawson, P. and Webb, J. 1989. 'New production arrangements: the totally flexible cage?'. *Work, Employment and Society*, 3, 2, 221–38.

Drucker, P. F. 1990. 'The emerging theory of manufacturing'. *Harvard Business Review*, 68, 3, May–June, 94–102.

Dumaine, B. 1990. 'Who needs a boss?'. *Fortune*, 7 May, 10, 40–7.

Elger, T. and Fairbrother, P. 1990. 'Inflexible flexibility: case study evidence and theoretical considerations'. Paper presented to the British Sociological Association Annual Conference, University of Surrey, April.

Emery, F. E. 1963. 'Some hypotheses about the ways in which tasks may be more effectively put together to make jobs'. Tavistock Institute of Human Relations. Reprinted in Hill, P. 1971. *Towards a New Philosophy of Management*. Aldershot: Gower Press, 208–10.

Emery, F. E., Thorsrud, E. and Lange, K. 1965. 'Field experiments at Christiana Spigerverk'. *Industrial Democracy Project Paper*, No. 2, Phase B. Tavistock Institute Document T807. London: Tavistock Institute of Human Relations.

Ford, R. N. 1969. *Motivation Through the Work Itself*. New York: American Management Association.

Gallagher, C. and Knight, W. 1973. *Group Technology*. London: Butterworth.

Golzen, G. 1991. 'Let the shop floor manage itself'. *Sunday Times*, 6 January, 6.10.

Gooding, J. 1970a. 'Blue collar blues on the assembly line'. *Fortune*, July, 68–71.

Gooding, J. 1970b. 'It pays to wake up the blue collar workers'. *Fortune*, September, 132–5.

Grayson, D. 1990. *Self Regulating Work Groups: An Aspect of Organizational Change*. Work Research Unit Occasional Paper, 46, July. London: Work Research Unit.

Gyllenhammar, P. G. 1977. *People at Work*. Reading, MA: Addison-Wesley.

Hackman, J. R., Oldham, G. R., Janson, R. and Purdy, K. 1975. 'A new strategy for job enrichment'. *California Management Review*, 17, 4, 57–71.

Hammarstrom, O. and Lansbury, R. D. 1991. 'The art of building a car: the Swedish experience re-examined'. *New Technology, Work and Employment*, 6, 2, 85–90.

Harding, D. W. 1931. 'A note on the subdivision of assembly work'. *Journal of the National Institute of Industrial Psychology*, 5, 5, 261–4.

Hertog, F. J. den. 1976. 'Work structuring'. In Warr, P. (ed.) *Personal Goals and Work Design*. London: Wiley, 43–65.

Herzberg, F. 1966. *Work and the Nature of Man*. London: Staples Press.

Herzberg, F. 1968. 'One more time: how do you motivate employees?'. *Harvard Business Review*, 46, 1, 53–62.

Herzberg, F. 1987. 'Workers' needs the same around the world'. *Industry Week*, 21 September, 29–30, 32.

Hill, P. 1971. *Towards a New Philosophy of Management*. Aldershot: Gower.

Hirschhorn, L. 1984. *Beyond Mechanization*. Cambridge, MA: MIT Press.

Hoerr, J. 1989. 'The payoff from teamwork'. *Business Week*, 10 July, 56–62.

Hoerr, J., Pollock, M. A. and Whiteside, D. E. 1986. 'Management discovers the human side of automation'. *Business Week*, 29 September, 60–5.

Huczynski, A. A. and Buchanan, D. A. 1991. *Organizational Behaviour: An Introductory Text*. Hemel Hempstead: Prentice Hall International.

Industrial Relations Review and Report. 1990. 'Change to cell-based working, multi-skilling and teamworking at Digital Equipment VLSI'. 2 November, 5-5-8.

Kirosingh, M. 1989. 'Changed work practices' *Employment Gazette*, August, 422–9.

Kroll, A. R. 1989. 'New working practices for blister packaging lines'. *Manufacturing Chemist*, November, 33, 35 and 38.

Land, D. 1990. 'Is this the best place to work in Britain?'. *Business World*, December 1990.

Lawler, E. E. 1976. 'Conference review: issues of understanding'. In Warr, P. (ed.) *Personal Goals and Work Design*. London: Wiley, 225–33.

Lawler, E. E. 1986. *High Involvement Management: Participative Strategies for Improving Organizational Performance*. San Francisco: Jossey-Bass.

Lin, X. 1989. 'Saab gives its workers their heads'. *Eurobusiness*, December, 68.

Lupton, T. 1971. *Management and the Social Sciences*. Harmondsworth: Penguin.

Lupton, T. 1976. ' "Best fit" in the design of organizations'. In Miller, E. J. (ed.) *Task and Organization*. London: Wiley, 121–49.

Maslow, A. 1943. 'A theory of motivation'. *Psychological Review*, 50, 4, 370–96.

Mitrofanov, S. P. 1955. *Scientific Principles of Group Technology*. Boston Spa: National Lending Library. (Translated from the Russian in 1966.)

Myers, J. B. 1985. 'Making organizations adaptive to change: eliminating bureaucracy at Shanandoah Life'. *National Productivity Review*, Spring.

Oliver, N. 1991. 'The dynamics of just-in-time'. *New Technology, Work and Employment*, 6, 1, 19–27.

Oliver, N. and Wilkinson, B. 1988. *The Japanization of British Industry*. Oxford: Basil Blackwell.

Parnaby, J. 1988. 'A systems approach to the implementation of JIT methodologies in Lucas Industries'. *International Journal of Production Research*, 26, 3, 483–92.

Paul, W. J. and Robertson, K. B. 1970. *Job Enrichment and Employee Motivation*. Aldershot: Gower.

Pauling, T. P. 1968. 'Job enlargement: an experience at Philips Telecommunications of Australia Ltd'. *Personnel Practice Bulletin*, 24, 3, 194–6.

Perry, B. 1984. *Enfield: A High Performance System*. Bedford, MA: Digital Equipment Corporation, Educational Services Development and Publishing.

Personnel Management Plus, 1991. 'The managerless shop', 2:11, November, 3.

Peters, T. 1987. *Thriving on Chaos: Handbook for a Management Revolution*. London: Macmillan.

Philips Report. 1969. *Work Structuring: A Survey of Experiments at NV Philips, Eindhoven, 1963–68*. Eindhoven: NV Philips.

Piore, M. and Sabel, C. 1984. *The Second Industrial Divide: Possibilities for*

Prosperity. New York: Basic Books.

Reich, R. B. 1983. *The Next American Frontier*. New York: Times Books.

Rice, A. K. 1953. 'Productivity and social organization in an Indian weaving shed'. *Human Relations*, 6, 4, 297–329.

Rice, A. K. 1958. *Productivity and Social Organization*. London: Tavistock Publications.

Ruehl, G. 1974. 'Work structuring: part 1'. *Industrial Engineering*, January, 32–7.

Schoderbek, P. P. and Reif, W. E. 1969. *Job Enlargement: Key to Improved Performance*. Ann Arbor: Bureau of Industrial Relations, Graduate School of Business Administration, University of Michigan.

Schonberger, R. J. 1982. *Japanese Manufacturing Techniques*. New York: Free Press.

Schonberger, R. J. 1986. *World Class Manufacturing: The Lessons of Simplicity Applied*. Illinois: Free Press.

Smith, C. 1989. 'Flexible specialization, automation and mass production'. *Work, Employment and Society*, 3, 2, 203–20.

Stevens, B. 1987. 'Integrated working at Blue Circle'. *Industrial Participation*, 594: Summer, 10–12.

Storey, J. (ed.) 1989. *New Perspectives on Human Resource Management*. London: Routledge.

Taylor, F. W. 1911. *Principles of Scientific Management*. New York: Harper.

Thornely, D. H. and Valantine, G. A. 1968. 'Job enlargement: some implications of longer cycle jobs on fan heater production'. *Philips Personnel Management Review*, 12–17.

Trist, E. L. and Bamforth, K. W. 1951. 'Some social and psychological consequences of the longwall method of coal-getting'. *Human Relations*, 4, 1, 3–38.

Trist, E. L., Higgin, G. W., Murray, H. and Pollock, A. B. 1963. *Organizational Choice: Capabilities of Groups at the Coal Face Under Changing Technologies*. London: Tavistock Publications.

Turnbull, P. J. 1988. 'The limits to "Japanization" – just-in-time, labour relations and the UK automotive industry'. *New Technology, Work and Employment*, 3, 1, 7–20.

Valery, N. 1974. 'Importing the lessons of Swedish workers'. *New Scientist*, 62, 4 April, 27–8.

Vernon, H. M., Wyatt, S. and Ogden, A. D. 1924. *On the Extent and Effects of Variety in Repetitive Work*. Medical Research Council Industrial Fatigue Research Board Report 26. London: HMSO.

Walker, C. R. 1950. 'The problem of the repetitive job'. *Harvard Business Review*, 28, 3, 54–8.

Walker, C. R. and Guest, R. H. 1952. *The Man on the Assembly Line*. Cambridge, MA: Harvard University Press.

Walton, R. E. 1985. 'From control to commitment in the workplace'. *Harvard Business Review*, March–April, 77–84.

Walton, R. E. and Susman, G. E. 1987. 'People policies for the new machines'. *Harvard Business Review*, March–April, 2, 98–106.

Wagner, R. C. 1989. 'Shenandoah Life Insurance Company: improving productivity and service through self-managed work teams'. *Quality and Productivity Management*, 7, 3, 33–4.

Weil, R. 1981. *General Motors Corporation: Organizational Development by Improving the Quality of Working Life*. Occasional Paper 18. London: Work Research Unit.

White, G. 1983. *Redesign of work organization – its impact on supervisors*. Work Research Unit Report, August.

Wickens, P. 1987. *The Road to Nissan: Flexibility, Quality, Teamwork*. Basingstoke: Macmillan Press.

Wild, R. 1975. *Work Organization: A Study of Manual Work and Mass Production*. New York: Wiley.

Wilson, N. A. B. 1973. *On the Quality of Working Life*. Department of Employment Manpower Papers No. 7. London: HMSO.

Zuboff, S. 1988. *In the Age of the Smart Machine: The Future of Work and Power*. Oxford: Heinemann Professional Publishing.

4

The Working Environment

Stephen Bach

In recent years there has been a flurry of activity as employers have given increasing attention to the creation of a safe and healthy working environment. While still predominantly concerned with accidents at work, a broader agenda has emerged as employers have acknowledged employee concerns about occupational ill-health and work hazards such as passive smoking and stress. This process has been reinforced by the accelerating pace of European economic integration, with the European Community (EC) emerging as the dominant player in launching new initiatives to regulate the working environment. Health and safety has been the least contentious area of EC social policy and, as a result, a stream of EC proposals has required modifications to existing health and safety legislation.

There have been more immediate reasons for renewed interest in health and safety. In the UK there has been a lengthening register of disasters with an associated heavy loss of life, including the 167 fatalities in the Piper Alpha catastrophe and the 35 deaths in the Clapham rail disaster. This climate of unease has been fanned by the stubbornly high numbers of workers killed at work each year and the seemingly weak legal redress available to bolster managerial interest in health and safety.

The dominant message of public enquiries into workplace deaths and major disasters has been the responsibility that employers must accept for these disasters and the need for them to give greater priority to safeguarding health and safety at work. In some quarters this message has been taken seriously. The Confederation of British Industry (CBI) has argued that the development of a safety culture enhances business performance and is an integral part of competitiveness (CBI, 1990). Although discussions of human resource management rarely mention the working environment, its emphasis on enhancing employees' commitment indicates the importance of safeguarding the health and welfare of employees. There is also a striking similarity between many of the practices associated with total quality management and the effective management of the working environment.

This chapter will examine the management of the working environment concentrating on health and safety at work, which has been the dominant focus of managerial concern. The chapter begins by examining the UK health and safety record over the last decade. The second section discusses the limitations of the legislative framework and the prospects of EC regulation altering this situation. The third section examines the role of employers and trade unions in shaping the working environment, leading to discussion of future trends and prospects. The central argument of this chapter is that there need to be clear incentives for employers before health and safety becomes a management priority. In some organizations health and safety is seen as central to the overall management approach and the importance of safety is reinforced through specific managerial incentives. However, this does not appear to be the norm and, in the absence of management commitment, a tougher regulatory framework is required to ensure health and safety moves up the management agenda.

Health and Safety at Work

Managerial concern with health and safety in the UK has until recently been largely confined to the prevention of accidents at work. This reflects the agenda that was set by the Robens report of 1972 (Robens, 1972) which predominantly defined health and safety in terms of accident prevention. This has not been the experience of other countries, such as France and Germany, where the establishment of occupational health services has been prominent, with works councils consulted on their establishment (Waters, 1990). Despite British managements' narrower agenda compared to those on the Continent, and its emphasis on accident prevention, it did not ensure falling levels of accidents during the 1980s.

Scale of the problem

The extent of accidents and occupational ill-health at work indicates that there is little room for complacency. The Health and Safety

Executive (HSE) collates information on injuries at work through data gained from employers under the Reporting of Injuries, Diseases and Dangerous Occurrences Regulations (RIDDOR) 1985. This information does not provide a comprehensive record of accidents at work as it is concerned with three categories of accident: fatal injuries; major injuries such as amputations and injuries which require 24-hour hospitalization; and injuries resulting in more than three days off work. Consequently the bulk of more routine accidents at work are excluded from the figures.

Moreover even the categories of accidents that have to be reported in order to comply with RIDDOR represent a gross underestimation of the true extent of these types of accidents. The Health and Safety Commission (HSC) has argued that only one-third of reportable accidents are actually reported by employers. The agriculture and service sectors were the worst offenders, reporting a mere 15–25 per cent of the accidents reportable by law (Department of Employment, 1992: 12). Under-reporting occurs not only because of ignorance of the law and the complexity of RIDDOR but also because managerial emphasis on accident-free operations may perversely discourage the reporting of accidents at work (Makin and Sutherland, 1991).

During 1991–2 an estimated 295 employees were killed by work or by work activity (Health and Safety Commission, 1992a). The level of fatalities finally started to level off at the start of the 1990s, but this is after consistent rises during the 1980s. Furthermore, considering the sharp decline in traditionally high-risk industries such as coal mining, the HSC acknowledges the position is much less favourable than the figures imply (Health and Safety Commission, 1992a: ix). Indeed the fatal injury rate for 1991–2 was virtually unchanged from the previous year at an estimated 1.5 per 100,000 (see figure 4.1). The estimated rate for injuries which caused absence from work for more than three days in 1991–2 was 795 per 100,000, a slight fall from the 1990–1 level of 816. Nonetheless the 1991–2 figure still represents 23.3 million working days lost.

There remain significant differences between sectors in terms of the number of fatalities. The safety record of the construction industry is particularly poor and it continues to account for high levels of fatalities, despite intensive efforts by the HSE to target the construction industry for higher levels of inspection in the last few years. The HSC has expressed concern about the rising number of accidents in the service sector which could not be accounted for simply by the growth in this sector (Health and Safety Commission, 1991: ix).

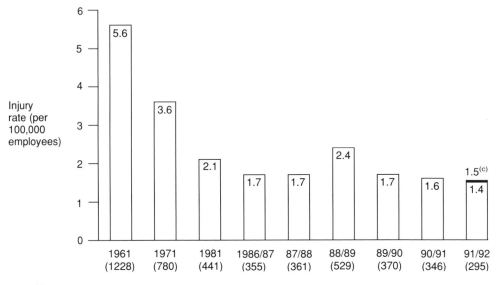

(a) As reported to all enforcement authorities
(b) Provisional
(c) Expected rise from provisional to final
Numbers in brackets are deaths in each of the years.
1988/89 figure includes the 167 deaths in the Piper Alpha disaster.
Source: *HSC Annual Report 1991/92*

Figure 4.1 Fatal injury incidence rates(a) 1961–1991/2(b)

The extent of occupational ill-health at work is even less well documented than accidents at work. The HSC in its 1989/1990 annual report commented: 'We can measure the extent of ill-health quite roughly. Our current best estimate suggests it directly gives rise to at least 2000 premature deaths a year, and contributes to a further 8000. We estimate that at least 80,000 new cases of work-related disease occur each year and that more than 500,000 people suffer continuing damage to health from work' (Health and Safety Commission, 1990: ix). The HSE does provide some discussion of the most important forms of occupational disease. Lung diseases are the most prominent form of occupational ill-health. The balance of ill-health has shifted away from disease caused by traditional hazards such as coal dust towards ill-health caused by asbestos dust, which may account for over 1000 deaths a year.

In an attempt to gain a better understanding of the extent of occupational ill-health, the 1990 Labour Force Survey asked respondents whether they had experienced any health problems in the last 12 months which they attributed to work. Although clearly subjective, the survey revealed in addition to anticipated diseases, such as upper limb disorders and deafness, an estimated 100,000 cases in the UK attributed primarily to work (cited in Health and Safety Commission, 1992a: 96). However, these occupational ill-health figures concentrate on diseases that are already known to be linked to particular work occupations. They do not provide information on hazards at work which have not yet been officially recognized as causing occupational ill-health. This is a worrying omission as the history of hazards, such as asbestos, indicate that dangers are ignored until the evidence on ill-health is patently obvious, leaving a legacy of disease (Willis, 1989: 322).

When comparison is made with other European countries the UK position appears more favourable (Health and Safety Executive, 1991a). This HSE study concluded that Britain had a lower level of fatal accident rates, both for individual industrial sectors and for all industries combined, than in France, Spain and Italy. The position with respect to Germany was also favourable, with a somewhat lower rate than the German manufacturing and service sector. However, there is evidence that France and Germany have achieved more rapid reductions in accident rates than Britain over the last two decades. The HSE warned that Britain's more favourable accident record could not be taken for granted, as the experience of the 1980s demonstrated.

The record of the 1980s

The re-election of a Conservative government for a fourth term of office has ensured the continuation of the policies of deregulation and privatization that characterized the 1980s. The Conservatives presided over the decline of manufacturing industry, the growth of small companies and the continuing trend to subcontract activities. These changes in industrial structure made it more difficult to ensure a safe working environment and exerted a significant impact on the health and safety record of the last decade.

During the 1980s the number of small firms increased very dramatically (Bannock and Daly, 1990). The HSE has expressed concern about the adequacy of safety arrangements in small firms and has increasingly targeted literature and campaigns specifically at small firms. During 1990 the HSE swooped on 1614 small firms in the North of England and as well as frequent breaches of the law found that one-third of these firms were not registered with the HSE (*Financial Times*, 10 October 1990). These failings are indicated by the evidence that employees in establishments of under 50 people are 20 per cent more at risk of major injury than those in medium-size enterprises and some 40 per cent more at risk than those in very large enterprises (Thomas, 1991). These higher risks seem to stem from poor training, inadequate guarding of machinery and the use of less experienced operators.

A major feature of the 1980s was the emphasis within firms on the restructuring and decentralization of their activities to ensure greater responsiveness to market signals. The emphasis on devolving greater responsibility for personnel policy to line managers to ensure greater alignment between human resource policies and product market conditions has important implications for the management of health and safety. As James (1992: 86) points out, these developments tend to reinforce pressures towards the achievment of short-run financial results in which safety measures are given a low priority, as the tangible benefits are hard to define.

A related trend has been the growth of subcontracting during the 1980s. Subcontracting operations has passed on functions to small firms which have no particular health and safety expertise or which do not invest in adequate training of their staff (Anderson, 1990: 16). The most striking example of where a complex set of subcontractual arrangements has jeopardized safety is in the construction industry. The high accident rates bear witness to the lack of clear responsibility for safety when a number of subcontractors are working on one site, which is exacerbated by the prevalence of temporary and self-employed workers (Dawson et al., 1988; Incomes Data Services, 1990a). Similar concerns apply to the public sector where the advent of compulsory competitive tendering has reinforced cost measures, jeopardizing health and safety standards (Bach, 1989; *Labour Research*, 1991).

These changes in industrial structure have not been the only legacy of the 1980s. The Conservative decade ended as it began, with the economy in severe recession. Dawson et al. (1988: 253, 258–60) have argued that recession influences the ability to maintain a safe and healthy workplace in a number of ways. Firstly, a harsher financial climate intensifies competition for resources within organizations, which may detract from health and safety matters. Secondly, pressure to contain labour costs and to raise productivity has been associated with an increased accident incidence rate. Finally, employees may tolerate working in hazardous conditions due to the fear of losing their jobs if they complain. This was graphically illustrated by the Chief Inspector of Factories who cited the case of a 17 year old worker who in stopping a machine that had trapped his arm damaged the conveyor. His parents offered to waive their claim for compensation as long as their son did not lose his job (Department of Employment, 1984: 506).

The 1980s therefore witnessed a reversal of the trend towards the reduction of accidents at work in an altered economic and political landscape. This worsening health and safety record raised doubts about the adequacy of the system of self-regulation introduced in 1974 to maintain health and safety standards and the extent to which employers would give sufficient attention to health and safety in the absence of strong legal regulation.

The Legislative Framework

The need for legislative intervention to safeguard health and safety at work has been recognized since the passage of the early Factory Acts in the wake of the industrial revolution. The legislation developed in a piecemeal manner in response to particular trade union demands and public concern (Wedderburn, 1986: 413). The plethora of legal regulations and statutes indicates acceptance of state intervention to ensure a healthy and safe working environment. Nonetheless this has neither dampened controversy about the most appropriate type of regulation nor has it diminished debate about the effectiveness of the current framework to regulate a safe and healthy working environment.

The Health and Safety at Work Act

The current UK regulation of the working environment stems from the 1972 Robens Committee Report on Safety and Health at Work (Robens, 1972), which focused on accidents at work. The establishment of the Committee of Inquiry arose out of increasing public concern about the level of accidents at work. The ensuing legislation was closely modelled on the Robens recommendations, which diagnosed the cause of accidents at work as apathy. Robens argued that the existence of a mass of complex regulations encouraged reliance on state regulation and discouraged individuals from taking personal responsibility for health and safety (ibid.: para. 28). It followed from this interpretation that responsibility for safety had to be fostered among individuals and it was axiomatic that as individuals caused accidents at work, their voluntary efforts could reduce them.

The Committee therefore believed that the amount of law was counter-productive. They advocated the establishment of a broad enabling framework, which would place primary responsibility for improving health and safety on 'those who create the risks and those who work with them' (ibid.: para. 28). This required management to take primary responsibility for health and safety, as they were in the best position to discharge this duty, but it was imperative that employers involved their employees in safety management. Robens felt this co-operation was unproblematic because of his oft repeated dictum that 'there is a greater natural identity of interest between the two sides of industry in relation to safety and health problems than in most other matters' (ibid.: para. 66).

The Robens Report was given legislative form in the 1974 Health and Safety at Work (HASAW) Act. It mirrored the Committee's emphasis on self-regulation by ensuring that the legislative framework acted as a catalyst for employers and employees to improve health and safety through their own endeavours. The HASAW Act placed responsibility on employers, so far as is reasonably practicable, to ensure the health, safety and welfare of all their employees, while employees were required to take reasonable care of their own health and safety (HASAW Act section 2[1], section 7). (For a detailed discussion of the legal provisions, see James and Lewis, 1986.)

In addition, the HASAW Act reformed the piecemeal system of administration and enforcement that had also been subject to criticism in the Robens Report. The HASAW Act established the Health and Safety Commission, which was charged with carrying out the Act and providing guidance on its application. Its executive arm, the Health and Safety Executive, has responsibility for enforcing the Act through the appointment of Factory Inspectors.

In one sense the HASAW Act has been peculiarly successful in that it survived the Thatcher decade when much of the protective employment legislation of the 1970s was being dismantled. The HASAW Act has also spawned similar legislation in other countries (Gunningham, 1985: 26). In the years following its adoption it was hailed as bringing eight million workers within the scope of the law and for stimulating greater interest in health and safety amongst employers and trade unions (Barrett and James, 1988: 30). A comparative study of the regulation of health and safety in the USA and the UK also drew favourable conclusions, arguing for the superiority of the self-regulatory approach in reducing accidents at work over the more interventionist and adversarial approach of the US authorities (Wilson, 1985).

Nonetheless the limitations of the HASAW Act have come into sharper focus in recent years. In particular, a series of major disasters and horrific individual deaths has widened the constituency that has urged reform of the HASAW Act to include solicitors, disaster support groups, trade unions and the Labour Party. The HSE, the target of much criticism for its lenient stance on enforcement, felt obliged to argue for tougher legal remedies. The criticism of the HASAW Act has focused on two issues. Firstly, in the altered economic and political circumstances of the 1980s, there has been criticism of the philosophy of self-regulation which underpins the HASAW Act. Secondly, the lack of adequate enforcement of the legislation has been highlighted and has been linked to broader questions about the adequacy of existing legal provisions.

The self-regulation philosophy of Robens is based on two questionable assumptions. Firstly, that managers and workers share a common interest in maintaining a safe workplace and, secondly, that apathy causes accidents. The unitary view that management and employees share a common interest in a safe workplace is not borne out in practice as inquiries into major disasters have testified (e.g. Cullen, 1990). Nichols and Armstrong (1973) in their examination of a series of accidents demonstrated that accidents were associated with a fault in the production process and employees' attempts to keep up production. They concluded that the pressure to maintain production from managers anxious to make an adequate return led to situations in which unsafe working practices flourished. Thus the need to maintain production coupled with the cost of ensuring a safe work environment may conflict with an emphasis on making safety a priority.

This has implications for the causes of accidents. Robens attributed accidents at work to workers' apathy and indifference to safety. This focus on the individual and the tendency to blame the victim for the accident has been widely endorsed. In the case of the Purley train crash, the driver received a prison sentence, while the pilots involved in the Kegworth air crash were sacked. The implication is that workers need to be encouraged to be less apathetic about safety through better training and strict enforcement of safety standards.

As the analysis by Nichols and Armstrong has shown, it is necessary to place the analysis of accidents in the social context in which they occur. Instead of focusing exclusively on individual attributes, the incentives within organizations that affect safety need to be considered. Take the case of construction sites where employees may be encouraged to collude in the maintenance of unsafe working practices. Dwyer's case studies found that certain employees consented to dangerous working conditions in return for higher wages. For management these higher wages were a relatively small expenditure to incur compared to the higher expenditure that would have resulted in making the whole site safe (Dwyer, 1983). Financial incentives therefore existed for management and employees to downplay the importance of safety. The implication is that unless organizational incentives exist, such as incorporating safety objectives within appraisal systems, no amount of cajoling of employees and managers will make them give priority to safety.

In the absence of incentives within organizations which emphasize safety, these conditions could be encouraged externally by the state through tough enforcement of the legislation. In practice this has not been the case. The HSE, in accordance with its emphasis on self-regulation, has preferred to secure compliance with the law through education and persuasion rather than by prosecution. It has felt the need to defend this stance, most recently in its 1991/1992 annual report, in the face of continuing criticism of this position. This reluctance to use prosecutions to enforce the law has been reinforced by the inordinate amount of inspectors' time needed to bring prosecutions and the difficulties of achieving successful prosecutions (*Health and Safety Information Bulletin*, 1991a).

The HSE has also traditionally been deterred from bringing prosecutions because of the low levels of fines meted out to offenders. Health and safety offences can be tried either summarily in a magistrates court or in a Crown court once the agreement of a magistrate has been gained. The maximum fine possible in a magistrates court has risen sharply from £2000 to £20,000 since 1991 and in the Crown court companies face unlimited fines. There have been higher fines in a few highly publicized cases. Tate and Lyle were fined a total of £100,000 after an employee died while clearing out a sugar silo and Nobel Explosives were fined the same amount in 1990 after an explosion on an industrial estate in Peterborough

(*Health and Safety Information Bulletin*, 1991a: 10). Nonetheless, these remain the exception rather than the rule. In 1991/1992 the average penalty per conviction amounted to just £1134 (table 4.1). It would appear that magistrates share the reluctance of the HSE to view breaches of the HASAW Act as normal criminal offences.

The possibility exists in law that a charge of manslaughter can be brought against a company or an individual. This is, however, rare in practice due to inadequate investigation of workplace deaths by the police and the HSE (Bergman, 1991). Nonetheless, in the case of George Kenyon, who was killed when he was sucked into a plastic

Table 4.1 Enforcement action, prosecutions and notices issued by all enforcing authorities (excluding local authorities) 1981–1991/2[a]

Prosecutions	Total informations laid[b]	Informations where result recorded[b]	. . . of which Convictions	Average penalty per conviction
1981[c]	1892	1838	1654	£189
1982[c]	2351	2261	2065	£233
1983	2238	2133	1941	£252
1984	2209	2130	1944	£313
1985	2321	2258	1915	£436
1986/7	2199	2120	1771	£410
1987/8	2337	2337	2053	£792[d]
1988/9	2328	2328	2090	£541
1989/90	2653	2653	2289	£783[e]
1990/1	2312	2312	1991	£903[f]
1991/2	2407	2405	2122	£1134[g]

[a] 1981–5, calendar years; 1986/7 onwards, year commencing 1 April; 1991/2, provisional

[b] Includes, for Scotland, charges preferred

[c] Data for HSE's Factory, Agricultural and Mines and Quarries Inspectorates only. Data for other enforcing authorities, namely Explosives, Nuclear Installations, Railways Inspectorates and Department of Energy (Petroleum Engineering Division), are not readily available

[d] Includes fines totalling £750,000 imposed on BP. If these convictions are excluded, the average fine for 1987/8 would be £427

[e] Includes a fine of £100,000 imposed against Nobels Explosives. If this conviction was excluded, the average for 1989/90 would be £739

[f] Includes fines of £250,000 against Nobels Explosives and £100,000 against Tate 8 Lyle (reduced from £250,000 on appeal in November 1990). If these were excluded, the average fine for 1990/1 would be £728

[g] Includes fines of £250,000 against British Rail and £100,000 against both Shell UK and British Gas. If these were excluded, the average fine for 1991/2 would be £923

Figures for average penalty are in current price terms not adjusted for inflation

Source: HSC Annual Report 1991/2

crushing machine, the HSE pressed for manslaughter charges to be brought against the directors of David Holt Plastics Ltd. An HSE investigation revealed that the machine had been rewired in a way that would allow it to operate with the lid open. This immobilized the safety mechanism, enabling increased output, and provides a grisly reminder of the relative priorities assigned to production as opposed to safety (*Health and Safety Information Bulletin*, 1991a: 11; Bergman, 1991: 23). One of the directors pleaded guilty to manslaughter charges and received a suspended 12-month prison sentence, while another had his plea of not-guilty accepted by the Crown Prosecution Service. Yet the fact that even in such a serious case, a non-custodial case was returned indicated the reluctance of the judiciary to criminalize health and safety offences.

The Conservative government also weakened the enforcement of health and safety regulations by the inadequate funding provided to the HSE during the 1980s. This was reflected in stagnant staffing levels and the decrease in planned preventative inspection which was giving way to reactive investigation of serious accidents (Tombs, 1990: 334). This situation has been exacerbated in recent years by the HSE taking on additional responsibilities, such as railway safety and responding to European Community initiatives. The HSE has also had to contend with the requirement to inspect a growing number of workplaces (Tombs, 1990: 333).

Despite a growing workload, the funding situation of the HSE deteriorated and it has increasingly been expected to make up the shortfall by income generated by its own activities (Institute of Professionals, Managers and Specialists (IPMS), 1992: 5). The most visible sign of this deteriorating position was the reduction in the number of Factory Inspectors over the course of the 1980s. Although this position is now beginning to be reversed, the number of inspectors remains below the 1979 level and the recruitment of inexperienced people has created the need to train these staff, thereby diminishing the actual operational capacity of the HSE (ibid.: 7).

European Community regulation

At the same time as the limitations of the HASAW Act were becoming more apparent, initiatives to regulate all aspects of the work environment were emanating from Brussels. As the HSC noted in 1990: 'The European Community has now to be regarded as the principal engine of health and safety law affecting the UK, not just in worker safety but also in major hazards and most environmental matters' (Health and Safety Commission, 1990: viii). There has been an accelerating stream of Directives from the EC which is modifying the current regulation of the working environment.

In line with more general concern to avoid 'social dumping', the European Commission aimed to reduce the differences between countries in health and safety standards, which formed one of the barriers to the establishment of a Single European Market. The passage of the Single European Act (SEA) was the catalyst for a more interventionist approach in the sphere of the working environment by the European Commission. Firstly, the incorporation of Article 118A into the SEA provided for EC jurisdiction over the work environment and encouraged 'improvements in the work environment as regards the health and safety of workers' by member states. Secondly, these legislative developments could be adopted though qualified majority voting, allowing more rapid progress to be made.

This led to a new emphasis on the work environment and in 1988 the European Commission unveiled an ambitious programme of change which included 15 new Directives (Eberlie, 1990: 90). The most significant changes resulted from the adoption by the Commision of a Framework Directive on health and safety together with five other Directives. Regulations to implement the Directives came into force at the start of 1993. The Framework Directive has been empowered by the Management of Health and Safety at Work (MHSW) Regulations which impose more specific requirements on employers than under the HASAW Act. A central feature is the requirement to carry out 'suitable and sufficient' risk assessment in order to decide what safety measures are needed. The Workplace (Health, Safety and Welfare) Regulations establish a series of minimum requirements on a range of health and safety matters, such as ventilation of workplaces. There are also regulations concerned with the manual handling of loads, provision of personal protective equipment and the use of work equipment. The greatest publicity has surrounded the Health and Safety (Display Screen Equipment) Regulations which are the first set of UK regulations which provide minimum health and safety standards for the use of VDU workstations. There are further Directives in the pipeline targeted at particular sectors, such as the construction industry, and at specific groups, for example, pregnant women.

It is the detailed nature of the initiatives that mark a departure from the traditional more flexible regulations in Britain, as can be seen in the Work With Display Screen Equipment Directive and the HSC proposals for implementation (Health and Safety Commission, 1992b). Firstly, whereas previously there were no specific legal requirements on employers concerned with VDU work, the Directive places responsibilities on employers to assess risks and to conform with minimum requirements for workstations, demonstrating the more prescriptive approach of European Directives. Secondly, it provides users with entitlements to eye and eyesight tests whose costs have to be borne by the employer. Thirdly, employers have to provide health and safety information and training to users, highlighting the need to amend existing regulations on employee participation in health and safety matters. Consequently, the HSC has estimated that employers could face costs of £300 million in the first year in implementing the Framework Directive and the related daughter Directives (*Financial Times*, 12/13 October 1991).

Although the EC proposals have stimulated renewed employer interest in health and safety, it is important not to equate the volume of regulation in the health and safety area with the likely impact of these measures. Firstly, the primary objective of the EC proposals is to harmonize rather than to improve health and safety standards across the Community. This is to prevent different health and safety standards acting as a barrier to free competition. As UK safety standards are viewed as relatively advanced, the impact of the regulations is likely to be less significant in Britain than in many other EC countries. Indeed the willingness of the UK government to go along with the health and safety measures while vociferously opposing EC social initiatives indicates that the government feels that health and safety measures pose little threat to the policy of labour market deregulation.

Secondly, while the HSC has drawn up proposals to comply with the EC Directives, its aim has been to avoid increasing obligations on employers and to maintain the basic structure of regulation established by the 1974 Act. This has led to controversy as some of the Directives extend existing arrangements in the UK, but the detailed regulations which implement the Directives adopt a minimalist interpretation of what is required. The HSE has continued to emphasize that requirements on employers apply the 'as far as reasonably practicable' test which has been criticized as diluting the potential impact of the 1974 law (James, 1992: 86). However the

EC Directives do not include the 'as far as reasonably practicable' proviso, so this is a clear attempt to limit their intent. Controversy also surrounds the narrowness of the definition of 'users' in the display screen equipment regulations, and this has limited their scope (*Health and Safety Information Bulletin*, 1993).

Finally, doubts remain about the commitment of the HSE to enforce the new regulations. The HSE has done little to dispel these concerns – for instance, in its 1991/1992 annual report, the HSE indicated its willingness to tolerate employers who did not comply with the regulations, stating 'in general, inspectors can be expected to recognize that employers will need time to take sensible action when requirements are completely new. Formal enforcement measures are not likely unless the risks to health and safety are evident and immediate . . .' (Health and Safety Commission, 1992a: para. 1.31).

Consequently, it remains to be seen whether European regulation can remedy the limitations in the existing system of self-regulation. The number of Directives coupled with reliance on the existing overstretched system of enforcement may simply reinforce the gap between firms committed to maintenance of a safe and healthy working environment and those who choose not to comply. The approach of employers and employees will therefore remain crucial in ensuring the maintenance of a safe and healthy working environment.

The Management of the Working Environment

The management of the working environment has long been associated with the personnel management function. Indeed the Institute of Personnel Management grew out of the welfare movement which in 1913 had founded the Welfare Workers Association (Niven, 1967). During the 1980s, however, personnel practitioners were exhorted to downplay their welfare legacy and to focus more directly on the way that personnel practice could contribute to the achievment of competitive advantage.

It is therefore scarcely surprising that personnel practitioners have not viewed management of the working environment as a priority. In a ranking of 14 personnel activities the category, 'Health, Safety and Welfare' was judged as only number 11, both in terms of importance and in respect of whether it would increase in importance

(Torrington et al., 1985: 14). Other groups have also occupied the terrain that personnel managers have relinquished. Safety advisers, whose primary role has been to provide advice on safety matters and monitor safety in the organization, have increased in numbers since the passage of the HASAW Act (Grayson, 1981: 5). Nonetheless safety advisers have encountered difficulties in fulfilling their function, not least because their advisory role means they have frequently lacked power (Dawson et al., 1988: 78). This is particularly the case when safety advisers have been located in production or production related departments, where concern for safety was more likely to come into conflict with the work of the department, rather than when they came under the auspices of personnel (Jones and Tait, 1992: 39).

If there is evidence of the increasing importance attached to safety advisers, it has not detracted from an emphasis on line management obligations. The CBI in its guidance on developing a 'safety culture' states 'it must be a line management responsibility' (CBI, 1990: 53). Companies including Esso and Conoco argue that integral to their successful management of the working environment, is the central responsibility placed on line management to maintain good safety performance (*Health and Safety Information Bulletin*, 1991b; *Occupational Safety and Health*, February 1990: 36–9). These organizations believe that this ensures that line managers take personal responsibility for the working environment and prevents safety advisors or external enforcement agencies being seen as the guardians of the safe working environment.

The attention given to the role of line management should not be viewed as an affirmation that greater importance will be attached to health and safety; nor is it new, as is often implied. Twenty years ago the Robens Report emphasized that 'safety and health must be the direct operational responsibility of line management' (Robens, 1972: para 54). However, it can't be assumed that line managers will give priority to safety unless it is clear to these managers that they will be judged on their safety performance (Dawson, 1986: 3). In practice, line managers are more likely to be judged against productivity and budgetary targets, particularly with the spread of budgetary devolution in both the private and public sectors.

Rarely is there recognition of these conflicting pressures facing managers and the contradictory signals this sends to employees about the importance of safety. The Cannon Street rail crash inquiry revealed these conflicting management priorities. Although train drivers were instructed not to report for duty if not fully fit, absence beyond a certain level resulted in dismissal, indicating that safety considerations were subservient to managerial attempts to discourage absenteeism and control costs (Makin and Sutherland, 1991). It is therefore evident that emphasis on line management responsibility is insufficient to ensure a safe and healthy working environment without support and encouragement throughout the organization, the provision of adequate resources and clear monitoring. This monitoring is required to ensure that health and safety is treated as a priority by line managers, even when faced with competing claims on their time and resources.

The role of trade unions

The questionable willingness of management to make safety a priority might be expected to be offset by trade unions acting as a positive force for safety in the workplace. Although the traditional focus of trade union activity was negotiating additional payments for dangerous work and gaining adequate compensation for injuries at work this has started to change. During the 1980s there was a shift towards an emphasis on accident prevention and improvements to the working environment gained greater prominence on the trade union agenda.

The passage of the HASAW Act and the subsequent Safety Representatives and Safety Committees (SRSC) Regulations 1978 boosted trade union activity. The SRSC Regulations introduced the right for recognized trade unions to appoint safety representatives and conferred on them a number of legal powers. These included the right to inspect workplaces and to investigate accidents or other hazards at work. They were also expected to be aware of employers' safety policy, assisting with updating the policy as well as ensuring compliance by employees. To assist safety representatives in performing their functions, they were entitled to paid time off for health and safety training. The regulations also allowed for the establishment of a safety committee where requested by two or more safety representatives.

However, the effectiveness of the safety representative regulations has been questioned. An early trade union critic (Gee, 1980) noted that safety representatives were isolated from other shop stewards, who neither had the training to tackle working environment issues nor viewed them as a priority. The effectiveness of safety representatives was dependent on trade union organization and thus, in industries where organization was weak, as in contruction, safety representatives had little impact (Codrington and Henley, 1981). These difficulties have been exacerbated by declining trade union membership and the impact of recession, which has led to tacit agreement to downplay safety concerns (Dawson, 1986). A comprehensive review of the operation of the SRSC Regulations, based on a survey of 4761 workplaces, confirmed this picture as well as highlighting other weaknesses, including declining levels of safety representatives' training and the lack of employee involvement in smaller workplaces (Waters and Gourlay, 1990).

During the 1990s the position of trade union safety representatives will be squeezed further. The confinement of safety representatives to unionized workplaces reflected an earlier era when trade union influence was at its height. During the 1980s, the decline in trade union membership and the reduction in the amount of small workplaces with safety representatives contributed to a decline in the number of workplaces covered by safety representatives from 16 per cent in 1979 (employing 79 per cent of employees covered) to 9 per cent in 1987 (employing 75 per cent of employees covered) (*Health and Safety Information Bulletin*, 1990a). Evidence from the 1990 workplace industrial relations survey confirmed this trend, indicating large increases in the proportion of workplaces where management dealt unilaterally with health and safety matters (Millward et al., 1992: 162).

The continuation of a Conservative government for a fourth term of office will further challenge trade union dominated representation on health and safety matters. A precedent has already been established. In 1989 the Department of Energy, in the aftermath of the Piper Alpha disaster, formalized employee participation arrangements on North Sea oil and gas installations which did not limit statutory rights to consultation to trade union representatives (Department of Energy, 1989). This permitted the workforce to elect safety representatives who have similar rights to carry out investigations and to form a safety committee as their trade union counterparts. Finally, the EC regulations place great emphasis on the provision of information and consultation rights to employees on a range of health and safety issues, further weakening the dominance of trade union appointed safety representatives.

The impact of a break with the trade union monopoly on health and safety representation has been viewed in different ways. For some commentators (Dawson et al., 1988: 275–8; Waters and Gourlay, 1990) the lack of statutory employee representation in non-union workplaces could be remedied by the election of safety representatives where there is no recognized trade union and this would have a positive impact on health and safety standards. Yet Waters (1990: 20–1), in contrast to his earlier stance, has argued that there is a danger that the Conservative government would use wider participation by non-unionized employees to undermine trade union effectiveness. He argues that this would not enhance health and safety standards because safety representatives can only be effective with strong trade union backing.

Ultimately the effectiveness of employee representation, whether it be through trade union channels or not, will depend crucially on the degree of management commitment. This has been the experience of the SRSC Regulations, particularly as they left wide discretion to management as to how they chose to implement the regulations. Management actions have also shaped the effectiveness of safety committees. As Waters and Gourlay note, where management had established a clear system for the reporting of routine hazards, it allowed the safety committee to concentrate on a wider health and safety agenda and not get bogged down by trivia (Walters and Gourlay, 1990).

Trends and Prospects

1992 is usually associated with the completion of the Single European Market. However, it also marked another EC inititiative, the European Year of Safety, Hygiene and Health Protection at Work. The purpose of the safety year was to promote awareness about European Commission measures in this area. Does the establishment of a EC year for safety symbolize the growing importance of health and safety during the 1990s or is it simply a gimmick that disguises the overall lack of concern about the working environment? The extent to which maintenance of a safe and healthy working environment becomes a priority for employers will be influenced by a number of factors: the willingness of management to adopt a safety culture; the ability of trade unions to assert their influence over health and safety; the extent to which occupational health matters gain more prominence; and the impact of the green agenda.

Towards a safety culture?

Commentators have suggested that management's concern for the working environment makes good business sense (Health and Safety Executive, 1991b; CBI, 1990; Stranks and Dewis, 1986). There is a striking similarity between the rationale and techniques associated with human resource management and the successful management of the working environment. Although the working environment is rarely mentioned explicitly in the human resource management literature, there is increasingly the same emphasis on cost effectiveness, commitment, quality and strategic integration that permeates the human resource management paradigm.

Firstly, the cost effectiveness of managing the work environment is stressed. The HSE examined the costs of accidents at work and showed the huge potential savings for firms with better than average safety records. The starkest example is of a transport company that was jeopardizing 37 per cent of its profits due to accidents at work and the resulting costs of ill-health and damage to property. The true cost of accidents at work is often hidden in maintenance and training budgets (Health and Safety Executive, 1993). As noted earlier, some companies have faced fines in excess of £250,000, and major accidents may also affect a firm's share price, as occurred after the Exxon Valdez oil spillage. The growing proportion of companies that include some form of environmental statement in their annual accounts is testimony to the costs of remedying environmental mistakes.

Secondly, firms noted the cumulative costs associated with a poor working environment. The HSE estimates that work-related injuries and ill-health account for 29 million days lost per annum, almost 15 times the number lost through strikes (Health and Safety Commission, 1991: x). In addition to expenditure caused by the absence of staff and the costs of repairs to damaged machinery, there are the less visible costs associated with the investigation of accidents. The CBI has noted the impact on insurance premiums. For one company, the reduction of lost time injuries meant 'the rate of employers' lost liability insurance dropped from an equivalent of £90,000 per annum in 1975 to £20,000 in 1985' (CBI, 1990: 12). Similarly, Conoco, in evidence submitted to the Cullen Inquiry, reported that the low level of lost day work injuries boosted profits by £6 million in 1985 through reduced compensation claims (*Health and Safety Information Bulletin*, 1991b: 2).

Thirdly, as quality has become the watchword of the 1990s, companies have capitalized on the links between quality and safety. The ability of companies to produce quality output consistently is jeopardized by a poor working environment. Similarly, the attention to detail needed to achieve a quality product is integral to creating a safe and healthy working environment (CBI, 1990: 14–15). A central objective for BP when it introduced total quality management was to raise awareness and commitment to safety, viewing safety as a central element within total quality management (*Health and Safety Information Bulletin*, 1988: 2).

Fourthly, companies emphasize that careful management of the working environment signals to employees that management is seriously committed to their well-being. This is particularly important as safety cannot be imposed on employees. As firms have reduced their layers of management, it has placed the onus on employees to take greater responsibility for creating a safe and healthy working environment. It is not surprising, therefore, that firms such as Esso and British Airways emphasize the working environment in their mission statements and annual reports.

Increasingly the guidance issued by the CBI (1990) and the HSE (1991b) urges managers to concentrate on 'software' as opposed to 'hardware' concerns. Hardware concerns focus on designing safety into work systems, for example by securing safe installation. Software concerns focus on the behaviour of individuals within the organization and the influence of leadership, communication, and training in securing a safe and healthy work environment. These latter concerns have increasingly dominated the management agenda.

An attempt has been made to rank the most important of these characteristics by Lines and Smith (1990). They used the safety elements of the *International Safety Rating System* (*ISRS*) as the basis of their comparison. Their results indicated that effective leadership and administration was emphasized as the most important element in securing a good working environment. This was defined as 'clear evidence of a management initiated safety policy, with defined standards and management commitment to implementation' (*ISRS*, 5th edn).

Under the HASAW Act, all employers with more than five employees have to write a statement on their general policy towards health and safety at work. By 1984, 89 per cent of establishments surveyed had a formal health and safety procedure (Millward and

Stevens, 1986: 170). This high level of coverage, however, masks the inadequacies of many of the documents. Policies may frequently be copied from other organizations with differing needs and may lack adequate detail about the organizational requirements needed to implement the policy effectively. There are also marked differences between organizations in the extent to which their terms are observed (Booth, 1985; Dawson et al., 1988).

While legislative requirements focus on formalized written procedures, some employers have used human resource management techniques to foster greater awareness of hazards at work. Safety circles have been used by employers to encourage employees to identify and implement proposals to meet the requirements of the Control of Substances Hazardous to Health (COSHH) Regulations (CBI, 1990: 38). Team briefings are another favoured approach. At Esso's Fawley refinery, meetings are held every Friday to discuss any incidents in the previous week. These discussions are converted into a team brief which is used by the supervisors in their weekly briefings with their staff. For management this ensures that key messages are passed to the workforce in a consistent manner and provides supervisors with material to run the meeting (*Occupational Safety and Health*, February 1990: 38). However, in addition to the usual warnings that are made about the effectiveness of these techniques (see other chapters in this volume), safety experts themselves have not ranked communication very highly (Lines and Smith, 1990).

It has become a commonplace to argue that Britain needs to improve its training record and this has increasingly been acknowledged as an important element in attempts to improve the working environment. The HSC made training a priority in its Plan of Work for 1991–2, arguing that inadequate training has contributed to major disasters such as at Zeebrugge and Kings Cross (Department of Employment, 1991: 373). The CBI argued that the companies in its survey viewed training as a priority to instill the company philosophy into employees. BP has placed considerable emphasis on ensuring adequate management training (*Health and Safety Information Bulletin*, 1988: 2). Nonetheless the picture remains mixed: Booth (1985: 38) maintains that organizations frequently lack the expertise to train their staff adequately. There has also been a sharp decline in levels of safety representative training (Walters and Gourlay, 1990).

There is an emergent consensus on the type of initiatives that help to sustain a safety culture, with the emphasis firmly on software concerns. The CBI typifies this approach with an emphasis on clear top management commitment, as indicated by the presence of a main board director responsible for safety. Great emphasis is also placed on building responsibility and accountability for health and safety throughout the organization through appraisal and emphasis on line management responsibility. It is evident that only by building positive incentives within organizations to give priority to health and safety can generalized concern for health and safety be translated into an integral part of the general management process.

Trade union initiatives

Employees and their trade unions have become increasingly safety-conscious. This reflects a continuing move away from an emphasis on gaining compensation for employees' injuries and ill-health, towards an emphasis on preventing accidents and eliminating hazards at work. Trade unions, in developing strategies to revitalize their dwindling ranks, have sought to broaden their appeal through greater emphasis on the working environment as a negotiating issue. This has spilled over into industrial action, notably in the North Sea oil industry during 1990, where improvements to health and safety were at the centre of a prolonged and acrimonious dispute. This itself had been triggered by a helicopter crash resulting in six fatalities.

Trade unions have responded to the broader health and safety concerns of their members which extend beyond accidents to include occupational ill-health. The priority concern for 45 per cent of trade unions has become 'repetitive strain injuries' (RSIs) (*Labour Research*, 1991). This is associated with making rapid repetitive movements and has afflicted workers who pluck chickens as much as keyboard operators. RSI has been associated with incentive schemes that require keyboard operators to undertake a certain number of keystrokes per hour. Data entry staff in major insurance companies have been able to raise their salaries by as much as two-thirds above their basic salary if they achieve 15,000–20,000 keystrokes an hour (Incomes Data Services, 1990a: 15). Although some banking and finance employers have issued guidance to employees which encourage them to take breaks, this guidance will be ignored if work incentives within organizations are not altered. The same difficulties will arise with the use of ergonomics specialists who have been employed particularly in the newspaper industry (Incomes Data Services, 1990a: 15). The pressure to produce a newspaper to a tight deadline will undermine efforts to improve the working environment by ergonomic means, as work pressures will reinforce hazardous work practices.

Frustration at the response of management to workplace hazards led journalists to vote to take industrial action at the *Financial Times* during 1991, to win reprieve for nine of their colleagues who faced mandatory ill-health retirement arising from their RSI. Trade unions have backed damages cases and achieved some success: two former keyboard operators were awarded £6000 damages for pain and suffering against BT during 1991 (*The Guardian*, 17 December 1991). The irony for trade unions is that despite their attempts to sign agreements with management to prevent workplace hazards, they have had most success in gaining compensation through the courts rather than achieving preventative measures. Until employers develop more imaginative approaches to tackling hazards at work, for example through job rotation and consideration of the whole work environment rather than solely the technology, trade unions will be forced to concentrate on gaining compensation for their members.

A greater opportunity to pursue preventative strategies at work has arisen from the introduction of the COSHH Regulations which came into force in October 1989 as a result of an EC Directive. The Regulations are designed to identify and control occupational hazards from the use of hazardous substances before these risks become manifest through ill-health. COSHH therefore makes explicit employer responsibilities to create a safe system of work and the way to achieve these objectives in a manner that was absent from the HASAW Act. Consquently the COSHH Regulations when introduced were hailed by the government as the most important legislation on the working environment since the 1974 legislation (Powley, 1989).

Although a review of the first year of operation revealed that an estimated 80 per cent of people worked in 'COSHH aware' organizations, the HSE was critical of the standards of assessment, which are central to the Regulations (Health and Safety Commission, 1991: 30). Purnell (1991: 30) has noted the lack of confidence among in-house assessors in gauging the health risk posed by hazardous substances. COSHH has therefore enabled trade unions, such as the General, Municipal and Boilermakers' Union, with a strong commitment to the work environment, to shape management practice by assisting them to comply with the COSHH regulations

(Incomes Data Services, 1990a: 13). Furthermore, the emphasis that COSHH places on the assessment, control and monitoring of hazards has provided an opportunity for trade unions to broaden this process to incorporate environmental objectives.

Trade unions in their attempts to attract new members have viewed the working environment as an important campaigning and negotiating issue. Take the case of the Transport and General Workers Union which, as part of its membership drive, campaigned for work-based cervical cancer screening facilities and the time off for women to attend sessions (Morris, 1989: 41). Nonetheless, while trade unions have had some success, it has usually been in situations where management has demonstrated its commitment to work jointly with trade unions. Overall, in the harsh economic and political climate faced by employees and their representatives, real progress has been dependent on management goodwill.

Occupational health and welfare

At the start of the 1990s, the neglect of occupational health issues has started to be reversed. The COSHH regulations and EC initiatives required employers to move beyond a narrow focus on accidents at work to a broader concern with the well-being of employees. This stimulus coincided with employers' concerns to develop more individual ways of managing the employment relationship as part of their attempt to adjust to more competitive trading conditions. The Conservative government encouraged employers to take greater responsibility for the well-being of employees as it proclaimed the desirability of a mininimalist role for the state.

Employers have also responded to pressure from employees to create healthier workplaces, the spread of no smoking policies being a good example of employee pressure for change. This has coincided with employers' attempts to improve the health of their workforce and has been reinforced by moves to improve employee relations (Sigman, 1992). There may also be the stirrings of what has become a dominant concern of US human resource managers, namely the rising cost of health insurance and attempts to curtail it by not employing high risk employees. In the UK there is also developing concern amongst employers about the cost of private health insurance premiums for their employees (*Financial Times*, 11 May 1992) and this has further encouraged attempts to keep employees healthy.

The most widespread health promotion initiative has been the rapid growth in the number of companies adopting policies that restricted or banned smoking at work (*Industrial Relations Review and Report*, 1992). A survey for BUPA of 104 large companies indicated that there had been an increase in the number of companies introducing smoking restrictions from 67 per cent in 1987 to 79 per cent in 1989 (cited in Incomes Data Services, 1991a: 2). This trend is likely to further accelerate in the light of recent legal claims from employees who have claimed that their employers were responsible for their poor health caused by passive smoking at work. Since the publication of the Frogatt report which highlighted the risks to health of passive smoking, employers have been concerned that they could be in breach of the HASAW Act if they allowed smoking at work (*Industrial Relations Review and Report*, 1992).

Prior to the introduction of a smoking policy, employers have frequently gauged the opinions of employees and their representatives. Opportunities are also usually provided to help employees stop smoking before the policy is introduced. While the spread of smoking policies has been most pronounced, employers have also developed policies to tackle alcohol and substance abuse at work. A number of companies, including Shell, IBM and United Biscuits, prohibit the consumption of alcohol at work (Incomes Data Services, 1991b: 5), while others have provided advice and information to ensure sensible drinking at work.

Fewer organizations are willing to acknowledge that their staff daily face the threat of violence from their customers or from other employees in the form of sexual harassment. It is difficult for organizations that are trying to be more customer oriented to admit that customers may be uncooperative, violent or may not wish to receive the service being offered. Furthermore, employers may be concerned at the negative portrayal of the organization if it is admitted employees are at risk from assault. Nonetheless employers not only have statutory obligations under the HASAW Act but also face poorer work performance from employees faced with the threat of violence at work (Incomes Data Services, 1990b: 2).

The extent of the problem of violence in the workplace has been quantified by a number of organizations as the first step to devising a strategy to tackle violence at work. A survey by the HSE's Health Services Advisory Committee indicated that in one year 19 per cent of ambulance staff suffered some injury from assault, while a further 17 per cent claimed to have been threatened with a weapon (cited in

Poyner and Warner, 1988: 56). A number of factors have been identified in different work environments that can increase the risk of assault including the presence of alcohol, handling of cash and people having to wait for a service, such as at social security offices (ibid.: 5). Publicans would therefore seem to be one high-risk group and Whitbread Inns have recognized this situation. Whitbread claims to have reduced the number of violent attacks on staff by one-third since 1987 (Trollope, 1991). This has been achieved by the introduction of seminars to train staff how to diffuse difficult situations and to understand the effects of alcohol on behaviour. The work environment has also been altered by designing pubs that break up large spaces where groups could gather.

Additional measures to reduce the risk of violence to employees may be harder to implement when they run counter to commercial interests. Adequate staffing levels both help to provide a service that prevents the frustration associated with violence at work and ensures that staff have greater protection if an attack occurs (Incomes Data Services, 1990b: 4). But trends in private and public sector organizations towards reduced staffing levels suggest it may be difficult to ensure adequate protection for employees.

The green agenda

Organizations have also been battling to establish their green credentials. Increased public awareness, the passage of the 1990 Environmental Protection Act and a series of Directives from Brussels have moved green issues up the managerial agenda. The amalgamation within companies, such as Texaco, of environmental matters with safety indicates the degree of overlap that is seen between the two issues (*Health and Safety Information Bulletin*, 1990b). For example, as workplaces are a major source of general pollution, it is evident that control of the general environment and of the working environment are closely interrelated.

In particular, there is a shared emphasis on the importance of audit systems. EC regulations, with their stress on the importance of risk assessment, have encouraged the growing use of audit systems designed to assess and eliminate work-based hazards. Environmental audits take this process further, examining the environmental impact of the firm's activities and proceeding to make recommendations on how to alter company practice to improve the environment and to reduce expenditure. British Airways has examined the impact of its activities at Heathrow Airport, detailing noise levels, fuel consumption and emissions (Jack, 1992), while National Westminster Bank has noted the potential savings revealed through the exercise (Lascelles, 1992).

Trade unions have also launched initiatives on the environment, with some unions beginning to appoint environmental representatives. The priority for trade unions has been to establish their legitimacy with employers in tackling green affairs. A policy document from the MSF trade union argues for environmental issues to be placed on the bargaining agenda and for the negotiation of environmental agreements (Manufacturing, Science, Finance, 1990). Employers have resisted signing environmental agreements (*Labour Research*, 1992) and favour more direct forms of employee involvement. Consequently, as with the more traditional health and safety agenda, trade unions will need to campaign to make the environment a trade union issue.

Conclusions

The importance attached by the European Commission to the working environment and the need for organizations to be more sensitive to the environmental consequences of their actions has stimulated renewed employer interest in the working environment in recent years. What is less clear is the extent to which this generalized concern has been translated into clear managerial commitment to give greater priority to health and safety at work. The deteriorating health and safety record of the 1980s and the stagnation of the early 1990s casts doubts on any simple conclusion that we are seeing the widespread development of a safety culture.

As with so many areas of human resource management, small numbers of companies are repeatedly identified as exemplars of this new approach. Yet if the majority of companies accepted that concern for the working environment made good business sense, the need for evangelical advice from the CBI and the HSE would be redundant. In addition, these exemplar companies are clustered in industries such as chemicals and oil, where not only are the hazards clearly evident, but where disasters such as the Flixborough explosion have reiterated the catastrophic human and financial costs of a disaster. Even in these cases, commitment to a safe and healthy working environment can still leave conflicts of interest unresolved.

For management, the primary emphasis in these organizations is the avoidance of a major disaster while for employees 'minor' accidents, such as those arising from slippery floors which result in days off work or long-term discomfort, are of more immediate concern.

In the absence of clear organizational incentives for employers to give greater priority to health and safety at work there is a need for a tough legislative framework that ensures employers give adequate attention to the working environment. The last decade has exposed the underlying flaws in the current system of self-regulation. The deregulation of the labour market, the growth of small firms and subcontracting, with the associated pressures to reduce costs, has jeopardized safety standards. This situation has been exacerbated by the weak enforcement of the HASAW Act by the HSE.

This situation has spawned demands that the law be strengthened to allow more effective prosecution of companies that breach health and safety laws. Additional strands of these reform proposals include enhanced rights for workers to refuse to carry out dangerous jobs and the establishment of a work environment fund to aid research and training on the working environment which would also move policy beyond the current concentration on accidents at work (for details of these proposals, see Bergman, 1991; Dalton, 1991; Moore, 1991).

The strengthening of the law would enhance rather than negate the importance of the role of management in health and safety at work, which has been a central theme of this chapter. For example, the legal establishment of named directors responsible for safety would mirror current best practice and provide clear signals to employers about the need to give greater emphasis to health and safety at work. In the absence of these stronger organizational and legal incentives, for most employers the rhetoric about the importance of the working environment will remain just that, with the resultant toll in ill-health and accidents at work.

Bibliography

Anderson, P. 1990. 'Tender Traps'. *Occupational Safety and Health*, April, 15–20.

Bach, S. 1989. *Too High A Price Too Pay? A Study of Competitive Tendering for Domestic Services in the NHS*. Warwick Papers in Industrial Relations, 25. Coventry: Industrial Relations Research Unit, University of Warwick.

Bannock, G. and Daly, M. 1990. 'Size Distribution of UK Firms'. *Employment Gazette*, Vol. 98, No. 5, 255–8.

Barrett, B. and James, P. 1988. 'Safe Systems: Past, Present, and Future?'. *Industrial Law Journal*, Vol. 17, No. 1, 26–41.

Bergman, D. 1991. *Deaths at Work: Accidents or Corporate Crime*. London: Workers' Educational Association.

Booth, R. 1985. 'What's New in Health and Safety Management'. *Personnel Management*, April, 36–9.

CBI. 1990. *Developing a Safety Culture*. London: Confederation of British Industry.

Cockburn, C. 1983. *Brothers: Male Dominance and Technological Change*. London: Pluto Press.

Codrington, C. and Henley, J. 1981. 'The Industrial Relations of Injury and Death: Safety Representatives in the Construction Industry'. *British Journal of Industrial Relations*, Vol. 19, No. 3, 297–315.

Cullen, Lord. 1990. *The Public Inquiry into the Piper Alpha Disaster*. London: HMSO.

Dalton, A. 1991. *Health and Safety. An Agenda for Change*. London: Workers' Educational Association.

Dawson, S. 1986. 'Self-Regulation: the Myth and the Reality'. *Health and Safety Information Bulletin*, 126, 2–5.

Dawson, S., Willman, P., Bamford, M. and Clinton, A. 1988. *Safety at Work: The Limits of Self-Regulation*. Cambridge: Cambridge University Press.

Department of Employment. 1984. 'Factory Inspectorate Warns Against Corner Cutting on Safety'. *Employment Gazette*, Vol. 92, No. 11, 506–7.

Department of Employment. 1991. 'Training is the Key'. *Employment Gazette*, Vol. 99, No. 7, 373.

Department of Employment. 1992. 'Accidents that Never Happen'. *Employment Gazette*, Vol. 100, No. 1, 12.

Department of Energy. 1989. *Safety Representatives and Safety Committees on Offshore Installations: Guidance Notes*. London: HMSO.

Dwyer, T. 1983. 'A New Concept of the Production of Industrial Accidents'. *New Zealand Journal of Industrial Relations*, Vol. 8, No. 2, 147–60.

Eberlie, R. F. 1990. 'The New Health and Safety Legislation of the European Community'. *Industrial Law Journal*, Vol. 19, No. 2, 81–97.

Financial Times. 1990. 'Health and Safety Executive Swoops on Small Businesses'. 10 October.

Financial Times. 1991. 'Cost of EC safety rules runs at nearly £300 million a year'. 12/13 October.

Financial Times. 1992. 'Losing Patience with Private Medicine'. 11 May.

Gee, D. 1980. 'Notes on the October Revolution'. *Trade Union Studies Journal*, No. 2, 14–16.

Guardian. 1991. 'Women Win £6000 for keyboard injuries'. 17 December.

Gunningham, N. 1985. 'Workplace Safety and the Law'. In Creighton, W. B. and Gunningham, N. (eds) *The Industrial Relations of Occupational Health and Safety*. Sydney: Croom Helm.

Grayson, J. 1981. *Safety and the Experts*. London: Workers' Educational Association.

Health and Safety Commission. 1990. *Annual Report 1989/1990*. London: HMSO.

Health and Safety Commission. 1991. *Annual Report 1990/1991*. London: HMSO.

Health and Safety Commission. 1992a. *Annual Report 1991/1992*. London: HMSO.

Health and Safety Commission. 1992b. *Work with Display Screen Equipment. Proposals for Regulations and Guidance*. London: HSE.

Health and Safety Executive. 1985. *Deadly Maintenance: a Study of Fatal Accidents at Work*. London: HMSO.

Health and Safety Executive. 1988. *Blackspot Construction*. London: HMSO.

Health and Safety Executive. 1991a. *Workplace Health and Safety in Europe*. London: HMSO.

Health and Safety Executive. 1991b. *Successful Health and Safety Management*. London: HMSO.

Health and Safety Executive. 1993. *The Costs of Accidents at Work*. London: HMSO.

Health and Safety Information Bulletin. 1988. 'Prioritising Safety at BP'. 155, 2–3.

Health and Safety Information Bulletin. 1990a. 'HSE Study on Employee Participation'. 179, 8–10.

Health and Safety Information Bulletin. 1990b. 'Coordinating Safety and Environmental Protection at Texaco'. 174, 4–6.

Health and Safety Information Bulletin. 1991a. 'The Role of Prosecution in Health and Safety Enforcement'. 186, 9–11.

Health and Safety Information Bulletin. 1991b. 'Safety Management at Conoco UK'. 182, 2–4.

Health and Safety Information Bulletin. 1993. 'Display Screen Equipment'. 205, 14.

Incomes Data Services. 1990a. *Safety First*. Focus No. 56. London: IDS.

Incomes Data Services. 1990b. *Violence Against Staff*. Study No. 458. London: IDS.

Incomes Data Services. 1991a. *Smoking at Work*. Study No. 474. London: IDS.

Incomes Data Services. 1991b. *Health Promotion at Work*. Study No. 487. London: IDS.

Industrial Relations Review and Report. 1992. '*Smoking at Work 1*'. 506, February.

Institute of Professionals, Managers and Specialists. 1992. *Health and*

Safety: an Alternative Report. London: IPMS.

Jack, A. 1992. 'Green Accounting and Competitive Advantage'. *Financial Times*, 19 March.

James, P. 1990. 'Holding Managers to Account on Safety'. *Personnel Management*, April, 54–8.

James, P. 1992. 'Reforming British Health and Safety Law: a Framework for discussion'. *Industrial Law Journal*, Vol. 21, No. 2, 83–105.

James, P. and Lewis, D. 1986. 'Health and Safety at Work'. In Lewis R. (ed.) *Labour Law in Britain*. Oxford: Basil Blackwell.

Jones, S. and Tait, R. 1992. 'Practice Makes . . . ?'. *Occupational Safety and Health*, January, 36–9.

Labour Research. 1990. 'Safety at All Costs'. Vol. 79, No. 12, 15–16.

Labour Research. 1991. 'Are Members Safe in Union Hands?'. Vol. 80, No. 9, 13–14.

Labour Research. 1992. 'Green Unions Face Red Light'. Vol. 81, No. 2, 13–14.

Lascelles, D. 1992. 'Paper Chase'. *Financial Times*, 26 February.

Lines, I. G. and Smith, A. J. 1990. *Analysis of the Results of a Paired Comparison Test on Management and Organisational Influences for Use in Quantified Risk Assessment*. London: HMSO.

Makin, P. and Sutherland, V. 1991. 'A Fatal Inversion?' *Occupational Safety and Health*, November, 41–3.

Manufacturing, Science, Finance. 1990. *MSF and the Environment*. London: MSF.

Millward, N. and Stevens, M. 1986. *British Workplace Industrial Relations 1980–1984: the DE/PSI/ACAS Surveys*. Aldershot: Gower.

Millward, N., Stevens, M., Smart, D. and Hawes, W. R. 1992. *Workplace Industrial Relations in Transition*. Aldershot: Dartmouth.

Moore, R. 1991. *The Price of Safety: The Market Workers' Rights and the Law*. London: Institute of Employment Rights.

Morris, B. 1989. 'The Challenge Facing British Trade Unions'. *Industrial Tutor*, Vol. 4, No. 9, 36–44.

Nichols, T. 1989. 'The Business Cycle and Industrial Injuries in British Manufacturing over a Quarter of a Century'. *The Sociological Review*, Vol. 37, No. 2, 538–50.

Nichols, T. 1990. 'Industrial Safety in Britain and the 1974 Health and Safety at Work Act: the Case of Manufacturing'. *International Journal of the Sociology of the Law*, Vol. 18, No. 3, 317–42.

Nichols, T. and Armstrong, P. 1973. *Safety or Profit: Industrial Accidents and the Conventional Wisdom*. Bristol: Falling Wall Press.

Niven, M. 1967. *Personnel Management 1913–1963*. London: Institute of Personnel Management.

Occupational Safety and Health. 1990. 'Refining Safety', February, 36–9.

Powley, D. 1989. '*Life Under the COSHH*'. *Manufacturing Engineer*, September, 24–31.

Poyner, B. and Warner, C. 1988. *Preventing Violence to Staff.* London: HMSO.

Purnell, C. 1991. 'Dotting the I and Crossing the T of the COSHH Regulations'. *Health and Safety at Work*, August, 29–30.

Robens Report 1972. *Safety and Health at Work.* Cmnd. 5034. London: HMSO.

Sigman, A. 1992. 'The State of Corporate Healthcare'. *Personnel Management*, February, 24–32.

Stranks, J. and Dewis, M. 1986. *Health and Safety Practice.* London: Pitman.

Thomas, P. 1991. 'Safety in Smaller Manufacturing Establishments'. *Employment Gazette*, Vol. 99, No. 1, 20–4.

Tombs, S. 1990. 'Industrial Injuries in British Manufacturing Industry'. *The Sociological Review*, Vol. 38, No. 2, 191–211.

Trollope, K. 1991. 'Worried at Work'. *Personnel Today*, 19 February, 35.

Torrington, D., Mackay, L. and Hall, L. 1985. 'The Changing Nature of Personnel Management'. *Employee Relations*, Vol. 7, No. 5, 10–16.

Waters, D. 1990. *Workers Participation in Health and Safety – A European Comparison.* London: Institute of Employment Rights.

Waters, D. and Gourlay, S. 1990. *Statutory Employee Involvement in Health and Safety at the Workplace: a Report of the Implementation and Effectiveness of the Safety Representatives and Safety Committees Regulations 1977.* HSE, Contract Research Report No. 20/1990. London: HMSO.

Wedderburn, B. 1986. *The Worker and the Law.* London: Penguin.

Willis, E. 1989. 'The Industrial Relations of Occupational Health and Safety: A Labour Process Approach'. *Labour and Society*, Vol. 2, No. 2, 317–33.

Wilson, G. K. 1985. *The Politics of Safety and Health.* Oxford: Clarendon Press.

PART III

Planning and Resourcing

5

From Manpower Planning to Strategic Human Resource Management?

Keith Sisson and Stuart Timperley

Interest in manpower or human resource planning, to use the term increasingly preferred, appears to have waxed and wained over the past 30 years, reflecting the changing context. Thus the early traditions of manpower planning owed much to the circumstances of the 1950s and 1960s: unemployment was low; economic growth appeared to be continuous and there was a considerable increase in public spending, notably on an expansion of higher and further education, in keeping with a growing working population; organization structures were highly centralized and relatively stable, with the emphasis on promotion and upward mobility; and the main concerns were recruitment and retention. In the 1980s the context changed and so did the concerns. Overall unemployment grew and, although there was much talk of the 'demographic timebomb' and substantial skill shortages, has remained stubbornly high into the 1990s. Competition has intensified. Senior managers in the large enterprises especially are continuously rethinking their business strategies and many have turned their backs on the diversification of the early 1980s, looking instead towards more 'focused' activities in the 1990s. Rationalization and restructuring have become the order of the day, and there has been considerable decentralization of operations to create semi-autonomous business units.

As well as the implications of this changing context, two problems have to be faced in discussing human resource planning in Britain. One is that there is no clear-cut definition of what the process involves. Thus the traditional view of manpower planning as a highly precise technology seems to have been rejected. Instead, it has come to be seen as 'a loose assemblage of ideas, tools, and techniques, which can be applied as necessary to the individual needs of a particular organization, and reflect its particular circumstances' (Bennison and Casson, 1984: 298). The same could be said of strategic human resource management which, for many commentators, has become the new orthodoxy in matters of planning: there is, as a later section will explain in more detail, a number of different models.

Second, of all the topics considered in this book, human resource planning is probably the one about which least is known in practice. The small number of case study collections (IPM, 1972; Manpower Services Commission/National Economic Development Office, 1978) are of relatively large organizations, such as the Civil Service, the Royal Air Force, National Westminster Bank, Ford, and International Computers, and are very old. The only major survey, carried out by the IPM, took place as long ago as 1975. Similarly, apart from those of Storey (1992) quoted in chapter 1 and of Pettigrew and his colleagues (e.g. Pettigrew and Whipp, 1991; Hendry et al., 1989; Hendry et al., 1991), there are very few studies of strategic human resource management in practice in Britain.

In the circumstances this chapter is therefore as much concerned with the changing ideas, tools and techniques of planning as with the practice. The first section reviews the stages typically involved in the two main processes of human resource planning, namely manpower planning and career planning. The second section discusses what is involved in, for some commentators, the new orthodoxy of strategic human resource management. The third and fourth sections are concerned with the practice of human resource planning in Britain. The third section looks at the evidence for the view that there is more 'muddling through' than planning, and the fourth discusses a number of the missing links which are important in explaining why so little planning appears to take place.

The Processes of Human Resource Planning

For present purposes, the processes of human resource planning can be considered under two headings: 'manpower planning' and 'career planning'. As will become apparent, apart from some of the techniques involved in forecasting supply, there is nothing intrinsically difficult about the activities involved.

Manpower planning

Manpower planning has been related to a variety of activities, from simple forecasting techniques to the whole range of activities in the personnel function. It can also involve individual posts, in which case the term succession planning is most often used, or large groups of employees. In any event, there is a pervasive view of the 'sequencing' of the major stages, namely stock-taking; forecasting supply and demand; the development of plans; and implementation and control. In simple terms, the first and second relate to the area of prediction and the third and the fourth to the area of control.

Stock-taking In models developed in the 1960s and 1970s, this stage was seen largely in numerical terms. Thus, the Department of Employment's first 'Manpower Paper', *Company Manpower Planning*, published in 1968, saw two main activities involved: first, an estimation of existing resources and, second, a calculation of the anticipated losses of these by the end of the forecasting period. More recent formulations (e.g. West Midlands Regional Health Authority, 1989; Mayo, 1991), involve qualitative as well as quantitative approaches: jobs analysis, which involves information on the number and type of jobs as the basis for determining the knowledge and skills required; a skills audit, which covers core competences in relation to skills knowledge and aptitude, and an inventory of the skills and experience of the existing staff; and a performance review, which identifies potential as well as future training needs, gives a measure of performance, plus an analysis of the factors underlying current levels, and the processes by which it can be improved.

Forecasting supply The forecasting of internal supply was the centre-piece of manpower planning in the 1960s and early 1970s. It was in this area that mathematical techniques were applied and models developed to highlight what was happening and what, given certain assumptions, would happen in the future to labour turnover and stability. As Bell (1989: 41; see also, Bryant, 1965) reminds us, this reflected the origins of many of the early pioneers of manpower planning. Significantly, the group which formed the Manpower Society in 1968 and then the Institute of Manpower Studies, started life as a study group of the Operational Research Society. Many were also drawn from large organizations such as BP, ICI, Shell and, in

---

particular, the Royal Navy, Royal Air Force and the National Coal Board.

The models developed included:

1 'renewal' or 'pull' models, where people are assumed to be 'pulled through' as a vacancy occurs through wastage or promotion and where vacancies in any grade are defined by outflows (wastage or promotion use of grade);
2 'linear programming' models for recruitment and deployment;
3 'camel' models based on assessing promotion chances in a hierarchy, using age distribution and estimates about the future size of the manpower system; and
4 'Markov' or 'push' models which model the flow of people.
(For further details, see Bartholomew, 1969; Lawrence, 1973.)

Taking one of these as illustration, Young (1976) used 'Markov' or 'push' models in the prediction of future manpower structures. The basis of this approach can be understood by reference to two demographic models of staffing: the first is a model of staff wastage based on the 'log normal law of distribution', and the second is a model of the hierarchical staff structure of institutions based on 'status profile analysis'. The log normal law of wastage asserts that staff leave an organization according to a clearly definable pattern of length of service, that this pattern may be recognized early in service, and survival rates deduced, from which losses of staff can be predicted. If total staff requirements are known, then recruitment needs can be predicted. The second approach is based on the assumption that recruitment, promotion and wastage patterns are stable over reasonable periods of time, so the probability that someone in a particular grade at any time will be in some other grade at a later time can be established from the detailed recent career histories of staff. Using these probabilities the possible distribution of the numbers of staff in each status or category (the status profile of the organization) at future dates can be inferred from the status profile at one particular time: thus, institutions pass through staffing cycles. This process involves the expansion and contraction of organizations and considers the effect this has on promotion and wastage, and the subsequent behavioural effects of such changes.

Forecasting demand   For reasons which will emerge later, this has proved to be the most difficult stage in manpower planning. Typically, most of the approaches deal with lists of factors emanating from the business plan and assume a direct link with manpower requirements via the operating plans which contain the budgets for the plan. Such factors would usually include the general pattern of trading and production, product demand, technology and administrative changes, capital investment plans, market strategies, acquisitions, divestments, mergers, product diversification, and centralization–decentralization. Thus, Mayo (1991: 202) writes: 'We would expect to find manpower and broad skill requirements and, whether explicitly stated or not, should be able to draw conclusions about

- changes in requirements for management, geographically or in 'new business' areas;
- new subsets of the organization that may be required as the plan progresses, and those that will no longer be required;
- changes in the number of particular types of jobs;
- the knowledge, skills, attitudes and experience that will be required of particular types of job;
- requirements for joint venture and collaborative management; and
- changes needed in career structures.'

This stage is in other words largely a reactive process. Very rarely is it recognized that the process might be developed in reverse, namely that the existing skills might influence the strategic plan, or even that it might be sensible to integrate manpower with strategic decision-making processes so that it is not simply a question of responding in a short-term fashion.

Plans and policies   This stage involves the reconciliation of the supply and demand forecasts and involves the developments which will help the organization to fill the gaps. Key areas have been selection and recruitment, training, career planning, payment systems and redeployment. This is not a simple administrative process, however. The issues raised by increasingly rapid changes in the needs of businesses create the necessity for equally rapid changes in the manpower system: any plans developed in the key manpower areas need to be both broad in principle and flexible in execution. Also, the plans developed in specific areas not only affect the nature, rate and direction of manpower flow, but also have an impact on the plans in other areas. Thus, a change in recruitment policy would influence promotion and create different pressures for rewards. Changes in promotion policy would have an impact on rewards and recruitment. Therefore, is it necessary to think not only within a planning framework, but also in terms of the interrelatedness of plans in each of the corporate personnel policy areas.

It is for these reasons that there has been a significant move in manpower planning to integrate personnel plans with the needs of the business, and, in addition, to address manpower questions within the relationship between corporate strategy and organizational structure. To anticipate the discussion in the next section, if the strategy of a business requires the development of an organization designed to provide for innovation, not only will the structural characteristics of the new organization be different from those of an operating organization, but the people requirements will be equally different. Similarly, if an organization creates a matrix structure, the requirements for matrix managers will differ from those of functional managers. This then creates pressure for planning processes that are able to ensure that the organizational requirements for manpower are met, not least the need for bigger investment in training and development.

Implementation and review   This final stage received little, if any, attention in the early manpower planning literature. Certainly there was a recognition of the need to have the confidence and commitment of decision-makers and of chief executives in particular; there was also some discussion about the most appropriate location for the manpower activity (IPM, 1975: 27–9; Bennison and Casson, 1984: 302), with the personnel and management services (or corporate planning) departments both having their advocates. As with the early planning literature more generally, however (see, for example, Taylor's comments, 1986: 17), the assumption seems to have been that manpower planning was a rational process and that, as long as they were presented and communicated properly, the plans would be accepted automatically.

Only recently, and then in literature dealing more generally with the management of change (Kanter, 1984; Pettigrew, 1985), has there been any serious discussion of the difficulties that even supposedly powerful chief executives have in translating plans into action and the way they seek to overcome them. Accordingly, an emphasis in recent approaches is the need to undertake regular review of the effectiveness and efficiency of the organizations' approach to managing human resources (e.g. Manpower Services Commission/National Economic Development Office, 1987; North Western/West Midlands Regional Health Authorities, 1991). Effectiveness involves judgements about the extent to which the organization is meeting the objectives it has set for itself. One way in which senior managers themselves, either individually or in teams, can undertake a regular and systematic audit across the full range of policies and practices is by questionnaire. For each significant activity or process, paired statements are prepared which describe the potential extremes of a performance range. Performance is then rated by using a discrete numbered scale, with an odd number of intervals, so that an average standard of performance can be identified. Efficiency is a measure of the costs and benefits, if possible in monetary terms, of the organization's policies and practices. An example would be the costs of a particular recruitment drive or of a training programme (e.g. Cannon, 1979). Organizations are also increasingly encouraged to undertake benchmarking exercises which means comparing the organization's performance with that of others, notaby close competitors, to see how it can be improved (e.g. Holberton, 1991).

Career planning

In principle, like manpower planning, career planning is applicable to employees in general. In practice, however, it has been largely confined to managers and professional staff. Mayo (1991: 168) suggests that, for each individual, it should involve a chosen career direction, for example, in 'functional' or 'general' management; a current perception of potential; a career plan, with aiming point; and a personal development plan – embracing knowledge, skills and attitudes plus experience – for the immediate future. The approach can be either organization-centred or individual-centred. In the first case, the emphasis is on the organization's needs in terms of jobs and career paths. In the second, it is on the individual's goals and skills. Either way, career planning means seeking to achieve some fit between organizational and individual goals. One attempt to show such a model diagrammatically is that of Schein (1977) which appears in modified form in figure 5.1.

Career planning is not new – it has been strongly linked with appraisal and management development, which are discussed in later chapters – but there has been a considerable upsurge in interest in recent years. One reason is the changing requirements for mana-

Organizational needs   Matching processes   Individual needs

Primarily initiated and managed
by the organization

Planning for staffing   *Career or job choice*
Strategic business planning
Job/role planning   Job analysis
'Manpower' planning and   Recruitment and selection
  human resource inventorying   Induction, socialization,
                                           initial training
                                         Job design and job assignment

Planning for growth and
development   *Early career issues:* locating
Inventorying of development   Supervising and coaching   one's area of contribution,
  plans   Performance appraisal and   learning how to fit into the
Follow-up and evaluation of   judgement of potential   organization, becoming
  development activities   Organizational rewards   productive, seeing a viable
                                         Promotions and other job   future for oneself in the
                                           changes   career
                                         Training and development
                                           opportunities
                                         Career counselling, joint
                                           career planning, and
                                           follow-up

Planning for levelling off
and disengagement   *Mid-career issues*: locating
                                         Continuing education and   one's career anchor and
                                           retraining   building one's career
                                         Job redesign, job enrichment,   around it, specializing
                                           and job rotation   *v.* generalizing
                                         Alternative patterns of work
                                           and rewards
                                         Retirement planning and
                                           counselling

Planning for replacement and
restaffing   *Late career issues*: becoming
                                         Updating of human resource   a mentor, using
                                           inventorying   one's experience and
                                         Programmes of replacement   wisdom, letting go and
                                           training   retiring
                                         Information system for job
                                           openings
                                         Reanalysis of jobs and job/   -
                                           role planning   New human resources from
                                         New cycle of recruitment   inside or outside the
                                                                            organization

Source: Reprinted from 'Increasing Organizational Effectiveness through Better Human
           Resource Planning and Development', by E. H. Schein (1977) *Sloan Management*
           Review, Fall, p. 7, by permission of the publisher. Copyright © 1977 by the Sloan
           Management Review Association. All rights reserved

Figure 5.1 A developmental model of human resource planning and
development

gerial staff. Kanter (1989), for example, talks in terms of the balance shifting away from the 'corpocrats', who maintain the organization, towards the 'professionals', who provide generic skills and expertise, and the 'entrepreneurs', who supply the creativity to run newer developing activities. Hence, there has also been a move from length of service criteria and attitudinal assessment to performance criteria and behavioural assessment discussed in other chapters. A second reason is the need to do something to maintain morale and commitment in a situation of declining opportunities within organizations, especially at middle levels, due to rationalization, low voluntary wastage and 'down-sizing/right-sizing' (i.e. the reduction in the number of hierarchical levels). Even large organizations, it is argued, can no longer guarantee an individual employment for life, but it can help to improve his or her 'employability' in the labour market more generally. This helps to explain why, in some organizations (e.g. BP), managers are said to have retitled personal development plans as personal departure plans (quoted in Lorenz, 1992).

Varieties of Strategic Human Resource Management

Having looked at the processes of human resource planning, we now turn to the influential idea of 'strategic HRM' which first came to prominence in the early to mid-1980s in the United States. As chapter 1 has pointed out, central to this idea is an all-embracing approach to the management of people. This means planning resources not only in quantitative terms, which has tended to be the main preoccupation with manpower planning, but in qualitative terms as well. It means seeking to integrate the full range of policies with one another and with business planning. An ever increasing number of books and articles in the UK proclaim these features (e.g. Armstrong, 1992a; 1992b; Manpower Services Commission/ National Economic Development Office, 1987; North Western/ West Midlands Regional Health Authorities, 1991).

Contrary to the impression given in much of the prescriptive literature, however, there is not just one model of strategic HRM, but several. As this section will reveal, there are also important differences between them, notably between what might be described as the 'best practice' models on the one hand and the 'contingency' models on the other.

'Best practice' models

The Harvard model   One of the most popular formulations, widely discussed in the UK (e.g. Guest, 1987; Boxall, 1991), has been the Harvard model (Beer et al., 1984). This suggests that HRM policy choices will be influenced by a set of 'stakeholders' (shareholders, government, trade unions etc.) and by the particular set of situational factors which will surround any particular case (such as product market conditions, the production technology and so on). Management's strategic task is to make certain fundamental policy choices in the light of these factors. Four clusters of choices are seen as especially important: these relate to the degree and nature of influence which employees will have; decisions about resourcing, throughflow and outflow of personnel; reward systems; and the organization of work. Figure 5.2 shows the suggested elements and their interconnections.

Ostensibly, the Harvard model allows for considerable variation and appears to contrast itself with situational determinism. In fact

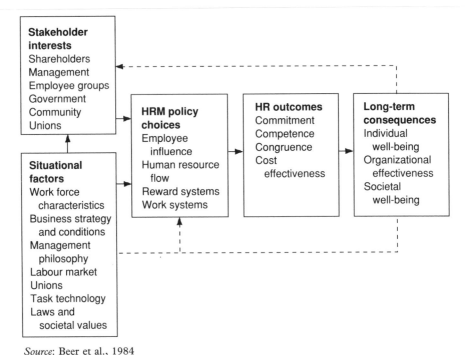

Source: Beer et al., 1984

Figure 5.2 The Harvard analytical framework of HRM

the model posits what Guest (1987: 510) has termed an 'implicit theory'. In other words, the analysis of strategic choice contained herein has a strong prescriptive overtone. The specified desirable outcomes of commitment, competence and the like can be seen as the elevation of one particular strategic approach over all others. This model appears to suggest that there is, in effect, one preferred and superior set of HR 'policy choices'.

The MIT model   The formulation advanced by Kochan et al. (1986) at the Massachusetts Institute of Technology (MIT), which has also appeared in abbreviated form in the UK (e.g. McKersie and Capelli, 1987; Storey, 1989), is a descriptive account of the transformation of industrial relations in leading US companies. Under competitive pressure in the product markets, these companies had made sub-stantial changes in the way they ran their businesses. Some had opted out of the the highly regulated arrangements of the so-called 'New Deal' model, which is outlined in the first column of figure 5.3, in favour of the HRM practices and policies of the 'non-union' model outlined in the second column. Many, however, were in the process of combining the 'New Deal' and 'non-union' models to produce the 'new industrial relations' model outlined in column three of figure 5.3. At the business unit level, there had been major changes in the content of work rules, with collective bargaining taking place on a more continuous basis, as it does in the UK, rather than just at the fixed intervals of the master contract negotiations. At the workplace level, the emphasis was increasingly on achiev-ing greater flexibility and the ability to adapt to changing circum-stances through communication systems, quality circles, and joint management–union teams. At the company level, in sharp contrast

Levels of activity	'New deal' model	'Non-union' model	'New industrial relations' model
Business strategy and policy-making	*Management prerogative*	*Management prerogative*	*Joint consultation*
Collective bargaining and personnel	*Comprehensive contracts*	*Comprehensive HRM policies*	*(Enabling agreements)*
Workplace	*Job control*	*Individual commitment*	*Co-operation and flexibility*

Source: based on Kochan et al., 1986

Figure 5.3 Models of US industrial relations

to the 'New Deal' model, under which they were more or less excluded, trade unions were being involved on a consultative basis in key business decisions, such as new investment, new technology, workforce adjustment strategies and new forms of work organization.

Like the Harvard model, however, the analysis is not purely descriptive or analytical. The 'new industrial relations' model emerges very clearly as the preferred route for the authors. The traditional 'New Deal' model is castigated because it proved 'inadequate in meeting the contemporary needs of employers for efficiency, flexibility and adaptability and of unions for organizing and representing workers' (Kochan et al., 1986: 224). But the 'non-union' model is, on its own, insufficient as a substitute – 'instead what is needed is a blending of traditional representation and newer participatory processes along with perhaps additional, more individualized forms of voice and representation' (ibid.: 225).

The flexible firm model This model has been primarily associated with Atkinson (1984) and his colleagues at the Institute of Manpower Studies. Its status has been the subject of considerable controversy (e.g. Pollert, 1987; Hunter and MacInnes, 1991). Like the MIT model, it is descriptive but with strong prescriptive overtones. At its heart is an organizational structure, which many British firms are supposedly trying to introduce, offered as a model for others to follow. This structure involves 'the break-up of the labour force into increasingly peripheral, and therefore numerically flexible, groups of workers, clustered about a numerically stable core group which will conduct the firm's key, firm-specific activities' (Atkinson, 1984: 29). In the case of the core, which will be made up of managers and groups whose skills cannot readily be bought in, terms and conditions are designed to promote task or functional flexibility: they are likely to include, for example, single status conditions, employment security and performance assessment. In the case of the periphery, the emphasis is on numerical flexibility and the relationship is essentially market-based. Here several groups are involved: those which are full-time, but have a job rather than a career; part-time and temporary workers; and those involved in subcontracting operations.

Contingency models

The models in the second group emphasize the variability of strategic human resource management policy choices under different business conditions. Three main types of contingency model have so far dominated: one links human resource strategic choices to different 'stages' in the business life cycle; the second, following Chandler (1962), emphasizes different 'strategy/structure' configurations; and the third follows Porter (1980; 1985) in suggesting that different business strategies are the key factors.

Business life cycle   The business life cycle approach essentially seeks to tailor human resource policy choices to the varying requirements of a firm at different stages of its life cycle, i.e. from business start-up, through early growth and maturity and eventually on to business decline. At each stage a business might be supposed to have different priorities. These different priorities in turn require their own appropriate human resource strategies (e.g. Lengnick-Hall and Lengnick-Hall, 1988; Kochan and Barocci, 1985; Baird and Meshoulam, 1988).

At the start-up stage, for instance, a business is posited as requiring recruitment and selection strategies which quickly attract the best talent; a reward strategy which supports this by paying highly competitive rates; a training and development strategy which builds the foundations for the future; and an employee relations strategy which draws the basic architecture and puts in place the underlying philosophy for the new business.

Under mature conditions, by contrast, the emphasis in HRM is on control and maintenance of costs and resources. Hence, the recruitment and selection stance might be geared to a trickle-feed of new blood into vacant positions created by retirements. There might also be a policy of encouraging enough labour turnover so as to minimize the need for compulsory lay-offs. Meanwhile the pay and benefits policy is likely to be geared to a keen control over costs. Training and development might be expected to have as their priority the maintenance of flexibility and the adequate provision of skill levels in an ageing workforce.

Strategy and structure   The most noted example of this type of contingency model is the work of Fombrun, Tichy and Devanna (1984): this shows a range of 'appropriate' HR choices suited to five different strategy/structure types, ranging from single product businesses with functional structures, through diversified product strategies allied to multi-divisional organizational forms and on to multi-product companies operating globally.

For each of the five types of situation the key HR policy choices in the spheres of selection, appraisal, reward and development are delineated. For instance, a company following a single-product strategy, with an associated functional structure, is likely to have an HRM strategy which is traditional in appearance. Selection and appraisal may well be conducted in a subjective fashion and reward and development practices may veer to the unsystematic and the paternalistic.

By way of contrast, a company pursuing a diversification strategy, with a multi-divisional structure, is likely to be characterized by a human resource strategy which is driven by impersonal, systematic devices which are, however, adaptable to the different parts of the organization. Reward systems are likely to be formula-based with a tendency towards a built-in response to return on investment and profitability. Selection and even appraisal may be found to vary between the different constituent business divisions. However, in circumstances where the multi-divisional strategy is accompanied by a business strategy built around interrelated, interdependent businesses, it is postulated that it is more likely that the human resource management strategy will foster and take advantage of that interrelationship.

Matching business strategy and HR strategy   The third type of contingency model links policy choices with different types of business strategy. Arguably, the most extreme example is that of Miller (1989). He seeks to tighten-up what he sees as the rather loose usage of the term HR strategy by suggesting that a human resource approach is only 'strategic' if it 'fits' with the organization's product-market strategy and if it is proactive in this regard. Most of the theorists in this category, however, draw on Porter's distinction between innovation, quality-enhancement or cost-reduction strategies (e.g. Schuler and Jackson, 1987) or on Miles and Snow (1984).

Thus, Schuler and Jackson's (1987) model suggests that, where a firm has opted for innovation as a means to gain competitive advantage, this sets up certain predictable required patterns of behaviour. Prime among these requisite 'role behaviours' are creativity, a capacity and willingness to focus on longer term goals, a relatively high level of collaborative action, a high tolerance of ambiguity and a high degree of readiness to take risks. On the other hand, concern for quality and for achieving output need only be at moderate levels.

As a way of illustrating the contrasts with other strategic choices, one might note that where a cost-reduction business strategy is chosen then the behaviour patterns at a premium will conversely hinge around a short-term focus and a willingness to perform and tolerate repetitive and predictable job cycles in a standardized undeviating way. The associated HRM policy choices to encourage this set of behaviours will include job design principles, close monitoring and control, and an appraisal system which rewards and punishes in accord with short-term results.

Conclusion

The various models identified in the section share a common approach: policies and practices need to be internally consistent with one another. Otherwise, however, there are significant differences between them which have been ignored in much of the discussion of strategic HRM. The sharpest contrast is between the 'best practice' and the 'contingency' models. The 'best practice' models, albeit in their different ways, put a premium on the quality of the human resources. The 'contingency models', by contrast, admit a number of possibilities, some of which are very far removed from the quality option. There are also fundamental differences in the treatment of trade unions. Most of the models are silent on trade unions, the implication being that they are either unimportant or unnecessary. Only the MIT model attempts to integrate the collective as well as the individual aspects of the employment relationship.

Muddling Through Rather Than Human Resource Planning?

The limited evidence available suggests that, in Britain, the practice of human resource planning is very different from the theory. Certainly there was no doubting the sombre mood of commentators on manpower planning in the 1980s. The talk was of a 'lack of application of manpower planning' (Torrington and Hall, 1987: 159) and of 'the lack of manpower policies in many organizations, and the brittle nature of these policies in others' (Bennison and Casson, 1984: 6). Purkiss, who was director of the Institute of Manpower Studies for a number of years, was even more forthright:

> Manpower planning has a reputation for being academic, if not tedious. It has been written about for over twenty years, every new book the definitive version. It failed in the 1960s and 1970s. It belongs to

the world of calculation, computers and big bureaucracies. (Bennison and Casson, 1984: ix)

Even the advent of computerization of personnel records and systems, which has received considerable attention in the personnel journals, does not seem to have had the impact that might have been expected. The regular 'Computerfile' survey carried out for *Personnel Management* (for the most recent results, see Richards-Carpenter, 1993) found increasing use of computerized personnel information systems (CPIS). For the most part, however, these systems involved individual applications such as absence control, training and development administration, and person and post data. Less than one-third of respondents used such systems for planning purposes and between 20 and 25 per cent even said that it was not required for these activities. Significantly, too, only 36 per cent of line managers and 27 per cent of senior managers made frequent use of the CPIS. In Richards-Carpenter's words, 'It seems that CPISs are still primarily seen as a way of enhancing the administrative efficiency of the personnel department . . .'.

Other surveys, concerned to establish whether or not there appeared to be any strategic direction to personnel management practice in Britain, have come to equally negative conclusions. Marginson and his colleagues, for example, after surveying senior managers in major companies with 1000 or more employees in 1985 concluded:

> It is difficult to escape the conclusion that, although the great majority of our respondents claim that their organizations have an overall policy or approach to the management of employees, with the exception of a number of companies which are overseas owned, or financially centralized, or operating in the service sectors, it would be wrong to set very much store by this . . . the general weight of evidence would seem to confirm that most UK owned enterprises remain pragmatic or opportunistic in their approach. (Marginson et al., 1988: 120)

The early signs are that a similar picture will emerge from the second Company Level Industrial Relations Survey, carried out in 1992.

Two recent case studies provide further evidence for these general conclusions. One involves the changing demographic trends in the labour force and the other the model of the flexible firm discussed in the previous section. In both cases, despite widespread publicity attaching to the issues and the emphasis of government agencies on the dangers of 'muddling through', most British managements seemed to be incapable of developing a more strategic approach.

The case of the demographic timebomb

In the late 1980s the implications of the lower birth rate in the 1960s and the prospect of a sharp reduction in the number of young people in the 16–19 age group coming on to the labour market in the 1990s became an issue of major public policy concern. Historically, young people in this age group had been one of the main sources of recruitment. Until the late 1980s they had been in oversupply – youth unemployment had been one of the major policy problems of the early 1980s, as chapter 9 describes in more detail – and employers were able to recruit in what was essentially a buyer's market. In the second half of the 1980s, however, a number of government agencies and other research institutions warned that this buyer's market was going to disappear. Overall, it was estimated that the number of young people was going to decline, on average, by 25 per cent across the country with steeper reductions in regions such as the south-east. Further reductions in the proportion of this group coming onto the labour were also predicted as a result of the government policy of increasing the relatively low numbers in higher and further education.

It proved extremely difficult, however, despite dire warnings from government agencies such as the National Economic Development Office (NEDO) and the Training Agency (TA), to get many British managements to become aware of the problem. In a major survey of 400 organizations in 1988, for example, only one in seven admitted to being well-informed about the demographic changes (NEDO/ TA, 1988). A year later, a survey of 2000 organizations suggested that the level of awareness had increased significantly (NEDO/TA, 1989). Many more, approximately two-thirds, knew about the decline in the number of young people. A significant proportion, however, continued to see the problems in terms of a decline in the labour force overall rather than in the specific 16–19 age group.

More worrying still was the response. Some organizations, such as the major retailers and the National Health Service, had showed considerable imagination, but the great majority had not. Less than one-third of the 2000 organizations surveyed in 1989, for example, considered seriously looking at alternative sources of recruitment such as women returners or older workers over 50 and less than 20 per cent were prepared to consider the unemployed. Fewer still considered making radical changes in the existing working arrangements or provisions for retraining to help deal with the problem. This was above all true of manufacturing companies. For the great majority, the preferred solution seemed to be to 'compete' rather than 'adapt', that is to say, to try to compete more effectively for the dwindling pool of young people. Unsurprisingly, there were considerable fears of a wage spiral.

Other research confirmed that the approach of most organizations had been tactical rather than strategic.

> Firms' responses to shortage . . . tend to be sequential (introduced only slowly as the full seriousness of the shortage problem become apparent to firms). They tend to be hiererachical (with more difficult/ expensive responses deployed only when easier/cheaper ones have proved inadequate). (Atkinson, 1989: 22)

The initial reaction was to 'take it on the chin', passively responding in the hope that something would turn up. In a second stage, when the first stage did not appear to be working, they began to compete more effectively for the same group of labour. Only the third and fourth stages involved strategic responses, such as seeking alternative supplies of older workers or restructuring existing working arrangements. Very few managements, anticipating the results of the NEDO/TA study, had progressed to these stages, however, and even then they had only done so by working through the other stages rather than thinking through the most appropriate solution for their own circumstances.

In the circumstances, the lament of the Director General of the National Economic Development Office, is perfectly understandable,

> The disappointing results indicate . . . that we are in for a bout of 'muddling through' British-style . . . many companies are chucking money at the problem and assuming that will do the trick. Given that level of complacency, can hysteria be far behind? The unfortunate truth is that, at any rate in personnel matters (because labour is so cheap?), most employers live hand-to-mouth and the idea of taking a strategic view and of doing so at board level is quite alien. (Cassells, 1989: 6)

There is a postcript to this case study. In 1990 the British economy turned into a deep recession. Unemployment grew rapidly in 1991 and reached nearly three million by 1992. Talk of the demographic timebomb disappeared even from the pages of such specialist journals such as *Personnel Management* and many of the innovations, such as the creation of greater equal opportunities, seemed to fall by the wayside. Yet the underlying demographic considerations remain the same as they were.

The case of the flexible firm

Our second case study involves the 'flexible firm' discussed in a previous section and, in particular, the 'core–periphery' model which is central to it. The model not only received a tremendous amount of publicity from academics and consultants. It became *de facto* a key element in government policy. In local authorities and the National Health Service, compulsory competitive tendering became enshrined in legislation; throughout the civil serice there was considerable emphasis on 'market testing', whereby government agencies were required to establish the comparative cost involved in putting out business to the private sector.

At first sight, changes in the patterns of working identified in chapter 1 seemed to offer empirical support for the widespread take-up of the approach. According to Casey's (1991) analysis of the Labour Force Survey, between 1979 and 1987, there was an increase from 1.76 million (7.3 per cent) to 3.0 million (12.4 per cent) in the number of self-employed and an increase from 4.4 million (18.3 per cent) to 5.4 million (22.4 per cent) in the number of part-time workers.

Closer inspection, however, suggested that these changes were primarily to be explained in terms of shifts in industrial structure, a reduction in the average size of establishments and regional distribution of employment rather than the development of a more strategic approach to employment matters. A survey of nearly 1000 establishments selected because they used peripheral labour reported that no more than one in nine had a manpower strategy which is consistent with the model. Most employed peripheral workers for 'traditional' reasons, such as matching manning levels to demand peaks, rather than 'new' reasons associated with the model, e.g. peripheral workers were cheaper or enjoyed fewer rights. They were also clustered in industries which already made considerable use of such forms of employment. Significantly, too, 'Only one-third of establishments reported having a manpower plan or strategy; the remainder made labour use decisions on a reactive, *ad hoc* basis' (McGregor and Sproull, 1991: 79).

Further insights came from a number of follow-up case studies (Hunter and MacInnes, 1991). Business concerns were the critical factor but this led to a predominantly pragmatic approach rather than one driven by deliberate manpower strategy. Traditional ways of doing things were the order of the day. Only when problems occurred did managers consider other possibilities. It was very rare, for example, for even large companies to have an ideal view about manpower strategy; the main concern of the centre was monitoring and control; and detailed decisions about the form of contract were left to individual units. It was also rare for companies to undertake detailed cost comparisons between different types of worker. The perceptions of what would work or would not work were far more important.

The authors' conclusions about the natue of the involvement of the personnel function in decision-making employment matters also make interesting reading. It was managers involved in operations, working within budgetary constraints, who made the key decisions rather than personnel. Personnel managers played a largely advisory and monitoring function: there was little evidence of them producing results in terms of cost outcomes.

> . . . decisions over labour use were rarely part of a coherent and articulate employment strategy, co-ordinated by a powerful personnel function which could identify and respond to changing labour market conditions. Instead the use of different forms of labour had usually built up in an *ad hoc* and pragmatic manner as general and line management responded to what they saw as the needs of the business. (Hunter and McInnes, 1991: 49)

A final point needs to be made before leaving this case study. The emphasis has been on the periphery because this is where the novelty has supposedly been. There is relatively little evidence of movement on creating the core as defined by Atkinson's model. First, as chapter 16 emphasizes, considerable status differences within the permanent workforce continue. Second, employment for those who might be thought of as 'core' staff has become far less secure; organizations have strongly resisted giving guarantees of employment security to most.

Missing Links

Much of the emphasis in discussing the lack of human resource planning focuses on the technical difficulties experienced in forecasting – especially in forecasting demand in the rapidly changing context of the 1970s and the 1980s. Torrington and Hall (1987: 158) paraphrase the example given by Lord Bowden in a lecture in 1978 appropriately entitled 'Is Manpower Planning Necessary? Is it Possible? What Next?':

> In 1972 and 1973, Mr Barber, the then Chancellor of the Exchequer, tried to reflate the economy. Restrictions on credit were removed so that the demand for television sets suddenly and dramatically increased. We began to import television sets from Japan as we were unable to make sufficient ourselves. In the expectation that this demand would continue, and using money borrowed from the government, a large factory was built to make television sets north of Manchester. It was several years between the time that some enterprising managers identified increasing demand for television sets and the time that the factory started to produce them in quantity. At the same time there was an economic crisis and a change of government. Mr Barber and then Mr Healey took measures to cut non-essential spending, and the demand for television sets dramatically fell by a factor of five. The factory closed just as it had started to work.

Gratton and Syrett (1990: 38) suggest that the main challenges confronting HR practitioners in designing an effective succession strategy are the changes in organization structures. Streams of mergers, acquisitions and international alliances have resulted in new structures and organizational demands making it more difficult to forecast demands.

Important though these difficulties of forecasting have been, they are not the only considerations. As well as assuming that managers actually have a choice of strategy, both the best practice and contingency theorists, despite their other differences, seem to build their cases on two assumptions which at first sight appear eminently reasonable. The first is that personnel managers will have easy recourse to a business strategy and, in particular, the operational plans that flow from it. The second is that the organization possesses the necessary personnel information to engage in meaningful human resource planning. Each of these assumptions, as this section argues, is in reality highly questionable.

Business planning and human resource planning

The first assumption – that personnel managers have easy recourse to the 'corporate strategy' of their employing organization – seems fair enough. In practice, however, nothing could be further from the truth. Where such strategies are available, they are often extremely vague. They may well take the form of financial targets which do not translate easily into operational terms. For example, the ambition of, say, a financial services institution to gain a 5 per cent market penetration in Europe for its range of products can carry numerous alternative meanings even for operational planning, let alone human resource planning.

The nature of business planning   A fundamental problem is that much of the strategic human resource management debate typically leans towards rational planning assumptions in its conception of corporate strategy. However, as a number of recent analysts have shown (see, for example, Pettigrew and Whipp, 1991; Johnson, 1987; Quinn, 1980; 1988; Mintzberg, 1978; 1987; 1988), the assumption that the formulation and implementation of business strategy occurs in linear fashion presents an unduly simplified and distorted view of strategic action. For these analysts, 'strategy' is understood in terms of 'processual' and 'incremental' models, i.e. it is seen to emerge through disjointed serial steps which are influenced by the social and political routines of organizational life. Strategy, in Mintzberg's (1978) classic formulation, may be best seen as 'a pattern in a stream of decisions'. By implication, strategic choices are often being made on an everyday basis and by people at many levels in an organization. The interplay of influential complex factors both external to and internal to the firm are seen as requiring managers to make continual assessments, and continual adjustments. Managing strategy is thus an interactive process. Objectives themselves are likely to be unclear and post-rationalized. Under these conditions it is naturally going to be extremely difficult for a personnel manager to simply reach out for *the* definitive corporate strategy and thence to construct a *congruent* personnel version.

A position which is even more distanced from the formalistic rational-planning view of strategy is to be found in the 'interpretive' model (Whittington, 1989; Johnson, 1987; 1990). Here strategy is seen very much as a social outcome shaped by the prevailing ideologies, rituals, myths and symbols of the organizational culture.

Changing the strategy entails an exercise in the manipulation or management of meaning. Effecting such a shift is difficult because managers and other organizational members operate within deeply-embedded 'causal maps', 'scripts' or 'ideologies' which may hardly be perceived at the conscious level. How managers come to be sensitized to the need for a change in direction, and what factors condition the formation of the range of options considered, along with other issues, are seen as crucially influenced by social and political forces. Managerial motivations, their circumscribed sources of information and their frames of reference all come centrally into the picture as critical factors in the shaping of strategic choices (Whittington, 1989; Johnson, 1987). Hence, the lack of interest among UK practitioners in the MIT model discussed earlier.

The process of business planning A second consideration is the dominance of the portfolio planning approach. This is especially important in the large diversified companies in Britain, but also has a pervasive influence more generally. Under this approach, business planning is seen essentially as making decisions about the mix (portfolio) of businesses or activities and the allocation of capital between them. Important implications, as Purcell (1989: 75–80) reminds us, are that the enterprise is seen not as a unified business but a collection of businesses; there is a limited role for headquarters in setting goals, values and missions; planning in the sense of the medium and long-term direction, including the area of personnel management, is delegated to the management of individual businesses; and the assumption is that policies and practices will reflect different business conditions, much as was discussed in an earlier section. Especially important is that performance controls tend to replace administrative controls. That is to say, the emphasis is on financial performance rather than on policies and guidelines from headquarters. Typically, for example, the managements of individual units have to work to extremely stretching financial tagets, backed up by performance pay, and strict short-term pay-back criteria spanning two to four years applied to investment decisions. They will also be very closely monitored on this financial performance on a regular basis, sometimes involving monthly reporting.

In practice, much of the balance of emphasis depends on the nature and extent of diversification. For example, the Goold and Campbell (1987) survey identified three main patterns. Of the 16 enterprises in the survey, relatively few – BOC, BP, Cadbury

Schweppes, Lex, STC and United Biscuits – indulged in the formal process of strategic planning. Courtaulds, ICI, Imperial, Plessey and Vickers, which the authors labelled the 'strategic controllers', had established planning procedures, but left the primary responsibility for doing it to the businesses. A third major group, notably those with a large number of businesses, such as BTR, Hanson Trust, GEC and Tarmac, claimed that discussion of business strategy was more or less continuous, but had no formal planning process as such. Instead, considerable emphasis was placed on the annual budgeting process in which the main focus was on financial control – on the sanctioning of expenditure, agreeing targets, and monitoring of performance against targets.

The strengths and weaknesses of portfolio planning, especially in so far as it encourages the 'financial control' model, have been hotly debated (see the discussion in Purcell, 1989). Many critics have been especially concerned about its wide adoption in the UK given the tradition of headquarter emphasis on monitoring and central rather than business development, and the pressure on short-term financial results. McKinsey and Co., which had a great deal to do with the introduction of multi-divisional structures in the UK, gives some flavour of these concerns in its report on the competitiveness of the UK electronics industry:

> Many UK electronics companies have structures and management processes which were 'state of the art' for the management of diversified portfolios in the 1960s and 1970s, but which have worked against the development of successful international businesses. Many (though not all) UK companies have highly decentralised structures, with divisions often run as relatively autonomous, budget driven, profit and loss centres. Management delegates strategy formulation to the lowest possible business unit level. GEC, Ferranti, Plessey, and Racal are the prime examples of this style. Each have lean corporate centres primarily playing the role of financial holding company, monitoring financial performance tightly but providing very limited planning and strategy formulation support.
>
> Decentralisation to small units has limited the scale of ambition to that of the units rather than the company as a whole. 'Numbers driven' rather than 'issue driven' planning has reinforced a focus on short term results rather than long term investment to create major new businesses. The limited role of the centre in many UK companies has meant that the potential synergies and scale benefits of a large company – in creating a customer franchise, in product development and in attracting and developing highly talented management – have not been achieved. (McKinsey & Co./NEDO, 1988: 49)

The net result is that, even in many large organizations, there is likely to be little which remotely resembles the business planning that is assumed in many of the prescriptive personnel management texts. Headquarters staff, to repeat, are primarily involved in planning the portfolio of the overall organization rather than with planning in the sense of the medium and long-term direction of individual businesses. Managers in the individual units, who nominally have the responsibility for this medium and long-term direction, usually have neither the time nor the expertise to take it seriously; nor is there any particular incentive given the extremely short-term pay-back criteria that headquarters is likely to insist on for investment decisions. The primary concern of business unit managers is to meet the demanding short-term financial targets that headquarters sets for them; their own pay and future career prospects are critically dependent on doing so. Similar pressures cascade down the individual business unit to affect departments and activities; they are also a key consideration within many independent organizations. Small wonder that the operational plans that the would-be human resource planner needs are missing.

In the light of the above analysis, it might be assumed that organizations in the public sector would be immune to the limiting pressures on HRM. In fact, while public sector organizations escape many of these forces they are nonetheless subject to others which can be equally limiting for the human resource management approach. Crucially, as chapter 1 pointed out, the managements in public sector organizations are under a great deal of pressure to adopt many of the practices associated with portfolio planning. These result from the break-up of organizations such as the civil service, National Health Service, and education into a number of quasi-independent organizations; a reduction in the number of headquarters staff; the delegation of much of the responsibility for business planning as well as operational management to unit managers; and the substitution of performance controls – with increasing emphasis on short-term financial performance – for administrative controls (see, for example, the discussion in Keep, 1992).

Human resource planning and personnel practice

As the Department of Employment (1968: 11) recognized a quarter a century ago, the quality of human resource planning depends on the 'adequacy of . . . personnel records and statistics'. The assumption implicit in many of the prescriptive texts is that not only will the quantitative data that the planner needs be readily available, but also the qualitative information. That is to say, the planner will supposedly have information about the competences of existing employees, their career preferences and aspirations and so on. More than that, it is increasingly assumed that much of this information will be computerized and, so, readily available at the press of a key. Thus, in a recent highly acclaimed text on career management, Mayo (1991: 201), director of personnel for ICL, summarizes the sources of data needed for effective planning as follows.

The Organization	The Individual
Strategic plan	Personal information records
Operating plan	Training records
Organization structure	Appraisal and development reviews
Organization demographics	CVs
Job grades/categories	
Person specifications	Personal growth profiles
Career structures	Career development plans
Career bridges	Test and assessment results
Development positions	Language capability
	Career history dynamics

The reality is that much of this information, especially that which appears in the right hand column, is very rarely available in the typical UK organization. The reasons are quite simple. Relatively few organizations, as the next chapter confirms, use such methods as bio-data and tests in selection; assessment centres are also very rare. This means that no systematic data are available on the validity of person specifications in most organizations. Similarly, as chapter 7 confirms, the use of appraisal is far from widespread – if there is no appraisal system, the organization has effectively cut itself off from the major source of information about individuals. Last but not least, very little training goes on, and there has therefore been little incentive to develop the kind of skills audits that are to be found in large companies in some other countries (see Keep, 1989: 181).

In short, the would-be planner in the typical UK organization is faced with a classic 'catch 22' situation. To plan effectively, he or she desperately needs the kind of data that Mayo is talking about. The problem is that, in the absence of practices such as appraisal and testing, the data are unavailable. In the absence of a plan, however, it is difficult to make sensible decisions about the kind of appraisal system that is needed. The result is the lack of integration of policies and practices which so many commentators have referred to.

It is not only the data which are missing, however. Few organizations in Britain have experience of these kinds of activities. Even if they do have such experience, it tends to be very fragmented. The result is that there has been little or no learning of the importance of the contribution that an integrated set of personnel policies can make.

The significance of these missing links, and the time it takes to put them in place, emerges in Whipp's summing up of a number of key points about Jaguar's experience in the 1980s:

> The first relates to the huge efforts required merely to 'catch-up' with the conventional personnel practices of other companies in the 1980s. Overcoming the inherited problems of the UK engineering sector with regard to the management of people took virtually a decade. Second, it is noticeable how HRM techniques were not developed to fit the company's strategy. Rather, Jaguar in the 1980s developed its capacity to think strategically and use HRM concepts and practices in parallel. It is the need to mobilise such a range of conditioning work and supportive secondary mechanisms which stands out. Nonetheless, by the end of the 1980s, even a company such as Jaguar – held up to be the epitome of the HRM approach – found it hugely difficult to make such an approach count in terms of competitive performance. (Whipp, 1992: 46)

Conclusion

It is almost certainly the case that the golden age, if there was one, of manpower planning has passed. Its context was the large bureaucracies of the 1950s and 1960s with relatively stable tasks and flows of standard jobs and activities. Clearly in some organizations, such as the armed forces or the banks, there will be a continuing need for such activities, although even here it is likely to be considerably less than it was. Elsewhere, however, change in business strategies, organization structures and job descriptions is too rapid.

In the circumstances it is understandable that the emphasis is shifting from the tools of planning to the disciplines of planning. The same seems to have happened in business planning more generally in the 1980s. In the one-hundredth issue of *Long Range Planning*, which has been the main publication in the field, the editor (Taylor,

1986: 17) talks in terms of a general disillusionment with corporate planning, of corporate planning departments being closed down, and of a shift to strategic management, as opposed to strategic planning, for which senior line managers are themselves responsible. The foundations of this are broad principles – some idea of vision – about where an organization is going etc.

Within the broad thrust of this shift towards strategic human resource management, two other understandable developments are discernible in the literature. One is a shift from the 'best practice' models towards 'contingency' models, which take into account the specific circumstances of the organization, such as the phase in its development or the nature and extent of diversification. The other is a greater stress on the individual in the form of succession planning and career planning: the individual, almost by definition, becomes more important as the numbers reduce and key posts assume greater importance.

The significance of any shift from manpower planning to strategic human resource management, however, should not be overestimated. Like manpower planning, the assumption underlying much of the thinking associated with strategic human resource management, whichever model is involved, is that the move to the desired state is relatively straightforward – it is simply a matter of the appropriate degree of will on the part of the managers concerned or of their enlightenment. The reality, especially in the UK, is very different. The processes as well as the nature of business planning are a major problem. So too is the relative underdevelopment of personnel management practice. Would-be planners do not possess much of the information they need because of the state of many aspects of personnel practice such as selection, appraisal and training. Until they do, the number of case studies of strategic human resource management in action is likely to remain extremely small.

Bibliography

Armstrong, M. (ed.) 1992a. *Strategies for Human Resource Management: A Total Business Approach.* London: Kogan Page.

Armstrong, M. 1992b. *Human Resource Management: Strategy and Action.* London: Kogan Page.

Atkinson, J. 1984. 'Manpower Strategies for Flexible Organizations'. *Personnel Management*, August, 28–31.

Atkinson, J. 1989. 'Four stages of response to the demographic downturn'. *Personnel Management*, August.

Baird, L. and Meshoulam, I, 1988. 'Managing two fits of strategic human resource management'. *Academy of Management Review*, 13, 1.

Bartholomew, D. J. 1969. *Stochastic Models of Social Processes*. London: Wiley.

Beer, M., Spector, B., Lawrence, P. R., Quinn Mills, D. and Walton, R. 1984. *Managing Human Assets*. New York: The Free Press.

Bell, D. 1989. 'Why Manpower Planning is back in Vogue'. *Personnel Management*, July, 40–3.

Bennison, M. and Casson, J. 1984. *The Manpower Planning Handbook*. Maidenhead: McGraw-Hill.

Boxall, P. F. 1992. 'Strategic human resource management: beginnings of new orthodoxy?' *Human Resource Management Journal*, Vol. 2, No. 3.

Bryant, D. T. 1965. 'A Survey of the Development of Manpower Planning'. *British Journal of Industrial Relations*, 3, November, 279–90.

Cannon, J. 1979. *Cost Effective Personnel Decisions*. London: Institute of Personnel Management.

Casey, B. 1991. 'Survey Evidence on Trends in "Non-Standard" Employment'. In Pollert, A. (ed.) *Farewell to Flexibility*. Oxford: Blackwell.

Chandler, A. D. 1962. *Strategy and Structure*. Cambridge, MA: MIT Press.

Department of Employment. 1968. *Company Manpower Planning*. London: HMSO.

Evans, P. and Lorange, P. 1989. 'The Two Logics Behind Human Resource Management'. In Evans, P., Doz, Y. and Laurent, A. (eds) *Human Resource Management in International Firms: Change, Globalisation, Innovation*. London: Macmillan.

Fletcher, C. and Williams, R. 1985. *Performance Appraisal and Career Development*. London: Hutchinson.

Fombrun, C. J., Tichy, N. M. and Devanna, M. A. 1984. *Strategic Human Resource Management*. New York: Wiley.

Goold, M. and Campbell, A. 1987. *Strategy and Styles Decision Making*. Oxford: Blackwell.

Gratton, L. and Syrett, M. 1990. 'Heirs Apparent: Succession Strategies for the Future'. *Personnel Management*, January, 34–7.

Guest, D. 1987. 'Human Resource Management and Industrial Relations'. *Journal of Management Studies*, 24, September, 503–22.

Guest, D. 1990. 'Human resource management and the American Dream'. *Journal of Management Studies*, 27, 4.

Haspeslagh, P. C. 1982. 'Portfolio Planning: Uses and Limits'. *Harvard Business Review*, January–February.

Hendry, C., Pettigrew, A. M. and Sparrow, P. 1989. 'Linking Strategic Change, Competitive Performance and Human Resource Management: Results of a UK Empirical Study'. In Mansfield, R. M. (ed.) *New Frontiers of Management*. London: Routledge.

Hendry, C., Jones, A., Arthur, M. and Pettigrew, A. M. 1991. *Human Resource Development in Small to Medium Sized Enterprises.* Employment Research Paper No. 83. Sheffield: Employment Department.

Hirsch, W. 1990. *Succession Planning: Current Practice and Future Issues.* Report 184. Sussex: Institute of Manpower Studies.

Holberton, S. 1991. 'How to help yourself to a competitor's best practices'. *Financial Times*, 24 June 1992, 24.

Hunter, L. C. and MacInnes, J. 1991. *Employer Use Strategies – Case Studies.* Employment Research Paper No. 87. Sheffield: Employment Department.

IPM. 1972. *Company Practice in Manpower Planning.* London: Institute of Personnel Management.

IPM. 1975. *Manpower Planning in Action.* London: Institute of Personnel Management.

Johnson, G. 1987. *Strategic Change and the Management Process.* Oxford: Blackwell.

Johnson, G. 1990. 'Managing strategic change: the role of symbolic action'. *British Journal of Management*, 1, 4.

Kanter, R. M. 1984. *The Change Masters.* London: Allen & Unwin.

Kanter, R. M. 1989. *When Giants Learn to Dance: Mastering the Challenge of Strategy, Management and Careers in the 1990s.* London: Unwin.

Keep, E. 1989. 'A Training Scandal?' In Sisson, K. (ed.) *Personnel Management in Britain*, 1st edn. Oxford: Blackwell.

Keep, E. 1992. 'Schools in the Marketplace – Some Problems with Private Sector Models'. *British Journal of Education and Work*, Vol. 5, No. 2, 43–56.

Kochan, T. A. and Barocci, T. 1985. *Human Resource Management and Industrial Relations: Text, Readings and Cases.* Boston, MA: Little Brown & Co.

Kochan, T. A. and Barocci, T. (eds) 1985. *Human Resource Management and Industrial Relations.* Boston, MA: Little Brown & Co.

Kochan, T. A., Barocci, T., Katz, H. C. and McKersie, R. B. 1986. *The Transformation of American Industrial Relations.* New York: Basic Books.

Lawrence, J. 1973. 'Manpower and Personnel Models in Britain'. *Personnel Review*, 2, 4–26.

Lorenz, C. 1992. *Financial Times*, 21 February.

Lengnick-Hall, C. A. and Lengnick-Hall, M. L. 1988. 'Strategic human resources management: a review of the literature and a proposed typology'. *Academy of Management Review*, 13, 3, 454–70.

McGregor, A. and Sproull, A. 1991. *Employer Use Strategies: Analysis of a National Survey.* Employment Research Paper No. 83. Sheffield: Employment Department.

Mackay, L. and Torrington, D. 1986. *The Changing Nature of Personnel Management.* London: Institute of Personnel Management.

McKersie, R. B. and Capelli, P. 1987. *Journal of Management Studies*, 24, September.

McKinsey & Co./NEDO. 1988. *Performance and Competitive Success: Strengthening Competitiveness in UK Electronics*. A report prepared by McKinsey & Co. London: NEDO.

Manpower Services Commission/National Economic Development Office. 1978. *Case Studies in Company Manpower Planning*. London: NEDO.

Manpower Services Commission/National Economic Development Office. 1987. *People: The Key to Success*. London: NEDO.

Marginson, P., Edwards, P. K., Martin, R., Purcell, J. and Sisson, K. 1988. *Beyond the Workplace: Managing Industrial Relations in Multi-Establishment Enterprises*. Oxford: Blackwell.

Mayo, A. 1991. *Managing Careers: Strategies for Organisations*. London: Institute of Personnel Management.

Miles, R. and Snow, C. 1984. 'Designing strategic human resource systems'. *Organizational Dynamics*, Summer, 36–52.

Miller, P. 1989. 'Strategic HRM: What it is and what it is not'. *Personnel Management*, February.

Mintzberg, H. 1978. 'Patterns in strategy formation'. *Management Science*, xxiv, No. 9, 934–48.

Mintzberg, H. 1979. *The Structuring of Organizations*. Englewood Cliffs, NJ: Prentice Hall.

Mintzberg, H. 1987. 'The Strategy Concept – Parts I and II'. *California Management Review*, Fall.

Mintzberg, H. 1988. 'Crafting Strategy'. *The McKinsey Quarterly*, Summer, 71–89.

National Economic Development Office/Training Agency. 1988. *Young People and the Labour Market*. London: NEDO.

National Economic Development Office/Training Agency. 1989. *Defusing the Demographic Timebomb*. London: NEDO.

North Western Regional Health Authority/West Midlands Regional Health Authority. 1991. *Human Resource Management Audit*. Birmingham: West Midlands Regional Health Authority.

Pettigrew, A. M. 1985. *The Awakening Giant*. Oxford: Blackwell.

Pettigrew, A. M. and Whipp, R. 1991. *Managing Change for Competitive Success*. Oxford: Blackwell.

Pollert, A. 1987. *'The Flexible Firm': A Model in Search of Reality (Or a Policy in Search of a Practice)?* Warwick Papers in Industrial Relations, No. 19. Coventry: Industrial Relations Research Unit.

Porter, M. 1980. *Competitive Strategy: Techniques for Analysing Industries and Competitors*. New York: Free Press.

Porter, M. 1985. *Competitive Advantage: Creating and Sustaining Superior Performance*. New York: Free Press.

Purcell, J. 1989. 'The impact of corporate strategy on human resource management'. In Storey, J. (ed.) *New Perspectives on Human Resource Management*. London: Routledge.

Quinn, J. B. 1980. *Strategies for Change: Logical Incrementalism*. Homewood, IL: Irwin.

Quinn, J. B. 1988. 'Managing Strategies Incrementally'. In Quinn, J. B., Minzberg, H. and James, R. M. (eds) *The Strategy Process: Concepts, Contexts and Cases*. Englewood Cliffs, NJ: Prentice Hall.

Richards-Carpenter, 1993. *Personnel Management*. February, 19–20.

Schein, E. H. 1977. 'Increasing Organizational Effectiveness Through Better Human Resource Planning and Development'. *Sloan Management Review*, 19, Fall, 1–20.

Schuler, R. S. and Jackson, S. 1987. 'Linking competitive strategies with human resource management practices'. *Academy of Management Executive*, Vol. 1, No. 3, 209–13.

Storey, J. 1989. *Developments in the Management of Human Resources: An Interim Report*. Warwick Pepers in Industrial Relations, No. 17. Coventry: Industrial Relations Research Unit.

Storey, J. 1992. *Developments in the Management of Human Resources*. Oxford: Blackwell.

Taylor, B. 1986. 'Corporate Planning for the 1990s: The New Frontiers'. *Long Range Planning*, 19, 13–18.

Timperley, S. R. 1974. 'Towards a Behavioural Approach to Manpower Planning'. *Personnel Review*, 2, Winter.

Torrington, D. and Hall, L. 1987. *Personnel Management: a New Approach*. London: Prentice Hall International.

Walker, J. W. 1981. *Human Resource Planning*. New York: NcGraw-Hill.

West Midlands Regional Health Authority. 1990. *A Human Resource Strategy*. Birmingham: West Midlands Regional Health Authority.

Whittington, R. 1989. *Corporate Strategies in Recession and Recovery: Social Structure and Strategic Choice*. London: Unwin Hyman.

Whipp, R. 1992. 'Human Resource Management, Competition and Strategy: Some Productive Tensions'. In Blyton, P. and Turnbull, P. (eds) *Reassessing Human Resource Management*. London: Sage.

Young, A. 1976. 'Demographic and Ecological Models for Manpower Planning'. In Bartholomew, D. J. (ed.) *Manpower Planning*. Harmondsworth: Penguin, 145–61.

6

Recruitment and Selection

Thom Watson

Recruitment and selection are conceived as the processes by which organizations solicit, contact and interest potential appointees, and then establish whether it would be appropriate to appoint any of them. This definition is meant to include seeking and appointing both internal and external candidates. This chapter will review these processes, drawing on both systematic evidence and informal knowledge of present practice.

The perspective adopted is that it is the task of managers to influence these processes to the advantage of the organization, but that there are other parties involved who have different interests and may have sufficient power to influence outcomes. Though they might express it differently, this notion is quite familiar to, and underlies some of the recruitment practices of, many British managers. They know that practical success depends on understanding what influences potential employees. It is therefore curious that British textbooks on personnel management have, until recently, tended to ignore the multiple roles of candidates and the impact of external influences on them in relation to seeking and accepting employment (e.g. Torrington and Chapman, 1983; Higham, 1983; Courtis, 1985). This issue is treated briefly by Thomason (1981: 154–8) and Atkinson and Purkiss (1983: 13–19). Herriot (1984: 97–131) offers thorough treatment in relation to graduates and Collinson et al. (1990: 68), reviewing existing managerial practices, comment: 'Implicit in these informal practices is the recognition that neither employees nor job candidates can be reduced simply to objects of control and evaluation.' Wanous raised this issue much earlier in the United States (1980: 71–8).

Analysing the Need

Retirement, resignation, promotion, transfer and dismissal, or changes in technology, procedures or markets, may all lead to a perceived need to make new appointments and thereby trigger the recruitment and selection process. Probably as a result of economic stringency and the adoption of perspectives which are being labelled 'human resource management', these changes are increasingly being seen as an opportunity to review the deployment of people in organizations. The issues to be faced in such a review are treated in other chapters, notably chapter 1, and will not be discussed further here. We might note, however, that this tighter control can also be counter-productive if middle managers tolerate unsatisfactory employees rather than take corrective action that could lead to the reduction of their work groups when an organization is 'freezing' all vacancies. However, the parallel trend towards performance-based assessment for managers (see chapters 7 and 14) seems likely to reduce this danger if the performance improvement plans work.

Assuming that this review has taken place, the next step towards recruitment is to define what kind of employee is required by describing and analysing the job and drawing up a job description and personnel specification. 'All recruitment must begin with a job specification and/or person specification' according to an IPM code of practice and this process is increasingly carried out formally. The Industrial Training Boards in the 1960s and 1970s promoted the use of job analysis to determine training needs. Economic pressure to use people effectively and increasing awareness of legal restraints on improper discrimination may also have contributed to the realization of the important contribution such specifications can make to recruitment and selection. Yet, 'despite these changes, occupational segregation by sex persists as a primary characteristic of the UK labour market' (Collinson et al., 1990: 3) and case studies have shown how the behaviour of line managers and personnel specialists may subvert the intention of this prescription while they appear to carry it out (ibid.: 96–108).

Both internal and external potential candidates need information to help them to gauge their interest in the job and their chances of being appointed. Initially they will probably want to know about the tasks, pressures and rewards of the job, and about the context of the work. Some of this is likely to be known to internal candidates. This information can provide a basis for advertising the vacancy to internal and external recruitment sources, for giving job details to candidates, and for briefing or reminding selectors of what is required. Such job descriptions typically include the following information:

- job title, reference, and other identifying features;
- relationships with other people inside and outside the organization;
- the key tasks;
- the purpose, aims or objectives of the job; and
- the performance standards which have to be met in performing these tasks to meet these objectives.

They may also include additional useful information such as:

- limits of authority over expenditure, working methods, sales, information, equipment, personnel matters, and so on;
- particular problems, difficulties, distasteful aspects, and constraints;
- working conditions and hours; and
- remuneration and benefits.

[These items are derived from a range of texts, such as Courtis (1985: 8), Torrington and Hall (1991: 245–61), Thomason (1981: 187–92), ACAS (1981: 4, 17), Cuming (1978: 71–3), Grant and Smith (1977: 30–4), Armstrong (1977: 86–8), Fraser (1971: 53–61) and Plumbley (1988: 16–19), which are taken to be representative of usual recommended good practice in Britain.]

None of the sources above mentions two very important items which could be added to the list as a reminder that recruitment and selection take place in a dynamic environment. An apparently trivial item, the date of preparation of the document, is a reminder that such documents can quickly become obsolete and that an undated document acquires a disturbing ambiguity. The second item, a prediction of the future changes likely to impinge on the job, may be difficult to estimate. However, as Burns and Stalker (1961) and Lawrence and Lorsch (1967) have shown, uncertainty and change are contingencies which call for changes in roles and organization structure if they are to be faced successfully. Awareness of possible job and organization changes should trigger thoughts about the demands these are likely to impose on the job holder and the characteristics that will be needed to deal with them. Herriot (1989: *passim*) has explored this issue.

Whatever system of headings is used, the purpose will be to identify and describe those aspects of the job which are crucial to success. This description will then provide a useful basis for identifying the critical attributes to be sought in candidates for appointment by revealing the particular demands which a job will make on the incumbent. This is not a mechanical process: the process of deduction requires imagination and the conclusions will be based on opinions and probability rather than certainty. People often feel 'certain' of their uncertain conclusions in such circumstances. It is, therefore, important to understand how difficult it is to constrain the effects of bias and prejudice which can lead to unfairness, even gross discrimination, and to errors with economic consequences.

Mackay and Torrington (1986: 41) reported that just under half of the companies in their survey used systematic job analysis as an aid to selection for white-collar jobs and about one-quarter for blue-collar jobs. Of these about three-quarters used the 'Seven Point Plan' (Rodger, 1970) and virtually all of the remainder used the 'Five-Fold Framework' (Fraser, 1971: 64–80) (see also the ACAS Advisory Booklet No. 6, 1981). Rodger's Seven Point Plan is 'a series of questions gathered together under seven headings':

1 physical make-up (health, physique, appearance, bearing, speech);
2 attainments (education, training, experience, degree of success in each);
3 general intelligence;
4 special aptitudes (mechanical, numerical, verbal, drawing, musical, manual dexterity);
5 interests (intellectual, practical, social, artistic, physical);
6 disposition (acceptability, influence, dependability, self-reliance); and
7 circumstances (domestic, family, special).

Rodger formulated his questions so that they relate the demands of the job to the personal characteristics needed for successful performance, emphasizing the need for a logical link between job description and personnel specification which is the basis for current research. If it is not clear what is to be expected from a suitable candidate, it is probable that there is a deficiency in the job analysis which should, therefore, be explored further.

Munro Fraser's 'Five-Fold Framework' considers:

1 impact on others (appearance, speech, manner, self-confidence);
2 acquired knowledge or qualifications (education, training, work experience);
3 innate abilities (speed of perception, special aptitudes);
4 motivation (goals, consistency, initiative, practical effectiveness); and
5 emotional adjustment (ability to stand up to stress).

It was developed specifically as an aid to selection interviewing. It can be viewed as a development of the 'Seven Point Plan' and there is considerable overlap between the two checklists. However, Fraser's highlighting of the use of job analysis to identify questions worth asking at interview (implicit in Rodger's work) and the provision of a scaled interview record form are also incorporated in Saville and Holdsworth's 'Work Profiling System' (1991).

As the relevant theory advances or fashions change, or even when developers find apparently clearer or more convenient ways of expressing the key ideas, further checklists emerge. A key problem with job analysis is its heavy reliance on judgement to identify key aspects of jobs, to assess their relative importance, and to deduce the human qualities associated with successful performance. Another problem is that at the same time as we are becoming less primitive in our understanding of jobs we are becoming more aware that our techniques are not socially and politically neutral. It would now be considered discriminatory to enquire about some of the factors listed under Rodger's heading 'circumstances', and 'acceptability' has strong potential to be used as a cloak for improper discrimination. Fraser (1971: 75) in his notes of guidance places more emphasis on the strength of motivation than on its direction. He is taking for granted that we are considering motives acceptable to management: this point will have to be taken up in more detail in relation to selection.

Techniques of job analysis are steadily developing in the attempt to provide a systematic framework which will minimize the danger of undesirable biases in the exercising of judgement and sharpen our ability to identify which behaviours make the critical difference between failure and successful job performance. Techniques such as 'Repertory Grid' have been used to elicit informants' views on the most important significant differences in the dimensions of jobs. The 'Position Analysis Questionnaire' (PAQ) (Mecham et al., 1977: *passim*) used factor analysis to identify 32 factors underlying the 194 questions relating to job content which are grouped under six headings: information input, mental process, work output, relationships, job context, and other. Analysts using carefully structured techniques like this reach a high level of agreement about jobs and inexperienced analysts achieve results quite similar to those of experts (Smith and Hakel, 1979).

These techniques have been imported to Britain but are not yet widely used. Saville and Holdsworth (1991), having developed a battery of personality questionnaires and ability tests, and having considered the use of PAQ by British users, went on to produce their 'Work Profiling System' (WPS). This combines the characteristics of the factor analysed job features questionnaire with those of a computerized expert system. The responses to the questionnaire provide a basis for job evaluation, designing training, the choice of appropriate selection techniques, even suggestions for interview questions. The need for subjective judgements was addressed directly: a panel of expert occupational psychologists helped design the questionnaire and suggested the recommendations encapsulated in the expert system. Reference was made to the Commission for Racial Equality and the Equal Opportunities Commission to minimize the risk of building improper discriminatory assumptions into the WPS. The system is designed so that key decisions about the relative importance of different aspects of a job can be made either by the parties who are directly affected by the consequences of these decisions, or by the user relying on the 'expert' judgements built into the system. All this is made clear in the training provided by the WPS's publisher but the sophistication and comprehensiveness of the system might too easily lead some users to abdicate their responsibilities by relying on it uncritically.

Methods of Recruitment

Having identified the characteristics of the person required for the vacancy, the next stage is to consider how to reach such people and cultivate their interest in the job. This requires consideration of the channels available for communication and the possible sources of information about such people, and the most cost-effective way of using either. These channels and sources overlap. Courtis (1985: 15) puts them in a single list: advertising; employment agencies and job centres/job points; *Professional and Executive Register*; registers; selection consultants; search consultants (head-hunters); outplacement consultants; introductions by existing staff or unions; people already known; people who have left the organization; people who applied last time; other 'volunteers' such as casual callers and correspondents; and university milkround and schools contacts. In terms of order of priority, one might expect an organization to look inside, use existing contacts, and then, after that, think about advertising, agencies or consultants.

Internal candidates may be sought by searching the records, asking managers or supervisors for recommendations, or through internal advertisements on notice-boards and/or in-house journals. It is difficult to know how extensively used or how effective the first method is. Its success will depend very much on the quality of the records and whether they are kept in a way which facilitates this kind of search. Keeping and searching manual records is very labour intensive and error prone and it is to be hoped that computerization will ease the problem. However, just as the cost of clerical time discouraged the elaboration of manual records in ways which would have assisted the search for internal candidates, it seems possible that, for a while at least, the Data Protection Act 1984 may inhibit companies from storing more than essential short-term operating information in computer processible form. Skills not necessary, and therefore under-utilized in a present job, maybe of key importance in a vacancy to be filled, but may be unrecorded.

Asking supervisors and managers for recommendations is similarly dependent on the quality of their information, but is likely to tap much more complex and up-to-date information. The danger is that this richer information is even more vulnerable to bias, leading to discrimination. Internal advertising is one way of reaching current employees who have unexpected and unrecorded skills or experience. Its use has spread in recent years and it is the most frequently used method for reaching blue- and white-collar workers (Torrington and Hall, 1991: 214–15). It may have the disadvantage of producing large numbers of applications, which are expensive to process, but this risk can be reduced by careful drafting. Internal recruitment is economical, and it highlights – or genuinely offers – opportunities for career development within the company, but it may also be required as a consequence of agreements with trade unions. It might also be conceived as a kind of passive discrimination which keeps out potential recruits who could be better qualified in terms of a personnel specification but do not conform to current stereo-types of 'acceptable employees'.

If there are no suitable internal candidates, an organization's records of former employees, applicants or casual callers may enable a vacancy to be filled quickly and economically. Again, the quality of the records will be of key importance: the Data Protection Act need not be inhibiting. The time between the last contact and the emergence of another relevant vacancy, and current levels of unemployment, affect the chance that people will be employed satisfactorily elsewhere, and, therefore, the amount which can justifiably be invested in retaining information. Both of these seem likely to increase in periods of high unemployment.

Contacts made through present employees may lead to very satisfactory appointments. The information made available to the candidate before accepting the position may be more comprehensive and, as Wanous (1980: 71–8) has shown in the United States, realistic job previews can reduce turnover. In some industries (printing, for example), the unions have exercised tight control over entry by agreement or custom and practice, in which case management may only be able to recruit through the relevant union. Management appears to have lost control in such circumstances, but recruitment will not be expensive and appointments may be no less satisfactory. However, recruiting through existing employees may be regarded as unacceptably paternalistic and, if the current workforce is not a fair cross-section of the local population, it may be held to be 'indirect discrimination' under the Race Relations Act and it could also lead to sex discrimination. It has been suggested, however, that the current legal definition of 'justifiability' is sufficiently vague for the legislation to be ineffective in such circumstances, and the workforce may be management's accomplice in discrimination (Collinson et al., 1990: 70–1).

Employment agencies and job centres can be useful subcontractors of recruitment work. As Courtis (1985: 16–17) reminds us, they vary in quality and their work is influenced by the quality of the brief they are given. He grouped the *Professional and Executive Register* (*PER*) with the agencies. *PER* advertising stressed its similarity with selection consultants. This is fair because it offers a similar service to employers, but also throws light on the issue of acceptability mentioned earlier. Professional and managerial candidates who had little or no contact with job centres preferred to deal with consultants rather than job centres. Changes in the labour market appear to be forcing changes in attitude: a job centre recently offered a business breakfast to senior people who might be considering a job change.

Executive selection consultancy began to grow in a significant way in the mid-1950s following a trend begun in the United States. The British pioneers did not believe that the UK was ready for US-style head-hunting or search consultancy in which promising candidates are sought out and approached directly. Developments in continental Europe were even slower. They were hindered by legislation

banning employment agencies which was intended to protect workers from having to pay anyone to find them a job, but was broadly
drawn and was construed to forbid the establishment of any agency
which maintained records of possible candidates. This situation is
changing. Clark (1991) identified 820 recruitment and search consultants operating in the UK. An IPM/Income Data Services guide
(1990) reveals a mixed picture across Europe. The number of consultants active is estimated to be: Belgium 110, France 122, Netherlands 360, Spain 45. There are 2000 personnel consultancies in
Germany, but the proportion carrying out executive search and
selection is not known. Major search and recruitment consultancies
are active in Denmark, Italy and Portugal and the general trend in
Europe is towards the relaxation of restrictive legislation.

Selection consultants in the UK sell their services on the basis of
offering:

- skills in recruitment, advertising and selection, which may be in short
  supply in the client firm;
- detailed and current knowledge of particular labour markets;
- access to a large file of candidates, which may save advertising costs; and
- brokerage between employer and applicants, so that jobs can be advertised without revealing the employer's identity and potential applicants
  need not have their identity revealed to the employer unless the post
  seems interesting after a fairly detailed discussion with the consultant.

It is argued that these factors will produce more appropriate candidates than would be prepared to apply directly to the employer. As
with agencies, competence varies. The best test is probably to get the
opinion of a former client for whom the consultants have handled a
similar task recently. Courtis (1985: 18) suggests reviewing *Executive
Grapevine* to identify firms claiming appropriate expertise: he then
suggests some useful questions to test their professionalism.

Search consultancy is very labour intensive and so the fees for an
assignment are correspondingly high. In consequence, it is mainly
used for positions at very senior levels, though here again acceptability may be a significant factor. To apply for a job may raise questions
concerning the need for the candidate to change, and this would not
be reassuring to potential future colleagues. The process must therefore be managed so that the prospective candidates can discuss the
possibility of joining the organization without having to make an
application. If the discussions are not fruitful, they can withdraw
gracefully and nobody suffers the ignominy of being rejected or

having their current positions undermined. Interestingly, head-hunting of a 'do-it-yourself' kind has long been practised at the highest levels in the public sector. Advertisements for some very senior positions in the public sector often indicate the willingness of the body concerned to have interesting names suggested by third parties. Search consultancy appears to have considerably strengthened its grip on senior management recruitment since 1980 (Heidrich and Struggles, 1985), and a *Personnel Management* (May 1993: 67) survey has suggested that 40 per cent of executive positions were filled without advertising in 1992.

Selection and search consultancy raise some interesting ethical problems. The purpose of much recruitment activity is to lure good employees away from other employers. Employers may not like it, but publicizing the availability of jobs shows employees the opportunities that are open to them. 'No poaching' agreements limit the freedom of workers for the short-run economic advantage of employers, though it might also be argued that the longer term effects are not in the employers' interests because they inhibit the development of a labour market in which critical skills are in adequate supply. In the case of selection and search consultants the problem is narrowed and sharpened. Both would normally begin an assignment by meeting a considerable proportion of the managers with whom the new person will have to work in order to understand the client organization's requirements. The difficulty arises because this means that they meet and are able to form an opinion of the competence of a group of exactly the sort of people their next client may be seeking. Naturally, the current client will want some reassurance that the consultant will not exploit this privileged access. The ethical selection consultant may undertake not to initiate any approach to the current client's employees, but is likely to point out that if any of these employees reply to an advertisement their applications will be treated no less favourably than those of other candidates. They will be recommended to the other client if they seem suitable and the consultant will not inform their present employer (the current client). An advantage that will probably be pointed out to the client is that the consultant is free to consider anybody who replies to an advertisement or who has already agreed to details being kept on file. The client generally agrees that it would be unsatisfactory for the strongest candidates for the position under discussion to be withheld because they were employed by another of the consultant's clients. The ethical search consultant, on the other hand, will reassure the client that no employee will be put forward for another job during the assignment and during some specified period afterwards, and that no direct competitor of the client will be accepted as a client during this period. The client thus has stronger protection with the search consultant than the selection consultant for a period of, probably, up to two years, and continually if the organization is large enough to be able to retain the search consultant regularly. Even so, the chief executive of a major unit of a multinational corporation once confided (or alleged) that he continuously retained three head-hunters who were considered particularly effective as an insurance policy to reduce the chance of the opposition getting to their best people.

Clark (1992) reports that virtually all of respondents in his survey of recruitment and selection consultants used unstructured interviews and over 80 per cent used references. He speculates that selection validity is not their prime consideration. Acceptability to the client will have greater economic significance for the intermediary in the short run than valid prediction of job performance. Interviews will thus in some cases be as much concerned with persuasion and negotiation as with assessment.

Schools, colleges, polytechnics, universities, 'outplacement' consultants who assist individuals with career planning or are retained by employers to help place staff made redundant, and registers may all prove to be fruitful sources of candidates. Registers ask for a relatively small fee if someone from their list is appointed; some universities at one time asked visiting recruiters to pay a fee or charged for interviewing rooms; otherwise these sources do not involve the direct payment of a charge. This is not to imply, however, that recruitment through these channels is free or even cheap. As in the other cases, careful thought is necessary to achieve cost-effectiveness. With approximately 80 universities and polytechnics in the UK, the travel and accommodation costs incurred in sending recruiters to visit all of them are considerable. Briefing their careers advisers to understand the ethos and requirements of the employing organization can also be quite expensive. Estimates of the total cost of 'milk round' recruitment have exceeded £10,000 per graduate appointed. For these reasons a number of employers have concentrated on building up a strong relationship with a small number of institutions which seem best able to assist them as a result of location, the existence of particularly good or relevant courses, prestige, or the competence of the careers staff.

Advertising is probably the recruitment channel which first comes to mind if internal candidates are not available to fill a job (although appropriate advertising may be necessary in internal recruitment too). Recruitment advertising is expensive. Fordham (1983: 48) considers that revenue from this source saved a large sector of the newspaper industry from financial collapse. Selling space to recruiters has become big and sophisticated business. They are being courted as never before. In 1957 *The Times* did not accept display advertisements for jobs, and refused to allow the pioneer selection consultants Management Selection Limited to advertise under their initials MSI: in May 1985 it was offering bottles of champagne to job advertisers.

In this new climate it is very easy to spend too much on recruitment advertising. Cuming (1978: 79) expressed strong opinions about wasteful advertising in the NHS, coupled with the suggestion that employers could get some coverage of 'stories' relating to job opportunities in the local press and use local direct mail shots much more cheaply as ways of reaching people who might not be reading the situations vacant columns. The force of Cuming's comments was underlined by a news item in *Personnel Management* (May 1985: 57) which reported a two-year trial period for restrictions on advertising designed to save the National Health Service £4 million.

To achieve cost-effectiveness in advertising it is necessary to consider the choice of media; the content of the advertisement; its presentation; and, finally, a simple but effective system of response analysis to monitor the results. These are discussed in turn below.

The aim of advertising will generally be to attract a sufficient number of suitably qualified applicants so that a good appointment can be made, and to do this at minimum cost. Effectiveness is the first consideration, and cost the second. When the Civil Service advertises a national competition for posts, fairness to all suitable potential candidates requires wide publicity for the competition. In other cases, such as medical appointments at consultant level in the NHS, it is a statutory requirement that the appointment be advertised in more than one journal. These are special cases and it has been more usual to aim close to the minimum coverage necessary. For positions that are difficult to fill, and when there is the danger of discrimination by restrictive advertising, there may be a need for wider advertising. The question is, therefore, how can the organization reach the people it needs? Recruitment officers are nowadays deluged with readership information by the press and advertising agents. Courtis (1985: 26) points out that 'the media which people read often bear no resemblance to the ones they look at for jobs'. An old example should make this clear. In the 1950s there was a shortage of draughtsmen. The majority of draughtsmen read the *Daily Mirror* and there would always be a considerable number of copies of that paper in a large drawing office. In addition, there was very often one copy of the *Daily Telegraph* which passed from hand to hand so that the jobs column could be scanned. The question is therefore not, what do they read? but, where will they see a job advertisement? Knowing the market and analysing the past responses to advertising will give the best guidance. The *Daily Express* and *Daily Mail* both have larger circulations than the broadsheet dailies but carry much less job advertising. The difference is partly explained by the difference in the social class profile of the readers of these papers but the habit of non-readers to consult the paper when searching for jobs assisted the *Daily Telegraph* to maintain its ascendency in job advertising until about 1990. In spring 1993 the leading position appeared to be held by *The Guardian*, with over 40 per cent of the market, while *The Times*, *Daily Telegraph* and *Sunday Times* each had about 10–15 per cent and *The Independent* 9 per cent, according to *Personnel Management* (1993: *passim*).

In addition to the press, trade and specialist publications, there are other possibilities for the recruiter to bear in mind. Some companies use slides at the local cinema. These do not seem likely to reach very large audiences at present, but may meet special needs. Posters are not widely used but may well be effective for some grades of staff when used on the London Underground trains or in similar situations. Television is relatively expensive and little used at present. However, the point made by Courtis in relation to the local press could be even more important in relation to television while job losses and job creation are national news. When numbers of new jobs are created, this is reported, naming the employer and the location: such very wide publicity can produce large numbers of applications which may be expensive to process. Professional conferences have long been used like the medieval hiring fairs. In Germany major trade fairs provide the opportunity for employers and job hunters to meet. In the UK careers fairs are becoming widely used as a way of recruiting school-leavers and graduates.

Television advertising through Prestel (Ray, 1980: 66–9) or Oracle and similar networks may become useful to recruiters. It seems likely, however, that recruiters will not rush to use new media unless they are potentially cost-effective substitutes for those currently used. (Computer bulletin boards might come into this category as an economical well-targeted means of reaching some IT professionals.) The *Sunday Telegraph* was launched during a job advertising boom. Initially, it offered very favourable terms to prestigious advertisers whose example was likely to be followed by others. At least one such advertiser declined to support the new paper on the grounds that if an additional place were created where people would look for jobs it would become necessary to use it and this would increase the costs of reaching the people who were already being recruited through the existing Sunday papers. It is interesting to note that in March 1985 the *Sunday Times* had 15.7 per cent, the *Observer* 3.7 per cent, and the *Sunday Telegraph* only 0.2 per cent of recruitment advertising in the quality papers. By March 1993 these shares had declined to *Sunday Times* 13.6 per cent, *Observer* 1.6 per cent, *Sunday Telegraph* 0 per cent. The *Independent on Sunday* also failed to establish itself in this market (*Personnel Management*, May 1985: 57; May 1993: 67).

Other media worth a brief mention are radio, films and video cassettes. Local radio can compete directly with local papers and can be very effective in persuading people to make a preliminary contact. It has the disadvantage that the listener has to note or remember where and how to respond, so the message is best kept very simple. Films and video cassettes seem most likely to be of value for large-scale recruitment, recruitment when a requirement is likely to remain unchanged over a number of years, or collaborative recruitment to a profession. Video cassettes have been supplied to universities in this latter connection for use in careers advisory work.

The message contained in the advertisement is crucial. The essence of preparing an effective message was given very pithily by Parkinson (1986: ch. 2) who argued that the ideal advertisement produced only one applicant but that applicant would be ideally qualified for the job. To achieve this, the message would balance the attractive and unattractive features of the job. It would avoid stating the requirements in terms of vague qualities which most people would claim to possess such as initiative, integrity, intelligence and tact. Instead it would set out a realistic thumb-nail sketch of the job from which the reader would be able to deduce the skills and qualities required. The difficulties and unpleasant features would not be minimized and the pay and benefits would be set out clearly. Allowing for the humorous exaggeration, this advice is based on a more searching analysis of some of the key issues than is found in most contemporary texts: Fordham (1983) and Courtis (1985) are exceptions.

Overall, an effective advertisement is likely to include:

- information concerning the organization;
- the location of the job;
- significant developments which may have an impact on the job;
- job preview;
- qualifications and experience required;
- outline of the remuneration and benefits; and
- instructions for responding.

People usually want to know who the advertiser is before revealing their own identity. Horror stories used to be told about people applying to their current employers who had advertised under a box number. Agencies and consultants now offer protection to both parties and the box number has almost disappeared from recruitment advertising. In specifying the requirements, it is useful to keep in mind both the ideal and the minimum-standard candidate (Courtis, 1985: 37) and to consider whether it is desirable to encourage or discourage candidates near the minimum standard. The statutory requirements concerning the employment of disabled people should be kept in mind, though the evidence suggests that their observance is not a significant aspect of employers' policies.

Many companies are reluctant to state clearly what pay they are offering, though this coyness seems to have diminished over recent years and the intermediaries provide a way of separating salary information from company identity in an initial advertisement. Courtis (1985: 38–9) demolished four stock arguments for coyness: first, if a company has a sound pay structure it does not have to worry about jealousy among existing employees; second, existing employees know more about supposedly secret salaries than management cares to acknowledge; third, if you do not reveal the salary you will not meet some of the most promising potential candidates; and, fourth, appointments are frequently made at salaries below the advertised maximum starting salary. At times when there is a shortage of particular skills, employers may be inhibited form advertising salaries either by agreement or a shared belief that this will lead to an escalation of salary costs. In West Germany after the Second World War there was legislation prohibiting the inclusion of salaries in job advertising. Some organizations circumvented this by arranging that the diagonal measurement across a display advertisement for a managerial position was directly proportional to the salary in Deutschmarks but it is not known how widely this convention was understood.

Instructions about responding can help applicants and selectors. The illiterate, the highly literate but very busy, and those who use the telephone a great deal in their work may use the telephone in the first instance. This might be welcome, but could introduce an unnecessary stage into the selection process. Firms using graphologists may ask for hand-written applications. If application forms are to be used, applicants can be discouraged from writing long letters: if they are not to be used, the task of comparing initial letters can be made easier by asking for specific information to be included. In either case the selector is left to decide how to interpret the failure of candidates to follow instructions.

A final and very important consideration when drafting copy and planning supporting illustration is to be aware of the considerable range of relevant legislation and to avoid infringing any of it. Wording (and, of course, illustration) which states or implies an intention to discriminate against some candidates in ways which contravene the Sex Discrimination or the Race Relations Acts are obviously to be avoided, and guidance on such points is readily available from the Equal Opportunities Commission (1977; 1985) and the Commission for Racial Equality. Ray (1980: ch. 10) discusses not only these Acts but nine others, from the Criminal Justice Act 1925 to the Control of Pollution Act 1974 'which prohibits the use of loudspeakers in the street for advertising purposes'. The range of prohibitions still varies quite widely across Europe (IPM/Incomes Data Services, 1990: *passim*).

An advertisement can deliver its message only when it has caught attention. Recruitment advertisements can be seen to be trying to do this in several ways. The first is size. This may convey more about the importance and resources of the employing organization than it does about the specific vacancy or vacancies that are being advertised: it may also indicate the scale of the recruitment need. The armed services are among the few organizations with the resources and the need to use both full-page advertisements in the national press and quite substantial commercials on television. The economy campaign in the NHS referred to earlier is aimed very largely at reducing expenditure on the features which attract attention. In journals where the majority of the advertising is for NHS jobs only, lineage or semi-display advertising is to be used. Logos which were also used as eye-catching devices were banned (*Personnel Management*, May 1985: 57). Other aspects of presentation that assist an advertisement to draw attention are the use of artwork, special type, and the position on the page or within the publication. Competent space sales managers recognize the value of the positions facing editorial matter and charge a premium which may be worth paying because the advertisement has a better chance of being noticed by people who are not actively job hunting, as well as those who are.

The style in which an advertisement is written can be significant in two ways: it affects the impression which is created and it can also affect costs. Ray (1980: 150–3) discusses indifferent, interesting, influential, impressive, and gimmicky styles. The indifferent should be avoided but each of the others can be appropriate when matched to the circumstances with increasing care as one progresses through the list. Creating an impression which is attractive to some candidates but discouraging to others who judge they would not fit in can be a cost-effective way of providing a realistic job preview which enables candidates to practise self-selection. It might also be improperly discriminatory. Costs are inflated when the copywriter uses an unnecessarily verbose style or adds redundant phrases such as 'Applications are invited for the post of' when the heading 'Computer Programmer' serves quite well on its own.

Consideration of the cost-effectiveness of advertisements requires the setting up of a monitoring procedure. It is common practice to ask candidates to quote a reference number which indicates both the position being sought and the publication in which the advertisement was seen. Analysing the responses is, of course, different from merely counting them. Two hundred replies to an advertisement might sound impressive, but if the applicants are not suitable the advertisement is of less value than another which produces two applicants and both are appointable. Good practice requires identifying the sources of the short-listed and appointed candidates.

Employers may feel the need for outside help in presenting their recruitment message. Ray (1980: ch. 16) reviews the role of agencies in recruitment advertising. A good agency will have a range of skills which only the largest employer could hope to match. It will have experience with a wider range of media and will have up-to-date knowledge of costs, print and artwork requirements, copy dates and so on; and it will be able to relieve the recruiter of the tedious and very detailed administrative work necessary to ensure that instructions are correctly carried out by a range of different publications, and that their bills are correct.

It has been stated above that the recruiter must know the market. This is fundamental. As recruitment has become more professional, more data have become available about trends in the job market. As a public relations and publicity device, Hay-MSL have been publishing an index of recruitment advertising for managerial staff since 1960. This was based on an analysis of the advertisements in six publications and for a time gave the best available impression of general trends in this job market. A wider analysis is now prepared by *The Guardian* and very detailed analyses are published by Media Expenditure Analysis Ltd. All of these are reported in *Personnel Management*, which also reports data from search consultants. Any tendency to rely on any one of these as indicating the state of a job market should be corrected by considering two headlines in the Recruitment Report (*Personnel Management*, September 1983: 45–6): one, based on advertising, said 'Demand for executives highest since 1974'; the other, based on head-hunters' data, declared 'Executive jobs down'. There is clearly an ebb and flow between the channels that are being used for recruitment as well as fluctuations in the number of vacancies to be filled. The implication, if this trend continues in times of high unemployment, is that recruitment from outside by the larger companies will be aimed at lower level jobs seen as entry grades. The developing concept of core jobs and peripheral work that can be handled by contractors or temporary staff seems likely to sustain this trend, and discussion of the 'demographic timebomb' seems to have been unhelpful in that it led many recruiters to associate 'entry grades' only with younger applicants at a time when there were very many experienced people unemployed. Perhaps there was a shortage of imagination rather than a shortage of suitable people, and too much consideration given to short-term rather than ongoing job requirements. The growing discussion of 'agism' may be one of the consequences of this behaviour.

An organization setting up a unit in a new location may find that successful recruitment of a new labour-force requires activities beyond those discussed above. It may have to convince the local community that its employment practices, the nature of its work and its impact on the district are consistent with it being accepted as a good citizen. Much of this will be done in discussion with trade unions, but it will probably also be necessary to cultivate the goodwill and support of civic, social and religious leaders, depending on the context. That this is merely a special case of a general issue is illustrated by the Annual Report for 1984 of the Civil Service Commission which describes how careers in the Civil Service have become less attractive to able undergraduates. This is reported to be influenced by 'how well-regarded the employment is seen to be by the community as a whole' (*Personnel Management*, May 1985: 16).

Negotiation of the terms on which a new incumbent will be accepted into a position is part of the recruitment and selection processes. Indeed, recruitment and selection would not be regarded as having been successful until such negotiations, too, had been satisfactorily concluded. Moreover, these processes are not in practice separate and distinct: the first statement made about remuneration or conditions of employment in an advertisement may also be the opening phase of the bargaining which leads to the offer and acceptance of appointment.

It is, of course, true that for positions covered by collective agreements the bargaining takes place between management and unions. It is not part of the recruitment process, but nevertheless it can affect recruitment considerably. Even in such circumstances some individual negotiation may still take place, as for example when a recruit is offered 'guaranteed' overtime or placed at a high level within a fixed salary scale. And, when the strength of the unions is weaker, management may respond by offering more flexible terms of employment: Storey cites such a response in the face of skills shortages (1992: 98).

Finally it is worth comment that this chapter is still relatively unusual among chapters in British texts on personnel management in devoting so much space to recruitment (Torrington and Hall, 1991 also give recruitment fuller treatment). The justification is that recruitment provides the candidates for the selector to judge. Selection techniques cannot overcome failures in recruitment; they merely make them evident.

The Selection Process

Selection is a decision-making process. Torrington and Chapman (1983: 70) point out that it is a reciprocal process, with both candidates and employers making decisions. They claim that, with one exception (French, 1974: 267), which turns out to be a single sentence and diagram, there is no discussion of this issue in major

US personnel management texts. It does emerge in the literature of industrial and organizational psychology (Rodger, 1971; Wanous, 1980) and is basic to the preceding discussion of recruitment and to the comments on realistic job previews and self-selection below. Makin and Robertson (1983: 21, 24) have also aired this issue in the personnel management literature.

Selection processes require the collecting and ordering of the data, opinions and inferences on which the decisions will be based. What follows will be largely concerned with the methods employers use. The methods selected are influenced by the employers' view of what is required to provide a satisfactory basis for decision making and awareness of the appropriateness of particular techniques to provide what is sought. Astrological analysis was reported by Clark (1991) as being used by two continentally owned search consultants. The author has encountered a French merchant bank consulting a Sorbonne professor who used physiognomic ratios to analyse character and IPM/Incomes Data Services (1990) report this technique being used in Italy. The polygraph has been widely used in the US to screen out potentially dishonest employees, but controversy led to legal limits being placed on its use (Sinai, 1988). UK practice is relatively conservative.

Parkinson (1986) in another of his pithy over-simplifications suggests that all selection methods can be reduced to two basic methods and combinations or elaborations of these. Each method requires asking the candidate only one question. In the Chinese method the candidate is asked 'What do you know?': the English method is to ask 'Who is your father?'. The 'English method' is blatantly discriminatory. The question does not have to be asked aloud and is an encapsulation of much racial and class discrimination. The United States version of the question is 'Where did you go to school?' which can be used in an elitist discriminatory way familiar in Britain. The Civil Service Commission is said still to be concerned that Oxbridge graduates are over-represented in the higher grades of the Civil Service. The 'Chinese method' is the basis of attempts to collect objective information about job-relevant knowledge, skills and abilities. It can also be used in ways which are as discriminatory as the 'English method' if the information collected is not job-relevant or consists of biased subjective judgements. McIntosh and Smith (1974) reported that the level of racial discrimination had declined since the passing of the 1967 Race Relations Act, but it was still substantial and considerably exceeded the level indicated by official complaints. A point worth underlining is that the adoption of systematic selection techniques designed to reduce racial and sex discrimination by focusing on valid job-relevant selection criteria would probably also reduce the number of selection errors affecting members of groups who are not discriminated against at present.

Reliability and validity

Before examining the techniques used to collect the data used in making selection decisions, there are some general principles to consider. Rodger told generations of his students that in considering the use of any psychological technique they should check that it is technically sound, administratively convenient and politically acceptable. This roughly means that it should really work, be cost effective and not run into so much resistance that it will be impossible to introduce with any hope of success. This is sound advice in relation to any managerial or administrative technique. Comments will be made on administrative convenience and political acceptability below. Technical soundness is, however, fundamental and will be considered separately before moving on to more detailed consideration of data-gathering techniques.

The two key requirements for selection methods to be technically sound are 'reliability' and 'validity' (Kline, 1993: 5–28). Reliability means that the method should not be influenced too much by chance factors, and should be consistent in the results it gives if used to assess a person on more than one occasion. Validity has traditionally been taken to mean that the method measures the characteristic or ability that it purports to measure and, what is more important from a practical point of view, predicts the future behaviour or performance that it is required or assumed to predict. Recently it has been suggested (Scholarios et al., 1993) that the ability of a test battery to classify applicants according to their suitability for different occupations may be of greater value than simple predictive validity.

Validity and reliability can only be established by practical empirical testing. A test may appear to be useful (this is called having high 'face validity') but properly controlled comparisons of scores with measures of work performance may show that an apparently less relevant test has higher 'predictive validity'. If the scores gained in a selection test, or awarded by a panel of interviewers, for a group of candidates are compared with a measure of their performance on the job, the correlation between these two sets of scores is a measure of the validity of the predictor. Until recently it was considered that this measure, the coefficient of validity, could only be interpreted in relation to the group of candidates from which it was obtained. A new approach called meta-analysis groups the results from similar studies to derive validity coefficients which it is argued have more general applicability. Nevertheless, a test may have different validities for males and females, or for different ethnic groups, which means that selection procedures to be used with mixed groups of applicants should be separately validated for each constituent sub-group. A strict interpretation of the anti-discrimination legislation in Britain would seem to call for this if it is to be shown that selection criteria are job related. Up to the present time this has not been demanded in Britain, but litigation in the USA has included some highly technical arguments on validation, and some test developers in the UK are taking steps to avoid using test items which discriminate on grounds of sex or race.

There are probably at least three reasons why validation of tests has not been widely practised in Britain (Sneath et al., 1976). Firstly, the users have not realized the need, or had assumed that tests acquired through reputable agencies were already validated (not understanding that validity may be affected by the context in which the test is used). Secondly, true predictive validation is a very lengthy process. It requires candidates to be tested, but selected on grounds other than the test results. These should remain unknown to anyone who will assess the candidates in any way so that the assessor's judgement is not influenced by knowledge of the test results. The results are reviewed and the validity of the test calculated when a sufficiently large group of candidates has been in employment long enough for there to be good measures available of their performance in the job. Because this process takes so long it is often replaced by applying the test to a group of existing employees whose performance is already recorded. This is known as concurrent validation. It is less satisfactory because test performance may have been influenced by experience of the job; the motivation of present employees and applicants taking the test may be different; and the variability of the validation group may have been reduced by promotions and separations. Thirdly, validation of measures to predict job performance requires that criteria of job performance are available which are themselves valid and reliable. These may not be available for service or advisory jobs. Even in production and sales jobs, where performance seems more readily measurable, there may be differences in the volume or quality of production which are attributable to the condition of equipment rather than worker performance, and sales volume can be influenced by the special factors in a particular territory as well as by an employee's selling skills.

Brotherton (1980) has drawn a distinction between measures of 'organizational performance' and 'job performance' and emphasized that successful non-discriminatory selection requires validation based on job performance. It is clear, however, that many employers are looking to select personnel for careers and so are trying to predict something much more complex than performance in a specific job. Additionally, as was noted earlier, jobs change over time in a way that is difficult to predict, so selectors may be trying to hit a target which will currently be moving in an unknown direction. The validation of such predictions will necessarily be an even lengthier and more difficult task.

Frequently, selectors are faced with sets of subjective judgements such as interview records and references when they come to make their final selection decisions. These may seem difficult to combine logically which leaves the decisions dangerously open to the effects of knowing or submerged discrimination. Fuzzy set theory has been suggested as a systematic way of combining qualitative judgements taking into account their subjectively assessed relative importance (Alliger et al., 1993). This work suggests a possible approach for dealing with the problem presented when the only data available for test validation are a series of subjective measures.

Methods of selection

Six methods of collecting information about candidates can now be considered: letters of application, application forms, references, interviews, tests and assessment centres.

Letters of application These are probably of little significance in selection for many manual jobs. If they are used at all, they probably serve only to provide a statement of the candidate's interest, identity and address, and possibly an indication of literacy if this is a requirement of the job. They probably also include some statement of previous experience which could assist a selector.

It must be true that millions of decisions to reject candidates are made every year on the basis of letters alone, yet there seems to be practically nothing in the contemporary British personnel literature on this subject. McIntosh and Smith (1974) showed discriminatory responses to application letters, Knollys (1983: 237) acknowledges that letters can be of critical importance, and Duxfield (1983: 247) is of the opinion that 'good potential salesmen are often poor performers in the art of letter-writing'. This all suggests a need for some systematic research, particularly as careers consultants, outplacement consultants, careers teachers and others are engaged in training applicants to write better letters.

Graphology, the study of handwriting characteristics in order to assess aspects of the personality or character of the writer, is claimed to provide a way of deriving additional information from application letters. It has been used in the Netherlands for a considerable period but less than 10 per cent of employers currently use it; use in Belgium is widespread and employers customarily seek candidates' consent to do so (IPM/Incomes Data Services, 1990: *passim*); reports of use by French companies vary from almost 50 per cent (Fowler, 1991) to 70 per cent (Gooding, 1991); and there is some use of it in Italy. However, the use of graphology is controversial in Britain. *Personnel Management* has featured the subject on a number of occasions recently and in the March 1985 issue Lynch reports that it is being used in Britain, citing Petrofina, Warburgs, Price Waterhouse Associates and a leading advertising agency as users. A cautionary note from Fletcher of the British Psychological Society is printed alongside, and the editor seems to be sitting on the fence. Graphology will be worth using if it can be shown that there is a series of characteristics which are a basis for valid predictions and can be applied with some objectivity by any suitably trained selector. The literature does not yet seem to offer this evidence. A small-scale unpublished study supervised by the author found a low positive correlation with global performance ratings of marketing managers but factor analysis did not identify rating factors corresponding to those used by the graphologist.

Application forms   The usefulness of letters to the selector will overlap with the usefulness of application forms. In particular, both can state claims to education, experience, and qualifications which can be compared with the recruitment specification. A candidate has more freedom of choice over what is presented in a letter. This may be either an advantage or a disadvantage to the selector. The possible disadvantage is that candidates may be difficult to compare because they have submitted different patterns of information. This is turned to advantage by some selectors who try to give a clear picture of the job in an advertisement which invites concise statements of relevant information. Candidates are then judged on their grasp of what is likely to be relevant. Some recruiters combine the advantages by inviting applicants to request a form and further particulars. The selector then does not have to make any decisions until information is available in a convenient format. However, a good letter and curriculum vitae (CV) can make a form unnecessary and thus reduce postage and printing costs.

Application forms have several purposes. Edwards (1983: 64) lists seven which should be taken into account in designing an application form. They may be paraphrased as:

1 selection of candidates for interview;
2 foundation for planning interview;
3 basic personnel record;
4 candidate file for other possible vacancies;
5 labour market analysis;
6 analysis of advertising and recruitment sources; and
7 improvement of public relations.

These might be considered to have been arranged in order of importance. It is economical to collect the factual information required for preliminary selection by using application forms: interviews can then be used to investigate the most promising candidates more fully. The data to be collected should, of course, be derived from the job analysis and employee specification. Because jobs vary, some organizations use different forms for distinct groups of employees, such as technicians, clerks, managers, from whom they may need to collect different information. Indeed, it can prove economical to have supplementary questionnaires for single specific appointments.

There has been considerable interest in the USA in attempting to apply the rigorous methods used for validating tests to the validation of items of biographical data as predictors of job success: Owens (1976) quotes work dating back to 1925. However, this seems not to have been carried over into practice on a large scale: a 1983 survey of 437 firms showed only 11 per cent using the weighted application forms such work is intended to generate (Mathis and Jackson, 1985: 245). Jewell (1985) points out that, of the items which had statistical significance in one study, 'a number of questions fall into the Equal Employment Opportunities Commission's suspect group'. One of these, 'marital status', would be considered dubious in Britain. The approach and its jargon label 'biodata' are being discussed in Britain: Torrington and Chapman (1983: 72) point out that not only will validation take time and require large samples, but also it may not be acceptable because 'it smacks of witchcraft to the applicants who might find it difficult to believe that success in a position correlates with being, *inter alia*, the first born in one's family'. Clark (1991) reported that 12–16 per cent of search and recruitment consultants were claiming to use biodata, but he seemed to doubt whether they understood the term as he intended.

References   There would appear to be wide variation in the practices followed by companies when they take up references. Some ask for no more than a few perfunctory ticks on a short pro forma, whereas others ask a series of searching open-ended questions that require careful thought. As a first generalization, it would be reasonable to say that the public services are more likely to use a searching procedure than manufacturing companies. Among commercial concerns, subsidiaries of US companies are more likely to have a carefully thought-out enquiry procedure than British companies. The present trend, while not dramatic, appears to be to tighten up the reference enquiry and, where it is possible to obtain candidates' permission, to take up references earlier in the selection process. The advantage of doing so is that some of the candidates who seem suitable when judged by their own account of themselves can be eliminated without incurring the cost of an interview. Economic stringency also seems to be causing some employers to present their requirements to referees much more carefully. For example, in 1985 the Atomic Energy Authority told the referees of graduate applicants what proportion of candidates it intended to interview, and asked them to frame their reports with this in mind. For search consultants, references are part of both the recruitment and selection processes.

An effective reference procedure needs to make clear what the selector wants. It should ask for information the referee can reasonably be expected to supply, and should make it as easy as possible for this to be done. Early in the selection process the selector can check critical facts and solicit opinions. There will always be a problem in assessing what weight to attach to opinions given by someone nominated by the candidate: some companies ask for supporting evidence. Later in the selection procedure it is possible to ask referees about any points that remain doubtful. Companies often do this by telephone rather than by letter, and a personal meeting is also used when the significance of the appointment justifies it. Some companies invariably take up references and do so very carefully. Experience suggests that being informed that references will be taken up encourages candidates to avoid making claims that will not hold up. It has also shown that the candidate who seems excellent when assessed by the techniques reviewed above may turn out to have feet of clay.

Interviews Employment interviewing is like driving: most people rate themselves highly; the consequences of mistakes can be serious; and when something goes wrong there is a tendency to blame the other party. Other parallels include the small amount of rigorous research in relation to the importance of the topic and the large amount of prescriptive advice that is available. Three main types of approach to interviewing may be identified (Torrington and Chapman, 1983: 86–7): the 'biographical', in which the interviewer questions the candidate about incidents in previous experience; the 'problem solving', in which the interviewer presents the candidate with a hypothetical 'what if?' type problem and asks for the candidate to offer his or her solution; and the 'stress' interview in which the interviewer may become aggressive and put the candidate under some pressure, perhaps criticizing an aspect of their career or performance. Typically, a single interview may involve elements of each of these approaches.

Little research is available on the different approaches to the interview. As far as the form of the interview is concerned, the Mackay and Torrington (1986: 39) survey of personnel managers suggests that the single interviewer was very much the norm in the case of manual workers. In the case of non-manual and managerial employees, however, the single interviewer was less in evidence, and having three or more interviewers is common in Greece and Spain. In the case of non-manual employees, the predominant form was for a line manager and a personnel specialist to be involved, although it has been reported that personnel specialists prefer a purely advisory role (Collinson et al., 1990). In the case of managers, the panel interview was the single most important type: indeed, no less than one-third of respondents confirmed this.

If the survey evidence suggests that the interview is the most widely-used method of selection, it also confirms that it is the most abused. It is not simply that the interview is subjective. The research evidence (e.g. Wanous, 1980; Honey, 1984; and Collinson et al.,

1990) suggests that interviewers are systematically prone to adopting certain stereotypes: they deem people from a particular background to be of a certain 'type'; they emphasize similarities with themselves; they tend to give undue emphasis to first impressions – the 'primacy effect'; they are influenced by accents; and they relate candidates to one another rather than to agreed criteria – the 'contrast effect'. They also tend to give overwhelming importance to negative features – selection, in other words is essentially a process of rejection.

Testing   A selection test is no more than a method of collecting a sample of behaviour under standardized conditions. The behaviour sample may be written or spoken answers to questions or the carrying out of a mental or physical task. This sample is then taken to be representative of how the person will behave generally, or used to predict how the person will perform in the future in some job. Part of the debate about tests, therefore, concentrates on whether the samples used provide a sensible basis for the generalizations and predictions made. This is an alternative way of raising the key issues of validity and reliability which have been discussed above (and, therefore, relates to all selection techniques).

Tests are variously classified according to what they purport to test (intelligence, aptitude, skill, trade knowledge, personality) or by the way they are carried out or administered (performance tests, paper and pencil tests, questionnaires, group tests, individual tests). In all cases, if the results are to be satisfactory in the sense that they can be compared with results obtained from other people on the same test, three requirements must be met: first, the subject must fully understand what is required; second, the subject must be motivated to perform in the way that the interpreter of the test will be assuming to be the case (i.e. motivated to achieve the best possible result on a test of ability, or to reply openly and honestly to a personality questionnaire); and finally, the test must be administered under standardized conditions, every subject being given exactly the same instructions. If these conditions are not met, it is not safe to generalize or make predictions from the text results.

Occupational testing began in a systematic way in Europe and Britain shortly before the First World War. It quickly spread to the USA where it was given a tremendous boost by the success of the Army Alpha and Army Beta tests in classifying and allocating recruits. Testing continued and developed in Britain and Europe but not as rapidly as it did in the USA, where the prevailing culture emphasized a combination of quantification, objectivity and a pragmatic approach which led to the rapid development and application of a wide range of tests, particularly paper and pencil tests for simultaneous assessment of groups of people. The European tradition was more inclined to qualitative approaches to individual psychology and that is reflected in the tests which were developed (Drenth, 1978: 144). Also, since individual tests are more expensive to administer, their economic appeal to employers is probably not as great.

Interest in the use of testing appears to be growing in the UK. Over 50 companies contributed to the cost of developing a British personality questionnaire by the consultants Savill and Holdsworth (Savill and Holdsworth Ltd, 1987). Concern about the possible misapplication of tests and the difficulty experienced by employers in judging the competence of testers led to a joint initiative involving the British Psychological Society (BPS) and the IPM, resulting in a certification and registration scheme administered by the BPS. This was supported by a code of practice published by the IPM in the summer of 1993. In mid-1993 about 5000 people held a statement or certificate of competence from the BPS and of these about 2500 appeared in the register. There is also a directory of advisers on testing which is available from the BPS and lists over 300 chartered psychologists with specialist competence in this area. This may offer some assistance to employers wishing to retain psychometric consultants, but not all competent practitioners have sought registration.

The extent to which tests are being used is not clear. In the 1960s and 1970s IPM surveys suggested that less than half of 696 respondent organizations used psychological tests and just over 60 per cent of 281 respondent organizations used tests of any kind (Sneath et al., 1976). Mackay and Torrington (1986: 42) suggested a much lower figure, with 20 per cent using tests for managerial appointments and about 25 per cent for manual and non-manual appointments, but Torrington and Hall (1991: 294), apparently using the same survey data, report 'almost two-thirds of our respondent organisations used tests in some way for selection'. Williams (1993: 67), in a study of local government, reported that about 40 per cent of authorities were using cognitive tests.

A study carried out in 1985, which draws on a survey of 108 organizations in *The Times* 'Top 1000' companies (Makin and Robertson, 1986) confirms the findings of the much larger survey carried out by the IPM (Gill, 1980) in conjunction with the British Institute of Management (which possibly sampled a different constituency) in suggesting that the great majority of companies rely almost exclusively on the interview and references in selecting managers. Nearly two-thirds of the organizations in the sample never used psychological tests and over 70 per cent never used cognitive tests of critical reasoning or perceptual ability. The proportion of organizations using assessment centres (discussed below), although on the increase, was also similarly low at 21 per cent. Test use varies across Europe and is reported to be declining in France (IPM/Incomes Data Services, 1990: 45–6).

Given that no test is perfect, how imperfect can a test be and still be useful? Critics of tests (and other selection methods) make perfectly sound comments about the shortcomings of tests but do not stop to carry out a hard-nosed evaluation of the costs and benefits. The value of a test depends on the accuracy of its prediction (validity), and also on the proportion of applicants that are capable of performing the job satisfactorily (if all were satisfactory there could be no gain from using a test, only costs incurred) and finally the proportion of applicants it would be necessary to take to fill all vacancies (the higher the proportion that have to be taken, the lower the value of the test). Some texts provide tables of the interaction of these factors which show that tests with low validities can have considerable practical value (McCormick and Ilgen, 1980).

Physical tests, which have received relatively little attention in the selection literature, are also subject to the problems of validity and reliability. For example, in one study of reliability two medical examiners testing the same items by the same methods achieved only 16 per cent agreement. In another study of pilots who were re-examined after passing the Civil Aeronautics Administration fitness examination, 43 per cent were found to have a disqualifying defect. A study of the validity of the physical screening procedure for RAF pilots compared 106 pilots who met the standards with 106 who had defects. After ten years half of each group were still flying and there was no statistically reliable difference in their accident rates. Some of these findings might be accounted for at least in part as resulting from the wise use of clinical judgement by medical practitioners.

Assessment centres   These are essentially an amalgam of several of the methods discussed above. They seem to be in fashion again but are by no means new, having been invented by the German and British armies during the Second World War. The British version, the War Office Selection Board (WOSB) was considered a success (Vernon and Parry, 1949) and a useful model for selecting fairly large numbers of graduates for the civil service (Vernon, 1950). The Civil Service Selection Boards (CSSBs) were followed up for 36 years and the boards' final assessment had a very high correlation with the positions being held at the end of the study (Anstey, 1977).

The essence of these group selection methods or assessment centres is that they use a variety of techniques, and observe the candidates in interaction over a period of two or three days (Macrae, 1970; Toplis and Stewart, 1983). It was the work of Bray at American Telephone & Telegraph which focused most attention on the industrial applications. Toplis and Stewart (1983) sound a note of caution. Copying the superficial features of an assessment centre may not improve selection: the key feature of the successful major studies is that they were based on very careful studies of the jobs or careers for which people were being selected. CSSB was based on a whole series of complex and interrelated exercises which simulated in some detail the type of work undertaken by senior and junior civil servants. In addition, the candidates were interviewed by panels and individual members of the assessment team, and completed ability, aptitude and personality tests.

Concluding Remarks

The pressures on British management to adopt recruitment and selection procedures that are sound and defensible, as well as job related, appear to have grown considerably in recent years. Legislation, dealing in particular with sex and race discrimination, requires organizations to develop procedures which, at the very least, are defensible against the charge that individual applicants have been unfairly treated. This has brought about some reduction in discrimination on grounds of sex, race, and religion but widespread discrimination remains. The legislation to protect the disabled is ineffective. The IPM *Statement on Age and Employment* (1993) attempts to discourage discrimination on grounds of age: economic pressures might work in the same direction as exhortation, but dramatic change seems unlikely. Whatever the economic situation, there is a premium on having the required number of people with the appropriate levels of attainment at the right time. In recession, recruitment is not necessarily easier in all categories, because people with key skills may be reluctant to move in uncertain times. Selection may become more costly because there are larger fields of candidates to be processed and there is anecdotal evidence that more candidates are willing to overstate their qualifications (making more careful scrutiny necessary) than was the case in the 1960s, even though fewer employers or their advisers in the private sector bothered to verify qualifications in those days. In a recovering or growing economy recruitment is competitive and, as the growth of vacancy advertisements in good times shows, expensive. At all times, the costs of mistakes in recruitment and selection, which have always been considerably underestimated, can be very expensive indeed.

Prescriptions have long been available which, though imperfect, could contribute to fairer and more cost-effective decision making. They are being improved, but are still under-utilized, perhaps because their introduction could shift the balance of power between line managers and personnel specialists and conflict with the line managers' image of themselves as decision makers (Collinson et al., 1990: *passim*). The development of tests that can be presented in a controlled standardized way by computer, and the development of computerized scoring systems with built-in expert systems for interpretation, may offer both technical and cost advantages, and political opportunities.

Alec Rodger's (1970) three criteria for the selection of psychological techniques might also be viewed proactively. Tests of improved validity and cost-effectiveness are being developed: the progress is not dramatic but it could contribute to both organizational effectiveness and the reduction of improper discrimination. Technical solutions will never solve all recruitment and selection problems, and tests valid in one situation might be used improperly elsewhere. Indeed, there is a fourth criterion to be considered and that is 'moral defensibility'. The proactive response, therefore, also requires the development of the political will to use the best available techniques and to be responsible in recognizing and seeking to overcome their shortcomings. The consequences of failing to do this have been described by many commentators but this central problem is difficult, and it has been tackled in only a minority of organizations.

Bibliography

ACAS. 1981. *Recruitment and Selection*. Advisory Booklet No. 6. London: Advisory, Conciliation and Arbitration Service.

Alliger, G. M., Feinzig, S. L. and Janak, E. A. 1993. 'Fuzzy sets and personnel selection'. *Journal of Occupational and Organizational Psychology*, June, 163–9.

Anstey, E. 1977. 'A 3-Year Follow-Up of the CSSB Procedure, with Lessons for the Future'. *Journal of Occupational Psychology*, 50, September, 149–59.

Armstrong, M. 1977. *A Handbook of Personnel Management Practice*. London: Kogan Page.

Atkinson, S. and Purkiss, C. 1983. 'Recruitment and Mobility of Labour'. In Ungerson, B. (ed.) *Recruitment Handbook*, 3rd edn. Aldershot: Gower, 10–22.

Brotherton, C. 1980. 'Paradigms of Selection Validation'. *Journal of Occupational Psychology*, 53, March, 73–9.

Burns, T. and Stalker, G. M. 1961. *The Management of Innovation*. London: Tavistock.

Clark, T. 1991. 'A survey and critique of selection methods used by executive recruitment consultancies in management recruitment'. Paper presented to the 1992 Occupational Psychology Conference of the British Psychological Society.

Collinson, D. L., Knights, D. and Collinson, M. 1990. *Managing to Discriminate*. London: Routledge.

Commission for Racial Equality. 1989. *Indirect Discrimination in Employment – A practical guide*. London: CRE.

Courtis, J. 1985. *The IPM Guide to Cost-effective Recruitment*, 2nd edn. London: Institute of Personnel Management.

Cuming, M. W. 1978. *Personnel Management in the National Health Service*. London: Heinemann.

Drenth, P. 1978. 'Principles of Selection'. In Warr, P. B. (ed.) *Psychology at Work*, 2nd edn. Harmondsworth: Penguin, 140–64.

Dulewicz, V. 1984. 'Uses and Abuses of Selection Tests'. *Personnel Management*, January, 16, 1, 46–7.

Duxfield, P. 1983. 'Sales Staff'. In Ungerson, B. (ed.) *Recruitment Handbook*, 3rd edn. Aldershot: Gower, 239–47.

Edwards, B. J. 1983. 'Application Forms'. In Ungerson, B. (ed.) *Recruitment Handbook*, 3rd edn. Aldershot: Gower, 64–82.

Equal Opportunities Commission. 1977. *Guidance on Employment Advertising Practice*. Manchester: EOC.

Equal Opportunities Commission. 1985. *Code of Practice*. London: HMSO.

Equal Opportunities Commission. 1988. *Avoiding Sex Bias in Selection Testing*. London: HMSO.

Fordham, K. G. 1983. 'Job Advertising'. In Ungerson, B. (ed.) *Recruitment Handbook*, 3rd edn. Aldershot: Gower, 46–63.

Fowler, A. 1991. 'An Even-Handed Approach to Graphology'. *Personnel Management*, March, 40–3.

Fraser, J. M. 1971. *Introduction to Personnel Management*. London: Nelson.

French, W. L. 1974. *The Personnel Management Process*, 3rd edn. Boston, MA: Houghton Mifflin.

Gill, D. 1980. 'How Britain Selects Its Managers'. *Personnel Management*, October, 49–52.

Gooding, J. 1991. 'By Hand, by Jove'. *Across the Board*, 28, 12 December, 43–7.

Grant, J. V. and Smith, G. 1977. *Personnel Administration and Industrial Relations*, 2nd edn. London: Longman.

Heidrich and Struggles. 1985. Consultants publicity leaflet.

Herriot, P. 1984. *Down from the Ivory Tower*. Chichester: Wiley.

Herriot, P. 1989. *Recruitment in the 90s*. London: Institute of Personnel Management.

Higham, T. M. 1983. 'Choosing the Method of Recruitment'. In Ungerson, B. (ed.) *Recruitment Handbook*, 3rd edn. Aldershot: Gower, 23–38.

Honey, J. 1984. 'Accents at Work'. *Personnel Management*, January, 16, 1, 18–21.

IPM. 1990. *The IPM Recruitment Code*. London: Institute of Personnel Management.

IPM. 1993. *The IPM Statement on Age and Employment*. London: Institute of Personnel Management.

IPM/Incomes Data Services. 1990. *European Management Guide – Recruitment*. London: Institute of Personnel Management.

Jenkins, J. F. 1983. 'Management Trainees in Retailing'. In Ungerson, B. (ed.) *Recruitment Handbook*, 3rd edn. Aldershot: Gower, 248–64.

Jewell, L. N. 1985. *Contemporary Industrial and Organisational Psychology*. St. Paul, MN: West.

Kline, P. 1993. *The Handbook of Psychological Testing*. London: Routledge.

Knollys, J. G. 1983. 'Clerical Staff'. In Ungerson, B. (ed.) *Recruitment Handbook*, 3rd edn. Aldershot: Gower, 230–8.

Lawrence, P. R. and Lorsch, J. W. 1967. *Organization and Environment*. Boston, MA: Harvard University Press.

McCormick, E. J. and Ilgen, D. 1980. *Industrial Psychology*. Englewood Cliffs, NJ: Prentice Hall.

McIntosh, N. and Smith, D. J. 1974. *The Extent of Racial Discrimination*. PEP Broadsheet No. 547. London: Political and Economic Planning.

Mackay, L. and Torrington, D. 1986. *The Changing Nature of Personnel Management*. London: Institute of Personnel Management.

Macrae, A. 1970. *Group Selection Procedures*. London: National Foundation for Education Research.

Makin, P. J. and Robertson, I. T. 1983. 'Self Assessment, Realistic Job Previews and Occupational Decisions'. *Personnel Review*, 12, 3, 21–5.

Makin, P. J. and Robertson, I. T. 1986. 'Selection the Best Selection Techniques'. *Personnel Management*, November, 38–43.

Mathis, R. L. and Jackson, J. H. 1985. *Personnel*, 4th edn. St. Paul, MN: West.

Mecham, R. C., McCormick, E. J. and Jeanneret, P. R. 1977. *Position Analysis Questionnaire Manual*. W. Lafayette, IN: The University Bookstore.

Miller, K. M. and Hydes, J. 1971. *The Use of Psychological Tests in Personnel Work*. London: Independent Assessment and Research Centre.

Owens, W. A. 1976. 'Background Data'. *Handbook of Industrial and Organizational Psychology*. In Dunnette, M. D. (ed.) Chicago, IL: Rand-McNally, 609–44.

Parkinson, E. N. 1986. *Parkinson's Law*. London: Sidgewick & Jackson.

Personnel Management. 1985. 'Two-Year Trial Period for Cuts in NHS Recruitment Ads'. May, 57.

Personnel Management. 1993. 'Executives find posts in hidden job market'. May, 67.

Plumbley, P. R. 1988. *Recruitment and Selection*, 4th edn revised. London: Institute of Personnel Management.

Pratt, K. J. and Bennett, S. G. 1985. *Elements of Personnel Management*, 2nd edn. Wokingham: Van Nostrand Reinhold (UK).

Ray, M. 1980. *Recruitment Advertising*. London: Institute of Personnel Management.

Rodger, A. 1970. *The Seven Point Plan*, 3rd edn. London: National Foundation for Education Research.

Rodger, A. 1971. 'Recent Trends in Personnel Selection'. *NIIP Bulletin*, Spring, 3.

Rodger, A. 1983. 'Using Interviews in Personnel Selection'. In Ungerson, B. (ed.) *Recruitment Handbook*, 3rd edn. Aldershot: Gower, 161–77.

Saville and Holdsworth Ltd. 1987. Consultants Publicity Booklet. London: Saville and Holdsworth.

Saville and Holdsworth Ltd. 1991. *Work Profiling System Manual*. London: Saville and Holdsworth.

Scholarios, D. M., Johnson, C. D. and Zeidner, J. 1993. 'Maximising the efficiency of personnel assignment'. Paper presented to the annual Occupational Psychology conference of the British Psychological Society. Brighton.

Sinai, L. 1988. 'Employee Honesty Tests Move to New Frontiers'. *Business Insurance*, 22, 3, September, 14–16.

Smith, M., Gregg, M. and Andrews, D. 1989. *Selection & Assessment: A New Appraisal*. London: Pitman.

Simth, J. E. and Hakel, M. D. 1979. 'Convergence among data sources, response bias, and reliability and validity of a structured job analysis questionnaire'. *Personnel Psychology*, 32, 677–92.

Sneath, F., Thakur, M. and Medjuck, B. 1976. *Testing People at Work*. IPM Information Report 24. London: Institute of Personnel Management.

Storey, J. 1992. *Developments in the Management of Human Resources*. Oxford: Blackwell.

Thomason, G. 1981. *A Textbook of Personnel Management*, 4th edn. London: Institute of Personnel Management.

Toplis, J. and Stewart, B. 1983. 'Group Selection Methods'. In Ungerson, B. (ed.) *Recruitment Handbook*, 3rd edn. Aldershot: Gower, 178–94.

Torrington, D. and Chapman, J. 1983. *Personnel Management*, 2nd edn. London: Prentice Hall.

Torrington, D. and Hall, L. 1991. *Personnel Management – A New Approach*, 2nd edn. London: Prentice Hall.

Vernon, P. E. 1950. 'The Validation of Civil Service Selection Board Procedures'. *Occupational Psychology*, 24, April, 75–95.

Vernon, P. E. and Parry, J. B. 1949. *Personnel Selection in the British Forces*. London: University of London Press.

Wanous, J. P. 1980. *Organizational Entry*. Reading, MA: Addison-Wesley.

Williams, R. 1993. 'Management Selection in Local Government'. *Human Resource Management Journal*, Vol. 3, No. 2, Winter 1992/93, 63–73.

7

Employee Appraisal

Gerry Randell

Employee appraisal can be seen as the *formal* process for collecting information from and about the staff of an organization for decision-making purposes. From an analysis of many organizations' procedures and a detailed review of the literature on the topic, one overriding purpose of this decision making emerged, *improving people's performance in their existing job*. This purpose is made explicit in most descriptions of employee appraisal schemes. When it is not explicitly stated, it is clearly implied that the scheme aims at least to maintain the level of effectiveness of people at work, and hopefully to add to their performance and satisfaction.

Consequently employee or staff appraisal can be defined as the process whereby current performance in a job is observed and discussed for the purpose of adding to that level of performance. Even though this is a simple definition of an everyday managerial activity it is a controversial topic. In the above description three contentious issues are implied:

1 What and how are observations made?
2 Why and how are these observations discussed?
3 What determines level of performance in a job?

When these issues are misunderstood and their implications misapplied then employee appraisal can be seen as 'dysfunctional' in that it can then detract from performance and satisfaction. Such outcomes have been observed and discussed by McGregor (1957) in the US, and Rowe (1964) and Pym (1973) in Britain. The more the above issues are analysed, the more complex they appear to be. The literature abounds with different analyses and conclusions that arise from how the process of appraisal is viewed and how it is seen to fit in with business strategy, personnel policy and individual managerial philosophies. It has been often regarded as a tool for managerial control: as Townley puts it, 'contributing to an overall approach to the handling of labour relations' (1991: 92). From the employees and their unions' point of view, it is frequently seen as a means of maximizing the financial rewards for individual workers' efforts. Employee appraisal can be both, but need not be either, of these processes. So, how the employee appraisal process is seen to fit in with an organization's development is a key issue. This can be seen in the debate on what is now known as 'performance management'. This is described in an Institute of Personnel Management publication as the approach that 'construes personnel management in a holistic sense . . . firmly set within the context of business planning and strategy. Individual objectives are dealt with as a part of the objectives of the organization as a whole. Managers are encouraged to coach, counsel and train people to improve their performance. Appraisal is seen as a continuing, year round dialogue, and pay is recognized as only part of the process' (Neale, 1991: 2). This is all easier said than done. Also, by concentrating on the macro issues of strategy and planning, and all the organizational politics that are involved, the need to get right the micro processes of the actual techniques and procedures of each of the component parts of performance management could get lost. This point can also be applied to the debate on the difference between the meaning of 'personnel management' and 'human resource management' (Guest, 1987; Torrington, 1988; Molander, 1989). Human resource management (HRM), as chapter 1 points out, is seen as a holistic process, integrating all the functions of personnel management into business strategy and planning. Again, the intention is commendable, but when the 'politics' of it leads to a disregard of the details of the management of people at work, then the intention fails. It is comparable to concentrating on the architecture of a building and ignoring the importance of the bricks. What adds further to the confusion is the fact that work organizations are dynamic. It is not the purpose of this chapter to review the topic of organization analysis but, when deciding exactly how an employee appraisal scheme should be designed, consideration must be given to the nature of the organization and the way it is intended to change.

This chapter aims to help the understanding of the key issues and implications of employee appraisal. It tries to achieve this first through a historical review, then by a conceptual analysis of the process of employee appraisal and, finally, by deriving from this the implications for practice, thus making it possible to design schemes which bring about increased performance and satisfaction.

The Development of Employee Appraisal

The formal observation of an individuals' performance at work by an appointed member of the organization and the communication of this observation to the individual for the purpose of improving his or her performance probably began in Scotland in the early 1800s. Robert Owen hung over employees' machines in his New Lanark textile mills a multicoloured block of wood, the front colour of which indicated the superintendent's assessment of the previous day's conduct, from white for excellent through yellow, blue and then black for bad. As Cole (1925) reports, Owen believed that letting employees know what was thought of them through his 'silent monitors', would have the effect of recognizing the worthy, and encouraging the less good to improve. To add to the pressure, Owen also recorded yearly assessments in a 'book of character', the beginning of annual staff reporting. It is these twin objectives of concern for satisfaction and performance that is now known as employee or staff appraisal, or performance appraisal or performance review, all terms that can be seen in contemporary personnel management systems. One of the great problems of staff appraisal over the years since Owen's time is how these two criteria have been diluted or even lost. Even Owen, with all his human concern, saw that work was about profit as well as human well-being. In his essay to factory managers (quoted by Cole, 1925) he said 'many of you have long experienced in your manufacturing operations the advantages of substantial, well-contained and well-executed machinery. If, then, due care as to the state of your inanimate machines can produce such beneficial results, what may not be expected if you devote equal attention to your vital machines, which are far more wonderfully constructed?' Hanging signs over employees' machines or desks in the 1990s may not be a way of achieving equal care and attention for people and work, but this review will continue to explore how 190 years of personnel management in Britain has helped the understanding and practice of what is required to help people to be better at their jobs.

The literature of performance appraisal is sparse during the remainder of the 19th century. Owen's utopian dreams were replaced by the realities of 'scientific management', for at the turn of the century performance measurement began to receive a great deal of attention through the work of F. W. Taylor and the 'scientific management' movement. Although extremely well-intentioned, the use of quantitative measures to understand and to increase productivity at work ran into difficulties with the inept application of otherwise useful concepts. In his testimony before a US Government Special House Committee in 1912, Taylor (1964) was vehement that work measurement was just a part of the whole philosophy of 'scientific management' and could and should not be regarded as an end in itself. Further, as the Hawthorne studies carried out by Mayo and his colleagues in the 1920s in the USA subsequently revealed (Roethlisberger and Dickson, 1939), even apparently objective measures of work performance were influenced by subjective factors and social control.

No doubt many attempts at performance appraisal were widespread in work organizations in the first half of this century and probably reached a pinnacle, as is often the case, during the mobilization of people for war. In the inter-war years the techniques of time and motion study matured into the discipline of 'work study' and were then incorporated into 'production engineering', but, as will be seen later, the legacy of seeking precision in measuring work performance remained.

Many people gained their first management responsibilities and experience through work in government and the armed forces during the two World Wars. The special circumstances of this work led to great advances in the techniques of personnel management, notably in the field of selection. Even so the systematic study of performance for the purposes of improving performance received scant attention. Vernon and Parry (1949) devote two pages to performance assessment in the military setting and say about 'gradings or assessments' that 'such judgements are extremely liable to be biased by the social qualities or conformity to discipline etc., of the people being graded' (ibid.: 107). The Royal Navy form S206 of 1940 gave 21 attributes to be graded using nine point scales as well as extensive provision for narrative information. Such assessment and reporting procedures were probably appropriate for that kind of organization at that stage in its development for the kind of work that it was expected to do. No doubt forms of a similar kind were introduced to British and American work organizations as officers returned to civilian managerial life. It took a little time to realize that such approaches were inappropriate for both post-war organizations and post-war people.

This realization began the attack on the concepts and practice of staff appraisal in the 1950s.

The attack was spearheaded by an article by McGregor (1957). This 'uneasy look' was followed by his 'critique' in 1960, in which he saw the main purposes of appraisal as 'administrative', 'informative' and 'motivational', and concluded that 'it appears to be something of a tribute to the adaptability of human beings that these procedures work at all!' (McGregor 1960: 88). This conceptual attack was followed by an empirical study in Britain by Rowe (1964) which exposed considerable reluctance by managers to use mainly personality trait-based appraisal procedures. These findings were further supported by Stewart's (1965) study illustrating the ineptness of appraisal interviewers.

Undoubtedly the classic compendium of relevant work in this period was *Performance Appraisal* edited by Whisler and Harper in 1962. Their own review of the history and the work of their colleagues lead them to conclusions which still have much relevance for current practice. They observed that 'many appraisal systems have failed simply because staff people responsible for planning the systems have become engrossed in trying to achieve technical perfection' (Whisler and Harper, 1962: 437), and that 'concentration on specific job-related activities and forms of behavior is the best substitute for quantitative performance standards where the latter cannot be formulated' (ibid.: 438).

While McGregor was making his attack, Maier (1952; 1958) was trying to give support to and guidelines for an approach to appraisal that would help it to be regarded as an essential feature of personnel management. Maier (1952) had already set out his philosophical position which had developed on the basis of the earlier work of social psychologists who were studying 'democratic leadership'. He had also foreseen how these concepts should be put into practice by saying 'skills must supplement this knowledge. In order to develop skills, practice on the job, interviews with trainees, and role playing are needed' (Maier, 1952: 18). Later that decade Maier further recognized the place of skill in management by saying: 'the skill of the interviewer is one of the more important determiners of the success of this plan; and since the interviews are conducted by all supervisors at all levels, this skill factor becomes a general managerial requisite' (1958: 1). Maier went on to contrast three styles of appraisal interviewing in great detail. He brushed aside the use of evaluation ratings with what he thought could be regarded as an 'insincere suggestion' (1958: 175) and condemned the use of personality trait approaches by stating: 'when a person's traits are discussed from the point of view of appraisal, a deficiency in a desirable characteristic takes the form of devaluation of the individual' (1958: 206). Instead, he strongly advocated the 'problem-solving' approach to appraisal interviewing and training for it using role playing. Regrettably, Maier did not give any insight into exactly how such skills should be inculcated or acquired. Nor did he display any awareness of just how difficult it was to bridge the gap between theory and practice in staff appraisal. Also, Maier's deep concern about the skills of management has not been carried forward by his colleagues or students, a point that will be returned to later as a key issue in understanding how to bring about improvement in the performance and the leadership of organizations. In 1974, the *Harvard Business Review* collected together the 13 key articles they had published since 1955 in the Performance Appraisal Series. Starting with the classic 1957 McGregor paper, it covers all the key conceptual issues. No doubt more recent US practitioners would criticize this collection for its lack of empirical studies, but it cannot be faulted for its lack of good sense. It is useful to note that the issue of ratings and how they can be improved is hardly touched upon in the whole issue, except in a critical way.

In Great Britain a more developmental approach to staff appraisal was first shown in the 1970s by Randell (1971) in Fisons Limited, and by Anstey et al. (1976) in the civil service. Randell had developed the point about skill being an essential component of management in an earlier article (1971) and had subsequently used the opportunity of helping a company with their staff appraisal scheme to formulate a 'skills approach' to staff development. Together with Packard, Shaw and Slater of Fisons (Randell et al., 1972) he first presented a conceptual analysis of staff appraisal which cut through all the conflicting issues of purposes and measurement. Although an over-simplification of the process – the three elements of development, reward and potential were separated out – it did facilitate the adoption of thorough training as the way to cope with the problems of staff appraisal, starting at the top of the organization and working progressively through all managers and supervisors who have responsibility for the work of staff. Perhaps reflecting the nature and needs of their employing organization, Anstey, Fletcher and Walker (1976) emphasized assessment and reporting in their account of staff appraisal. They saw the way forward in the subject was to take a 'dynamic' approach. Although they agreed with separating discussion of pay from development, they were against any further 'fragmentation' on grounds of extra complications and costs of time and effort. They were, however, strong on the need for training and, in particular, the use of practice interviews under guidance from trained tutors.

The growth of interest in performance appraisal in the 1960s and 1970s is further illustrated by the publication in both Britain and the USA of numerous surveys of companies' practices and managers' opinions of employee appraisal. In Britain, there were two surveys by the BIM and three by the IPM. In the USA, the more influential surveys were carried out by the US Bureau of National Affairs and the National Conference Board.

The most recent IPM survey, by Long (1986), covered 306 organizations, of which 18 per cent had no formal appraisal schemes. Her main findings were that there had been a substantial overall increase in systems for appraising non-management employees; the shift in emphasis in performance review towards concern for current rather than future performance had continued; appraisal for performance-related pay had remained at about 40 per cent of schemes, with only 15 per cent of organizations carrying out a salary review at the same time as the performance review; and there had been a sharp increase of 22 per cent of organizations providing appraisal skills training, to 78 per cent of the sample surveyed. Taking a case study approach, Yeates (1989), through an Institute of Manpower Studies project with 22 of the most prestigious work organizations in Britain, attempted to identify issues central to good appraisal practice. This study displayed the very considerable range of approaches to employee appraisal currently being followed in Britain.

The problem with such surveys is that they only display the current conventional wisdom. To discover what really is good practice requires the application of more conceptual ability by the researchers. In recent years the main output of textbooks on performance appraisal has been in the USA rather than in Britain. After the Whisler and Harper classic (1962) probably the next most impressive text was by Cummings and Schwab (1973). Their analysis is thorough and at a high level of abstraction. They attempt to integrate both ability and motivation development into a single model of performance determinants. They are succinct on measurement techniques, leaning heavily towards objectives setting and self-appraisal procedures. They are extremely thin on training managers to appraise, however, saying 'managers should be given specialized skill training along the lines (eight short guidelines) just suggested' (ibid.: 116).

A far-ranging and thorough British text is by Fletcher and Williams (1985) who place their analysis into both a historical and economic context and also relate performance appraisal to the wider issues of career development. But this breadth dilutes the depth of their conclusions for they do not adequately tackle the conflicts between evaluation and development in appraisal. Nor do they stress just how important interpersonal skills are to successful appraisal schemes. Perhaps the most useful account of current British views and practice is the final section of *Assessment and Selection in Organizations*, edited by Herriot (1989). The eight chapters in the 'Performance Appraisal and Counselling' section range from a detailed analysis of the characteristics of rating scales to what is required to train appraisers. Again, all the writers display confusion concerning the place of ratings in appraisal, and consequently they obfuscate the real issues of bringing about behaviour change in individuals and organizations. They do not seem able to stand back and ask the fundamental questions about appraisal which would then allow them to give a thorough analysis of the issue they are considering and provide precise conclusions and recommendations.

Unlike the British trend towards more person-centred, skills-based approaches to staff appraisal, American texts display a distinct leaning towards work-centred, mechanistic, ratings-based procedures, with hardly a reference to the interpersonal skills training that is required to support a staff appraisal scheme. Thus, Latham and Wexley (1981) devote most of their book to the criterion problem and to measuring work performance. They give a detailed account of the use of 'behavioural observation scales' (BOS), including the legal aspects of using them in the US, and conclude with many guidelines about 'making the system work'. Carroll and Schneier (1982) follow a very similar line, concentrating on the use of 'behaviourally anchored rating scales' (BARS). They take more of a contingency approach, arguing the need to match appraisal systems to organizational and individual differences. But they conclude that in future more emphasis should be put on to interpersonal and behavioural rather than psychometric issues. In a more insightful text, DeVries et al. (1981) analyse the history and use of performance appraisal under all the main issue headings. With a slight tone of despair they conclude that their analysis at least showed the need for appraisal systems to be constantly adaptive to changing economic and social developments. To achieve this they advocate that performance appraisal should be broken down into its manageable parts, each serving a critical purpose and that these parts should be planned according to the particular needs and resources of any given organization.

Of the numerous 'how to do it' books and articles produced by US consultants, two are commendable by showing awareness of the wider conceptual and practical issues. Both cover the legal and equal opportunity issues which are considerable in the US but both spend two-thirds of their text on rating issues, no doubt reacting to demands from their clients for a box-ticking rating system. Henderson (1984) puts much effort into job analysis, which he calls the 'bedrock for performance appraisal', and from this base he builds up to a computer-aided system. Rausch (1985) is more influenced by managerial theory and advocates a transactional analysis approach to appraisal interviews. Both writers end their texts emphasizing the need for developing the interpersonal skills of appraisal but, beyond describing exercises and audio-visual aids, show little insight into just what is required to inculcate the necessary skills. In contrast, the academic articles tend towards empirical investigations of performance analysis and rating. The August 1992 volume of the *Journal of Applied Psychology* contained seventeen articles, seven of which bore upon employee appraisal. None of these articles discussed the use of ratings to improve performance.

This review of the US literature gives the impression of a widening rift in their publications on appraisal between the consultants who write up their own personal experiences with their clients, with little awareness of the real *purposes* of appraisal, and the academics who endlessly dissect the minutiae of the rating process but who display little awareness of the practical issues and desired outcomes. In contrast, the British literature displays a continuing disagreement about the place of assessment in appraisal, ranging from ratings and performance measurement being placed first in the process to a denial of the need for any assessment, beyond a skilled diagnosis, being required at all in employee appraisal. What this literature survey has shown is the muddle and confusion that still surrounds the theory and practice of employee appraisal. This would appear to stem either from studies of inept organizational practice or from unrealistic 'laboratory' studies. Neither of these approaches can provide a precise understanding of what should be done to make appraisal an effective process for individual and organizational development. What is required is a more thorough conceptual analysis of the issues and then a set of guidelines to help the application of the concepts. This will now be attempted.

Issues in Employee Appraisal

As can be seen from the preceding surveys and analysis of research, the term 'employee or staff appraisal' means different things to different people. What can be said is that its use has grown to include all those formal processes for observing, collecting, recording and using information about the performance of staff in their jobs. Unfortunately, an emotive tone has also grown up around the term and many organizations prefer to use the term 'employee or staff development' or 'job appraisal review' to minimize hostility to the process. The previous section has also shown that confusion and controversy still surround this topic. There are many unresolved issues, which will now be considered in detail.

Conflicts of purpose

The overriding purpose of employee appraisal is the improvement of the performance of people in their jobs. However, this broad purpose can be interpreted in many ways, both from a theoretical and a practical standpoint. For example, following Randell et al. (1972), the main functions of appraisal, each of which can be seen to some degree in all appraisal schemes, can be summarized as follows:

- to enable the organization to share out the money, promotions and perquisites apparently 'fairly', i.e. *evaluation*;
- to discover the work potential, both present and future, of individuals and departments, i.e. *auditing*;
- to construct plans for manpower, departmental and corporate planning, i.e. *succession planning*;
- to discover learning needs by exposing inadequacies and deficiencies that could be remedied, i.e. *training*;
- to ensure that employees reach organizational standards and objectives, i.e. *controlling*;
- to develop individuals through advice, information and shaping their behaviour with praise or punishment, i.e. *development*;
- to add to employees' job satisfaction through understanding their needs, i.e. *motivation*; and

- to check the effectiveness of personnel procedures and practice, i.e. *validation.*

Behind these operational purposes lie more significant theoretical issues. An examination of an organization's employee appraisal scheme can show a great deal about how the organization 'sees' its staff and how it should be managed and developed. So the overall broad purpose of performance improvement can both be influenced by theories about people at work, and contribute to those theories. In practice, the format of an employee appraisal scheme is perhaps determined more by how senior managers who design the system see the *causes* of work performance than by specific objectives for the scheme.

Beliefs about the determinants of human behaviour at work can be grouped in four ways which encompass the academic theories about the probable causes of performance. These theories can be seen to be reflected, more often implicitly than explicitly, in the various approaches to staff appraisal.

If it is believed that the past is the main determinant of the present and the future, then this is given emphasis in an information-gathering and decision-making procedure through some kind of comprehensive assessment of past strengths and weaknesses. Implicit in this view is that if good performance is observed and then rewarded, the chances of it being repeated are increased, while poor performance is discouraged or even punished to decrease the chance of it happening again.

Psychologists will notice a connection with the ideas of 'reinforcement theory' associated with the work of Skinner (1972). These concepts have been very influential in all branches of psychology and have been very usefully and practically set out under the general descriptive heading of 'behaviour modification' by Martin and Pear (1978), and more explicitly in relation to changing managerial work by Goldstein and Sorcher (1974) under the rubric 'behaviour modelling'. This 'past patterns of behaviour' approach has been taken to the limits of atheoretical pragmatism by Rackham and Morgan (1977) in their work on interactive skills development. The approaches to staff appraisal based on these ideas usually lead to an emphasis on providing praise and recognition, and, even in special circumstances, to 'token economies', where immediate rewards are handed out for extra effort and performance. As Skinner (1972) has pointed out, it takes a great deal of skill on the part of the manager

to shape human behaviour through appropriate 'schedules of reinforcement'. When this can be achieved, however, it can be a very
powerful approach to developing performance at work.

If the 'here and now' is seen as the most important source of
causes of behaviour then such factors as understanding and learning
will be the focus of observation and decision making in an employee
appraisal procedure. These beliefs fit in with the more 'cognitive'
theories in psychology, such as those of Festinger (1957) and Lawler
(1973), and can be elaborated through using the additional concept
of 'equity' as put forward by Adams (1964). The point about much
of this work is that it is how the member of staff *perceives* the work
situation that is important, rather than what actually exists. Techniques for getting a better match between what a member of staff
perceives and what actually exists have been put forward by Mager
and Pipe (1970), but their rather pragmatic approach does not get
much reference in the appraisal literature, sound and useful as it is.
Evidence for the usefulness of this approach comes from studies by
Meyer et al. (1965) in the General Electric Company. They surveyed 92 employees who heavily criticized the existing mechanistic
pay-related appraisal system. On the basis of this, they developed
alternative 'work planning and review' discussions that took place
more frequently and had no summary judgements, ratings or pay
bargaining, and instead discussed specific work goals that could be
achieved immediately. A controlled follow-up study showed that the
staff who experienced the 'WP and R' method had significantly
better attitudes to their work than those who experienced the traditional GEC appraisal scheme. The attractiveness of this approach to
many practitioners is its non-evaluative, non-threatening tone.

If the 'pull' of future events desired by individuals is seen as the
pervading influence then employee appraisal schemes will emphasize
the work that has to be achieved for the organization and the reward
and promotion prospects and opportunities for the individual. The
more advanced 'expectancy' theories, such as those of Vroom
(1964), and concepts of self-actualization and self-fulfilment, as
discussed by Maslow (1970), fit in with such approaches to employee appraisal. Further, the enthusiasm for objective-setting procedures can be explained in terms of belief in future-oriented
theories of human behaviour. The practical aspects of objectives
setting have been analysed well by Odiorne (1965; 1979) and are
widely used. The theoretical aspects have been set out by Locke
and Latham (1984) who wisely integrate the use of goal setting

with behavioural observation scales in appraisal interviewing to counteract the relative paucity of truly objective indices of work performance.

As a footnote, it is important to point out that management by objectives, which is often associated with this school of thought, has been widely criticized because of its unhealthy emphasis on quantitative rather than qualitative or behavioural objectives. However, a more fundamental theoretical criticism can be made of objectives or goal setting as a method for performance improvement. Just setting targets does not necessarily change behaviour. It may provide pressure to change but, unless a person *knows* what to do differently, it is chance that determines whether or not the appropriate behaviour is produced. This is why there has been the trend away from quantitative target setting procedures in appraisal towards more qualitative behavioural objectives, as it is now realized that target setting, like financial budgets, is a method of control rather than development.

Many senior managers are inclined towards beliefs about human behaviour that can be regarded as transcending time. They believe that if an individual values, and is committed to, a certain doctrine then all their behaviour stems from this. Such doctrines are usually religious or political in nature, but not necessarily so, as can be seen by membership of certain semi-secret societies: the phrase 'Is he one of us?' can be the key question asked in employee appraisal. The theories underpinning this approach to understanding and predicting human behaviour are more sociological, or even philosophical, than psychological. It could be that there is a pervading influence of Jung's (1958) ideas of the 'collective unconscious', or just the influence of age, as many psychologists, such as Skinner (1971), Maslow (1965), Argyris (1964), and Herzberg (1966), turn in their later years to higher levels of abstraction to explain human behaviour. These rather abstract ideas are a long way from the day-to-day problems of employee appraisal and perhaps are best understood and placed in context by sociologists such as Sorokin (1966).

The above analysis of the *theoretical* basis of staff appraisal shows that the stated explicit purposes can be in conflict. However, what can be seen is that *implicitly* there are just two main purposes for all staff appraisal schemes. The first is to add to the individuals' capacity for doing their existing job, and the second is to maintain and, if possible, add to their motivation. The above section is mainly concerned with the motivational theories behind staff development, none of which adequately explains how people come to put the effort that they do into their work. Where the theories can help is to signal to a manager just what should be done *next* for a member of staff to increase the chances of his or her most pressing need being met. People's motivation is maintained or enhanced by having their needs met, or at least worked on, by another individual or their employing organization. Theoretical stand-points can either hinder or help this process.

This chapter is concerned with changing individual behaviour at work – over and above the change which would occur as a result of ordinary work experiences and the passage of time – through the personnel management techniques that can be termed 'employee appraisal'. As the above analysis has shown, there are many conflicting purposes so it is not possible to advocate or prescribe any particular technique. All those that exist can have their place in the overall scheme of employee appraisal: what is used, how and when, will have to be decided by the designers. Getting such decisions appropriate to the needs of the organization, and of the employees, is one of the key problems of personnel management.

This conflict of organizational needs and employee needs can be looked at another way, from either a *macro* or *micro* point of view. If a work organization is analysed in terms of its economic purpose or historical structure then its development is seen in those terms. If, however, it is seen as an organization of people assembled around a set of purposes (e.g. making things or money or providing a service) then its development is seen through changes in behaviour of its people. Clearly, some kind of balance is required between organizational and individual needs. The concept and achievement of such a balance must be at the upper limits of skilled management.

Methods of assessment

An analysis of the various approaches to employee appraisal to be found in Britain reveals that the main area of controversy is the part that the evaluation or measurement of work performance plays in the process. On the one side are railed those managers who are philosophically inclined towards McGregor's (1960) Theory X or Likert's (1961) System 1. They see, as Likert would put it, that the leading variable is work. People go to work and if the amount of work that is performed is assessed, and the person told about how much more they could and should do, then more work will result.

Alternatively, this 'work-centred' position can be explained by the observation that many managers have had some kind of systematic, or even scientific, education. Such managers would argue that if employee appraisal is about changing performance at work, then the first step is to define the headings under which performance can be assessed, then it should devise measurements of those categories, apply the 'treatment' (i.e. some kind of employee development process), and then reassess to see if the 'treatments' have taken effect. It is this paradigm that underpins most employee appraisal schemes that exist in Britain today. It can be called the 'performance control approach' to appraisal.

A complication in the performance control approach is defining what it is that should be assessed. Managers who are inclined to more abstract sets of beliefs about the determinants of work performance can be seen to be disposed to scales that attempt to measure the personality traits that are regarded as crucial to effective work. Examples appear in many employee appraisal forms, such as integrity, honesty, determination, drive, initiative and other labels of human behaviour that are used in everyday life but lack precise psychological meaning. These kinds of staff appraisal schemes result in an individual being told at an annual interview to go and get more 'integrity' and perhaps show a bit more 'initiative', so that things are better next year!

Locke and Latham (1984: 89) summarize the position by saying 'performance is typically appraised in one of three ways: by the use of trait scales, by objective outcome measures, or by Behavioral Observation Scales. Trait scales are inherently ambiguous and are not recommended. Outcome measures can be extremely useful when they are available and relevant to the job. Behavioral Observation Scales are always recommended, so that the means as well as the ends receive proper attention.' Consequently, a key question to be faced by designers of employee appraisal schemes is whether any kind of assessment or quantitative evaluation should take place within the scheme. As has been pointed out, this decision is more often determined in practice by the background or training of the designers rather than on any conceptual analysis of the purpose of the staff appraisal procedure. The need to measure is the basis of methodology in science but, as it happens, not in technology. Managers trained in scientific disciplines find it difficult to accept that change, albeit less certain, can be arranged to take place in other ways.

The further observation can be made that measurement-based methodology is more appropriate to the raw material of the 'hard' sciences and technologies than to the 'soft' behavioural sciences. Here the raw material is people. Unlike inanimate objects they can have their own views and, in particular, feelings about the processes of measurement and change to which they are subjected. If the process is seen as inept or unfair they can feel strong resentment and reject the whole procedure. Unfortunately, in performance assessment, the probability that the measurement process is inept and unfair is very high because the technical problems in designing rating scales and the observational problems involved in using them are considerable. This makes it virtually certain that the assessment process will be seen as uncertain by the appraisees. Hence, references to the need for accuracy in ratings abound in the appraisal literature.

So the key question must be, why take this approach if it creates so many problems? If 'assessment' is the main purpose of the procedure, and as data are required to feed some kind of control or merit-rating scheme, then the risks may be seen as acceptable. Under such circumstances the stages and techniques set out by Bailey (1983) would appear to be the least that should be attempted. These are the establishment of dimensions for performance measurement, and controlling subjectivity in judgement and ratings. If the purpose is employee development (i.e. bringing about committed behaviour change), then the dangers in going through an assessment stage are not likely to be justifiable no matter how technically competent the measurement devices are.

A further important point about the use of assessment of employees arises from its relationship to organization development. Many managers see an *employee* development scheme as a means to *organizational* development. Where the ability and willingness to change behaviour exist, setting organizational objectives and quantitative criteria of performance could well work as a strategy for bringing about change in performance through the pressure of an assessment method. However, if the causes of non-obtained objectives and poor performance are *behavioural*, then such *structural* solutions are not likely to work. It can be argued that to solve organizational problems requires organizational solutions, and to solve behavioural problems requires behavioural solutions. This is why the techniques of target setting and management by quantitative objectives can be effective with able and committed staff but ineffective with inept and alienated staff. In such circumstances, to attempt to change individual behaviour through the means of a so-called employee development procedure with targets or rating scales is highly misguided. All it does is let employees know how poor their performance is rather than what they should do to correct it, probably with alienation rather than motivation being the outcome.

This is not to say that methods of assessment do not have their place in personnel management. They clearly are crucial to many organizational *control* activities, e.g. payment systems, production and sales planning, and manpower planning. This is the position taken by Whitaker (1991: 26) who states 'the measurement of performance is, therefore, the foundation on which performance management is built. If the foundation is flawed, the whole structure is suspect.' The review of 190 years of literature has shown that ways of measuring performance are always flawed: consequently, there is little hope for building a sound structure for performance measurement. The holistic approach to employee appraisal is therefore itself seriously flawed. Traditionally in employee appraisal, and now in performance management, the sequence is seen as from *performance assessment* to *performance change*. What is being argued here is that it should be from *performance development* to *performance assessment*. In other words, employee appraisal and performance management should be development led rather than assessment led.

This section argues that there may not be a need to have any formal scheme for the assessment of employee performance at all. If this is so, all the difficulties of designing rating scales and ensuring their accuracy in use disappear! In particular, as Randell (1991) points out, all the problems associated with legal issues and equal opportunities in appraisal evaporate. No one would sensibly deny, whatever their sex, orientation, ethnic origin, religion or age, that they could be better or happier in their job. To have a personnel management process that is aimed to achieve this must be acceptable. It is the place of performance measurement in the process that causes all the problems and, as this is neither necessary nor sufficient to achieve the objectives, its use should be thoroughly questioned.

The alternative to rating can be called *qualitative assessment*. At the most simple level, all that a qualitative approach demands is the diagnosis of what an individual should be doing differently *next* in their job. This can be checked and discussed with the individual in an interview and this diagnosis turned into an 'action plan'. Randell et al. (1972) call this agreed next action a 'development step'. All manner of observation forms and scales could be used in this process, as long as they aid the diagnosis and commitment to an action plan. With a skilled observer/interviewer as a manager, all the paperwork support that is required at this conceptually simple but technically difficult level is a blank sheet of paper. In practice, however, some kind of paperwork procedure is required for all the kinds of formal employee appraisal that take place within an organization.

Forms and reporting

As the previous sections imply, the kind of support system that is designed for an employee appraisal procedure more often than not reflects the beliefs of the designers about the determinants and control of behaviour at work, rather than serving the main purposes of the scheme. The literature already quoted abounds with examples of forms and paperwork. Such systems often become ends in themselves: their biggest indictment comes when managers are heard to say to a member of staff that the time has come to complete an appraisal form because 'they have to'.

In many cases there is no need for more than a blank sheet of paper. However, to lay down guidelines, give support and to signal organizational sanction of time and effort, something more than that is usually required. What exactly, bearing in mind the different purposes of appraisal, is appropriate to the current needs of the organization? As the diversity and history of the design of employee appraisal systems reveals, getting the design right is fraught with difficulty, and requires great care to match the objectives and the commitment and skill of the managers and managed who are going to use it.

One of the first design decisions that has to be made is how the different purposes of a scheme are to be separated in time, training and paperwork. Many workers in the field (Maier, 1958; Sokolik, 1970; Randell, 1973) have argued for separation of purposes into separate procedures, for example, 'reward review', 'potential review' and 'performance development'. Others, for example, Anstey et al. (1976) and Stewart and Stewart (1977), advocate integration and attempting to achieve as much as possible in a single procedure.

A further aspect of diversification is designing separate procedures for different types and levels of staff. Such separation, if done ineptly, may cause misunderstandings among the various levels, but can, if the organization is flexible, provide useful variations of approach. A less obvious variation is having schemes for people of the same grade but different levels of ability. This has quite a long history, going back to Miner (1965) and then Steinmetz (1969), who both analyse and prescribe ways to manage the unsatisfactory performer.

It is probable that, with growing understanding of the concepts of appraisal, and increasing sophistication in techniques, this trend to designing different kinds of systems and paperwork for different types and levels of staff will become more strongly apparent and applied. In the meantime, the exhortation that appears frequently in the literature to 'keep it simple' would appear the best current advice on form design.

The other main use for forms is as the vehicle for transmission of information to other managers, and to the 'files'. This use is of considerable concern to the larger, perhaps more bureaucratic, organization. Smaller organizations may not see this as much of a problem, as there is sufficient general knowledge about the individuals making up the company. There has been much debate about open versus closed reporting, as Anstey et al. (1976) display in their work based on the British Civil Service. Such difficulties as who should see, sign, countersign and file the forms cause considerable heart-searching and discussion in many organizations.

Clearly, in large organizations, where staff may be spread among different locations and are relatively mobile between them, some kind of central file is an important human resource management need. However, if care is not applied, this central file can become more important to the appraisal system than the behavioural effects on the employees involved. The issue is how to match the needs of a report with the need for open, frank and purposeful discussion between a manager and member of staff.

The main problem to be resolved is whether or not the system requires regular reports. Again, at the lowest level of reporting, a note on the file that a formal meeting has taken place between a manager and a member of staff may well be sufficient. However, at the extremes of performance some kind of report will be important. If performance is so poor that a formal warning to the member of staff has to be given, then a central record of this is necessary, especially for any subsequent stages in a disciplinary procedure. If performance is outstanding, then some kind of formal recognition may be desirable, or important to a procedure for identifying management potential. But, for the usual range of interactions between a manager and a member of staff it is probably better for no detailed report to be submitted at all on the appraisee. However, what may be justifiable is some kind of self-report by the managers, if only for their own files, commenting on the level of skill they displayed, what they think they achieved and how they could do better in future in managing that particular employee.

The significance of interpersonal skills

An issue that has run through the whole history of employee appraisal is the place of interpersonal skills in the process. The survey and analysis of practice has shown that attempts to resolve the problems of employee appraisal by the design of systems and forms have not been successful. The complexity of the process explains why such simplistic approaches probably fail. The alternative is to regard purposeful interactions between managers and staff as nothing more or less than a high-level sensorimotor skill. Even though Maier (1958) laid the foundations for this skills approach to staff development, the American practice since then has been to emphasize systems and assessment techniques, whereas in Britain the skills approach was taken up by Randell and his colleagues (Randell et al., 1972, 1984; Wright and Taylor, 1984). Although most workers in the field recognize the need for training support for employee appraisal procedures, they seem reluctant to start from the premise that it is the skill that is crucial and the systems and forms should be designed in support. Perhaps it is the practical implications of regarding employee appraisal as primarily a skill that deters organizations from taking this approach: skills can only be acquired by people who want to obtain them; they can only be learnt by practice and with some kind of guidance or feedback from skilled tutors; and they cannot be acquired easily in a matter of days. In fact, the long-term development of the skill can only be achieved by training managers in how to be their own source of guidance and feedback – that is, to be a 'self-tutor' – which is perhaps the most difficult kind of training of all.

Not only have the difficulties of taking a skills approach to staff appraisal been underestimated, so too have the benefits. It has been argued by Randell (1978) that training in the skills of staff appraisal can be used as the vehicle for getting managers to develop their skills of interviewing that form the basis of all interpersonal decision making at work. Many writers in Britain, such as Argyle (1981),

Randell (1981), Guirdham (1990) and Hayes (1991) have argued, following Maier's (1958) original plea, that these skills should form the basis of all management training. A conceptual structure for inculcating such skills in managers has also been propounded by Randell (1980). It is probably the shortage of skilled tutors that now hinders the advance of this skills-based approach to employee appraisal. A detailed analysis of what is required by tutors to be effective trainers of managers in staff development skills has been set out by Taylor (1976). A thorough analysis of the concepts and practice of interpersonal skills training for managers has been provided by Taylor and Wright (1988). In the US, the connection between staff appraisal and interpersonal skills has been taken up by Sashkin (1981) who asserts that not only are such skills necessary for effective implementation of performance appraisal but they are also basic to long-term sound management practice. Then, in a highly detailed and descriptive way, Whetton and Cameron (1984) give a useful account of management skills but, although they identify and emphasize the key concepts, they do not show how the motor component of such skills can be inculcated. Robbins (1989) makes up for this deficiency by giving a wide range of examples and exercises for interpersonal skills training. However, he falls short on the process of giving feedback and guidance in skills acquisition, describing how this can be achieved only by means of a 'short quiz' and a 'behavioural questionnaire'. This may well, however, be a way to get around the considerable difficulties involved in selecting and training sufficient interpersonal skills tutors for large groups of trainees. It is McKnight (1991) who really faces up to the considerable problems and demands of developing managerial skills in large groups, describing a cascading method for supplying one tutor for every eight students in a large university business school skills training programme. This account is in a book edited by Bigelow (1991) that may well come to be regarded as the turning point in the US approach to employee appraisal. When all the students of management who have experienced the various kinds of skills training described in this book reach positions of influence in work organizations, they will demand from consultants and academic researchers advice and data that will really help them to manage their employees more effectively, using the skills-based approach that they know is crucial to staff and organization development.

More recently, in Britain in particular, similarities have been noticed between what is required for successful 'leadership' on the part of a manager and what is required for effective appraisal. Alban-Metcalfe (1984) has called these activities the 'micro-skills of leadership', and they are seen to form an essential part of any effective relationship *behaviour* between managers and staff. This skills-based view is now known as the 'Bradford Approach' to staff and management development and has been described by Randell et al. (1984), and Wright and Taylor (1984). The theoretical and practical implications of this approach are wide ranging. As Wright and Taylor say:

> We would rather supply managers with a set of behavioural tools from which they can select the one most appropriate to handle a particular leadership situation, than develop a grand theory which explains everything but has few real practical implications. Unfortunately much of modern leadership theory seems to fall into the latter category. (1984: xi)

This view has been taken up by Makin et al. (1989) who place their account of staff appraisal in their chapter on Leadership and Management Style. They argue that all those interactions when a manager tries to influence subordinates' behaviour 'are in fact mini-appraisals' (ibid.: 78).

The powerful implication of this position is that employee appraisal can be used, if an organization is so inclined, as the vehicle for the development of what most of them search for – i.e. better leadership for their human resources, which results in more effective use of the capacities and inclinations of their employees.

Evaluation

The evaluation of the effectiveness of any process or technique of personnel management is both highly desirable and exceedingly complex. It is notoriously difficult to design such validation studies and then to generate data of sufficient quality to enable causal conclusions to be drawn. There is the further complication of 'bias of auspices', when the promulgators of the concepts and training produce evidence of its effectiveness themselves. Obtaining 'independent' evaluation data is methodologically more respectable, but difficult to achieve in practice. Nevertheless, even though data generated from such studies may be suspect for validation purposes, the act of carrying them out can have two important beneficial effects. By authorizing a survey into the effectiveness of a staff appraisal scheme an organization can signal how seriously it is taking its application and effects. Second, by completing a questionnaire, or by being interviewed, a manager can be reminded of the main principles, purposes and practices of the procedure, and hopefully be encouraged in their further application.

Problems arise when these twin aims of maintenance for the process and the evaluation of its effectiveness become entwined. The designers of a scheme require the data for their systems' development, whereas senior managers require evidence that the scheme is working. In practice it is extremely difficult to disentangle these two aims. Fletcher and Williams (1985) allow the two requirements to merge. In a survey of seven organizations, totalling 5940 appraisees and 1332 appraisers, they give indices describing details of the process: one on overall assessment of the scheme by the appraisee (9 per cent on average against it), and two on outcomes (30 per cent of appraisees saying the appraisal interview had increased job satisfaction and 40 per cent saying it had resulted in improved job performance). No information was given about the training the appraisers had received in appraisal skills.

The trouble with such overviews is that they do not help the real issue. The long history of employee appraisal and the conceptual analysis given in this chapter should convince any manager that it is a necessary and useful part of personnel management: what is not known is just how effective a particular technique or application really is. As Meyer et al. (1965) demonstrated, different kinds of appraisal procedures can have different effects in the same organization. What, then, is required is a detailed study of the effects and effectiveness of each particular scheme.

An example of this is a study carried out within the Civil Service and reported by Anstey et al. (1976). It involved the detailed analysis of 3239 *post-facto* questionnaires from appraisees and 564 from appraisers. The study concentrated on the effects of the appraisal interview and showed that 51 per cent of appraisees reported 'encouraged performance' as a result of the interview, 79 per cent of appraisers reported 'useful outcomes' and only 6 per cent of respondents 'saw no value in it'.

An ingenious study has been carried out within Fisons, with a three stage hierarchical/corroborated evidence design, involving questionnaires from 640 managers. As reported by Allinson (1977), the 103 managers who had received appraisal skills training not only reported on themselves, but were also reported on by their own managers and staff. The three overlapping and interlocking samples provided a total of 220 corroborating questionnaires and their analysis showed that the managers had improved their skill levels on all the nine rating scales of 'before' and 'after' behaviour as a result of the training. Managers in mid-career seemed to gain most from such skills training. It did emerge, however, that the appraisal scheme raised hopes and expectations in employees about being managed more skilfully.

At the simplest level of evaluation, it would appear that most organizations which undertake training in the structure and content of their appraisal scheme at least ask participants at the end of the course to give their 'reaction' to the training. Although reactions data are scientifically suspect they can have considerable social significance. If senior managers say that such training works for them and authorize further investment of money and staff time in it, then this will be interpreted by staff as hard evidence for the effectiveness of the procedures. As far as line managers are concerned, such evidence is regarded as far more 'significant' than any statistical tests. If this outcome is widely felt, then the climate can be established in which the delicate and sensitive skills of interpersonal interaction can grow and develop within an organization. It is this that could well be the main use of evaluation studies of employee appraisal within an organization, rather than the generation of suspect validation data.

The Need for a Contingency Approach

It can now be noted that the study of employee appraisal has turned full circle. Robert Owen can be seen as one of the first great leaders of industry, someone who, in his early work and within the constraints of his time, skilfully balanced the needs of profit making and human well-being to develop an effective work organization. F. W. Taylor, although working from a different philosophical base and in a different economic climate, attempted much the same. Douglas McGregor, spurred on by Alfred P. Sloan of General Motors, was working under different conditions again, but at a similar level of managerial balance and success. Today all these efforts and themes can be recognized in the work of contemporary leadership theorists. Leaders are currently judged mainly on how well they make use of and develop the human resources of their organization. As can be seen from the information and analysis in this chapter, employee appraisal is one of the major processes available to help them to achieve this. However, the problem of choosing what particular approach to take to human resources development remains. As has been emphasized many times in this chapter, to be successful, an employee appraisal scheme has to reflect the current needs and skills of the appraisers and appraisees of the organization. This is not easy as there are invariably many different expressions of needs and skills, and the vested interests of groups and individuals colour their perception. In a remarkably succinct, thorough and insightful booklet, the Advisory, Conciliation and Arbitration Service (ACAS, 1988) gives very useful advice on establishing employee appraisal schemes. Although commendably comprehensive, this advice lacks sufficient precision to be of real help to a particular organization trying to revise or design a scheme.

So how should an appraisal scheme be designed to take into account the demands of the organization, the expectations of the appraisees and the skills of the appraisers? The first conclusion of this chapter is that it is essential to separate *performance assessment* from *performance development* and to devise two distinct processes, concentrating on development first. Once this is achieved, then the two procedures can run in parallel, if both are needed by a performance management strategy.

The next conclusion is that a *contingency approach* is required. An appraisal scheme must match the needs of the organization and the expectations of the employees at its particular stage of development. The remaining conclusion is that employee appraisal can only be effective if appraisers possess the interpersonal skills required for its practice. It is of little use designing or improving any personnel management system if the participants in it are unable or unwilling to work it *skilfully*. Of course, as the contingency approach implies, the nature and timing of the skills training depends on the existing skills and attitudes of the employees, if they are not ready or prepared for it then a 'shake-up' approach may be required. Or, if sufficient skill exists, a very direct approach can be taken. To help designers of employee appraisal schemes to decide what is appropriate for their organization, or how an existing scheme can be categorized, four approaches to appraisal, described in simple and rather prescriptive terms in table 7.1, are put forward. In practice a particular scheme may turn out to be a 'blend' of these approaches.

Radical staff development might be for organizations where employees are inclined to be inept and alienated, and where the objective is to provide a psychological shake-up. This is a very 'organization/work-centred' approach to appraisal, and is not to be undertaken lightly. Several variations of this approach can be seen in practice: it could even be regarded as the 'traditional' approach that emerges when a committee of tough-minded managers decides on an appraisal scheme for their organization. However, many of the attacks

Table 7.1   Types of employee development

Radical staff development	*Passive staff development*
1. Establish quantitative or operational performance criteria	1. Agree a staff reporting policy based on fixed interval reports and discussions of staff performance
2. Design behaviourally anchored scales to assess the criteria	2. Design a comprehensive form, usually through meetings of widely representative committees
3. Establish training in staff assessment concepts and include rating exercises	3. Prepare a thorough manual describing the scheme and distribute it widely throughout the organization
4. Introduce the staff assessment and reporting procedure, by decree, and supply a set of authoritative guidelines or manual of operation	4. According to the agreed wishes of the staff, establish the distribution and filing of the reports
5. Give recognition and/or reward to those who are assessed as excellent and assurance to those who are regarded as adequate	5. Establish training opportunities for learning needs arising from the scheme
6. Give counselling and, if necessary, warnings to those who are assessed as inadequate	
7. Provide opportunity for reassessment and arbitration	
8. Provide training opportunities for learning needs arising from the reports	
9. File all data arising from the system	

Table 7.1 *(cont.)*

Dynamic staff development	*Active staff development*
1. Agree a quantitative target – objective setting management policy 2. Brief managers on 'management by objectives' concepts and techniques, preferably incorporating behavioural standards as well as quantitative 3. Distribute MBO paperwork systems and exhort managers to use them 4. Monitor procedure by reviewing targets and the realism of objectives set	1. Agree a 'performance improvement' policy based on a 'work review and action plan' (WRAP). This plan leads to a capacity development step being taken by a member of staff, hopefully with commitment but, failing that, complicance and a 'motivation development step' being taken by the manager, hopefully with sincerity, but failing that, reluctance 2. Gain acceptance of the policy at all levels in the organization, particularly with the trade unions and staff associations 3. Establish a workshop in the interpersonal skills of staff development, and make sure that the managers who most need the training attend the course first, and all others subsequently 4. Design paperwork procedures, *supportive* of the staff development system, probably of a narrative kind 5. Establish training opportunities for learning needs arising from the scheme 6. Establish reporting channels that will enhance change and commitment, both by the individual members of staff and the management of the organization 7. Monitor progress, and change the content and emphasis of the scheme according to the follow-up data that are generated

on appraisal are directed at schemes like these because they are known to antagonize or alienate employees.

Passive staff development   might be appropriate for those organizations that are working satisfactorily but where the maintenance of performance is regarded as important and where some provision is thought necessary to cope with the occasional ineffective or highly able member of staff. Such an approach can lead to a 'cosy', rather bureaucratic system. If care is not taken a great deal of paperwork can be generated, with not much use made of it. One of its main virtues is the comfort it can provide by letting employees know where they stand and by opening a channel of communication with the central personnel administration.

Dynamic staff development   might be for organizations where able employees are already highly committed to short-term organizational objectives, and where the organization is growing and changing rapidly. This approach may well be appropriate for a relatively young organization, where the selection procedure has attracted very able and highly motivated employees. A danger here is over-stressing the staff with unrealistic or inappropriate objectives, so that the commitment turns to breakdown and alienation.

Active staff development   might be for those organizations that have a satisfactory level of performance, where morale and industrial relations are sound but where there is a desire to increase productivity and job satisfaction as much as possible within the constraints of economic conditions and existing quality of staff. It is this approach that demands most of the management of an organization in time, effort and cost, which is probably why it is not chosen as often as it should be. It is built on the interpersonal skills of bringing about behaviour change, rather than the pressure of rating forms or reporting procedures. It works from the premise that employees *want* to get better at their jobs and to see their employing organization improve and succeed. If this premise is flawed, then this approach is inappropriate and more of a 'shake-up' policy may have to be chosen.

The task for personnel managers is to diagnose what approach is most appropriate for their organization, and to take astute steps to get it accepted and applied.

Bibliography

ACAS. 1988. *Employee Appraisal.* Advisory Booklet No. 2. London: HMSO.

Adams, J. S. 1964. 'Inequity in Social Exchange'. In Berkowitz, L. (ed.) *Advances in Experimental Social Psychology*, Vol 2. New York: Academic Press.

Alban-Metcalfe, B. M. 1984. 'Micro-skills of Leadership: A Detailed Analysis of the Behaviour of Managers in the Appraisal Interview'. In Hunt, J. G., Hosking, D., Schriesheim, C. A. and Stewart, R. (eds) *Leaders and Managers: International Perspectives on Managerial Behavior.* New York: Pergamon, 179–91.

Allinson, C. W. 1977. 'Training in Performance Appraisal Interviewing: An Evaluation Study'. *Journal of Management Studies*, 14, 179–91.

Anstey, E., Fletcher, C. and Walker, J. 1976. *Staff Appraisal and Development.* London: Allen & Unwin.

Argyle, M. (ed.) 1981. *Social Skills and Work.* London: Methuen.

Argyris, C. 1964. *Integrating the Individual and the Organization.* New York: Wiley.

Bailey, C. T. 1983. *The Measurement of Job Performance.* Aldershot: Gower.

Bigelow, J. D. (ed.) 1991. *Managerial Skills.* Newbury Park, CA: Sage.

Carroll, S. J. and Schneier, C. E. 1982. *Performance Appraisal and Review Systems.* Glenview, IL: Scott, Foresman.

Cole, G. D. H. 1925. *Robert Owen.* London: Benn.

Cummings, L. L. and Schwab, D. P. 1973. *Performance in Organizations: Determinants and Appraisal.* Glenview, IL: Scott, Foresman.

DeVries, D. L., Morrison, A. M., Shullman, S. L. and Gerlach, M. L. 1981. *Performance Appraisal on the Line.* New York: Wiley.

Festinger, L. 1957. *A Theory of Cognitive Dissonance.* Evanston, IL: Row, Peterson.

Fletcher, C. and Williams, R. 1985. *Performance Appraisal and Career Development.* London: Hutchinson.

Goldstein, A. P. and Sorcher, M. 1974. *Changing Supervisor Behavior.* New York: Pergamon.

Guest, D. E. 1987. 'Human Resource Management and Industrial Relations'. *Journal of Management Studies*, 24, 5, 503–21.

Guirdham, M. 1990. *Interpersonal Skills at Work.* London: Prentice Hall.

Hayes, J. 1991. *Interpersonal Skills.* London: Harper Collins.

Henderson, R. I. 1984. *Performance Appraisal*, 2nd edn. Reston, VA: Reston.

Herriot, P. (ed.) 1989. *Assessment and Selection in Organizations.* Chichester: Wiley.

Herzberg, F. 1966. *Work and the Nature of Man.* London: Staples Press.

Jung, C. J. 1958. *The Undiscovered Self.* Boston, MA: Little Brown.

Latham, G. P. and Wexley, K. N. 1981. *Increasing Productivity Through Performance Appraisal.* Reading, MA: Addison-Wesley.

Lawler, E. E. 1973. *Motivation in Work Organizations.* Monterey, CA: Brooks.

Likert, R. 1961. *New Patterns of Management.* New York: McGraw-Hill.

Locke, E. A. and Latham, G. P. 1984. *Goal Setting: A Motivational Technique That Works.* Englewood Cliffs, NJ: Prentice Hall.

Long, P. 1986. *Performance Appraisal Revisited.* London: Institute of Personnel Management.

McGregor, D. 1957. 'An Uneasy Look at Performance Appraisals'. *Harvard Business Review*, 35, 3, 89–95.

McGregor, D. 1960. *The Human Side of Enterprise.* New York: McGraw-Hill.

McKnight, M. R. 1991. 'Management Skill Development: What It Is Not'. In Bigelow, J. D. (ed.) *Managerial Skills.* Newbury Park, CA: Sage.

Mager, R. F. and Pipe, P. 1970. *Analyzing Performance Problems.* Belmont, CA: Fearon.

Maier, N. R. F. 1952. *Principles of Human Relations.* New York: Wiley.

Maier, N. R. F. 1958. *The Appraisal Interview.* New York: Wiley.

Makin, P. J., Cooper, C. L. and Cox, C. J. 1989. *Managing People at Work.* London: British Psychological Society and Routledge.

Martin, G. and Pear, J. 1978. *Behavior Modification: What It Is and How To Do It.* Englewood Cliffs, NJ: Prentice Hall.

Maslow, A. H. 1965. *Eupsychian Management.* Homewood IL: Irwin Dorsey.

Maslow, A. H. 1970. *Motivation and Personality*, 2nd edn. New York: Harper & Row.

Meyer, H. H., Kay, E. and French, J. R. P. 1965. 'Split Roles in Performance Appraisal'. *Harvard Business Review*, 43, 123–9.

Miner, J. B. 1965. *The Management of Ineffective Performance.* New York: McGraw-Hill.

Molander, C. 1989. 'Personnel Management – From "Welfare" to Human Resource Management'. In Molander, C. (ed.) *Human Resource Management.* Bromley: Chartwell-Bratt.

Neale, F. (ed.) 1991. *The Handbook of Performance Management.* London: Institute of Personnel Management.

Odiorne, G. S. 1965. *Management by Objectives: A System of Management Leadership.* New York: Pitman.

Odiorne, G. S. 1979. *Management by Objectives II: A System of Managerial Leadership for the 80s.* Belmont, CA: Fearon Pitman.

Pym, D. 1973. 'The Politics and Rituals of Appraisals'. *Occupational Psychology*, 47, 231–5.

Rackham, N. and Morgan, T. 1977. *Behaviour Analysis in Training.* Maidenhead: McGraw-Hill.

Randell, G. A. 1971. 'The Motor Skills of Man-Management'. *Manage-

ment Decision, 9, 31–9.

Randell, G. A. 1973. 'Performance Appraisal, Purposes, Practices and Conflicts'. *Occupational Psychology*, 47, 221–4.

Randell, G. A. 1978. 'Interviewing at Work'. In Warr, P. B. (ed.) *Psychology at Work*, 2nd edn. Harmondsworth: Penguin.

Randell, G. A. 1980. 'The Skills of Staff Development'. In Singleton, W. T., Spurgeon, P. and Stammers, R. B. (eds) *The Analysis of Social Skill*. New York: Plenum.

Randell, G. A. 1981. 'Management Education and Training'. In Singleton, W. T. (ed.) *Management Skills: The Study of Real Skills*, Vol. 3. Lancaster: Medical and Technical Publishing Co. Ltd, 239–53.

Randell, G. A. 1991. 'The Nonsense of Staff Appraisal'. In Randell, G. A., Ford, J. and Rennie, S. (eds) *Appraisal of Staff: An Equal Opportunities Approach*. Bradford: Work and Gender Research Unit, University of Bradford.

Randell, G. A., Packard, P. M. A., Shaw, R. L. and Slater, A. J. 1972. *Staff Appraisal*. London: Institute of Personnel Management.

Randell, G. A., Packard, P. M. A., Slater, A. J. 1984. *Staff Appraisal: A First Step to Effective Leadership*, 3rd edn. London: Institute of Personnel Management.

Rausch, E. 1985. *Win-Win Performance Management/Appraisal*. New York: Wiley.

Robbins, S. B. 1989. *Training in Interpersonal Skills*. Englewood Cliffs, NJ: Prentice Hall.

Roethlisberger, F. H. and Dickson, W. J. 1939. *Management and the Worker*. Cambridge MA: Harvard University Press.

Rowe, K. B. 1964. 'An Appraisal of Appraisals'. *Journal of Management Studies*, 1, 1–25.

Sashkin, M. 1981. *Assessing Performance Appraisal*. San Diego, CA: University Associates.

Skinner, B. F. 1971. *Beyond Freedom and Dignity*. New York: Knopf.

Skinner, B. F. 1972. *Cumulative Record: A Selection of Papers*, 3rd edn. New York: Appleton-Century Crofts.

Sokolik, S. L. 1970. *The Personnel Process*. Scranton, NJ: International Text Book Co.

Sorokin, P. 1966. *Sociological Theories of Today*. New York: Harper & Row.

Steinmetz, L. L. 1969. *Managing the Marginal and Unsatisfactory Performer*. Reading, MA: Addison-Wesley.

Stewart, R. 1965. 'Reactions to Appraisal Interviews'. *Journal of Management Studies*, 2, 1, 83–99.

Stewart, V. and Stewart, A. 1977. *Practical Performance Appraisal*. Aldershot: Gower.

Taylor, D. S. 1976. *Performance Reviews: A Handbook for Tutors*. London: Institute of Personnel Management.

Taylor, D. S. and Wright, P. L. 1988. *Developing Interpersonal Skills*

Through Tutored Practice. New York: Prentice Hall.

Taylor, F. W. 1964. *Scientific Management*. London: Harper & Row.

Torrington, D. 1988. 'How Does Human Resources Management Change the Personnel Function?'. *Personnel Review*, 17, 6, 3–9.

Townley, B. 1991. 'Selection and Appraisal: Reconstituting "Social Relations"?'. In Storey, J. (ed.) *New Perspectives on Human Resources Management*. London: Routledge.

Vernon, P. E. and Parry, J. B. 1949. *Personnel Selection in the British Forces*. London: University of London Press.

Vroom, V. B. 1964, *Work and Motivation*. New York: Wiley.

Vroom, V. B. and Yetton, P. W. 1973. *Leadership and Decision Making*. Pittsburgh: University of Pittsburgh Press.

Whetton, D. A. and Cameron, K. S. 1984. *Developing Management Skills*. Glenview, IL: Scott, Foresman.

Whisler, T. L. and Harper, S. F. (eds) 1962. *Performance Appraisal: Research and Practice*. New York: Holt, Rinehart & Winston.

Whitaker, C. 1991. 'Measurement – the Foundation of Performance Management'. In Neale, F. (ed.) *The Handbook of Performance Management*. London: Institute of Personnel Management.

Wright, P. L. and Taylor, D. S. 1984. *Improving Leadership Performance*. Englewood Cliffs, NJ: Prentice Hall.

Yeates, J. D. 1989. *Performance Appraisal: A Self-Help Manual*. Brighton: Institute of Manpower Studies.

8

Wasted Resources? Equal Opportunities in Employment

Linda Dickens

Introduction

It is becoming a commonplace statement that people are the most important organizational asset. Human resources, we are told by many commentators, can provide organizations with competitive advantage. At the same time, however, we have continuing discrimination in the labour market on grounds of sex, race, disability or other arbitrary factors, and a lack of equality of opportunity in employment. This prevents the full and effective utilization of all human resources. This chapter explores this apparent contradiction, arguing that, despite some progress in 'equal opportunities', resources are being wasted. It also offers an explanation of why this is the case.

In the next section signs of progress towards greater equality of opportunity in employment are considered in the context of data which reveal continuing employment disadvantage for particular groups in Britain. The initiatives which organizations might take to tackle this differential distribution of opportunities and rewards are outlined in section three, drawing on guidance from the equality commissions. Section four considers the factors which might encourage an organization to adopt such guidance, identifying two main categories of reason why equality action might be taken: positive organizational self-interest and penalty avoidance through compliance.

These potential motivating forces have not been sufficient to produce a universal adoption of equality initiatives, however. Some organizations have taken equality initiatives but have achieved relatively little in terms of substantive outcomes. Section five accounts for the unevenness of action by considering the limited and contingent nature of the self-interest and compliance pressures, and the existence of countervailing pressures, while section six discusses problems in translating the equal opportunity (EO) prescription into practice, highlighting issues relating to the distribution of power within organizations. It goes on to argue, however, that even if the good practice 'equality model' were to be implemented adequately, this would not necessarily produce equity in terms of distributional outcomes.

Much of the prescription in the employment equality area, it is argued, rests on an inadequate conceptualization of the 'problem', underplays the resistance which equality initiatives can generate and simplifies the reasons for it. The adoption and implementation of such prescription will deliver only limited progress. Although such progress is well worth achieving, the concluding section argues for the need to shift the currently predominant emphasis on measures designed to help members of the disadvantaged groups progress within existing organizations towards an approach centred on changing the nature, structure and values of organizations themselves.

Progress but Continuing Disadvantage in Employment

Signs of apparent progress towards greater equality of opportunity in employment can be seen in the large number of organizations declaring (in recruitment advertising and elsewhere) that they are an 'equal opportunity employer'; in the adoption of 'equal opportunity policies' (EOPs); in the appointment of equal opportunity officers by both public and private sector employers; in such campaigns as 'positive about disabled people' (whereby companies displaying the campaign logo agree, *inter alia*, to interview all disabled applicants who meet the minimum criteria for a job vacancy); and in the existence of various well publicized initiatives.

One such initiative is 'Opportunity 2000' which is a business-led campaign launched in October 1991 to 'increase the quality and quantity of women's participation in the workforce'. Employers who participate in the initiative set themselves qualitiative or quantitative goals for the year 2000. They need not have an existing EOP but some of the first members were organizations already well known for their EO initiatives. After one year, membership had grown to 141 public and private sector organizations, employing nearly one-quarter of the workforce. Almost one-third of those in membership now offer flexible work arrangements; half provide some kind of childcare or career break option; and almost all provide some kind of training or education designed to increase women's opportunities at work (*Employment Gazette*, 1992a: 597). No single set of goals was proposed for Opportunity 2000 members: organizations declared their own objectives (some of which were rather general – for example, 'monitoring all recruitment and development practices for equal access and treatment') or set themselves qualitative or numerical targets (*Equal Opportunities Review*, 1992a: 20–23). Among those setting numerical targets were TSB Group (women to constitute 21 per cent of managers by the end of 1992), IBM (UK) (aiming for 30 per cent of graduate hires to be women) and Kingfisher (to increase the percentage of women in management of Superdrug from 14 per cent to 20 per cent within five years and to have 50 per cent more women at senior management level).

Employer initiatives specifically aiming to promote equal opportunities for ethnic minorities can also be identified. A recent survey of 750 subscribers to *Equal Opportunities Review* found these most commonly included provision of guidance on race equality to selectors, ethnic monitoring of applicants and recruitment schemes to encourage ethnic minority applicants, such as placing job advertisements in ethnic minority publications and using ethnic minority images in publicity material (*Equal Opportunities Review*, 1993a: 14–20). Less common steps, taken by only a minority of respondents, included the setting of recruitment targets (usually reflecting local labour market composition) and pre-recruitment training schemes. Those surveyed might reasonably be expected to exhibit a predisposition to EO initiatives: of 166 respondents (a 22 per cent return), 63 per cent were from the public sector (mainly local authorities), 33 per cent were from the private sector (mainly finance and retail) and 4 per cent were voluntary organizations.

Equality initiatives are being taken, therefore, but the evidence suggests that they are not necessarily very widespread or running very deep. It is still the case that a majority of private sector companies and almost half of all local authorities do not claim to have an EOP (*Equal Opportunities Review*, 1989: 13; Equal Opportunities Commission, 1988). While the absence of an EOP need not mean necessarily that no steps are being taken to promote equal opportunities (Aitkenhead and Liff, 1991), it seems unlikely that an organization which was doing something to promote equality of opportunity would respond to surveys by saying it had no such policy, not least when many of those who do claim to be EO employers do little beyond adopting that label.

The existence of an EO statement or policy (and not all organizations recognize the difference) says little about what is actually happening in the organization. Adoption of a policy may have little impact, even at the minimal level of awareness of the policy's existence (Jewson et al., 1990; Colling and Dickens, 1989). In the NHS, for example, although 93 per cent of health authorities and Boards investigated by the Equal Opportunity Commission (EOC) in 1990 stated they had an equal opportunity policy or statement, for many this amounted to little more than paying lip service to equality: 10 per cent had not committed their EOP to paper; 30 per cent had not communicated the policy to their employees; 60 per cent did not have an equal opportunities committee to plan or evaluate progress; and 75 per cent did not monitor their policy (Equal Opportunities Commission, 1991). Other surveys of self-declared EO employers similarly find that there may be little behind the declaration (e.g. Equal Opportunities Commission, 1988; Hitner et al., 1981).

In some organizations, where the adoption of a policy is not seen as an end in itself, and equality initiatives have been taken, there have been achievements, although these may appear relatively small. In the Greater London Council between 1981 and 1985, when the promotion of EO was given a high profile, the proportion of women employed increased from 16 per cent to 21 per cent and the proportion of black people from 7 per cent to 11 per cent. Most of the gains were at the lower levels (Coyle 1989: 46). In the Civil Service a 'Programme of Action' to achieve equality of opportunity for women was implemented in 1984, followed by a second programme in 1992, with a similar programme for ethnic minorities being introduced in 1990. The representation of women in the top three grades of the Service (which employs 265,685 women) increased from 28 (9 per cent) in 1984 to 53 (17 per cent) in April 1992 (Cabinet Office, 1992: 3). The overall representation of ethnic minority staff in the Civil Service increased by half a percentage point in the two years to April 1992 to reach 5 per cent. While this figure is in keeping with the proportion of ethnic minorities of working age in the general population (4.9 per cent), ethnic minorities remain under-represented in all management grades in the Civil Service and it appears that 'ethnic minority candidates are not being recruited and promoted to more senior grade levels in the same proportions as those who are white' (*Equal Opportunities Review*, 1993b: 9).

Thus, while it appears EO is firmly on management agendas in a number of organizations, and a range of initiatives is being taken, with some examples of imaginative and often thoroughgoing approaches, progress in terms of significant aggregate distributional outcomes (that is to say changes in the representation and distribution of various disadvantaged groups within organizations and in the workforce as a whole) is less easy to identify. There clearly have been gains for some people in certain areas but this must be placed in the context of little change in long-standing patterns of job segregation and pay disadvantage.

Aggregate labour force statistics show patterns of continuing disadvantage for women, with vertical and horizontal job segregation and continuing inequalities in pay and conditions. Women constitute 43 per cent of persons in employment in the UK and 47 per cent of those classified as employees. There has been considerable growth in female labour force participation but it has been of a particular kind. The Labour Force Survey (*Employment Gazette*, 1992b) indicates that the number of women in employment increased by nearly 20 per cent between 1979 and 1991, a continuation of earlier upward trends, but this growth has been unevenly spread, with much of it concentrated in part-time work in the service sector. Of those women in employment (as employees and self-employed) in 1991, 57 per cent worked full time and 42 per cent part time (the remainder were on government schemes).

The great majority of women (82 per cent overall and 89 per cent of women working part time) are employed in the service sector, compared with just over half of men. They form the majority of workers in many service industries but they are the minority (often a small minority) in most manufacturing industries. Manufacturing accounts for just 14 per cent of working women, against 28 per cent of men.

There is marked occupational, as well as industrial, segregation. Men outnumber women by 58:1 in skilled construction trades; by 9:1 in science and engineering professions; and there are three male corporate managers/administrators for every one woman (the women managers/administrators being found disproportionately in the hotels and distribution sector). Conversely, women outnumber men by 7:1 in healthcare professions; by 4:1 in personal services occupations; and by 2:1 in clerical occupations (*Employment Gazette*, 1992b: 440).

Women's pay position relative to that of men has improved over the past few years but women still receive only 79p for every £1 earned by men. Whereas in 1992 just under one-quarter of men earned £420 or more each week, only 7 per cent of women did. At the other end of the pay ladder, while only 10 per cent of men earn less than £170 per week, this is the case for just under one-third of women (*Equal Opportunities Review*, 1992b: 31). Women (particularly those working part time) also receive fewer employment benefits than men.

The aggregate data available on the employment distribution and pay position of ethnic minorities is less detailed than that available for women, although surveys and analysis have revealed considerable disparities in pay and working conditions to the detriment of black men (e.g. Brown, 1984) and lower pay and fewer employment benefits for black women when compared to white women (Breugel, 1989). A relatively small-scale investigation of occupations where it was possible to collect detailed data on earnings by ethnic group found that 'even when ethnic minority workers have higher education and training, their wages tend to be lower when compared with their white counterparts' and that 'ethnic minorities do not get promoted and in relative terms tend to stay on in lower grades relative to their education and qualifications' (Pirani et al., 1992: 40–1).

Labour Force Survey data (*Employment Gazette*, 1993) reveal certain differences in the sectoral distribution of ethnic minority and white workers. For example, ethnic minority women are more likely than white women to work in the medical and health services, and ethnic minority men are more concentrated in distribution, hotels, catering and repairs compared to their white counterparts. Self-employment is higher among ethnic minorites (16 per cent) than the corresponding white population (13 per cent). Most marked, however, are differences in unemployment. Overall unemployment rates are significantly higher for ethnic minority groups (13 per cent) than for the white population (7 per cent), with highest rates among the Pakistani/Bangladeshi (21 per cent) and West Indian (14 per cent) groups. Unemployment was twice as high among ethnic minority groups than among white people with the same broad level of qualification.

Doyle (1991: 94) cites research estimates that there are 2.3 million disabled adults below pension age in Britain. Of these 31 per cent were in paid employment (compared to an economic activity rate of 69 per cent for the general population). The rate and length of disabled unemployment is twice that for the population in general.

As well as the continuing disadvantage displayed in the survey statistics, research reveals continuing employment discrimination. For example a study by Brown and Gay (1985) found black applicants matched with white applicants by gender, experience and qualifications were much less likely to be called for interview for a variety of skilled manual, secretarial, clerical, office junior and sales representatives jobs. Investigations by the Commission for Racial Equality (CRE) found applicants from ethnic minorities were disadvantaged compared to their peers in access to various professions, including accountancy (Commission for Racial Equality, 1987) and medicine (Commission for Racial Equality, 1988). St George's Hospital Medical School was found to have discriminated against women and black applicants for a number of years. A computer program had been devised to score applications, using past interview decisions as a guide. To replicate these past decisions, the program awarded lower scores to females and to black applicants as compared with similarly qualified white applicants.

A study of black graduates found them less likely than matched white graduates to be employed 12 months after graduation; more likely to be in jobs at levels below their qualifications and to be receiving lower salaries (Brennan and McGeevor, 1987 and 1988, cited in Iles and Auluck, 1991: 304). Even within organizations which declare themselves to be equal opportunity employers, discrimination may continue. Bradford Metropolitan Council, for example, one of the first local authorities to declare itself an EO employer, had legal action taken aginst it by the CRE in 1991 for persistent discrimination.

From an outcomes-oriented perspective, therefore, it would appear that EO initiatives have been too few or have failed in practice. Reasons for this are explored later. First, consideration is given to what is generally meant by EO initiatives, based on guidance issued by the equality commissions.

Equal Opportunity Initiatives

EO initiatives concern policy and practice designed to tackle the differential distribution of opportunities, resources and rewards (jobs, wages, promotions, employment benefits) among workers, based on their membership of a social group. For organizations wishing to take some action to address this differential distribution, there is no shortage of guidance on what to do and how to do it. Much comes from the two equality commissions – the EOC and the CRE – which publish Codes of Practice, guidance on developing and implementing EOPs, and on particular aspects such as ethnic monitoring. There is also a code of good practice on the employment of disabled people, published by the Manpower Services Commission. Guidance is offered, too, by the Institute of Personnel Management (IPM) and management consultants, and the specialist press (such as *Equal Opportunities Review*) regularly publish examples of good practice.

The centre-piece of the equality commissions' guidance concerns the adoption of an EOP. As described by the CRE (1984: 8), this is a policy which aims to ensure

> ... that no job applicant or employee receives less favourable treatment than another on racial grounds; that no applicant or employee is placed at a disadvantage by requirements or conditions which have a disproportionately adverse effect on his or her racial group and which cannot be shown to be justifiable on other than racial grounds, and that, where appropriate and where permissible under the Race Relations Act, employees of underrepresented racial groups are given training and encouragement to achieve equal opportunity within the organisation.

The EOC guidance is similar, presenting an EOP as ensuring no direct or indirect discrimination operates to the detriment of women or married people in any area of employment, including access to it, and that positive action measures (encouragement to apply, single sex and 'special needs' training, childcare provision, flexible hours, return to work schemes, etc.) are introduced.

On implementing EOPs, the CRE guidance (1983) is for the allocation of responsibility to a suitably qualified member of senior management; consultation with trade unions or employee representatives; a statement of the policy and publicity to all employees and job applicants; training and guidance on law and company policy to supervisory staff and other relevant decision makers; an examination of existing procedures and criteria for indirectly discriminatory effect, implementing change where this is found; and monitoring of policy through analysis of the composition of workforce and job applicants, and positive action/remedial action (e.g. language training), as permitted under the legislation.

The equality commissions' advice centres on developing fair procedures and fair practice, with some 'compensatory' measures for members of disadvantaged groups. It emphasizes developing unbiased criteria and formal procedures, and guiding and training responsible staff to ensure that these are followed, with monitoring to be undertaken of process and outcomes. This forms the core of many EO initiatives.

Reasons for Taking Equality Initiatives

A variety of external and internal factors can be identified which might encourage an organization to adopt the advice proffered and implement equality initiatives. These can be divided roughly into two categories: the positive pursuit of organizational benefits (self-interest) and penalty avoidance through compliance.

This is not to deny that initiatives to promote greater employment equality can arise from a sense of social justice or moral responsibility. Key individuals in an organization, indeed, may be motivated by concerns for social justice. The role of John Moores in Littlewoods is often cited as such an example (Hackett, 1988: 49; Hansard Society Commission, 1990: 53). Social justice or altruistic considerations, however, probably have most purchase when operating in combination with the organizational self-interest or compliance factors discussed below, or where they are stimulated by external factors such as the link sometimes made in popular discourse between 'race riots', inner-city problems and high black youth unemployment.

Organizational self-interest

A number of, sometimes linked, factors encouraging an interest in equality initiatives can be grouped under this heading: competition in the labour market; efficient management of human resources; better employee relations; positive company image; and gaining from diversity. What they have in common is that EO is promoted as being in the best interests of the company, providing positive organizational benefits.

Competition in the labour market Recently, labour market changes have provided an external stimulus of this organizational self-interest kind. Concern in late 1980s with the 'demographic timebomb' (the decline in numbers of young people entering the labour market), and with labour and skill shortages, led to increased consideration being given to 'non-traditional' recruits. The link to EO is that disadvantaged groups constitute an untapped or under-utilized labour supply. For example, women constitute the largest single group of under-utilized workers, with some six million women of working age not in paid employment (Metcalf and Leighton, 1989). Black workers are disproportionately represented among the unemployed within every age and sex group, but particularly in the male 16–24 age group (*Employment Gazette*, 1993).

The emphasis is not only on widening recruitment, but also on better retention of existing staff. In some companies this stimulated an interest in such initiatives as enhanced maternity provisions, career breaks and flexible working as ways of holding on to valued female staff (*Industrial Relations Review and Report*, 1990a: 2).

The efficient use of labour also concentrates on not wasting available resources by implicitly assuming that white, 'non-disabled' men have a monopoly of talent, or that older workers have no contribution to make, and involves identifying untapped skills within existing workforces. There is evidence that part-time workers and workers from ethnic minorities, for example, are often overskilled for the jobs they do (e.g. Horrell et al., 1989). One stark example of this is the radiologist found working as a cleaner in the National Health Service (NHS) (Parkyn, 1991).

In the early 1990s, the demographic trends are masked by economic recession, but the underlying features remain and skill shortages are predicted to emerge as soon as recovery gets underway.

Efficient management of human resources Discriminatory practices are often attacked as part of a web of poor personnel procedures and bad management policies while EO is presented as good, professional management which encourages the efficient use of human resources (e.g. Seear, 1981: 295).

Organizations may gain from the development of a more professional approach to the management of people, but this professional rationale for EO action may have a particular impact on personnel professionals within organizations. The IPM stresses 'personnel managers have a special leading role in combating discrimination' (IPM, 1989: 2) and recommends that personnel managers 'should promote the publication and adoption of positive equal opportunity programmes in their organizations'. Further, as Young notes (1987: 100), 'the procedural implications that follow are consonant with their own professional values . . . personnel managers stand to reap both the psychological rewards of establishing good practice and the material rewards of increased responsibility and resources within the organization.'

Better employee relations   Where disadvantaged groups (and/or those claiming to represent them) channel demands for social justice into industrial action (actual or potential), EO action may be instituted in a search for better industrial relations. The EOC (1986: 1) claims that other industrial relations benefits which accrue to EO employers include 'an improvement in motivation and performance which, in turn, can reduce turnover levels'. It says 'employers have also found that by focusing attention on the treatment of all staff at work, the implementation of equal opportunities policies stimulates a healthy and more productive atmosphere and creates a better quality of working life.'

Image   A further 'self-interest' pressure to EO action is concern for the organization's image. Clearly a company's image can be harmed by its being found to have unlawfully discriminated, but, more positively, EO can be presented as a selling point for the organization.

The audience or customers in question might be electors. In local authority employment political pressure from elected councillors, plus an awareness of diversity among recipients of council services, stimulated a number of EO policies. In some retail and other service sector companies, a need to have a staff more representative of the customer base has been an incentive to act. This may arise where the company is based in areas of high ethnic minority population or, more generally, where organizations are developing a greater customer service orientation and attempting to 'get close to the customer'.

The concern may also be with how the organization is perceived by potential applicants and existing staff. In this case, an EOP may be adopted to project the image of a 'good employer' which 'puts people first', thereby presenting the company as a quality organization in order to attract and retain quality people.

Particular organizations may be expected to have variants on this aspect of self-interest. For example, the BBC sees itself as holding others accountable and so must demand high standards of itself. The Corporation also perceives a need for a workforce representative of the community at large to contribute to diversity in programme making (*Industrial Relations Review and Report*, 1990b), a way the organization can gain from having diversity among its employees.

Gaining from diversity   The theme of organizational self-interest being served by recognizing that there is value added by having blacks, women etc. fully represented at all levels within the organization is more dominant at present in the American personnel management literature than in the British. In the US there has been a move away from a concern with equal employment opportunity, seen as largely compliance based, towards valuing diversity (Copeland, 1988a; 1988b). The idea is that organizations recognize the benefits that multi-culturalism can bring to them, 'including, for instance, the challenging of stereotypical opinions and traditional assumptions . . . (T)he talents and attributes of people from different backgrounds and heritages are fully valued, utilized and developed' (Greenslade, 1991). This argument has particular self-interest appeal to organizations operating in a context where minority groups are important customers and in a country, like the USA, where they constitute the fastest growing segment of the population.

Compliance and penalty avoidance

Law   The major external factor underpinning the compliance approach is equality legislation. There is extensive national legislation operating in the UK within the context of European law (which is particularly concerned with equality between men and women since the Treaty of Rome does not explicitly cover racial discrimination). Figures 8.1 and 8.2 provide a summary overview of relevant European and national legislation. Figure 8.2 merely sketches some key legal provisions and does not attempt to provide comprehensive coverage nor detail of the legislation. Figure 8.3 indicates how direct

---

Article 119 of the EEC Treaty. Directly applicable. Equal pay for equal work between men and women

Equal pay Directive 1975 (75/117/EEC). Extends Art. 119 to include equal pay for work of equal value

Equal Treatment Directive 1976 (76/207/EEC). Outlaws sex discrimination in all aspects of employment

Equal Treatment Directive (state social security) 1978 (79/7/EEC). Equality of treatment in all state benefits except pensions

Equal Treatment Directive (occ. social security) 1986 (86/378/EEC). Equality in occupational benefits except pensions (now overridden by the *Barber* case where ECJ ruled definition of pay under Art. 119 includes pensions)

Equal Treatment Directive (self employed) 1986 (86/613/EEC)

Protection of Pregnant Workers Directive (92/85/EEC). Requires 14 weeks' paid maternity leave, right to return and protection from dismissal for all pregnant workers, regardless of service, and special health and safety provisions.

Figure 8.1 Relevant key European provisions

and indirect discrimination are defined and the legal penalties which apply when a claim of sex or race discrimination is upheld.

As figure 8.1 indicates, the major legislative focus in Britain is on sex and race discrimination. Legal intervention in the area of disability falls far short of outlawing discrimination. These legislative priorities are reflected in voluntary EO initiatives. But other forms of discrimination exist (for example, age, class, sexual orientation) and some EOPs attempt to embrace other disadvantaged groups also. The impact of the legislation in shaping equality agendas and practice is indicated by the continuing extent of overt age discrimination (even by equal opportunity employers) in the UK compared to other countries where this form of discrimination has been outlawed (Tillsley, 1990; *Equal Opportunities Review*, 1993b).[1] The main focus of this chapter is sex and race.

Individuals may complain of discrimination on grounds covered by the legislation and seek to enforce their statutory rights through the industrial tribunal system. The equality commissions have statutory investigative powers as well as a role in aiding individual complainants and in giving advice and issuing guidance on the legislative requirements and the promotion of EO. The legislative threat therefore centres on the adverse publicity and the direct and indirect costs that a tribunal claim or commission investigation would involve.

Threatened or actual investigations by the equality commissions have helped stimulate progress in a number of sectors. In 1983, for

---

Equal Pay Act 1970 (amended by ***Equal Value (Amendment) Regulations 1983***).
Equal pay and other contractual conditions for men and women where engaged on
same or similar work; work rated as equivalent by job evaluation, or where work is of
equal value.

Sex Discrimination Act 1976, SDA 1986. Prohibits direct and indirect discrimination in
all areas of employment on grounds of sex or married status. Sex may be a genuine
occupational qualification (GOQ) in specified circumstances (including for reasons of
authenticity, decency and privacy; delivery of a personal welfare service; certain
employment in a single sex establishment). Special treatment permitted in respect of
pregnancy and childbirth; and to encourage applications from, and to provide training
for, under-represented sex. Discriminatory terms in collective agreement or employers'
rules rendered void.

Social Security Act 1989. Equality in occupational benefit schemes (including health
insurance and pensions).

Employment Protection (Consolidation) Act 1978 (as amended). Maternity rights
(maternity leave, with pay; right to return after leave); time off for ante-natal care.

Race Relations Act 1976 (not applicable in Northern Ireland). Prohibits direct and
indirect discrimination in all areas of employment on grounds of race, colour, nationality,
ethnic or national origins (includes some religious groups, e.g. Sikhs and Jews). Race
may be a GOQ in specified circumstances (including authenticity, delivering welfare
service). Special treatment permitted to encourage applications from, and to provide
training for, under-represented group. Particular action allowed by local authorities.

Fair Employment (Northern Ireland) Act 1989 (not applicable in Great Britain).
Outlaws discrimination on grounds of religious belief or political opinion. Employers
required to register with Fair Employment Commission, to monitor religious composition
of their workforce and, in the case of employers of over 250, applicants submit
monitoring returns annually. Required to take 'affirmative action' where imbalances are
evident, such action enforceable by the Commission.

Disabled Persons (Employment) Act 1944. Duty on employers with 20 or more staff
to employ a quota of 3 per cent registered disabled people. Registration is voluntary.
Provides for reserved and sheltered employment.

Companies Act 1985 requires employers with over 250 staff to state in the directors'
annual report how their policy has operated with respect to people with disabilities,
registered or not.

Figure 8.2 Key aspects of UK legislation

example, the possibility of an investigation by the EOC in Barclays
bank led to reform of the bank's recruitment and selection practices,
and an EOC formal investigation into Leeds Building Society helped
stimulate a reconsideration of mobility requirements in the finance
industry. CRE investigations into Yorkshire Passenger Transport
Authority had spin-offs for other areas of passenger transport, including in London (Hackett 1988: 51). Its investigation policy
was to target high profile, household name companies to provide
examples likely to encourage more widespread action.

In the case of equal pay, the disruption to an organization's whole
pay structure which a single claim potentially could involve is an

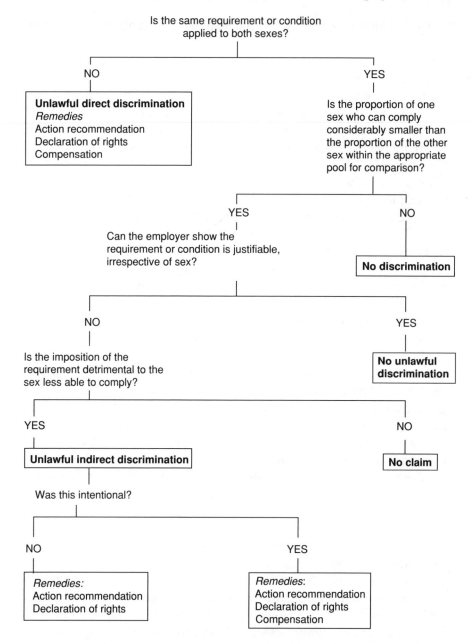

Note: The same approach applies to determining direct/indirect race discrimination

Figure 8.3 Discrimination: definition and remedies

added incentive for employers to take pre-emptive action rather than wait for legal challenge. An example of the potential impact of the use of the law by an individual employee can be seen in supermarket retailing. In 1987 a checkout operative employed by the major food retailer, J. Sainsbury, compared her job to that of a warehouseman and claimed equal pay for work of equal value. The company agreed an out of court settlement and reviewed its pay structure, leading to an increased salary bill for the company of 4 per cent above the annual wage settlement. Grading and pay structure revisions followed in other major food retailers. A recently agreed scheme for employees in the Co-operative Retail societies has upgraded checkout operators, with their pay rising 6.8 per cent, and checkout operators will also gain from a new pay structure agreed in Asda. Marks and Spencer is among other leading employers who reviewed their pay structures also, although they have frozen the pay of the male warehouse staff as a means of helping achieve pay equality.

The threat of numerous individual claims for equal pay has been a tactic used by some unions to persuade employers to review grading structures (for example, in respect of ancilliary workers in the NHS and in parts of the electricity industry). The major regrading exercise in the local authority manual sector provides a good example of how the incorporation of equal value considerations into a grading structure (with value being attached, for example, to caring skills and responsibility for people) can improve women's relative pay position in terms of basic rates if not take-home pay, since the latter can be distorted by differential bonus payments which favour male occupations (Dickens et al., 1988; LEVEL, 1987).

Contract compliance Externally imposed standards with which organizations have to comply may be imposed by means other than legislation. For example, an organization can use its economic power (as purchaser of goods or services) to force those who deal with it to conform to minimum standards, whether in respect of health and safety measures or EO promotion. A number of local authorities used contract compliance effectively in this way (*Equal Opportunities Review*, 1990: 26–8) but their ability to do so has been limited by the Local Government Act 1988 which prevents non-commercial factors from being taken into account in the award of a contract. The Act does allow specific questions (approved by the Minister) relating to the employment of ethnic minorities to be asked of contractors but only a small number of local authorities are using this limited provision (Commission for Racial Equality, 1992: 30).

In Northern Ireland a limited form of legally backed contract compliance is in operation in respect of religious discrimination. Loss of government contracts is used as a legislative sanction of last resort where employers fail to comply with obligations under the Fair Employment Act 1989 (McCrudden, 1991).

The existence of organizational self-interest and compliance driven pressures of the kind just outlined may be necessary to produce action for equality, but, for reasons discussed in the next section, they may not be sufficient.

Non-Adoption of EO Initiatives

Arguments that EO is good for business (organizational self-interest factors) or that discrimination is bad for business (the threat of penalties for non-compliance) clearly have not been sufficient to produce a universal adoption of equality initiatives. In trying to account for the absence of initiatives designed to promote greater equality in employment, the limitations and contingent nature of the self-interest and compliance pressures indicated above need to be recognized.

Organizational self-interest

The self-interest considerations will be experienced differently by different organizations and, indeed, pursuit of organizational self-interest may run counter to, rather than support, EO initiatives. Further, if the organizational benefits argument does promote an interest in EO, it may encourage only a selective approach. The legal compliance threat, although present, is generally weak in the UK in terms of risk of legal action and the penalties for discrimination, and it too is variable and contingent. Further, pressures potentially detrimental to EO may be in operation alongside the potentially positive factors just outlined.

The variable appeal of the self-interest arguments as between organizations can be seen, for example, in the case of changing demographics and labour market composition. Skill and labour shortages are not experienced in the same way everywhere. Even where they are perceived as problems, responses other than those favourable to promoting EO are possible, and are taken – for example, competing for scarce male labour through pay increases or by contracting out work (Atkinson, 1989; Dickens, 1989). Further, the segmentation of labour markets means that the various groups are not seen by employers as interchangeable. For example, a lack of skilled (male) labour will not necessarily lead to women being seen as a potential resource where skill is itself a male gendered concept (Philips and Taylor, 1980). Where equality initiatives are taken in response to labour market pressure, they may not be secure when those pressures cease to apply. The 'defusing' of the demographic timebomb in the recession of the early 1990s led to some backsliding in the detail and extent of equality provisions – for example, removing guarantees of re-employment after a career break and cutting childcare facilities (Dickens, 1993).

An organization's capacity to respond to changing labour markets in ways likely to be beneficial for EO requires an awareness of the situation, which is often lacking, and adequate, qualitative human resource planning. The effective and full utilization of the labour force also calls for investment in training. As is described elsewhere in this volume, UK organizations rarely score highly in these areas. Women and ethnic minorities are often disadvantaged in access to training, whether provided by employing organizations or the state (Clarke, 1991; Lee and Wrench, 1987; Pollert, 1985) and the training provided may reinforce rather than challenge job segregation (Cockburn, 1987).

Part of the argument that EO is good for business is that 'equal opportunities are cost-effective' (Equal Opportunities Commission, 1986: 1). Unfortunately, economic rationality does not necessarily point to EO practice. There can be cost advantages to the employer, for example, in the undervaluing of women's labour. It can be cheap to use ethnic origin, or other group characteristics or stereotypes, as screening devices in selection, a practice which helps reproduce patterns of gender and race segregation. Informal recruitment methods, such as word-of-mouth recruiting, often constitute indirect race and sex discrimination yet they may be attractive as cheap options for employers, particularly in times of recession where there is a reluctance to use open advertising because of the cost and difficulty in processing lots of applications (Wood, 1986). Recruitment costs are saved also by allowing workers to seek applicants through use of their social and familial networks rather than undertaking active, open recruitment (Fevre, 1989). Cost advantages for employers accrue from having disadvantaged groups on the labour market, as can be seen in respect of employers' ability to gain numerical flexibility cheaply through atypical working (Dickens, 1992a).

Atypical working (part-time, temporary and home-work) is disproportionally performed by women. This in part reflects a constrained choice for women (particularly those with children) in the absence of equality in the labour market and in the home, influenced by broader state and social policies (for instance, on childcare, welfare and taxation (Dex and Walters, 1989)). Institutional and ideological constraints on women's labour market choices facilitate their use as cheap disadvantaged labour (Brannen, 1989; Dickens, 1992a: 34–7). For some employers in the finance sector, for example, the use of part-time workers, including bringing back mothers who have previous work experience in the industry, offers several advantages: lower salary costs, more flexibility, reduced staffing levels and lower training costs (Ashburner, 1988). But such part-time jobs are not necessarily tied into career structures and regular grading schemes, and may not be rewarded in proportion to full-time jobs.

Because cost benefit analysis is not always likely to favour the adoption of EO measures (at least in the short run), an appeal to 'the bottom line' may not stimulate EO action, particularly as the cost of thoroughgoing EOPs can be high. The BBC estimated the short-term annual cost of its EO programme (covering race, gender and disability) at £2–2.5 million (*Industrial Relations Review and Report*, 1990b). Any financial returns on cost in under four years were seen as unlikely and it was recognized that it would be impossible probably ever to show in accounting terms that the full cost of investment had been recouped. The BBC can point to other gains to justify its expenditure, such as the image of the company in the labour market and wider community, and a positive impact on quality of broadcasting output, but such compensating gains are not going to be perceived by, or be relevant to, all organizations.

Although smaller organizations will face smaller costs than those just cited, many of them, starting off with undeveloped personnel policies and practices and an absence of detailed personnel records, will have to bear considerable costs simply to get to first base.

The cost–benefit equation, however, is not static. Publicity given to successful tribunal claims and high awards against employers for discrimination, or to a formal investigation by one of the equality commissions, may have an impact, particularly on employers in the same sector. The cost–benefit equation will be affected also by the reaction of those who are discriminated against. Large costs may be incurred through not taking equality action where disadvantaged groups push their demands through industrial action, as black workers and women (and, indeed, black women) have done (e.g. Wrench, 1987).

Trade unions, of course, can exert pressure for equality through collective bargaining, but, again, this is variable. Unions historically do not have a good record in tackling discrimination, and the exclusion strategies of unions against women and blacks have helped underpin job segregation and employment disadvantage (e.g. Boston, 1987; Phizacklea and Miles, 1987: 124). Unions in some areas have been negotiating for improvements in women's pay and conditions and pushing for EOPs, and equality structures for women, ethnic minorities and, at times, other groups (for example, gay and lesbian members) have been established within unions (Dickens, 1993; Ellis, 1988; SERTUC, 1992; Labour Research Department, 1988). On the other hand union officials, often at local level, have been found condoning or colluding in management discrimination against women and ethnic minorities despite national level statements of commitment to equality (Snell et al., 1991; Colling and Dickens, 1989; Commission for Racial Equality, 1981; *Equal Opportunities Review*, 1993c: 9). Elsewhere unions may not take action because those with power within the union or in negotiating positions (disproportionately white men) share management's complacency that there is no problem, do not prioritize equality issues and/or lack detailed knowledge of how indirect discrimination occurs and how it might be tackled (Colling and Dickens, 1989; Heery and Kelly, 1988).

Although unions can apply positive pressure for EO through collective bargaining, thereby increasing the costs to employers of doing nothing, they also can exert countervailing pressure. Unions may defend the status quo by protecting the interests of male white workers, defining such interests as 'members' interests' and classifying the divergent interests of women or other disadvantaged groups as 'special', 'sectional' or even trivial (e.g. Lee, 1987; Colling and Dickens, 1989; Cunninson, 1983). Unions' ability to exert pressure for the adoption of equality initiatives also depends on their organizational and bargaining strength which has been weakened in the 1980s and 1990s through adverse economic conditions, legislative attack and some employer strategies.

Arguing for equality initiatives on the grounds that the promotion of greater employment equality makes good business sense in fact may be problematic for EO achievement. Such arguments may encourage action, but only in areas where it is clear that EO and business needs do immediately coincide. Further, once the debate about equality is conducted in terms of what is in the company's best interests, EO initiatives can be contested and resisted as irrelevant or marginal to the best or real interests of the organization, as defined by those currently in positions of power, or as measured in terms of short-term contribution to the bottom line.

Equality initiatives motivated by a search for organizational benefits can lead to the targeting of initiatives to reflect employer needs rather than the needs of the disadvantaged groups. An organization can benefit from a selective approach to equality, perhaps addressing only one particular problem: a general approach may be more costly, and thus less clearly in the interests of the organization. For example, enhanced maternity provision and career breaks targeted at women in higher grades, or 'high flyers', helps keep those women in whom training has been invested, thereby retaining scarce skills for the organization, and at the same time provides a positive image for the company. The extension of such provision to all women in the organization, including those in low level jobs where no labour or skill shortages exist, although potentially a good move for EO, would be more costly, less attuned with the needs of the organization and, thus, can be argued against using the 'best interests of the business' rhetoric.

Often, targeted EO initiatives seem to be about clearing the way for the advancement of individual blacks or individual women rather than about changing the position for significantly large groups of blacks or women within the organization. In studying an organization where initiatives had been taken which had increased the proportion of women in management, Cockburn (1991: 74) notes that if the concern had been the value of the labour of women at the bottom of the organization, the issues raised would have been different, namely, training for less skilled women, harmonization of part-time and full-time terms and conditions, job re-evaluations and regrading, and narrowing of pay differentials.

Compliance and penalty avoidance

Turning to the second cluster of factors providing pressure for equality initiatives, those to do with avoiding penalties for non-compliance, we have already noted the weakening of the contract compliance lever. It is indisputable, however, that the enactment of equality legislation and key decisions by the national and, particularly in recent years, the European courts, have provided an important stimulus to action in respect of the removal of race and sex discrimination and in the area of equal pay between men and women. However, the nature and extent of that action varies.

Legislation can be a lever to wider reform, especially if it operates in conjunction with other factors. It provides an important statement of public policy as well as providing for rights and remedies and imposing duties. But the action stimulated by law as an external factor operating on organizations may be that of avoidance rather than compliance, with organizations seeking to minimize the likely impact of the law.

This happened, for example, in response to the original Equal Pay Act (Snell et al., 1981), with some employers ensuring that male and female workers were not employed on work that might be seen as the same or similar under the provisions of the Act. While this tactic is no longer open, following the equal value amendment, which allows comparisons of dissimilar jobs to be made, some employers have sought to protect themselves through adopting job evaluation schemes. Formalizing and making explicit the basis for payment structures and pay differences through job evaluation can help expose and remove discrimination. There is, however, the risk that the introduction of job evaluation may serve to legitimate or obscure discrimination rather than remove it and make an equal pay challenge less likely to be made or to succeed. Outside the pay area, there is evidence of direct discrimination giving way to more covert, indirect discrimination (e.g. Collinson and Knights, 1985).

Even if compliance action is taken in respect of the law, little is actually required by way of positive action from employers and, at times, as Gregory notes (1989: 101), the judiciary have seemed more concerned 'with policing the equality laws to ensure they do not ride roughshod over employers than with policing employers to ensure that the laws are observed'. An example of this is provided by the scope allowed to employers by the national courts to justify indirect discrimination (with small advantages to the employer sufficing to make the discriminatory requirement justifiable) until a more robust interpretation of the concept emerged following a lead given by the European Court of Justice (Dickens, 1992b: 119–20).

Compliance with the letter of the equality law does not take an organization far along the EO path. The law requires an end to discrimination: it does not actually require that employers do anything to promote equality. Although an EOP might be a useful defence in any legal claim against an organization, the development of such a policy is not required by law. Apart from religious monitoring in Northern Ireland, there is no requirement for employers to audit or monitor their workforces (although recent decisions indicate it is advisable to do so). Most forms of positive action to aid disadvantaged groups are prevented by the legislation, which equally protects white males, and which is concerned with halting present discrimination but does nothing to overcome the effects of past discrimination.[2]

Apart from the now little used investigation powers of the equality commissions, rights in Britain are conferred on individuals to challenge discriminatory behaviour rather than responsibilities being imposed on administrative, employing, governmental and other organizations to take action to tackle disadvantage. The emphasis is on action by victims rather than action by power-wielders (Lustgarten, 1987; Dickens, 1986), an approach less likely to lead to EO action.

Although the legal requirements are limited (for a more detailed discussion, see Dickens, 1992b), arguably the full potential of what compliance with the *spirit* of the law requires is not reflected in current practice. Potentially the concept of indirect discrimination is a far-reaching one, which could be utilized to throw into question much of the taken-for-granted practice in organizations and to tackle structural discrimination. But research shows a lack of understanding of the concept of indirect discrimination, and many companies which feel they have done enough to comply with the law have focused only on the more obvious direct discrimination. Similarly, in respect of equal pay for equal value work, many organizations consider the changes they made at the time of the original equal pay legislation to be sufficient, despite the subsequent important legislative change, about which many negotiators are ill-informed (Colling and Dickens, 1989; Industrial Relations Services/Equal Opportunities Commission, 1991).

Although organizations may be vulnerable to legal challenge, in practice the risk appears small. Investigations by the equality commissions are infrequent (especially since judicial interpretation of their statutory powers restricted their scope for action) and individual applications to industrial tribunals remain relatively scarce and meet with limited success, as shown in table 8.1.

Table 8.1 Discrimination claims to industrial tribunals 1990–1991

	Sex discrimination	*Equal pay*	*Race discrimination*
ACAS conciliated			
settlement	335	64	185
Withdrawn	424	246	371
Total not heard	759	310	556
% of all cases	*70*	*61*	*60*
Case dismissed by tribunal	220	25	269
Otherwise disposed of	21	163	54
Case successful at tribunal	78	10	47
% success rate★	*24.5*	*5*	*13*
Total cases heard	319	198	370
Total cases disposed of	1078	508	926

★ proportion of heard cases which were successful at tribunal hearing
Source: *Employment Gazette* 1991: 682

As the table indicates, only a small proportion of cases is actually determined by the industrial tribunals and success rates for applicants are not very high. About one-third of race discrimination claims were determined by tribunals in 1990–1, with 15 per cent (47) being upheld. In 27 cases, awards were made: the median compensation award was £1749. Five people received awards of £3000 and over. Twenty-eight per cent of sex discrimination claims were determined by tribunals in the same period: 26 per cent of these (78) were successful and compensation was awarded in 50 cases. The median compensation was £1142, with three people receiving awards of £8000 and over. Compensation awards in discrimination cases include an element for 'injury to feelings' and average awards under this head, particularly in race discrimination and sexual harassment cases, have increased in recent years following two Court of Appeal decisions in 1988 which made it clear that such awards should not be nominal (*Equal Opportunities Review*, 1992c: 30–5). However, as the median figures indicate, awards in practice still fall far short of the maximum permitted in the statute.[3]

Thirty-five equal pay claims were heard by tribunals in 1990–1: ten (29 per cent) were successful. The large number of withdrawals under this jurisdiction may reflect the use of the legislation by trade unions as a tool in bargaining, as indicated earlier.

Where discrimination is found, the emphasis in the statute is on compensating the individual rather than requiring the employers to change their behaviour. There have been repeated calls by the commissions (e.g. Equal Opportunities Commission, 1990), and lobbying groups, for the law to be strengthened, since the risk of a legal challenge at present is seen to provide an inadequate deterrent to discriminatory behaviour, and for the enforcement procedures and mechanisms to be made more 'user friendly'.

Countervailing pressures

As well as indicating the sometimes weak and contingent nature of the organizational self-interest and compliance factors in providing a pressure for EO action, we need to note that there are also external pressures which are making it less likely that equality initiatives will be taken.

Public policy may send contradictory signals to employers on equality. The UK government is urging various EO actions on employers, supporting EOPs and action plans, and as an employer (in the Civil Service) has developed a number of equality initiatives. Yet it has been found in breach of European equality law on more than one occasion, and has opposed or weakened European Commission initiatives which many see as beneficial to women. The recent Directive on pregnant workers which, among other things, extends the coverage and length of paid maternity leave, was adopted, with the UK abstaining, only in a weakened form after UK opposition. The adoption of Directives on atypical workers, which seek to extend pro rata rights and benefits to part-time and temporary employees, who are disproportionately women, is being blocked by UK opposition (Dickens, 1992a). Further, the UK continues to be one of the worst providers of publicly funded childcare in Europe, which constrains women's employment choices (Moss, 1990).

Deregulationary labour law policies pursued by governments since 1979 have weakened statutory employment rights, pushing more women in particular outside employment protections. Although government ministers publicly deplore continuing race and sex discrimination, no government action has been taken on the detailed legislative reform proposals made by EOC and CRE, and both agencies have complained of underfunding and inadequate resources to cope with an increasing demand for their services (Equal Opportunities Commission, 1992).

A context of economic recession is also unfavourable to EO progress. Equality initiatives may seem a luxury in a time of job loss, reduced employment opportunities and financial restraint. Those employers, for example, trying to alter the ethnic composition of their workforces will find it particularly difficult to do so in a time of little or no recruitment. Indeed ethnic minority workers appear to be disproportionately affected by current job losses, in part a reflection of their particular regional and industrial distribution.

In the public sector, restructuring, growing commercialism and financial restraint provide reasons or opportunities for limiting or abandoning EO initiatives rather than affirming or building on them. A number of local authority equality units are under threat. Abolishing equality units does not necessarily save a lot of money but, argues Cooper (1991), often their controversial demands are seen as a nuisance and readily expendable in a time of cuts.

As noted, the government severely curtailed contract compliance in the public sector. It also has imposed compulsory contracting out requirements on public sector employers which have led to a deterioration in women's jobs, hours and conditions (Coyle, 1985; Public Services Privatisation Research Unit, 1992). Equality initiatives which have been taken in the public sector may be under threat from decentralization and fragmentation and from developments such as contracting out and market testing (where equality measures may add to the cost of in-house provision when compared to external tenders). Parkyn (1991: 33) notes 'at least one trust hospital has already chosen to remove the General Whitley Council equal opportunities agreement from its employment package and has scrapped its own career break scheme'.

This section has explored factors which may provide pressure towards the adoption of equality initiatives and sought to explain why, despite such factors, initiatives may not be taken. The next section looks at why achievements might be limited, even where EOPs are adopted.

Limited Achievements of EO Initiatives

It was noted earlier that equality initiatives in some organizations go no further than a declaration that they are EO employers. This may reflect complacency – a public declaration that there is 'no problem here'. The mere presence of ethnic minorities or women in an organization may be pointed to as evidence of no unfair discrimination or the existence of equality since many organizations fail to recognize that global numbers may mask marked disparities in distribution (Jewson et al., 1990: 11). Adopting a policy, therefore, does not necessarily indicate an intention to change the status quo. It can be seen, rather, as a declaration or symbolic ratification of current practice, an 'affirmation that customary behaviour conforms to the cannons of acceptability' (Young, 1987: 98).

Many organizations, however, do seek to go beyond applying the label and follow the steps indicated in the guidance from the equality commissions and elsewhere. And yet, as we have seen, there may be relatively little achievement in terms of distributional outcomes. In seeking to explain this relative lack of achievement when EO initiatives *are* taken, I shall first look at the problems of translating EO prescription into practice, and then consider the inadequacies of EO prescription itself.

EO policy and practice

The intention of EOPs can be neutralized through procedures being neglected or allowed to atrophy, or by being followed in the letter but not in the spirit. As Jenkins (1986) found in recruitment and selection, 'espoused' models (what we say we do) and 'operational' models (what we actually do) can differ considerably.

Part of the explanation for the inadequate translation of the EO prescription into practice is the distribution of power within organizations. Procedures operate within an organizational context and power in decision making may not be in the hands of the guardians of good practice, namely the personnel managers, who are likely to have developed the espoused model. Personnel managers, for example, are often marginal to selection decisions, with real power being vested in line managers (Collinson et al., 1990; Jenkins, 1986). Some organizations appoint EO managers, who may or may not be based in the personnel department, but their power and status can be just as problematic and the EO function is often understaffed and under-resourced. 'They are sometimes beleaguered, lonely figures, who have to steer a course between trying to get line managers to understand how discrimination works and not being labelled a feminist or a loony lefty' (Hackett, 1988: 52).

Line managers may resist the formalization, accountability and monitoring required by EOPs as interference with their discretion in decision making. Any change can be threatening and unwelcome but this may be exacerbated in the case of EO in that it may be seen as a challenge to personal attitudes and traditional local norms or values. EO may be experienced as criticism of those in power: managers and others can be affronted by assumptions that they discriminate. As Jones (1988: 43) notes, even fairly low-key initiatives, such as redesign of application forms, 'implicitly and overtly cast aspersions on and criticize management'.

The personnel function, or the EO office, may be viewed as 'external' by line managers. EO initiatives then become seen as external imposition and, therefore, dismissed as not relevant. In such circumstances procedures are likely to suffer from neglect or manipulation and decision makers are likely to use the discretion inevitably left to them within procedures to continue as before.

Problems with the prescription

Focusing on the reasons why prescription may be translated inadequately into practice might suggest that adequate implementation would produce desired outcomes. This is not so. Fair procedures do not necessarily produce fair (distributive justice) outcomes, as Jewson and Mason (1986) and others have argued cogently.

The prescriptive model of recruitment and selection embodied in EOPs, for instance, advocates a focus on unbiased assessment: assessing individuals against relevant, job related criteria rather than according to their membership of a particular social group. The emphasis is on suitability criteria (technical ability to do the job) rather than acceptability criteria (attitudinal, behavioural, personality factors), a distinction made by Jenkins (1986) whose research showed how the latter tend to interact with racial stereotypes and lead to discrimination.

But strict adherence to suitability criteria can still lead to the continued appointment of white men (Webb and Liff, 1988; Jewson and Mason, 1986; Liff, 1989). The emphasis in the prescriptive model is on the assessment of an individual's skills, attributes and qualifications against the suitability requirements of the job and the assumption is that this will remove unfair discrimination and produce EO outcomes. Given the construction of such skills and the current distribution of skills, attributes and qualifications in society, however, not all individuals will be able to demonstrate their suitability for the job to the same extent and the composition of the current workforce is likely to be reproduced. Individuals within disadvantaged groups may be able to meet criteria developed around the usual incumbents – white able-bodied men – but, at best, this is EO as individual advancement rather than the advancement of social groups: it is an exclusive or selective equality which may aid a few 'honorary white men' but leaves the position of the many untouched.

Further, as Jenkins (1986) acknowledges, and Curran's work clearly demonstrates, in practice suitability and acceptability criteria may overlap. Curran (1988: 348), investigating the filling of vacancies in the service sector found recruiters' selection criteria of 'acceptability' and 'suitability' were inextricably linked and these linkages were operationalized in the perception of specific job vacancies as gendered jobs. Both gender and a variety of personal attributes (social and tacit skills) in which gender (and possibly race) is embedded are regarded by many employers as specific and functional attributes and as requirements for the effective performance of particular jobs.[4] The prescriptive model urges attention to whether selection criteria are 'relevant' to the job but, because of the way in which jobs are gendered, masculinity, or a typical male working and domestic life pattern, can constitute an 'essential' qualification and necessary quality for occupancy of key positions.

Implicit in much good practice equality prescription is an argument that discrimination arises from actions of prejudiced individuals, that it is irrational behaviour, indicative of poor management practice, and that it can be curbed by detailed instructions, training and policing. This neglects the fact that organizational ends can be served by not following the prescription and that, as a result, unfair discrimination can be rational and efficient for an individual and the organization.

Perceived cost advantages to organizations in continuing discriminatory practices have been discussed earlier. Other advantages for the employer in terms of control of the labour force or in the organization of the labour process also may be secured by continuing such practices as recruitment through existing employees, utilizing the extended internal labour market (Maguire, 1986; Manwaring, 1983); or through emphasizing acceptability ('fitting-in') criteria, for example in the search for multi-skilling and flexibility through team-working. Despite the problematic nature of acceptability criteria for EO, organizations may consider it easier to add suitability (in terms of technical skill) to acceptability (in terms of behavioural characteristics and fitting in with co-workers and with organizational cultures and control systems) rather than the other way round.

Since there can be an organizational rationality in continuing discrimination, it becomes rational for individuals within the organization to act in ways detrimental to EO. This is not necessarily a conscious process. Where sexism and racism have become institutionalized, it is simply adherence to normal practice – 'the way things are done around here'. An organization may have adopted an EOP but individuals will respond to signals (formal and informal) about what 'really matters' in the organization and, therefore, what behaviour is likely to ensure success within it. This applies as much to those in personnel management as elsewhere.

Personnel managers, particularly at local level, may play a role in recruitment and selection but their involvement is not always likely to foster the professional EO model. Local personnel managers 'often contribute to the reproduction of both highly vague and informal selection criteria, channels and procedures, and sex discriminatory practices' (Collinson, 1991: 58). This links in part to the fact that many local personnel managers are transferred line managers with 'no allegiance to those principles and ideals of the personnel profession that could conflict with the more immediate and short-term managerial priorities or profit and production' (ibid.: 59). But even those who are professionals (members of the IPM) may elevate their organizational identity over their professional identity in order to be viewed as effective and to promote personal career progress. The alternative on offer is what many EO managers experience: 'a very unpopular and stressful role . . . (which) . . . offers little reward in terms of career development' (Holland, 1988: 20).

Personnel managers and EO staff need to be seen to contribute to the core values of the organization. This conflicts with the promotion of EO because only rarely is it a core value. EO tends to be marginal in organizations rather than mainstream; a bolt-on rather than a strategic objective. It is regarded often as the concern of those discriminated against, or as the concern of the EO officer, rather than an organizational concern, and equality objectives are not often integrated into general appraisal, reward or disciplinary mechanisms. EO structures, if they exist, are often isolated from other structures. In such circumstances it becomes possible, as Cockburn (1989) found, to argue the 'main aim' (what the business is really about) *against* EO.

EO may be advocated as good management practice but, unless it is a mainstream objective, priority will be given to other good management practices which serve organizational objectives and which may conflict with the tenor or requirements of EO. This can be seen in a range of current personnel developments. For example, monitoring and pursuing equal pay becomes difficult in the context of the individualization of pay systems and the spread of merit and individual performance-related pay. Performance-related pay is often spread unevenly in an organization and contains scope for subjective appraisal which may lead to discriminatory pay practices (Townley, 1990: Industrial Relations Services/Equal Opportunities Commission, 1991; Kessler, this volume, ch. 14). Attempts to impose an EO policy and monitor it from a central personnel department are hampered by increased decentralization in organizations, an emphasis on devolution and power to the line, with management 'owning' their own decisions, etc. In short, a number of practices currently associated with the 'human resource management' approach may be at odds with the promotion of equal opportunity.

It can be organizationally 'rational' to continue to discriminate despite the adoption of an EOP. Managers prioritizing organizational loyalties, or seeing their personal success linked to so doing, will also find it rational to discriminate for reasons other than, or in addition to, individual prejudice. Problems in implementing EOPs also reflect vested interests in the status quo within organizations which confer further rationality on discrimination – these tend to be underplayed by prescriptive models.

A key implementation problem in respect of EO 'is that support for taking action designed to improve prospects for women, ethnic minorities and the disabled must come from an overwhelmingly white, male and 'non-disabled' dominant group who may well regard equal opportunities as a threat' (Lovenduski, 1989: 15). The threat comes in part from the fact that white men's characteristic career paths are implicitly predicated on the existence of 'unpromotable' categories, including women and blacks (Crompton and Jones, 1984: 248). EO is not necessarily the win-win game portrayed in the prescriptive literature.

The threat is not simply to career opportunities. Work is a place where identities are shaped and lived out. For men, work can be an affirmation of their masculinity: equal opportunities, the entry of women into that work, or paying women equivalent wages, can seem like an attack on that identity. Few organizations have attempted to tackle the issue of gender conditioning (for one example, see Cameron, 1987). The entry of 'outsiders' may be seen also as a threat to valued social organization and social group identity in the workplace (Salaman, 1986). Such social organization is often homosocial (Lipman-Blumen, 1976) and exclusion tactics include sexual harassment.

To take another example, sexual harassment is an issue which is increasingly on the EO agenda. An EC Code of Practice has been issued and the Employment Department has produced an employer's guide to combating sexual harassment (*Industrial Relations Review and Report*, 1992: 6). But the link between sexual harassment and occupational segregation and the perpetuation of male power within organizations is not often acknowledged in the practitioner literature, the problem being presented rather as one of protecting individual women from deviant individual men. Those who seek to cross gender boundaries by entering non-traditional work often find their masculinity or femininity questioned, as with young people attempting to take up training for non-traditional jobs (Cockburn, 1987), or find themselves subjected to harassment. A Leeds-based survey (cited in Purcell, 1988: 174) found that women working in typically male environments were twice as likely to report having experienced sexual harassment at work than other women. Such pressures help keep women 'in their place' (Seddon, 1983) and give women who are interested in retaining their femininity and avoiding harassment a vested interest in the perpetuation of the status quo.

Masculinity is not only shaped by work; it is shaped too by men's power over women in the home. The promotion of equality in employment can challenge this power. The potentially revolutionary nature of the demands being made under the banner of EO should not be underestimated in seeking to locate and explain resistance to it. As Cockburn (1991: 63) argues, for example, the claim for equal pay for work of equal value 'potentially undermines the whole strategy of exploiting women sex-specifically'.

Of course, individual white men may not feel particularly powerful or see themselves as 'the problem'. One important criticism of racism awareness training, for example, is that it is experienced by whites as a personal attack, putting individuals in the dock on behalf of white society, and is thus resented, contributing to opposition to EOPs (see the discussion in Iles and Auluck, 1989: 27–8). As Coyle (1989: 77) notes, however, although individual men may not feel powerful, 'men's strength lies in the way in which an ideology of gender, of expectations of masculinity and femininity, is lived out in the collective practice of an organization'.

But resistance to EO does not come only from white, non-disabled men. There may be resistance from within the disadvantaged groups which an EOP 'is designed to help', and this can be particularly dispiriting for the personnel or EO manager. Such resistance may arise through conflicting expectations of 'equal opportunities', a term which can mask multiple and conflicting meanings. There may be agreement at the symbolic level giving an illusion of common cause, but underlying differences in understanding and expectations can lead to feelings of betrayal (Young, 1987: 4; Jewson and Mason, 1986: 309). Opposition to EO initiatives may be occasioned through fear of blacklash, or of being seen to have achieved a position based on grounds other than 'merit'. Those few from disadvantaged groups who have 'made it' within organizations may resist EO initiatives on the grounds that as they did it 'unaided', anyone should be able to.

Resistance may arise also because there are divisions between disadvantaged groups. The assumption of shared interest implicit in much universalistic EO prescription is misplaced. For example, seniority rules may advantage ethnic minority men in an organization where there is low turnover, but may not be of advantage necessarily to women with interrupted employment patterns. Certain disadvantaged groups, in particular circumstances, may have an interest in the EO prescription *not* being followed. Jewson and Mason (1986), for example, found in their study that the formalization of recruitment and selection in the name of EO damaged existing informal channels of communication valued by the ethnic minorities and there was resentment over the refusal of a new personnel manager to recognize traditional links with an Asian broker.

Divisions also exist within any one disadvantaged group and, consequently, interests may differ. Women are divided by class, ethnicity, age, occupational status, etc. Ethnic minorities are far from homogeneous, as the difficulty even in finding an adequate definition and acceptable terminology demonstrates (Iles and Auluck, 1991). Not only are there different groups (Asians, Africans, Caribbeans, Greeks and so on), but the situation and experience of men and of women within these diverse groups also differs, and other factors contribute further to diversity of interests. Among people with disabilities there is great diversity depending on the nature of disability, as well as other factors such as their gender, ethnicity etc. What all these diverse groups do have in common, however, is that they do not conform to the standard which informs and shapes formal and informal organizational structures and norms in Britain, namely, the white, non-disabled male.

Changing the Focus

The discussion so far indicates how problems of implementing equality initiatives and of obtaining substantive outcomes are rather more complex than suggested in much of the guidance literature and prescriptive equality models. The problems of obtaining desired substantive outcomes through procedural approaches has led some to argue for positive discrimination to effect distributional change. The 'radical' approach, outlined by Jewson and Mason (1986) in the context of a study of race discrimination, favours appointing candidates from disadvantaged groups regardless of the fact that they are 'less well qualified' in order to achieve desired outcomes in terms of proportional representation of various groups in the occupational hierarchy.

This approach, however, has been criticized (e.g. Webb and Liff, 1988) for sharing with the 'liberal' procedural approach, an acceptance of jobs and organizations as they are currently constructed. What is required is more than putting a black person into a white person's job (Jones, 1973, cited in Iles and Auluck, 1991). As Cockburn (1989) has noted, the radical approach focuses on gaining power not changing it: it is about attempting to advance disadvantaged groups within existing organizational structures whereas those organizational structures are what needs to be changed to better accommodate all. The 'valuing diversity' approach, discussed earlier, potentially might contain the seeds of this alternative approach in that it could open the way for different formal and informal organizational cultures and structures, reflective of diverse contributions, needs and attributes.

The changing perception of disability provides a useful pointer to what is required. Leach (1989: 65) notes a shift in focus from physical 'defects or deficiencies' to a recognition that most of the difficulties encountered by disabled people arise not from their impairment but from the systematic ignoring of their needs. Access ramps can help those with certain physical disabilities play a full part in organizational life but are necessary only because buildings have been designed originally with only the non-physically disabled in mind. Similarly, positive action for equality of opportunity for women and ethnic minorities at present usually consists of 'special measures' to help individuals in these groups compete for jobs designed with only white men in mind within organizations whose norms, values and structures are similarly shaped around the traditional incumbents and power holders, again, white men.

Initiatives such as job sharing, presented as an advance in EO for women, are such 'special measures' focused on finding ways to enable women to cope with working patterns shaped around the typical domestic circumstances of men. Various 'flexibility' initiatives such as home-working or part-time working, which are often cited as evidence of an EO approach, may be double edged in that they are seen as 'atypical' because they differ from the (male) norm (Dickens, 1992a). Developments such as career breaks and part-time work, while recognizing the current reality of women's lives, attempting to juggle waged work and domestic work, can be seen as initiatives which in practice take women out of competition for jobs or reduce labour force attachment and thus 'save' full-time jobs for men (Figart, 1992: 43). They also help perpetuate the assumption that women bear the primary responsibility for caring for and raising children. Also, the more that women are granted various kinds of work flexibility to enable them to cope with motherhood and other domestic responsibilities the more they can be dismissed as 'different', less serious than male employees (Cockburn, 1991: 92).

Opening flexible arrangements to men as well as women is preferable to seeing them as open to women only but, without further change, this may not solve the problem. Even if career breaks, for example, are open to, and taken by, both men and women (and they rarely are) they are likely to be taken for different reasons and to be regarded differently by the organization: career enhancing if time out is taken to study but career detracting if used for childcare, reflecting the low value currently placed on women's experience in household and family management despite the organizational, managerial and interpersonal skills involved.

The current focus is on helping ethnic minorities, the disabled and women compete 'on equal terms' with white non-disabled men for jobs which have been shaped around the typical circumstances of white, able-bodied men, within organizations where the culture, norms, values, notions of merit, formal and informal structures all reflect the attributes, needs, work and life patterns of the typical white non-disabled male. That is to say, there is a template for employment shaped around white, non-disabled men against which those seeking to get in and get on are measured. Rather than adopting this Procrustian approach (Dickens, 1992c), with its focus on changing individuals to fit the template in order to obtain distributive justice, the template should be abandoned.

This argument for a different focus, for what has been called by Cockburn (1989) a 'transformative EO strategy', concerned with the nature, culture, relations and purpose of the organization, should not be taken as an argument against attempting the kind of EO initiatives indicated earlier, which, as noted, can produce gains for members of disadvantaged groups. Rather, the attempt here has been to explain why such initiatives generally fail to produce substantive change in the aggregate picture of disadvantage and discrimination, and to indicate the limitations of much current prescription.

The exhortation and guidance from official bodies and personnel management manuals tend to imply that the formulation and implementation of EOPs is relatively straightforward. Ambiguities in the concept of equal opportunities tend to be glossed over: the procedural emphasis is dominant but often with the promise of substantive outcomes in terms of change in the distribution of jobs. The application of professional bureaucratic models of good practice is advocated, which it is argued will produce benefits for employers and be cost-effective. Adherence to such models is to be secured by monitoring, training and controls to counter prejudiced, irrational behaviour and 'traditional' practice. The promotion of EO is presented as a technical problem for which technical solutions (monitoring systems, rational selection criteria etc.) are appropriate.

What is neglected, as Jenkins and Solomos argue (1987: 118), is the highly political nature of the process, the need for (and difficulty in achieving) sustained commitment for 'measures whose legitimacy, either in the nation at large or in the public domain of politics, cannot by any stretch of the imagination be regarded as either secure or consensual'. Considerable investment of time, labour and other resources is called for in a context where EO may appear to conflict with, rather than serve, what the company (or key people within it) define as its best interests; where discrimination may be organizationally and individually 'rational'; and where other objectives which are accorded more importance may run counter to equality initiatives.

Much EO prescription rests on an inadequate conceptualization of the 'problem'; assumes unitary interests where divergent interests exist; pays inadequate attention to the resistance EO generates; and simplifies the reasons for it. Furthermore, what is called for generally focuses on helping individuals from disadvantaged groups get in and get on within existing organizations, with no real challenge being mounted to the nature, structure, and values of the organizations themselves.

Without acknowledging through action that current organizational cultures, norms, structures, rules and notions of merit etc. have been shaped around white, non-disabled men, and without a shift in focus away from, at best, helping people fit into jobs and organizations as presently constructed, towards changing the construction of jobs and organizations to accommodate all, achievement will always fall short of equality in employment.

Notes

1 It may be possible to argue that age discrimination constitutes unlawful (indirect) sex discrimination (e.g. *Price* v. *Civil Service Commission* [1977] IRLR 291 EAT) but cases may not succeed because of difficulties in showing that the age requirement has a disproportionate impact on women and because employers can argue age discrimination is 'justifiable' (*Jones* v. *University of Manchester* [1993] IRLR 218 EAT).
2 Although the Fair Employment Act 1989 provides for 'affirmative action' to secure 'fair participation' in the employment of Protestants and Roman Catholics, this goes little further than the sex and race discrimination legislation, adding redundancy selection in pursuance of affirmative action to the usual provisions permitting outreach recruitment and training provision for the under-represented group (McCrudden, 1992: 179–81).
3 A 1993 decision of the European Court of Justice (Marshall no 2, Case C-271/91) requires the removal of fixed upper limits on the amount of compensation recoverable for unlawful sex discrimination. Such limits are contrary to the Equal Treatment Directive as they prevent loss and damage actually sustained as the result of discrimination from being fully compensated. The decision is likely to have important implications for discrimination on other grounds also.
4 Although women's tacit skills may be sought by employers, they are

rarely positively rewarded. This is part of the systematic undervaluing of women's work. The skills which tend to be recognized and rewarded as such (for example, in job evaluation) are those normally associated with work done by men.

Bibliography

Aitkenhead, M. and Liff, S. 1991. 'The effectiveness of equal opportunity policies'. In Firth-Cozens, J. and West, M. A. (eds) *Women at Work*. Milton Keynes: Open University Press.

Asburner, L. 1988. 'Just inside the Counting House: Women in Finance'. In Coyle, A. and Skinner, J. (eds) *Women and Work: Positive Action for Change*. Basingstoke: Macmillan Education.

Atkinson, J. 1989. 'Four stages of adjustment to the demographic downturn'. *Personnel Management*, August, 20–4.

Boston, S. 1987. *Women Workers and the Trade Unions*. London: Laurence and Wishart.

Brannen, J. 1989. 'Childbirth and Occupational Mobility: Evidence from a longitudinal study'. *Work Employment and Society*, Vol. 3, No. 2, 179–201.

Brennan, G. and McGeevor, P. 1987. *The employment of graduates from ethnic minorities*. London: Commission for Racial Equality.

Brennan, G. and McGeevor, P. 1988. *Graduates at work: degree courses and the labour market*. London: Jessica Kingsley.

Breugel, I. 1989. 'Sex and race in the labour market'. *Feminist Review*, Vol. 32, Summer.

Brown, C. 1984. *Black and White in Britain*. London: Heinemann.

Brown, C. and Gay, P. 1985. *Racial Discrimination 17 Years after the Act*. London: Policy Studies Institute.

Cabinet Office. 1992. *Equal Opportunities for Women in the Civil Service: Progress Report 1991–2*. London: HMSO.

Cameron, I. 1987. 'Realising the Dividends from Positive Action'. *Personnel Management*, October.

Clarke, K. 1991. *Women and Training. A Review*. Manchester: Equal Opportunities Commission.

Cockburn, C. 1987. *Two-Track Training*. Basingstoke: Macmillan Education.

Cockburn, C. 1989. 'Equal opportunities: the short and long agenda'. *Industrial Relations Journal*, Vol. 20, No. 3, 213–25.

Cockburn, C. 1991. *In the Way of Women. Men's Resistance to Sex Equality in Organisations*. Basingstoke: Macmillan Education.

Colling, T. and Dickens, L. 1989. *Equality Bargaining – Why Not?* London: HMSO.

Collinson, D. 1991. ' "Poachers turned Gamekeepers": Are Personnel Managers One of the Barriers to Equal Opportunities?'. *Human Resource Management Journal*, Vol. 1, No. 3, Spring.

Collinson, D. and Knights, D. 1985. 'Jobs for the boys: Sex discrimination in Life Insurance Recruitment'. *EOC Research Bulletin*, 9, Spring, Manchester: Equal Opportunities Commission, 24–44.

Collinson, D., Knights, D. and Collinson, M. 1990. *Managing to Discriminate*. London: Routledge.

Commission for Racial Equality. 1981. *BL Cars Ltd: Report of a Formal Investigation*. London: CRE.

Commission for Racial Equality. 1983. *Implementing Equal Employment Opportunity Policies*. London: CRE.

Commission for Racial Equality. 1984. *Race Relations Code of Practice*. London: CRE.

Commission for Racial Equality. 1987. *Chartered Accountancy Training Contracts: Report of a formal investigation*. London: CRE.

Commission for Racial Equality. 1988. *Medical School Admissions: Report of a formal investigation*. London: CRE.

Commission for Racial Equality. 1992. *Annual Report 1991*. London: CRE.

Cooper, D. 1991. 'Equal Opportunities Work: After the boom, the gloom and doom?'. *Everywoman*, April, 16–17.

Copeland, L. 1988a. 'Valuing Diversity I'. *Personnel*, June, 52–60.

Copeland, L. 1988b. 'Valuing Diversity II'. *Personnel*, July, 44–9.

Coyle, A. 1985. 'Going Private: The implications of privatisation for women's work'. *Feminist Review*, No. 21, Winter.

Coyle, A. 1989. 'The limits of change: local government and equal opportunities for women'. *Public Administration*, Spring, 39–50.

Coyle, A. and Skinner, J. (eds). 1988. *Women and Work: Positive Action for Change*. Basingstoke: Macmillan Education.

Crompton, R. and Jones, G. 1984. *White collar proletariat: deskilling and gender in the clerical labour process*. London: Macmillan.

Cunninson, S. 1983. 'Participation in Local Union Organisation. School Meals Staff: A case study'. In Gamarnikow, E., Morgan, D., Purvis, J. and Taylorson, D. (eds) *Gender, Class and Work*. London: Heinemann Educational Books.

Curran, M. 1988. 'Gender and Recruitment: People and Places in the Labour Market'. *Work, Employment and Society*, Vol. 2, No. 3, September, 335–51.

Dex, S. and Walters, P. 1989. 'Women's occupational status in Britain, France and USA: explaining the difference'. *Industrial Relations Journal*, Vol. 20, No. 3, 203–12.

Dickens, L. 1986. 'Equal Opportunity – A More Encouraging Approach'. *Employee Relations*, Vol. 8, No. 4, 27–32.

Dickens, L. 1989. 'Women – a rediscovered resource?'. *Industrial Relations Journal*, Vol. 20, No. 3, Autumn, 167–75.

Dickens, L. 1992a. *Whose Flexibility? Discrimination and Equality Issues in Atypical Work*. London: Institute of Employment Rights.

Dickens, L. 1992b. 'Anti-discrimination Legislation: Exploring and Explaining the Impact on Women's Employment'. In McCarthy, W. (ed.) *Legal Intervention in Industrial Relations: Losses and Gains*. Oxford: Blackwell.

Dickens, L. 1992c. 'Employment: a Procrustean bed for women'. *The Journal: Women in Organisations and Management*, Issue 5.

Dickens, L. 1993. *Collective Bargaining and the Promotion of Equality for Women in the UK*. Geneva: International Labour Organization.

Dickens, L., Townley, B. and Winchester, D. 1988. *Tackling Sex Discrimination through Collective Bargaining*. London: HMSO.

Doyle, B. 1991. 'Disabled Workers: Legal Issues'. In Davidson, M. and Earnshaw, J. (eds) *Vulnerable Workers: Psychological and Legal Issues*. Chichester: Wiley.

Ellis, V. 1988. 'Current trade union attempts to remove occupational segregation in the employment of women'. In Walby, S. (ed.) *Gender Segregation at Work*. Milton Keynes: Open University Press, 138–43.

Employment Gazette. 1991. 'Industrial Tribunal Statistics 1991'. December, 681–4.

Employment Gazette. 1992a. 'Drop Unfair Practices'. December.

Employment Gazette. 1992b. 'Women and the labour market: results from the 1991 Labour Force Survey'. September.

Employment Gazette. 1993. 'Ethnic Origins and the Labour Market'. February.

Equal Opportunities Commission. 1986. *Guidelines for Equal Opportunities Employers*. Manchester: EOC.

Equal Opportunities Commission. 1988. *Local Authority Equal Opportunities Policies: Report of a Survey by the EOC*. Manchester: EOC.

Equal Opportunities Commission. 1990. *Equal Pay for Men and Women: Strengthening the Acts*. Manchester: EOC.

Equal Opportunities Commission. 1991. *Equality Management*. Manchester: EOC.

Equal Opportunities Commission. 1992. *Annual Report 1991*. London: HMSO.

Equal Opportunities Review. 1989. 'Discrimination at work, BIM finds'. March/April, 3.

Equal Opportunities Review. 1990. 'Contract compliance assessed'. No. 31, May/June, 26–8.

Equal Opportunities Review. 1992a. 'Opportunity 2000'. No. 41, Jan/Feb, 20–6.

Equal Opportunities Review. 1992b. 'Women earn 79% of men's pay'. No. 46, November/December.

Equal Opportunities Review. 1992c. 'The rising cost of injury to feelings'. No. 41, January/February, 30–5.

Equal Opportunities Review. 1993a. 'Action for race equality: An EOR survey of employer initiatives'. No. 48, March/April.

Equal Opportunities Review. 1993b. 'Ethnic minorities losing out on jobs and training'. No. 48, March/April.

Equal Opportunities Review. 1993c. 'Age Discrimination – no change!'. No. 48, March/April.

Equal Opportunities Review. 1993d. 'CRE warns rail union over race bias'. No. 48, March/April.

Fevre, R. 1989. 'Informal Practices, Flexible Firms and Private Labour Markets'. *Sociology,* Vol. 23, No. 1, February, 91–109.

Figart, D. M. 1992. 'Is positive action "positive"? Collective bargaining and gender relations in the Irish civil service'. *Industrial Relations Journal,* Vol. 23, No. 1, 38–51.

Greenslade, M. 1991. 'Managing diversity: Lessons from the United States'. *Personnel Management,* December.

Gregory, J. 1989. *Sex, Race and the Law.* London: Sage.

Hackett, G. 1988. 'Who'd be an equal opportunity manager?'. *Personnel Management,* April, 48–55.

Hansard Society Commission. 1990. *Women at the Top.* London: Hansard Society for Parliamentary Government.

Heery, E. and Kelly, J. 1988. 'Do Female Representatives Make a Difference?'. *Work Employment and Society,* December.

Hitner, T. et al. 1981. 'Races at Work: Equal Opportunity Policy and Practice'. *Employment Gazette,* September.

Holland, L. 1988. 'Easy to say, hard to do: managing an equal opportunity programme'. *Equal Opportunities Review,* No. 20, July/August, 16–21.

Horrell, S., Rubery, J. and Burchell, B. 1989. 'Unequal jobs or unequal pay?'. *Industrial Relations Journal,* Vol. 20, No. 3, 176–91.

Iles, P. and Auluck, R. 1989. 'From racism awareness training to strategic human resource management in implementing equal opportunity'. *Personnel Review,* Vol. 18, No. 4, 24–32.

Iles, P. and Auluck, R. 1991. 'The Experience of Black Workers'. In Davidson, M. and Earnshaw, J. (eds) *Vulnerable Workers.* Chichester: Wiley.

Industrial Relations Review and Report. 1990a. 'Recruiting and Retaining Women Workers'. Recruitment and Development Report 6, June. London: Industrial Relations Services.

Industrial Relations Review and Report. 1990b. 'Ethnic monitoring – policy and practice'. December, No. 478, 4–11.

Industrial Relations Review and Report. 1992. 'Sexual Harassment at the Workplace'. June, 6–15.

Industrial Relations Services/Equal Opportunities Commission. 1991. *Pay and Gender in Britain.* London: IRS.

IPM. 1989. *The IPM Equal Opportunities Code.* London: Institute of Personnel Management.

Jenkins, R. 1986. *Racism and Recruitment: Managers, Organisations and Equal Opportunity in the Labour Market.* Cambridge: Cambridge University Press.

Jenkins, R. and Solomos, J. 1987. 'Equal opportunity and the limits of the law: some themes'. In Jenkins, R. and Solomos, J. (eds) *Racism and equal opportunity policies in the 1980s.* Cambridge: Cambridge University Press.

Jewson, N. and Mason, D. 1986. 'The theory and practice of equal opportunities policies: liberal and radical approaches'. *Sociological Review,* Vol. 34, No. 2, 307–33.

Jewson, N., Mason, D., Waters, S. and Harvey, J. 1990. *Ethnic Minorities and Employment Practice. A Study of Six Organisations.* Research Paper 76. London: Employment Department.

Jones, P. 1988. 'Policy and Praxis: Local Government, a Case for Treatment?'. In Coyle, A. and Skinner, J. (eds) *Women and Work: Positive Action for Change.* Basingstoke: Macmillan Education.

Labour Research Department. 1988. 'Are unions working for black members?'. *Labour Research,* July, 11–13.

Labour Research Department. 1990. 'Union Reserved Seats – Creating a Space for Women'. *Labour Research,* March.

Leach, B. 1989. 'Disabled People and the Implementation of Local Authorities'. Equal Opportunities Policies'. *Public Administration,* Vol. 67, Spring, 65–93.

Lee, G. 1987. 'Black Workers and their Unions'. In Lee, G. and Loveridge, R. (eds) *The Manufacture of Disadvantage.* Milton Keynes: Open University Press.

Lee, G. and Wrench, J. 1987. 'Race and gender dimensions of the youth labour market: from apprenticeship to YTS'. In Lee, G. and Loveridge, R. (eds) *The Manufacture of Disadvantage.* Milton Keynes: Open University Press.

LEVEL. 1987. *A question of earnings: a study of earnings of blue collar employees in London local authorities.* London: London Equal Value Steering Group.

Liff, S. 1989. 'Assessing Equal Opportunities Policies'. *Personnel Review,* Vol. 18, No. 1, 27–34.

Lipman-Blumen, J. 1976. 'Toward a Homosocial Theory of Sex Roles: An Explanation of the Sex Segregation of Social Institutions'. In Blaxall, M. and Reagan, B. (eds) *Women and the Workplace.* London: University of Chicago Press.

Lovenduski, J. 1989. 'Implementing equal opportunities in the 1980s: an overview'. *Public Administration,* Spring, Vol. 67, 7–18.

Lustgarten, L. 1987. 'The politics of anti-discrimination legislation: planned social reform or symbolic politics?'. In Jenkins, R. and Solomos, J. (eds) *Racism and equal opportunity policies in the 1980s.* Cambridge: Cambridge University Press.

McCrudden, C. (ed.) 1991. *Fair Employment Handbook.* London: Industrial Relations Services.

McCrudden, C. 1992. 'Affirmative Action and Fair Participation; interpreting the Fair Employment Act 1989'. *Industrial Law Journal*, Vol. 21, No. 3, September.

Maguire, M. 1986. 'Recruitment as a means of control'. In Purcell, K. et al. (eds) *The Changing Experience of Employment*. Basingstoke: Macmillan Educational.

Manwaring, T. 1983. 'The extended internal labour market'. *Cambridge Journal of Economics*, Vol. 8, No. 2, 166–9.

Metcalf, H. and Leighton, P. 1989. *The Underutilisation of Women in the Labour Market*. Brighton: Institute of Manpower Studies.

Moss, P. 1990. *Childcare in the European Community 1985–90*. Brussels: European Commission Childcare Network.

Public Services Privatisation Research Unit. 1992. *Privatisation – disaster for quality*. London: PSPRU.

Parkyn, A. 1991. 'Operating equal opportunities in the Health Service'. *Personnel Management*, August, 29–33.

Philips, A. and Taylor, B. 1980. 'Sex and Skill: Notes Towards a Feminist Economics'. *Feminist Review*, Vol. 6.

Phizacklea, A. and Miles, R. 1987. 'The British trade union movement and racism'. In Lee, G. and Loveridge, R. (eds) *The Manufacture of Disadvantage*. Milton Keynes: Open University Press.

Pirani, M., Yolles, M. and Bassa, E. 1992. 'Ethnic pay differentials'. *New Community*, Vol. 19, No. 1, 31–42.

Pollert, A. 1985. *Unequal Opportunities: Racial Discrimination and the Youth Training Scheme*. Birmingham: Trade Union Resource Centre.

Purcell, K. 1988. 'Gender and the Experience of Employment'. In Gallie, D. (ed.) *Employment in Britain*. Oxford: Blackwell.

Salaman, G. 1986. *Working*. Chichester: Ellis Horwood.

Seddon, V. 1983. 'Keeping women in their place'. *Marxism Today*, July, 20–2.

Seear, N. 1981. 'The Management of Equal Opportunities'. In Braham, P., Rhodes, G. and Pearn, M. (eds) *Discrimination and Disadvantage in Employment*. London: Harper Row.

SERTUC (South East Region Trade Union Congress) Women's Rights Committee. 1992. *A Step Closer to Equality*. London: TUC.

Snell, M. et al. 1981. *Equal Pay and Opportunities*. Department of Employment Research Paper 20. London: HMSO.

Tillsley, C. 1990. *The Impact of Age upon Employment*. Warwick Paper in Industrial Relations No. 33. University of Warwick: Industrial Relations Research Unit.

Townley, B. 1990. 'A Discriminating Approach to Appraisal'. *Personnel Management*, December.

Webb, J. and Liff, S. 1988. 'Play the white man: the social construction of fairness and competition in equal opportunities policies'. *Sociological*

Review, Vol. 36, No. 3, 532–51.

Wood, S. 1986. 'Personnel Management and Recruitment'. *Personnel Review*, Vol. 15, No. 2.

Wrench, J. 1987. 'Unequal comrades: trade unions, equal opportunity and racism'. In Jenkins, R. and Solomos, J. (eds) *Racism and equal opportunity policies in the 1980s*. Cambridge: Cambridge University Press.

Young, K. 1987. 'The space between words: local authorities and the concept of equal opportunities'. In Jenkins, R. and Solomos, J. (eds) *Racism and equal opportunity policies in the 1980s*. Cambridge: Cambridge University Press.

PART IV

Employee Development

9

Vocational Education and Training for the Young

Ewart Keep

Introduction

Britain's training effort has been perceived as inadequate relative to that of other countries for over a hundred years. This has been as true for provision for the young as for almost every other facet of vocational education and training (VET) activity. Progress in tackling this problem has been slow in coming. Only during the 1980s were attempts finally made, through the Youth Training Scheme, to address Britain's persistent failure to provide a 'permanent bridge between school and work', a problem which had been highlighted as long ago as the late nineteenth century by Philip Magnus, Director of the City and Guilds London Institute (CGLI), when he suggested that 'the real aim of school education should be to establish such a relationship between school instruction and the occupations of life as to prevent any break in continuity in passing from one to another' (quoted in Dale et al., 1981: 180).

For reasons that will be discussed below, the last 15 years have witnessed major attempts to solve long-standing weaknesses in the provision of VET for the young, whether employed or unemployed. The result has been a considerable number of schemes, initiatives and new institutions, such as the Youth Training Scheme (YTS), the General Certificate of Secondary Education (GCSE), the Certificate of Pre-Vocational Education (CPVE), the Technical Vocational Education Initiative (TVEI), and Compacts, many of which have gone through frequent changes of character and administrative structure during their often brief lives.

Developments in VET provision for young people have attracted more interest by researchers than any other aspect of the long-running debate concerning Britain's training provision. Furthermore, the process of transition from school to work is a tremendously complex one, involving the individual in the creation of a range of identities concerned with gender, home and social life, career patterns, and beliefs and values. The transition is affected by a series of interlinked and interacting factors, such as geographic location and local labour market conditions, gender, ethnicity, and educational attainment (for a detailed discussion of these processes, see Banks et al., 1992; Bynner and Roberts 1991). This process is also mediated by class and cultural attitudes towards the value of education and training (Willis, 1977; Halsey, Heath and Ridge, 1980; Bennett, Glennerster and Nevison, 1992).

This chapter does not attempt detailed coverage of every facet of the debate about the transition from school to work. The aim is to outline the strategies which policy-makers have adopted, to review critically the resultant major developments, and, where appropriate, to point readers towards more detailed discussion of some of the chief issues. The main focus is vocational training for the young, but the chapter perforce also examines educational provision. This chapter differs from those that follow, which deal with other aspects of training, in that its focus lies primarily beyond the individual firm and centres on the wider operation of the youth labour market. The reason for this is simple. Whereas other aspects of change in training provision, such as that for adult workers and supervisors, have occurred largely as individual companies have attempted to grapple with changing markets and increased competitive pressures, reforms in the training of young workers have chiefly been driven by government policies and programmes.

The chapter opens with a brief review of the reasons why changes in British VET provision for the young came to be seen as necessary. It then examines some of the major developments within training and education, and then proceeds to analyse some of the major obstacles to reform. The chapter concludes with some general remarks about the direction which policy has taken, and future prospects for progress.

The Need for Reform

Problems in education

British provision of VET for young people has been marked by two distinctive features. The first of these has been early school leaving.

Table 9.1 International staying-on rates in full-time education (%)

Country	16 year olds	17 year olds	18 year olds	16–18 year olds
UK (1988)	50	35	20	35
W. Germany (1987)	69	43	33	57
France (1986)	78	68	52	66
USA (1986)	94	87	55	79
Japan (1988)	92	89	50	77

Source: Finegold et al., 1990: 50

Until very recently the majority of young people left education at the first opportunity (at age 16) and entered the labour market. This situation has been in sharp contrast with practice in most other developed countries, where a far higher proportion of the 16–18 age group remain in full-time education.

One measure of the scale and nature of the UK's deficit is that here the problem has been defined in terms of low staying-on rates, while in most other countries problems with post-compulsory schooling are defined in terms of the scale of dropping-out rates (Spours, 1992).

This situation has reflected an exclusionary academically oriented examination system, and, as a corollary, a persistent failure to create a coherent vocational pathway through post-compulsory vocational education. The Higginson Committee (1988: 2) report on the reform of A levels indicated that one of the fundamental problems with English and Welsh educational qualifications has been the persistent tendency to view their primary purpose as being to act as filters to sieve out those deemed unsuitable for progression to the next stage of the educative process. Thus O levels, and now GCSEs, have been used to determine who might progress to A levels, and A level results in their turn decide who goes on into higher education. As Cassels (1990: 30) points out, 'it is . . . extraordinary that we should have set out in the post-war era with a secondary school system in which the only school examinations (GCE O levels) were intended for 20 per cent of pupils only'. The result has been an examinations system with relatively high drop-out rates (about one-third of all A level candidates either drop out or fail), a system that establishes hurdles that have to be surmounted rather than encouraging young people towards sustained participation (Finegold et al., 1990: 16).

Finegold et al. (1990), the authors of the Institute of Public Policy Research report *A British Baccalaureat*, characterize the British education system as one founded on early selection and low participation. They suggested that its design has been

> based on the assumption (a) that abilities are largely fixed throughout life, (b) that only a relatively small proportion of the population need to be qualified, and (c) that the qualified people would continue to come predominantly from one social class. The education system that developed on the basis of this view was and to a large extent still is dominated by exclusion. (ibid.: 14)

It is important to note that the position in Scotland is very different from England and Wales. Scotland maintains an education system separate both in administrative control and qualifications structure from that the rest of mainland Britain, and the Scottish system has been able to achieve higher post-compulsory participation rates. It also encompasses a less significant gap between vocational and academic qualifications than exists in England and Wales (Raffe, 1991).

The lack of structured training provision

The failings in the English and Welsh educational system have been compounded by the second distinctive feature of British VET provision – the widespread failure of employers to offer structured training to young entrants to the workforce. In manufacturing industry, formalized training was traditionally restricted to the small segment of the age cohort who entered craft apprenticeships. In the service sector, with the major exception of hairdressing, there was even less training for school leavers. Thus the vast majority of those entering employment were offered little more than unstructured, on-the-job training, which provided no qualifications and no real foundation for future progression.

Forces triggering reform

Although over the years numerous official reports questioned the wisdom of this state of affairs, little progress in tackling the problem occurred until the late 1970s (Reeder, 1981; Perry, 1976; Sheldrake and Vickerstaff, 1987). Two factors acted as the catalyst for change. First, increasing levels of international competition forced British employers and government to confront the possibility of a link between levels of VET and the productivity of national workforces. Through officially commissioned reports, such as *Competence and Competition* (National Economic Development Office/Manpower Services Commission/Institute of Manpower Studies, 1984), the proposition that there was a positive link between levels of VET and national economic success became commonplace during the 1980s (see also Worswick, 1985; Daly, 1986; Prais, 1990). As a result, increasing attention was directed towards overseas provision.

Study of overseas VET systems indicated that, for young people not going directly into higher education, there are two basic models of provision. The first is an education-based system, with the broad mass of young people gaining vocational education within education, as in France and Sweden. The second model is employment-based, as in Germany, the Netherlands and Switzerland, with young people being engaged as trainees in the workplace, and the education system providing an element of off-the-job education. Of these systems, the German model proved by far the most influential in Britain during the mid to late 1980s, with considerable interest by both employers and government in the operation of the 'dual system' of apprenticeship (for details of the operation of this system and how it compares with provision in Britain, see Prais, 1990; Bynner and Roberts, 1991; Her Majesty's Inspectorate, 1991a; Casey, 1991).

The second trigger for reform was the massive increase in youth unemployment that occurred from the late 1970s onwards. In 1978, 85 per cent of 16 year old school leavers found work. By 1982 this figure had declined to 50 per cent, and by 1985 was only 27 per cent (Ashton, 1988: 419). This surge in youth unemployment posed a serious political challenge to government, and demanded a visible and large-scale response.

The Reform of Youth Training

The Youth Opportunities Programme

The first major attempt to tackle rising youth unemployment was the Youth Opportunities Programme (YOP), which commenced in April 1978. The YOP offered the young unemployed periods of work experience (normally six months) on employers' premises (WEEP), but provided 'little in the way of training' (Atkinson 1985: 29). The YOP grew extremely rapidly. In 1978 one in eight school leavers went onto the YOP. By 1982 nearly half of all school leavers were on the programme.

The result of this rapid growth was a sharp decline in the YOP's effectiveness. By 1981 only one in three ex-YOP graduates were gaining employment, and the Manpower Services Commission's failure to put in place adequate quality monitoring mechanisms led to mounting accusations that the programme was often doing little more than provide cheap labour for employers. As a result, the YOP was becoming increasingly discredited. The still rising tide of youth unemployment and the shock effect registered by the youth riots of the summer of 1981 led to a political decision that further measures were required as a matter of urgency (Keep, 1986).

In response, the tripartite Manpower Services Commission (MSC) formulated the New Training Initiative (NTI). The NTI (MSC, 1981) laid down three strategic goals for training policy in the 1980s: to reform and revitalize existing craft apprenticeships, to provide vocational training for all young people not covered by apprenticeships, and to improve the provision of training for adult workers (see chapter 10 for details). From the second of these objectives sprang the Youth Training Scheme (YTS).

The Youth Training Scheme

The MSC's planning of the YTS took place within a number of budgetary, time and political constraints (for a detailed account of the YTS planning process, see Keep, 1986). The major issue confronting the scheme's architects was whether it was to be a measure aimed at ameliorating youth unemployment or securing lasting improvements in the provision of vocational training for all young people. The MSC decided that the later objective should be the scheme's goal, and that the YTS should form a 'permanent bridge between school and work'.

In its original form the YTS was designed to offer a one-year traineeship, providing 13 weeks' off-the-job training combined with on-the-job training and work experience on employers' premises. Design and supervision of each YTS scheme was to be undertaken by 'managing agents', who might be individual employers, particularly larger firms, or private training providers, chambers of commerce, Industrial Training Boards, local authorities, or group training associations. To supervise the operation of the YTS, the MSC established a network of local 'Area Manpower Boards'

(AMBs) made up of education representatives, employers and trade unionists, reporting to a national Youth Training Board.

In 1986 the decision was made to move to a two-year scheme, offering 20 weeks' of off-the-job training, and this brought with it changes to the managing agent structure. Managing agents were expected to pass through an MSC-controlled vetting procedure whereby they converted themselves to 'Approved Training Organisations' (ATOs). Efforts were also made to increase the contribution made by employers to the cost of the scheme (see Chapman and Tooze, 1987; Jones, 1988).

The Young Workers' Scheme

A complementary development was the Young Workers' Scheme (YWS), started in 1982, which paid employers £15 a week for every young person that they took on to whom they paid less than £45 per week. The aim of the scheme was to help price young people back into jobs. While the YTS was a one-year scheme, the YWS 'tended to function as the second year of YTS' (Ainley and Corney, 1990: 78). With the move to the two-year YTS, the YWS was renamed the 'New Workers' Scheme' and retargeted to deal with 18–25 year olds, so as not to compete with year two of the revamped YTS.

In 1987 the government removed the rights of unemployed young people to claim benefits if they had refused the offer of a YTS place. This was coupled with a guarantee of a place on the scheme for all unemployed 16 and 17 year olds.

Youth Training programme

In 1989, the two-year YTS was revamped to create the Youth Training (YT) programme. The main changes were moves to make the scheme far more 'flexible'. This meant, for example, the abandonment of the two-year fixed duration for the traineeship, and the guarantee of 20 weeks' off-the-job training. The new YT scheme was to be 'outcomes driven', these outcomes being expressed in the form of trainees' achievement of 'National Vocational Qualifications' (NVQs). (The development of NVQs is discussed later in this section.)

With the demise of the MSC and the move to a training system based, in England and Wales, on local, employer-led 'Training and Enterprise Councils' (TECs), and in Scotland upon similar 'Local

Enterprise Companies' (LECs), responsibility for the delivery of YT has passed to individual local bodies. This shift of responsibility to locally controlled TECs and LECs has fragmented the training system and, thereby, increased the bureaucracy in arranging YT places faced by large companies operating nation-wide. There is now a central 'National Providers Unit' (NPU), but even this has not removed all the difficulties of dealing with more than 100 local training bodies, and some large companies have withdrawn from the YT programme, such as B&Q (Evans, 1992), Woolworth, W. H. Smith and the Halifax Building Society.

At the same time, YT funding has experienced progressive cuts. In the three years to January 1992 the unit cost for each YT trainee fell from £218 per month to £188 (*The Guardian*, 22 January 1992). The TECs have made clear their desire for the government to free them of a contractual obligation to meet the 'guarantee' to all unemployed 16 and 17 year olds of a YT place (*Times Educational Supplement*, 15 May 1992). The TECs believe that government funding for YT is inadequate to deliver sufficient quality training places, and would prefer to abandon the guarantee and allocate their limited funds to a smaller number of higher quality traineeships.

The legacy of the YTS and YT

The YTS and YT were central to the government's training strategy during the 1980s. As Geoffrey Holland, the then director of the MSC commented, 'if the two-year YTS fails then we are at the end of the road. There is nowhere else to go' (*Times Educational Supplement*, 3 September 1985). Substantial claims were made about its positive effects. For example, Atkinson (1985: 32) argued that the YTS provided 'a solid basis for a comprehensive and lasting system for a more effective transition from education to employment', and Lord Young, the then chair of the MSC (*MSC Youth Training News*, February 1986) commented that, 'the new two-year Youth Training Scheme stands comparison with any training system for young people in the world'. What are we to make of these claims?

On the credit side of the balance sheet, the sheer scale of the YTS was impressive, particularly given the speed with which provision was built up. In 1983–4 the average number of trainees on the YTS during the year was 162,000. By 1986–7 this had risen to 296,000, and by 1988–9 was 389,000. In 1985 no less than 29.4 per cent of all 16 year old males, and 23.9 per cent of all 16 year old females, were on a one-year YTS, and, in 1989, 15.5 per cent of the entire 16–18 population was on the two-year YT scheme. In terms of cost, between 1983 and 1992 central government expenditure on the YTS and YT reached a cumulative total of £7.86 billion (Employment Department, 1992a).

Moreover, the YTS introduced systematized vocational training provision into areas of the economy where previously little or no such training had existed (Witherspoon, 1987). Examples of sectors where this was the case include healthcare, retail and catering. It is also the case that, despite the current recession, YT remains far more successful than its predecessor, the YOP, in helping young people subsequently to gain employment, with just under 60 per cent of YT leavers gaining employment (Employment Department's *Labour Market Quarterly Report*, February 1992: 6). Perhaps most importantly of all, the YTS and YT moved forward the debate about training for the young. There is now no going back to the state of affairs that existed before the YTS.

On the debit side, while the YTS and YT undoubtedly changed the quantity of youth training being provided, there are doubts about the quality of provision and the effectiveness of quality control mechanisms within the scheme (Marsden and Ryan, 1991: 268–71). In some industries, such as construction and engineering, the YTS could be built into an existing, well-established training infrastructure centred on craft apprenticeships. In other sectors, and among small employers, the YTS represented the first attempt to provide any form of structured training experience for young entrants to the labour force. In some sectors that had previously provided no training for their young employees, employers failed to accept the basic tenets of the YTS (Lee et al., 1990). Thus there was often little structured supervision or on-the-job training. Moreover, the off-the-job element of the scheme was not valued by employers and was rarely integrated into the trainees' work placement.

Another problem has been the relatively modest proportion of the YTS and YT trainees gaining qualifications. It was originally intended that the YTS leaving certificate would 'come to be regarded as the most valuable piece of paper that young men and women possess – more valuable than any O level or CSE from an employer's point of view' (Young, 1982: 35). This did not happen, and attempts have subsequently been made to gear the YTS and YT instead to the attainment of NVQs (for further details of which, see below). Unfortunately the proportion of YT trainees gaining qualifications has fallen during the past two years (Employment Department, *Labour Market Quarterly Report*, November 1992: 4), and now stands at a national average of 33 per cent of trainees gaining some form of qualification (as compared with 41 per cent in December 1990). Employment Department estimates suggest that of the 58,000 YT trainees who achieved qualifications in 1991–2, 48,000 gained the comparatively low NVQ levels one or two, and only 10,000 the higher NVQ levels 3 and 4 (Employment Department, 1992a). Furthermore, it is argued that many of these qualifications are often too low, and narrowly job-specific (Jones, 1988; Steedman and Wagner, 1989; Jarvis and Prais, 1989; Prais, 1989).

Employer-led YTS provision tended to reproduce rather than challenge existing patterns of discrimination and disadvantage within the youth labour market. Lee et al.'s (1990) study of the YTS in one south-eastern town suggests that the scheme witnessed the creation of a 'surrogate' labour market for youth, which often replicated the segmentation by gender, ability and class normally experienced in the traditional youth labour market. YTS provision was also heavily stratified, with the least employable and the most disadvantaged finding themselves on the 'low-skill fringe of YTS' (Lee et al., 1990: 58). Thus, 'the least responsible and unsympathetic employers, whose placements carried the most minimal training opportunities and job prospects, were likely to be offered to the YTS trainees who were most disadvantaged and worst motivated' (ibid.: 59).

Furthermore, the YTS encountered difficulties in trying to confront gender discrimination in youth training provision. (Cockburn, 1987). The Training Agency (a later manifestation of the MSC) admitted that 'although some progress has been made in providing non-traditional occupational training in individual areas, this has had little effect on the broad occupational groups' (Training Agency, *Youth Training News* No. 55, June/July 1989: 24).

More fundamentally, it can be argued that the YTS and YT failed because they never became the 'permanent bridge between school and work' that was intended. The two-year YTS was 'to become a permanent feature of vocational education and training provision in this country' (Employment Department, 1985: 7). Yet the government has now decided to replace YT with 'Training Credits' by 1996. The underlying reason for this failure was the refusal by most employers to see the YTS and YT as being concerned with training rather than youth unemployment (Bevan and Hutt, 1985; Rainbird and Grant, 1985; Roberts et al., 1986; Coopers and Lybrand, 1985; Sako and Dore, 1986; Lee et al., 1990). Because of this, employers often offered trainees jobs and then promptly removed them from the scheme. In 1988 only about 20 per cent of trainees actually finished their traineeship (Marsden and Ryan, 1991: 267), and by 31 March 1990, after the YTS and YT had been in operation for more than six years, only 33 per cent of trainees had employed status. In 1988, official estimates suggested that as many as 100,000 young people each year still entered jobs offering little or no formal training (Goulbourn, 1988: 14).

Training Credits

Training Credits, which are to replace YT, originated from CBI proposals made in its 1989 report *Towards a Skills Revolution – A Youth Charter*. Credits are essentially a form of voucher, given to every school leaver to pay for further education or training. The aim is to create a system in which public funding for training is routed through the individual young person rather than the training provider (such as an FE college or employer). The advantages claimed for this new arrangement are the 'empowerment' of young people through giving them greater choice and control over training provision and 'by making obvious to them the scale of investment available to support their training' (Employment Department, 1992a: 16), and through the creation of what the CBI termed a 'training market', in which providers will compete for young people and their credits. The control of credits is vested in TECs and LECs, and all credits are aimed at the achievement of NVQ level 2 qualifications and above.

Credits were initiated during April 1991 in nine TECs. In May 1991 the government announced the extension of Training Credits to a nation-wide scheme which will, by 1996, replace YT.

The launch of credits has been adversely affected by the recession, with the attendant collapse of the youth labour market, and the limited take-up of credits (*The Independent*, 23 October 1991; *Personnel Management*, December 1991: 8; Employment Department, 1992c; Her Majesty's Inspectorate, 1992). Credits were designed during a period of tight youth labour markets, and employers' willingness to offer all young employees jobs with training was supposed to have been driven by competition for scarce youth labour.

The decline of apprenticeships

What of the NTI's other youth training measure – the reform of apprenticeships? The NTI aimed to replace the tradition of schemes based on serving a set training period with training to specific, tested standards, and also to ease the restrictions that limited entry to apprenticeships to 16 year olds. Reform proved slower than was hoped for (Sako and Dore, 1986: 201), especially with regard to ending the limits on age of entry, and did not halt the collapse of apprenticeship numbers (for details of reformed apprenticeship provision in a sample of large companies, see *Industrial Relations Review and Report* 354, 22 October 1985: 2–7). As table 9.2 indicates, the decline in apprenticeship provision was sharp.

To take the example of one industry, in 1981 there were 5500 apprentices in the chemical and man-made fibres industry. By 1984 there were 2500, and by 1990 only 1700 (see Keep and Mayhew, forthcoming).

These reductions have outstripped the falls in manufacturing employment. For example, in all manufacturing industry in 1980, apprentices accounted for 2.3 per cent of the total workforce. By 1990 this figure had fallen to 1 per cent. In the chemical and man-

Table 9.2 The decline in apprenticeship
numbers in Great Britain

Year	Number of apprentices
1970–	218,000
1975–	155,300
1980–	149,500
1981–	147,600
1982–	123,700
1983–	102,100
1984–	82,000
1985–	73,200
1986–	63,700
1987–	58,000
1988–	55,700
1989–	53,600
1990–	53,600

Source: Employment Gazette

made fibre industry the percentage of apprentices within the workforce fell from 1.3 per cent in 1980 to 0.6 per cent in 1990. It might be argued that technological change and shifts in the skill requirements of industry could account for these falls (Wilson, 1987: 4). In the engineering industry between 1978 and 1987 total employment fell by 35 per cent, while craft employment fell even faster, by 38.5 per cent (Senker, 1992: 100). However, falls in craft apprentice numbers outstripped even the decline in overall craft employment by a significant margin. Between 1980 and 1983 the annual intake of apprentices fell by 55 per cent, whereas craft employment in the sector diminished by only 26 per cent during the same period (ibid.: 101).

The official view is that these falls are deceptive, as more and more apprenticeships have been absorbed within the umbrella of YT. For example, Guy suggests that:

> In the latter part of the decade, as the focus moved towards vocational qualifications (through the NVQ process) the scheme gradually converged with the traditional vocational apprenticeship; the principle difference being that now such an apprenticeship is available in all sectors and occupations and is not based on time serving but on the acquisition of standards of competence. (1991: 52)

The data on the qualifications achieved by YT trainees do not entirely bear out this optimistic view. The YTS and YT have accompanied, and in some cases hastened, the decline of apprenticeships but, arguably, without creating an adequate substitute in terms of training quality (Marsden and Ryan, 1989).

National Vocational Qualifications

A further element of the government's plan to reform training provision was the restructuring of vocational qualifications. Following a review of the existing vocational awards, it was concluded that the jungle of competing, overlapping qualifications – in 1990 there were 279 different vocational secretarial qualifications offered by 11 examination boards at five levels (Employment Department, 1992d) – should be rationalized so that trainees and employers were provided with a system that was easily comprehensible. A new National Council for Vocational Qualifications (NCVQ) was established in 1986 to oversee this task. Its mission was outlined in the White

Paper, *Working Together – Education and Training* (Employment Department, 1986).

The NCVQ has constructed a national framework within which it recognizes and approves existing and new qualifications submitted by awarding bodies. These qualifications are known in England and Wales as National Vocational Qualifications (NVQs) and in Scotland as Scottish Vocational Qualifications (SVQs), and initially cover four levels (a fifth level embracing professional qualifications is being developed). NVQs differ from previous vocational qualifications in a number of ways. They are designed by Lead Industry Bodies (LIBs), made up of employer representatives rather than educationalists, are based on standards of competence required to perform specific jobs, and assessment is normally to be made in the workplace, rather than through written examinations (see Jessup, 1991). NVQs and SVQs are also based on the *outcomes* of learning, rather than the *process* of learning. They are therefore specified independently of any particular mode, location or duration of study. Training provided under YT and Training Credits is aimed towards the achievement of NVQs and SVQs, and funding is increasingly related to achievement of these qualifications.

NVQs have not been without their critics. Some commentators suggest that employers have defined NVQ skill levels in a very narrow and task-specific way, in contrast to their European counterparts who desire a broader mix of training and general education (Prais, 1989; Steedman and Wagner, 1989; CBI, 1989; Raggatt, 1991; Callender, 1992). The ability of NVQs to cope with changing technology, skill requirements and methods of work organization has also been questioned (Raggatt, 1991; Field, 1992). Finally, there has been concern that the levels of skill being specified in NVQs are very low (Jarvis and Prais, 1989).

Changes in Education

In parallel with the changes taking place in training provision, the 1980s and the early 1990s witnessed massive changes in the structure and control of state education in Britain. These have included the replacement of O levels and CSEs by a unified 16-plus examination, namely the General Certificate of Secondary Education (GCSE); the imposition of a national curriculum; the weakening of the power of local education authorities (LEAs); the delegation of financial responsibility to individual schools through the introduction of Local Management of Schools (LMS); and the ability of schools to 'opt out' of LEA control. The government has claimed that the overall objectives of these changes have been to raise standards and to increase parental choice and influence. A further change has been the government's decision to remove sixth form and further education colleges from LEA control. These institutions have been placed under the control of a new national FE funding council.

From school to work

A number of developments have been aimed specifically at improving provision for vocational preparation and at smoothing the transition from school to work. The first of these was the Technical and Vocational Education Initiative (TVEI) introduced by the MSC into schools on a pilot basis in 1983. The TVEI was an attempt to develop a more practical and relevant curriculum, especially with regard to the study of technology; to foster increased personal effectiveness among students; to reduce barriers at 16-plus; to increase community (employer) involvement in schools; to change assessment methods; and to promote a cross-curricula (rather than subject-based) approach to learning.

In 1986 the government announced the extension of the TVEI to cover all schools. This 'extension' programme now operates in all 106 Local Education Authorities (LEAs) in England, and every authority will have completed the extension phase by 1997. By 1993 about 70 per cent of all 14–18 year olds – more than a million students – were participating in the initiative. After 1994 the numbers involved will start to decline as the TVEI projects reach completion and funding is terminated (Education Department, 1992a: 21). In total, the TVEI and TVEI-Related In-Service Training (TRIST) programmes for teaching staff will have incurred direct costs of approximately £1.2 billion over a 15-year period. Nearly 75 per cent of this total has been accounted for by staffing and training and development costs. In many ways, therefore, the TVEI might be viewed as acting as a research and development fund for curriculum and organizational development within state schools (National Foundation for Educational Research, 1992a). For further details about and discussion of the TVEI, see Her Majesty's Inspectorate, 1991b; Dale et al., 1990; Ainley and Corney, 1990.

17-plus qualifications

A second development was the replacement in 1985 of the Certificate of Extended Education (CEE) with the Certificate of Pre-Vocational Education (CPVE) – a one-year full-time general pre-vocational course aimed at those staying on in school after 16 who were not studying for A levels. In 1989 the CPVE was made more flexible, so that it could be taken part time over two years alongside other qualifications, such as A levels, or as part of the YTS or TVEI. City and Guilds is currently developing a new diploma to replace the CPVE.

School – industry liaison

Problems with the transition from school to work have triggered major efforts by many companies to improve liaison between the worlds of work and education via a variety of school–industry initiatives. For a review of such initiatives, see Warwick, 1989.

One example is the development of 'compacts'. Local compacts between schools and employers are a North American invention (Richardson, 1992), and were first pioneered in Britain in East London by the now-disbanded Inner London Education Authority (ILEA). Under a government programme, local Training and Enterprise Councils now offer funding for a four-year period to support the establishment of compacts in inner city areas.

The aim of compacts 'is to motivate young people to achieve more at school and to continue education and training once they have left school'(Employment Department, 1992a: 21). Within a compact, students work towards agreed goals, such as improved school attendance, punctuality, and completion of course work. In return local employers offer guarantees of a job, or training that leads to a job, to those students that achieve their goals.

A network of 49 inner city compacts has been established in England, involving 7800 employers collectively committing around 20,000 jobs a year (Employment Department, 1992a: 21). It is now intended to extend the coverage of compacts beyond inner city areas. Evaluation undertaken in the first East London compact shows that compact schools registered increases in post-16 'staying-on' rates that outstripped the general rises recorded in post-compulsory participation, despite the compact schools being located in some of the most deprived areas of inner London (ibid.). However, the recession has brought problems for compacts because employers are often unable to meet job guarantees (see National Foundation for Education Research, 1992b; 1992c). Many compacts have had to abandon the agreed targets and job guarantees, and turn themselves into more general school–industry liaison programmes (*Times Educational Supplement*, 31 January 1992).

Vocational qualifications in schools

There have been two major initiatives on the provision of vocational qualifications within schools. First, the government has announced the introduction of General National Vocational Qualifications (GNVQs) which are to be a vocational route running parallel to academic A levels, and are intended to have 'parity of esteem'. GNVQs are being developed under the aegis of the NCVQ and will initially cover five areas – business, manufacturing, art and design, health and social care, and leisure and tourism (see Jessup, 1992). Second, schools will be able to offer vocational courses during the period of compulsory schooling (i.e. up to 16). Initially these will take the form of Business and Technician Education Council (BTEC) first diplomas (roughly equivalent to several GCSEs).

The government also aims to achieve parity of esteem between academic and vocational qualifications by grouping academic and vocational awards under new umbrella diplomas. There will be an 'Ordinary Diploma' covering GCSEs and their vocational equivalents, and an 'Advanced Diploma' covering A levels, GNVQs and other qualifications.

The first pilot GNVQ courses commenced in September 1992 but only 137 schools then offered BTEC first diplomas, and only 40 the higher level BTEC National (equivalent to A levels) (Adonis and Wood, 1992). It is therefore difficult to make more than tentative forecasts about their likely success. One difficulty that has yet to be fully resolved is the assessment methods that will apply to these new courses. It is not clear how the NCVQ's predilection for assessment of competences in the workplace can be married to the delivery of NCVQ-accredited qualifications in schools. There is also doubt about the ability of many schools to offer pre-16 vocational qualifications. Adonis and Wood (1992) ask where schools can find appropriately trained staff, teaching materials, equipment and facilities to provide vocational courses, particularly at a time when LMS and general funding constraints are inhibiting school's ability to recruit experienced staff or invest in teacher development and training to support the introduction of new courses (Spours, 1992: 3–4). Perhaps most importantly of all, the ability of vocational awards to achieve parity of esteem with traditional academic qualifications remains in doubt.

Rising post-compulsory participation

Underlying these various initiatives has been a rise in the proportion of young people engaged in post-compulsory education. During most of the 1980s this rise was relatively slow but steady. If both full- and part-time participation are counted together, in 1991 58 per cent of the 16–18 population were involved, compared with 52 per cent in 1980–1 (Department of Education and Science, 1992). In terms of full-time participation of 16–18 year olds the figures are rather less comforting, though even here there has been an improvement. In January 1990 36 per cent of all 16–18 year olds were in full-time education, compared with 32 per cent in 1988 (Department of Employment, *Labour Market Quarterly Report*, February 1992: 1).

More recently, with the onset of the recession, staying-on rates in schools and colleges have risen dramatically. The 1991 Careers Service school leavers destination survey, which covered 94 per cent of all those eligible to leave school in 1991, revealed the extent of the recession's impact. In 1989 the full-time participation rate by 16 year olds was 48 per cent; in 1990 this had risen to 53 per cent; and in 1991 it had further increased to 61 per cent (Association of County Councils, 1992). In some local authorities, the post-16 staying-on rate has now reached 80 per cent (Spours, 1992: 3). Increases in staying-on rates were particularly marked in those areas of the country most severely affected by the recession – London and the south-east (Association of County Councils, 1992). In Tower Hamlets in East London, post-compulsory participation rates have doubled in the past five years (Spours, 1992). Most of this growth in participation has occurred in schools rather than FE colleges, although the Employment Department (1992b: 40) suggests that 'there are indications that further growth will mainly be concentrated in the FE sector' (for further details of provision in FE, see Employment Department, 1992b).

As Raffe (1992) and Spours (1991; 1992) make clear, however, this improvement has been very patchy between and even within

LEAs. It is also the case that the quantitative growth in post-compulsory participation has not been fully matched by a quantitative shift in provision. Much of the participation can be viewed as compensatory, in that youngsters are remaining within the education system in order to try and achieve qualifications not attained during the period of compulsory schooling (Spours, 1992: 2). It is also uneven across the ability range of the age group, participation often being concentrated in the top and bottom quartiles (ibid.). Participation also tends to be short term. Figures for participation by 17 and 18 year olds have improved – from 32 per cent in 1987–8 to 47 per cent in 1991–2 for 17 year olds, and from 18 per cent to 28 per cent for 18 year olds over the same period (Employment Department, 1992b: 38) – but there remains a sharp dip after 17. This reflects the fact that many students are enrolling for one-year, low-level courses that are unlikely to lead to further progression (Spours, 1992).

Despite doubts about the consistency of the qualitative improvement, the impact of the quantitative change outlined above should not be underestimated. Sharp increases in post-16 participation, coupled with the declining size of the age group due to demographic change, means that the size and age profile of the pool of young people entering the labour market is undergoing structural change. Thus, whereas 400,000 16 year olds left education and sought work in 1988–9, less than 250,000 did so in 1991–2. The result will be that 'employers face the prospect of fewer but more mature, and potentially better qualified, young recruits by the mid-1990s' (Employment Department, 1992b: 39).

Why has this change taken place? There is a wide variety of explanations. Gray (1992) discusses no less than 18 causes that have been advanced to explain the increase (see also, Gray, Jesson and Tranmer, 1992). Of these, perhaps the most important are: a compositional effect dictated by changing class structure in the UK, particularly with the decline of manual working class occupations and the growth of those which might be defined as 'middle class'; easier access to higher education; rising unemployment, which dissuaded young people from leaving education only to enter a hostile labour market (what is termed the discouraged worker effect); the benefit changes of 1988, which removed young people's right to claim unemployment benefit, thereby forcing those without jobs to choose between education and participation in YT; a decline in the appeal of YT; and, finally, the fall in the size of the age cohort, which meant that increasing participation could be accommodated at more or less marginal cost through 'spare' capacity within schools and FE colleges.

The National Education and Training Targets

The developments described in the foregoing sections, their proponents claim, are sufficient to provide the foundations for a significant change in both the quantity and quality of British VET provision for young people. An overarching objective for these reforms is provided by the National Education and Training Targets (NETTs), which were established by the CBI in conjunction with a variety of other organizations (including the TUC) and subsequently endorsed by the government. The targets relating to VET for young people were outlined by the Employment Department (1991a) in its guidance to TECs:

- By 1997 at least 80 per cent of all young people should attain NVQ/SVQ Level 2 or its academic equivalent during their foundation education and training.
- All young people who can benefit should be given an entitlement to structured training, work experience or education leading to NVQ/SVQ Level 3 or its academic equivalent.
- By the year 2000 at least half the age group should attain NVQ/SVQ Level 3 or its academic equivalent as the basis for further progression.
- All education and training provision should be structured and designed to develop self-reliance, flexibility and broad competence as well as specific skills.

As the Employment Department makes clear in *Labour Market and Skills Trends, 1993/94* (1992b), these 'world class' targets are ambitious and, to meet them, major improvements in current education and training provision will be required. For instance, in order to meet the first attainment target by 1997, the annual rate of growth in the number of 18 year olds achieving NVQ/SVQ level 2 or its academic equivalent (four GCSEs at grades A–C) between 1990 and 1997 would need to be double the rate achieved between 1985 and 1990 (Employment Department, *Labour Market Quarterly Report*, February 1992: 17). Furthermore, the CBI is certain that to achieve the targets means eliminating all employment for 16–18 year olds which offers no training that leads to nationally recognized qualifications (ibid.: 19).

Just how achievable are these targets, and, more generally, what are the prospects for the success of recent reforms of youth training and education? The section that follows examines some of the obstacles to progress.

Obstacles to Progress

Problems with educational reform

Turning first to the prospects for current educational reforms, it is apparent that there is a deep-seated tension within government educational policy between what might be termed the progressive, vocationalist school, as exemplified by the TVEI, and the traditional academic model of education as enshrined in the national curriculum. Whereas the TVEI was concerned with student-centred, cross-curricula work, providing incentives to achieve, and embraced course-work and flexible assessment methods, the national curriculum stresses subject-based learning, the primacy of academic standards, assessment by written examination, and traditional didactic learning methods. To some extent, the battle between vocationalists and traditionalists can be characterized as one between the MSC (and subsequently the Employment Department) and the Department of Education and Science (now the Department For Education – DFE) (Ainley and Corney, 1990). The nation-wide extension of the TVEI probably represented the high-water mark of vocationalist influence. Since then, the DFE and traditionalist influences within the Conservative party have sought to reassert their influence.

Evidence of these tensions comes in the controversy that has marked rising levels of examination success at GCSE. These have been seen by, traditionalists, not as a vindication of examination reform and slowly rising standards of education, but as a dilution of standards (see Richardson, 1991: 18–19). The government's response was to limit course-work and to launch an enquiry into rising GCSE pass rates. This reaction betrays an underlying belief that rising levels of attainment are impossible without a drop in standards because only a more or less fixed percentage of the age group can ever achieve any given standard (Bolton, 1992) – a belief encouraged by independent schools (see Richardson, 1991: 43–6).

More immediately, the government's refusal to contemplate re-form of the A level system has raised questions about the ability to fashion a vocational route offering genuine parity of esteem along-side what the government terms the 'gold standard' of A levels. Reform of the A level system has the support of the CBI, the TUC, the British Institute of Management, the Royal Society, and the vast majority of head teachers, and has been recommended by successive official enquiries, but has been opposed by traditionalists and by the powerful public school lobby (for an account of this complex debate, see Richardson, 1991).

Government concern about rising success rates in GCSEs and a continued enthusiasm for A levels suggest that there is still the belief that only a fixed proportion of the population can achieve qualifica-tions, and the associated exclusionary view of academic examina-tions discussed earlier has not disappeared. Such attitudes render it difficult to make substantial progress towards increasing educational attainments for the broad mass of the population, and are also blighting attempts to introduce new forms of more vocationally oriented provision. Thus, efforts to develop modular A levels and GCSEs, and to promote credit transfer between them and voca-tional courses, have faced ministerial opposition in the form of objections to the use of course-work assessment (Nash and Purchon, 1992). Attempts to put in place vocational GCSEs have also run into problems because the School Examination and Assessment Council (SEAC) turned down syllabuses from vocational examining bodies (City and Guilds) because they featured too great an element of course-work (*Times Educational Supplement*, 15 May 1992). In such a climate, parity of esteem between vocational and academic quali-fications appears problematic.

Issues concerning training reform

One of the most vexed issues in youth training is that of trainees' pay. Some commentators, such as Marsden and Ryan (1991) argue that British apprenticeship pay has been high compared with that in Germany, and has tended to discourage employers from offering high quality training to a broad mass of young people. At the same time, the relatively high pay available to young people entering 'dead end' jobs which offer little in the way of training or opportunities for progression has attracted young people away from staying on in education, or entering jobs with better training opportunities

(Cassels, 1990; Finegold et al., 1990). With the exception of the now-defunct YWS, little beyond exhortation has been directed at this problem.

More broadly, moves towards the establishment of a training market raise the issue of the long-term pay-offs available to the individual young people who invest in their own education and training. Usually this investment will take the form of time, effort, and income foregone by continued participation in education or some form of traineeship that carries with it a lower wage than a full-time job without training. Unless pay-offs are positive, in terms of higher subsequent lifetime earnings, a training market is unlikely to produce significant increases in the supply of skills and qualifications.

The financial returns that a young person might expect from a decision to invest in obtaining post-16 vocational and academic qualifications have been probed in a report undertaken by Bennett, Glennerster and Nevison (1992). The picture which they reveal is not encouraging. Among their chief findings are that the returns to post-compulsory education and training are mixed, with degrees and higher level vocational qualifications generally enhancing lifetime earnings, but with low-level vocational qualifications (and, for many males, even A levels) producing only modest and in some cases negative returns. For example:

> The expected lifetime earnings associated with lower level vocational qualifications, such as apprenticeships, NVQ IIs and clerical qualifications, generally fall below those of school leavers with only GCSEs. (Bennett et al., 1992: 16)

The report also underlines that family background continues to play an important part in conditioning young peoples' choices.

The report's authors conclude that low demand for skills from employers produces inadequate returns to young people who invest in skills and qualifications, and that this situation reduces the demand of young people for post-compulsory education and training. Thus 'many young people are quite rational in not pursuing training – it does not give them great enough reward' (Bennett et al., 1992: 2). Hence the message that employers have been sending the youth labour market via their pay and recruitment structures has directly contradicted their calls for more and better post-16 education and training. The overall result is that the low level of education and training in Britain 'is not primarily the result of supply constraints, but is caused by a low level of demand' (ibid.: 15). These findings are reinforced by research commissioned by the Employment Department and undertaken in 1990 which indicated that vocational qualifications figured eighth out of nine in the ranking of attributes that employers desired of school leaver job candidates (Employment Department, 1991b).

In the face of weak demand from employers for qualifications, attempts to increase the incentives to young people to invest in learning have assumed something of an air of desperation. The Royal Society of Arts (RSA) in its report, *Profitable Learning* (Ball, 1992) went so far as to suggest that students who passed their exams early should be given the vote, allowed to apply for provisional driving licences six months or a year early, or allowed to see adult-rated films. That such proposals have been advanced is testimony to the continued failure of the labour market to provide sufficiently powerful incentives to the young to raise their achievements.

Given the absence of adequate incentives, it is not surprising, as Banks et al. (1992) underline, that one of the fundamental difficulties facing attempts to increase training for young entrants to the workforce is the low status which many young people attach to the idea of training – it is often seen as 'a poor substitute for work' (ibid.: 44). The priority is to get a job, with or without training.

Besides the lack of visible pay-offs from training, these attitudes also stem in part from youngsters' negative perceptions of government-sponsored training schemes, such as the YTS and its successor, YT (Banks et al., 1992; Lee et al., 1990). Young people interviewed by Unwin in south and east Cheshire in 1991 tended to see training as something that happened to the less able. Typical comments by school pupils were: 'I am doing A levels, I do not intend to do any training', 'it only affects people who do practical jobs', and 'it is of little use to intelligent students who intend to go into university' (Unwin, 1992). It is important to note that the attitudes of many British youngsters to the value of training contrast sharply with those of German teenagers, a divergence which largely reflects the differing availability of jobs without training in the two countries, and also the varying priority which British and German employers attach to skills and qualifications (Bynner and Roberts, 1991).

This brings us to the fundamental problem facing current attempts at reform – the weakness and patchiness of demand for skills and qualifications within the British youth labour market. One of the clearest restraints on progress towards achieving widespread high quality foundation training for young employees is the fact that many firms continue to believe in the necessity of only very limited amounts of training for youngsters. This was illustrated when the YTS was extended from a one-year to a two-year scheme (Pointing, 1986; Chapman and Tooze, 1987: 60). One personnel director commented:

> Given the nature of many of the jobs available, it is already hard to provide sufficient content for the one-year scheme and still be credible in the eyes of those concerned. Youngsters are quick to see the difference between the training being given and the tasks which they will be required to do . . . the crux of the issue on the move from one-year to two-year YTS is that we are moving from building a bridge between education and business, something most businesses can cope with, to real vocational education and training, something many of the schemes may have difficulty in coping with. (Milton, 1986: 29).

Such comments reflect the reality that the product market strategies of many UK businesses place greater stress on the price-based competition, and the provision of standardized, low-cost, relatively low-quality goods and services, than on quality-based competitive advantage and higher value-added products (Prais, 1990). The result is that demand for skills within the British economy is by no means uniform. While some companies, such as Rover Group (Muller, 1991) and British Steel (Morris et al., 1991), see a highly skilled, flexible and autonomous workforce as an integral part of their drive for quality production, many others, particularly within sectors characterized by low pay, have product market strategies and Taylorist methods of work organization that require a cheap, relatively lowly skilled workforce which follows orders (Keep, 1990). Even within organizations following the high-skill, high-quality route, work organization may create substantial pockets of lowly skilled employment.

This divergence of demand poses problems for plans to reform both the education and training of young people. As Bash, Coulby and Jones remark:

> the stratification of the labour market is such that public and private employers actually require young people with different skills at different levels. Industry, commerce, the professions and service facilities

need some young people with a high level of specific specialised skill. They also need people with low-level skills or virtually no skills at all. If schools do not produce unskilled and unqualified young people, then they will fail to meet one of the demands of the labour market. (Bash et al., 1985: 136)

Yet during the 1980s attempts to increase the vocational relevance of education, such as the TVEI, aimed to encourage all young people to take the initiative, make decisions, manage resources, influence others, monitor progress and show drive and determination. At the same time significant efforts were made to eradicate the unqualified school leaver. It is open to question how far such initiatives chime with the real demands of significant segments of the youth labour market.

Beyond creating potentially conflicting demands which any comprehensive system of vocational education may find hard to meet, the presence of a substantial pool of low-skill jobs for young people currently poses serious problems for training policy. For example, the successful introduction of Training Credits as a universal foundation traineeship for those young people entering employment is crucially dependent upon the removal of all jobs without training from the youth labour market (CBI, 1989: 15) and, in the absence of a statutory duty upon employers to provide training for all young employees, there are good reasons for doubting whether employers in low-skill sectors will co-operate (Cassels, 1990: 32–7; Banks et al., 1992).

Hopes of this occurring have certainly been reduced by the return of high levels of youth unemployment at a time when official policy had anticipated that demographic trends would be producing a tight youth labour market. The resulting competition between employers to recruit and retain scarce young people was to have been the motor that powered the new training market to success (CBI, 1989). Given current reductions in demand for young workers it is open to question whether Training Credits can operate as anything other than the YTS in yet another guise, dealing largely with the young unemployed and existing alongside a residuum of jobs for young people which offer little or no training. Thus, the continued prevalence of jobs without training coupled with the belief on the part of many youngsters that training is low-quality, exploitative, and associated with the less able – is likely to mean that the prediction that almost all 16–18 year olds will be in education or training by the end of the decade 'will almost certainly be proved wrong' (Economic and Social Research Council, 1992: 3).

Future Prospects

It is difficult to reach definitive conclusions about British progress towards erecting a VET system that ensures a smooth transition from school to work in the 1990s. Perhaps the most important reason is the transitory nature of schemes and initiatives in this area (Evans and Watts, 1985) and the degree to which education and training provision for young people finds itself once again in a state of flux. The failure of the YTS and YT to form the promised 'permanent bridge between school and work', coupled with increasing pressure for examination reform, the introduction of a new national structure of vocational qualifications, the gradual winding down of the TVEI, and moves to a locally based system of training delivery via TECs, has meant that a state of permanent revolution has pervaded British attempts over the last 12 years to arrive at a workable system.

One fundamental difficulty that has underlain these attempts has been a government strategy that has seen the chief problem as one of inadequate supply of flexible education and training provision to young people. As the experience of the YTS demonstrated, attempts to improve supply tend to founder on a fundamental lack of widespread demand within the UK labour market for a mass of more highly qualified young workers. As a result the incentives to train are limited, not least because there continues to be a supply of comparatively well-paid dead-end jobs for young people that require little in the way of qualifications to obtain. The weak demand for skill arguably reflects the adoption by many British organizations of a low-skill, low-quality product market strategy that relies on price-based competitive advantage (Finegold and Soskice, 1988; Prais, 1990). Unless, and until, product market strategies come to rely far more upon high-quality goods and services, and job design alters accordingly to stress the exercise of higher level skills and to offer chances for progression and development, the demand for education and training both from employers, and from young people, is likely to remain limited.

A second problem has been the nature of policy making in the field of youth VET, which has tended to be fragmented, *ad hoc* and incremental (see Evans and Watts, 1985; Keep, 1986; 1987; Ainley and Corney, 1990). Such a policy style is a problem because, as Bennett, Glennerster and Nevison (1992: 15–16) argue, the interdependence of education, training and the shape of the youth labour market make the creation of a unified VET policy for young people vital. Such a unified policy for Britain has been very slow to emerge.

One crude characterization of overseas VET systems for young people is that they are either education or employer based. It is notable that the pattern of provision developed in Britain during the 1980s has attempted simultaneously to incorporate elements of both models. For those remaining in education there has been the development of a better defined vocational route and GNVQs, buoyed by rising post-compulsory participation; while for those who decide to enter employment there has been first the YTS and YT, and then Training Credits and NVQs. Thus, as Raffe (1992) and the authors of *A British Baccalaureat* (Finegold et al., 1990) argue, during the 1980s Britain pursued a mixed model of VET for the 14–19 age group. This model, to some extent at least, reflected the pursuit of two parallel and relatively uncoordinated streams of VET policy, one education based, the other training based, whose existence has in turn reflected competition between the Employment Department and the Department of Education and Science (now the Department For Education). Raffe concludes that 'the mixed model has come to reflect divided control, and the absence of a clear strategy' (Raffe, 1992: 4). Such policies have been met by a persistent demand for greater co-ordination and coherence in provision for the age group (e.g. National Association of Head Teachers, 1987; Evans and Watts, 1985; Cantor, 1985).

In the longer term, the mixed model may not be sustainable. The general slump in employment caused by the onset of recession in the early 1990s has masked underlying shifts in the structure of demand for young people from the labour market. Technological change, two recessions and broad compositional alterations in the structure of UK employment all mean that the number of employment opportunities for 16–18 year olds is being reduced (see Ashton, 1988: 422–3). It is particularly noticeable that many of what might be termed the premium employers are either not recruiting young people or are sharply reducing numbers. For example, recruitment by the big four clearing banks is down to one-seventh of the levels in the mid-1980s (*Financial Times*, March 1992). Barclays' youth intake (normally the largest of the four) was down from 11,000 in 1988 to 2000 in 1991.

The effects of these trends are ambiguous. On the one hand, the declining size of the youth labour market could mean, in the long term, a reduction in the supply of dead-end jobs with no training for young people. On the other hand, and perhaps more crucially, high-quality, formalized training for the young has largely been provided by large employers. If their demand for young people is being reduced, so too may the amount of structured training opportunities available.

Should the changes currently occurring in employers' demand for young workers continue, this could force a greater emphasis upon the provision of VET through increasing post-compulsory educational participation. Recent sharp increases in participation rates at 16-plus may indicate that such a shift is already under way. This change has served to strengthen post-compulsory educational participation and to increase the underlying rationale of an education-based solution to vocational provision for the 14–19 age group. It may be, therefore, that Britain is moving towards the situation advocated by Raffe (1992) where the vast majority of the age group receive their VET via education, with employers responsible for training above that age, and Training Credits targeted at 18 year olds (ibid.: 4). The long-term success of these developments, however, is dependent upon a clear post-compulsory vocational route within education which carries a reasonably high status with both higher education and with employers. A great deal will hence rest upon the success of GNVQs in establishing a vocational pathway that genuinely commands 'parity of esteem' with A levels.

Thus, while one possible VET structure for young people may be emerging from the current round of change, it is by no means certain that this model will achieve permanence and stability. An editorial in the *Financial Times* (9 May 1990) commented that 'the history of British vocational training and education is largely a history of failure'. Whether the 1990s will mark a decisive break with this tradition remains to be seen. Given the deep-seated nature of the attitudes and employment structures that have created the problem, it is perfectly possible that Britain will find itself entering the first decade of a new century still lacking an adequate and comprehensive system of education and training for the young.

This chapter draws on material prepared by the author and K. Meyhew for their forthcoming volume, *The British Vocational Education and Training System – A Critical Analysis.*

Bibliography

Adonis, A. and Wood, L. 1992. 'Lessons to be Learnt in Vocational Training'. *Financial Times*, 27 April.

Ainley, P. and Corney, M. 1990. *Training For the Future: the Rise and Fall of the Manpower Services Commission*. London: Cassell.

Ashton, D. 1988. 'Educational Institutions, Youth and the Labour Market'. In Gallie, D. (ed.) *Employment in Britain*. Oxford: Blackwell.

Association of County Councils. 1992. *The School Leavers Destinations Survey 1991*. London: ACC Publications.

Atkinson, K. N. 1985. 'National Programmes to Promote Youth Training'. *Long Range Planning*, 18, 3, 26–32.

Ball, C. 1991. *Learning Pays*. London: Royal Society for the Encouragement of Arts, Manufactures and Commerce.

Banks, M., Bates, I., Breakwell, G., Bynner, J., Emler, N., Jamieson, L. and Roberts, K. 1992. *Careers and Identities*. Milton Keynes: Open University Press.

Bash, L., Coulby, D. and Jones, C. 1985. *Urban Schooling: Theory and Practice*. Cambridge: Cambridge University Press.

Bennett, R., Glennerster, H., and Nevison, D. 1992. *Learning Should Pay*. Poole: British Petroleum.

Bevan, S. and Hutt, R. 1985. *Company Perspectives on the Youth Training Scheme*. Report 104. Sussex: Institute of Manpower Studies.

Bolton, E. 1992. 'Visions of Chaos'. *Times Educational Supplement*, 31 July.

Bynner, J. and Roberts, K. 1991. *Youth and Work: Transition to Employment in England and Germany*. London: Anglo-German Foundation.

Callender, C. 1992. *Will NVQs Work? – Evidence from the Construction Industry*. IMS Report No. 228. Sussex: Institute of Manpower Studies.

Cantor, L. 1985. 'A Coherent Approach to the Education and Training of the 16–19 Age Group'. In Worswick, G. D. N. (ed.) *Education and Economic Performance*. London: Gower.

Casey, B. 1991. 'Recent Developments in the German Apprenticeship System'. *British Journal of Industrial Relations*, 29, 2, 205–22.

Cassels, J. 1990. *Britain's Real Skill Shortage and What to Do About It*. London: Policy Studies Institute.

CBI. 1989. *Towards a Skills Revolution*. London: Confederation of British Industry.

Chapman, P. G. and Tooze, M. J. 1987. *The Youth Training Scheme in the United Kingdom*. Aldershot: Avebury.

Cockburn, C. 1987. *Two-Track Training*. Basingstoke: Macmillan.

Coopers and Lybrand Associates. 1985. *A Challenge to Complacency: Changing Attitudes to Training*. Sheffield: Manpower Services Commission/National Economic Development Office.

Dale, R., Esland, G., Fergusson, R. and MacDonald, M. (eds) 1981. *Education and the State, Volume 1: Schooling and the National Interest*. Lewes: Falmer Press.

Dale, R., Bowe, R., Harris, D., Loveys, M., Moore, R., Shilling, C., Sikes, P., Trevitti, J. and Valasecchi, V. 1990. *The TVEI Story, Policy Practice and Preparation for the Work Force*. Milton Keynes: Open University Press.

Daly, A. 1986. 'Education and Productivity: A Comparison of Great Britain and the United States'. *British Journal of Industrial Relations*, 24, 2, 251–67.

Department of Education and Science. 1992. *Education Statistics for the United Kingdom 1991*. London: HMSO.

Employment Department. 1985. *Education and Training for Young People*. Cmnd 9482. London: HMSO.

Employment Department. 1986. *Working Together – Education and Training*. Cmnd 9823. London: HMSO.

Employment Department. 1991a. *A Strategy for Skills: Guidance from the Secretary of State for Employment on Training, Vocational Education and Enterprise*. London: Employment Department.

Employment Department. 1991b. 'Into Work'. *Skills and Enterprise Briefing*, Issue 15/91, October.

Employment Department. 1992a. *The Government's Expenditure Plans, 1992–93 to 1994–95*. Cm 1906. London: HMSO.

Employment Department. 1992b. *Labour Market and Skill Trends, 1993/94*. London: Employment Department.

Employment Department. 1992c. *Training Credits progress report*. Sheffield: Employment Department.

Employment Department. 1992d. 'Clerical and Secretarial Skills: A Neglected Resource?'. *Skills and Enterprise Briefing*, Issue 33/92, November.

Economic and Social Research Council. 1992. *Careers and Identities*. ESRC Research Briefing 4, Swindon: ESRC.

Evans, J. 1992. 'The DIY Approach to Youth Training'. *Personnel Management*, April, 47–8.

Evans, K. and Watts, A. G. 1985. Introduction in Watts, A. G. (ed.) *Education and Training 14–18*. Cambridge: Careers Research and Advisory Centre.

Field, J. 1992. 'The Pedagogy of Labour'. Paper delivered to the University of Warwick VET Forum, February. University of Warwick, Department of Continuing Education (mimeo).

Finegold, D. and Soskice, D. 1988. 'The Failure of Training in Britain: Analysis and Prescription'. *Oxford Review of Economic Policy*, 4, 3, 21–53.

Finegold, D., Keep, E., Miliband, D., Raffe, D., Spours, K. and Young, M. 1990. *A British Baccalaureat – Ending the Division Between Education and Training*. Education and Training Paper No. 1. London: Institute of Public Policy Research.

Gouldbourn, T. 1988. 'The Way Forward – NTI Objective 2'. *Youth Training News*, 49, September/October, 14–15.

Gray, J., Jesson, D. and Tranmer, M. 1992. *Boosting Post-16 Participation: A Study of Some Key Factors*. Sheffield: Department of Employment Research and Development Series.

Gray, J. 1992. 'What's Driving the Recent Increases in Post-16 Staying On Rates? Some Propositions for Review and Debate'. Paper presented to the ESRC Research Seminar on Participation in Education and Training: Age Group 16–19, June. Sheffield: University of Sheffield, Division of Education, QQSE Research Group (mimeo).

Guy, R. 1991. 'Serving the Needs of Industry?'. In Raggatt, P. and Unwin, L. (eds) *Change and Intervention – Vocational Education and Training*. London: Falmer Press, 47–60.

Halsey, A., Heath, A. and Ridge, J. 1980. *Origins and Destinations: Family Class and Education in Modern Britain*. Oxford: Clarendon Press.

Her Majesty's Inspectorate. 1991a. *Aspects of Vocational Education and Training in the Federal Republic of Germany*. London: HMSO.

Her Majesty's Inspectorate. 1991b. *TVEI in England and Wales 1983–1990*. London: HMSO.

Her Majesty's Inspectorate. 1992. *The Implementation of the Pilot Training Credits Scheme in England and Wales*. London: HMSO.

The Higginson Committee. 1988. *Advancing A Levels*. London: HMSO.

Jarvis, V. and Prais, S. 1989. 'Two Nations of Shopkeepers: Training for retailing in Britain and France'. *National Institute Economic Review*, 128, 58–74.

Jessup, G. 1991. *Outcomes: NVQs and the Emerging Model of Education and Training*. Brighton: Falmer Press.

Jessup, G. 1992. 'Towards a Coherent Post-16 Qualifications Framework'. In Finegold, D., Richardson, W. and Woolhouse, J. (eds) *The Reform of Post-16 Education and Training in England and Wales*. London: Longman.

Jones, I. 1988. 'An Evaluation of YTS'. *Oxford Review of Economic Policy*, 4, 3, 54–71.

Keep, E. 1986. *Designing the Stable Door: A Study of How the Youth Training Scheme was Planned*. Warwick Papers in Industrial Relations, 8. Coventry: Industrial Relations Research Unit.

Keep, E. 1987. *Britain's Attempts to Create a National Vocational Education and Training System: A Review of Progress*. Warwick Papers in Industrial Relations, 16. Coventry: Industrial Relations Research Unit.

Keep, E. 1990. 'Training for the Low-Paid'. In Bowen, A. and Mayhew, K. (eds) *Improving Incentives for the Low-Paid*. London: Macmillan/National Economic Development Office.

Keep, E. and Mayhew, K. forthcoming. *The British Vocational Education and Training System – A Critical Analysis*. Oxford: Oxford University Press.

Lee, D., Marsden, D., Richman, P. and Duncombe, J. 1990. *Scheming For Youth. A Study of YTS in the Enterprise Culture*. Milton Keynes: Open University Press.

Manpower Services Commission. 1981. *A New Training Initiative – An Agenda for Action*. London: Manpower Services Commission.

Marsden, D. and Ryan, P. 1989. 'Employment and Training of Young People: Have the Government Misunderstood the Labour Market?'. In Harrison, A. and Gretton, J. (eds) *Education and Training UK*, Policy Journals, 47–53.

Marsden, D. and Ryan, P. 1991. 'Initial Training, Labour Market Structure and Public Policy: Intermediate Skills in British and German Industry'. In Ryan, P. (ed.) *International Comparisons of Vocational Education and Training for Intermediate Skills*. London: Falmer Press, 251–85.

Milton, R. 1986. 'Double, Double, Toil and Trouble: YTS in the Melting Pot'. *Personnel Management*, April, 26–31.

Morris, J., Bacon, N., Blyton, P., and Franz, H. W. 1991. 'Beyond Survival: The Implementation of New Forms of Work Organisation in the UK and German Steel Industries'. Paper prepared for the Employment Research Unit Conference, Cardiff, September (mimeo).

Muller, F. 1991. 'A New Engine of Change in Employee Relations'. *Personnel Management*, July, 30–3.

Nash, I. and Purchon, V. 1992. 'A-level limits will hamper reform'. *Times Educational Supplement*, 10 January.

National Association of Head Teachers. 1987. *NAHT Action Plan – a policy 14–18*. Haywards Heath: National Association of Head Teachers.

National Economic Development Office/Manpower Services Commission/Institute of Manpower Studies. 1984. *Competence and Competition*. London: NEDO.

National Foundation for Education Research. 1992a. *TVEI and the Management of Change: An Overview*. Slough: NFER.

National Foundation for Education Research. 1992b. *The Impact of Compacts 1991*. Slough: NFER.

National Foundation for Education Research. 1992c. *The Contribution and Views of Employers*. Slough: NFER.

Perry, P. J. C. 1976. *The Evolution of British Manpower Policy*. London: British Association of Commercial and Industrial Education.

Pointing, D. 1986. 'Retail Training in West Germany'. *MSC Youth Training News*, April, 2–3.

Prais, S. J. 1989. 'How Europe would see the new British initiative for standardising vocational qualifications'. *National Institute Economic Review*, 129, 52–4.

Prais, S. J. (ed.) 1990. *Productivity, Education and Training*. London: National Institute of Economic and Social Research.

Raggatt, P. 1991. 'Quality Assurance and NVQs'. In Raggatt, P. and Unwin, L. (eds) *Change and Intervention – Vocational Education and Training*. London: Falmer Press, 61–80.

Raffe, D. 1991. 'Scotland v England: The Place of Home Internationals in Comparative Research'. In Ryan, P. (ed.) *International Comparisons of Vocational Education and Training for Intermediate Skills*. London: Falmer.

Raffe, D. 1992. *Participation of 16–18 Year Olds in Education and Training*. National Commission on Education, briefing paper 3. London: National Commission on Education.

Rainbird, H. and Grant, W. 1985. *Employers' Associations and Training Policy*. Coventry: Warwick University, Institute of Employment Research.

Reeder, D. 1981. 'A Recurring Debate: Education and Industry'. In Dale, R., Esland, G., Fergusson, R. and MacDonald, M. (eds) *Education and the State, Volume 1: Schooling and the National Interest*. Lewes: Falmer Press.

Richardson, W. 1991. *Education and Training Post-16: Options for Reform and the Public Policy Process in England and Wales*. University of Warwick, Warwick VET Forum Report No. 1, June.

Richardson, W. 1992. 'Employers as an Instrument of School Reform: Compacts in Britain and America'. In Finegold, D., MacFarland, L. and Richardson, W. (eds) *Something Borrowed, Something Blue? An Analysis of Education and Training in the U.S. and Great Britain*. Oxford: Triangle Books.

Roberts, K., Dench, S. and Richardson, D. 1986. 'Firms' Uses of the Youth Training Scheme'. *Policy Studies*, 6, January, 37–53.

Sako, M. and Dore, R. 1986. 'How the Youth Training Scheme Helps Employers'. *Employment Gazette*, June, 195–204.

Senker, P. J. 1992. *Industrial Training in a Cold Climate*. Aldershot: Avebury.

Sheldrake, J. and Vickerstaff, S. 1987. *The History of Industrial Training in Britain*. Aldershot: Gower.

Spours, K. 1991. *Student Destinations 1991: Towards a Tower Hamlets Post 16 Participation Study*. London: Borough of Tower Hamlets, December (mimeo).

Spours, K. 1992. 'Studies of post 16 Participation in Tower Hamlets'. Paper presented to the ESRC Research Seminar Group on Participation in Education and Training: Age Group 16–19, June (mimeo).

Steedman, H. and Wagner, K. 1989. 'Productivity, machinery and skills in Britain and Germany'. *National Institute Economic Review*, 128, 40–57.

Unwin, L. 1992. Presentation on Training Credits Pilot Evaluation (SE Cheshire) to ESRC Research Seminar Group on Participation in Education and Training: Age Group 16–19. Workshop on Pilot Training Credits Evaluation, University of Warwick, March.

Warwick, D. (ed.) 1989. *Linking Schools and Industry*. Oxford: Blackwell.

Willis, P. 1977. *Learning to Labour*. Farnborough: Saxon House.

Wilson, T. 1987. 'Opinion'. *Transition*, May, 3–4.

Witherspoon, S. 1987. *YTS: A Second Survey of Providers*. London: Social and Community Planning Research.

Worswick, G. D. N. (ed.) 1985. *Education and Economic Performance*. London: Gower.

Young, D. 1982. 'Worried About Unemployment? How You can Help . . .'. *The Director*, October, 34–5.

10

Continuing Training

Helen Rainbird

Introduction

Continuing training is increasingly recognized as contributing to productivity and to the management of change through the adaptation and extension of skills, on the one hand, and in facilitating new patterns of work on the other. Recognition of the need to extend continuing training to broader sections of the working population is due, in part, to structural changes in the British labour market and to the fact that 80 per cent of the workforce in the year 2000 will already have been in employment since the beginning of the decade (Cassels, 1990: 27). Consequently, many future skill requirements will have to be met by retraining current employees rather than through the recruitment and training of young people as discussed in chapter 9. In addition, there is an emerging consensus (not always supported by the evidence in practice) that changes in production processes and in the nature of product markets require a more highly trained workforce. This has been translated into the policy debate as requiring 'a different approach to education and training, one which puts emphasis on building up not only technical competence but also personal capacity and self-reliance' (Cassels, 1990: 27). Moreover, if the objective of 'human resource management' is to improve the motivation and effectiveness of employees, then an extension of access to continuing training and development across the entire workforce might demonstrate the seriousness of management strategy in this area.

Employers as well as interest groups such as the CBI, the TUC, individual trade unions and professional organizations have begun to recognize the significance of continuing training. However, the British training system, which is essentially voluntarist, has few mechanisms for encouraging and influencing its development. If chapter 9 demonstrated the restricted influence of the state over initial training, except through publicly funded programmes aimed at the unemployed, then the scope for influencing company decisions with respect to the training of existing employees is even less. This contrasts with the more highly regulated training systems found in other European countries, which ensure higher levels of investment in training and are less prone to cyclical fluctuation (Campinos-Dubernet and Grando, 1988).

Both France and Germany have provisions for encouraging continuing training. In France, a significant feature of the training system is the 1971 law on continuing vocational training. Employers with more than ten workers are obliged to spend 1.2 per cent of their annual wage bill on staff training. This is divided into 0.15 per cent to be spent on individual training leave, 0.3 per cent to be spent on youth training and 0.75 per cent to be spent at the employer's initiative under a company training plan (Dubar, 1990). In 1991 a new national agreement was reached whereby employers' contributions were to be increased to 1.5 per cent of payroll from January 1993. For the first time, too, small companies are required to make a contribution towards training, and provisions have also been introduced for employee 'co-investment' in training. These provisions are based on the principle of company decision making, but include a process of consultation with the works council on the company training plan (*European Industrial Relations Review*, September 1991).

Méhaut (1988) reports that the legislation, along with a series of other measures designed to promote restructuring processes in companies, has resulted in the allocation of funds above the legal minimum to further training: firms now spend an average of 2.6 per cent of their wage bills on training. However, Amadieu (1992: 62) reports that although there has been a significant upgrading of skills in the French labour market since the mid-1970s, many low-skill jobs remain. Moreover, continuing training has not provided a 'second chance' for unskilled workers, but has been concentrated on engineers, managers and, to a lesser extent, technicians and supervisors (Tanguy, 1991: 35).

In Germany, continuing training is regulated at federal level by the Vocational Training Act of 1968/9. A distinction is made between continuing vocational training, retraining and on-the-job training. Most courses of continuing training are of short duration and do not lead to recognized qualifications. The structures for regulation at national level are similar to those for initial training and the Chambers of Commerce can issue examinations (Streeck et al., 1987). Despite this formal situation, in practice it is only supervisory training, under the *Meister* system, which is effectively regulated. Mahnkopf argues that there is no clear system of regulating training at plant level and that decisions made on it are fully at the discretion of the employer. Unions have not exploited their consultation rights to exercise influence over further training (Mahnkopf, 1992: 69–70). Despite a more highly regulated initial training system, unskilled workers in Germany have as little access to continuing training as those in Britain (Campbell and Warner, 1991: 156).

The examples of France and Germany demonstrate that, even in more regulated training systems, access to continuing training is restricted and tends to favour those employees who already have the highest levels of qualifications. What, therefore, is the nature and extent of continuing training in Britain, where there are no such external influences on company practices? This chapter considers the evidence. The first section will examine the literature on continuing training, one which is fairly limited because very few data are collected on company training on a systematic basis. The second will examine the institutional structures and interest groups which influence the adoption of policies on continuing training. The third will consider the ways in which the state can support and promote it. The fourth will examine case study evidence on continuing training, considering factors which are supportive of the development of continuing training.[1] The conclusion will return to the theme of the limitations of a voluntarist training system.

The Nature and Extent of Continuing Training

There are two main sources of evidence on continuing training: that derived from surveys of individuals, and surveys and case studies of companies. Neither of these sources collects data on training on a systematic basis which would allow conclusions about company policy to be drawn. Since the abolition of the majority of the Industrial Training Boards in 1981 and the privatization of the remainder in 1991, data on training have ceased to be collected on an industry-wide basis. The annual 'Labour Force Survey' is the only major source of information about patterns of individual's experience of training, but its reliability is uncertain and it cannot be used as a basis for making anything more than general inferences about company policies. This is because what individuals recognize and experience as training may differ from what personnel and training departments recognize and value as training. For example, in the case of open learning, which is being widely adopted as a cost-effective means of training staff, Fuller and Saunders (1990: 9) have pointed to the distinction between what they call the 'use value' and the 'exchange value' of learning. The former refers to the development of competences directly beneficial to the performance of jobs, while the latter refers to the perceived value of training in relation to potential internal and external mobility. While training which has use value may be valued by employers because it rapidly increases productivity, it may be accorded low status by employees because it brings no immediate reward and is not externally recognized. Therefore, employees and employers may have different perceptions of the quantity and quality of training, especially where it is associated with open learning, on-the-job instruction or induction into corporate culture. A further problem associated with such forms of training is how their volume and cost are estimated.

Individuals' experience of training

The main sources of information about individuals' experience of training are the 1975 'National Training Survey', the 1987 'VET Funding Study' and the annual 'Labour Force Survey'. The 1975 survey found that most people experienced training in the early part of their working lives, and that men were 50 per cent more likely than women to have received it and for a longer period. Training on a part-time basis and at evening classes was less common than full-time training for all employees (Payne, 1992: 4). In the VET Funding Study, one-third of the sample reported having received some vocational education or training in the previous three years. Of the remainder, one-third could not recall ever having received training and the other third had received some training, but not in the last three years (ibid.: 5). Three-quarters of training received in the previous three years and lasting at least three days was employer-provided. Receipt of training dropped off sharply with age except for that provided for managers and professionals (ibid.: 5). Regardless of whether training is provided by the employer or whether self-motivated individuals take up education and learning, similar patterns emerge. The survey, 'Londoners Learning', conducted by the National Institute for Adult Continuing Education, demonstrated that 'adult learning opportunities are available and taken up by those who enjoy an extended initial education, and by those who come from professional and managerial backgrounds' (NIACE, 1990: 1).

The Labour Force Survey records training received by individuals in the four weeks prior to the survey. Continuing training accounted for one-third of all training reported in the 1989 Labour Force Survey. Table 10.1 shows the main location of this training activitity and participation by gender and employment status. For both women and men, employer-provided training accounts for approximately one-third of continuing training, with 40 per cent of men's and nearly 50 per cent of women's continuing training being provided by education institutions.

Patterns of labour market segmentation exercise considerable influence on individuals' access to continuing training. Analysing the same Labour Force Survey data, Clarke (1991: 28) found that women with higher level qualifications (A level and above) were more likely to have received training than men. However, highly qualified women are concentrated in lower age bands and in the public sector, where higher levels of training provision are found. She concludes: 'The pattern of training provision for adult employees is a complex one, with different groups of women and men having very different access to continuing training. Women part-timers in all occupations have substantially less access to training than full-time employees, both women and men. Since a high proportion of women spend at least part of their working life in part-time employment, and over two-fifths of all women employees currently work part-time, this is a major source of disadvantage for women in the labour market. Other groups of adult workers who are disadvantaged in terms of access to training are manual workers (the majority of whom are men), employees in small workplaces (who are disproportionately women) and employees in the private manufacturing sector (the majority of whom will be men)' (ibid.: 41–2). A recent survey reported by Lovering (1992) confirms that: few employees have experience of explicit training beyond initial induction and that semi-skilled production operatives have the least access to continuing training; operatives, clerical and secretarial staff are most likely to be offered technical training only to meet immediate production needs (ibid.: 18); employees had ambivalent attitudes towards the employer-provided training they had experienced because

Table 10.1 Main location of off-the-job training by sex and
economic activity status

	Full time (%)	Part time (%)	Unemployed (%)	Economically inactive (%)
Men				
Premises of:		—		—
own employer	31	—	3	—
another employer	5	—	1	—
Private training centre	10	—	4	—
Govt./LA workshop or centre	1	—	6	—
Open Univ./correspondence course	9	—	12	—
College of further education	22	—	37	—
Other educational institution	9	—	15	—
No information	14		20	
Total	100	100	100	100
(Weighted N)	(2572)	(29)[1]	(112)	(50)[1]
Women				
Premises of:				
own employer	32	26	4	*
another employer	3	4	1	0
Private training centre	7	6	4	4
Govt./LA workshop or centre	1	2	5	4
Open Univ./correspondence course	7	8	16	15
College of further education	26	29	34	44
Other educational institution	14	18	20	25
No information	10	8	16	7
Total	100	100	100	100
(Weighted N)	(1653)	(480)	(110)	(227)

Figures cover work-related education/training received in the past four weeks by GB
population aged 16–49 excluding full-time students, apprentices, people doing initial training
under dual systems, and trainees on the YTS and other government schemes
* Less than 0.5%
[1] Number too small for analysis

Source: Payne, 1992 (calculations based on the Labour Force Survey, 1989)

it was not certificated (ibid.: 15); and much of the training provided
consisted of measures to improve the personal performance, presentation and commitment of employees, rather than promote transferable skills, along with 'devices to impart corporate ideology down the
line' (ibid.: 28).

Even within the occupational groups which do have access to continuing training, the British workers have relatively limited access and their experience compares unfavourably with that of other countries. Research carried out by the National Institute for Economic and Social Research demonstrates that, outside the engineering industry, 90 per cent of supervisors have no formal qualifications. Even in engineering, they have craft rather than supervisory qualifications.[2] In response to concerns about the quality of supervision in this industry, a course modelled on the German *Meister* system was set up through a joint initiative of the Engineering Industry Training Board (EITB), the National Economic Development Office (NEDO), the Gauge and Toolmakers' Association and the City and Guilds of London Institute. However, the EITB reported a disappointing response from employers (Incomes Data Services 1988: 22).

These findings are probably not surprising given the experience of continuing training of the professionals who are themselves responsible for decisions about training and development. Management's own lack of training has been seen as resulting in poor attitudes to the training of employees more generally (Crockett and Elias, 1984). Line management, in particular, has been seen as the weak link in the implementation of training and development policies (Centre for Corporate Strategy and Change/Coopers and Lybrand Associates, 1989: 15–16). Although the Institute of Personnel Management (IPM) published a code on training and development – *Continuous development: people at work* – in 1984, it was only in May 1991 that the IPM Council voted to require evidence of continuing professional development from all those applying to upgrade corporate membership and fellowship, and to introduce a policy on continuing professional development for all corporate members from 1994 (Whittacker, 1992: 28).

Companies' provision of continuing training

Company practices compound the difficulties of assessing the nature and extent of their training provision. There is no requirement for companies in Britain to publish finanical data on training in their annual reports. In addition, the 'Training in Britain' survey found that few employers attempt to cost their training activities and only 40 per cent have a training budget (Incomes Data Services, 1990: 5). Furthermore, they favour on-the-job training, the cost of which is notoriously difficult to assess (Ryan, 1991). While there are well-publicized examples of companies which have introduced innovative training policies and agreements, it is harder to analyse the effectiveness of wider practice. Finally, although continuing training and professional development schemes may be available for managerial and professional grades in some organizations, these rarely extend to the majority of the workforce.

Unlike other countries which collect systematic data on training expenditure under the terms of their training legislation, there is little survey evidence in Britain on expenditure on training in general and continuing training in particular. Since the abolition of the Industrial Training Boards' requirement on companies to complete levy returns, no longitudinal industry-level data have been collected. The major sources of information are the Training in Britain survey and case studies commissioned by the Training Agency (Deloitte, Haskins and Sells, 1989; Centre for Corporate Strategy and Change/ Coopers and Lybrand Associates, 1989). More recently, the Employment Department has conducted the 'Employers' Manpower and Skills Practices Survey' which should prove to be a useful data source.

The failure of British employers to train their workforces has been recognized since the nineteenth century (Perry, 1976). Surveys conducted in the early 1980s suggested that British employers spent between 0.15 and 0.5 per cent of turnover on training compared to 3 per cent spent by leading employers in Japan, West Germany and the USA (Keep, 1989a: 179). The Training in Britain survey of employers' activities (Deloitte, Haskins and Sells, 1989) estimated that they spent £14.4 billion on 125.4 million person days of training in 1986–7, which, allowing for factoring up to include categories of employer not covered by the survey produced the claim that British employers annually spend £20 billion on training. Since this is equivalent to 8.6 per cent of payrolls and 5.4 per cent of national income, it contradicts previous assumptions about employers' lack of commitment to training (Ryan, 1991: 55). However, an analysis of the methodology of the survey finds that while it provides comprehensive and reliable statistics on employers' spending on off-the-job training, for on-the-job training 'the estimates of durations and costs . . . are highly unreliable and in all probablity seriously upward biased – almost certainly so for less skilled occupations' (ibid.: 71). Therefore, one of the major sources of information on employers' spending on continuing training is of dubious reliability. Twenty

Table 10.2 Training received by British employees in
the past four weeks*

	1984	1989	1990†	Change 1989–90	Change 1984–90
All of who received training (000s)	1806	3097	3339	241	1533
of which:					
Aged 16–19	333	390	405	15	72
20–24	369	588	607	18	237
25–34	491	868	958	90	467
35–49	481	980	1063	83	582
50–64	131	272	306	34	175
As a percentage of all employees in the age group:					
All who received training	9.1	14.4	15.4		
of which					
Aged 16–19	20.2	23.0	25.3		
20–24	13.5	19.4	20.5		
25–34	10.7	16.0	16.9		
35–49	7.1	13.3	14.2		
50–64	5.4	7.0	7.8		

* Time series estimates, adjusted for cases where training information was not known
† Prelimary estimates (1990 only)
Source: *Employment Gazette*, April 1991, 188

case studies of companies conducted at the same time showed that in 1986–7 the average spend per employee was £337 with a range of £24–1146. This produced figures of 0.76 per cent of turnover spent on training, within a range of 0.1 and 2.52 per cent of turnover among the case study companies (Centre for Corporate Strategy and Change/Coopers and Lybrand Associates, 1989: 16).

Clearly, it is difficult to obtain accurate information on employers' spending on training over time. Evidence on trends is only available from the Labour Force Survey, which was initiated in 1984 and refers only to individuals' experience of training in the four weeks preceding the survey. Table 10.2 shows that between 1984 and 1990 the percentage of employees receiving training in this period increased from 9.1 to 15.4. It has gradually increased for all age groups, but the increase was greatest among older age groups, indicating a rise in continuing training. However, overall, the greatest proportion of training activity was concentrated on the 16 to 24 age group (*Employment Gazette*, April 1991: 188). By 1991, the Labour Force Survey demonstrated that training budgets were being cut in the recession and the numbers of employees calculated to be receiving training on the basis of the survey findings had fallen from 3.3 million to 3.2 million (*Financial Times*, 11 March 1992). While this decline is partly accounted for by a reduction in initial training resulting from cut-backs in recruitment, a proportion of it must also be attributable to a drop in continuing training and development.

Strategies towards training

A study of training strategies in six private sector companies was conducted in 1990 (Incomes Data Services, 1990). It found that increasing numbers of companies were attempting to integrate training strategies with business objectives and to assess the effectiveness of their training investment on a more systematic basis. Although numerous training activities, particulary those related to initial training and induction continued to be of a routine nature, a number of activities reported had implications for continuing training. Nevertheless, many of the training strategies continue to be a short-term response to market conditions aimed at attaining business objectives rather than a development of long-term strategic approaches to training.

The major way in which business strategies and training were integrated in the IDS study was through the development of total quality management techniques and customer care initiatives, and as a means of facilitating organizational and cultural changes (ibid.: 2). These developments had implications for both the means for identifying training needs and for the organization of the training function and training methods themselves. Techniques such as skills audits, succession planning and appraisal had been introduced to identify individual and corporate training requirements. Although corporate structure clearly influences the organization of the training function, there was some evidence of decentralization of training functions in the companies examined, along with a greater integration of training into the responsibilities of line managers and other non-specialist training staff. Trainers themselves were becoming more like internal consultants and were leaving behind their role of instructors. Training methods were moving in two distinct directions: on the one hand, a greater tailoring of instruction towards business needs, and, on the other, an individualization of the training experience. This was occurring through on-the-job training, and open, distance and action learning methods (ibid.: 3–4).

In addition to these partial accounts of company training strategies there is also some direct evidence of specific initiatives taken by companies on continuing training. These include the retraining of employees for different jobs within the same company and developments in flexible working practices, some of which concern multi-skilling and others a narrower process of job enlargement.

A study of retraining published by Incomes Data Services draws on the experience of seven companies, the Engineering Industry Training Board (EITB) and technical training courses provided by the Electrical, Electronic, Technical and Plumbing Union (EETPU). The report comments: 'The growing awareness of re-training has sparked a lively debate on the "management of change" and how workers should be equipped to deal with it' (Incomes Data Services, 1988: 1). Among this sample, organizations engaged in retraining for different major reasons. Some saw training as a continuous process and made no distinction between initial and further training. Others engaged in retraining for a specific purpose, such as to overcome a skill shortage or to impart the skills required to operate new technology or to accommodate changes in production processes. In other instances the objective of retraining was to increase flexibility. Among the case study companies there was evidence of some limited progression from semi-skilled to skilled status (Sony) and from manual to professional work (*Financial Times*, where print workers were retrained as journalists). Retraining had resulted in job enlargement but full flexibility between trades had not been achieved (Swan Hunter). The EITB had a policy of encouraging adult training and awarded grants for updating, particularly in relation to new technology. The EETPU provides courses in electronics and computing to members and also sells them on a commercial basis to employers.

A study by *Industrial Relations Review and Report* (1989: 2) of multi-skilling agreements in 15 companies distinguished between agreements which link reward to skill acquisition and others which traded a pay award for 'a commitment, some time in the future, to co-operate with training and flexibility programmes'. Two main approaches were adopted to agreements: one was a system of skills-based rewards, whereby progression to new grades was conditional on obtaining additional skills, and the other a system of rewards for dual or multi-skilling, often achieved in steps. Although multi-skilling agreements are linked to rewards, they were timed separately from general pay awards. The reason for this lies in 'the frequent intention that much of the cost of multi-skilling agreements will be recouped from the gains in productivity, such as the sharp reduction in "down time" that moves to team-working can bring' (ibid.: 2).

A more recent survey by Incomes Data Services of the operation of skill-based pay in six companies found employers using it as a mechanism for developing the skills base of the workforce. The advantages were perceived as lying in the increased flexibility of labour, in a leaner and more productive workforce, in increasing pay competitiveness and in motivating staff (Incomes Data Services, 1992: 1). In some of the companies skill-based pay was applied to the whole of the workforce, whereas in others it was more closely targeted. However, the schemes had a finite life. There was the question of how employees' development would continue once they had reached the ceiling of skill levels required, and how the pay system would evolve once the immediate objectives had been met (ibid.: 3). Perhaps more importantly, a long-term strategy towards training and development presupposes the existence of a business plan which allows future skill needs to be anticipated.

Institutional and Policy Context of Continuing Training

A voluntarist system

Both initial training and continuing training are affected significantly by influences from outside the workplace, the major ones being corporate ownership and the state. Insofar as the state creates the regulatory framework of employment law and is responsible for the education system and policy towards vocational training, it may exert influence over decisions made within companies on investment in training. Although the 1964 Industrial Training Act and the 1973 Employment and Training Acts regulated training in companies through the imposition of a training levy, since the Conservative government came to power in 1979 these powers have been progressively eroded and the majority of the boards abolished. The only sectors to retain statutory powers are construction and engineering construction. Therefore, within a voluntarist system, the state has few instruments with which to influence company practices. The exception has been where health and safety, and food hygiene legislation impose standards which require the training of workers.

In contrast to the state's assumption of responsibility for the training of unemployed workers through schemes such as Employment Training, the continuing training of employees has been perceived as the reponsibility of the employer, on the one hand, and the individual employee, on the other. The White Paper *Employment for the 1990s* argued that 'developing training through life is not primarily a government responsibility' (Employment Department, 1988: 49). Rather, employers have the primary responsibility for continuing training, though individuals are also responsible for developing their own careers. In a deregulated training system there are no opportunities for imposing sanctions on employers and individuals who fail to invest in continuing training. However, there are possibilities for encouraging it through financial incentives and the effect of exalting successful companies which do invest in training.

Even though the British training system is essentially voluntarist there are institutional mechanisms for encouraging training in the form of the Training and Enterprise Councils in England and Wales and the Local Enterprise Companies in Scotland which came into operation in 1990 and 1991. There are 82 of these bodies organized on a local basis and they are dominated by employer interests. They are now responsible for the delivery of state-funded training schemes for the unemployed and for a number of schemes fostering business development and self-employment. They operate databases of local labour market information and co-ordinate business/education partnerships. They offer support and guidance on the adoption of quality measures such as total quality management and BS5750 which require a systematic approach to training and are responsible for the implementation of the 'Investors In People' (IIP) award (Incomes Data Services, 1991).

Even before this, a number of different schemes had been introduced to encourage employers to update their employees' skills by investing in continuing training. These have included national grant schemes operated through industry training organizations, local grants operated through Manpower Services Commission (MSC) area offices, training for enterprise schemes aimed at small businesses and support for partnership activity between industry and educational institutions (Hillier, 1989). The Local Collaborative Projects programme, which was jointly funded by the MSC and the Department of Education and Science (DES), was an example of the latter and aimed to establish networks of collaborators between training providers and users in order to make provision more responsive to employers' needs. The programme funded pilot projects, which thereafter were to be self-financing. However, the intended objective of fostering long-term collaboration was not met and formal institutional collaboration occurred in only one-third of the projects funded (Cheshire and Pemberton, 1988: 322). The PICKUP scheme, run by the DES in England and Wales, and the Scottish Education Department, operated on a similar basis and had the objective of increasing the provision of updating and retraining courses offered to employers by institutions of higher education (Stephens, 1988: 597). A review conducted of publicly funded programmes in 1987 resulted in the phasing out of grants for training individuals and a concentration on developing business skills and organizational capabilities. Subequently, in 1989, the Business Growth Programme was launched, its objective being 'to help individual companies to improve their capability to invest effectively in the skills of their workforce' (Hillier, 1989: 220). Government expenditure must be complemented by a financial contribution from the participating companies and the programme is sold 'on the basis of the business benefits which BGP is expected to confer' (ibid.: 223).

In addition to programmes which aim to increase companies' organizational capabilities, there are a number of schemes aimed at encouraging individuals to engage in their own training and development. Among its strategic priorities for action, the White Paper *People, Jobs and Opportunities* listed 'Young people must have the motivation to achieve their full potential and to develop the skills the economy needs' and 'Individuals must be persuaded that training pays and that they should take more responsibility for their own development' (Education Department, 1992: 24). Although the stress is on individual motivation and demand in a 'training market', a number of measures have been introduced to promote individuals' access to training. Among these are Career Development Loans, tax allowances for self-funded training and training credits for young people. In this context, measures to improve information about training availability through Training Access Points and the use of National Vocational Qualifications as a 'currency', providing information about the quality of training on offer, can be seen as mechanisms for improving the operation of the training market.

Nevertheless, there are a number of problems with an emphasis on the individual's responsibility for training and development. There is considerable evidence to demonstrate that in unregulated training systems existing patterns of labour market segmentation are reinforced (Equal Opportunities Commission, 1988; Payne, 1991; Clarke, 1991). Payne (1992: 1) argues that it has been the system of rationing training which has prevented wider access, rather than the problem of individual motivation. She points out that current levels of self-funding are extremely low and carry a high level of personal risk. Furthermore, 'there are indications that self-funding is to some extent the resort of people who cannot get training in any other way . . . It is possible that by shifting a greater proportion of training costs to private individuals, inequalities in access to training will be widened' (ibid.: 22).

There are much more fundamental problems about the processes whereby the state can influence employers' and individuals' training decisions in a deregulated training system. Keep and Mayhew (1994) point out that 'having accepted the primacy of the employer and of market mechanisms, and the counter-productiveness of any role for legislative underpinning, the range of choice available to policy-makers in designing institutional delivery mechanisms has been heavily circumscribed'. It seems unlikely that individuals' decisions regarding training will effectively meet employers' skill requirements, even if there were mechanisms in place to provide them with perfect information. This is not to argue that there is no place for individual decision making with respect to continuing training and development, since individual choice forms a powerful motivational factor, as the Ford Motor company's Employee Development and Assistance Programme (EDAP) – which concerns access to education and lifestyle courses rather than vocational programmes – has demonstrated (McCarthy, 1990).

At the same time, employers' decisions on training, which are often driven by short-term skill requirements, are unlikely to produce the planning of a longer term training strategy. Incentives in the form of grants, advice and the evidence of good examples may provide some motivation to train, but can amount to no more than the fine-tuning of the market mechanism. Moreover, some questions have been raised concerning the basic direction of the government's chosen mechanisms – namely the development of the Training and Enterprise Councils and the system of National Vocational Qualifications – for the delivery of training objectives. These concern the possibility that 'money would be spent on marketing the idea of training rather than improving substance' and that 'new forms of certificate will give spurious recognition to the existing level of skills' (*Financial Times*, 2 April 1991, quoted by Beaumont, 1991: 118).

Indirect influences on continuing training

There are some areas where professional associations and trade unions perform a regulatory role and can therefore exercise a direct or indirect influence over training. Although professional organizations and trade unions are often excluded from a formal policy-making role (Rainbird, 1991; Rainbird and Smith, 1992), they nevertheless exert indirect influence over continuing training in the workplace. A survey for the IPM of 16 professional bodies found that three – the Law Society, the Royal Institute of Chartered Surveyors and the Institute of Chartered Accountants – had mandatory schemes of continuing professional development. The Engineering Council plans to introduce a voluntary scheme and the Royal College of Veterinary Surgeons strongly recommends that members allow a minimum of five days a year for developmental activities (Arkin, 1992: 29). The Institute of Civil Engineers and the Institute of Structural Engineers also require members to attend training courses in order to retain membership (Green et al., 1992: 20). In recent years, trade unions have attempted to put training on the bargaining agenda in view of the absence of statutory rights to training. For example, MSF has argued: 'As long as access to training is not a statutory entitlement, employees depend to a large extent on trade unions to secure this right for them as part of their contract of employment' (Manufacturing, Science, Finance, 1988: 20). Although a Labour Research Department survey of shop stewards in 1989 found relatively little progress on the establishment of workplace training committees and agreements on training (Labour Research Department, 1990: 7), by 1992 a number of unions, including those organizing unskilled workers, were increasing the priority they attached to training. An illustration of this is the joint policy document issued by the GMB and the TGWU in 1992 calling for workers' entitlement to a minimum of five days' training a year (*Industrial Relations Review and Report*, 1992: 5). Other unions run courses for their members allowing them to update their vocational and professional skills, the EETPU and NALGO being examples of this. Despite the exclusion of trade union interests from a formal policy-making role with respect to training, the CBI and the TUC have engaged in dialogue on the achievement of training targets for the future. The development of 'social dialogue' on training at European level seems likely to support the inclusion of training in collective bargaining (Milner, 1992).

Even in the absence of a formal trade union role in workplace training, there is evidence that a trade union presence contributes indirectly to the provision of training. The unions' influence is significant 'not so much in exerting active pressure on companies to train, but in the way they secure companies' commitment to existing staff, either through agreements or, tacitly, through membership density. Trade unions exercise a positive, though indirect, influence also through co-operation in changes which they recognize lead to training and increased marketability of their members' (Centre for Corporate Strategy and Change/Coopers and Lybrand, 1989: 16). Econometric analysis of the Labour Force Survey suggests the impact of unions on training is 'positive and substantial' in the case of non-manual workers in small establishments (Claydon and Green, 1992: 7).

Case Study Evidence of Continuing Training

Given the weakness of institutional regulation of training in Britain, it is useful to examine case study evidence of organizations' continuing training practices. This allows the rationale for policies towards continuing training to be investigated. It also provides a basis for examining which organizations are investing in it and which groups of employees benefit from it. Five case studies have been selected to illustrate different aspects of continuing training and, in particular, to address the question of the linkage between business and training strategies. They draw on examples from the private and public sectors and aim to illustrate differences in market strategies as well as the impact of patterns corporate ownership.

Training for flexible working

In this vehicle components manufacturer it was estimated that the company spent 8 per cent of payroll on training, which included a consideration of outlay and training staff time alongside a subtraction of the benefits of having trainees working on production. In this company, training was viewed as an investment, linked to the quality of work, which was required by all employees, from the board members through to operators. In addition to its initial training for youth employees and for graduate recruits, the company had received support from the European Social Fund to undertake retraining of adults in high-technology skills. This had involved a minimum of 100 hours' training for operators and 200 hours for young people on courses developed jointly with the manufacturers of new equipment. In addition, the company had been developing definitions of performance standards for maintenance workers and toolmakers so that they could work across trades. Although there was some resistance by workers in these areas to flexible working, the management view was that in terms of their skills they were already highly flexible but that the process of assessment, skill recognition and identification of additional training needed formalization.

The reason for this high level of investment in training appeared to lie in three main factors: firstly, the company operated in an international market and had to train to compete; secondly, it had taken on the engineering design function and had acquired a product design authority requiring a higher level of engineering skills throughout the organization; and, thirdly, following a management buy-out, it had undergone a process of recapitalization in the 1980s, acquiring a CAD system compatible with that of the major motor manufacturers, which it supplies on a 'parts-on-time' basis. It has adopted a system of recognizing skills, and employees' ability to train other workers in them, modelled on that of Nissan, one of its major customers. This system has been described in detail by Wickens (1991).

This training system was linked to the development of team-working. Although there was no direct pay incentive to acquiring the new skills certified in this way, the fact that it made workers more proficient at their jobs was seen as providing an incentive insofar as this could increase bonus earnings. Although these were currently calculated on an individual basis it was envisaged that bonuses would eventually be calculated on a group basis as team-working became more established.

The company was seeking to achieve flexible working practices and team-working through its training programme. Although investment in training was considerable and new systems had been introduced to facilitate the generalization of new production skills, the process of upskilling and constant updating of skills was only in its initial stages.

Training for Taylorism

This specialist vehicle manufacturer operates in an international market covering the UK, Western Europe, the Middle East and North Africa. It employs a total of just over 1000 workers at its production site, alongside a further 200 employees in the marketing and service engineering departments at separate locations. In 1987 it was bought by a US-owned conglomerate which was perceived by the staff in the personnel department as having a positive attitude to training. The company was reported to be moving towards a flexible manufacturing system, though it was at the 'islands of automation' phase. Although there was a flexibility agreement with the hourly paid staff, this was primarily aimed at a reduction of down time rather than multi-skilling, a degree of specialization being perceived as desirable.

In this company the training budget was £120,000, compared to a payroll of £10 million (i.e. a budget of 1.2 per cent of payroll). The main focus of training was on apprenticeship, management and supervisory courses. As far as continuing training was concerned, this was restricted to line managers, who were only just beginning to receive training on a systematic basis, and technicians, who were receiving training with support from the European Social Fund. Although a training audit was planned, it was estimated that it would take three to four years before there would be an effective training organization. Training policy was reactive rather than planned.

The absence of forward planning and policies on continuing training can be ascribed to a number of different factors. Firstly, this was a traditional manufacturing company using Taylorist methods of work organization. Secondly, the US parent company was more concerned with improving management and supervisory training than with that of the shop floor and, in fact, was impressed with the quality of craft training provided in the company. Moreover, the local labour market was economically depressed and there was a pool of skilled workers who could readily be recruited in the locality. Finally, there was the possibility that the corporate parent would sell the company at short notice since it was only one in a large portfolio of investments. Therefore the commitment to increased management and supervisory training was probably transitory and aimed at increasing short-term profits. The parent company had no interest in the long-term development of a training strategy extending to the workforce as a whole.

Training for organizational development

In this contract catering company the devolution of operating strategy to unit managers was accompanied by the devolution of training responsibilities. While training remained part of the personnel function at the corporate centre, training had become a part of every manager's day-to-day responsibility. Senior management's view was that previously the personnel and training department had often served as a prop for the shortcomings of management. In this company, the objective was to build up training and development skills throughout the organization, which would create a mechanism for transferring competences down the line.

The way in which this objective was implemented was through a 'Trainer Development Scheme', a programme to develop training skills which leads to the issuing of trainer licences. This involved two three-day programmes, one for the development of one-to-one coaching skills, the other in the development of group training techniques. Initially an external consultant was brought in to set the scheme up, but the significance of the scheme was that of creating a system for cascading information and competences down the management hierarchy. The two parts of the scheme involve the development of project work which is geared to displaying managerial skills. They are run in-house with external certification. The course has enabled the company to identify high flyers, who are then designated as possible tutors for others. As senior managers passed through the scheme a network of senior trainers was created, effectively made up of unit managers with responsibilities for training other managers of units within their districts. In this way, peer groups work together in developing skills and the disadvantages of a top down approach imposed by a central training unit are avoided. Nevertheless, initially there was some resistance to the programme from regional personnel officers who believed that they did not have the staff with the abilities to implement it. By the end of 1989 it was estimated that about one-third of the units within the organization had been affected by the training programme and the company was embarking on an evaluation exercise.

Alongside the development of these trainer skills is a system of modular training packages, with closely targeted content and objectives related to health and safety, hygiene etc. which can be adapted to the requirements of individual business units. They can be used either on-the-job or, in combination, as an off-the-job programme.

The objective of the scheme is for operational managers to train unit managers. The system is linked into performance review objectives and is perceived as being part of a process of cultural change that the senior trainers have responsibility for communicating downstream. In other words, it is a programme which is capable of achieving internal organizational development and, in particular, transmitting a new organizational ideology linked to customer service and quality assurance.

Training for customer service

In the early 1980s this high street supermarket chain had greatly increased investment in training as a means of moving up market. This increase was spread across all types of staff, from shop-floor workers and checkout operators through to management, and was accompanied by improved staff facilities on site. Even so, training for most of the staff was in customer service and was company-specific. Although it may have increased the staff's sense of commitment to the company and, in theory, opened up potential internal career routes for them, the training did not impart transferable skills. Moreover, the employment of large numbers of women on a part-time basis meant that although these career paths were open in theory, in practice there was very little job mobility for shop-floor employees. In contrast to this, the management training consisted of courses which were both company-specific and general, the latter being externally certified and transferable.

The supermarket chain has six regional training teams, which operate in parallel with, but are separate from, the regional structure of the personnel function. New projects in training development are organized nationally, such as a new national foundation training scheme aimed at youth recruits, involving registration for the retail certificate, introduced in 1989. Responsibility for the training of staff for the opening of new stores, including team-building programmes, are also organized nationally. However, the main responsibility for implementation lies at the regional level, which is responsible for co-ordination with stores.

A regional structure also enables some measure of adaptation to local labour market conditions. Although a decision was made at national level to replace trainee status and allowances by employee status and wages in 1989, specific initiatives – for example, the recruitment of older people and their integration into the company through induction and departmental training programmes – were possible through the element of managerial discretion at store level.

In this instance, a reorientation in market strategy had produced a major investment in training, linking organizational development, corporate culture and the development of career development paths within the organization. Although in theory they are open to all, in practice, the fact that a major part of the staff are part-time women employees means that training and development opportunities are restricted. Nevertheless, in this example there is a clear relationship between corporate strategy and human resource strategy.

Training for public service

In 1989 this large local authority had a total workforce of over 30,000, of which just over one-third were part-time workers. Its activities are organized into 18 major departments of different sizes, each of which are affected to varying degrees by government reforms of public service provision. Many departments are now having to introduce more commercial working practices into their operations and are having to compete or collaborate with the private sector to deliver services. Therefore, a major objective of the authority has been to improve the quality of its service delivery so as to retain contracts and maintain the workload of its directly employed workforce. The authority is Labour-controlled and sees itself as a 'good employer'.

The local authority had a large central personnel and training function which was undergoing a period of decentralization to departmental level. The objective of decentralization was to integrate departmental training plans with the business objectives of service delivery. Although this process was linked to the imposition of compulsory competitive tendering (CCT) by central government, it affected departments to varying degrees. Whereas the Works Department had been obliged to compete for contracts since the passing of the 1981 Local Government Land and Planning Act, it was not to affect the Leisure Services Department (running swimming pools, sports centres and public amenities) until 1992. In contrast, other departments were unlikely to be affected by CCT, though their relationship with the private sector provision of services was changing – for example, the need to regulate the growth of private sector provision of care for the elderly in the case of the Family and

Community Services Department. The Housing Department was similarly unaffected by CCT but, with council house sales and moves to joint ventures with the private sector and housing associations, it was having to move towards a reassessment of the services it provided. Changes in organizational culture and the ethos of service delivery were putting the local authority services increasingly on a commercial basis. This produced a new emphasis on the ideology of customer service and the quality of service which the authority sought to achieve through the integration of its training programme with its business strategy. It attempted to introduce total quality management through performance review of senior managers while attempting to link improved service delivery to staff development programmes for employees.

Overall, the local authority spent approximately 1 per cent of the wages bill on training, although this budget was unevenly distributed, with a major proportion of it being devoted to craft training. However, attempts were being made to tailor courses provided externally more closely to the organization's needs through closer liaison with external providers. This was particularly the case with management and supervisory courses, where general courses were seen to be required to enable the authority to operate in the new culture while operating within the constraints of local government legislation and national agreements in a highly unionized environment.

Improvements in the delivery of services were targeted through the introduction of performance management. There was no formal appraisal scheme, but some departments had introduced staff development interviews. Trainers were seen as having a key role in building the counselling skills managers required to conduct such interviews.

The development of a customer care orientation also required the establishment of links between client and service departments. Training officers played a key part in facilitating this linkage through their consultancy role. The central personnel department did retain a role in managerial training, as this had spin-offs in terms of internal and external linkages as well as leading to the development of joint courses between departments. Training has also been a vehicle for improving communications and understanding between departments and has, in some instances, led to substantial cost savings.

Discussion

As can be seen from these examples, there are differences in the extent to which business and training strategies are integrated within these organizations. In some cases, factors intrinsic to the nature of the product or services offered structure the extent to which continuing training has been introduced into the organization. For example, with the supermarket chain the delivery of a fairly uniform range of products across a broad geographical spread of retailing outlets allowed training procedures to be standardized. The company's decision to move up market prompted the adoption of a customer service orientation as a means of differentiating products from those of competitors. Since its competitors stock a similar range of products, it is the quality of service which becomes a key factor in differentiating one supermarket chain from another. In contrast to this, the variety and specialized nature of the vehicle components manufacturer's products, alongside its need to satisfy the quality specifications of large corporate clients, produced a different emphasis on training. The same components manufacturer also provides an interesting contrast with the specialist vehicle manufacturer. Both operate in international markets, but it is the production process itself which differentiates the emphasis on training provision. The components manufacturer produces small batches and is moving towards team-working and flexible working practices while the vehicle manufacturer, which produces longer runs of more standardized goods, will be dependent on specialization in the division of labour for the foreseeable future. It was the need for lean production techniques and flexible working practices which was driving higher levels of investment in training in the components firm for manual and white collar workers alike, although it was concentrated on the highly skilled. In contrast, continuing training in the specialist vehicle manufacturer was focused on management development, with some provision for maintenance staff, among whom more flexible working practices were being developed. Production workers were not affected. There are two further factors influencing the strategy observed in the components manufacturer: the role of the integration of the CAD/CAM system with that of major clients and the integration, as opposed to externalization, of the design function.

Nevertheless, corporate structure can be seen to be crucially important in the degree to which organizations are able to co-ordinate and integrate their approaches to training and human resource management. As an independent company, the components manufacturer has a much greater degree of discretion over training policies and the capacity to plan a longer term strategy than the specialist vehicle manufacturer which has to satisfy financial targets set by its conglomerate parent. Carey (1992) draws the distinction between companies which are able to integrate their training function and those whose structures inhibit or even discourage central co-ordination and integration. She argues that 'strategic planning' companies have the greatest capacity to develop centralized strategies, while 'strategic control' companies exhibit tension between central control and the local or even client orientation of the business unit. 'Financial control' companies, which exhibit a restricted role for corporate strategy outside the setting of financial objectives, are least capable of influencing training. Similarly, Keep (1989b: 121) has noted that the leading examples of human resource management are companies producing single or closely related products, rather than conglomerates or holding companies.

The local authority, the contract caterers and the supermarket chain all demonstrate the use of continuing training for the purposes of organizational development. Training is used as a means of conveying changes in corporate culture and, linked to developments such as team briefing and the use of in-house newsletters, can be utilized to 'cascade' corporate objectives down the management line. This may also be linked to the reorganization of the training function. In the contract caterers, training was devolved to line management and although some centralized functions were retained in the local authority, the devolution of training responsibilities to departmental level was closely linked to the objective of getting business strategy to drive training strategy.

What is less clear from these examples is the extent to which staff development accompanied strategies for organizational development. In the local authority the extensive use of professional staff imposed certain requirements for continuous training, as did the need to impart more commercial values to senior and line management. However, outside these groups of employees, though some resources were committed to the training and development of manual and clerical staff, with one scheme aimed at women in particular, the bulk of expenditure continued to be on the initial training of craft workers. In both the supermarket chain and the contract caterer, resources were being devoted to management development, but the 'exchange value' to staff of customer service training, on the one hand, and basic operational skills training, on the other, on the external labour market must be questioned.

The evidence concerning the ways in which continuing training is used to motivate and retain staff is limited. Although training and development are widely recognized as contributing to motivation, it appears to be provided mainly for managerial grades and for professional staff, particularly those whose skills are in short supply or whose professional organizations require it as a condition for membership. During the fieldwork period there was widespread concern about skill shortages and this had had the effect of releasing funds for training as a means of reducing levels of turnover among the most highly qualified staff. In this respect, individuals were temporarily in a strong market position which enabled them to accept employment where the best opportunities for training and career progression were offered. However, it is uncertain whether the same funds continue to be available for professional development in less favourable market conditions.

There was considerable evidence in the case study organizations of restructuring, both internal corporate restructuring and divestments and takeovers. There was widespread use of training as a means of imparting a new organizational culture, whether imposed by a new parent organization or through changes in corporate strategy and identity.

Finally, although much lip-service was paid to the significance of human resource management in corporate strategy, there was some evidence of moves towards a more systematic identification of training needs through the integration of training and business strategies. Training in many instances had facilitated the introduction of appraisal and performance assessment which, in turn, were leading to the identification of training and development needs. These techniques, however, tended to be restricted to managerial and administrative staff and were seldom extended to manual and clerical staff. There was evidence in particular of a growth in in-house training provision and a greater tailoring of externally provided courses to organization-specific needs.

In addition, many of the developments observed concerned the transmission of corporate culture. This was related to processes of restructuring, changes in corporate ownership or the development of new business strategies. This raises the question of whether levels of investment in training are retained once the initial requirements to transmit a new corporate culture have been satisfied. Moreover, will they be maintained under further changes in corporate ownership? The relationship between corporate culture, transmitted through training programmes, and broader skill development programmes has yet to be investigated, alongside employees' perceptions of the usefulness and transferability of competences attained through their socialization into corporate culture.

Conclusion

In this chapter the consequences of a weak system of institutional regulation of continuing training have been documented. The evidence suggests that there may have been some extension of access to continuing training in recent years from managerial and professional groups, which have traditionally had greatest access to it, to skilled workers, especially where employers are attempting to introduce multi-skilling and where changes in production processes require the updating of skills. However, this is strongly influenced by product markets, production methods and corporate structure. It is also important to emphasize that the case study organizations all have established training practices. They are therefore representative of the 40 per cent of employers who were found to have a training budget in the 'Training in Britain' survey (see Incomes Data Services, 1990: 5) rather than the 60 per cent which did not. As Streeck (1989) has argued, the problem of a market-driven system is not the 'islands of excellence' such as these organizations, but the fact that good training practices are not generalized more widely. In a deregulated training system there are few mechanisms available to the government for exerting influence over either employers or individuals. This surely begs the question of the role of regulation with respect to both initial and continuing training.

Even among the case study organizations, access to continuing training is concentrated among managers, professionals and the highly skilled. This suggests that even where organizations are developing a training strategy in tandem with their business strategy, the major part of these organizations' human resources are not being developed to their full potential. As such, the market-driven training model reproduces existing patterns of occupational inequality. This failure to extend continuing training to all sectors of the workforce is also found in the more highly regulated training systems in France

and Germany, which suggests that regulation provides a framework
for, but not the essence of, effective practice.

Notes

1 This draws on the research conducted by the author and Malcolm
Maguire of the Centre for Labour Market Studies, University of Leicester, under the ESRC's initiative 'The Institutional Determinants of Adult
Retraining'.
2 Contribution by Hilary Steedman to the Warwick VET Forum workshop
on higher intermediate skills, University of Warwick, 6 April 1992.

Bibliography

Amadieu, J.-F. 1992. 'Labour-Management Cooperation and Work Or-
ganisation Change: Deficits in the French Industrial Relations System'.
New Directions in Work Organisation: The Industrial Relations Response.
Paris: Organization for Economic Co-operation and Development.

Arkin, A. 1992. 'What Other Institutes are Doing'. *Personnel Management,*
March, 29.

Beaumont, P. B. 1991. 'Annual Review Article 1991'. *British Journal of
Industrial Relations,* Vol. 30, 1, March, 107–25.

Campbell, A. and Warner, M. 1991. 'Training Strategies and
Miocroelectronics in the Engineering Industries of the UK and Germany'. In Ryan, P. (ed.) *International Comparisons of Vocational Education
and Training for Intermediate Skills.* London: Falmer Press.

Campinos-Dubernet, M. and Grando, J.-M. 1988. 'Formation
professionelle ouvrière: trois modèles européenes'. *Formation/Emploi,*
No. 22, 5–29.

Carey, S. 1992. 'Given a Committment to the Strategic Integration of
Training Within an HRM Framework, What Kinds of Structures Enhance or Inhibit the Training Capability of an Organisation? What are
the Implications for the Training Function and Training Personnel?'.
Paper presented to the conference 'Multinational Companies and Human Resources: A Moveable Feast?'. University of Warwick, 22–4 June.

Cassels, J. 1990. *Britain's Real Skill Shortage and What to Do About It.*
London: Policy Studies Institute.

Centre for Corporate Strategy and Change/Coopers and Lybrand Associates. 1989. *Training In Britain. A Study of Funding, Activity and Attitudes.
Employers' Perspectives on Human Resources.* London: HMSO.

Cheshire, P. and Pemberton, J. 1988. 'Restructuring Training – Evaluation
of the Local Collaborative Projects Programme'. *Employment Gazette,*

June, 319–23.

Clarke, K. 1991. *Women and Training: A Review*. Research Discussion Series, No. 1. Manchester: Equal Opportunities Commission.

Claydon, T. and Green, F. 1992. *The Effect of Unions on Training Provision*. Discussion Papers in Economics, No. 92/3. University of Leicester, Department of Economics.

Crockett, D. and Elias, P. 1984. 'British Managers: A Study of Their Education, Training, Mobility and Earnings'. *British Journal of Industrial Relations*, Vol. 22, 34–46.

Deloitte, Haskins and Sells. 1989. *Training In Britain. A Study of Funding, Activities and Attitudes*. London: HMSO.

Dubar, C. 1990. *La Formation professionelle continue*. Paris: Editions La Découverte.

Employment Department. 1990. *Employment For The 1990s*. London: HMSO.

Employment Department. 1992. *People, Jobs And Opportunity*. Cm 1810. London: HMSO.

Equal Opportunities Commission. 1988. 'Submission'. House of Lords Select Committee on the European Communities. *Vocational Training and Re-Training*. London: HMSO.

Fuller, A. and Saunders, M. 1990. 'The Paradox in Open Learning At Work'. University of Lancaster, Institute for Post-Compulsory Education (mimeo).

Green, F. et al. 1992. 'Training in the Recession'. Paper presented to the conference 'Vocational Training in Britain and Europe Post-1992'. Oxford, 7–8 September.

Hillier, R. 1989. 'Making Training a Key Factor in Business Success'. *Employment Gazette*, May, 219–24.

Incomes Data Services. 1988. *Retraining*. Study No. 405.

Incomes Data Services. 1990. *Training Strategies*. Study No. 460.

Incomes Data Services. 1991. *TECs – Training and Enterprise Councils*. Study No. 485.

Incomes Data Services. 1992. *Skill-based Pay*. Study No. 500.

Industrial Relations Review and Report. 1989. 'Multi-skilling – Linking Pay to Skill Acquisition'. No. 451, November.

Industrial Relations Review and Report. 1992. 'TGWU and GMB Unite in Training Claim'. February.

Keep, E. 1989a. 'A Training Scandal?' In Sisson, K. (ed.) *Personnel Management In Britain*. Oxford: Blackwell.

Keep, E. 1989b. 'Corporate Training Strategies: The Vital Component'. In Storey, J. (ed.) *New Perspectives in Human Resource Management*. London and New York: Routledge.

Keep, E. and Mayhew, K. 1994. 'UK Training Policy – Assumptions and Reality'. In Booth, A. and Snower, D. J. (eds) *The Skills Gap and Economic Activity*. Cambridge: Cambridge University Press.

Labour Research Department. 1990. *Bargaining Report.* January.

Lovering, J. 1992. 'The Institutional Determinants of Employers' Training Strategies'. Paper prepared for the Economic and Social Research Council.

Mahnkopf, B. 1992. 'The Skill-Oriented Strategies of German Trade Unions; Their Impact on Efficency and Equality Objectives'. *British Journal of Industrial Relations*, Vol. 30, 1, 61–81.

Manufacturing, Science, Finance. 1988. *Training For The Future. Can Britain Compete?* London: MSF.

McCarthy, J. 1990. 'In Pursuit of Jointness. The Ford EDAP Programme'. Unpublished MA dissertation. University of Warwick, Industrial Relations Research Unit.

Méhaut, P. 1988. 'New Firms' Training Policies and Changes in the Wage-Earning Relationship'. *Labour and Society*, Vol. 13, 4, 443–56.

Milner, S. 1992. 'European Community Training Policy and Social Dialogue At European Level: A New Agenda?'. Paper presented to the British Sociological Conference, 'A New Europe?'. University of Canterbury, 6–8 April.

NIACE. 1990. *Annual Report, 1989–90.* Leicester: National Institute Of Adult Continuing Education.

Payne, J. 1991. *Women, Training And The Skills Shortage. The Case For Public Investment.* London: Policy Studies Institute.

Payne, J. 1992. 'Motivating Training'. Paper presented to the Centre for Economic Performance's Project on Vocational Education and Training. January.

Perry, P. J. C. 1976. *The Evolution of British Manpower Policy. From the Statute of Artificers 1593 to the Industrial Training Act 1964.* London: Eyre and Spottiswoode.

Rainbird, H. 1991. 'British Trade Unions and the Possibility of a Skill-Oriented Modernisation Strategy in a Low Skill Economy'. Wissenschaftzentrum Discussion Paper. Berlin: WZB.

Rainbird, H. and Smith, J. 1992. 'The Role Of The Social Partners in Vocational Education and Training in Great Britain'. Report prepared for the Italian Ministry of Labour. University of Warwick, Industrial Relations Research Unit.

Ryan, P. 1991. 'How Much Do Employers Spend on Training? An Assessment of the "Training in Britain" Survey'. *Human Resource Management Journal.* Vol. 1, No. 4. Summer.

Stephens, M. 1988. 'PICKUP – Where Two Worlds Merge'. *Employment Gazette*, November, 596–8.

Streeck, W. et al. 1987. *The Role of the Social Partners in Vocational Training and Further Training in the Federal Republic of Germany.* Berlin: CEDEFOP.

Streeck, W. 1989. 'Skills and the Limits of Neo-Liberalism: The Enterprise of the Future as a Place Of Learning'. *Work, Employment and Society*, Vol.

3, No. 1, 89–104.

Tanguy, L. 1991. *Quelle formation pour les ouvriers et employés en France?* Rapport au Secrétaire d'Etat a l'Enseignement Technique. Paris: La Documentation Française.

Whittacker, J. 1992. 'Continuing Professional Development. Making a Policy of Keeping Up-To-Date'. *Personnel Management*, March, 28–31.

Wickens, P. (1991) 'Innovation in Training Creates a Competitive Edge'. In Stevens, J. and Mackay, R. (eds) *Training and Competitiveness*. London: Kogan Page.

11

Management Development

John Storey

Activity in the field of 'management development' has been particularly intense in the past few years. Numerous initiatives have been
launched at every level of the British personnel system. Meanwhile,
debate among practitioners and analysts has taken off in new directions: the idea of the 'learning organization' has been thrust to the
fore; the dichotomy between 'manager' and 'leader' has been extensively explored; and various models of 'informal learning' have been
subjected to close analysis. In these, and many other ways, the
management development scene has moved on considerably since
the chapter on management development was written for the first
edition of this book.

But the increased activity has raised as many questions as it has
answered. How are managers really made? What, indeed, are the
skills, competences, capabilities and expertise required of managers?
Are there ways to engender those which can be regarded as more
effective than other ways? What are the principal current techniques
in management development and what evidence is there of effective
use?

These are the main issues addressed in this chapter. The first
section discusses the nature of management development. This at-
tends to matters such as how the activity is conceptualized and its
various perceived purposes. It also reviews the changing ways in
which management development has been viewed over time. The
second section examines the main methods and techniques which
are used in management development. The third section reviews the
work of the 'Management Charter Initiative', focusing, in particular,
on the idea of 'competences' and the accreditation of learning. The
fourth section is concerned with the factors which shape the provision and effectiveness of management development. The chapter

concludes with a look at possible scenarios for development in the future.

The Nature of Management Development

Conceptualizations about what management development *is* are obviously closely intertwined with what it is deemed to be *for*. As many senior managers can increasingly be heard to say, it is not an end in itself. There is an interesting tension in the provision of developmental opportunities. On the one hand economic utility is frequently demanded of it: it must be shown to 'meet the needs of the business'. To this end, there has been an increasing interest in attempts to evaluate the outcome of 'investments' in management development activity. Yet on the other hand one finds much talk of the inherent value of developmental opportunities and even open declarations of the willingness to take its beneficial outcomes on trust.

Another equally fundamental issue which runs throughout the theory and practice of management development turns on the question of whether there is a known body of knowledge and set of generic skills which management professionals must have, in the same way as must, say, qualified accountants, lawyers, doctors or skilled tradesmen. This is by no means a trivial issue. The controversial 'competences' debate hinges on this point. Much of the defence of the idea of codifying, and itemizing, generic managerial competences at each main level of management is based on the assumption that certain demonstrated areas of expertise must be attained and recorded if progress is to be made manifestly observable. There are many laudable aspects to this endeavour, but the inherent problem associated with a fixed list of competences in the sphere of management work is the extent to which the needed role behaviours are subject to such tremendous variation. The source of variability may lie in the divergent business strategies (Schuler and Jackson, 1987) and it may lie in the periodic change in priorities concerning what is required of managers and workers as paradigms of 'good practice' change over time (Storey, 1992). For example, in the large relatively stable industrial bureaucracies which grew up after the Second World War, the prized behaviours were efficient performance, conformity with rules, cost reduction, and an understanding of and activity within the prescribed role. Under later conditions of instability and heightened international competition, which made traditional industrial bureaucracies look moribund, the new managerial competences hinged around the capacity to foresee new developments. Hence, the ability to identify threats and opportunities became salient, as did the demonstration of creativity, of being a self-starter, and of capability to get things moving and manage change within large organizations – in other words, the competences of entrepreneurship and political acumen.

So significant was this movement that it became increasingly common to treat management development itself simply as a device to engineer organizational change and in particular to engineer 'culture change' (Marsh, 1986). Thus, Lippitt (1982), for example, talks of management development as 'the key to organizational renewal'. This link between culture change and management development has been particularly noticeable in the finance sector. Banks, building societies and insurance companies – where managers are traditionally unlikely to be innovators or risk-takers – have all been subjected to broadly similar treatment involving management development interventions (see, for example, Smith, 1987; Stemp, 1987). Similar attempts to use management development as a tool to engineer wide-ranging culture change are reported from other sectors such as railways (Thackway, 1987) healthcare (Annandale, 1986) and telecommunications (Smith et al., 1986).

Another related theme is the objective of using management development as a tool in pursuit of quality, cost reduction and 'profitability through excellence' (Alexander, 1987; Nagler, 1987; Wagel, 1987). Companies increasingly declare that their training activities are to be seen as explicitly linked with establishing 'company values' such as 'existing for the customer'. Following the famed British Airways example, chief executives are now routinely drawn into training programmes to signal symbolically 'top management commitment' to the message being conveyed. Management development may also be used as a means to forge a common identity following a takeover or merger. Fulmer (1986) describes how it was used by Bendix Corporation to reduce resistance to a merger and to build a 'positive, blended corporate culture'.

If, then, these are among the wide-ranging and ambitious objectives of 'management development', how has the phenomenon itself been defined? A much-quoted definition conceives of it as 'an attempt to improve managerial effectiveness through a planned and deliberate learning process' (cited by Mumford, 1987: 29). But interestingly Mumford now avers that, despite an erstwhile attachment to this definition, his recent empirical research and consulting activity leads him to conclude that it is defective. His main objection now is that it over-emphasizes the importance of deliberate planning in the process of management learning.

The fact that formal definitions are now out of favour serves to highlight the fashions and trends within the field of management development. As Pedler et al. (1991) remind us, managerial training and development has evolved through a number of recognizable phases. Immediately following the Second World War the perceived urgency of upgrading skills in order to meet productivity targets led to an emphasis on systematic training. The limitations of this planned, formalistic approach, they suggest, led to the emergence of 'organizational development' (OD), discussed in more detail in the next chapter, as an antidote to bureaucracy. Another 'reaction' was the coming into favour of self-development methods and action learning.

These latter approaches have in turn been subjected to criticism. They are now sometimes perceived as all very well for 'personal growth', but as less functional for moving forward the organizational needs. This same point can be found embedded in the popular and useful distinction between 'manager development' and 'management development'. The former can include all manner of educational and training experiences which enhance the individual, while the latter denotes an upgrading which is seen to have a more direct impact on the functional capability of the managerial stock as a whole in a manner relevant to business needs.

The current state of play is seen as reaching its apotheosis in 'the learning organization'. This is defined as 'an organization that facilitates the learning of all its members and continuously transforms itself' (Pedler et al., 1991: 1). These authors go on to claim:

> We have seen, then, that the Learning Company is here, in the time-space era of the early 1990s in the UK. This is because the ideas of organization, training and development and of quality management, have evolved to that point. It is no coincidence that an increasing number of organizations are faced with the true bureaucratic crisis phase in their developments such that the Learning Company is needed. (ibid.: 16)

The tension between two fundamental and divergent 'models' of management development can be seen today and throughout its formative history. The first model sees appropriate management development as being provided in a formal top-down and highly structured manner. The emphasis is placed therefore on formal training programmes. Associated with this approach are corporate training colleges, a corporate training department staffed with qualified trainers, a well-publicized programme of 'core' and optional training courses, and an integrated system of appraisal which identifies both training needs and candidates for the training programmes. The opposite, 'informal' model is decentralized and places the emphasis on self-development.

It is not possible, in the abstract, to claim that one or other is more effectual in all circumstances. It can, however, be observed that the *profile* of management development activity is more pronounced when a more formalized posture is adopted. This prominence should not, however, be confused with impact or efficacy. In particular, the maturity and embeddedness of developmental activity in an organization is not necessarily related to the degree of visibility which the management development function itself might or might not have.

A more finely drawn way to conceptualize levels of maturity in management development provision has been drawn by Burgoyne (1988). He identifies six main 'levels' or 'stages' in organizational management development. At the first level there is no systematic development in any sense of the term. Whatever development of talent may happen does so in a totally unplanned way. At the second level there are isolated fragmentary activities, perhaps in sporadic responses to identified acute problems. At the third level a range of development activities do occur and are to a degree co-ordinated and integrated with each other. At stage four the integrated approach is taken further in that management development is treated strategically and plays its part in implementing corporate policies – for example, through human resource planning to meet the pre-ordained corporate strategy objectives. At stage five the practice becomes even more sophisticated in that management development in turn makes an input into corporate strategy formulation. The final stage is really an embellishment of number five: management development processes enhance the nature and the quality of corporate policy formulation and they are also used to implement these enhanced policies (see also Barham, 1988). So much for the conceptualization of management development, but how, in particular, can it be achieved?

Management Development: Techniques and Approaches

There are innumerable ways in which managers and potential managers might be trained, educated and developed. It would be impossible and not particularly helpful to attempt to describe them all here. What is useful to note, however, is that the variety of methods can be classified as follows.

1 Formal, directed, structured methods such as centrally provided training programmes which all managers must progress through in order to rise up the ranks.
2 Self-development through informal, unstructured ways of learning.
3 Self-development which is guided and supported by various organizationally provided mechanisms.

Using these three categories it is possible to illustrate the features associated with them by focusing on examples from each one. Thus, the prime example of the first approach is the provision of structured training. The informal, unstructured approach can be illustrated through self-development. The third, 'middle way' of guided self-development can be illustrated by reviewing the method known as 'mentoring'.

Structured training

Sending managers away on courses represents a relatively simple and yet high-profile way for management development to be seen to be happening. The efficacy and appropriateness of such activity is dependent on a range of factors. Many a training and development department has degenerated into a state where its function is merely to administer training course programmes. Course details are circulated and the department simply handles the paperwork by matching nominees and volunteers to the available places. At worst there is no real investigation of whether the courses offered are really the ones which are most needed by the business – nor is there any proper investigation of who would benefit most from the courses. The handling of follow-through and impact is likely to be a further area of weakness in such cases. In these circumstances training may be seen as being offered as a *substitute* for effective management development.

The problems often associated with management training are fairly well known. Managers, especially at senior levels, may be reluctant to accept the idea that they have weaknesses which require rectification through training. Managers may maintain they are simply always too busy to spend the time away on a course. Training content and process may themselves come under attack. Courses may be described as 'irrelevant', too 'academic' and insufficiently practical. They may not be appropriately tailored or targeted to the particular audience. If they are provided in-house then they may, conversely, be attacked as too simplistic and too insular. Finally, there is the seemingly perennial problem of transferring learning back into the work situation. Even if end-of-course measures do reveal considerable learning, there is no guarantee that this will be carried over into subsequent work behaviour. In the absence of such behaviour change, questions are inevitably raised about the value of this investment of time and money.

These problems highlight certain key points in the management training and development debate. Although training can constitute an integral and critical element of a management development programme, it is as well to acknowledge that in some circumstances these sorts of complaints may be fully justified. Not all training courses are valuable. The training lobby may imply that training *per se* is 'a good thing' but time spent on an inappropriate course can be a waste. The problem is that having acknowledged these instances there is divergence of judgement about the appropriate nature and place of training. One currently very popular position is that training should be demonstrably related to 'business needs' and that its outcome should be measurable in specific terms of business improvement.

Self-development

Given the varied nature of managerial work and the wide range of individual strengths and weaknesses which every individual manager brings to it, there are some strong advocates of the view that formal training approaches are simply inappropriate. Moreover, in reaction to disappointment about the overall impact of formal training courses – and perhaps as a way to avoid their costs – the enthusiasm for 'self-development' grew apace. Dunnell (1987) proselytized a self-development scheme at the insurance company Guardian Royal Exchange under the title 'Management Development on a Tight

Budget'. Others have preferred to emphasize the motivational effects of individuals devising their own development plans, taking responsibility for their own development and in effect 'owning' the problem. A popular idea has been the notion of 'learning contracts' (Boak and Stephenson, 1987a; 1987b; Garfield, 1987) whereby company and individual act in partnership on the development question. Burgoyne and Germaine (1984) see 'mutual benefits' in linking self-development and career planning while Nixon and Allan (1986) emphasize the need to create a conducive organizational climate if self-development is to have any chance of taking off in practice.

There are, however, some cautionary notes struck among the general enthusiasm for the concept. Pedler (1986) observes that many managers may not really be capable of self-development and that, where packages are provided, those who need them least are paradoxically the ones most likely to make use of them. There are also attendant dangers of isolation if self-development becomes too heavily relied on. Consequently, he suggests some form of 'group support' to underpin self-development.

The main mechanisms of self-development might be regarded as comprising initial activity in 'self-awareness' – e.g. through assessment or development centres – followed first by familiarization with career development options, including a realistic view of possible career paths, and then by the preparation of an individual development plan (IDP). An IDP should ideally incorporate the preferences of the individual, objective assessments of his or her capabilities, and a realistic view of opportunities within the organization. The unfolding of events may involve ongoing lobbying (by subordinate and boss) relating to emerging opportunities and amended action-plans to develop skills in preparation for desired options.

The self-development mode of approach is given vigorous support by the exponents of the virtues of 'self-managed learning' (Cunningham, 1991). The person-centred approach to learning with the 'trainer' recast as a 'resource' to assist others in their learning through counselling and coaching is the philosophical basis for self-development. Cunningham describes how self-managed learning (SML) can operate in practice using illustrations from the postgraduate diploma in one of the new London universities and the MBA at Roffey Park Management College. Much of the emphasis is placed on the learner identifying his or her own goals, using groups, known as 'sets', to help them clarify these into learning objectives and, in turn, translate these objectives into 'contracts'.

The extent to which those contracts are fulfilled forms the basis of final assessment. But even in these experimental instances it would appear that the main delivery vehicles for learning still take place on pre-existing 'modules' such as marketing, accounting and the like.

Mentoring and action learning

This third category of approaches to development includes methods which are designed to combine the merits of informal self-development with more formal organizational support mechanisms. Here a key distinction is drawn between informal and incidental. As Marsick and Watkins (1990) observe, the former refers to self-directed conscious attempts to learn using, for example, coaching or networking, and in these instances learning itself may well be the main purpose. Incidental learning occurs, however, as a by-product of everyday worklife: it arises out of work tasks where learning is not the main purpose. Marsick and Watkins' research-based argument is that the quality of both types of learning can be enhanced by proactivity, by critical reflexivity and by creativity. Thus, as suggested also by Mumford (1989), an individual or group can plan work tasks so that one of the required outcomes is further learning. There can be an aim to foster collaborative learning and this itself can be aided by the creation of a learning community with appropriate norms. Supportive climates will encourage managers to invite a focus on the way they formulate problems as well as the problem-solving phases.

A management mentor is a senior 'father (or grandfather) figure' who, although not the direct line manager, takes a relatively long-term interest in the development of a promising individual. The mentor acts as a guide on developmental issues and can provide orientation with respect to longer term career matters. A set of prescriptive guidelines is furnished by Clutterbuck (1987).

It is claimed that research supports the thesis that mentoring, along with achievement motivation, is highly predictive of ultimate success both for fast-track and steady-track managers (Willbur, 1987). There are many articles which argue that 'recycling' the experience of older senior managers is cost effective (Tack, 1986). Other reports suggest that older managers who are left out of corporate training schemes may be found useful alternative roles as mentors (Skapinker, 1987). But this contradicts Clutterbuck's advice which is only to use as mentors those managers who are currently highly active and who are at the height of their credibility, standing and influence. These people are more likely to be in their forties and early fifties than in their sixties.

Two separate American studies argue that what matters is not so much the detail of any particular mentoring scheme but the general quality of the boss–subordinate relationship (London, 1986; Clawson, 1985). Indeed, Clawson suggests that career planners should concentrate on improving existing 'supportive relationships' rather than being deflected by attending to the details of mentoring arrangements. But just how an organization might encourage the recommended 'supportive behaviours' among its senior managers without using structural devices and semi-formal schemes remains somewhat elusive.

Action learning

A range of varied approaches to developing managers can be put under the heading of action learning. Their common theme is the view that 'management' is a cluster of practices which can best be upgraded and honed by direct exposure to problem-solving situations. Much of the credit for bringing recognition to the concept of action learning is given to Revans, a business professor who made widely known his disenchantment with traditional business education methods. Revans pioneered an approach which engaged managers in 'programmes' wherein they were assigned problem-solving situations, often in organizations other than their own, and for which they were given various types of support. For example, the participating managers would meet regularly with each other in a self-help group and with a facilitator. The analysis of issues was thus problem-directed and closely aligned to felt need.

Action learning projects may involve more than one inducement on a given problem assignment. But whether tackled by individual or group, the key point is to move beyond debating possible solutions to problems and to try out favoured options as soon as possible. Learning is also designed to continue beyond the implementation of successful solutions through the explicit analysis of why something worked as it did. This emphasis on review stems from Revans' conviction that 'the true learner is he who constantly examines his beliefs'.

This process of 'learning by doing' is clearly adaptable to many situations and it can take many forms. One key mode adopted by Revans himself was to initiate an exchange programme which involved collaboration between a consortium of collaborating companies and universities. The participants spent a period of months in their receiving organizations interspersed with university-based periods to discuss and analyse the problems they had encountered and their other experiences. The package was designed to 'constantly challenge each manager to review and reinterpret his previous experience'.

Action learning is defined by Pedler as

an approach to the development of people in organizations which takes the task as the vehicle for learning. It is based on the premise that there is no learning without action and no sober and deliberate action without learning . . . The method has been pioneered in our work organizations and has three main components – people, who accept the responsibility for taking action on a particular issue; problems, or the tasks that people set themselves; and a set of six or so colleagues who support and challenge each other to make progress on problems. (1991: xxii)

Pedler's depiction of the main elements of action learning postulates the process as a 'learning spiral'. Arising out of previous activity emerges a new 'problem'. As Pedler observes, the ability to 'problematize', i.e. to construct appropriate questions which are neither too overwhelming nor too trivial, is a crucial skill which influences a person's ability to learn through action. A second stage, 'ownership', relates to the acceptance of problems as having both a personal and public dimension. A third step involves building a 'set' or work group that can help tackle problems. Other stages in the learning spiral entail various reworkings of the problem, dealing with conflict, and the handling of negative feedback. Significant learning events will involve an amendment in identity and a move on to new problems.

Currently, action learning is marketed under a range of forms. It is possible for the in-company trainer to purchase off-the-shelf packages containing guidebooks, videos, case notes and learning instruments. Workshops are also offered to familiarize clients with these materials. A particular form of action learning which has received widespread publicity in recent years is 'outdoor learning'. The underlying principle here is that managers will benefit speedily by the character-forming experiences which can be engineered by pitting them against the elements in the great outdoors. A range of varied tasks can be set over a short residential period. Through these experiential learning opportunities it is postulated that managers will develop such fundamental managerial tools as planning, organizing, having effective communication, working in a team, having appropriate leadership and so on – i.e. most of the essential elements of what are widely thought to constitute 'management principles'.

Integrated training, education and development

The significance of bringing into alignment the systems for monitoring and evaluating managers, the setting of goals and targets for managers, the way they are developed and the way they are rewarded can perhaps best be illustrated by drawing upon the comparative Britain–Japan study conducted by the Industrial Relations Research Unit (Storey et al., 1991). The study was conducted in four British companies in Britain and matched with four Japanese companies operating in Japan. In all, 239 managers were studied using a detailed self-completion questionnaire followed by a personal interview. The objective of the study was to uncover how these managers were 'made' in practice and in particular to trace the relative influence of national cultural differences and sectoral differences.

The results of the study are relevant on a number of levels: they allow comparisons between Japanese and British management practices and they permit comparisons between and within particular companies. The major difference between British and Japanese managers is educational attainment, frequency of job change and the age at which they become managers. Not one of the Japanese managers had entered the workforce before age 18, whereas 45 per cent of the British sample had. Almost all of the Japanese managers (94 per cent) had undergraduate or postgraduate qualifications compared with 42 per cent of their British counterparts.

But the main message, apart from this higher level of education at start-up, was the consistent, careful and systematic way in which the Japanese went about making their managers. Many British managers may have experienced a greater volume of job change but it was more random than was occurring in Japan. The British were more likely to encounter a deep-seated preconception that people either 'have what it takes' or they do not. In consequence, a certain sink-or-swim philosophy was allowed to prevail. A corollary was the emphasis placed on being exposed to responsible positions at an early age for a select few. The assumed power of this practice finds support in current conventional wisdom in Western management development literature (e.g. Margerison and Kakabadse, 1985). What it neglects, however, is the often happenstance nature of the process. Those given such early challenges often just happened, as our respondents admitted, to be 'in the right place at the right time'. The corollary of this lack of planning is that large numbers of an equally talented cohort became disillusioned and key talents may consequently be lost to the company as those who were not plucked out leave to look for opportunities elsewhere. In contrast, the Japanese were far more likely to give weight to the importance of continuous development for the whole cohort of entrants over a prolonged time.

Another factor was the consistency with which Japanese companies stayed within the broad contours of a recognizable training and development system over many years. Continuous adjustments might be made but the system remained essentially intact and known to all. The notable feature in Britain, by contrast, was the propensity to chop and change. New programmes and initiatives were launched and old ones swept away almost in entirety. There were two damaging consequences: managers at all levels saw little point in committing themselves too heavily to a prevailing system because it was thought likely to be temporary; second, there was little inclination to invest time in learning about the current pattern of provision and so British managers (especially those out in the divisions away from corporate HQ) were often remarkably unclear about what training packages and related development devices were available. Sometimes the centrally provided core courses were of the highest world standards but their promulgation often left a lot to be desired.

A related feature was that Japanese training and development was on the whole better integrated with their manpower planning and deployment systems. For example, in a Japanese retailing company which was studied, progress through the grades occurs through an interlocking series of steps which embrace training, examinations, interviews and performance evaluation methods. Appointment to particular posts is a separate issue because the candidate first needs to reach the appropriate grade via the qualification system. In contrast, in Britain, training was often only loosely connected with human resource planning. Indeed, it is not unusual to find management training coming after appointment to a managerial post. Finally, in Japan it was the accepted responsibility of every line manager or staff manager to develop his or her staff. This idea was deeply imbued in everyone's expectations. Learning on the job was therefore an embedded part of everyday work. Performance against this criterion of subordinate development was typically found to be a critical issue at the manager's own appraisal.

So much for the particular techniques used within companies. It is important now to gain an understanding of the key developments which are being driven above company level.

The Management Charter Initiative and Competences

Following a string of influential reports in the mid- to late 1980s (Constable and McCormick, 1987; Handy, 1987; Mangham and Silver, 1986) an atmosphere of acute concern about the state of management development and the quality of British managers was engendered. The reports revealed the poor state of training, education and development for Britain's managerial workforce. There were approximately three million people in managerial jobs with about one-third of these being in senior and middle managerial posts. On average it was found that these three million received only about the equivalent of one day's formal training per year. The majority received no training. Worse still, of the 100,000 persons entering managerial roles each year, the majority had received no formal management education or training.

The Handy report puts this record in international context. Although some organizations were doing a lot for the development of their managers and were doing it well, the main conclusion was that, overall, the main competitor countries were doing more and doing it better. A key feature of 'doing it better' was that while other countries followed varied and discrepant models they were relatively consistent in their application of these models. Thus, for example, the Americans placed considerable emphasis upon the provision of formal business education in colleges and universities. The output of MBAs, for example, was high. In contrast, the Japanese output of MBAs was close to zero but in the place of the business education approach the Japanese had a successful formula of recruiting potential managerial talent from well-educated graduates from the elite universities followed by a highly systematic approach to in-company development. In contrast, Britain followed neither the 'external' nor the 'internal' model but toyed ineffectively with elements of both. The overall message was that Britain should not import wholesale any particular foreign system but it should attend to the provision of some coherent and logical approach which fitted its home circumstances. As it was, the general state of affairs for management development in Britain was summarized as 'too little, too late, for too few'.

Both the Handy and the Constable and McCormick reports made a number of recommendations. The Handy report suggested that leading companies should commit themselves to a 'Development Charter' of good practice. This would include, for example, a benchmark standard of five days off-the-job training per annum for all managers. Other recommendations related to the provision of education. The most far-reaching of these was Constable and McCormick's call for the establishment of an apprenticeship or 'articles of management' approach in the form of a new national Diploma in Business Administration and an expansion in MBA programmes. They suggested a target output of 10,000 MBA graduates per annum by the late 1990s.

It was also recommended that access to both of these courses should be made more easily available to working managers through the wider provision of part-time modular courses. The hallmark of these would be flexibility. Their character would be shaped by a careful melding of academic and work-based activity.

In many respects the Mangham and Silver report (1986), which was a major survey of the nature and extent of management training, anticipated many of the findings of Constable and McCormick. Over half of British companies were discovered to be making no training provision for their managers. Even the larger companies with over 1000 employees figured in this group: one-fifth of these were simply failing to train and among those that did train the extent of provision was, in the main, found to be small. The median expenditure per annum was only £600 per manager – senior managers were apportioned even less. There were other interesting findings emerging from this report. Difficulty was encountered in establishing a statistical link between the incidence of training and company performance. Perhaps one reason for this was that few respondents were able to articulate the competences which were required of senior, middle and junior managers. This is a key issue to which we return later in this section.

The report by Mumford (1987) drew on a survey of 140 directors from 45 organizations. The main finding was that although some companies could point to considerable systematic management development (and some could even claim a direct linkage with subsequent performance by the recipients) others had no schemes in place. Mumford also tracked those instances where provision had been made but had been perceived to fail. His assessment was that failure occurred where schemes were insufficiently related to the real concerns of these senior managers, were insufficiently related to other planning processes in the companies and offered too little perceived return to the individual. Most directors interviewed appeared to judge that the formal processes of management development had not been very influential. Most claimed to have learnt more effectively from an admix of accidental and unstructured experiences.

In the light of his survey and associated previous work on how managers learn, Mumford and his colleagues go on to advocate what they term an 'integrated' approach to management development. Under this model they recommended that the kind of learning by experience which occurs without planning and without clear objectives being set could be much enhanced if it was underpinned by certain rather more formal interventions. For instance, they refer to the need for the setting out of developmental objectives; the 'owning' of development by the individual managers themselves; the making it happen within the context of everyday managerial problem-solving activities; and the need to undertake conscious reviews of what has been learnt. In short, they recommended a judicious blend of planned learning and learning by doing. This learning from the accomplishment of ongoing tasks lends itself to self-development guided by a coach or mentor.

Clearly, the reports, and the Mumford report in particular, are not without messages for individual organizations. In the main, however, they are largely concerned with questions of national policy. They imply a need for concerted action at the supra-organizational level. This has traditionally been an area in which British provision has been characteristically weak. Following the publication of this unprecedented cluster of reports, the challenge to take action was, in part at least, taken up on this occasion. The most immediate response was the establishment of the Management Charter Initiative

(MCI). This was launched in 1988 by a consortium comprising the CBI, the British Institute of Management (BIM), and the Foundation for Management Education. The new consortium body was named the National Forum for Management Education and Development. The MCI is an employer-led initiative which is backed by the Employment Department and the Department of Trade and Industry. It is the designated lead industry body for the development of standards in management. Its precise relationship with the Training and Enterprise Councils (TECs) remains, however, somewhat unclear and problematical.

The MCI started out with three major items on its agenda: (1) the founding of a mass movement of organizations prepared to commit themselves publicly to a code of good practice to promote the development and application of high standards in modern management (the Management Charter Movement); (2) the construction of a set of management qualifications designed to provide recognizable steps of accreditation for professional managers (the Chartered Manager); (3) the formation of a Chartered Institute of Management with a Royal Charter to advance the 'profession' of management (the Chartered Institute).

This became a highly controversial agenda. There was considerable internecine strife among the membership of the original Council for Management Education and Development. Moreover, other interested parties outside the MCI, such as the Association for Management Education and Development, contested the aspiration for codification and standardization. The whole future of the MCI at certain points in the late 1980s looked to be in some doubt. However, the MCI has survived though progress on the threefold agenda has been variable.

The first thrust, towards the signing-up of major employers to form a critical mass of champions of management development has been the easiest part to achieve. By July 1991 more than 900 employers, representing 25 per cent of the UK workforce, had joined the MCI. These major employers, including companies such as ICI, Marks and Spencer, Sainsbury, IBM and the major clearing banks have thus publicly committed themselves to a ten-point code of good practice and paid a subscription fee.

Despite the rapid progress in numerical terms on this first leg of the MCI agenda, there is some scepticism about the significance of organizational membership. There is a certain suspicion that some companies have signed-up mainly for public relations reasons. A particularly important facet of this is the projection of a training and development image to the graduate market.

The second leg of the MCI agenda has been concerned with the definition of national standards of managerial competence and the establishment of a naturally recognized hierarchy of management qualifications. In 1990, the MCI published a comprehensive set of guidelines for the 'certificate level' aimed at all providers of training for first level managers. Also published were draft guidelines for the 'diploma level', which is deemed appropriate for middle level managers. The MCI endorses management training arrangements which meet its declared quality standards and in other ways conform to its promulgations. These arrangements relate to training and assessment procedures and validation processes. The MCI endorses qualifications and training providers. Qualification awarding bodies and professional institutes have to demonstrate that their arrangements meet the MCI requirements. The MCI will then help these bodies gain endorsement from the National Council for Vocational Qualifications.

At each of the three main levels, key competences are being investigated, refined and codified. The emphasis is on demonstrated capability to do rather than the possession of knowledge or the amount of time spent on courses. The MCI likes to stress, in other words, its interest in 'outputs' rather than 'inputs'.

Part of the initiative is the Accreditation of Prior Learning (APL) launched in 1990. APL allows candidates to receive formal recognition and credit for 'competences' already built-up through work experience. This allows for individuals to be accredited for demonstrated capabilities or competences regardless of how these were gained. The MCI has now piloted a methodology for APL. Pilot centres have been established – ranging from colleges and other training providers to MCI networks and employers – to engage in the assessment of individual managers' prior learning. The MCI will act as the co-ordinating and overseeing body for this national string of centres and trained assessors. The centres will offer a competence accreditation service directly to employers. It is expected that some 50–70 centres, each handling about 100 candidates, will operate in the first year (*Employment Gazette*, March 1991). The concept is that managers must 'reflect on their own experience, analyse the units of competence they have gained against national standards, and develop a portfolio of evidence to demonstrate that competence (ibid.: 403). APL and competence crediting have won government backing and £11 million has been allocated over three years to TECs in order to implement the process nationally.

The third leg of the MCI, the formation of a professional Chartered Institute, was the one which ran into the fiercest opposition. Established professional groups such as the IPM and the Institute of Industrial Managers were particularly alarmed. It would appear that this idea has now been quietly dropped.

The main recent development for the MCI has been the establishment of local networks. There are currently over 50 of these, with a target of 90 to cover the whole country. Many local networks are based in Chambers of Commerce and similar existing bodies. Local networks are supposed to recruit new members and service their needs. An annual fee is charged to all members. The local networks encourage the adoption of the MCI national standards, endorse providers, engage in assessment and they also offer a consultancy service.

So far we have reviewed what management development is and the provision made at company and supra-company levels. But how effective is this pattern of provision and what factors influence effectiveness?

Factors Shaping the Provision and Effectiveness of Management Development

There is a wide measure of agreement among specialists that the 'climate' or 'culture' of an organization is a vital factor in successful management development activity taking root. The quality of particular courses may wax and wane but if the underlying climate is perceived to encourage development then this will be the more important consideration. Such an observation is, however, somewhat nebulous: what in practice constitutes such an environment and how can it be fostered?

This was the concern of one company in the financial services sector. Sun Alliance has sought over a period of years to foster in-company management development using a variety of devices. It began with individual-based approaches and then, in the mid- to late 1980s, relied increasingly on OD techniques. But the key lesson from this example of 'creating the right climate' appears to be the demonstrated success of the central development unit whose work triggered independent initiatives by divisions which set up their own training and development units. In this way, Sun Alliance claims to have succeeded in meeting a key target – to have management development genuinely accepted as a line management function.

As earlier sections have implicity if not explicitly made clear, there has been extensive debate about the most favourable conditions to enable effective management learning and development. While the issue is still hotly contested there are some signs of a measure of consensus around a few vital points. In brief, these are:

- that management development will be most effectual when it is recognized and accepted as a strategic business activity;
- that the design of management training programmes recognizes the nature of managerial work;
- that account is also taken of the varied needs and capacities of individual managers;
- that education, training, selection, career planning, reward systems, and managerial evaluation are recognized as all part of an interlocking 'system'; and
- that evaluation is itself a vital part of the system of development.

Each of these is worth reviewing in turn.

Management development as a strategic business activity

One of the most hackneyed aphorisms is that there must be top management commitment to the activity of development. If this is not to be an empty declaration it must be demonstrated in a number of ways. These include the attendance of top managers on training programmes; the appointment of highly able and respected executives to specified management development posts; and the allocation of sufficient reserves to the management development function, reserves which must not be the first target of cuts in a recession.

The 'strategic' connection can also be established in a number of ways. The task of overseeing and managing the process of development and succession planning can be assumed directly by the chief executive and the most senior executive body. Their serious and consistent handling of this part of their many responsibilities will send a signal to all other managers about the significance or otherwise of developmental activity and its supporting mechanisms.

Whatever the precise terminology used – 'competences', 'skills', 'expertise', or 'capabilities' – the significance of the idea of identifying and clarifying the nature of effective management practice has certainly caught hold. In a major article in the *Harvard Business Review*, three vice-presidents of the Boston Consulting Group suggest that while 'time' and 'speed' were the popular keys to competitive advantage in the late 1980s the key for the 1990s is 'capabilities' (Stalk et al., 1992). Their understanding of 'capabilities' is wide-ranging – it encompasses expertise at all points along the value-chain including, for example, design, production, logistics, customer-service and so on. They illustrate their argument with respect to the American retailing super-success story of Wal-Mart. Its success is normally attributed to consistent low prices and friendly customer service including staff who stand and greet customers as they enter the stores. But, as Stalk et al. rightly say, the real question is: why is it that Wal-Mart alone has the cost structure which *allows* consistent low pricing and the employment of greeters? The answer they suggest lies deep in a set of strategic decisions which have 'transformed the company into a capabilities-based competitor' at all points in its service cycle. Foremost here is the strategic status allotted to development, especially management development. Hence, at Wal-Mart, 'senior management's job is to help individual store managers learn from the market and from each other' (ibid.: 59). This commitment is backed by heavy investment: 'a fleet of airplanes regularly ferries store managers to the Bentonville, Arkansas, headquarters for meetings on market trends and merchandising' (ibid.: 59). The key lessons are plain: capability is the underlying source of any manifest 'competitive edge'; this capability has to be worked at; and the activity of developing capability is therefore a (possibly, the) strategic role of top management. As Stalk et al. (1992: 63) observe, 'a CEO's success in building and managing capabilities will be the chief test of management skill in the 1990s'.

Taking account of the nature of managerial work

The relevance and impact of training and development provision will be shaped also by the extent to which it is in tune with the true nature of managerial work. The classic accounts of this work have been drawn by Stewart (1976; 1991) and Mintzberg (1973). These research-based accounts reveal managerial work to be fragmented, with the day's activities being broken up into a large number of disparate activities: managers are revealed to prefer 'action' over contemplation; they prefer to communicate directly rather than submitting ideas to paper; their time horizons are short; and they operate within complex social networks. On the basis of how different managers balanced these role characteristics, Mintzberg classified a number of key typified roles: 'spokesperson', 'negotiator', 'reserve handler' and 'leader'.

These research findings have direct implications for managerial training and education. The design of programmes needs to take into account these characteristics. Managers may require some help in learning how to manage their own time effectively. The techniques of delegation and of planning so as to avoid constant short-term fire-fighting may also be worth adding to the agenda. Conversely, the selection of topics and the way they are handled on training courses may need to be amended in recognition of the fact that managerial work has these characteristics and that, if effective learning is to occur, courses need to be seen to connect with this reality. One example would be the shift towards action learning as described in a previous section – i.e. the adoption of learning methods which involve active rather than solely passive processes. It may also mean therefore moving to the abstact level from a specific instance on problems grounded in experience. A further implication may be seen in the shift towards course units which take account of these characteristics of managerial work as witnessed, for example, in courses devoted to interpersonal skills, project management skills, managing in teams, handling stress and similar other courses which mark a departure from the traditional rational-planning model of management education.

But there is another dimension to this whole question of the nature of managerial work. As has been signalled already, the normative basis of the 'true' nature of this work is fiercely contested. While it may be the case that most managers behave in practice in a way characterized 'by brevity, variety and fragmentation' (Mintzberg, 1973: 5), this may not necessarily be the most effective behaviour to which high performers should aspire. Lessom (1990), for example, urges a decisive shift from the conventional management thinking which leads to this pattern of behaviour. It is based, he suggests on traditional thinkers such as Fayol, Taylor and Drucker while, in contrast, his preferred 'developmental' style draws inspiration from sources such as Schumacher and Yamamoto. Likewise, Hickman (1990) suggests that 'managers' and 'leaders' are types at opposite ends of a continuum. 'Managerial types' behave in structured, analytical, controlled, deliberate and orderly ways.

'Leader types' lean to the experiential, visionary, flexible, uncontrolled and creative aspects of work. The appropriate behaviour for current work organizational circumstances, Hickman suggests, is a balanced 'management-leader' work behaviour pattern. Developmental activity thus needs to promote this configuration.

Management teams

A further aspect of managerial work which is of critical relevance is the extent to which so much of it is done not by isolated individuals but by members of a team. Working often in increasingly complex technological and economic settings, managers cannot be skilled in all relevant areas: they must therefore rely on team-work. The theory and practice of successful work teams (Belbin, 1981; Margerison and McCann, 1990) hinges around the idea of complementary roles or, as Margerison and McCann would term it, 'balanced teams'. These latter authors and consultants claim to have identified nine generic functions which all teams have to perform in one way or another if they are to be effective. The nine functions which have to be accomplished are: advising, innovating, promoting, developing, organizing, producing, inspecting, maintaining and linking. Advising is about collecting and transmitting relevant information; innovating means creating new ideas or thinking of new ways to tackle old problems; promoting refers to the task of selling a new idea in an up-front way; developing is about taking the idea forward in a realistic way; organizing refers to setting up structures and setting deadlines; producing is the core activity of making the goods or actually delivering the service; inspecting refers to the quality checking of details; maintaining roles ensures that the infrastructure is in place and it typically relates to various support services; the final role, linking, is about co-ordination of all of the other roles.

The identified 'team roles' purport to describe not only the work function being performed but also the behavioural characteristics of those persons preferring these functions. Hence, the team roles carry descriptions such as 'thruster-organizer', 'assessor-developer', 'creator-developer' and 'concluder-producer'. Margerison and McCann, and Belbin, have devised a questionnaire in order to measure individuals' typified team-work preferences.

The implications of team management theory for management development are varied. One usage is where a company may base part of its selection decisions for a team-management position on the revealed individual 'type'. Margerison and McCann (1990: 47) are quite explicit in claiming

> the most successful teams are those composed of members who, between them, are comfortable working in all eight sectors of the team management wheel as well as the 'linker' role. In other words, successful teams are multi-preference teams. We have worked with many teams that are not multi-preference and invariably they run into difficulties.

Management development specialists who collect this kind of data on their people in development workshops tend to look for any 'bunching' of people at certain points on the wheel. Where this is found, they will frequently seek to correct for this, both through subsequent selection and promotion decisions and through developmental and training activity. Another training implication is that when team members themselves understand the different work orientations or 'frames of reference' which people have they may make allowances which result in the utilization of interlinked skills and balanced contributions.

Margerison and McCann (1990: 53–5) quote a specific case of the use of the team wheel in management development. They report how the Group Training Manager of St Ivel Ltd used it to transform the strategy of a general manager and his executive team in one of St Ivel's subsidiaries. All executive team members completed the team questionnaire and engaged in various training and assessment exercises. Overall results were checked against the wheel and action plans were agreed to ensure that in future executive group meetings the 'missing work preferences' would be given some exposure.

Management development related to the capabilities and needs of the individual

Management development will only be effective if it fits with the motivation, needs, and potential of the individuals who are the 'clients' of the system. And yet assessing these characteristics has been shown to be extraordinarily difficult. As chapter 7 has revealed, conventional appraisal by the immediate boss can be a highly flawed and subjective activity. Even if more objective measures of actual performance are introduced these may give little guidance as to the potential for more senior roles which an individual may or may not have.

In an attempt to grapple with these sorts of problems an increasing number of organizations are turning to assessment and/or development centres. These devices typically expose a small group of 'candidates' to a battery of varied tests, exercises, interviews, role plays and group activities over an intensive two-day period. Each individual during the period will be closely monitored by a designated observer. At the end of the two-day period, and possibly prior to the end as well, the group of observers will meet to compare notes and to relate the outcome of the varied tests and exercises one with another.

Management development as part of a 'system'

Key sustainable messages are transmitted to individual managers in multifarious and complex ways. The messages conveyed on training courses may be speedily discounted if they conflict with the everyday 'messages' received through task assignment, the selection and promotion process, the reward pattern and many other aspects of the totality of ways in which the management stock is itself managed.

A recent Institute of Manpower Studies study based on 12 leading cases (Hirsch, 1990) suggested that there is a discernible trend away from the more limited approaches to succession planning, such as just planning one step (or job layer) ahead, towards a wider ranging development of potential across a broad front. This draws a far larger number of people into the scope of developmental activity and marks a departure from the reliance on fast-track methods for a select group of presumed 'high potentials'. If this trend means that managers who have already experienced a considerable degree of job mobility both within and between companies (Alban-Metcalfe and Nicholson, 1984) will need to rely less on informal sources of information about how to do these jobs, then a great many more managers can be expected to record higher levels of satisfaction in future.

The evaluation process

Evaluating the effectiveness of management training, education and development has become a realm of practice in its own right in recent years. Current thinking maintains that the way in which evaluation is structured into the total package of development is a critical issue: evaluation becomes part of the development process. Wallace (1991), formerly head of the management development branch of the International Labour Organization in Geneva, illustrates well the shift in emphasis internationally towards the themes of cost-effectiveness in management development activity and the associated ability to demonstrate quantifiable results from the investment in management training. His central model depicts management development as a 'cycle'. The central elements in this cycle are problem definition, aim setting, needs analysis, design and delivery, and review. The last of these also includes 'diplomatic' advertising of the success and the receiving of recognition for achieving business improvement by using training. On the back of this, a new cycle can begin. The key points along the way, suggests Wallace, drawing on extensive international case research, are the preparatory stages where managers must justify the actions they plan to take and get permission to take them. This preparatory phase involves diagnoses and needs analysis of the knowledge, attitudes and skills of managers so as to reveal what training should be provided. Wallace sees the 'new MD professional' as someone who possesses the skills, can raise awareness of the need for training, can work in harmony with decision makers and can, above all, *evaluate and report results*' (ibid.: 18, emphasis in original).

One specific methodology for evaluating or 'auditing' management development activity is described by Easterby-Smith (1985). The essence of the method is the collection of data from managers about their experience of management development and the feeding back of these data to those who are responsible for the management development function. Questionnaires or 'checklists' are provided as the basis for the conduct of audits.

Preparing Managers for Tomorrow

Among the shifts in thinking about management development theory and practice in tomorrow's organizations, a certain momentum has built up around the idea of the 'learning organization' (Pedler, et al., 1991; Garratt, 1988; 1990). For Garratt this implies, *inter alia*, the rise of the 'learning leader', that is, someone who will champion learning as a key facet of organizational life. In practice, this will entail intelligent and authoritative reviews of the management development interventions used by line managers, such as coaching, energizing staff and so on.

Another approach to dealing with the problem of management development needs for the future is the attempt to foresee the critical new skills which will be required. Barham et al. (1988) set out to study 'leading international companies' such as Shell, ICI, Burton Group and BMW who were envisaging the future demands on their management. As might be expected the pattern emerging from these visions placed prime emphasis on themes such as quality and customer service; flexibility with integration; internationalization; commitment and motivation; leadership, corporate culture and the management of change. These have a familiar ring and seem to resonate with, for example, the Peters and Waterman (1982) and Kanter (1984) message from the early 1980s. The exercise indicates the extreme difficulties of using leading practitioners to produce a map of the future; the lists invariably seem to reflect familiar current concerns.

On the basis of this picture of the corporate future, Barham et al. then proceed to draw out the implications for managerial competences which can be expected to be at a premium in that future. The future manager, they suggest, will be a 'sensor' (i.e. will be highly alert to environmental messages); will move from vertical to horizontal concerns (will cut across specialisms); and will be proficient in mobilizing and energizing. The future manager will therefore be characterized by a set of 'doing skills' (good technical specialist, analytical, capable of planning) and also by a 'being' profile (e.g. resilient, flexible and decisive). The key indicators are:

Key positive indicators	*Negative indicators*
Active analyst	Shallow, unthinking
Willing to take risks	Stays in comfort zone
Strong personal goals	Lacks direction
Constructive	Defensive
Wide vision	Tunnel vision
Sensitive to others	Aggressive
Aware of strengths and weaknesses	Ego-oriented

The management development system which is needed to produce people with these 'doing' and 'being' characteristics will be different from the formalized approaches of today. The predicted profile looks similar to that described earlier as constituting the ideal of the 'learning organization' – an organizational setting where learning is continuous and intrinsic; where learning is linked to corporate strategy and is seriously treated as a source of competitive advantage; where on-the-job development is emphasized; where training is generally 'non-directive'; where there is much greater concern to measure effectiveness; where the main ownership and responsibility rests with line managers; and where training specialists adopt a much wider role than hitherto and become close partners with line managers. This list of themes is reflective of many of the key ideas flagged in earlier parts of this chapter. It usefully draws the currently favoured ideas together into a package of recommended practice for leading contemporary and future organizations.

A similar exercise was conducted by consultants Korn/Ferry International (1989) in conjunction with Columbia University Business School. This report draws on a survey of over 1500 chief executive officers (CEOs) across 20 countries. Its focus was on an assessment of how CEOs envisage the shape of business in the twenty-first century and expected crucial top management skills which will be required as a consequence of these changed priorities. While there were regional differences expressed by American, European, Japanese and Latin American CEOs there was a broad consensus about the need for visionary leadership. This translated into a need for CEOs to be able to imbue the organization with energy and to inspire employees to realize their potential. The key recommendations arising from the study were for CEOs preparing for the twenty-first century to:

1 define, create and nurture a corporate culture that attracts the talent best suited to corporate goals;
2 invest in people: their recruitment, development and training;
3 protect that investment by designing long-term compensation programmes which reward corporate goal achievement;
4 track the pool of the most promising executives and implement an ongoing audit;
5 develop these people systematically using functional rotation, movement across business units and executive education; and
6 confront the issue of succession planning.

Beneath these generalities there were some interesting regional differences relating to management development in the report. The Japanese, for example, were the least worried about the supply of qualified manpower. The Japanese also were distinctive in the priority they were according to product innovations as the key to competitive edge, and in the extent to which they rated highly the importance in the future of technological skills and an international outlook for the ideal CEO in the year 2000.

A final theme in looking to the future of management development is the increasing willingness to question the dominance of
conventional Western development models. For example, Davies et
al. (1989) highlight the variety of approaches in different parts of the
world and raise the issue of methods which are 'appropriate' to
particular cultural circumstances. In terms of management learning
for instance, while there may be a trend towards active learning
(such as projects and action learning in Britain), this is not necessarily reflected in other countries. In the USA there still appears to be
a preference for the interactive case method and in African countries
the role of the teacher as expert is still more highly valued and
preferred.

While Sadler (1989) draws out the distinctive activities of the
'new management' in post-industrial society (using IT, managing
the knowledge and service economies), more radical postulates are
made by those who discern the emergence of 'post-modernism'. The
phenomenon of post-modernism is notoriously difficult to define but
it suggests a systemic break as in the progression feudalism – mod-
ernism – post-modernism. Clegg (1992) detects key elements of it in
the Japanese model: empowerment rather than disempowerment in
organizations; diffusion rather than specialization in missions, goals
and main functions; flexible rather than inflexible skills; and trust
rather than mistrust in leadership style. Certain implications for
management development fall out from the post-modernist paradigm. For example, Fox and Moult (1990) see in it a fundamental
challenge to the certainties of the sciences, and to the legitimacy of
hierarchy and authoritative knowledge. Cunningham (1990) draws
from this an endorsement of his advocacy of self-managed learning.
He sees post-modernism as conducive to an approach to management learning in which managers 'explore the development of wisdom rather than attempting to learn truths about management'
(Cunningham, 1990: 216). In this new era 'the wise use of competence and knowledge may require a post-modern transcendence
of current practice' (ibid.).

At the outset of this chapter it was observed that activity in the
field of management development has been fairly intense in recent
years. The number of MBAs has increased fourfold, the MCI has
been launched and managers in general have enjoyed greater exposure to a range of learning opportunities. There are insufficient signs
to support the idea of self-managed 'post-modern' learning but the
quality, diversity and volume of management education, training

and development seems on balance to have increased since the time of the first edition of this book. To that extent the message of this chapter is optimistic. However, it must be borne in mind that management development in Britain in recent years has been growing from an insubstantial base and that even now the plant is best described as fragile rather than robust.

Bibliography

Alban-Metcalfe, B. and Nicholson, N. 1984. *The Career Development of British Managers*. London: British Institute of Management.

Alexander, G. P. 1987. 'Establishing Shared Values through Management Training'. *Training and Development Journal*, Vol. 41, No. 2.

Annandale, S. 1986. 'The Four Faces of Management Development'. *Personnel Management*, Vol. 18, No. 10.

Barham, K. 1988. *Management for the Future*. Ashridge Management College/Foundation for Management Education.

Belbin, R. M. 1981. *Management Teams*. London: Heinemann.

Boak, G. and Stephenson, M. 1987a. 'Management Learning Contracts'. *Journal of European Industrial Training*, Vol. 11, No. 4, 4.

Boak, G. and Stephenson, M. 1987b. 'Management Learning Contracts'. *Journal of European Industrial Training*. Vol. 11, No. 6, 17.

Burgoyne, J. 1988. 'Management development for the individual and the organisation'. *Personnel Management*, June.

Burgoyne, J. and Germaine, C. 1984. 'Self Development and Career Planning: An Exercise in Mutual Benefit'. *Personnel Management*, Vol. 16, No. 4.

Clawson, J. G. 1985. 'Is monitoring necessary?'. *Training and Development Journal* (USA), 39/4, 36.

Clegg, S. 1992. 'Modernist and Postmodernist organization'. In Salaman, G. (ed.) *Human Resource Strategies*. London: Sage.

Clutterbuck, D. 1987. *Everyone Needs a Mother*. London: Institute of Personnel Management.

Constable, R. and McCormick, R. J. 1987. *The Making of British Managers: A Report of the BIM and CBI into Management Training Education and Development*. London: British Institute of Management.

Cunningham, I. 1990. 'Beyond modernity: is postmodernism relevant to management development?'. *Management Education and Development*, 21, 3, 207–18.

Cunningham, I. 1991. 'Self-managed learning'. In Mumford, A. (ed.) *Handbook of Management Development*. Aldershot: Gower.

Davies, J., Easterby-Smith, M., Mann, S. and Tanton, M. 1989. *The*

Challenge to Western Management Development: International Alternatives. London: Routledge.

Dunnell, R. 1987. 'Management Development on a Tight Budget'. *Personnel Management* (UK), 48–50.

Easterby-Smith, M. 1985. *Evaluating Management Education, Training and Development.* Aldershot: Gower.

Fox, S. and Moult, G. 1990. 'Postmodern culture and management development'. *Management Education and Development*, 21, 3, 241–61.

Fulmer, R. 1986. 'Management Development after the Merger'. *Journal of Management Development*, Vol. 5, No. 4.

Garfield, C. A. 1987. 'Peak performance in business'. *Training and Development Journal* (USA), 41/4, 54–9.

Garratt, R. 1988. *The Learning Organisation.* London: Fontana.

Garratt, R. 1990. *Creating a Learning Organization: A Guide to Leadership, Learning and Development.* Cambridge: Director Books.

Handy, C. B. 1987. *The Making of Managers.* London: NEDO.

Hickman, C. 1990. *Mind of a Manager, Soul of a Leader.* New York: Wiley.

Hirsch, W. 1990. *Succession Planning: Current Practice and Future Issues.* IMS, Report No. 184. Sussex: Institute of Manpower Studies.

Kanter, R. M. 1984. *The Change Masters.* London: Allen & Unwin.

Korn/Ferry. 1989. 'Reinventing the CEO'. *21st Century Report.* New York: Korn Ferry and Columbia University, Graduate School of Business.

Lessom, R. 1990. *Development Management.* Oxford: Blackwell.

Lippitt, G. 1982. 'Management development as the key to organisational renewal'. *Journal of Management Development*, Vol. 1, No. 2.

London, M. 1986. 'The boss's role in management development'. *Journal of Management Development*, Vol. 5, No. 3.

Mangham, I. and Silver, M. S. 1986. *Management Training: Context and Practice.* London: Economic and Social Research Council.

Margerison, C. and Kakabadse, A. 1985. 'What Management Development Means for CEOs'. *Journal of Management Development*, Vol. 4, No. 5.

Margerison, C. and McCann, R. 1990. *Team Management: Practical New Approaches.* London: Mercury.

Marsh, N. 1986. 'Management development and strategic management change'. *Journal of Management Development*, Vol. 5, No. 1, 26–37.

Marsick, V. and Watkins, K. 1990. *Informal and Incidental Learning in the Workplace.* London: Routledge.

Mintzberg, H. 1973. *The Nature of Managerial Work.* New York: Harper & Row.

Mumford, A. 1987. *Developing Directors: the Learning Process.* Sheffield: Manpower Services Commission.

Mumford, A. 1989. *Management Development: Strategies for Action.* London: Institute of Personnel Management.

Nagler, B. 1987. 'Cummins' Efforts to Cut Costs'. *Managing Automation*, Vol. 2, No. 7.

Nixon, B. and Allen, R. 1986. 'Creating a Climate for DIY Development'. *Personnel Management*, Vol. 18, No. 8.

Pedler, M. 1986. 'Management Self Development'. *Management, Education and Development*, Vol. 17, No. 1.

Pedler, M. 1991. *Action Learning in Practice*. Aldershot: Gower.

Pedler, M., Burgoyne, J. and Boydell, T. 1991. *The Learning Organization*. Maidenhead: McGraw-Hill.

Peters, T. J. and Waterman, R. H. 1982. *In Search of Excellence: Lessons from America's Best Run Companies*. New York: Harper & Row.

Sadler, P. 1989. 'Management development'. In Sisson, K. (ed.) *Personnel Management in Britain*, 1st edn. Oxford: Blackwell.

Schuler, R. S. and Jackson, S. 1987. 'Linking competitive strategies with human resource management practices'. *Academy of Management Executive*, Vol. 1, No. 3, 209–13.

Skapinker, M. 1987. 'Cookson Seeks a Common Management Style'. *Financial Times*, 22 April.

Smith, D. 1987. 'Culture and Management Development in Building Societies'. *Personnel Review*, Vol. 15, No. 3.

Smith, P. E., Barnard, J. M. and Smith, G. 1986. 'Privatisation and Culture Change'. *Journal of Management Development*, Vol. 5, No. 2.

Stalk, G., Evans, P. and Shulman, L. 1992. 'Creating capabilities: the new rules of corporate strategy'. *Harvard Business Review*, March–April, 57–69.

Stemp, P. 1987. 'Improving Management Effectiveness'. *Management, Education and Development*, Vol. 18, No. 3.

Stewart, R. 1976. *Contrasts in Management*. New York: McGraw-Hill.

Stewart, R. 1991. *Managing Today and Tomorrow*. Basingstoke: Macmillan.

Storey, J. 1992. *Developments in the Management of Human Resources*. Oxford: Blackwell.

Storey, J., Okazaki-Ward, L., Edwards, P. K., Gow, I. and Sisson, K. 1991. 'Managerial careers and management development: a comparative analysis of Britain and Japan'. *Human Resource Management Journal*, 1, 3.

Tack, W. L. 1986. 'Management Recycling'. *Sloan Management Review*, 27/4, 63.

Thackway, J. 1984. 'Educating for a Commercial Railway'. *Management, Education and Development*, Vol. 15, No. 3.

Wagel, W. H. 1987. 'Leadership Training for a New Way of Managing'. *Personnel*, Vol. 64, No. 12.

Wallace, J. 1991. *Developing Better Managers: Creating Change Through Effective Training*. London: Kogan Page in Association with the International Labour Office.

Willbur, J. 1987. 'Does monitoring breed success?' *Training and Development Journal*, 41/11, 38.

12

Managing Culture: Fact or Fiction?

Karen Legge

In recent years senior managers, in both the private and the public sectors, have launched a number of wide-ranging initiatives such as 'total quality management' (TQM), 'working with pride', and 'customer care', as well as the leadership programmes of management development discussed in the previous chapter. Central to these initiatives is the belief that a key task of those in senior positions is to develop an organizational culture – a set of shared meanings, or taken-for-granted assumptions – consistent with and supportive of the organization's strategic objectives (Peters and Waterman, 1982; Storey, 1989; Thomas, 1985; Whipp et al., 1989). The logic is that, through acts of 'transformational leadership', employees will exchange a 'resigned behavioural compliance' (Ogbonna and Wilkinson, 1988; 1990), maintained by externally imposed bureaucratic control systems, for an internalized commitment to the organization and its mission. Replace compliance with commitment, to paraphrase Walton (1985), and organizational performance will be improved: commitment will deliver to the 'bottom line'.

This chapter assesses the theory and practice of managing culture involved in such initiatives as TQM. It begins by briefly outlining the historical antecedents to the interest in culture management and why it emerged in the 1980s as such a strong theme of the prescription to senior managers. The second section discusses the problematic nature of the key concepts involved – notably organizational culture, commitment and performance – and the difficulties in establishing their interrelationships. The third section reviews recent British case study evidence and considers what it tells us about the aims, impact and the feasibility of managing culture. The fourth and final section of the chapter asks whether the development of a strong organizational culture – even if it is feasible – is necessarily a good thing for either senior managers or their employees.

The Human Side of Enterprise

Well before the publication of McGregor's (1960) book of that name, organization theory was concerned with the tensions between the instrumental rationality of bureaucratic systems and the affective needs of complex (wo)man (Schein, 1980), or, to put it somewhat differently, the tensions inherent in a major contradiction in capitalist systems, namely the need to achieve both control and consent of employees in order to secure not only the extraction but also the realization of their surplus value. The influence of Taylor's (1911) scientific management and the subsequent development of Fordism in the 1920s (see Rose, 1975), based on notions of rational-economicman and formal organization, had been counterbalanced by that of the Hawthorne studies in the 1930s (Mayo, 1933; Roethlisberger and Dickson, 1939) and the Ohio/Michigan studies of the 1940s and 1950s (Katz and Kahn, 1966; Stogdill, 1974) which revealed the importance of employees' social affective needs and of informal organization – relationships and values within small unofficial work groups. Erstwhile unquestioned assumptions about the rightness of rational management embedded in hierarchy were challenged by research that pointed to the effectiveness of open participative leadership (Likert, 1961; 1967; McGregor, 1960) and the dysfunctional side-effects of Fordist work system design and bureaucracy generally (Blauner, 1964; Selznick, 1949; Merton, 1957; Gouldner, 1954).

This research – both that of the neo-human relations writers (McGregor, Likert, Argyris, and motivation the-orists such as Maslow, Herzberg, Vroom, Porter and Lawler) and the structural-functionalist sociologists (Selznick, Merton and Gouldner) – anticipated present interest in organizational culture in two ways. The neo-human relations school expanded the early concern with groups into a broader, organization-wide perspective, focusing on how organizations might be developed to achieve a high-trust climate in which employees would see the achievement of organizational goals as the route to achieving their own aspirations. From this grew the work of the organizational development consultants in the 1960s and 1970s which will be discussed below. The structural-functionalist sociologists – particularly Gouldner (1954) in his study of a gypsum mine – identified the existence and process of emergence of subcultures within an organization, which could oppose and subvert the instrumental rationalism of the formal organization.

Organizational development

Organization development (OD), in vogue in the 1960s and 1970s in the UK and US, had much in common with present-day strategies of cultural management, but also had some significant differences. Like present-day strategies it was largely a response to the problem of organizational adaptation to rapid changes, both in technologies and social values, in the 'swinging sixties' (Beer, 1972; Toffler, 1970). The rhetoric, though, as befitted the era of 'flower power', was more in terms of self-development and the challenge of innovation than of achieving competitive advantage. Furthermore, many managers (and some academics) found it difficult to define precisely what OD involved that was different to normal operational activities conducted through bureaucratic channels. In theory, OD referred to systems of three interrelated elements: humanistic values, change processes (i.e. data gathering, organizational diagnosis and action interventions, such as sensitivity training or team building or work system redesign) and technology (i.e. techniques and methods emerging primarily from the behavioural sciences) (French and Bell, 1973). The processes and technology aimed to implant humanistic values throughout the organization, which, by placing organizational relationships on a new basis of openness, trust and collaboration, would (in theory) create a climate conducive to absorbing or even welcoming the challenge of change. Hence, in the main, the emphasis was on human process issues – team building, communications, interpersonal relationships – rather than on task-centred initiatives or specific work goals. To obtain a feel for the idealistic, not to say naive (and unconsciously sexist) intentions of OD practitioners, it is worth reading the florid texts of supporters of that time (Tannenbaum and Davies, 1969).

Even in its heyday, much scepticism was expressed by both managers and academics about the feasibility of implanting such 'sweetness and light' values into hard-nosed organizations that operated both as bureaucracies and political jungles. This scepticism was reinforced by encounters with managers who had experienced sensitivity training in 'T-groups' (for further details, see Lippitt, 1975) as a supposed path to greater self-awareness and openness. They tended to fall into two categories: those who rejected the experience and dismissed it as a pseudo-psychoanalysis, totally inappropriate to organizational realities, and those who 'saw the light' and exuded an air of religious conversion. As a result, OD was seen either as a form of devious manipulation, managers describing the activities as 'propaganda', 'brain washing' and, in one extreme case (referring to T-groups), 'wholly wrong and almost evil', or as 'wishy-washy', 'being nice', 'not to be taken seriously' and 'without a proper concern for profit' (Blackler and Brown, 1980: 54; Pettigrew, 1985: 295).

Furthermore, major OD initiatives in British companies such as Shell, Pilkington and ICI were far from being unqualified successes, as evinced by some of the titles of books and chapters reporting their evaluation (Klein, 1976; Blackler and Brown, 1980; Warmington et al., 1977; Pettigrew, 1985). Hence, of Shell, Blackler and Brown (1980) were constrained to ask 'Whatever happened to Shell's New Philosophy of Management?', while Pettigrew's account of OD in ICI's (then) Plastics Division is entitled 'The change strategy without political support'. Even of the relative success story of value change in ICI's (then) Mond division, Pettigrew (1985: 375) queries

> whether the halting, meandering, some might say inefficient, process of connecting developmental thinking and resources to issues of structure, systems, culture and management processes in Mond, needed to be as meandering as it surely was.

Furthermore – and perhaps this should stand as a warning to the present generation of 'transformational leaders' – he quotes Harvey-Jones' (initiator of OD in ICI's (then) Petrochemicals division and subsequently Chairman of ICI) wry comments about its demise in that division:

> I think P.C.D. organization is a sad case, because I really believed that I had started an irreversible force. I knew there would be attempts to halt it, but I really believed it wouldn't be easy to halt it. I was dead wrong – well 80% . . . (ibid.: 257)

The relative lack of success of OD initiatives in effecting major and lasting cultural change in the relatively small number of UK organizations in which it was tried may be put down to several factors.

First, the industrial relations climate in the 1960s and 1970s was one of strong union power, backed up by (generally) tight labour markets. The OD philosophy of trust and collaboration, in spite of urging the need for openness and confrontation, essentially assumed an ultimate identification of organization members' interests. This implicitly unitarist position flew in the face of the rampant pluralism of industrial relations in the 1960s and 1970s. Secondly, in spite of much talk of OD signalling the 'death of bureaucracy' (Bennis, 1966) in order to cope with an increasingly complex and changing environment, many of the initiatives were, in retrospect, surprisingly inward looking, involving schemes of management development, work system design and attempts at participation, but without close attention as to how they were to deliver against market-driven organizational success criteria. The long-term nature of OD activities, combined with difficulties in demonstrating clearly to sceptics their contribution to organizational success criteria (and within a UK culture of financial short-termism) (Sisson, 1990: 8), rendered the initiatives marginal to mainstream personnel management activities, at best being regarded as 'deviant' innovation (Legge, 1978) and, at worst, being treated with a cynical contempt. Pettigrew (1985: 255), for example, in discussing the 'ambivalence and rejection' the OD unit encountered in the (then) Petrochemicals division of ICI, cites an OD practitioner's observation that captures well this marginality:

> I asked the managers what they thought the OD unit does? It wasn't a question of them saying, 'Oh my God. They're way out.' Wasn't that at all. Either they didn't know, or somebody had done a study on transport drivers for them, or somebody had sat in, as a process resource. Or nothing had happened, and they didn't have the faintest idea or interest in the OD unit.

Against this background of only very limited success of OD initiatives in the 1970s, how do we account for the resurgence of interest in cultural management in the 1980s and 1990s?

Models of excellence and the enterprise culture

It is generally considered (e.g. Sisson, 1989; 1990; Storey, 1989) that the emergence of a rhetoric of HRM in the 1980s in the US and UK may be seen as the result of several changes experienced in both product and labour markets, changes brought about by technological development and a swing to right-wing ideologies. Several 'buzz' words signify these changes: intensification of international competition, the Japanese Janus (threat/icon), cultures of excellence, information technology, knowledge working, high value-added, and the enterprise culture. The phrase that encapsulates them all is 'the search for competitive advantage'. Here, the focus is on two – models of excellence and the enterprise culture – that have been particularly influential in identifying cultural management as a major potential contributor in delivering competitive advantage.

Models of excellence Given that international competition has intensified and made the search for competitive advantage more urgent, it is not surprising that people looked for answers from those that appeared to be achieving just that: the Japanese and 'household name' successful companies. In so doing, managers and academics alike were alert to culture as a potentially significant factor. Was it something about Japanese culture that enabled a country decimated by allied bombing and nuclear attack, in the space of 40 years, to emerge phoenix-like as the second most powerful world economy? What distinguished successful companies from the less successful? Was it something about their 'feel', their 'ethos'? The message from both sources pointed not only to the fact that values and beliefs were a contributing factor to competitive advantage, but also to what these values might be. Both the Japanese and US 'excellent' companies appeared to share a similar set of values, whether derived from a Confucian ideology, a Protestant work ethic, or national culture. As stereotyped in numerous publications (e.g. Peters and Waterman, 1982: 285) such 'strong' corporate cultures emphasized the values of 'being the best', of flexibility, initiative and innovation, of superior quality and service, of open, participative communications and, above all, of the organizations' employees being its most important asset.

Hence the lesson learnt in the early 1980s from such influential publications as Ouchi's (1982) *Theory Z* and Peters and Waterman's (1982) *In Search of Excellence* was that American management practice (and by inference that of the UK too) had traditionally placed too much emphasis on a centrally imposed rationality, expressed through excessive emphasis on the measurable, involving the manipulation of complex structures to achieve compliance and results.

The Japanese, on the other hand, prioritized creating a shared vision, a culture of collective commitment to achieving organizational goals, often expressed in philosophical ('quality', 'being the best') rather than quantitative terms. The Americans had neglected this 'transformational' leadership in favour of a shorter term 'harder' transactional style. But the comforting message was that all was not lost. Where US companies *had* adopted management practices that resembled those of the Japanese (Theory Z, Peters and Waterman's 'eight attributes') they had achieved financial success. The lesson was clear: cultural management that secured the commitment of employees as valued assets – hallmarks of the 'soft' HRM model (Legge, 1989; Hendry and Pettigrew, 1990) – should be the order of the day. Supported by the six pillars of Japanese employment practice (lifetime employment, company welfare, quality consciousness, enterprise unions, consensus management and seniority-based reward systems) – all suitably adapted to local context, of course – this would facilitate the adoption of other Japanese practices (e.g. *Kanban* [JIT] and *Kaizen* [continuous improvement]) that call for flexible utilization of resourceful humans.

It should be noted that the idea of equating the use of Japanese management techniques, including human resource management practices, with success in US companies is shaky to say the least. First, the design and empirical basis of Peters and Waterman's research is highly suspect, raising doubts as to the genuine excellence (even financial) of the companies identified, and the reliability of the eight attributes (for an excellent critique, see Guest, 1992). Second, the typification of Japanese management practice rests on crude stereotypes that neglect such important qualifications as Japan's dualistic industrial structure and the extent to which traditional HRM policies have never been universally applied and, indeed, are in the process of erosion in the light of demographic change, internationalization, and technological development (for a short summary, see Thompson and McHugh, 1990: 202–6; for longer accounts, see Clark, 1979; Godet, 1987; Mroczkowski and Hanoaka, 1989; Bartlett and Yoshihara, 1988; Whittaker, 1990; Okubayashi, 1988). Nevertheless, the imagery of the Japanese Janus and the rhetoric associated with models of excellence resonated with core values embedded in the UK and US national culture, those of a Protestant 'work ethic' and the 'American Dream' (Hofstede, 1980; Guest, 1990).

The enterprise culture At a macro level, in the UK and US, government ideology and resultant policies reinforced an emergent belief that appropriate management of the corporate culture might be the key to securing competitive advantage. The reason for this was that the political rhetoric in both societies extolled many of the virtues – being the best, initiative, innovation and the sovereignty of the customer – that were also being promoted in the Japanese management/excellence literature. The promotion of an enterprise culture, the very notion that stimulating a 'rugged entrepreneurial individualism' (Guest, 1990: 31) would foster national economic well-being, placed cultural management to the forefront of many organizational as well as political agendas. We can explore this idea further.

Enterprise, as Keat (1991) and Fairclough (1991) point out, has a dual meaning. It can act as a noun (the commercial 'enterprise') as well as an adjective or adverb (to be 'enterprising'). In the latter sense, it has connotations of initiative, energy, independence, boldness, self-reliance and a willingness to take risks and to accept responsibility for one's actions. In this sense an enterprise culture is one in which the acquisition and exercise of these qualities is valued and encouraged.

The two meanings of the enterprise culture come together in the view that management of commercial enterprises is the field of activity in which enterprising qualities are best put to use and developed. As enterprising qualities are seen as virtues, this justifies and validates the workings of a free market economy. At the same time, in order to maximize the benefits of a 'free enterprise' economic system, firms and their participants must be seen to act in ways that express enterprising qualities (Keat, 1991: 3–4).

Although major criticisms can be raised about many of the assumptions the lie behind this vision of enterprise culture and the politico-economic policies that have been adopted in its pursuit (e.g. Keat, 1991: 7–9), its message is consistent with the values embodied in both the 'soft' and the 'hard' models of HRM (see Legge, 1989 and Hendry and Pettigrew, 1990 for a full discussion of the distinctions between 'hard' and 'soft' models of HRM). The individualistic values (and anti-union bias) that pervade the rhetoric of the enterprise culture are consistent with individualistic and unitarist values of the 'soft' HRM models. Its emphasis on the primacy of the market and the need to create enterprising individuals and firms to compete successfully in the market-place finds echoes in the 'hard' model's emphasis on external integration – of the match between strategy and environment, and of HRM policy, procedures and practices with business strategy. The image of enterprising individuals as those who are keen to take responsibility, goal-oriented and concerned to monitor their progress towards goal achievement, motivated to acquire the skills and resources necessary to pursue these goals effectively, and see the world as one of opportunity rather than constraint (Keat, 1991: 5–6) is consistent with the values of commitment and flexibility embodied in the 'soft' model. One could argue, too, that the rhetoric about the sovereignty of the consumer is consistent with the ideas about quality, which are also central to the 'soft' model. Finally, the ideas about competitive advantage that pervade HRM and the models of excellence are part of the rhetoric of a free market economy, the bedrock of the enterprise culture.

The efforts of senior managers in UK companies to manage corporate culture in the 1980s might cynically be seen as a reflection of the domination of the government leader's charisma over her most faithful followers. What Mrs Thatcher attempted at societal level (if she had believed in that concept), business leaders attempted in their own organizations – both with an eye to competitive advantage.

Culture, Commitment and Performance

What is organizational culture?

If senior managers seek to manage 'organizational culture', what exactly is it that they are seeking to manage? Up to this point, organizational culture has been defined in the most minimal way as a 'set of shared meanings, or taken-for-granted assumptions'. Such a simple definition cloaks a wide-ranging debate about the problems in arriving at an adequate conceptualization of organizational culture (Pettigrew, 1979; Deal and Kennedy, 1982; Pondy et al., 1983; Gregory, 1983; Smircich, 1983; Frost et al., 1983; Meyerson and Martin, 1987; Meek, 1988; Whipp et al., 1989; Turner, 1990). For example, is 'corporate' culture the same as 'organizational' culture? Are organizational 'climate' (often talked about in the 1970s by OD practitioners) and organizational 'culture' one and the same? How inclusive a concept is it – i.e. what is *not* organizational culture?

For the purposes of this discussion, two issues appear central: the epistemological position taken with regard to the concept, and its inclusivity. The position adopted with regard to epistemology determines whether one considers that culture can be 'managed' at all, or whether managers are merely deluding themselves. The issue of inclusivity determines what aspects of the organization managers might seek to manipulate when they attempt to change or reinforce its culture, assuming they believe such issues can be managed.

Organizational culture as variable or 'root metaphor' In a seminal early paper, Smircich (1983) made the valuable distinction that, depending on whether we lean towards a positivistic, structural-functional or a phenomenological world view, we can either conceptualize organizational culture as a variable (something an organization *has*) or as a process of enactment (something an organization *is*). Studies of culture in comparative management, and of corporate culture, treat it as something an organization *has*: either as an independent variable (e.g. when a national culture is imported into an organization via its membership), or as something produced by the organization (its values, language and rituals) as a by-product of the production of goods and services. As Meek (1988) points out, this conceptualization of culture derives squarely from the anthropological tradition of structural-functionalism which rests on a biological metaphor. This heritage gives rise to a particular focus: culture is seen as somehow unitary and the collective consensus of the organization. The organic analogy also suggests that culture is defined functionally, as an instrument serving human biological and psychological needs (e.g. giving employees a sense of identity and direction), and as an adaptive-regulating mechanism that effects system stability (through facilitating integration). Furthermore, the organic functionalist perspective encourages the view that the 'head' of the organism (its senior management) has a directive role in developing the collective consciousness, and that 'healthy' (strong) cultures are both reflective and facilitative of organizational adaptation and growth (success). Given this epistemological perspective, it is not surprising that Schein (1985a; 1985b, cited in Meek, 1988: 196, 198) can state both that

> 'strong' cultures are somehow more likely to be associated with effectiveness than are 'weak' cultures, and that strong cultures can be deliberately created
> (and)
> organizational cultures are created by leaders, and one of the most decisive functions of leadership may well be the creation, the manage-

ment, and – if and when that may become necessary – the destruction of culture.

In using the term 'corporate' culture, many writers seem to be imputing a culture created by senior management for the lower orders to swallow (e.g. Schein, 1985b; Martin, 1985; Lorsch, 1985; Gordon, 1985). This approach to conceptualizing organizational culture *as* corporate culture has been termed the 'integration' paradigm by Meyerson and Martin (1987). In it, the emphasis is on that which is shared, consistency across cultural manifestations, consensus, among cultural members, a denial of ambiguity and a focus on leaders as culture creators.

In contrast, culture may be conceptualized as something emerging from social interaction – something an organization *is* (Smircich, 1983; Gregory, 1983). According to Smircich (1983) it may be regarded as a system of shared cognitions, knowledge and beliefs, or as a system of shared symbols and meanings, or even as a projection of the mind's universal unconscious infrastructure. It is both produced and reproduced through the negotiating and sharing of symbols and meanings – it is both the shaper of human action and the outcome of a process of social creation and reproduction (Meek, 1988; Whipp et al., 1989). If culture is seen in these terms, it is questionable to what extent – or even whether – senior management can successfully manipulate or unilaterally change it. As Meek (1988: 293) puts it:

If culture is regarded as embedded in social interaction, that is as something that is socially produced and reproduced over time, influencing people's behaviour in relation to the use of language, technology, rules and law, and knowledge and ideas (including ideas about legitimate authority and leadership) then it cannot be discovered or mechanically manipulated; it can only be described and interpreted. The researcher adopting the social emergent view of culture cannot suggest how it can be created or destroyed, the researcher can only attempt to record and examine how culture may be altered in the process of social reproduction. People do not just passively absorb meanings and symbols; they produce and reproduce culture and in the process of reproducing it, they may transform it. The social emergent approach to culture also moves the researcher away from the political and ideological interests of management, towards those of the organizational community as a whole.

To adopt this position is not to imply that senior managements can have no influence at all on their organizations' cultures. Indeed, given shared understandings in industrial organizations about the meaning of hierarchy, it is likely that their voices will be more audible and influential than those of subordinate employees. But it does imply that theirs will not be the only voice, nor will it *necessarily* be listened to and internalized. As there are likely to be competing voices, the process of social production and reproduction may spawn a variety of cultures, given people's different experience of reality. Corporate culture – that shared by senior management and presented as the 'official' culture of the organization – may be only one of several subcultures within any organization, and may be actively resisted by groups who do not share or empathize with its values. If the corporate culture makes no sense of the organizational realities experienced by the employees other than senior management, it will not become internalized outside that small subgroup.

But the distinction between culture as variable or root metaphor still leaves unanswered how it is to be demarcated from other social aspects of organization. So, what is, and is not, organizational culture?

Inclusivity Substantive definitions of culture range from the all inclusive to those that exclude all but taken-for-granted assumptions. Thus, on the one hand we have Deal and Kennedy's (1982) 'it's the way we do things around here' and, on the other, Gregory's (1983) 'a system of meanings'. Deal and Kennedy's definition would view organizational culture as meshed into organizational structure, while Gregory's would see organizational culture as distinct from structure. Such a distinction is of more than academic interest. If management is to manage culture, it needs to know what aspects of organizational life cause, comprise or are manifestations of organizational culture.

First, following Meek (1988), it is important to remember than both 'culture' and 'structure' are abstractions of regularities from observations of actual behaviour, not tangible entities. Hence, we can define either abstraction as we find appropriate to our purpose. To define organizational culture so as to include all organizational behaviour is self-defeating when our purpose is to assess the feasibility of cultural management, for the latter then becomes equivalent to 'managing behaviour in organizations' – the focus of all the chapters in this text. Geertz's (1973) distinction (cited by Meek, 1988: 204) seems more helpful – namely, that culture may be viewed as an ordered system of meanings and of symbols, in terms of which social interaction takes place, and that structure can be seen as the pattern of social interaction.

Such a distinction is not inconsistent with Schein's (1984) well known conceptualization of organizational culture. Schein defines it as 'the pattern of basic assumptions that a given group has invented, discovered or developed in learning to cope with its problems of external adaption and internal integration, and that have worked well enough to be considered valid, and therefore, to be taught to new members as the correct way to perceive, think and feel in relation to these problems'.

Schein goes on to distinguish three levels of culture and their interaction (see figure 12.1). Visible artifacts – the organization's architecture, technology, office layout, dress codes, visible or audible behaviour patterns and public documents – are the surface level of culture, and are easy to identify but difficult to interpret without an understanding of the underlying logic. The 'why' of how a group behaves is explained by identifying the values that govern behaviour, the second level of culture. Yet such values, being identified through

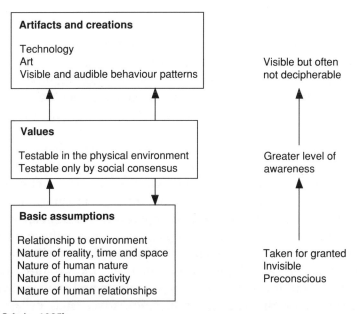

Source: Schein, 1985b

Figure 12.1 Levels of culture and their interaction

interviewing key members of the organization and content analysing artifacts such as documents, are likely to represent accurately only the manifest and espoused values of the organizational culture. To understand a culture, Schein argues, it is necessary to penetrate the third level, the underlying taken-for-granted assumptions that determine how group members perceive, think and feel. These assumptions are learned responses that originate in espoused values and have resulted in successful adaptive behaviour, such that the original values become so habitually validated that they drop from conscious recognition. The basic assumptions which refer to the organization's relationship to its environment, the nature of truth and reality, the nature of human nature, activity and relationships, are, in Schein's view, the essence of organizational culture, the artifacts and values being just manifestations of that culture.

Schein goes on to make the point that a culture only exists in the context of there being a group to 'own' it, defined as a set of people who have been together long enough to have shared significant problems, to have had the opportunity to solve those problems and observe the consequences, and who have taken in and socialized new members. The latter point is an important test of whether a given solution is shared and perceived as valid, i.e. that a culture has developed.

Implications of definitional issues for cultural management If organizational culture is seen as a variable rather than as a 'root metaphor', clearly there is far more room for senior management to mould it consciously. If organizational culture is seen as an inclusive catch-all concept, including artifacts and espoused values as well as taken-for-granted assumptions, there are more ways in which management can manipulate it than if the former are considered merely as manifestations of culture. If culture is seen as being embedded in sets of people with a shared history and relative success in coping with problems of external adaptation and internal integration, then it argues for the likely existence of organizational subcultures and points to the time factor in enacting any change in culture. Hence it is not surprising that the management initiatives that will be considered later have invariably, if often implicitly, conceptualized culture as a variable and focused on changing artifacts and espoused values. When evaluating the success of such initiatives, it is necessary to consider potential resistance from competing subcultures and to be aware of the resources invested in socialization, including time.

But, before turning to the case study evidence, we need to briefly consider the nature of commitment to an organizational culture and its potential relationship to performance.

What is commitment?

In much writing about cultural management (e.g. Peters and Waterman, 1982; Tichy, 1983), it is assumed that the intention is to develop a strong, unitary, corporate culture, whereby organizational members share a commitment to values, beliefs and taken-for-granted assumptions that direct or reinforce behaviours considered to be conducive to organizational success. But as Coopey and Hartley (1991) have recently pointed out (echoing an earlier analysis by Salancik, 1977) 'commitment' in organizational behaviour has been conceptualized in two distinct ways.

The orthodox approach is to see commitment as referring to an individual's psychological bond to an organization; as 'affective attachment and identification' (Coopey and Hartley, 1991: 19). In the same vein, Porter et al. (1974) define commitment as the relative strength of the individuals' involvement with, and in, a particular organization. This is operationalized in terms of three factors: a strong desire to remain a member of the organization; a firm belief in, and acceptance of, the values and goals of the organization; and a readiness to exert considerable effort on behalf of the organization.

In contrast, other commentators, notably Becker (1960), Kiesler (1971) and Salancik (1977; 1982), see commitment as 'the binding of the individual to behavioral acts' (Kiesler and Sakumura, 1966). This approach, which has its roots in theories of cognitive dissonance and consonance (Festinger, 1957), argues that the degree of commitment a person develops derives from the extent to which behaviours are experienced as binding. Individuals are more likely to be bound to their acts if such acts are highly visible and their outcomes are irrevocable, and when they perceive their acts as voluntary (Salancik, 1982).

From the point of view of attempting to manage corporate culture, these contrasting definitions have very different implications. In spite of its orthodoxy, the 'affective identification' conceptualization, as Salancik (1977: 3) points out, can only be used after the event to classify persons (via the 'organizational commitment questionnaire' (OCQ)) as committed or not committed. Its implicit emphasis, though, that existing attitudes influence behaviour, would suggest that managers interested in changing or reinforcing a culture should opt for re-educative approaches (development and training, persuasive communications, role-modelling, counselling) or replacement strategies (recruitment, selection, intensive socialization) designed to change beliefs (or recruit compatible beliefs) in the assumption that appropriate behaviour will follow. In contrast, if the 'behavioural acts and consistencies' (Coopey and Hartley, 1991: 19) conceptualization is adopted, the preferred strategy might be to induce behavioural change, but through minimal use of material rewards (to inhibit behavioural compliance rationalized through instrumentality), and rely on the individuals involved to develop (and hence reinforce) attitudes consistent with their new desired behaviours. For example, if the organization wishes its employees to internalize the value of quality, a strategy might be to abolish the role of the specialist on-line quality inspector, and redesign jobs so that each operator is held responsible for monitoring and achieving a work standard of 'right first time'. Based on theories of cognitive consistency, the argument would go that, assuming the operator had some choice in adopting the new role, and assuming that new behaviour was not elicited through promise of great rewards or threat of sanctions, the very enactment of the new behaviour would result in attitudes consistent with it and, hence, reinforce it (see Salancik, 1977: 21–7 for a more detailed discussion).

But this is to consider only half of the generally linked concepts of 'organizational commitment'. Assuming commitment is secured, what is the employee committed to? We will return to this issue at the end of the chapter. Suffice to say here that if we assume a pluralistic model of organization, following Coopey and Hartley (1991), multiple and potentially competing 'organizational' foci of commitment might be identified: job, profession, department, union, quite apart from that monolithic abstraction 'the organization'. Normative HRM models, in their preference for unitaristic rather than pluralistic frameworks, overcome this difficulty by playing down enacted subcultures in favour of managed corporate cultures.

Culture, commitment and performance

As already stated, there is an assumption in much of the popular 'excellence' literature (Peters and Waterman, 1982; Peters, 1987; Waterman, 1987; Morgan, 1988; Kanter, 1989) that strong cultures, possessing resolute values, contribute to exceptional levels of organizational performance. Let us leave aside for the moment the host of problematic issues embodied in such an assumption, namely: the questionable equating of performance with dubious selected financial measures (Guest, 1992); the worry that 'strength' is a dimension antithetical to the nature of culture as an interpretational phenomenon (Van Maanen and Barley, 1984); or that the trait-strength approach suffers from overreliance on modal cultural pro-files, ignoring the complex interaction of multiple sub-cultures to influence outcomes (Saffold, 1988). Let us assume that employees share a commitment to a range of values espoused by senior manage-ment, and that we can treat this as synonymous with a strong culture. In attempting to demonstrate a linkage between strong cultures and organizational performance, several issues have to be considered that are frequently neglected in much of the extant research.

First, as Saffold (1988: 549–50) points out, the relationship be-tween culture and performance is not necessarily monotonic. Citing total institutions (Goffman, 1969) as a case in point, he argues that

> . . . as cultural values are more fully elaborated, a greater range of organizational behavior is brought under control. Initially this may enhance performance by ensuring that organizational priorities are uniformly established. But, if cultural controls multiply too greatly, resistance is likely to develop, causing performance to decrease.

Secondly, it is possible that a particular cultural value may not affect all performance-related organizational processes in the same direc-tion. Sharing meanings may have a positive integrative effect, but at the same time inhibit an organization's ability to learn and adapt (Janis, 1972; Shrivastava, 1985; Coopey and Hartley, 1991).

Third, even if we assume a monotonic, unidirectional effect of certain shared values on performance, attention (often lacking) must be paid to validation measures. Contrasting comparison groups, for example, are necessary to show that a cultural profile generally characteristic of high performing organizations (however defined) is not equally evident in average or low performing ones (Saffold, 1988; Guest, 1992).

These problems stand even before we consider the immense dif-ficulties of isolating the effects of any corporate culture from those of simultaneously interacting intervening variables on performance.

Needless to say, if culture is treated as an all inclusive variable (and hence a meaningless one) much of this latter problem is circumvented, but to little analytical point.

Can Culture be Managed?

There exist numerous accounts of cultural change in newly privatized industries, such as British Telecom and British Airways (e.g. Clark et al., 1988; Young, 1989; Höpfl, 1992); in those public services, notably the NHS, newly subject to quasi-markets and managerialism (e.g. Coombs and Green, 1989; Kelly, 1991; Strong and Robinson, 1990); in engineering and in car manufacturing, whether on greenfield (Wickens, 1987) or brownfield sites (Hendry and Pettigrew, 1987; Pettigrew and Whipp, 1991); in banking and financial services (e.g. Hendry and Pettigrew, 1987; Pettigrew and Whipp, 1991; Knights and Willmott, 1987); and in retailing (Ogbonna and Wilkinson, 1988; 1990; Marchington, 1993).

What do such programmes aim for? How do they seek to achieve cultural change (or reinforcement)? On what assumptions are their strategies based? What is achieved?

The aim of cultural change programmes

The aim of cultural change programmes is to achieve employee commitment to those values which senior management considers conducive to improved organizational performance. Following Ray (1986), cultural change strategies may be seen as an addition to other forms of control which organizations have tried to implement. Whereas bureaucratic control focuses on the social and organizational structure of the firm (e.g. structures of the internal labour market, appraisal and reward) (Edwards, 1979) and humanistic control on matching employee needs to 'satisfying task or work group life' (Mayo, 1933; 1945) – both strategies aiming to increase worker loyalty and, ultimately, productivity – cultural control

> ... implies that the top management team aims to have individuals possess direct ties to the values and goals of the dominant elites in order to activate the emotion and sentiment which might lead to devotion, loyalty and commitment to the company (Ray, 1986: 294).

First, cultural control can supplement the other two forms. This is often done implicitly in broad-brush HRM initiatives where performance-related pay may go hand in hand with enhanced communication and participation, and with training (e.g. in quality circles aimed at the internalization and implementation of espoused values, as at British Telecom). But, secondly, 'more than other forms of control . . . corporate culture elicits sentiment and emotion, and contains possibilities to ensnare workers in a hegemonic system' through treating the organization, à la Durkheim, as an appropriate site for an integrative moral order (Ray, 1986: 287).

On the whole, cultural change programmes over the last decade have promoted the values of quality (of product or service) and the pre-eminence of the market-place, sanitized into 'customer awareness/customer care'. The other major values of cost-effectiveness and flexibility (read labour intensification?) are promoted largely through systems of bureaucratic control, although their rhetoric may enter cultural change programmes.

It is instructive to compare the statements of espoused values emanating from the range of organizations identified above and note their similarity. Privatized British Gas (in a patriotic red and blue booklet, *Banishing Gripes*, sent free of charge to all customers) asserts 'British Gas is totally committed to giving you the best possible service' and specifies its standards, as does British Rail in its *Passengers' Charter* (also in patriotic blue and red) which declares 'The *Passengers' Charter* is a statement of our commitment to provide a high quality service for our passengers'. (One can only assume that British Rail dropped the recently acquired designation 'customer' in response to passengers' irritation at being so labelled, with the implications of consumer choice.)

An early advertising slogan of British Telecom – 'We answer to you' – also asserts the primacy of the customer. Indeed, the whole concept of the *Citizen's Charter* is indicative of the government's desire to bring concepts from the market-place (i.e. the sovereignty of the customer) into the erstwhile non-market public sector.

Private companies have echoed the same message, although with the competing one of cost-control. In the cases explored by Pettigrew and Whipp (1991) – in the automobile, merchant banking, book publishing and life assurance industries – the pervading themes are a search for quality that will satisfy more discriminating customers (e.g. Jaguar) or the provision of the diversified range of services required by clients (e.g. Hill Samuel and Prudential). In retailing, too, 'customer care' combined with the provision of an up-market range of high value-added products (e.g. Marks and Spencer, Sainsbury and Tesco) is the espoused value although, with the persistence of recession and recognition of market segmentation, some firms (e.g. Kwik-save) have interpreted 'customer responsiveness' as involving a reconsideration of the 'Pile 'em high, sell 'em cheap' philosophy. Marchington (1993), in his research on the retailing sector, cites one company's message, which was pinned up on the employee notice board: 'Customer Care is the Number One skill that employees must have. Our future success will depend on how well you apply this skill'.

Nevertheless the emphasis on quality has gone hand in hand with the espoused value of cost-control because, in an environment of (at the time of writing) high interest rates and slowing of customer demand, it is perceived that even customers who demand quality are not insensitive to price. The message of cost-control may be conveyed symbolically (as was done by Castleman, chief executive of Hill Samuel, who questioned division heads in 'public' regarding their cost projections and overruns, made the bank dining room self-service and cut the number of company chauffeurs), but the real thrust generally lies in the messages conveyed by bureaucratic controls (e.g. appraisal systems, promotion policies, performance-related pay and the use of numerical flexibility).

Strategies to achieve culture change

In talking of cultural change, given the epistemological and inclusivity assumptions made earlier, it is assumed that senior managers attempt to change two *manifestations* of organizational culture, viz. artifacts (including overt behaviour) and espoused values. At best they seek to bind individuals to behavioural acts that are coherent with (newly) espoused values. This inevitably, then, involves the use of bureaucratic controls (e.g. structuring of the internal labour market, appraisal and promotion systems, training and payment systems) *as well* as managing meaning through rituals, symbols and so forth.

Hence the techniques used are those common to any strategy aimed at changing behaviour but with particular emphasis on their symbolic content. In most cultural change strategies one can recognize an implicit adherence to Lewin's (1951) change model and Chin and Benne's (1976) change strategies. In other words, the social system is viewed as a force field of driving and restraining forces in equilibrium: change is effected through a process of 'unfreezing' this system (by showing inadequacies of current beliefs), introducing change (via empirical-rational, normative re-educative and power-coercive strategies) and 'refreezing' it in its changed state (by developing reinforcing structures and control systems).

Unfreezing may occur through skilfully managed organizational trauma. In 1980, Edwardes, the BL chief executive, announced that Jaguar would close within a year, unless the unit broke even. In the same year, a new managing director and chairman, Egan, was appointed. One of his early acts was to create a 'Black-Museum', displayed at plant level, of the worst product defects of the 1979–80 period and invite US dealers to the tracks to put the case directly of the quality problem with the Series III model. (In this, Egan was assisted by the rising levels of unemployment in the early 1980s.)

Change can be introduced through empiricist-rational strategies (assumption: that individuals are rational and will follow rational self-interest given 'correct' information); normative re-educative strategies (assumption: that people's rationality and behaviour is influenced by social and subgroup norms, and that, therefore, re-education should not only provide correct information about the 'facts' of the situation, but address socially supported beliefs and norms by working through groups rather than individuals); and power-coercive strategies (assumption: that power can be used to enforce behavioural change, by exercise or threat of sanctions). Translated into management practice, this generally results in three strategies, often applied simultaneously, but to different groups of people, at different levels in the hierarchy and at different stages in the change process. These are re-education (including participative communication such as briefing groups, role-modelling, quality circles, training and management development generally), replacement (e.g. selection, promotion and redundancy) and reorganization (e.g. new structures, appraisal and reward systems).

Many companies have attempted to promote the values of quality and customer service through re-educative methods. Notable are British Airways' 'Putting People First' programme (Young, 1989; Höpfl, 1992; 1993), ICL's major management education programme in the early 1980s (Sparrow and Pettigrew, 1988; Sparrow, 1991), the 'new tech' training at GKN (Hendry and Pettigrew, 1988; Hendry, 1991), British Rail's 'Customer Care' and TQM programmes (Storey, 1992b; Guest et al., 1993), Lucas' TQM and JIT initiatives (Storey, 1992b) and the team building at Grampian Health Authority (Fullerton and Price, 1991). Role-modelling examples abound – not only the now legendary story of Marshall, at

British Airways, assisting at the check-in on the first day of the Super Shuttle service (Young, 1989), but also of Turnbull, at Peugeot-Talbot, receiving customer complaint calls personally in 1990 (Pettigrew and Whipp, 1991).

Role-modelling too plays a part in training initiatives, as in the use of senior managers, known for their participative style, taking question and answer sessions in Royal Bank of Scotland training courses – or even the use by Sainsbury of group role-play exercises, with checkout staff role playing the customers. Briefing groups and quality circles, it is claimed, have been used effectively in car assembly particularly and in engineering generally (e.g. Hardy Spicer, Jaguar, Nissan, Rover) (Hendry and Pettigrew, 1988; Wickens, 1987; Pettigrew and Whipp, 1991). In summary, recent research by Storey (1992a; 1992b) based on a sample of 15 'household name' organizations (including Rover, British Rail, ICI, the NHS, Plessey and Whitbread) found most were engaged in intensive and direct communications with employees as part of 'wide ranging cultural, structural and personnel strategies', aimed at 'conflict reduction through culture change'.

Replacement strategies are also in evidence. Well known are the selection policies of major engineering companies (e.g. Rover, Nissan, Toshiba and Pirelli) (Willman and Winch, 1985; Wickens, 1987; Yeandle and Clark, 1989) that select not only for staff potential but for appropriate attitudes and values, namely those supportive of flexibility and team-working. The TSB and Abbey National have steadily increased the number of graduate trainees recruited in an effort to become more commercially oriented (e.g. Hendry and Pettigrew, 1987). Selective early retirement of senior or middle managers, perceived as averse to new, more commercially oriented values, has also been used in many organizations, such as TSB, Shell, Smith and Nephew (e.g. Hendry and Pettigrew, 1987; Storey, 1992b).

Finally, major structural changes have been used to align organizations closely with the market-place. In general terms, this has involved decentralization and increased operational autonomy for identified separate business units, and their change from cost to profit centres. In erstwhile public sector industries (e.g. British Gas, British Telecom) this has often resulted in a (relatively late by industrial standards) move from functional organization to business/market centred structures. The same is true of British Rail before privatization (see Guest et al., 1993). The post-Griffiths reforms of the NHS and the opting-out of schools involve structural change similarly aimed at increased market responsiveness (e.g. Reed and Anthony, 1993; Fullerton and Price, 1991).

Such initiatives are often reinforced by the implantation of the new 'espoused values' into appraisal systems, backed up by the introduction of various forms of performance-related pay – see, for example, the 'new contracts' at British Telecom and in the polytechnics/higher education section, and the use of performance-related pay on the shop-floor at Black and Decker and Birds Eye Walls (Kinnie and Lowe, 1990; Kessler and Purcell, 1992). Further details of the combinations of re-educative, replacement and reorganization strategies may be found notably in Pettigrew and Whipp, 1991; Storey, 1992b and Gowler et al. 1993.

Most of these strategies have received symbolic as well as instrumental expression. Identification with the organization and its values is expressed by the vast expansion of company-specific workwear, particularly in areas where there is direct contact with the customer (e.g. banks and building societies). Commercial orientation has resulted in changes in physical artifacts, as evidenced by the redesign of banks and building societies, moving away from images that convey the safeguarding of money (metal grilles, high counters, mahogany and real marble) to ones of selling money (carpets, glass screening, personal banking, open-plan area). Language has changed in the same direction too: British Rail passengers are now 'customers', as shall shortly be the students in institutions of higher education. Checkout personnel at supermarkets and fast-food outlets are now encouraged to smile at customers and wish them a 'nice-day' (Ogbonna and Wilkinson, 1988; 1990). Above all, the transformational leaders have learnt the value of symbolic acts – as referred to earlier in this chapter and exemplified in the writing of that erstwhile supporter of OD, Sir John Harvey-Jones (Harvey-Jones, 1988).

Paradoxes of cultural management

It may be argued that the paradoxes embedded in the intentions and implementation of cultural management render it self-defeating. As Anthony (1993) points out, if cultural control ('hegemonic' in Ray's terms) is regarded as a more effective substitute for rational bureaucratic control, it is interesting that the mechanisms by which messages of initiative, autonomy, innovation, risk-taking and personal responsibility are conveyed – e.g. organization-wide cascaded briefings, training days, appraisal systems – are themselves highly bureaucratic. Might not this, in itself, negate the messages that are being preached? And what of the infrastructures set up to monitor the success of team building, multi-skilling and so forth?

Second, the development of a new strong culture is often seen as the task of the new leader (e.g. Egan at Jaguar, Castleman at Hill Samuel, Turnbull at Peugeot, Birch at Abbey National) as part of a strategy for revitalizing the organization. Such leaders, at least in the first instance, are often regarded as organizational deviants, representing a small subculture in battle with the strong (but perceived as ineffective) dominant culture (e.g. Harvey-Jones at ICI, see Pettigrew, 1985). A classic example is the battle presently raging between post-Griffith's style NHS managers, representing the espoused management values of the primacy of the efficient allocation of resources, and the professional clinicians arguing the primacy of the delivery of best patient care as defined by clinicians. Which is the legitimate strong culture?

To quote Anthony (1990: 6)

> ... there is no doubt that the allegiance of the [professionals] to a common culture is reinforced by a tradition of moral concern. In the National Health Service and the universities the internal values of health or education are shared by the inhabitants who influence the culture of their organizations because they regard its institutions as instrumental to their practices and to their concern with internal values. In these instances, culture is based upon identifiable values widely shared; they are not imposed by the institution although they may be reinforced by it. *Historically, the institution is secondary to the practice. In managed organizations the opposite is true: the institution comes first in time* and any culture that follows is likely to have been imposed, often coercively, by a leader or founder, who may have charismatic qualities attributed to him or her. And the values and the culture are, of course, likely to be changed or obliterated with a change in the leadership; in the professions, culture is more likely to abide. (Added emphasis)

So here we have the paradox that a small subgroup (senior managers) is being called on to create a strong subculture to confront and overwhelm an existing, more widely shared strong culture, one that is rooted in moral rather than instrumental values. Questions inevitably must be raised about the ethics of such initiatives, if only in the interests of democracy. And, in this context, Anthony (1993) reminds us of Jackall's (1988: 195, 133) words: 'The fundamental requirements of managerial work clash with the normal ethics governing interpersonal behaviour' . . . [and] . . . 'The logical result of alertness to expediency is the elimination of any ethical lines at all'. Perhaps we should consider these words as a prophetic warning of the role of a charismatic leader bent on the creation of his own strong organizational culture in opposition to that of a strong occupational community.

Third, Anthony (1990) argues that when a small senior management group attempts to superimpose a new set of espoused values on subordinates that are discordant with the latters' sense of reality, the result may be that they act out the surface signals of the 'new culture' but cynically and without internalization. Existing bureaucratic structures (hierarchy, appraisal, promotion ladders) ensure that negative, critical, even whistle-blowing feedback is unlikely to occur. On the contrary, the skilled performance enacted by employees such as the checkout assistants quoted above may confirm senior management in its view that the new culture has taken, when all that is on show is a 'resigned behavioural compliance' (Ogbonna and Wilkinson, 1990: 14) supported by bureaucratic controls. Without negative feedback, senior management is reinforced in the delivery of a message that may become increasingly at odds with employees' perceptions of organizational reality, and engender an increasing cynicism. In such circumstances the paradox will exist that as senior management becomes increasingly convinced that cultural change has taken place, other organizational members may become increasingly cynical and resistant to such attempts to influence behaviour. (Hence, Harvey-Jones' rueful retrospective reflections on the failure of OD in ICI's Petrochemicals Division, cited earlier.)

What is achieved?

It is difficult to answer this question because, although we have accounts of such 'cultural change' initiatives, there are few, if any, systematic evaluations of them. Has the reviving engineering culture of Jaguar, for example, survived takeover by Ford? Has the diversified, cost-conscious ethos that Castleman tried to develop in Hill Samuel survived his departure and its acquisition by TSB? We have no systematic evaluations that can answer these questions. The answers, one way or the other, await detailed longitudinal case studies and follow-up studies a decade later. Even then, for reasons already outlined, it is probable that researchers will find it easier to identify long-term changes in the manifestations of culture than in basic assumptions.

Recent case study evidence appears to suggest that cultural change initiatives appear more successful among its initiators (senior management) and its immediate collaborators (surviving middle managers) than further down the hierarchy. On the basis of his 15 core cases, Storey (1992b: 215), for example, concludes that 'while there was very considerable evidence of transformation with line managers as the objects of change . . . there was much less evidence that this had as yet been carried through into similar behavioural and attitudinal changes at shopfloor level'.

In a passage that echoes Salancik's (1977) comments about conditions facilitative or inhibiting in the achievement of commitment as 'behavioural acts and consistencies', Storey (1992b: 241) states, with reference to supervisory reaction to the newly designated 'first line manager' role at Whitbread, that

> . . . in consciously seeking to manage a change of culture, senior managers had manipulated some symbols to signify a new order, but these were insufficient to counterbalance the range of signs which persuaded the sceptical that things were pretty much the same. Hence the name change to 'first line manager' was not accorded very much significance by those who could glimpse little realistic future as a 'manager'. Without that glimpse even training courses on 'leadership' could make little impression. Those F.L.M.s who had 'caught the management bug' had been receptive to the new set of symbols because they relished the planning and data-handling aspects of the role and they could envisage a future in a management career. It was those who had gone to the trouble of taking the old 'shift supervisor' name plates off their office doors. For the rest, the companies' paradigmatic shift (in Birds Eye, Whitbread and Eaton) had been too ambivalent to persuade most supervisors that they personally should buy into a new mode of operating. There were, on balance, simply too many contra-symbols (including middle and senior managers' general demeanour towards them) to overcome the power of inertia.

In the retailing sector, too, we have some evidence (admittedly of a less longitudinal nature than would be methodologically desirable) that points in the same direction. Ogbonna and Wilkinson (1990) point to the likelihood of 'resigned behavioural compliance' rather than changes in espoused values – let alone basic assumptions – among checkout staff when the managerial rhetoric of the 'customer is king', 'quality and service' is at odds with their experience of work as involving rude customers, monotony, and intense pressure for speed. While employees take pride in their ability to act out the espoused values of 'service with a smile' ('We are told to smile all the time . . . sometimes it's very hard . . . I succeed because I try to put up an act . . . my mother thinks I'm very good at it and that I should have been an actress') Ogbonna and Wilkinson (1990: 13) claim that rarely do such values appear internalized.

> Rather, the motives behind the behaviour patterns displayed on the shopfloor were almost invariably either instrumental ('this disarms the customer') or under threat of sanction ('I smile because I'm told to'; 'you have to be very careful and polite because they can report you to the manager'). The check-out operator's job is, of course, highly visible and not smiling or even 'putting on a false smile' can result in being 'called into a room for a chat' with the supervisor. Random visits by bogus shoppers and head office managements reinforce the threat of sanctions for undesirable behaviour or expressing one's true feelings to difficult customers.

While the connection between bureaucracy and acting has been well made before (MacIntyre, 1981), following Salancik, these accounts raise two questions. Does continuous acting finally internalize the values being enacted? Possibly 'yes' where, as in the case of Whitbread's supervisors who were 'caught by the management bug', behaviour was voluntary. Or, does the process of acting out a part at odds with perceptions of reality, merely enhance cynicism and, paradoxically, a deeper rejection of the newly proselytized values? This may well be true for Ogbonna and Wilkinson's checkout operators. Either way, it might be argued that the manipulation of values and symbolism to facilitate the extraction and realization of surplus value raises issues about the mobilization of bias and false consciousness as well as more general ethical issues (see Anthony, 1993).

What we can say on the evidence that we have is that the internalization of any value demands its testing and reinforcement by relatively stable groups of employees over time, and their socialization of newcomers into these values. The amount of delayering and redundancy in British industry since the late 1980s raises doubt as to whether these conditions have prevailed. Further, the assertion of the values of quality and customer care were very much part of the 'rejuvenation' of manufacturing, the high street boom, and the privatization of public sector industries and services in the mid-1980s. While market-place competition probably maintains support for these values in manufacturing (note the number of household-name manufacturing companies – Shell, Ford, ICI, Rover, etc. – heavily involved in TQM and the securing of BS 5750 'Quality Assurance'), there is the issue of the extent to which such values may be undermined by the competing ones of cost-control, with the recession of the late 1980s and early 1990s and the intervention of regulatory bodies (Ofgas, Oftel) affecting profitability.

What could be argued, if we take the 'behavioural consistencies' view of commitment, is that the *bureaucratic* controls (restructuring, redesign of working practices and control systems) that have induced new behaviour patterns *may* result in the eventual internalization of the values embedded in the new structures and resultant behaviours. However, as argued earlier, in theory this internalization is only likely to occur if the individuals involved feel they have some choice and discretion over their new behaviours and that the consequences of engaging in them are positive. If the individual has no choice (other than redundancy), or is heavily 'bribed' to participate, the required behaviour may result, but even espoused values of all but senior management remain unchanged. As for the taken-for-granted assumptions, it is debatable whether many of the work groups involved in cultural change programmes have had sufficient time to test and be reinforced in the new espoused values for these to be absorbed into unconscious assumptions. For example, to what extent did British Airways' espoused values of 'Putting People First' stand the test of the redundancy programme and the Gap Closure and Sprint cost cutting exercises, in the light of revenue losses due to recession and the Gulf War?

Are Strong Cultures Desirable?

Strong culture can act as a 'moral glue', binding together a (possibly) differentiated organization. This is particularly relevant when a penchant for tight-loose structures dissolves bureaucratic centralizing controls other than the financial ones. Also, widely shared basic assumptions and espoused values can act as guidelines to facilitate co-ordinated and rapid decision making. Commitment to shared values is particularly important when the relationship between an individual's actions and outcomes are uncertain or the instrumental pay-offs are likely to be low. Furthermore by co-opting an individual's commitment to espoused values and courses of action, and inducing a sense of personal responsibility for them, senior management inhibits that individual's ability to find fault with the same (Salancik, 1977: 445). However, the downside of a strong organizational culture is an inward looking, conformist, complacent organization, sunk into a morass of group-think, and rigid, rather than flexible, in its outlook.

According to Brunsson (1982), 'objective' ideologies (defined as ideas shared by all organizational members), when 'conclusive' (i.e. clear, narrow and consistent), in one sense – speed of response – can promote adaptability. This is because decisions can be made quickly as the conclusive ideology (read 'strong culture') acts as an effective seal of approval on the acceptability of an action, thereby eliminating lengthy discussion and generating commitment to implementing it. Weick (1987: 125) points out the advantages, in high-risk systems, such as air traffic control and nuclear power stations, of a rich culture of horror stories, aphorisms and histories that 'register, summarize, and allow reconstruction of scenarios that are too complex for logical linear summaries to preserve'. This assumes though that either the stories 'hold the potential to enhance requisite variety among human actors' or, failing that, that the action required involved no radical departures from tenets of the strong culture, as conclusive ideologies rule out changes that challenge their assumptions.

Weick (1969; 1987) and Coopey and Hartley (1991) point out the dangers of strong culture in developing rigid and conformist thinking among its members. While strong cultures imply a convergence of goals and values, adaptability to rapidly changing conditions relies on people having different perceptions of environmental data (Weick, 1969). Coopey and Hartley argue for the advantage of multiple commitments within organizations – to job, career, profession, department and trade union. They suggest that competing ideologies 'stimulate individuals to think meaningfully about themselves and the world around them' (1991: 26), and that creative tensions between heterogeneous viewpoints are ultimately more facilitative of flexibility and innovation than the complacency engendered by a shared, unchallenged view of reality.

The danger of the latter may be illustrated by the much quoted example of IBM in the early 1980s. IBM's narrow ideology of 'IBM is service' contained particular assumptions about the nature of product and service (mainframe, customized systems, salesmen as management consultants to customer-as-end-user, seeking quality of product and service) which were inappropriate when strategy dictated an entry into the personal computers market (standardized product, cost competition, dealer as customer) (Mercer, 1987). The very success of the service ethic in its traditional markets inhibited an adaptive response from employees to new market opportunities.

Yet, conclusive ideologies, reflecting strong cultures, Brunsson argues, in the long term may be more amenable to radical shifts than the broad, ambiguous ideologies, often taken as symptomatic of weak culture. Superficially, while the latter might appear to allow more flexible responses on the part of the employee, their very vagueness fails to generate the necessary commitment for effective action. Nevertheless, such ideologies tend to survive as they are difficult to disconfirm, being apparently applicable to a wide range of situations. In contrast, the very precision of conclusive ideologies allows their disconfirmation as individuals' own experience of changed circumstances cannot be reconciled with their unequivocal prescriptions and justifications. In these circumstances, the ideology (culture) is likely to be questioned and replaced. Until a new ideology is in place, Brunsson suggests, it will be impossible for the organization to take effective action as the period of transition will be marked by conflicts and uncertainties that will inhibit individuals' willingness to make a commitment to any one course of action and hinder co-ordination.

Hence, it could be said that the relationship between strong cultures, employee commitment and adaptability contains a series of paradoxes. Strong cultures allow for a rapid response to familiar conditions, but inhibit immediate flexibility in response to the unfamiliar, because of the commitment generated to a (now) inappropriate ideology. Weak cultures, in contrast, when equated with ambiguous ideologies, allow flexibility in response to the unfamiliar, but cannot generate commitment to action. Yet, strong cultures, through disconfirmation and eventual ideological shift may prove ultimately more adaptive to change, assuming the emergence of a new, strong yet appropriate culture. This may be at the cost of a transitional period when ability to generate commitment to any course of action, new or old, is minimal.

Given the different levels of culture that need to be penetrated if genuine cultural change is to be effected, it is tempting to ask whether it is worth it. Certainly, once values are internalized, organizational members have the desired controls 'built in' and they are self-maintaining. But, as evidenced by the case studies cited, this is both expensive and not always successful. There is a case to be made that, where boundaries are to be specified to a relationship, behavioural compliance achieved through instrumentalities and external pressure may be more cost-effective. Developing a strong culture for peripheral employees may be an ineffective use of resources. The best strategy is probably to build on existing deeply held beliefs in such a way that the new message (e.g. 'customer service') resonates with an old belief (e.g. 'how I like to be treated as a customer') and the connections and positive consequences are spelt out.

Bibliography

Ackroyd, S. A. and Crowdy, P. A. 1990. 'Can Culture be Managed? Working with "Raw" Material: The Case of the English Slaughtermen'. *Personnel Review*, Vol. 19, No. 5, 3–13.

Anthony, P. D. 1990. 'The Paradox of the Management of Culture or "He Who Leads is Lost"'. *Personnel Review*, Vol. 19, No. 4, 3–8.

Anthony, P. 1993. Managing Culture. Milton Keynes: Open University Press.

Bartlett, C. A. and Yoshihara, H. 1988. 'New Challenges for Japanese Multinationals: Is Organization Adaptation Their Achilles Heel?'. *Human Resource Management*, Vol. 27, No. 1, 19–43.

Becker, H. S. 1960. 'Notes on the Concept of Commitment'. *American Journal of Sociology*, Vol. 66, 289–96.

Bennis, W. G. 1966. *Changing Organizations*. New York: McGraw-Hill.

Beer, S. 1972. *Brain of the Firm: The Managerial Cybernetics of Organization*. London: Allen Lane.

Blackler, F. H. M. and Brown, C. A. 1980. *Whatever Happened to Shell's New Philosophy of Management? Lessons for the 1980s from a Major Socio-Technical Intervention of the 1960s*. Farnborough: Saxon House.

Blauner, R. 1964. *Alienation and Freedom*. Chicago: University of Chicago Press.

Brunsson, N. 1982. 'The Irrationality of Action and Action Rationality: Decisions, Ideologies and Organizational Actions'. *Journal of Management Studies*, Vol. 19, No. 1, 29–44.

Chin, R. and Benne, K. D. 1976. 'General Strategies for Effecting Changes in Human Systems'. In Bennis, W. G., Benne, K. D., Chin, R. and Corey, K. E. (eds) *The Planning of Change*. New York: Holt, Rinehart and Winston.

Clark, J., McLoughlin, I., Rose, H. and King, R. 1988. *The Process of Technological Change*. Cambridge: Cambridge University Press.

Clark, R. 1979. *The Japanese Company*. New Haven: Yale University Press.

Coombs, R. and Green, G. 1989. 'Work Organization and Product Change in the Service Sector: The Case of the U.K. Health Service'. In Wood, S. (ed.) *The Transformation of Work?* London: Unwin Hyman.

Coopey, J. and Hartley, J. 1991. 'Reconsidering the Case for Organizational Commitment'. *Human Resource Management Journal*, Vol. 1, No. 3, 18–32.

Deal, T. E. and Kennedy, A. 1982. *Corporate Cultures*. Reading, MA: Addison-Wesley.

Edwards, R. 1979. *Contested Terrain. The Transformation of the Workplace in the Twentieth Century*. London: Heinemann.

Fairclough, N. 1991. 'What Might We Mean By "Enterprise Culture"?'. In Keat, R. and Abercrombie, N. (eds) *Enterprise Culture*. London: Routledge.

Festinger, L. 1957. *A Theory of Cognitive Dissonance*. Stanford, CA: Stanford University Press.

French, W. L. and Bell, C. H. 1973. *Organization Development*. Englewood Cliffs, NJ: Prentice Hall.

Frost, P. J., Moore, L. F., Louis, M. R., Lundberg, C. C. and Martin, J. (eds) 1983. *Organizational Culture*. Beverly Hills: Sage.

Fullerton, H. and Price, C. 1991. 'Cultural Change in the NHS'. *Personnel Management*, Vol. 23, No. 3, 50–3.

Geertz, C. 1973. *The Interpretation of Culture*. London: Hutchinson.

Godet, M. 1987. 'Ten Unfashionable and Controversial Findings on Japan'. *Futures*, August, 371–84.

Goffman, E. 1969. 'The Characteristics of Total Institutions'. In Etzioni, A. (ed.) *A Sociological Reader on Complex Organizations*. New York: Holt, Rinehart and Winston.

Gordon, G. G. 1985. 'The Relationship of Corporate Culture to Industry Sector and Corporate Performance'. In Kilmann, R. H., Saxton, M. M. and Serpa, R. (eds) *Gaining Control of the Corporate Culture*. San Francisco: Jossey Bass.

Gouldner, A. W. 1954. *Wildcat Strike*. New York: Antoich Press.

Gowler, D., Clegg, C. and Legge, K. (eds) 1993. *Case Studies in Organizational Behaviour and Human Resource Management*. London: Paul Chapman.

Gregory, K. 1983. 'Native View Paradigms: Multiple Cultures and Culture Conflicts in Organizations'. *Administrative Science Quarterly*, Vol. 28, No. 3, 359–76.

Guest, D. 1990. 'Human Resource Management and the American Dream'. *Journal of Management Studies*, Vol. 27, No. 4, 376–97.

Guest, D. 1992. 'Right Enough to be Dangerously Wrong: An Analysis of the "In Search of Excellence" Phenomenon.' In Salaman, G. (ed.)

Human Resource Strategies. London: Sage.

Guest, D., Peccei, R. and Fulcher, A. 1993. 'Culture Change and Quality Improvement in British Rail'. In Gowler, D., Clegg, C. and Legge, K. (eds) *Case Studies in Organization Behaviour and Human Resource Management*. London: Paul Chapman.

Harvey-Jones, J. 1988. *Making it Happen: Reflections on Leadership*. London: Collins.

Hendry, C. 1991. 'Manufacturing Change at Belma Joints'. In Legge, K., Clegg, C. and Kemp, N. (eds) *Case Studies in Information Technology, People and Organizations*. Oxford and Manchester: NCC/Blackwell.

Hendry, C. and Pettigrew, A. 1987. 'Banking on H.R.M. to Respond to Change'. *Personnel Management*, Vol. 19, No. 11, 29–32.

Hendry, C. and Pettigrew, A. 1988. 'Multi-skilling in the Round'. *Personnel Management*, Vol. 20, No. 4, 36–43.

Hendry, C. and Pettigrew, A. 1990. 'Human Resource Management: An Agenda for the 1990s'. *International Journal of Human Resource Management*, Vol. 1, No. 1, 17–44.

Hofstede, G. 1980. *Culture's Consequences*. Beverly Hills: Sage.

Höpfl, H. 1992. 'The Making of the Corporate Acolyte'. *Journal of Management Studies*, Vol. 29, No. 2, 23–33.

Höpfl, H. 1993. 'Culture and Commitment: British Airways'. In Gowler, D., Clegg, C. and Legge, K. (eds) *Case Studies in Organizational Behaviour and Human Resource Management*. London: Paul Chapman.

Jackall, R. 1988. *Moral Mazes: The World of Corporate Managers*. New York: Oxford University Press.

Janis, I. 1972. *Victims of Groupthink*. Boston: Houghton Mifflin.

Kanter, R. M. 1989. *When Giants Learn to Dance*. New York: Unwin.

Katz, D. and Khan, R. L. 1966. *The Social Psychology of Organizations*. New York: Wiley.

Keat, R. 1991. 'Introduction, Starship Britain or Universal Enterprise?'. In Keat, R. and Abercrombie, N. (eds) *Enterprise Culture*. London: Routledge.

Kelly, A. 1991. 'The Enterprise Culture and the Welfare State: Restructuring the Management of the Health and Personal Social Services'. In Burrow, R. (ed.) *Deciphering the Enterprise Culture*. London: Routledge.

Kessler, I. and Purcell, J. 1992. 'Performance Related Pay: Objectives and Applications'. *Human Resource Management Journal*, Vol. 2, No. 3, 16–33.

Kiesler, C. A. 1971. *The Psychology of Commitment: Experiments Linking Behavior to Belief*. New York: Academic Press.

Kiesler, C. A. and Sakumura, J. 1966. 'A Test of a Model for Commitment'. *Journal of Personality and Social Psychology*, Vol. 3, 349–53.

Kinnie, N. and Lowe, D. 1990. 'Performance Related Pay on the Shopfloor'. *Personnel Management*, Vol. 22, No. 11, 45–9.

Klein, L. 1976. *A Social Scientist in Industry*. Epping: Gower Press.

Knights, D. and Willmott, H. 1987. 'Organizational Culture as Management Strategy: A Critique and Illustration from the Financial Services Industry'. *International Studies of Management and Organization*, Vol. 17, No. 3, 40–63.

Legge, K. 1978. *Power, Innovation and Problem-Solving in Personnel Management*. London: McGraw-Hill.

Legge, K. 1989. 'Human Resource Management – A Critical Analysis'. In Storey, J. (ed.) *New Perspectives on Human Resource Management*. London: Routledge.

Lewin, K. 1951. *Field Theory in Social Science*. New York: Harper.

Likert, R. 1961. *New Patterns of Management*. New York: McGraw-Hill.

Likert, R. 1967. *The Human Organization*. New York: McGraw-Hill.

Lippitt, G. L. 1975. 'Guidelines for the Use of Sensitivity Training'. In Taylor, B. and Lippitt, G. L. (eds) *Management Development and Training Handbook*, 1st edn. London: McGraw-Hill.

Lorsch, J. W. 1985. 'Strategic Myopia: Culture as an Invisible Barrier to Change'. In Kilmann, R. H., Saxton, M. J. and Serpa, R. (eds) *Gaining Control of the Corporate Culture*. San Francisco: Jossey Bass.

McGregor, D. 1960. *The Human Side Of Enterprise*. New York: McGraw-Hill.

MacIntyre, A. 1981. *After Virtue: A Study in Moral Theory*. London: Duckworth.

Marchington, M. 1993. 'Close to the Customer: Employee Relations in Food Retailing'. In Gowler, D., Legge, K. and Clegg, C. (eds) *Case Studies in Organizational Behaviour and Human Resource Management*. London: Paul Chapman.

Martin, H. J. 1985. 'Managing Specialized Corporate Cultures'. In Kilmann, R. H., Saxton, M. J. and Serpa, R. (eds) *Gaining Control of the Corporate Culture*. San Francisco: Jossey Bass.

Mayo, E. 1933. *The Human Problems of an Industrial Civilization*. New York: Macmillan.

Mayo, E. 1945. *The Social Problems of an Industrial Civilization*. Cambridge, MA: Harvard University Press.

Meek, V. L. 1988. 'Organizational Culture: Origins and Weaknesses'. *Organizational Studies*, Vol. 9, No. 4, 453–73.

Mercer, D. 1987. *IBM: How the World's Most Successful Company is Managed*. Homewood, IL: Irwin.

Merton, R. K. 1957. *Social Theory and Social Structure*. New York: Free Press.

Meyerson, D. and Martin, J. 1987. 'Cultural Change: An Integration of Three Different Views'. *Journal of Management Studies*, Vol. 24, No. 6, 623–47.

Morgan, G. 1988. *Riding the Waves of Change: Developing Managerial Competencies for a Turbulent World*. London: Sage.

Mroczkowski, T. and Hanaoka, M. 1989. 'Continuity and Change in Japanese Management'. *California Management Review*, Winter, 39–53.

Ogbonna, E. and Wilkinson, B. 1988. 'Corporate Strategy and Corporate Culture: The Management of Change in the U.K. Supermarket Industry'. *Personnel Review*, Vol. 17, No. 6, 10–14.

Ogbonna, E. and Wilkinson, B. 1990. 'Corporate Strategy and Corporate Culture: The View From the Checkout'. *Personnel Review*, Vol. 19, No. 4, 9–15.

Okubayashi, K. 1986. 'Recent Problems of Japanese Personnel Management'. *Labour and Society*, Vol. 11, No. 1.

Ouchi, W. 1981. *Theory Z: How American Business Can Meet the Japanese Challenge*. Reading, MA: Addison Wesley.

Peters, T. J. 1987. *Thriving on Chaos*. London: Pan.

Peters, T. J. and Waterman, R. H. 1982. *In Search of Excellence: Lessons from America's Best Run Companies*. New York: Harper & Row.

Pettigrew, A. M. 1979. 'On Studying Organizational Cultures'. *Administrative Science Quarterly*, Vol. 24, No. 4, 570–81.

Pettigrew, A. M. 1985. *Awakening Giant*. Oxford: Blackwell.

Pettigrew, A. M. and Whipp, R. 1991. *Managing Change for Competitive Success*. Oxford: Blackwell.

Pondy, L., Frost, P. J., Morgan, G. and Dandridge, T. 1983. *Organizational Symbolism*. Greenwich, CT: JAI.

Porter, L., Steers, R., Mowday, R. and Boulian, P. 1974. 'Organizational Commitment, Job Satisfaction and Turnover among Psychiatric Technicians'. *Journal of Applied Psychology*, Vol. 59, 603–9.

Ray, C. A. 1986. 'Corporate Culture: The Last Frontier of Control?' *Journal of Management Studies*, Vol. 23, No. 3, 287–97.

Reed, M. and Anthony, P. 1993. 'Southglam: Managing Organizational Change in a District Health Authority'. In Gowler, D., Clegg, C. and Legge, K. (eds) *Case Studies in Organizational Behaviour and Human Resource Management*. London: Paul Chapman.

Roethlisberger, F. J. and Dickson, W. J. 1939. *Management and the Worker*. Cambridge, MA: Harvard University Press.

Rose, M. 1975. *Industrial Behaviour: Theoretical Development Since Taylor*. Harmondsworth: Allen Lane.

Saffold, G. S. 1988. 'Cultural Traits, Strength and Organizational Performance: Moving Beyond "Strong" Culture'. *Academy of Management Review*, Vol. 13, No. 4, 546–58.

Salancik, G. R. 1977. 'Commitment and the Control of Organizational Behavior and Belief'. In Staw, B. M. and Salancik, G. R. (eds) *New Directions in Organizational Behavior*. Chicago: St. Clair Press.

Salancik, G. R. 1982. 'Commitment is Too Easy!'. In Tushman, M. L. and Moore, W. L. (eds) *Readings in the Management of Innovation*. London: Pitman.

Schein, E. H. 1980. *Organizational Psychology*. Englewood Cliffs, NJ:

Prentice Hall.

Schein, E. H. 1984. 'Coming to a New Awareness of Organizational Culture'. *Sloan Management Review*, Winter, 3–16.

Schein, E. H. 1985a. 'How Culture Forms, Develops and Changes'. In Kilmann, R. H., Saxton, M. J. and Serpa, R. (eds) *Gaining Control of the Corporate Culture*. San Francisco: Jossey Bass.

Schein, E. H. 1985b. *Organizational Culture and Leadership*. San Francisco: Jossey Bass.

Selznick, P. 1949. *T.V.A. and the Grass Roots*. Berkeley, CA: University of California Press.

Shrivastava, P. 1985. 'Integrating Strategy Formulation with Organizational Culture'. *Journal of Business Strategy*, Vol. 5, 103–11.

Sisson, K. 1989. 'Personnel Management in Perspective'. In Sisson, K. (ed.) *Personnel Management in Britain*. Oxford: Blackwell, 3–21.

Sisson, K. 1990. 'Introducing the Human Resource Management Journal'. *Human Resource Management Journal*, Vol. 1, No. 1, 1–11.

Smircich, L. 1983. 'Concepts of Culture and Organizational Analysis'. *Administrative Science Quarterly*, Vol. 28, No. 3, 339–58.

Sparrow, P. R. 1991. 'Developing a Human Resource Management Strategy: International Computers Ltd.' In Legge, K., Clegg, C. and Kemp, N. (eds) *Case Studies in Information Technology, People and Organizations*. Oxford and Manchester: NCC/Blackwell.

Sparrow, P. and Pettigrew, A. 1988. 'Strategic Human Resource Management in the Computer Supplier Industry'. *Journal of Occupational Psychology*. Vol. 61, 25–42.

Stogdill, R. M. 1974. *Handbook of Leadership: A Survey of Theory and Research*. New York: Free Press.

Storey, J. 1987. *Developments in the Management of Human Resources: an Interim Report*. Warwick Papers in Industrial Relations, No. 17. IRRU, School of Industrial and Business Studies, University of Warwick, November.

Storey, J. (ed.) 1989. *New Perspectives in Human Resource Management*. London: Routledge.

Storey, J. 1992a. 'H.R.M. in Action: The Truth is Out at Last.' *Personnel Management*, Vol. 24, No. 4, 28–31.

Storey, J. 1992b. *Developments in the Management of Human Resources*. Oxford: Blackwell.

Strong, P. and Robinson, J. 1990. *The NHS: Under New Management*. Milton Keynes: Open University Press.

Tannenbaum, R. and Davies, S. M. 1969. 'Values, Man and Organization'. *Industrial Management Review*, Vol. 10, No. 2, 67–86.

Taylor, F. W. 1911. *Principles of Scientific Management*. New York: Harper.

Thomas, M. 1985. 'In Search of Culture: Holy Grail or Gravy Train?' *Personnel Management*, Vol. 17, No. 9, 24–7.

Thompson, P. and McHugh, D. 1990. *Work Organizations, A Critical*

Introduction. London: Macmillan.

Tichy, N. 1983. *Managing Strategic Change.* New York: Wiley.

Toffler, A. 1970. *Future Shock.* London: Bodley Head.

Turner, B. A. (ed.) 1990. *Organizational Symbolism.* Berlin and New York: de Gruyter.

Van Maanen, J. and Barley, S. 1984. 'Occupational Communities: Culture and Control in Organizations'. In Staw, B. M. and Cummings, L. L. (eds) *Research in Organizational Behavior.* Greenwich, CT: JAI.

Walton, R. E. 1985. 'From Control to Commitment in the Workplace'. *Harvard Business Review*, 63, March/April, 76–84.

Warmington, A., Lupton, T. and Gorfin, C. 1977. *Organizational Behaviour and Performance.* London: Macmillan.

Waterman, R. H. Jr. 1987. *The Renewal Factor: Building and Maintaining Your Company's Competitive Edge.* London: Bantam.

Weick, K. 1969. *The Social Psychology of Organizing.* Reading, MA: Addison-Wesley.

Weick, K. 1987. 'Organizational Culture as a Source of High Reliability'. *California Management Review*, Vol. XXIX, No. 2, 112–27.

Whipp, R., Rosenfeld, R. and Pettigrew, A. 1989. 'Culture and Competitiveness: Evidence from Two Mature U.K. Industries'. *Journal of Management Studies*, Vol. 26, No. 6, 561–85.

Whittaker, D. H. 1990. 'The End of Japanese Style Employment?' *Work, Employment and Society*, Vol. 4, No. 3, 321–47.

Wickens, P. 1987. *The Road to Nissan.* London: Macmillan.

Willman, P. and Winch, G. 1985. *Innovation and Management Control: Labour Relations at B.L. Cars.* Cambridge: Cambridge University Press.

Yeandle, D. and Clark, J. 1989. 'A Personnel Strategy for an Automated Plant'. *Personnel Management*, Vol. 21, No. 6, 51–5.

Young, D. 1989. 'British Airways: Putting the Customer First', Ashridge Strategic Management Centre, July.

PART V

The Wage–Work Bargain

13

Managing Pay in Britain

William Brown and Janet Walsh

The rewards from employment are far from clear-cut. For most employees, work offers a bitter-sweet mixture which cannot be simply added up: frustration, friendship, strain, self-esteem, boredom, satisfaction, and much else besides. These variable, unmeasurable, and very personal aspects of work are of profound motivational importance. Personnel policy is increasingly laying emphasis upon them in the design of jobs and careers, in training, and in policy on, for example, employee involvement.

Amid this complexity, pay stands out as by far the most conspicuous part of the reward package. By its nature quantifiable, and thus generalizable across all manner of jobs and employees, pay provides, however misleadingly, the only common language of reward. It provides the natural focus for collective bargaining and the obvious channel into which discontents over the more intangible aspects of work can be displaced. It may be only a part of the reward package, but it is the principal part open to transaction between employers and employees, and especially employee organizations. Consequently, the satisfactory management of remuneration is a necessary, if not a sufficient, precondition of the satisfactory management of employment.

This chapter is concerned with the problem of managing pay and, to a lesser extent, fringe benefits. Hours of work are dealt with in chapter 15. The intention is to make the reader sensitive to the tangled forces that affect management policy making. The starting point is the labour market, and the extent to which it guides or constrains management action. It is argued that employees' notions of fairness are of crucial significance, which leads into a discussion of the job evaluation techniques used to manage them. We describe the broader strategic issues shaping an enterprise's pay policy. The chapter then discusses payment systems, bearing in mind Ian Kessler's subsequent chapter on performance pay, and fringe benefits.

The Labour Market

In a perfect market for labour, management would have no discretion over what to pay. If pay fell below the 'going rate', or if the level of effort demanded rose above what was normal, then employees would, according to traditional economic theory, start to leave, and the employer would then have to move back into line in order to remain in business. The management of pay would be a wholly passive routine. In practice, however, such circumstances are unusual, the closest being those involved with casual, unorganized, unskilled labour such as, for example, in seasonal catering jobs. For most employment, the labour market is in varying degrees very imperfect.

A consequence of this is the vagueness, in practice, of the notion of a 'going rate' of pay. Surveys have been carried out of pay in many occupations in numerous local labour markets in several countries. There is generally a substantial spread of pay to be found among jobs within the same occupation within the same labour market. This applies whether one looks at gross earnings or at earnings standardized for hours worked. The median coefficient of variation of earnings in a single occupation in a local labour market in Britain and the USA is typically around 15 per cent (Brown, W. et al., 1980). If one takes into account non-wage benefits, the spread of total benefits is even larger, for it is generally the firms that pay their employees higher wages that also give them better non-wage benefits (MacKay et al., 1971). Far from there being an obvious local market rate for a given occupation, firms are faced with a broad range of options for pay.

The generally sluggish and unequally priced nature of the labour market stems partly from the behaviour of employees, and especially those who are older and more skilled. They tend to stick with the same employer for many years and, when they do move, it is rarely because of dissatisfaction with pay (Harris, 1966; Main, 1981). But employer behaviour also contributes. Many employers take pains to insulate their employees from the labour market to some degree. By showing preference for promotion and training of existing employees, rather than recruiting from outside, firms encourage the view that individual improvement is to be sought within the firm rather than by job search outside. Although this phenomenon is often refered to as an 'internal labour market', it a slightly misleading expression since there are no market-clearing mechanisms at work. Employees are encouraged to adapt their portfolio of skills and responsibilities in response to career and pay opportunities that are particular to their firm. It is an administrative and not a market process.

Many of the developments in training discussed in earlier chapters are tending to increase the imperfection of the labour market. The rapid decline of apprenticeship and other forms of industry-wide training in Britain is leading to greater emphasis being placed on in-house, company-specific training. One result is that employees are more than ever being recruited for their potential to acquire skills rather than for any skills that they might already possess. Another consequence is that job titles and job content are becoming increasingly specific to individual employers. Occupation and job descriptions, the essential language of the labour market, are losing public meaning and precision so that it is becoming harder to match employees' capabilities to employer needs outside the confines of the firm. No market can function satisfactorily without common terminology.

A market's imperfection does not, however, deny it influence. Labour scarcity may still become an acute managerial problem, even if its impact is blunt and is diffused by internal labour markets. In the late 1980s, employers in the south-east of Britain faced a serious shortage of skilled labour arising from a combination of housing difficulties, training deficiencies, and demographic change. The gravity of the problem they had to tackle was reflected in the radical nature of many of their responses. For some the problem was a major stimulus towards the introduction of performance-related pay and the decentralization of bargaining. One long-established device for meeting the higher living costs of the London area had been the 'London allowance' or 'London weighting', generally applied as a flat-rate allowance to all staff working within specific geographical limits. In the late 1980s many employers began to use local additions with much more discretion, targeting key professional and skilled occupations and individuals with extended salary ranges, merit payments, supplementary payments and fringe benefits.

An important feature of this sort of labour market shortage supplement is that it reduces the component of remuneration regulated by collective bargaining and extends managerial discretion over pay. But it is doubtful whether the large imbalances that developed in the south-east labour market in the late 1980s were alleviated by the *ad hoc* proliferation of supplements, even though the net effect was a substantial increase in the magnitude of the south-east regional pay differential (Walsh and Brown, 1991). There is also likely to have been longer-term damage. Exclusive reliance on the short-term palliative of local pay supplements tends to disrupt the internal coherence of firms' pay structures, with serious consequences for internal labour flexibility. Employers view such payments as discretionary at the time of their inception, and therefore consider them to be much cheaper than having to increase the pay of all staff when recruitment problems occur. But they generally prove to be irreversible in practice, and are rarely reduced or abolished when labour shortages decline.

The Problem of Effort

The market for labour is fundamentally different from markets for non-human things. This is because the act of hiring an employee is not sufficient to ensure that the job in question gets done in an acceptable way. Labour, unlike non-human goods, is sentient, and it is not necessarily committed to the same objectives as the employer. The employee has to be motivated – by encouragement, threats, loyalty, discipline, money, competition, pride, promotion, or whatever is deemed effective – to work with the required pace and care. Economic theorists since Alfred Marshall have tended to assume the problem away by theorizing that labour markets would cause earnings to equalize once the 'exertion of ability and efficiency' of the workers, and the equipment they work with, is taken into account (Marshall, 1920). This undue faith in the effectiveness of labour markets has thereby caused economic theory to overlook the importance of managerial competence in motivating employees.

No systematic British data exist relating effort levels in different firms to earnings and, as we shall see, there are sound practical reasons for this. There has been some study by sociologists of the relationship between pay and effort within individual establishments (Baldamus, 1957; Behrend, 1984). They have noted the local norms whereby managers and employees act as if there were an implicit 'effort bargain' between them that permits a trade-off between pay and effort: 'the definition of work obligations in everyday employment situations can usefully be understood as an example of negotiated order' (Hyman and Brough, 1975: 65). But this says nothing about the comparative terms of such 'bargains' in different establishments, and it certainly implies that their terms are far from the same nation-wide. Modern-day managers of multi-plant firms report substantially different norms of effort prevailing over periods of many years in different factories with similar pay levels in different parts of the country. The reduction of unit costs at laggardly sites within multi-plant concerns is a constant but difficult management objective.

A more fundamental reason for caution about the way in which traditional labour market theory assumes away the problem of effort lies in the nature of the concept. Effort is essentially a subjective notion, assessed in terms of the strain felt by the individual doing the work. But the fact that it is subjective does not mean that it is wholly private to the individual employee. The amount of strain perceived is to a considerable extent socially conditioned. People feel less strain when doing something they enjoy, or feel committed to, or proud of, than when it seems boring, futile, or unappreciated. The creation of the correct social conditions for employees to want to exert themselves is a constant and elusive goal for successful personnel policy.

More broadly, there are no objective means of comparing effort levels involved in different tasks such as, say, child-caring, stockbroking, rubbish collection, or soldiering. Societies differ markedly both between each other and between generations in the way effort is judged. There is, for example, substantial evidence that in Britain during the 1980s there was an increase in what was demanded as a 'fair' effort level (Guest, 1991; Edwards and Whitston, 1991; Nichols, 1991). But this absence of absolute values does not mean that there cannot be a parochial consensus, a negotiated order particular to a time and an organization. Nor does it deny the possibility of predictive calculations about the pace of working. Indeed, upon these two things depends the success of work study, to which we shall return.

It is also important that there is no simple connection between the number of hours worked and the amount of work done. A cut in hours may be accompanied by an improvement in the organization of work that achieves reduced unit costs. This underlies the fact that successive reductions in the length of the standard working week over the past century have done little to create new jobs (Nyland, 1985). Paid holidays can in part be seen as payment for not working in order to improve efficiency when working. Conversely, extra unplanned hours in the form of overtime may amount to little more than the intrusion of working into leisure time, with rising marginal unit costs. A question that has long interested economists is how a change in wage rates influences employees' trade-off between work and leisure and the intensity with which they work. The econometric studies are largely inconclusive. As one review puts it, 'the most intellectually defensible position is that after a decade and a half of effort we can say very little about labour supply elasticities' (Brown, C. V., 1983).

The purpose of this discussion has been to qualify rather than to reject the idea of a price mechanism in the labour market. Many personnel managers use and participate in local pay surveys. Sometimes market shortages may be the dominant force, as we have seen in the recent case of the south-east labour market, and as happens from time to time with particular occupations subject to a surge in demand, as was the case for welders and deep-sea divers when the North Sea gas and oil fields were being developed. But a more constant and immediate anxiety prompting personnel managers to scan their local and national pay surveys appears to be that, if their firm's pay levels were to fall too far out of line, existing employees might become discontented and less productive, or leave, or that recruitment problems might develop.

Managerial concern with competition focuses on the market for their product rather than that for their labour. The focus is thus on unit labour costs, which depends at least as much on nurturing labour productivity as on restraining pay. The battle for competitive unit costs is thus typically not fought by recruiting labour that is already technically competent, and doing so at the lowest wage rates possible, but rather by motivating the labour already employed to use and to develop its abilities, and to respond sympathetically to new methods of production (Nolan and Brown, 1983; Rubery et al., 1986). The constraints to managerial pay policy presented by labour market forces cannot be ignored, but they are in many respects easier to satisfy, and more forgiving of neglect, than are employees' conceptions of fairness.

The Problem of Fairness

Pay deserves more respect as a source of disincentive than of incentive. The most ingenious of bonus schemes and the best of supervision are of little use if the underlying pay structure is felt to be unfair. Consequently, the prudent personnel manager devotes far less time to devising new pay incentives than to tending old notions of fairness. This section discusses the ways in which fairness features in perceptions of pay. This leads on to the techniques of job evaluation that have been devised to cope with it.

There is nothing absolute about fairness in pay. It is a normative idea, the use of which varies from society to society and from generation to generation, from industry to industry and from workplace to workplace, much as does the notion of fairness of effort, or of a fair day's work. Fairness in pay is essentially concerned with the relationship between the pay of different individuals or groups: it is based on comparison. It is thus inextricably tied up with the valuation of social relationships and, of particular importance to individual motivation, with the way an individual perceives his or her work to be esteemed by others. This, in turn, has considerable significance for the individual's self-esteem. It is thus little wonder that arguments about fair pay arouse deep emotions, or that feelings of unfair treatment on pay issues can quickly lead to discouragement and dissent.

What sorts of comparisons matter in fairness arguments? There is no simple answer. Empirical studies have demonstrated how elusive, numerous and often contradictory are the reference groups with which individuals make their comparisons (Delafield, 1979; White, 1981a; Willman, 1982). One generalization that does seem fairly safe is that individuals appear to take comparisons more seriously when they are with those who are close to them, socially or geographically, than with those who are more distant. We have a far more discriminating and subtle evaluation of status within our own social class, our own workplace, and among those with whom we have regular face-to-face relationships, than elsewhere (Behrend, 1973). This is, after all, the part of our world upon which so much of our self-esteem depends. Consequently, employees tend to be far more upset if a pay differential deteriorates between themselves and others in their own department than if a similar deterioration occurs with respect to their company directors, or another company altogether. The most salient group within which comparisons are made is usually that of the individual administrative or bargaining unit (that is, the group of employees covered by a particular set of pay arrangements).

The question of which points of comparison are felt to be most pertinent leads on to that of the criteria whereby those comparisons are judged to be fair. The most abiding basis for accepting the fairness of a pay differential is convention. Or rather, more negatively, it is a change from the status quo which provokes anxieties about unfairness. In the absence of good reason to do otherwise, we tend passively to accept as fair that to which we have become accustomed (Wootton, 1955). Collective bargaining consolidates this view of fairness because the use of traditional comparisons provides the basis for employers and trade unions to maintain a *modus vivendi*, a basis of settlement which preserves honour for both sets of negotiators (Ross, 1948; Brown and Sisson, 1975). Historians of pay structures constantly stress their remarkable stability over many years and much economic change (Routh, 1980; Phelps Brown, 1977).

Despite this deep foundation of conservatism, pay structures – the patterns of relative pay – do alter and can be made to alter. New jobs are introduced, occupations suffer from technological decline, organizational structures are changed, groups develop new bargaining strength, and so on. By what criteria are new pay relationships judged to be fair? Here the key principles are those of legitimacy and consistency. Where trade unions are weak or non-existent, a new pay differential may be accepted as legitimate because management has decreed it. Under collective bargaining, however, it usually requires the use of formal negotiating procedures leading to an agreed settlement for the innovation to have sufficient legitimacy with the workforce to overrule past conceptions of fairness.

The principle of consistency refers to the normal sensitivity of any bureaucratic organization to the setting of precedents. Unless the criteria for establishing a new pay differential are clearly expressed at its initiation, and are adhered to subsequently, anomalies are likely to emerge which will provoke feelings of unfairness. Workforces are able to accept with enduring equanimity some highly idiosyncratic internal pay structures, so long as they are internally consistent. But it only needs a single, slight inconsistency of treatment to generate one anomalous pay rate, for all of the workforce to begin to have doubts about the fairness of the whole pay structure.

The management of the fairness of pay is of great importance for the achievement of satisfactory labour productivity. Before planning positive incentives for employees, it is necessary to guard against the demoralizing effects of feelings of unfair treatment. The basis for managing fairness lies in the characteristics that have been outlined: its normative, relative, conservative, and parochial nature, and the importance of consistency and procedural rectitude. The fact that individuals on their own may be ambivalent and inconsistent in the ways they form conceptions of fairness does not prevent their collectively being marshalled into an orderly consensus. This is the purpose of job evaluation.

Job Evaluation

Job evaluation is the generic term applied to a variety of techniques by which, through more or less systematic analysis, the relative pay of different jobs within an organization can be established in a way that is broadly acceptable to the employees concerned. It can only be implemented within the individual unit and it must cover the whole of the unit, otherwise inconsistencies of job definition and pay rate will begin to creep in. Particularly common in manufacturing industry and the nationalized industries, its incidence increases with establishment size, with a majority of workplaces of over 500 employees using job evaluation. Between 1984 and 1990, the proportion of workplaces with 25 or more employees using job evaluation rose from 21 to 26 per cent (Millward et al., 1992: 267).

The fact that the technique is generally applied to an individual bargaining unit has considerable significance. For the reasons discussed earlier, it is within the unit that the force of comparison is greatest and that attitudes to differentials are most sensitive. It is also within the unit, with its single management and union structures and its associated procedural framework, that it is possible to implement deliberate alterations of relative pay. A bargaining unit has the political infrastructure that permits the renegotiation of order. Furthermore, the visibility of different pay levels, and the understanding of different job contents, are far greater within the bargaining unit than outside. Pay structures are both more controllable and more in need of control within units than between them.

The techniques of job evaluation are described in detail elsewhere (National Board for Prices and Incomes, 1968b; Belcher, 1974;

Lupton and Bowey, 1983; Grant and Smith, 1984). The simplest and cheapest methods are those described as 'non-analytic'. In one of these, the 'ranking' method, either all or a selection of key jobs are described and then ranked in what is felt to be a 'fair' order. The employees involved in this may be asked to compare random pairs of jobs as a means of arriving at a ranking. Once ranked, the jobs are split into distinct job grades for which pay rates can subsequently be negotiated. An alternative method, called 'grading' or 'classification', starts with the grades and then fits the separate jobs into them, again using the judgement of those concerned as to the nature of the various jobs, each taken as a whole.

The crudeness of the non-analytic approach is its strength. It makes no pretence to do other than place the collective prejudices of the workforce on a consistent basis and, in workforces with strong traditions, that seems to work fairly well. These two non-analytic methods accounted for about 36 per cent of schemes in operation in Britain in 1990 (Millward et al., 1992: 267).

The 'analytic' methods of job evaluation seek to break jobs down into component parts and to assess these separately. 'Factor comparison' is a method which usually identifies five different aspects of manual jobs: mental, physical and skill requirements, level of responsibility, and working conditions. Key jobs are examined, factor by factor, and are ranked within each factor. If the existing wage structure is thought to be reasonably acceptable, it is related to the factor rankings of each key job and the deduced factor values are then applied to the remaining jobs and to any new ones. Both the assumptions involved and the process of deduction tend to be somewhat arbitrary. The technique accounted for a growing 15 per cent of schemes in 1990.

The most sophisticated analytic technique, accounting for 45 per cent in 1990, is 'points rating'. This comes in many varieties, some extremely complex. They use varied factors, sometimes several of them, and sometimes they are broken down into subfactors and the subfactors into degrees. Within these categories, jobs are assessed on a scale of points, the number of points allocated to each factor indicating its weighting with respect to other factors. The final relative position of different jobs is determined by the total number of points they have scored. For all its complexity, this is not an objective technique; the choice of factors and their weighting, quite apart from the assessment of points, are matters of judgement. What matters is that, in practice, the technique is found to be helpful in producing an acceptable and internally consistent pay structure. The process of analysis helps to discipline and make more dispassionate the comparison of jobs to an extent denied by the non-analytic techniques.

There are many circumstances, typically with weak or non-existent trade unions, where the complexity of the job evaluation technique, or the unexceptional nature of its results, are sufficient for it to be implemented without employee involvement. But these are unusual. Employee involvement is usually seen to be an essential feature for the establishment and maintenance of a job evaluation scheme. The seemingly endless committee meetings to discuss job descriptions, points ratings and factor weightings are doubly important. First, they provide a forum in which different employee interest groups can negotiate over differentials with each other. This intra-organizational bargaining between different employee groups, albeit mediated by the constraints of the technique, is more significant than any bargaining that might occur between unions and employer at this stage; the latter starts in earnest when the job evaluation is complete. Secondly, as an elaborate participative ritual, job evaluation helps bestow legitimacy upon the resulting pay structure for the employees represented. Adding to this stabilizing inertia is usually a cumbersome procedure for the maintenance of the scheme and for the review of individual appeals for job regrading.

Job evaluation, it should be emphasized, is best seen as a procedural aid to pay determination that has to be maintained, rather than as a one-off system to be installed and then insulated from individual and group pressures. It provides a flexible, disciplined, participative device for the management of the fairness of pay under what are usually changing circumstances. Hence the paradox, noted by Clark Kerr in 1950: 'The more exact, consistent, and rigid a description and evaluation plan, the less its survival value under collective bargaining. The more self-executing the plan, the more it is self-defeating' (Kerr, 1977).

The high tide of job evaluation is probably past. There will doubtless be continued elaboration of technique, and continued extensive use of job evaluation. But the centrality of the notion of a precisely defined job in the management of labour is in decline. The more that pay is linked to the careers and knowledge of individual employees, and the more that adjustment to changing technologies is seen to be a part of the employee's duties, the less appropriate it is to link pay rigidly to the particular basket of tasks currently being performed by an individual employee.

The Strategic Context of Pay Management

Pay cannot be considered in isolation. It is part of a wider set of job rules, a larger structure of industrial government, and a broader package of motivation and control. The basic component of industrial government to which a payment system is attached is the administrative or bargaining unit. The decision to alter the pattern of bargaining units cannot be taken lightly. Their profound influence in shaping notions of fairness was discussed earlier: they mould conceptions as to what constitute 'fair' bases of pay comparison. There is ample evidence that changes in bargaining units alter not only the comparisons pursued by unions, but also the pay outcomes of negotiations (Brown and Sisson, 1975). Reshaping bargaining units, like the redrawing of national frontiers, risks a lingering confusion of new alignments and old loyalties.

The last two decades have, however, seen unprecedented and accelerating change in the pattern of pay bargaining units in both private and public sectors in Britain. Why should employers have embarked on so hazardous a course?

The character of the change in the structure of pay bargaining is described elsewhere (Brown and Walsh, 1991). The long decline of the multi-employer, industry-wide agreements that once dominated private sector bargaining accelerated in the 1980s, spurred on by government encouragement. By the mid-1990s over 90 per cent of private sector employees will have their pay bargained or otherwise fixed within the single enterprise that employs them. Most firms that in the 1970s 'topped up' an industry-wide agreement with a company-level addition moved to complete autonomy in the 1980s. A further aspect of this fragmentation of bargaining became apparent in the 1980s. This was an increasing tendency for large multi-divisional and multi-plant firms to decentralize their internal bargaining structures. Similar developments are also underway, although to a lesser extent than in Britain, in most major industrialized market economies (Hegewisch, 1991).

What has been driving these changes in pay bargaining strategies? First, the withdrawal from multi-employer bargaining arrangements has been prompted by the desire of companies to utilize greater negotiating autonomy as a means to secure wider changes in the design of jobs and in employee performance. Second, the decentralization of bargaining within firms has been a consequence of the emergence of the multi-divisional enterprise whereby strategic decisions are formed at the corporate level while operational matters have been devolved to quasi-autonomous, often product-based, divisions. As operational responsibility and financial accountability have been increasingly devolved within companies, it has made sense to reshape bargaining arrangements around the countours of profit centres, divisions or individual sites.

The extent of decentralization of pay fixing within a firm is influenced by a variety of factors, among which product diversification and the intensity of competition stand out. The more heterogeneous is the range of goods and services provided by a firm, the greater is the scope for decentralization. Such scope is limited in, for example, banking, with its relatively standardized services and high staff mobility (Walsh, 1993). Decentralization can, however, render a company vulnerable to trade union strategies which use leap-frogging and comparability claims as bargaining levers. To counter this, employers may deliberately disrupt an established sequence of negotiations, or offer different length pay deals, or differentiate employment conditions, or reshape pay structures and job descriptions, in order to blur the pertinence of these internal pay comparisons.

Pay decentralization may be deceptive. The degree of decentralization of pay bargaining achieved in reality within a firm is usually substantially less than formal bargaining arrangements might imply. Corporate head offices play an important role behind the scenes in co-ordinating and monitoring the conduct and outcome of pay negotiations. A sample survey conducted in 1985 showed that two-thirds of the establishments which were ostensibly autonomous in pay bargaining were actually in thrall to a higher corporate policy which set out clear settlement limits or guidelines and similar evidence comes from the 1990 survey (Marginson et al., 1988; Millward et al., 1992). The central board in apparently decentralized companies generally retains strong control of pay planning and finance, often through control of the decentralized units' business plans. Adverse economic conditions can provoke intense monitoring activity by the centre. During the downturn of the early 1990s, for example, decisions at several large companies to postpone or stage pay rises were centrally imposed, despite their ostensibly decentralized pay bargaining structures.

Closer international economic integration and the advent of a single European market are likely to have some impact on company pay bargaining strategies. It is most likely to be of significance in companies with common European product divisions or with production integrated across more than one country (Marginson, 1992). But the signs so far are that the great majority of companies with businesses in Europe appear to favour nationally specific bargaining arrangements. The international equalization of pay structures within multinational companies is effectively constrained by the costs involved in raising occupational wage levels to the level of the highest paying country. Even when international pay levelling is restricted to managerial or technical personnel, this can provoke resentment among local employees doing similar work at lower, non-international pay levels (Ryan, 1991). The Europeanization of pay and of bargaining remains more in the realm of possibility than of reality.

Payment by Time

There is no necessity for pay to play a central role in motivating employees. Although haphazard pay administration can have a potent effect as a demotivator, the importance of pay as a positive incentive is generally exaggerated. Three-quarters of British employees are paid on pure time rates. For most of these people there will also be little opportunity for promotion. They work with whatever care and effort they bring to their job (and studies by psychologists suggest that most individuals judge their own contribution to be considerable (Porter et al., 1975)) for a mixture of reasons that varies from individual to individual, from job to job, and even from day to day.

The need for money may be the central motive for being employed at all, but it is rarely enough to ensure that work is done well. More important even than the fear of dismissal may be a mix of motives, including the desire for the manager's approval, pressure from workmates, force of habit, pleasure in helping customers and clients, fear of doing a bad job, pride in exercising a skill, and much else. This is true even for those successful innovative managers whom political mythology might suggest are most in need of money incentives. Their exceptional achievements spring primarily from a desire to solve difficult problems, to do justice to the confidence placed in them, and to prove pet projects, and it is the less effective managers who appear to be more concerned with eventual rewards such as promotion and salary increases (Kanter, 1983).

There is a substantial literature on the nature of different pay systems and the circumstances appropriate to their use (e.g. OECD, 1970; Department of Employment, 1971; Conboy, 1976; White, 1981b; Lupton and Bowey, 1983; Grayson, 1984; International Labour Organization, 1984; Cannell and Wood, 1992). It is a reflection of the perennial nature of the problem that some of the best books on the subject are the oldest (Schloss, 1892; Cole, 1919). There is, in any case, no such thing as the perfect payment system for a given situation: the choice between different options is usually reduced to selecting from the least problematic. Furthermore, no payment system continues to operate satisfactorily for ever. They tend to lose their edge and to develop anomalies with the passage of time. With growing familiarity, employees come to treat as an entitlement that which they once perceived as a reward. Time and changed circumstances tend to blur the rationale for once plausible grading structures. Minor loopholes become normal pathways. Consequently, most organizations periodically undertake a major overhaul of their payment systems, often switching into, and then out of, a payment by results scheme of some sort, perhaps every decade or so. Payment systems cannot, in short, be treated as mechanical constructs to meet fixed technical needs. They must be designed to meet the highly dynamic social task of eliciting labour productivity.

The majority of employees are paid according to a fixed rate per hour, shift, week, month, or year. There is an increasing tendency for simple wage rate systems, whereby a single rate is attached to all (typically manual) jobs of the same description, to give way to salary systems. In these (quite apart from other differences in terms of employment) there is a range of possible pay for each job grade, with different rules applying for an individual's movement within the grade range from those applying for promotion between grade ranges. Within the grade range the improvement in an employee's position is likely to depend on either a mechanical rule (such as an age increment) or the discretion of an immediate manager. Between grade ranges there is likely to be a more demanding and externally accountable promotion procedure.

Under time rate systems, the level of effort and quality of work is generally maintained by supervision, custom, or other social pressure. There has, in recent years, been a tendency in some industries to use work measurement as a basis for calculating and, sometimes, negotiating the workload and pace of work. Often no more than a planning device, this can be made a central feature of the payment system, as it was under the name of 'measured daywork' in the 1970s (Office of Manpower Economics, 1973). Work measurement of some sort may be applied to the workloads of time rated employees in locations as varied as architects' offices, haulage firms, banks, forestry sites and town halls.

The supreme virtue of time rate payment systems should be their simplicity. It is, however, a simplicity that is often denied in practice by the use of additional payments. The most pervasive addition is overtime, the payment at an enhanced rate for hours beyond the 'standard' week. Its persistence is extraordinary. The approximately one-third of manual male workers in manufacturing who work some overtime have averaged eight to nine hours a week for the last two decades, and they have done so despite the waves of job losses of the early 1980s and 1990s. In some industries it may be paid without being worked – this was normal until recently in commercial television. More widespread is the sort of regular overtime that is covertly protected by junior management as a source of discretionary payment.

One form of additional payment which declined in the face of collective bargaining pressure after the Second World War but made a rapid return in the 1980s is the individual merit rate. These provide the opportunity for individual employees to earn additional pay in the form of either a lasting increment or a one-off cash bonus, in recognition of management approval. Merit pay is usually linked to some form of appraisal procedure and may be tied into a well-defined salary structure.

Other additions to time rates may be linked to an ostensibly more objective principle, such as length of service or age, as in many salary systems, especially in the public services. Another form of addition may be designed to compensate for particular features of the job such as dirty working conditions or working away from home. The integrity of a time rate system can, however, quickly become threatened if these additional payments depend on the discretion of a junior manager. Bargaining pressure and supervisory prejudice can corrode the criteria for the application of an additional payment –

and, equally important, the criteria for its removal when, for example, the cleanliness of working conditions improves.

Grade drift is a term commonly applied to the tendency for individual jobs to bunch up, with the passage of time, into the higher levels of the grading structure. This typically occurs because individual managers, when dealing with a job grading decision that is marginal between two grades, generally give the benefit of the doubt to the employee concerned, and such actions become benchmarks for future decisions. It is thus common, in a grading structure that has not been overhauled for some years, to find the lowest grades quite empty and, within salary bands, to find most employees bunched up to the band maxima.

The proliferation of job grades is another feature of the management of time rate systems. The introduction of a new job grade with a slightly higher pay rate may often be used as an inducement to win employee acceptance of a slight alteration to an existing job, such as might arise from a new piece of equipment, or a reallocation of responsibilities, or extra training. In the mid-1980s many engineering firms were augmenting their once sacrosanct craft rate with 'supercraft' grades. In time the multiplicity of job grades becomes a major irritant. Distinctions which were once introduced to facilitate change can themselves become serious sources of job demarcation when the technology moves on. Since, however, the novelty of a job alteration fades quite quickly, it usually takes a fairly straightforward (if expensive) negotiation to shake the jobs back into a simpler grade structure. Many firms go through this 'pay restructuring' process every few years; others cope better through the active use of job evaluation maintenance procedures.

It would be wrong to conclude that evidence of this sort of manipulation of time rate systems was a sign of management failure. No bureaucratic system operates efficiently under changing circumstances unless its rules are open to judicious bending. For payment systems this is of particular importance because so much productivity change necessitates incremental job change. The fact that a time rate system makes no formal allowance for productivity-related pay does not remove the fact that employees are often disturbed by technological innovation and require some compensation to accommodate to it. Typically, however, the shock of a work innovation is a passing experience. The disruption that it brings to an employee's sense of competence, work habits, and work friendships usually heals quite quickly and, while the job may have altered, it is often

not, in the long run, 'harder' in any tangible sense. By tacitly allowing some grade drift, or the creation of a new grade, in the knowledge that these aberrations will be 'restructured' away in a few years,
the employer gives in effect a phased one-off payment, to compensate for a fading one-off shock to the employees, in return for lasting
benefits in terms of improved productivity. It is vastly preferable to
the sort of haggling over 'fair' cash shares from productivity improvements that caused so much difficulty in the late 1960s when
official incomes policies had the effect of encouraging dubious and
often divisive 'productivity deals'.

A time rate system, when sensitively administered, can thus provide a pay structure which is a sound basis for managing employees'
productivity. For this purpose the absolute cash difference between
grade rates is usually of less importance than the fact of the difference between them. Employees appear to aspire for promotion less
as a result of an economic calculation of the expected extra income,
duly discounted, that might result, and more in response to the
status rewards, among which the importance of the pay increase is
importantly symbolic. The manager who gives detailed attention to
perceptions of fairness within the organization by tending the internal pay structure, while at the same time keeping broadly in step with
prevailing pay trends outside, need have few anxieties about the
employees' incentive for promotion.

Payment by Results

In payment by results systems a proportion of the employee's pay,
typically between 10 and 20 per cent, is variable, linked to some
measure of the physical output of the individual or of a wider group.
It is to be distinguished from performance pay, discussed in the next
chapter, which depends on some formal appraisal or assessment of
individual behaviour. The intention is that payment by results linked
to physical output should act as an incentive to work harder, or with
less supervision. Such systems have been used since employment
began. There are many guides to them and there has been much
research into their effects (e.g. Shimmin, 1959; National Board for
Prices and Incomes, 1968a; Marriott, 1971; Lloyd, 1976; Incomes
Data Services, 1980; International Labour Organization, 1984).
Payment by results systems come in numerous varieties, with pay
linked to physical output in linear and non-linear, progressive and

regressive, lagged, cushioned, periodically contracted, and sometimes curious other ways. At best they offer a means of maintaining effort that is cheap to manage and popular with employees; at worst they provide the surest method imaginable of disrupting industrial relations.

The intention of payment by results is to raise and reward effort. But effort, as has been said above, cannot be measured. Consequently it is necessary to have a technique to link what is deemed to be an acceptable pace of work to the level of output. It is also necessary to be able to do this for all the very different sorts of jobs that might be performed in the same workplace, and to do so with sufficient consistency, so that workers end up earning approximately the same bonus despite their different tasks. If this is not achieved they will consider the payment system unfair. The set of techniques used to establish this are variously called time and motion study, work study, and industrial engineering (Department of Employment, 1971; Whitmore, 1976). For convenience we shall use the term 'work study'.

At the heart of these techniques is the skill of 'effort rating' through which the work study engineer, considering the task as a series of short elements, repeatedly observes its performance by a trained worker. He or she times each element and simultaneously makes a judgement about the pace at which it is being performed. The latter being expressed as a percentage of 'standard' effort. After rating a large number of cycles of the task, the work study engineer is then able to calculate a modal estimate of the time that would be taken by any adequately trained and practised worker putting in the sort of effort that is acceptable in that workplace (Brown, W., 1973). This provides a systematic method of gauging and thus of standardizing effort norms on different tasks. It makes it possible to predict how long jobs will take in future. Although norms do differ between different workplaces, as do the effort rating standards of work study engineers from different backgrounds, this does not matter as long as they are consistent within their own workplace and from one month to another (Lupton, 1961).

There are two ultimate justifications for this rather odd procedure. The first is that, in the right circumstances, it can provide consistent and predictively accurate results within a given workplace and thus serve as the basis for a satisfactory incentive scheme. The second justification is simply that there is usually no other practical way of predicting levels of output, and it is often necessary to do this for production engineering and cost-control purposes as well as for payment.

Of the many impediments that prevent payment by results systems from performing as intended, two deserve special mention. The first is that workers often subordinate the maximizing of individual earnings to the social objective of minimizing conflict among themselves. As a result they may place informal restrictions on effort which reduce or even nullify the incentive (Whyte, 1955). The second major impediment is that oversights (most commonly the neglect of tangential technical innovation) may cause some job times to be 'slacker' than others, with the result that bonus earnings are seen to differ between individuals in ways that bear no relation to individual effort. These anomalies are likely to give rise to discontent and a loss of confidence in the fairness of the whole payment system. Unless contained, this will result in the swamping of work study techniques by constant fragmented bargaining whenever jobs alter or groups feel their earnings are falling behind. Then it is not only the incentive effect that is corrupted but the control of production more generally. The covert efforts of employees and their supervisors to moderate pay anomalies may result in their distorting the rules governing, for example, the speed of machines, labour mobility, management information systems, and quality standards (Brown, W., 1973).

This is not the place to discuss the design of payment by results systems. Considerable thought has been given to the technical and industrial relations factors that enter into such decisions (Lupton and Gowler, 1969; Lupton and Bowey, 1983). Key variables in a scheme are the gearing of the reward to incremental changes in output; the manner by which 'output' is measured; the length of time allowed to elapse before output levels are reflected in payment; and the size of the group to be covered by a common incentive payment. Such choices are to some extent shaped by fashion, and during the 1970s this increasingly favoured schemes encompassing larger groups of workers and with less frequent and smaller earnings fluctuations than would previously have been normal. Since then three loosely related trends have become evident. The payment by results schemes discussed so far relate pay more or less simply to workers' physical output. Increasingly during the 1980s, it became popular, first, to relate the bonus to some indicator that takes into account the market circumstances of the employer, second, to experiment with a wider range of measures of employee performance than physical output and, third, to use performance-related pay more at the level of the individual employee.

The second and third of these developments are discussed in the next chapter. The first development focuses on the market circumstances of the employer, rather than the performance of the employee, however assigned and measured. It has often been felt that, by linking pay to a measure that fluctuates with external prices or with company performance, the employee is brought into closer contact with the risks and realities of the commercial world in which the company has to survive. The more a payment system focuses the employee's attention on the immediate task, it is argued, the greater the danger that the pursuit of individual self-interest might undermine the efficiently co-ordinated management of the enterprise as a whole. On the other hand, incentives related to the performance of the enterprise as a whole may be too remote from anything over which the individual employee feels any degree of control. But an incentive system that attempts to relate both to the immediate circumstances of the employee and also to the global circumstances of the firm runs the risk of confounding both objectives through complexity.

Schemes relating the incentive to some measure of the value (as opposed to physical quantity) of production have generally been more popular in the United States than in Britain. The Scanlon plan uses the relationship between the wage bill and the total value of sales as its indicator. The Rucker plan takes input costs into account by focusing on the relationship between the wage bill of the enterprise and total added value (for further details, see National Board for Prices and Incomes, 1968a: 44–7). In Britain there has been more interest in using employee share ownership and profit-related pay as incentives related to commercial performance. The newly found ability of companies to link bargaining units to their internal 'profit centres' has increased this interest. Governments have encouraged it further in a number of Finance Acts.

The first legislative stimulus, in 1978, was for approved profit-sharing (APS) schemes which give employees a distribution of shares. Under this, the Inland Revenue require the company to establish a trust fund and periodically pay money into it. The trustees use this to buy shares in the company which are allocated to individual employees (subject to an upper limit of 10 per cent of earnings) but held by the trustees on the employees' behalf. The shares are held in trust for at least two years before they can be sold, but employees must wait a further three years before they can sell their shares without tax liability. Such a scheme is 'non-discretionary' in the sense that it must be open to all full-time employees who have been with the company for at least five years. By 1993 there were over a thousand registered schemes in existence, covering 800,000 employees.

The second major encouragement was the 1980 Save-As-You-Earn (SAYE) share option scheme. Under this non-discretionary scheme the employee can enter a five-year savings contract with an option to purchase shares in the company at the end of the contract. The eventual lump sum can be used to acquire shares at a 20 per cent discount to the current market price prevailing at the outset of the scheme, with no income tax payable on the options exercised at the end of the five-year saving period. Over a thousand registered schemes in 1993 covered 470,000 employees.

In 1984 a Discretionary Share Option Scheme was introduced which provided tax incentives to companies to grant options to selected employees. Options can be granted to full-time employees over shares worth up to four times the individual's annual earnings, or £100,000, whichever is the greater. If the options are exercised more than three years but no more than ten years after they are granted, the proceeds will be tax free. This proved highly popular for a privileged few: the Institute of Management calculated that by 1993 as many as 35 per cent of senior managers and directors were covered.

In 1987 the Chancellor introduced a radical scheme for tax relief on profit-related pay, if it could be demonstrated that pay was linked to an audited measure of profits. The tax relief was doubled in 1991, providing the scheme with the potential to provide a tax free bonus equivalent to a 7 per cent pay rise. Between 1990 and 1993 the number of profit-related pay schemes registered with the Inland Revenue tripled to cover 1.3 million employees.

Whether or not registered with the Inland Revenue, in 1990 in the private sector 9 per cent of establishments had employee share-ownership derived from deferred profits, 24 per cent had SAYE schemes, 17 per cent had discretionary share option schemes, and 7 per cent had some other form of share-ownership scheme. In all, one in three private sector establishments had some sort of scheme (Millward et al., 1992: 263). A substantial number of profit-related schemes are not registered with the Inland Revenue because of difficulties in meeting its strict accounting requirements. By 1990 direct profit-related arrangements had become the most widespread type of financial arrangement and were reported in 40 per cent of establishments in the private sector, especially in larger, successful, service-providing establishments. Taking share-ownership and profit-sharing arrangements together, some sort of financial participation scheme was in use in 55 per cent of private sector establishments in 1990 (Millward et al., 1992: 262).

There was a marked rise in interest in employee share-ownership schemes in the mid-1980s, with macro-economists such as Weitzman (1984) and Meade (1982) arguing their theoretical advantages for economic stability and fuller employment, with an increasing number of employee 'buy-outs', and with the government's stimulus of wider share ownership through its privatization programme. The John Lewis Partnership remains a long-standing success in linking employee share ownership to measures for industrial democracy (Bradley and Taylor, 1991). A more conventional but impressive achievement has been the high level of employee share ownership achieved with the privatization of the National Freight Consortium, with two-thirds of the 30,000 employees owning two-thirds of the shares in 1990 (Bradley and Nejad, 1990). But the NFC has not been alone in playing down the centrality of employee share ownership in the 1990s. Experience tends to temper initial enthusiasm (Bradley and Gelb, 1986). Substantial employee shareholdings may constrain corporate decision making and may create serious difficulties in raising external capital.

The Fringes of Pay

Although, as was observed at the outset, pay is the most conspicuous aspect of the package of rewards from employment, other benefits are important. These 'fringe' benefits are hard to define precisely. They encompass both generally available benefits such as subsidized canteens and creches as well as more private benefits such as company cars and family health insurance.

Non-pay benefits are growing in importance. In British manufacturing industry, for example, pensions, sick pay, time off with pay, social security payments, benefits in kind and subsidized services rose rapidly in significance from adding 14 per cent of average pre-tax remuneration in 1960 to as much as 40 per cent in 1988 (Ray, 1987; 1990). Such benefits are very unevenly distributed across the population, with employees on high income getting substantially larger benefits than the low paid, both absolutely and as a proportion of income (Green et al., 1985).

Within organizations there is a systematic tendency for non-pay benefits to increase with job status. It is true that the 'harmonization' of manual and non-manual conditions is generally diminishing the once massive discrimination in non-pay benefits between them, but this mainly affects full-time adult men in reasonably secure jobs. Women, part-timers, and those in jobs of short tenure have much more limited non-pay benefits. It should not go without mention that almost all indicators of occupational health also show that health tends to improve with job status.

It has sometimes been argued that the disproportionate increase in non-pay benefits that comes with ascending hierarchical level reflects a conscious policy of attempting to conceal the full extent of inequality within an organization from its own members (Allen, 1969). But, against this, it is arguable that one managerial advantage of many non-pay benefits is precisely that they *do* reflect standing in the company: although they are less conspicuous when viewed from outside organizations, they may be very visible within them. By clearly signalling status within the social system of the organization, such finely differentiable 'perks' as company cars, catering, furniture, working hours, and orders of St Michael and St George, emphasize the managerial authority structure. In this respect, a relatively cheap allocation of symbolic differentiators can be seen to be not only a means of rewarding employees but also one of reinforcing management. In addition, the comparative lack of visibility of non-pay benefits outside the firm increases the difficulty of job search by their beneficiaries and ensures that the higher one is in an organization, the harder it is to break away from it.

In Britain the state has traditionally provided many benefits which in some other European Community countries would be part of the responsibility of the employer – family allowance and health insurance, for example. There is currently a tendency for the state to withdraw from such commitments, however, and to legislate in such a way as to transfer the obligation to employers. Elements of this are to be found in recent policy developments on, for example, health and safety at work, maternity leave, pensions, and training. The ageing of the population and electoral antipathy to taxation will ensure that this shift of obligations continues. Non-pay benefits will continue to grow in significance within the remuneration package.

Conclusion

A continuing theme of this chapter has been that labour is not something that can be hired in predictable quantities and fuelled on cash incentives. The remarkable quality of employees, which successful personnel management seeks to utilize, is their potential. Suitably motivated, employees have the capacity to acquire new skills, accept changed responsibilities, and adjust to more potent technologies. On the other hand, when discouraged or poorly-supervised, employees can often spend a great deal of time achieving very little.

The successful management of pay in an organization requires an internal structure of rewards that is consistent and acceptable to those covered. If this is achieved, the level of those rewards needs only to be kept roughly comparable with that provided by other employers. At the heart of the issue is the task of managing productivity. Pay is only a part of the motivational package. Two major requirements of pay systems are that they complement both a coherent managerial structure and a programme of competence acquisition. The sources of productivity growth increasingly lie less in getting employees to work harder, than in getting them to adapt to more productive ways of working. The potency of pay lies in its capacity, if mismanaged, to prevent this.

Bibliography

Allen, D. 1969. *Fringe Benefits: Wages or Social Obligation?* Ithaca, NY: Cornell University.

Baldamus, W. 1957. 'The Relationship between Wage and Effort'. *Journal of Industrial Economics*, 5, July, 192–201.

Behrend, H. 1973. *Incomes Policy, Equity and Pay Increase Differentials*. Edinburgh: Scottish Academic Press.

Behrend, H. 1984. *Problems of Labour and Inflation*. London: Croom Helm.

Belcher, D. W. 1974. *Compensation Administration*. Englewood Cliffs, NJ: Prentice Hall.

Bowey, A. M. (ed.) 1982. *Handbook of Salary and Wage Systems*, 2nd edn. Aldershot: Gower.

Bowey, A. M., Thorpe, R., Mitchell, F. H. M., Nicholls, G., Gosnold, D., Savery, L. and Hellier, P. K. 1982. *Effects of Incentive Payment Systems: United Kingdom 1977–80*, Research Paper No. 36. London: Department of Employment.

Bradley, K. and Gelb, A. 1986. *Share Ownership for Employees*. London: Public Policy Centre.

Bradley, K. and Nejad, A. 1990. *Managing Owners: The NFC in Perspective*. London: Cambridge University Press.

Bradley, K. and Taylor, S. 1991. *Business Performance in the Retail Sector*. Oxford: Oxford University Press.

Brown, C. V. 1983. *Taxation and the Incentive to Work*. Oxford: Oxford University Press.

Brown, W. 1973. *Piecework Bargaining*. London: Heinemann.

Brown, W. and Sisson, K. 1975. 'The Use of Comparisons in Workplace Wage Determination'. *British Journal of Industrial Relations*, 13, March, 25–53.

Brown, W., Hayles, J., Hughes, B. and Rowe, L. 1980. 'Occupational Pay Structures under Different Wage Fixing Arrangements'. *British Journal of Industrial Relations*, 18, July, 217–30.

Brown, W. and Walsh, J. 1991. 'Pay Determination in Britain in the 1990s: the Anatomy of Decentralisation'. *Oxford Review of Economic Policy*, 7, 1.

Cannell, M. and Wood, S. 1992. *Performance-Related Pay*. London: Institute of Personnel Management.

Cole, G. D. H. 1919. *The Payment of Wages*. London: Fabian Research Department.

Conboy, W. 1976. *Pay at Work*. London: Arrow Books.

Delafield, G. L. 1979. 'Social Comparisons and Pay'. In Stephenson, G. and Brotherton, C. J. (eds) *Industrial Relations: A Social Psychological Approach*. Chichester: Wiley, 131–51.

Department of Employment. 1971. *Training for Work Study Practice*. London: HMSO.

Edwards, P. and Whitston, C. 1991. 'Workers are Working Harder'. *British Journal of Industrial Relations*, 29, 4.

Grant, J. V. and Smith, G. 1984. *Personnel Administration and Industrial Relations*. London: Longman.

Grayson, D. 1984. *Progressive Payment Systems*. Occasional Paper 28. London: Work Research Unit.

Green, F., Hadjimatheou, G. and Smail, R. 1985. 'Fringe Benefit Distribution in Britain'. *British Journal of Industrial Relations*, 23, July, 261–80.

Guest, D. 1991. 'Have British Workers been Working Harder in Thatcher's Britain?'. *British Journal of Industrial Relations*, 28, 293–312.

Harris, A. 1966. *Labour Mobility in Great Britain*. London: HMSO.

Hegewisch, A. 1991. 'The Decentralisation of Pay Bargaining: European Comparisons'. *Personnel Review*, 20, 6.

Hyman, R. and Brough, I. 1975. *Social Values and Industrial Relations*. Oxford: Blackwell.

Incomes Data Services. 1980. *Guide to Incentive Payment Schemes*. London: IDS.

International Labour Organization. 1984. *Payment by Results*. Geneva:

ILO.

Kanter, R. M. 1984. *The Change Masters*. London: Allen & Unwin.

Kerr, C. 1977. *Labor Markets and Wage Determination*. Berkeley, CA: University of California Press.

Lloyd, P. A. 1976. *Incentive Payment Schemes*. London: British Institute of Management.

Lupton, T. 1961. *Money for Effort*. London: HMSO.

Lupton, T. and Bowey, A. 1983. *Wages and Salaries*. Aldershot: Gower.

Lupton, T. and Gowler, D. 1969. *Selecting a Wage Payment System*. London: Kogan Page.

MacKay, D. I., Brack, J., Boddy, D., Diack, J. A. and Jones, N. 1971. *Labour Markets under Different Employment Conditions*. London: Allen & Unwin.

Main, B. G. M. 1981. 'The Length of Employment and Unemployment in Greater Britain'. *Scottish Journal of Political Economy*, 28, June, 146–64.

Marginson, P., Edwards, P., Martin, R., Purcell, J. and Sisson, K. 1988. *Beyond the Workplace: Managing Industrial Relations in the Multi-Establishment Enterprise*. Oxford: Blackwell.

Marginson, P. 1992. 'European Integration and Transnational Management–Union Relations in the Enterprise'. *British Journal of Industrial Relations*, 30, 528–545.

Marriott, R. 1971. *Incentive Payment Systems*. London: Staples.

Marshall, A. 1920. *Principles of Economics*. London: Macmillan.

Meade, J. E. 1982. *Wage-Fixing*. Vol. 1 of *Stagflation*. London: Allen & Unwin.

Millward, N., Stevens, M., Smart, D. and Hawes, W. R. 1992. *Workplace Industrial Relations in Transition*. Aldershot: Dartmouth.

National Board for Prices and Incomes (NBPI). 1967. *Productivity Agreements (1)*. Report 36, Cmnd. 3311. London: HMSO.

National Board for Prices and Incomes. 1968a. *Payment by Results Systems*. Report 65, Cmnd. 3627. London: HMSO.

National Board for Prices and Incomes. 1968b. *Job Evaluation*. Report 83, Cmnd. 3772. London: HMSO.

Nichols, T. 1991. 'Labour Intensification, Work Injuries and the Measurement of Percentage Utilisation of Labour'. *British Journal of Industrial Relations*, 29, 4.

Nolan, P. and Brown, W. 1983. 'Competition and Workplace Wage Determination'. *Oxford Bulletin of Economics and Statistics*, 45, 3.

Nyland, C. J. 1985. 'Worktime and the Rationalization of the Capitalist Production Process'. PhD thesis, University of Adelaide.

OECD. 1970. *Forms of Wage and Salary – Payment for High Productivity*. Paris: Organization for Economic Co-operation and Development.

Office of Manpower Economics. 1973. *Measured Daywork*. London: HMSO.

Phelps Brown, E. H. 1977. *The Inequality of Pay*. Oxford: Oxford University Press.

Porter, L. W., Lawler, E. E. and Hackman, J. R. 1975. *Behaviour in Organisations*. Tokyo: McGraw-Hill Kogakusha.

Ray, G. F. 1987. 'Labour Costs in Manufacturing'. *National Institute Economic Review*, 120.

Ray, G. F. 1990. 'International Labour Costs in Manufacturing 1960–88'. *National Institute Economic Review*, 132.

Ross, A. M. 1948. *Trade Union Wage Policy*. Berkeley, CA: University of California Press.

Routh, G. 1980. *Occupation and Pay in Great Britain 1906–1979*. Cambridge: Cambridge University Press.

Rubery, J., Tarling, R. and Wilkinson, F. 1986. 'Flexibility, Marketing and the Organisation of Production'. University of Cambridge, Department Applied Economics (mimeo).

Ryan, P. 1991. 'The European Labour Market: Meaning and Prospects'. In Hantrais, L., O'Brien, M. and Mangen, S. (eds) *Education, Training and Labour Markets in Europe*. Birmingham: Aston University, Cross-National Research Group.

Schloss, D. F. 1892. *Methods of Industrial Remuneration*. London: Williams & Norgate.

Shimmin, S. 1959. *Payment by Results*. London: Staples.

Walsh, J. 1993. 'Internalisation v Decentralisation: an Analysis of Recent Developments in Pay Bargaining'. *British Journal of Industrial Relations*, 31, 409–432.

Walsh, J. and Brown, W. A. 1991. 'Regional Earnings and Pay Flexibility'. In Bowen, A. and Mayhew, K. (eds) *Reducing Regional Inequalities*. London: Kogan Page.

Weitzman, M. L. 1984. *The Share Economy: Conquering Stagflation*. Cambridge, MA: Harvard University Press.

White, M. 1981a. *The Hidden Meaning of Pay Conflict*. London: Macmillan.

White, M. 1981b. *Payment Systems in Britain*. London: Policy Studies Institute and Gower.

Whitmore, D. A. 1976. *Work Study and Related Management Services*. London: Heinemann.

Whyte, W. F. 1955. *Money and Motivation*. New York: Harper & Row.

Willman, P. 1982. *Fairness, Collective Bargaining and Incomes Policy*. Oxford: Clarendon Press.

Wootton, B. 1955. *The Social Foundation of Wage Policy*. London: Allen & Unwin.

14

Performance Pay

Ian Kessler

Forging a direct link between performance and pay has been a major preoccupation of personnel practitioners, policy-makers and commentators since the emergence of industrial organizations. It is a link, however, which has proved to be highly problematic and unstable. In contrast to time worked, which has remained a relatively uncontentious basis for reward, spawning few variations in practice and raising issues related more to the other techniques required to ensure employee compliance, pay for performance is a concept laiden with interpretative complexities and giving rise to a range of different structures and systems.

Despite the long-standing difficulties of establishing an effective link between pay and performance, and a catalogue of attempts which have often generated organizational disorder, a review of personnel management literature over the last decade suggests that performance pay is again attracting considerable managerial interest. It has been suggested, for example, that performance pay 'is one of the most dynamic issues in human resource management and arguably the most topical component of reward policy today' (Brady and Wright, 1990: 1).

What accounts for this resurgence of interest in performance pay? Has the focus of the interest changed in any way? Is renewed interest reflected in changed practices and if so to what extent have these changes fulfilled managerial expectations?

This chapter addresses these questions by reviewing recent developments in performance pay. The first section reviews trends in performance pay, the second assesses managerial objectives which have informed the use of performance pay and the third considers how performance pay has operated in practice. It will be argued that a new prescriptive rhetoric on the use and character of performance pay finds some support in changing managerial practices. The match between rhetoric and practice will be related in large part to changing economic, political and social circumstances which have encouraged the use of performance pay as a means of pursuing a wider range of managerial objectives than those traditionally associated with pay systems. While doubt will be cast upon the effectiveness of performance pay in motivating employees, the value of such a pay system in facilitating organizational change will be presented as a much more open question.

Trends in Performance Pay

Definitions and types

Performance pay can broadly be defined as the explicit link of financial reward to individual, group or company performance (Armstrong and Murliss, 1991: 211; Wright, 1991: 84). Such a definition covers a wide variety of performance-pay systems. Drawing on the various attempts which have been made to categorize these systems (Lawler, 1973: 129; National Research Council, 1991: 78), they can generally be seen as the institutional response to three basic questions: whose performance is being assessed?; how is it being measured?; and how is it being rewarded?

These questions imply a multidimensional model of performance-pay systems. The first question highlights variation in the coverage of performance-pay schemes. Thus, schemes can relate to the individual employee or to the group, however defined. The second focuses on performance measures. These can take the form of employee/group inputs or outputs and be expressed in 'hard' quantifiable terms or in 'softer' qualititative forms. The third concentrates on the performance–pay link. This directs attention to the distinction between a relatively fixed relationship, where a given level of output usually produces an automatic payout, and a less mechanistic link often founded on some assessment of individual performance. It also highlights the fact that the payment may be consolidated into base pay or remain an unconsolidated lump sum.

Drawing on these dimensions, three types of performance-pay system are typically distinguished (Casey et al., 1991; National Research Council, 1991). First, there are individual merit and performance-related systems based on some form of appraisal or assessment of the individual using various input (traits, skills, competences) or output (objectives) indicators. They often involve a payment which is integrated into the basic salary. The second type involves bonuses which provide unconsolidated payments to the individual employee. These are founded on a relatively mechanistic relationship between pay and the individual in terms of units of production, targets or sales. They include the differing forms of piecework as well as other traditional systems such as sales commissions. The third type is bonuses which are mechanistically geared to the performance of the group – the group being defined as the work group, section, department or establishment. These bonuses are often provided as unconsolidated payments and are paid on a collective basis to those within the measured unit. These collective bonuses include gain-sharing schemes which relate pay to changes in the sales value or the added value of a designated group within the organization.

Alternative sources provide further details on the systems which fall under these headings (e.g. Marriott, 1961; Smith, 1989; Armstrong and Murliss, 1991) and the mechanics of the more popular schemes will be returned to below. Nonetheless, for the moment, these categories provide the basis for an assessment of how the interest of policy-makers and practitioners has shifted over the years.

The shifting focus

For much of the post-Second World War period, the concern with performance pay was focused primarily on manual worker individual bonus systems, especially in the private manufacturing sector. This focus sprang from the importance attached to instability in industrial relations as a cause of the difficulties emerging in the British economy from the mid- to late 1960s. This instablity was traced in large part to traditional piecework systems that covered almost six million employees at that time. These systems were seen to have decayed in the face of workplace pressures, undermining ordered national bargaining, generating conflict, earnings drift and rigidities in working practices (National Board for Prices and Incomes, 1968).

Subsequent developments in performance pay were directed towards addressing the perceived weaknesses in piecework systems. The productivity agreements of the 1970s were based on a clearer reciprocal relationship between pay and broader organizational change while measured daywork schemes sought to establish a much more controlled, stable and fixed relationship between pay and output. Both approaches, however, met with limited success. The incomes policies of the period stimulated the use of productivity agreements as a means of bolstering earnings without necessarily creating a genuine link to revised working practices. Some of the management difficulties which had bedevilled piecework schemes, in particular, those related to the planning production and ensuring workflow, inhibited the operation of measured daywork, and such systems also ran the risk of simply replacing wage drift with effort drift. Indeed in the face of these difficulties some organizations moved away from incentives for manual workers altogether (Smith, 1989: 46–9; Tolliday, 1991: 95).

In the 1980s, there was a general revival of interest in pay systems which relate pay to performance, although this interest has had a different emphasis to that in the 1960s and 1970s. First, attention has generally concentrated far more on individual performance and merit related schemes and less on individual bonus schemes. Second, the focus has been primarily on non-manual rather than manual employees. As Smith (1989: 61) succinctly puts it: 'The only group not experiencing the changes brought about by the reward culture are shopfloor employees.' Third, the interest has concentrated particularly on schemes which relate pay to performance as measured by the achievement of specific individual objectives. These schemes can be distingushed from merit-based schemes which assess performance in terms of behavioural traits (Fowler, 1988). Fourth, and setting aside this distinction, both individual performance *and* merit-based schemes have been seen as appropriate to an increasing range of white-collar employees, throughout the managerial hierarchy and across the public and private sectors of the economy.

The prescriptive literature is by no means united on the viablity and value of these individual appraisal-based payment schemes. It is noteworthy, for example, that some of the higher profile 'management gurus' have been critical. Deming (1982: 102) refers to merit pay as a 'deadly disease' and includes, as one of his 14 points, the 'elimination' of such schemes; Kanter (1989: 233–5) is critical of the assumption that individuals alone are responsible for their performance and suggests that the establishment of a 'fair' link between pay and performance is difficult for many professional groups; while Peters (1988: 215) places greater store on group-based schemes as opposed to individual incentives as a means of improving organizational performance.

In the face of these reservations, however, alternative opinion leaders and policy-makers have provided a powerful supportive rhetoric for individual performance pay. The CBI (1988), for instance, has called for pay systems which 'focus on the performance and needs of individuals'. Equally significant, Conservative governments of the 1980s and 1990s have encouraged this type of performance system both generally and especially in relation to public sector workers. As the *Citizen's Charter* (1991: 35) states: 'Pay systems in the public sector need to make a regular and direct link between a person's contribution to the standards of the service provided and his or her reward.' It is a view echoed by policy-makers in specific parts of the public sector. The NHS Management Executive's booklet on hospital trusts (1990: 21) opens its chapter on human resource management by noting that:

> The ability of trusts to deliver improved health care will rest to a large extent on their ability to motivate staff to higher performance. This, in its turn, will depend on staff recognising . . . that achieving higher performance levels is directly linked to higher rewards.

While the focus of interest on performance pay among practitioners and policy-makers appears, therefore, to have shifted, it is important to assess the extent to which this interest and rhetoric has been reflected in changing practice.

The evidence

The renewed attention given to performance pay implies a number of developments: first, a growth of individual performance and merit-based schemes; second, the concentration of these schemes among non-manual rather than manual employees; third, the dispersal of these systems throughout managerial and white-collar hierarchies and across a range of sectors; and, fourth, a declining interest in individual bonuses and manual worker pay systems in general. These developments are reviewed by a reference to the main types of performance-pay systems distinguished above.

Individual merit and performance schemes   The evidence presents a generally consistent picture suggesting that this type of pay system covers a significant and increasing proportion of employees. Although Long (1986: 15) found that the 40 per cent of organizations in her survey which linked pay to appraisal in the mid-1980s represented only a very slight increase from a decade earlier, recent work indicates a more pronounced move in this direction. An ACAS (1988: 25) survey of private sector establishments concluded, for example, that there had been a 'substantial growth' in this type of system. One-third of establishments covered had merit schemes, with one-quarter of these being introduced in the last three years.

Other surveys suggest the coverage may be even broader. Research carried out for the Institute of Personnel Management (IPM) and National Economic Development Office (NEDO) (Cannell and Long, 1991; Cannell and Wood, 1992) found that over two-thirds of the private sector companies in the sample had schemes for some of their non-manual workers. Almost one-third of the companies with schemes had introduced them over the last ten years and a further 19 per cent in the last five years. A Policy Studies Institute (PSI) survey, more narrowly focused on pay in two distinctive regional labour markets, came to a similar conclusion, indicating that four out of five organizations had appraisal-based systems. It also noted that in over a third of establishments 'increased use' was being made of the assessment–pay link and concluded that an 'individualization of pay had indeed occurred' (Casey et al., 1991: 457). Furthermore, there is support for the contention that the coverage of these schemes has extended down the managerial hierarchy and across the range of non-manual occupation groups. A review of 125 companies concluded that 'only in recent years have we witnessed concerted attempts to change payment systems down the line to become more merit orientated' (Incomes Data Services, 1985: 9).

It is a contention reinforced by the IPM/NEDO survey which indicated that in almost half of their sample companies, performance pay covered all non-manual staff and by the PSI survey which found that in around two-thirds of their sample organizations merit pay operated for 'lower' professional and 'clerical/secretarial' staff. The 1990 Workplace Industrial Relations Survey found that while 40 per cent of establishments had merit pay for middle/senior managers, around one-third had it for clerical/administrative staff and almost one-quarter for skilled manuals (Millward et al., 1992).

Focusing more specifically on the public sector, the same trends are apparent although perhaps less sharply so. The IPM/NEDO survey found slightly fewer schemes in this sector and a narrower occupational coverage. Schemes were noted in 37 per cent of public sector organizations, with non-management grades less likely to be included than in the private sector. Certainly, for around 500,000 non-industrial civil servants (where the government has direct influence over pay determination), assessed performance is now integral to salary progression for most grades (Kessler, 1990). Moreover, at least one executive agency, Her Majesty's Stationery Office, has developed a pay system which relies even more heavily on performance, with other agencies pledged to follow suit (Kessler, 1992; Davies, 1991). In local government, however, performance pay is still filtering down from management levels. A Local Authorities Conditions of Service Advisory Board (LACSAB) survey (1990a) indicated that almost 40 per cent of authorities were using such a schemes, but only some 30,000 (4 per cent) of the local authority non-manual workforce were covered. Similarly, the recently introduced performance-pay scheme in the NHS, is largely restricted to general and senior managers.

Finally, the evidence lends weight to the contention that new approaches to performance pay have not reached the shop-floor. However, there are examples of organizations which have introduced appraisal schemes for manual workers (Kinnie and Lowe, 1990) and this is particularly apparent where companies have harmonized terms and conditions. In Johnson and Johnson (*Industrial Relations Review and Report*, 1986b) and a BP Chemicals factory in Wales (*Industrial Relations Review and Report*, 1986a), for instance, manuals moved to appraisal-related pay following the introduction of integrated grading structures. Nevertheless, the ACAS survey (1988) found that only one-quarter of organizations used merit pay for manual workers. This figure is put into perspective by developments in other countries and particularly in France where a recent Ministry of Labour survey found that over 50 per cent of employees in around 1300 companies had a merit element in their pay packets (*IDS Focus*, No. 61, December 1991: 11).

The one recent initiative for manual workers which can be classified as an appraisal-based payment scheme is that related to skills acquisition. Although the acquisition of skills is a relatively objective input measure which often triggers an additional payment, these schemes usually require some assessment to ensure that the new competences are applied at the workplace. Skills acquisition schemes appear particularly prevalent on 'greenfield sites' where their introduction is linked to the drive for flexibility in the context of technological change. Recent studies suggest that they have risen in popularity and around 100 companies now operate them (Incomes Data Services, 1992).

Individual and collective bonuses   Trends on bonuses in the light of the themes outlined above are less easy to interpret. *New Earnings Survey* data does suggest a general decline in the coverage of bonus schemes, especially among manuals. While just over 43 per cent of manual workers were covered by such bonuses in 1985, by 1991 the figure had fallen to around 35 per cent. Those surveys which allow for a disaggregation of individual and collective bonuses do, however, suggest a small but continuing core of piecework schemes and even indicate some growth. The ACAS survey (1988), for example, found that while only 12 per cent of its establishments had piecework, a small proportion of these (13 per cent) had introduced this system for the first time. Similarly the PSI survey (Casey et al., 1991) found that one in five of its sample was making 'increased use' of individual bonuses.

The incidence of collective bonuses or more specifically those covering the plant or the enterprise also remains relatively low. ACAS found only 13 per cent of establishments with such schemes, and the PSI suggested very little evidence of their growth. This is perhaps suprising given the recent attention accorded to group-based schemes as a way of overcoming the perceived divisiveness of some individual performance systems (*IDS Focus*, No. 49, December 1988: 8; No. 61, December 1991: 13). It is also somewhat unexpected in the light of the importance attached to group schemes which relate pay to group-based quality indicators as a means of reinforcing a 'quality culture'. The difficulty of identifying such indicators and more especially administering them may account for the apparent absence of quality-based bonus schemes (Incomes Data Services, 1991).

In general, therefore, the evidence appears to provide some support for the rhetoric. There has been a shift towards the greater use of individual performance or merit systems, covering an increasing range of non-manual employees. This in turn leads to a consideration of why such a shift has taken place. Before moving on, however, a number of points qualifying this trend need to be made.

First, time rates remain the single most important basis of payment. The ACAS survey, for instance, indicates that in two-thirds of their sample organizations, time was the basis for pay for at least some of their employees. Moreoover, while all merit increases are spreading, in many organizations they are still underpinned by general across the board increases: in other words merit pay remains the 'icing on the cake' (*IDS Focus*, No. 61, December 1991).

Second, the development of individual performance pay in Britain appears less dramatic when set against developments in the United States. A survey conducted by the American Management Association in 1986 found that practically all firms in their sample relied on annual performance appraisals by supervisors as an input to make pay decisions (Balkin and Gomez-Mejia, 1987: 159). This was confirmed by a major survey of salary practices in large companies which showed that 80 per cent of the companies had merit plans, with over 50 per cent saying that at least 95 per cent their employees received merit increases (Meyer, 1987).

Reasons for Growth

The selection of pay systems

Explanation of the growing popularity of individual performance pay directs attention to the broader question of why organizations select particular types of payment system. Two analytical approaches provide guidance on this issue: the first views selection as part of a relatively ordered and rational managerial process; the second sees selection as a far less ordered process, with pay becoming subject to political pressures within the organization and acquiring symbolic value in supporting distinctive internal interests.

Although the first approach has prescriptive undertones, it also has strong theoretical foundations, attempting to explain the link between the selection of a pay system and its likely effectiveness. It involves an evaluation of the 'fit' between different payment systems and organizational needs and circumstances. It is an approach which has a long pedigree. While crudely conceived, Taylor's techniques, forming the basis for work study and piecework, still rested on a mutual recognition of the company's aim to maximize output and profit and the employee's concern to maximize earnings potential. Even the human relations school's sceptism about piecework schemes in the context of work group dynamics was based on a careful consideration of how organizational goals might be fulfilled more effectively.

In its most sophisticated form, however, this approach is expressed through contingency theory. Recognizing that a variety of objectives might be pursued through pay systems, it is suggested that organizations need to follow a number of steps in selecting a pay system: identify the specific objectives to be pursued; consider the pay systems available to further these objectives; and, having identified the options, base the choice on the organization's internal and external circumstances (Lupton and Gowler, 1969).

The different stages of the contingency approach have been built on in various ways. Standard lists of managerial objectives to be pursued through payment systems are readily available in the textbook literature (Armstrong and Murliss, 1991: 211). The relationship between different types of pay systems and the achievement of various managerial goals has also been highlighted in a number of works (Grinyer and Kessler, 1967; Lawler, 1987). Moreover, considerable importance has been attached to organizational context in explaining payment system selection and effectiveness. Attention has been drawn, in particular, to influential external factors, including labour and product market position and legal regulation, as well as to internal considerations related to technology, workplace size and tasks or occupational composition (National Research Council, 1991: 135–66).

This emphasis on a considered evaluation of organizational circumstance and need has assumed particular importance as attention has focused on the development of more strategic approaches to personnel management. Building on one of the models discussed in chapter 5, it has been suggested that approaches to pay systems can be related to business strategy. The links are most explicitly drawn in the work of Balkin and Gomez-Mejia (1987: 1–6). They suggest that organizations which are pursuing 'growth orientated' strategies with an organic structure and are 'buying-in' an entreprenuerial workforce would be better served by performance evaluations linked to competitive organization-level performance indicators and pay systems based on group bonuses. In contrast, organizations which are pursuing cost efficiencies and the maintainence of market share with mechanistic structures and are concerned to develop internal skills would be better served if they used appraisal and merit plans recognizing long-term employee contributions.

The second perspective is more sceptical about the existence of any underlying rationality and unity to the management process. It is a perspective which similarly has a long tradition. Behrend (1959), for example, found that management support for manual worker incentives was based on a set of beliefs which remained unverified and arguably unverifiable. In such circumstances there was an inference that belief in incentive systems served to support covertly the ideology of managerial authority. More recently, Ahlstrand (1990) has emphasized the importance of symbolism as a means of explaining the continuation of an approach to pay determination which was clearly failing to meet management's stated objectives.

The assumption that pay objectives can readily be identified has also been challenged. Bowey et al. (1982), for instance, stress the need to assess the objectives of incentive pay schemes from different behavioural perspectives: a normative perspective, considering the objectives required to ensure organizational success; a perceived perspective, looking at the expressed objectives for introducing the scheme; and an operative perspective, reviewing what objectives those implementing the scheme are actually trying to achieve.

Within the context of these two approaches, it is pertinent to ask whether the move towards individual performance pay is the result of a considered managerial process, revolving around the systematic evaluation of objectives, options and circumstances, or whether it is the consequence of a far less ordered and rational process involving interaction between diverse objectives and competing interests.

There are very few studies which trace the influence of evolving company policy on the selection of pay systems. The emergence, however, of particularly intense competitive, political and labour market pressures during the 1980s encouraged moves toward the use of individual performance-pay systems which appeared to have distinctive qualities in allowing the pursuit of a broader range of objectives than those normally associated with pay systems.

There were some organizations which were caught by the fashion of performance pay and 'bounced into' its use without any rational assessment. It has been noted, for example, that: 'Many organizations were vague and uncertain about what they were doing; some were swept away by the mood of the times' (*IDS Focus*, No. 61, December 1991: 6). Nonetheless, those companies which have used individual performance pay in a more considered way have sought to pursue two sets of objectives. One set relates to the traditional objectives of pay systems related to recuitment, retention, motivation and fairness, and typically the concern of labour market analysis. The second concentrates on organizational change where pay systems are used as one means of 'transforming' the organization to satisfy the entrepreneurial needs of the 1980s and 1990s. This is a relatively new approach to the rationale for the design of pay systems and is related to the behaviour of the firm, not the labour market. In this sense such an approach to pay may form part of a strategic human resource management policy (Boxall, 1992). Distinguishing between these two sets of goals is crucial to any critical evaluation of individual performance pay because any assessment of effectiveness must be based on an identification of expected achievements. If the importance of enhanced employee motivation is highlighted as a central management goal, the practical difficulties facing such a pay system render it highly questionable whether it can be effective in these terms. If individual performance pay is being used as a vehicle for facilitating organizational change, however, a different set of criteria may well be the basis for assessment and the effectiveness of performance pay is much more open to debate. In this context, it is perhaps more appropriate to stress a number of dilemmas faced by management in introducing and operating performance pay rather than making any precipitative judgement.

Traditonal pay objectives and performance pay

Recruitment and retention   The value of using a pay system to address recruitment and retention needs is a matter of some debate. The prescriptive literature tends to stress the use of competitive labour market pay rates or market supplements as a means of dealing with such needs, while evidence on the positive impact of a pay system on attracting and keeping staff is limited (National Research Council, 1991: 90–2). Organizations have, however, attached considerable importance to the use of individual performance pay as a means of responding to labour market pressures. In the local government sector, for example, recruitment and retention objectives have been cited as primary reasons for the introduction of performance pay (LACSAB, 1990a).

The use of individual performance pay for this purpose in part reflects the intensity of labour market pressures from the mid- to late 1980s in certain occupations and in particular regions of the country. Indeed, some organizations were lulled into establishing new pay systems to deal with a cyclical problem (*IDS Focus*, No. 61, December 1991). Other companies, however, have seen a distinct value in individual performance pay which has allowed them to address recruitment and retention needs in a more refined and selective way. Thus this type of pay system has not only been viewed as a way of attracting the 'right' type of employee to the company, but also as a powerful mechanism for indicating who it wishes to keep and who it is prepared to lose. The Alliance and Leicester Building Society, for example, has noted that reduced staff turnover was one of the main benefits it derived from the introduction of an all-merit pay scheme in 1987. Turnover fell from 16 per cent to just over 11 per cent and almost half of the 'poor' performers identified under the scheme over the preceding three years had left the organization (Incomes Data Services Top Pay Unit, 1990: 6).

Motivation The significance of pay as a motivator has been subject to intense and ongoing discussion. While the importance of pay to employees as a reason for working is rarely questioned, its direct motivational impact is a more contentious issue. Brown and Walsh in the previous chapter, for example, have suggested that the incentive effect of pay has been much exaggerated and that it is therefore more important to guard against pay as a demotivator rather than promote it as a motivator.

Nonetheless, it is clear that the use of individual performance pay to enhance employee motivation and productivity has been a key objective. The seductive value of pay as a motivator has never perhaps been pushed more to the fore than over the last decade, during which commercial pressures have forced companies to seek improved employee performance as a means of establishing a competitive edge.

The assumption that motivation will be improved by linking pay directly to individual performance finds some superficial support in expectancy theory. This suggests employee motivation will be enhanced in circumstances where the employee understands performance goals and perceives them as achievable; where there is a clear link between the achievement of these performance goals and pay; and where the employee values the related pay as a means of fulfilling salient needs. It is an approach complemented by goal setting theory which relates improved individual performance to clear employee objectives and constant feedback on progress towards them (Thierry, 1992).

These conditions are more likely to characterize the operation of individual bonus schemes which relate pay directly to individual performance using clear and unambiguous output measures. Indeed, research has suggested that in these circumstances pay can have a positive effect upon employee productivity (Richardson and Wood, 1989; National Research Council, 1991: 80–4). It is equally apparent, however, that these conditions are restricted to relatively simple and highly structured jobs. In the case of individual performance pay applied to more complex occupational tasks, the link between pay and performance is distorted in a number of ways, as outlined below.

Fairness   Many managers have come to view individual performance as a 'fairer' means of reward. In part, this accords with an instinctive belief that employee contributions to the organization vary and that this should be reflected in their pay. It is noteworthy that even among employees, who have traditionally equated fairness with equality of treatment (the 'rate for the job'), *the principle* of pay for individual performance finds considerable support. It is only when attention turns to the operation of specific schemes that employee concerns about fairness begin to emerge.

The importance of individual performance pay as a means of 'fair' reward has also assumed significance, however, in the light of recent changes to organizational structure. The move to flatter structures has reduced promotion opportunities, leaving pay systems to take the weight of providing a 'fair' reward for the high performer.

Organizational change

In addition to the traditional pay objectives, it has also been suggested that individual performance pay has been used to pursue a number of objectives related to the behaviour of the firm. This is an observation which, in turn, implies that such systems may be integral to strategic human resource management approaches. It is important, however, to distinguish the aspects of the firm's behaviour which are addressed through the use of individual performance pay. In general, the focus has been on organizational change. More specifically this type of pay system has been used to facilitate changes in organizational culture; to weaken the influence of trade unions and undermine collective bargaining as the primary means of pay determination; to revitalize and strengthen the role of the line manager; to enhance employee commitment to the organization; and to strengthen financial control over payroll costs. Each is considered in turn.

Culture In general terms, the importance of pay as a means of changing organizational culture is well recognized in the academic literature. White (1985), for instance, has stressed the significance of pay as a medium for the expression of management style, while Schien (1985) views reward systems as a primary reinforcer of cultural change. The use of pay schemes for this purpose in earlier periods finds support in the suggestion that productivity agreements were used as a means of encouraging cultural change through promoting a better spirit of co-operation (Ahlstrand, 1990: 63). Individual performance pay is, however, a particularly powerful mechanism for changing organizational values and sending strong messages to employees and the outside world alike about the 'kind of company we are'. It promotes an image which stresses flexibility, dynamism, entrepreneurial spirit and the careful allocation of resources. This objective is reflected in the support given by Rankin (1988: 23) for the introduction of individual performance pay: 'Dynamic markets need dynamic organizations. Individual contributions in leaner, more goal orientated enterprises can be seen to have real importance.'

The significance of this particular objective is illustrated in circumstances where individual performance pay has been used as part of a concerted attempt to change organizational culture. Attention has been drawn to the manner in which it has been used in newly privatized companies as a means of generating a more market oriented culture. Batstone et al. (1984) have stressed the importance of individual performance pay as part of a managerial strategy designed to break down the Post Office ideology of corporate paternalism and bureaucratic centralism. Moreover, there are examples of greenfield sites where such a pay system has been specifically used to develop an organizational culture which emphasizes the role and importance of the individual (Kessler and Purcell, 1982).

Union influence and collective bargaining Individual performance pay involves more than simply sending messages to employees about organizational values and goals, however. The very mechanics of these schemes necessitate a fundamental restructuring of the employment relationship which can enhance managerial control. It is an approach which invariably isolates the individual from the work group and forces the personalized design and evaluation of work. Moreover, although performance criteria are often discussed and agreed with employees, the assessment, the final evaluation and certainly the pay decision remain firmly in management's hands.

The individualization of the employment relationship can be related to the managerial use of individual performance pay as a means of weakening the role of the union, particularly in the arena of pay determination. The introduction of these schemes is sometimes part of a package of measures focused on the individual and designed to foster the view that employee benefits are not soley dependent on union action.

Whether such a payment system is a cause or effect of union weakness will vary according to organizational circumstances. There are, however, examples including the well-publicized cases of British Rail (*Involvement and Participation*, Autumn 1990: 12–13), where the introduction of performance pay for around 10,000 middle and junior managers was accompanied by union derecognition for pay purposes, and British Telecom, where a 'substantial tranche' of senior managers were similarly withdrawn from the collective bargaining machinery (Petch, 1990). In the case of one national newspaper, performance pay was used to address union power in a more gradualist way, with the presentation of a non-negotiable performance-related pay element during annual wage bargaining being designed to impress upon the unions their reduced influence over the pay pot (Kessler and Purcell, 1992).

Line manager–employee relations   A further objective, also linked to the restructuring of the employment relationship relates to the role of the line manager. Individual performance-pay schemes are often designed to give managers considerable discretion and responsibility, in effect, forcing managers to manage. These schemes push the manager into a direct one-to-one, usually face-to-face, relationship with each of their employees. This is clearly designed to improve communication and feedback but, perhaps more importantly, it requires the line manager to make and defend 'tough' decisions about individual employee performance and pay. At some point in this decision-making process a degree of subjectivity must intrude (see below). While being a source of instability, this subjectivity is the basis for the exercise of managerial prerogative. The right of employee appeal against managerial assessments is widespread.

Nonetheless, in some organizations attempts to protect the prerogative have led to a denial of appeal rights.

Employee commitment   The mechanics of the system are designed
both directly and indirectly to strengthen employee commitment to
the organization. The personalized development of objectives, often
linked to cascading business goals, is directly aimed at enhancing
employee identification with the company. The discussion and
agreement with the line manager on the setting of objectives can be
seen as binding the employee to his or her achievement, while the
weakening of collective bargaining can lead to a transference of
allegiance from the union to management as the main source of the
pay increase. Both reinforce the authority of the line manager and
are intended to build new, more interactive relationships between
manager and subordinate.

Financial control   The pressure to contain labour costs in a period of
economic strain has also encouraged the use of individual performance pay as a means of tightening financial control. As suggested
above, it has been perceived as a way of targeting and directing
pay to 'those who deserve it' and in this respect has been seen as
providing better 'value for money' than inflexible, across the board
increases related to cost of living or service. The extent to which
individual performance pay has been effective in this respect is by no
means clear. There are suggestions, for example, that this type of pay
scheme actually inflates the wage bill, necessitating additional merit
elements to supplement the continued provision of a general cost of
living increase.

The question of costs need to be considered, however, in a
broader context. The cost of any pay system must be assessed
not only in terms of its direct impact on the pay bill but also in
terms of indirect costs related, for instance, to the administration
of the scheme and management time and effort. Furthermore,
any consideration of costs needs to be set against the productivity or unit labour cost benefits that might accrue from any
system not only in an absolute sense but relative to any other
pay system that might be used. It is only, however, by looking at
the implementation and operation of performance-pay schemes
that a fuller appreciation of cost in this broader sense can be
ascertained.

Performance Pay in Practice

There is a well-established body of literature which has focused on the pressures influencing the effective pursuit of managerial objectives when pay systems have been put into practice. This work has highlighted the difficulties which may arise at two stages: first, during the design and introduction of schemes and, second, when the schemes are actually put into operation. Individual performance-pay schemes are likely to be susceptible to pressures at both of these stages. As Hammer (1975) states:

> It is not the merit pay theory that is defective. Rather, the history of the actual implementation of the theory is at fault.

The introduction of performance pay

Researchers have attached importance to various dimensions of the preparation for the introduction of payment systems. It has been suggested, for example, that a significant relationship exists between the effectiveness of a scheme and the degree of employee consultation during its design and implementation (Bowey et al., 1982). Others have placed emphasis upon communication, noting that employee satisfaction with a scheme is related to understanding of the way it operates (Shimmin, 1958). Moreover, training for those who have to operate a system as well as those subject to it has been pinpointed as contributing to 'success' (Gupta et al., 1986). In a more general sense, attention has been drawn to the need for establishing trust between management and employees prior to the introduction of a scheme. Thus where management–employee relationships are 'good', pay changes have a chance for success but where they are 'bad' pay can become just another battlefield for the articulation of antagonistic interests (White, 1981).

The prescriptive literature on the introduction of individual performance pay reflects these research findings, with a particular emphasis on the need for training, consensus and involvement during the design and implementation stages. The ACAS advisory booklet on appraisal-related schemes (1990: 7), for example, states that:

> Adequate resources and suitable training should be provided;
> Employers should consult with managers, employees and their representatives before appraisal related pay is introduced;

All employees involved must receive full and clear information about how the scheme will operate.

In practice, however, following such advice has not always proved easy. The preparations may well reflect the circumstances leading to the introduction of performance pay. If it is a response to immediate pressures the time available for preparation may be limited. The LACSAB survey (1990a), for instance, found that where local authorities used performance pay to address recruitment and rentention needs, schemes were prepared less carefully. Furthermore, the use of performance pay to address union influence clearly has implications for the level of union involvement in the preparations.

Indeed, whether or not performance pay is being overtly used to weaken the trade union power, the introduction of such a system presents the unions with a dilemma. They can oppose on principle a pay system which often undermines their influence or 'swallow' the principle and, in so doing, affect and become involved in certain aspects of the scheme. Some unions, for example NALGO, have remained formally opposed. This perhaps helps account for that fact that only 10 per cent of the authorities in the LACSAB survey (1990a) ran schemes negotiated with the unions. There are, however, cases where performance schemes have been negotiated with the unions. The involvement of the civil service unions, for instance, after initial hostility, contributed towards a system which provided many procedural 'safeguards'. More generally a survey of some 40 schemes, particularly in the financial service sector, concluded that most organizations negotiated the introduction of schemes (*Industrial Relations Review and Report*, 1989). The unions have also been involved in the operation of schemes: still negotiating general increases where they underpin merit rises; bargaining over the size of the pay then distributed at management's discretion; monitoring individual markings and pay awards to ensure consistency and to prevent any form of discrimination; and representing members in related appeals and grievances. The concern of some unions to at least monitor these schemes is reflected in a number of Central Arbitration Committee cases where the disclosure of related information has been sought (*IDS Report*, No. 570, June 1990: 25–8).

The operation of performance pay

While the instability of payment systems can in part be related to difficulties faced in the design and implementation stages, greater attention has focused on the way in which they can decay over time. A number of the classic workplace studies have focused on the degeneration of individual and group bonus schemes, particularly piecework systems, within the context of workplace social and political pressures (Whyte, 1955; Lupton, 1963; Brown, 1973).

In understanding the operation of payment systems the concept of control has proved particularly important. White (1981), for example, has suggested that, like any control system, pay has to be continuously administered. This administration provides the focus for the ongoing articulation and pursuit of distinctive managerial and employee interests which can distort the original goals of a scheme.

The administration of individual performance pay is more sophisticated and complex than for many payment systems. As a consequence, it arguably provides greater scope for the exercise of managerial and employee interest. Thus any performance-pay scheme requires administrative mechanisms dealing with the establishment of performance criteria; the assessment of whether those criteria have been met; and the linkage between assessment and pay award. At each of these stages difficulties have been found to emerge.

Performance criteria   Three types of criteria are generally used singularly or in combination in individual performance-pay schemes: behavioural traits which the employee brings to the job or displays when working on it; skills and competence which the employee gains or brings to the post; and outputs from the job in the form of objectives or tasks sometimes linked to key accountabilities or job descriptions. Their use has, however, given rise to a number of managerial problems.

First, the establishment of performance criteria can be problematic. Over one-third of the respondents in a survey of almost 600 organizations conducted by Wyatt (*Personnel Today*, October 1990: 28–31) suggested that 'targets were hard to establish', while just under one-third indicated that there was 'no objective measure'. These difficulties are particularly apparent in certain sectors. In the private and public service sectors, for example, it may be very difficult to identify a tangible end product which is measurable in quantitative terms. Indeed in certain parts of the public service sector the difficulties are compounded by the existence of a wide variety of groups, including politicians, management, community groups, claiming a say in the performance criteria set and in the assessment of whether they have been met.

Similar difficulties have arisen in seeking to establish viable and valid performance criteria for certain occupational groups and for those at particular levels within the organizational hierarchy. Examples are available of organizations which have grappled with setting performance criteria for scientists involved in highly speculative research and for journalists on a national newspaper (Kessler and Purcell, 1992). In the case of clerical and technical workers, there is always a danger that, in jobs which simply do not provide scope for ongoing variation and improvement of performance, the establishment of criteria can become ritualistic and meaningless. It is noteworthy that for this type of worker there is often greater reliance on behavioural traits than on objectives or tasks. The Midland Bank scheme for clerical and junior staff, for instance, bases assessment primarily on such traits as judgement and reliability, initiative, co-operation and promoting the Bank's image (Incomes Data Services, 1985: 54).

Second, the character of the performance goals can create difficulties for employees in terms of how they relate to colleagues and how they order their own work priorities. Focusing on individual performance goals, it is conceivable that team spirit and group cohesion may be undermined. The Midland Bank along with many other organizations seeks to address this by including 'co-operation' as one of the factors taken into account in the assessment. Equally significant is the possibility that employees may focus on their objectives to the neglect of other aspects of their job. This was one of the major drawbacks to the scheme established and later abandoned by Coventry City Council. As a personnel manager in the authority noted: 'When the scheme was running staff were less concerned with their daily tasks than with their target sheets' (*Personnel Today*, August 1990: 23).

This raises the broader question of whether the performance goals relate to the normal job requirments or whether they are set over and above what is typically expected. Some organizations recognize this distinction. Kodak's scheme for senior and middle managers, for instance, distinguishes between 'standard' objectives which are quantifiable goals linked to the main aspects of the job, and 'targets', designed to stretch the employee (Incomes Data Services Top Pay Unit, 1989: 4–5). Such a distinction is not, however, always made, leading to uncertainty among managers as to what basis they should use for the establishment of performance criteria.

Finally, procedural difficulties may arise. These can take the form of variable managerial interpretations of how to set performance goals and what form they should take. Despite training and guidelines there is evidence to suggest that, even within the same organization, definition of an objective can vary significantly between the general statement of intent and the precise and measurable goal. More fundamantally perhaps, the procedure for setting performance criteria, particularly objectives, may undermine rather than enhance the pursuit of managerial flexibility and commitment. Pearce (1987), for instance, has suggested that the establishment of a pay plan places the employee in the position of a 'labour contractor' with performance solely reflected in the 'contract measures' and less account taken of performance outside of the established criteria, future performance and potential. He also notes that, if performance requirements are uncertain, the writing of a fixed-pay contract actually restricts the ability of managers to respond to change rather than providing for greater flexibility and discretion.

Performance assessment   The potential for distortion of the performance-related pay system is perhaps at its greatest at the assessment stage discussed in more detail in chapter 7. This arises in part from the subjectivity and inconsistency inherent in the process but also from the intensity of the workplace pressures at this particular point.

Subjectivity and inconsistency can enter the assessment process in a number of ways. First, within any dynamic organization, performance criteria, particularly those related to tasks or objectives, can be rapidly undermined and require revision. Some organizations seek to address this issue by having regular manager–employee meetings to revise targets in the light of changed circumstances. There is, nonetheless, still a managerial judgement to be made about whether and how objectives should be revised.

Second, an appraisal system for pay purposes requires some overall evaluation of performance as a means of establishing the pay link. Organizations normally use between three and six ratings (Incomes Data Services, 1985) with most choosing to attach descriptive labels characterizing performance. There are examples of schemes where the allocation of points to different features of the job performance allows an overall score to be used to determine a rating. Such schemes are not, however, common, being seen to lend a spurious objectivity to the process and allowing managers to 'blame' their decisions on 'the system' rather than take responsibility for them. In the absence of any viable technique for mechanistically relating assessment to overall rating there is scope for variation in approach between different managers and by the same manager in relation to different employees.

Third, subjectivity and inconsistency can become a problem in situations where appraisal is employed for different ends. In many organizations appraisal is used for career development as well as pay purposes (Bevan and Thompson, 1991). There is, nevertheless, a perceived tension between the two and a desire to keep them separate both in temporal and administrative terms. How distinct these processes can ever be or, in managerial terms, should be, is perhaps debatable. It is unrealistic to assume that a manager can separate the two processes easily and it could be argued that in a broad sense the evaluations should be congruent. There are, however, examples where performance review for development purposes is open and jointly conducted while the evaluation for pay purposes is closed. In such circumstances the linkage between the two becomes blurred, particularly in the employee's mind.

Many companies seek to address the difficulties outlined by monitoring assessments and ratings. In so doing, they hope to pick out marked variations and anomalies between managers in different parts of the organization. Nonetheless, inconsistency and subjectivity remain the major source of difficulty with schemes. The Wyatt survey, for instance, indicated that in 60 per cent of organizations inconsistency was a problem, while in almost half the companies subjectivity was seen as a problem.

Inconsistency and subjectivity are likely to assume increasing importance as a managerial concern, particularly if they lead to claims of discrimination on grounds of sex (Bevan and Thompson, 1992). In the case of the performance-related pay scheme for senior civil servants, for example, the First Division Association has already raised some concerns about the distribution of ratings between male and female employees (Kessler, 1992). The European Court of Justice ruling in the *Handels* v *Danfloss* case has more significant implications. It suggests that work quality cannot be used as a criterion for pay purposes if it reveals that the quality of women's work is consistently below that of men; it also excludes the use of adaptability and flexibility pay criteria unless these can be shown as important to the performance of the job (Ashtiany, 1992).

While the need for managers to make and defend decisions was highlighted as a key objective for individual performance-pay schemes, the social and political realities of the workplace make it far easier for the manager not to rate subordinates harshly. Managers often take the 'easy option' in marking employees at an average level or even allow the markings to drift upwards as a means of attracting better rewards for their staff. On the assumption that there should be a 'normal distribution' of performance some organizations have introduced systems which force managerial choice or at least provide managers with some guidance on 'prefered' distribution.

The realities of the workplace are also apparent in relation to what might seem to be the trivial issue of the rating label. The demotivating effect of being singled out as a 'satisfactory' rather than an 'outstanding' performer should not be underestimated. Attention has been drawn to the case of a national newspaper where journalists, so dependent on reputation for career development purposes, were particularly concerned about being labelled 'average' (Kessler and Purcell, 1992). Another example can be found in the Audit Commission where a decision was taken to replace terms such as 'outstanding' and 'below standard' by numbers which were seen as less inhibiting (Incomes Data Services Public Sector Unit, 1989: 14).

Workplace pressures in the form of the workload facing managers also raises question marks about the way the assessment process is carried out. Performance assessment is an extremely resource intensive procedure. The willingness of managers to meet the requirements of a scheme raises questions about ownership and acceptance in the context of what might otherwise be perceived as an imposed personnel bureaucracy.

The link to pay   The establishment of a clear and effective link between performance and pay is crucial to the achievement of certain management objectives. There are, however, a number of ways in which this link may become distorted. First, the mechanics of the scheme may obscure the relationship. In certain cases the link is straightforward – a particular performance rating will give rise to a number of increments on a fixed scale or to a specified percentage increase. Other schemes, however, are based on a much more variable and opaque link. This may involve, for instance, relating pay increase to the position on a scale as well as to the performance rating, or providing increases within a salary range rather than on a scale with fixed incremental points.

Second, and more significantly, distortion can arise from the financial constraints under which many schemes operate. The amount of money available for individual performance-related pay may be small, particularly if underpinned by a general cost of living increase. Even in cases where all merit increases are provided, employees may initially assess their rise against inflation and merely view any residual amount as related to their performance.

These financial constraints can also lead to incongruity between performance assessment and financial reward. The expectation raised by positive feedback from a performance review may simply not be translated into a significant pay increase. It is in these circumstances that employees with raised expectations are most likely to be demotivated. In addition, the limited money available may inhibit managers in differentiating sharply in pay terms between average and outstanding performers (Meyer, 1987: 183).

Financial constraints in circumstances where there are certain weaknesses in the organization's basic pay structure – for instance, where pay is no longer seen as competitive in comparison to external labour markets – may cause additional difficulties. This may arise, in particular, where the devolution of pay for performance-related purposes to line managers allows them to address these problems in their own way. In effect, pay can be diverted from its intended purpose to deal with these other pay issues. As far back as the early 1970s, the Commission on Industrial Relations provided an example of merit pay being used to retain particular employees in the engineering company Rubery Owen (Commission on Industrial Relations, 1974: 38).

Finally, the small amount of money available for performance pay and the recent financial constraints have led a number of writers to dismiss its incentive effects. Smith (1989), for instance, has suggested that anything less than 25 per cent of basic pay is unlikely to motivate or improve employee performance for long enough to justify a scheme.

To view the performance–pay link solely in quantitive and motivational terms, however, may be to completely miss the underlying rationale of these systems. Organizations may not actually be looking for a direct link between pay and performance. The size of the payout or the clarity of the link may be unimportant when set beside the benefits derived from the pursuit of broader organizational goals. It is interesting to note, for example, evidence from the local government sector which indicated that the simple existence of a performance–pay link rather than its size encouraged employees and managers to carry out appraisals and take the process seriously (Local Authorities Conditions of Service Advisory Board, 1990b).

The Future

Given the broad range of factors liable to influence individual and organizational performance, it is notoriously difficult to isolate and assess the impact of any pay system. This helps account not only for the fact that there has been very little research on the effectiveness of individual performance pay (National Research Council, 1991) but also for evidence indicating that few attempts have been made by organizations to assess the impact of their own schemes (Cannell and Long, 1991; Thompson, 1992).

The adoption of a pay system can therefore be seen as an act of faith (Shimmin, 1958), with the longevity of the individual performance-pay schemes unlikely to be based on a considered evaluation of effectiveness. Nevertheless, these schemes appear to have considerable life left in them yet. The Wyatt survey, reflecting many of the managerial concerns about such systems, still indicates that over half of the sample (54 per cent) felt performance pay was a 'major priority' with 40 per cent viewing is as being of 'emerging importance'.

This chapter has suggested that any discussion of impact must be based on a clear appreciation of objectives. Arguing deductively from the central principles of expectancy theory, it can be suggested that the value of individual performance pay in enhancing employee motivation is always likely to be limited. The establishment of clear and consistent performance goals is highly problematic as a general managerial exercise and particularly so when applied to certain occupational groups. Moreover, the link between pay and performance is liable to be distorted by a wide variety of company and workplace pressures.

If, however, the distinctiveness of individual performance pay is seen to lie in its use as a lever for promoting organizational change, perhaps as part of a broader human resource management strategy, with the emphasis on its symbolic and rhetorical value in generating a new performance-driven company culture and supporting the principles of managerialism and individualism, the issue of impact assumes an altogether different form. It remains no easier to measure impact but the effectiveness of individual performance pay may well be contingent on managerial responses to a number of dilemmas and questions which they face.

First, should individual performance pay stimulate change in organizational culture or follow from it? While a scheme may be used as a way of changing attitudes and values, if it runs counter to prevailing company norms it may prove unacceptable to employees as well as to line managers.

Second, should a scheme only be introduced when the necessary line management skills are in place or should a scheme be used as the best way of developing these skills? Although many schemes are designed with the express purpose of enhancing managerial discretion, if managers exercise their discretion in unintended ways a scheme can become discredited.

Finally, if individual performance pay is introduced as means of undermining the collective strength of the employees and as a way of addressing union power, does it become more difficult to meet some of the conditions necessary for a scheme to be accepted by the employees? The attempt by management to individualize the employment relationship and implement a scheme in the face of union opposition may reduce the level of employee–management trust and eliminate the possibility of consensual introductory procedures which have been perceived as essential to the establishment of an effective scheme.

Bibliography

ACAS. 1988. *Developments in Payment Systems*. Occassional Paper 45. London: Advisory, Conciliation and Arbitration Service.

ACAS. 1990. *Appraisal Related Pay*. Advisory Booklet 14. London: Advisory, Conciliation and Arbitration Service.

Ahlstrand, B. 1990. *The Quest for Productivity*. Cambridge: Cambridge University Press.

Armstrong, M. and Murliss, H. 1991. *Reward Management*. London: Kogan Page.

Ashtiany, S. 1992. 'European Law: Equal Treatment/Equal Pay'. Paper given at Templeton College, 27 January.

Balkin, D. and Gomez-Mejia, L. (eds) 1987. *New Perspectives on Compensation*. New Jersey: Prentice Hall.

Batstone, E., Ferner, A. and Terry, M. 1984. *Consent and Efficiency.* Oxford: Blackwell.

Behrend, H. 1959. 'Financial Incentives as the Expression of a System of Beliefs'. *British Journal of Sociology*, Vol. 10, No. 2, 137–47.

Bevan, S. and Thompson, M. 1991. 'Performance Management at the Crossroads'. *Personnel Management*. November.

Bevan, S. and Thompson, M. 1992. *Merit Pay and Performance Appraisal and Attitudes to Women's Work.* Sussex: Institute of Manpower Studies.

Bowey, A., Thorpe, R., Mitchell, F., Nicholls, G., Gosnold, D., Savery, L. and Hellier, P. 1982. *Effects of Incentive Payment Systems, United Kingdom 1977–80.* Department of Employment Research Paper No. 36. London: Department of Employment.

Boxall, P. 1992. 'Strategic Human Resource Management: Beginnings of a New Theoretical Sophstication?'. *Human Resource Management Journal*, Vol. 2, No. 3, 60–79.

Brady, L. and Wright, V. 1990. *Performance Related Pay.* Fact Sheet No. 30. London: Personnel Management.

Brown, W. 1973. *Piecework Bargaining.* London: Heinemann Educational Books.

Brown, W. 1989. 'Managing Remuneration'. In Sisson, K. (ed.) *Personnel Management in Britain.* Oxford: Blackwell.

Cannell, M. and Long, P. 1991. 'What's Changed about Incentive Pay?'. *Personnel Management*, October, 58–63.

Cannell, M. and Wood, S. 1992. *Incentive Pay.* London: Institute of Personnel Management.

Casey, B., Lakey, J., Cooper, H. and Elliot, J. 1991. 'Payment Systems: A Look at Current Practice'. *Employment Gazette*, August, 53–8.

CBI. 1988. *People at the Cutting Edge.* London: Confederation of British Industry.

Citizen's Charter. 1991. Cm 1599. London: HMSO.

Commission on Industrial Relations. 1974. *Rubery Owen Company Ltd. and Associated Companies.* Report No. 80. London: HMSO.

Davies, A. 1991. 'Restructuring Pay and Grading in a Civil Service Agency'. *Personnel Management*, October, 52–3.

Deming, W. 1982. *Out of Crisis.* Cambridge: Cambridge University Press.

Fowler, A. 1988. 'New Directions in Performance Pay'. *Personnel Management*, November, 30–34.

Grinyer, P. and Kessler, S. 1967. 'Systematic Evaluation of Methods of Wage Payment'. *Journal of Management Studies*, Vol. 4, No. 3, 309–20.

Gupta, N., Jenkins, G. and Curington, W. 1986. 'Pay for Knowledge: Myths and Realities'. *National Productivity Review*, Vol. 5, No. 2, 107–23.

Hammer, W., 1975. 'How to Ruin Motivation with Pay'. *Compensation Review*, Vol. 7, No. 3, 17–27.

Incomes Data Services. 1985. *The Merit Factor.* London: IDS.

Incomes Data Services. 1991. *Bonus Schemes, Part 2*. Study No. 492.

Incomes Data Services. 1992. *Skills Based Pay*. Study No. 500.

Incomes Data Services Public Sector Unit. 1989. *Guide to Performance Related Pay*. London: IDS.

Incomes Data Services Top Pay Unit. 1989. Review 104.

Incomes Data Services Top Pay Unit. 1990. Review 110.

Industrial Relations Review and Report. 1986a. 'BP Chemicals Barry: A Move to Staff Status'. 362, February, 9–11.

Industrial Relations Review and Report. 1986b. 'Johnson and Johnson: Integrated Payment Structure'. 378, October, 3–9.

Industrial Relations Review and Report, Pay and Benefits Bulletin. 1989. 'Merit Pay – The Big Growth Industry'. 226, February, 2–6.

Kanter, R. M. 1989. *When Giants Learn to Dance*. London: Unwin.

Kessler, I. 1990. 'Flexibility and Comparability in Pay Determination for Professional Civil Servants'. *Industrial Relations Journal*, Vol. 21, No. 3, 194–208.

Kessler, I. 1992. 'Pay Determination in the Professionl Civil Service'. *Templeton College Management Research Paper*, No. 1, January.

Kessler, I. and Purcell, J. 1992. 'Performance Related Pay – Objectives and Application'. *Human Resource Management Journal*, Vol. 2, No. 3, 34–59.

Kinnie, N. and Lowe, D. 1990. 'Performance Related Pay on the Shopfloor'. *Personnel Management*, November, 45–9.

Lawler III, E. 1973. *Motivation in Work Organisations*. California: Brook Cole.

Lawler III, E. 1987. 'New Approaches to Total Compensation'. In Steers, R. and Porter, W. (eds) *Motivation and Work Behaviour*. New York: McGraw-Hill.

Local Authorities Conditions of Service Advisory Board. 1990a. *Performance Related Pay in Practice*. London: LACSAB.

Local Authorities Conditions of Service Advisory Board. 1990b. *Performance Related Pay Case Studies*. London: LACSAB.

Long, P. 1986. *Performance Appraisal Revisited*. London: Institute of Personnel Management.

Lupton, T. 1963. *On the Shopfloor*. Oxford: Pergamon.

Lupton, T. and Gowler, D. 1969. *Selecting a Wage Payment System*. Research Paper III. London: Engineering Employers' Federation.

Marriott, R. 1971. *Incentive Payment Systems*. London: Staples Press.

Meyer, H. 1987. 'How Can We Implement a Pay for Performance Policy Successfully?'. In Balkin, D. and Gomez-Mejia L. (eds) *New Perspectives on Compensation*. New Jersey: Prentice Hall.

Millward, N., Stevens, M., Smart, D. and Hawes, W. 1992. *Workplace Industrial Relations in Transition*. Aldershot: Dartmouth.

National Board for Prices and Incomes. 1968. *Payment by Results Systems*. Report No. 65. Cmnd 3627. London: HMSO.

National Health Service Management Executive. 1990. *NHS: A Working Guide*. London: HMSO.

National Research Council. 1991. *Pay for Performance*. Washington: National Academic Press.

Pearce, J. 1987. 'Why Merit Pay Doesn't Work'. In Balkin, D. and Gomez-Mejia, L. (eds) *New Perspectives on Compensation*. New Jersey: Prentice Hall.

Petch, S. 1990. 'Performance Related Pay – Problems for the Trade Unions'. Paper to TUC Seminar on PRP, 21 January.

Peters, T. 1988. *Thriving on Chaos*. London: Macmillan.

Rankin, N. 1988. 'Performance and Pay: Making the Connection'. *Manpower Policy and Practice*, Spring, 23–38.

Richardson, R. and Wood, S. 1989. 'Productivity Change in the Coal Industry and New Industrial Relations'. *British Journal of Industrial Relations*, Vol. 27, No. 1, 33–56.

Schien, E. 1985. *Organizational Culture and Leadership*. San Fransisco: Jossey Bass.

Shimmin, S. 1958. 'Worker Understanding of Incentive Bonus Systems'. *Occupational Psychology*, Vol. 32, No. 2.

Smith, I. 1989. *People and Profits*. London: Croner.

Thierry, H. 1992. 'Pay and Payment Systems'. In Hartley, J. and Stephenson, G. (eds) *Employment Relations*. Oxford: Blackwell.

Thompson, M. 1992. *Pay for Performance in the Employer Experience*. Sussex: Institute for Manpower Studies.

Tolliday, S. 1991. 'Ford and "Fordism" in Postwar Britain: Enterprise Management and the Control of Labour 1937–87'. In Tolliday, S. and Zeitlin, J. (eds) *The Power to Manage*. London: Routledge.

White, M. 1981. *The Hidden Meaning of Pay Conflict*. London: Macmillan.

White, M. 1985. 'What's New in Pay?'. *Personnel Management*. February, 23–6.

Whyte, W. 1955. *Money and Motivation*. New York: Harper.

Wright, V. 1991. 'Performance Related Pay'. In Neale, F. (ed.) *The Handbook of Performance Management*. London: Institute of Personnel Management.

15

Working Hours

Paul Blyton

In the workplace, the duration and organization of working time have represented key themes in the development of relations between employers and employees. Historically, the working period – and specifically the campaigns for shorter working time – has been a focus for the development of trade unionism and union–management relations. This focus has hardly diminished in more recent times. In the 1980 Workplace Industrial Relations Survey (WIRS), for example, holiday entitlement and the length of the working week figured as the most common non-pay issues covered by collective bargaining among both manual and non-manual groups (existing as subjects for negotiations in over 90 per cent of establishments where unions were recognized) (Daniel and Millward, 1983: 197; Batstone, 1988: 220–1). The 1990 WIRS continued to show that in workplaces where collective bargaining took place, negotiation over working time issues was more common than for any other non-pay issue (Millward et al., 1992: 251). In British engineering, the issue of a shorter working week played a prominent role in the 1978–9 'Winter of Discontent', involving one and a half million workers and the loss of 16 million worker days in a series of one- and two-day national strikes. More recently, in the late 1980s and early 1990s, the issue of working time gave rise to arguably the most successful union campaign of industrial action for a decade, as engineering unions used selective strike action to achieve shorter hours (Blyton, 1992a). Working time has also been a prominent issue for trade unions in other countries. In West Germany in 1984, for example, a campaign for shorter hours in engineering led to the biggest strike in the Federal Republic's history (Bosch, 1986).

Yet while the question of *duration* has traditionally represented the focus of union–management relations on working time, in recent years this has been increasingly supplemented by a growing managerial concern with the more effective *organization* and *utilization* of working time. As a consequence, negotiations over the length of working hours have been increasingly tied to issues relating both to the arrangement of those hours (leading to agreements over shiftworking and 'flexible' rostering, for example), and a tighter definition of the working period (through, for example, changes to the taking of breaks and increased discipline over start and stop times). This increased attention on the arrangement and utilization of work hours reflects both general and specific managerial concerns: general issues, such as a search for improved productivity and competitiveness via closer control of labour costs, and specific issues such as improving capital utilization by maintaining or extending operating hours in a context of widespread reductions in the basic working week.

The upshot of these increasingly prominent managerial concerns is that it is no longer appropriate (if indeed it ever was) to seek an understanding of working time developments simply by charting changes in duration. Such changes are certainly worthy of our attention – indeed, developments such as the extension of paid holiday entitlement probably represent one of the main advances in conditions of employment over the past generation. However, these changes need to be seen in the context of a widening management agenda over working time, an agenda which raises important questions about the future pattern of working time, and its significance both for the way in which individuals experience work, and the way management pursues a more productive organization of the working period.

The arrangement of working time has also been given added moment in the early 1990s by the publication of the EC's draft Directive on working hours designed to limit employers' scope to compress work hours into longer shifts and rely on high levels of overtime working (Incomes Data Services, 1990: 5). The rejection of this draft Directive by the UK Conservative government in 1991 – part of a broader rejection of issues pertaining to the Community Charter of Fundamental Social Rights of Workers (the 'Social Charter') – is unlikely to mean that such issues will fade during the 1990s. On the contrary, as European integration is extended, there is likely to be increasing pressure on governments and employers in the UK to conform more closely with developments occurring on the European mainland.

To examine the changes taking place and their implications, the chapter is divided into four main sections. The first gives an overview of the developments in the duration of working time as a result of reductions in the basic working week, together with developments in overtime working, paid holiday entitlement and changes in the length of lifetime work hours as a result of shifts in the age of entry into, and exit from, the labour market. Following this, issues involving the arrangement of working time are considered, together with the growing management attention given to (though in many respects only limited formal development of) greater working time flexibility, through such arrangements as 'annual hours' contracts.

This discussion of temporal flexibility and the arrangement of working hours is followed by a brief examination of employers' increasing desire to improve the utilization of working time, primarily by reducing non-productive time and intensifying the working period through such practices as 'bell-to-bell' working. These developments are considered in the context of evidence that managements have previously shown a less than complete ability to impose their own time-reckoning system on the workforce, these systems being susceptible to significant modification by work groups imposing aspects of their own time-reckoning pattern on management's 'official' one.

In the concluding section, possible future developments in working time are considered, and the argument put forward that in pursuing a more extended, intensified and flexible working time pattern, managements are in danger of ignoring several important issues. Among these are that working time arrangements and flexibility are not simply employer concerns but have a direct and forceful impact on many aspects of employees' lives, including their job satisfaction, family responsibilities, social life and physical and mental well-being. In the long term, management's search for a more productive and variable working period needs to take closer account both of employee preferences over the arrangement of working time, and the possible harmful effects of particular schedules.

The Duration of Working Time

The working week

Of the various elements contributing to the duration of working time – including the age of entry into and exit from the labour market, the length of holidays and the amount of overtime and short-time work-ing – it is the duration of daily, and weekly working hours which has been the prime focus of attention in union–management negotia-tions. Britain is virtually unique in Europe in having no general legislation concerning the overall duration or arrangement of work-ing time. There is no statutory regulation, for example, governing the maximum length of the working day or minimum rest periods and holidays. Former legislation regulating the hours of women and young people was repealed under the Sex Discrimination Act 1986 and the Employment Act 1989 (Horrell and Rubery, 1991: 1). The little statutory regulation which continues to exist is confined to particular groups and occupations, such as mining and lorry driving (Hepple, 1988: 423). Thus, as with the case of pay determination in Britain, the main aspects of working time have been determined either by management action or collective bargaining.

Basic hours of full-time workers Following the gradual spread in the nineteenth century first of the ten-hour day, and later the 54-hour week, working time developments in the twentieth century have been characterized by a number of step-like reductions in the length of the basic working week.[1] The periods after the First and Second World Wars, and the early 1960s saw the widespread establishment in Britain of the basic 48-, 44- and 40-hour week for a majority of the manual workforce. Similarly, the period 1980–3 witnessed the intro-duction of a basic working week of below 40 hours (generally a 39-hour week) for over seven million manual workers (Department of Employment, 1984: 174). By 1986, 75 per cent of manual workers had a basic week of 39 hours, with 15 per cent working a basic 40-hour week and approximately 10 per cent with a basic week of below 39 hours (Blyton, 1989: 113).

Various explanations have been put forward to account for this periodicity in weekly hours reductions, rather than a more gradual and continuous trend. These include: an 'individual preference' argument, that a reduction in hours temporarily satisfies a demand for more non-work time and shifts preferences (temporarily) to improving wage levels (Hill, 1989); a 'conjunction of organizational and economic factors' argument, for example increasing productiv-ity and falling inflation, that encourages both a demand by the workforce for reduced hours (rather than higher income) and a greater willingness by employers to concede such a reduction

(Bienefeld, 1972); a 'work intensification' argument, that the adoption of more intensive production systems periodically forces employers to concede to demands for reduced hours to counter the effects of greater fatigue caused by the method of production (Nyland, 1989); and an 'employer resistance' argument, that employers are more reluctant to concede on hours than pay (and so concede much less frequently on the former than on the latter) because hours cuts are generally not reversible and reduced hours threaten output capacity (Bienefeld, 1972).

These different arguments focus attention on individual, organizational and societal level factors. In practice, however, the diverse social and economic conditions under which reductions in hours have occurred (contrast, for example, the early 1960s and early 1980s), the variety of organizational settings and production processes in which reductions have taken place, and the maintenance of a plurality of working week levels at any one point – not to mention international variations in weekly hours – indicate that no single explanation is likely to encapsulate fully the various factors involved in the agreement and timing of hours reductions. Further, it is evident that in between some of the weekly hours changes, organized labour has sought improvements to other aspects of working time duration – for example, in paid holiday entitlement (see below) – which cautions against explanations focusing exclusively on the conditions prevailing when basic weekly hours fall. In addition, what arguments such as the ones noted above tend to overlook are the practical issues for management (and employees) in terms of reorganizing work to accommodate changes in the basic week: for example, drawing up new shift rotas and rescheduling transport arrangements. Such additional work is also likely to encourage the concentration of changes into particular periods rather than a more gradual and continuous pattern of change.

Following the reductions in hours which took place in Britain in the early 1980s, the basic working week for the majority of both manual and non-manual workers has remained little changed over the past decade (though see below for developments in particular sectors). Over that period there has remained a clear difference between the average basic weekly hours of the two groups: on average, as table 15.1 shows, the basic hours of full-time non-manual workers are approximately two hours below those of their manual counterparts in Britain. This manual/non-manual difference is also evident outside Britain, though a notable exception to this is Germany where manual workers have tended to achieve hours reductions (such as the breaching of the 40-hour week) before their white-collar counterparts. Table 15.1 also indicates the extent to which the basic working week for full-time males tends to be higher than for full-time females, this difference being virtually identical among manual and non-manual occupations.

Reviewing agreements struck during 1989–90 covering 11.5 million workers, the Labour Research Department (1990) identifies 13 per cent of full-time manual workers with a basic working week of below 39 hours. This proportion is somewhat higher in the private than the public sector: particular industrial sectors where the shorter working week was most common included energy, coal-mining and water, chemicals, and paper, printing and publishing.

The most notable development in weekly hours in recent years, however, has come in the engineering industry. This follows a protracted period of negotiations dating back to 1983, and the commencement in 1989 of what became a two-year campaign of industrial action by the Confederation of Shipbuilding and Engineering Unions (CSEU), involving targeted strike ballots and strike action at selected plants. By November 1990 the CSEU claimed that over 1200 establishments (including many of the leading engineering companies such as British Aerospace, Lucas and Rolls Royce) had reached agreements on reduced hours, generally involving a phased reduction to 37 hours – half an hour more than had been originally offered by the Engineering Employers' Federation (EEF), though two hours less than the unions' original target of 35 hours (Blyton, 1992a; McKinlay and McNulty, 1991). The CSEU cam-

Table 15.1 Average basic weekly hours of
full-time adults in Britain – April 1992

	Normal basic hours
Manual males	39.0
Manual females	38.0
Non-manual males	37.3
Non-manual females	36.2
All males	38.1
All females	36.5

Source: New Earnings Survey 1992, Part D

paign was suspended in April 1991 (the second anniversary of the 'failure to agree' registered with the EEF), partly because of the increasingly adverse economic situation in the industry. The union position is that the 37-hour settlements represent an interim step to achieving a 35-hour week, a level which has now been agreed in the German engineering industry, to be introduced by 1995[2] (Bosch, 1990; Blyton, 1992b).

When the engineering industry had previously agreed a shorter working week (the 39-hour week introduced in 1981), it appeared to stimulate similar settlements in other industries. To date, however, the extent of the imitation effect outside engineering appears very limited, probably primarily reflecting the poor economic conditions during 1990–2. Indeed, even within engineering, the degree to which the 37-hour settlements have 'cascaded' down to other companies which had not made agreements before the campaign was suspended, appears only modest.[3] For example, in the vehicles sector, while manual workers at Rover, Jaguar, Rolls-Royce and Honda were working a 37-hour week by 1992, Ford, Vauxhall, Peugeot-Talbot and Nissan retained a 39-hour week, as does the new Toyota plant (Incomes Data Services, 1993: 26). Thus, prior to any union campaign in pursuit of a 35-hour week, a standardization at 37 hours will need to be secured.

Basic hours of part-time workers The overall distribution of weekly working hours reflects not only full-time, but also part-time workers who are a growing proportion of the workforce. In 1991 over 23 per cent of the workforce in Britain worked part time (up to 30 hours per week) (Watson, 1992). The distribution of part-time hours shows considerable diversity, both among manual and non-manual workers. In reviewing the hours of female part-time employees – who in Britain comprise more than nine out of ten of the total part-time workforce – almost two-fifths of female manual part-timers and over one-third of non-manuals work less than 16 hours per week (table 15.2). Shorter length part-time schedules are more evident in the service sector, and within certain industries. In catering, for example, almost half the female part-time workforce has a basic week of less than 16 hours, and this proportion reaches 66 per cent for bar staff (New Earnings Survey, 1992, tables 181 and 183). Similarly, in sections of retailing (such as checkout operators and sales assistants) the proportion of female part-timers on less than 16 hours is again around one-half, climbing to two-thirds for particular occupations,

Table 15.2   Basic hours of women working part time – April 1992 (%)

	<8 hours	8–16 hours	16–21 hours	>21 hours
Manual				
Production industries	3.8	15.4	28.4	52.4
Services	8.2	34.5	25.7	31.5
All industries and services	7.7	32.0	26.0	34.3
Non-manual				
Production industries	4.2	18.5	36.5	40.7
Services	13.4	24.1	30.3	32.0
All industries and services	12.9	23.7	30.7	32.7

Source: New Earnings Survey, 1992, Part D

such as shelf-fillers. As discussed below, this growth in the proportion of the workforce engaged on part-time schedules potentially provides employers with considerable scope to organize work hours to match operating needs, not least by employing part-time staff to cover busy periods and using part-time shifts to extend operating hours.

So far, the analysis of weekly hours has focused on basic hours. Yet, while for some groups of manual workers basic hours are beginning to fall below 39 hours, average *actual* weekly hours for male manual workers in April 1992 stood at 44.5 hours (New Earnings Survey, 1992). Indeed, the 1991 Labour Force Survey indicates that over three million employees (more than 15 per cent of the workforce) usually work more than 48 hours per week (Watson, 1992). This underlines the significant contribution to weekly hours which continues to be made by overtime working.

Overtime working   Overtime refers to those hours worked in addition to agreed basic weekly hours. A distinction may be drawn between contractual and non-contractual overtime, the former (as the term implies) being included as part of the individual contract of employment. Most information is available on overtime working which is paid, though according to recent estimates based on Labour Force Survey data, paid overtime may account for as little as 56 per cent of total overtime hours worked by employees (Watson, 1992: 542). Paid overtime is worked primarily by male manual workers in manufacturing, transport and communications. In 1992, 52 per cent of full-time manual men and 20 per cent of non-manual men worked overtime (or, at least, overtime that was paid for). Comparable proportions for full-time manual and non-manual female employees were 27 per cent and 16 per cent. Among full-time males covered by the 1992 New Earnings Survey, manual workers undertook an average of 5.5 overtime hours each week, compared to 1.4 hours among non-manual employees; comparative overtime hours among full-time female employees in 1992 were 1.9 hours (manual) and 0.6 hours (non-manual). Table 15.3 lists a number of occupations where average overtime working is particularly high.

Looking more closely at overtime working in manufacturing, it is evident that while aggregate levels of overtime working fluctuate considerably with the state of the economy – for example, dropping from an average of around 15 million hours per week in 1988 to approximately 10 million hours by 1991 – overtime remains a persistent and prominent aspect of working time in Britain, even when labour markets are comparatively weak. For example, even in the depths of the 1980–2 recession, an average of over 8.5 million overtime hours were worked each week in the UK manufacturing sector. Similarly, in 1991 just over one-third (34.5 per cent) of all operatives in manufacturing worked an average of 9.1 overtime

Table 15.3 Occupations with high incidence of overtime working – 1992

	Average weekly overtime (hours)
Mechanical plant drivers and operatives	12.2
Rail signal operatives	11.7
Railway station staff	10.4
Agricultural machinery drivers and operatives	10.3
Road construction and maintenance workers	10.3
Lathe setters and setter operatives	10.0
Seafarers (merchant navy)	9.9
Crane drivers	9.5
Furnace operatives	9.4
Bakery and confectionery process operatives	9.2
Drivers of road-going goods vehicles	9.2

Source: New Earnings Survey, 1992, Part D

hours per week, giving an average weekly total of 9.82 million overtime hours. Very similar levels were evident in 1992: in September 1992, for example, 34.2 per cent of operatives in manufacturing worked an average of 9.7 hours overtime, amounting to 9.65 million hours in total, per week (*Employment Gazette*, December 1992).

This high level of overtime working continues to be a major feature of working time patterns in Britain despite criticism from both national employer and union organizations, who in the past have been particularly critical of 'systematic' overtime as a regular feature of work patterns, rather than being employed on an *ad hoc* basis to cover extraordinary circumstances (Blyton, 1985). Unions, for example, have argued that high levels of overtime not only allows employers to set lower basic pay rates, but that it also engenders long work hours and may potentially undermine job creation. Employers' organizations on the other hand have criticized overtime on grounds of its cost and that the availability of overtime working can reduce productivity in normal work hours. These factors were prominent in many productivity negotiations in the 1960s. Reduction of overtime, for example, was a major issue in the path-breaking productivity agreement reached at Esso's Fawley plant in the early 1960s (Flanders, 1964). Yet returning to the same plant two decades later, Ahlstrand (1990) documents a series of subsequent attempts to curb overtime, each enjoying only relatively limited and short-term success.

The persistence of high levels of overtime despite espoused opposition to it from employer and union bodies is explained partly by the lack of incentive at local level to eliminate overtime. For employers, overtime provides a means of extending the normal day without incurring additional costs of recruiting and training extra labour. It also allows the operation of particular shift patterns which do not fit exactly with agreed weekly hours, and it provides a way of increasing employees' earnings without conceding a general wage rise. For many employees, overtime pay forms an important component in overall earnings. The 1992 New Earnings Survey data for example identified ten occupations where those on overtime received an average of over £60 per week overtime pay. For rail signal operatives, the average weekly value of overtime payments was as high as £88. Given this importance of overtime to total earnings for many workers, it is perhaps not surprising that, in what still remains the most extensive study conducted on overtime, in less than 0.5 per

cent of the 2000 establishments studied were local unions opposed
to the practice of overtime working (National Board for Prices and
Incomes, 1970). Yet despite the benefits which overtime may bestow
on local managers, its premium-paid rate represents a significant
cost, particularly where the level of overtime working is high. It is
partly the desire to reduce these costs that has led to some growth of
interest in 'seasonal hours' and 'annual hours' contracts. These are
examined in more detail in a later section.

Short-time working　While overtime expands the length of the working day, short-time working contracts it. Long used by employers in
periods of slack demand, in more recent times short-time working
has received a measure of specific state subsidy, being viewed as
preferable to the declaration of redundancies. As a temporary measure, short-time working does have a number of points in its favour.
For the workers involved, short-time working is likely to be seen as
both preferable and more equitable than selective redundancies,
particularly if pay is maintained at a reasonable level or subsidies are
available to make up a significant proportion of any lost income. For
employers, short-time measures help retain trained workers, and
avoid costs of redundancies and any later recruitment and training
costs.

In Europe, one of the most extensive state-subsidized short-time
working schemes operates in Germany where, under a 1969 Act, an
allowance is available equal to 68 per cent of lost earnings, payable
for up to three years depending on the industry and region (Meisel,
1984). A more restricted scheme operated in Britain between 1979
and 1984. The Temporary Short-Time Working Compensation
Scheme (TSTWCS) initially provided employees placed on short-
time working with an allowance of 75 per cent of pay for up to 12
months, though this was later cut to 50 per cent for up to six months.
By March 1981, 984,000 workers in Britain were on short time.
Overall, three million workers were placed on short-time working
during the operation of the Scheme. Despite its limitations (its
temporary nature, its non-applicability to very small firms, its take-
up disproportionately by a narrow range of industrial sectors, and its
increasingly restricted compensation levels), Szyszczak (1990: 127)
describes the TSTWCS as 'one of the most important special employment measures for adult workers'. Despite this, no comparable
scheme has been introduced during the 1990–2 recession. In 1991,
an average of 60,000 workers in manufacturing (2.1 per cent of all

operatives) were on some form of short-time working, on average working 12 fewer hours per week.

The working year

Paid holiday entitlement has increased significantly over the past generation. At the end of the 1960s, average annual holiday entitlement for manual workers in Britain was two and a half weeks. Over the following decade and a half this average rose to read almost four and a half weeks (22 working days) by 1985. Analysis of 1989/90 agreements by the Labour Research Department (1990) reveals only limited further gains in the later 1980s. Among agreements covering over six million manual workers, 22 days remained the most common basic entitlement (excluding public holidays). This level principally reflects entitlement levels in the public sector, however: in the private sector, 20 days was the most common entitlement. Overall, three-quarters of manual workers received between 20 and 22 days' holiday, while one in five received 23 to 25 days and 4 per cent over 25 days. Among many non-manual workers, holiday entitlement is somewhat higher. While 60 per cent of non-manuals were entitled to between 20 and 22 days' holiday in 1989/90, almost one-quarter (24 per cent) had 23–5 days, and one in ten non-manuals enjoyed an annual entitlement of more than 25 days.

In addition to the basic level of paid holidays, many workers (for example, around one-third of manual workers) receive an additional service-related entitlement. Typically this service-related element is applied in a single or small number of stages. An example is that of holidays at Vauxhall Motors where the basic entitlement for manual workers is increased by one day after five years' service and a further day at 10, 15 and 20 years' service. Service-related entitlement also operates for many non-manual groups. Post Office counter staff, for example, have a basic holiday entitlement of 23 days which rises in five stages to 29 days after 30 years' service (Labour Research Department, 1990: 27).

Two factors suggest that following several years when holiday entitlement has changed only slightly, the coming period could be characterized by greater demands for longer paid holidays. First, elsewhere in Western Europe, basic holiday entitlement of five weeks is now common: for example Austria, Denmark, Finland, France, Luxemburg, Spain and Sweden have a legal minimum of five weeks' paid holiday (Blyton, 1989: 119). Further, in Germany, which in some respects has been acting as a lead country in developments in working time (see below), over two-thirds of employees now enjoy six weeks' or more annual paid holiday. Second, in the late 1970s and early 1980s, many employers channelled part of the demand for shorter hours into additional leave days, viewing the option of arranging cover to maintain plant operating times as preferable to the effect of shortening the working day. Faced with demands for reductions below 39 hours, it is possible that a common employer counter-offer will again be some extension to holiday entitlement. If so, this will be consistent with the preferences of many groups within the workforce. In a survey of employee preferences towards working time arrangements, Rathkey (1990: 71) found younger workers and females particularly supportive of taking time reductions in the form of longer holidays rather than a shorter working week or earlier retirement.

The working life

The overall duration of working time for individuals is influenced not only by the length of the working week and working year but also significantly by the length of their working lifetime. Various factors can affect this – age of entry into the labour market; periods of unemployment, education, illness, child-bearing and other causes of temporary withdrawal from the labour market; and age of exit from that market. In combination, these factors exert a considerable influence on levels of lifetime work hours. There is insufficient space to deal with all influences on the working lifetime here, but some significant recent developments in patterns of entry into and exit from the labour market may be noted. First, over the past generation there has been a persistent trend towards later entry. Aspects of this include the raising of the school-leaving age, the expansion of further and higher education places and the introduction of government training schemes. The overall trend appears set to continue, particularly in the light of the marked expansion of post-school education which is planned over the next decade. In 1990, 52 per cent of 16 year olds in Britain were in full-time education, as were 38 per cent of 17 year olds and 21 per cent of 18 year olds. These reflect a significant increase during the 1980s: in 1984, for example, the corresponding proportions of those in full-time education were 45 per cent, 31 per cent and 17 per cent for 16, 17 and 18 year olds respectively (*Labour Market Quarterly Report*, December 1992: 10–

11). Further, the proportion of 15–18 year old school leavers entering full-time further or higher education is increasing. From a level of 28 per cent in 1980/1, this proportion increased to 35 per cent in 1988/9 and is projected to rise further to 38 per cent by the year 2000/01 (ibid.: 12).

At the other end of the working lifetime, developments are less clearly defined. Overall, the gradual expansion of occupational pension schemes, most of which contain an early retirement provision (albeit at a reduced pension), has facilitated an increase in retirement prior to the age at which a state pension is payable. This trend towards earlier retirement was significantly reinforced in the early 1980s as organizations sought to use early retirement as a means of reducing their workforce size. White (1980) for example, found that almost one-third of manufacturing companies had utilized early retirement to reduce workforce totals: among those who were also reducing their workforces by other means, this proportion rose to more than 50 per cent.

This trend to earlier retirement is likely to continue. Three factors, however, may act to partially counter this trend. First, it appears that following the experience of the early 1980s, many organizations found early retirement to be a comparatively expensive method of reducing workforce totals, particularly where this involved employers making up pension contributions to normal retirement age. Second, following European Court rulings on sexual discrimination, women in Britain now have a clearer right to work until 65 years should they wish, rather than being required to retire from their jobs at 60. Attempts by individuals to seek an interpretation of the ruling so as to allow men to retire at 60 years in Britain rather than 65, have made little progress. Third, in North America, legislation to prevent mandatory retirement at 65 on grounds of age alone has been passed in both the United States and Canada (Blyton, 1988). Though this has not led to a large surge of people wanting to work beyond 65 years, it is conceivable that as life expectancy increases, and general levels of health among older workers improves, interest in working up to and beyond 65 years may increase. While changes to mandatory retirement provision are not imminent in Britain, there is generally an increasing awareness of age discrimination in employment (for example, in advertisements which specify particular age ranges for applicants) which in the future could extend to the issue of retirement age.

The Arrangement of Working Time

While the duration of working hours remains a major issue in the negotiation of the effort–reward bargain, in latter years management has given increased attention to the general arrangement of working time and the extent to which time represents a source of labour flexibility. As we will examine in this section and the next, in a number of key negotiations over the length of the working week during the past decade, the issue of duration has been extended to incorporate the scheduling of any reduced work time. The nature of these scheduling discussions has taken various forms ranging from new shift-work patterns to variable work weeks and annual hours contracts. Before examining recent changes, however, it is useful to review the current situation regarding the arrangement of working hours. Employers have at their disposal a variety of possible means to arrange working time to match operating needs. These include various systems of shift-working, overtime and the scheduling of part-time hours within the overall working period. Issues relating to the arrangement of working hours have gradually taken on an added significance as employers have sought to maintain or extend operating hours against a background of agreed reductions in individual working time. These issues are at least as prominent in service industries as in manufacturing, particularly where services involve direct contact with the public and where operating hours have been extended as a result, for example, of longer opening hours in the retail sector.

The issue of the duration of working hours in Britain has been subject to little statutory intervention, and this is also the situation as regards the arrangement of working hours. This situation may change in the future, however. In July 1990, the EC published a draft Directive on working time, which set out restrictions on maximum daily working hours (13 hours), the provision of rest days (an average of at least one day in seven) and, most contentiously, limitations on night-working (not more than an average of eight hours in any 24, calculated over a 14-day period). Thus, the draft Directive represents an attempt to give further protection to employees by restricting the scope of employers to compress work schedules and extend normal shift times, particularly at night. When published, the draft Directive drew opposition from both the Conservative government and various employer organizations in the UK – the Engineering Employers' Federation, for example, commented that restrictions on night-working could have 'disastrous consequences' for the engineering industry in Britain (quoted in the *Financial Times*, 14 September 1990).

Shiftwork

In a recent study of individual work patterns, 15 per cent of respondents were engaged on shift-work, with more males (18 per cent) working shifts than females (11 per cent) (Wareing, 1992). The industrial distribution of shift-work is, however, heavily weighted towards certain industries, notably extractive industries, manufacturing, and transport and communication. In a study of 170 manufacturing companies in the late 1980s, the Confederation of British Industry (CBI, 1989) found shift-working to be operating for at least some employees in more than four-fifths (81 per cent) of them. Within these companies, the average proportion of manual grades undertaking shift-work was almost half (49.5 per cent); in one-quarter of the companies, over four-fifths of the manual workforce were on shifts. While double day shifts were the most common single pattern, when the various possible systems involving night-work are considered together (that is, various three shift continuous and discontinuous patterns) over half of the manufacturing companies in the CBI sample operated with some degree of night-working.[4]

Notable among the developments in shift-working in recent years have been the growing use of part-time workers on 'twilight' shifts and moves to five crew working patterns. Twilight shifts, as their name implies, generally involve evening working, typically by part-time employees working, say from 6.00 p.m. until 10.00 p.m. In a recent study of employers' working time policies, Horrell and Rubery (1991) found twilight shifts operating in almost one-third (31 per cent) of their sample companies.[5] The move from four to five crew working in situations of continuous production is partly linked to the accommodation of agreed reductions in weekly hours without resort to higher levels of overtime working. In four crew systems, any 24-hour period is normally covered by three crews working eight-hour shifts, with one crew taking a rest day. When weekly hours fall significantly below 40, however, this necessitates major changes in the way shift rotas are drawn up. In one study of five crew working in the chemical industry, Rathkey (1990) describes how this change was linked not only to reductions in the working week, but also to other changes in the patterning of working time, notably a compression of individuals' working week by moving from eight-hour to 12-hour shifts, with each worker rostered for 142 shifts a year.

As the duration of weekly hours falls, increased interest in more compressed work weeks may be anticipated. Compressed work weeks involve working a weekly hours pattern in less than a 'normal' work week (currently five days). Various arguments for and against compression have been put forward, though relatively little detailed research has been conducted into such issues as the impact in different situations on performance, production scheduling, maintenance of adequate cover, levels of overtime, job satisfaction, and absenteeism. Compressed work weeks also raise wider issues such as the potential impact on levels of traffic congestion and the fulfilment of family responsibilities (for a more detailed review of arguments and evidence on compressed work weeks, see Blyton 1985: 139–42). At present, compressed work weeks remain uncommon. In the study by Wareing (1992) referred to above, just over 4 per cent of the full-time employment sample worked a compressed work week. The main compression was that to a four and a half day week (commonly involving a half-day on Fridays), with four day weeks as the second most common pattern. Compressed work weeks were found to be more common in larger workplaces and in manufacturing and construction, rather than services. Outside the UK, particular compressions appear to be somewhat more common, such as the nine day fortnight in Australia (Symons, 1978). Further reductions in weekly hours in Britain, coupled with employers' desire to maintain or extend operating hours without extra reliance on overtime working, are likely to raise the level of compressed week working, possibly leading eventually to the establishment of a new 'norm' for the working week of four and a half or four days. As we discuss below, the introduction of annual hours contracts has also been widely associated with compression of working hours.

In contrast to compression of the working week, the growth of part-time working has seen the introduction of work schedules in some sectors which involve relatively short working periods each working day. While many jobs in areas such as cleaning have traditionally followed this pattern, the past decade has witnessed a rise in part-time work scheduled to cover busy periods in other activities, most notably in retailing. Many part-time retail positions are now scheduled to cover the busiest shopping periods (e.g. lunch-times, weekends and late-night shopping times).

Flexible hours

Both employees and employers have long valued temporal flexibility
– the ability to vary work time beyond a standard work period.
Thompson (1967) perceives industrialization as an important part of
the process of instilling time-discipline into a workforce which previously had operated a highly variable working pattern, interspersing
bouts of intense labour with periods of leisure time, partly revolving
around fairs and festivals and adherence to the tradition of 'Saint'
Monday – taking Monday as a second rest day after Sunday (Reid,
1976). This pattern is seen partly to reflect a pre-industrial value
system more supportive of non-work time once a subsistence income
had been earned, rather than a more materialist orientation emphasizing the maximization of earnings (Pollard, 1963: 254). As Whipp
(1987) has pointed out, however, the industrialization process has
not been as successful in imposing as strict a managerial time-
discipline on all groups in the labour force as Thompson seems to
believe. Note, for example, the traditionally high levels of absenteeism in coal-mining, partly reflecting miners' preferences for extra
leisure time rather than additional earnings. More generally, the
work of industrial sociologists such as Roy (1960) have pointed
to the retention of workers' own time-reckoning systems, including various periods for work and non-work activities, despite
management attempts to impose a single 'rational' system of time-
reckoning.

One means by which some employers have sought to formalize
employees' desire for greater choice over the working period is
through the introduction of flexible working hours or 'flexitime'
arrangements. These offer employees a degree of choice over start
and finish times, provided that agreed 'core' periods are worked.
Typically, workers on flexitime can begin work within a band of two
hours or so in the morning, and leave sometime within a similar size
band in the evening, providing that over a given period an agreed
number of hours is worked. Other conditions pertaining to particular
flexitime arrangements, such as the ability to block-up credited
hours into additional free days and/or carry credit or debit hours
forward from one settlement period to another, can significantly
influence the degree of temporal flexibility available to employees on
flexitime.

Flexitime schemes were first developed in Germany in the late
1960s and spread to Britain and elsewhere during the 1970s. A

major stimulus appears to have been the strong labour market and employers' desire to attract and retain staff by offering more favourable terms of employment. Though much of the study of flexitime arrangements has lacked scientific rigour, the overall impression is that it is well received by employees and can convey certain advantages to employers (such as reductions in minor absences and greater self-supervision of time-keeping) though potentially at the cost of reduced cover at the beginning and end of the working day (Blyton, 1985: 125–36). By the end of the 1970s, one estimate indicated that approximately one employee in twelve (excluding managers and professionals) were covered by flexitime arrangements in Britain (McEwan Young, 1982). A survey conducted in 1990 shows comparable levels of flexitime working (Wareing, 1992). Just over 9 per cent of respondents in the 1990 survey reported that they worked flexitime: this was more common among women (10 per cent) than men (8 per cent), and more common among full-time workers (11 per cent) than part timers (4 per cent). In addition, flexitime remains far more prevalent among non-manual than manual workers, in larger than smaller workplaces, in services than manufacturing and in the public and recently privatized sectors than the traditional private sector. Most notably, the coverage of flexible working hours in the recently privatized sector was found to involve more than one-quarter (26 per cent) of the workforce (ibid.: 92–3).

Wareing's study distinguishes between formal and less formal flexitime systems by the ability of employees to take any extra worked hours as blocks of leave at the end of a given period. When less formalized systems are also taken into account, just over one-fifth of employees indicated that they had a degree of choice over starting and finishing times. Those in higher status positions had greater access to this flexibility: for example, half of the employees in professional occupations enjoyed flexibility over their start and finish times, compared to less than one in ten of those in semi-skilled occupations. Other studies (e.g. Horrell and Rubery, 1991; Marsh, 1991) have similarly pointed to the significance of informal arrangements between employees and employers for modifying start and finish times.

If the 1970s were characterized by a growth in interest in *employees'* working time flexibility, the 1980s and 1990s have witnessed the emphasis shifting to *employers'* desire to secure greater temporal flexibility. This, of course, is not a newly embarked-upon quest. Employers have long recognized the cost advantages of modifying the pattern of work hours to match the level of work demand – hence the long tradition in some industries of offering seasonal rather than permanent employment, and the use of casual labour hired by the hour or the day (characteristic of industries such as dock-working), a practice which continues in some cases today. Overtime, short-time working and temporary shifts are other long-established sources of flexibility which give employers scope to extend or contract operating hours.

Most of this flexibility in the past has been achieved via informal co-operation and voluntary compliance rather than contractual obligation, and it is evident that this pattern continues to prevail in contemporary work organizations. Marsh (1991), for example, found that for over two-fifths of respondents in her survey, the length of their working week changed over the year. Further, more than three in ten of full-time male employees and over one-quarter of full-time females, together with one-fifth of female part-timers, indicated that they had worked extra hours at short notice in the previous four weeks. These proportions are considerably higher than the 6 per cent who indicated that they were required by their contract to do overtime (ibid.: 23).

Yet over the past decade there have been several notable developments by employers seeking to extend their access to temporal flexibility through more formalized agreements. The sum impact of these developments has so far been no more than modest. However, such developments may well point to the sort of changes which could develop in coming years as employers' search for this flexibility intensifies and, in this light, they are worthy of closer consideration. Three examples – flexible rostering, annual hours and the flexibility issue in the engineering hours dispute – indicate the type of developments occurring and also the sort of factors which so far have restricted the impact and spread of these developments.

In the early 1980s, the issue of working time flexibility became focused on the question of 'flexible rostering' in the railway industry. British Rail management sought to link a pay rise and a reduction in weekly hours (to 39) to an agreement to abandon the eight-hour standard working day in favour of variable length shifts (between seven and nine hours). The object of this was to increase shift utilization by reducing the degree of mismatch between train running times and employees' eight-hour shifts – a mismatch which gave rise both to a large degree of unproductive time on some shifts and large amounts of overtime working on others. The issue led to

a two-week strike in 1982, after which flexible rostering was conceded by ASLEF, the train drivers' union. Since then, flexible
rostering, together with issues such as seven-day rostering and the
calculation of working hours over periods of up to ten weeks, have
continued to be significant issues in the railway industry, not least
because of the industry's continued over-reliance on overtime working. To date, however, the outcomes of flexible rostering appear to
have been at best partially successful. Ferner (1985: 59) concluded
from his analysis of the early implementation of flexible rostering
that direct savings had been 'extremely meagre'. A Monopolies and
Mergers Commission Report in 1987 (quoted in Ferner, 1988: 129)
found that the proportion of driving time on rostered shifts on the
Southern Region had risen only slightly (from 45 to 47.5 per cent)
between 1980 and 1986. Moreover, the high levels of overtime
working still prevalent among railway employees (see table 15.2
above) indicates the continued heavy reliance on overtime within the
industry. Difficulties encountered in working with flexible rostering
have included problems of arranging cover for variable rather than
standardized shifts (Pendleton, 1991). The abandoning of long-
established working practices – the guaranteed eight-hour day for
train drivers dated back to 1919 (Ferner, 1985: 55) – and the
introduction of new working practices likely to be much more disruptive to domestic routines, could be seen to call for high levels of
co-operation to gain acceptance for the new system and steer its
introduction through effectively. In the event, the introduction of
flexible rostering only after strike action was an inauspicious beginning for what many employees regard as a major upheaval in their
pattern of working.

Annual hours

Just as flexible rostering acted as the focus of attention for working
time flexibility in the early 1980s, by the mid-1980s, much discussion was taking place over the issue of 'annual hours' as an alternative contractual means of increasing temporal variability and
reducing reliance on overtime working during busy work periods
(Brewster and Connock, 1985; Lynch, 1985; Desmons and Vidal
Hall, 1987). Under this arrangement, employees are contracted to
work an agreed number of hours per year, with working time schedules (including holidays) determined at the beginning of 12-month
cycles. Annual hours contracts are typically one of two main types

(though in practice many contain mixtures of the two): (1) where variability of weekly hours is detailed in agreements such that work periods are longer at busy periods and shorter during slacker times; and (2) where the number of shifts rostered in the annual hours schedule is less than the agreed annual working time, with the difference comprising non-rostered work time, during which employees are effectively 'on-call' and can be brought in to work to cover unforeseen circumstances.

A principal managerial objective behind both of these versions of annual hours agreements is a reduced reliance on overtime working and an improved utilization of normal work hours. The first version of annual hours has been applied particularly in organizations subject to a seasonal pattern of demand – examples discussed in the management literature include companies involved in vegetable freezing, milk processing, toy manufacture, photoprocessing and white goods manufacture (Abbs, 1991; Incomes Data Services, 1991; Lynch, 1991; Pickard, 1991). The vegetable freezing company, Frigoscandia, for example, introduced an annual hours system to counter a working pattern which involved work weeks of as long as 84 hours in particularly busy weeks in the summer – much of this paid as overtime – and slack periods from October onwards when workflow was insufficient to make full use of employees' basic 37.5-hour work week. The annual hours system of 1832 hours, divided into 12-hour shifts (plus a number of 'stand-by' shifts) is used as a way of rostering employees more in line with production demands without management incurring high levels of overtime costs. The employees' loss of overtime pay and the imposition of fixed holidays was seen by the general manager as being offset by increased time off, a more predictable work pattern and more guaranteed earnings levels (Abbs, 1991).

The second version of annual hours agreements has been most prominent in continuous process industries such as cement manufacture and paper-making, though more recently annual hours arrangements have been introduced in different service industries such as finance, local authorities and television companies (Incomes Data Services, 1991; Pickard, 1991). In continuous process, annual hours have been seen not only as a way to reduce dependence on overtime to cover for absence and holidays, but also to increase management's ability to stabilize labour costs, and to introduce five or six crew working systems linked to agreed reductions in weekly hours. A recent example of an annual hours agreement in continuous processing is that introduced by Wiggins Teape in January 1992 at its paper mill in Cardiff. Driven by a desire to reduce overtime and accommodate an agreed reduction in working time, the system involves individual contract hours of 1740 per year (145 12-hour shifts based on a five crew shift system). Production hours are set at 1684, the difference representing 'reserve' hours which are used for training, cover for absence or housekeeping. In the shift rota which is issued annually, each crew has only two types of time: working time or rest time; all holidays (annual or statutory) are rostered into the rota and taken during shut and/or rest periods.

Despite the apparent advantages to managers of reducing their dependence on overtime, while maintaining a degree of temporal flexibility by agreed variations or via the reserve shifts arrangements, take-up of annual hours systems has so far been relatively low. Various surveys (ACAS, 1988; CBI, 1989; Marsh, 1991) have indicated around 3 per cent of organizations or employees working with annual hours contracts. A more recently published study (Wareing, 1992) suggests a somewhat larger take-up, with 6 per cent of people in employment reporting that their working time was based on a system of annual hours. This latest subsample was fairly evenly spread across different industries (both manufacturing and service) and likewise spread between those working shifts and those not. Nevertheless, even at 6 per cent of the workforce, the take-up of annual hours arrangements still remains modest. Several factors may account for this: the reluctance of employees (and possibly many employers) to forego access to overtime working; the desire among employees to maintain existing schedules since other arrangements such as childcare might not easily be changed to cope with being 'on call'; the difficulty of introducing annual hours arrangements, with 12-month schedules, in highly unpredictable work situations (Pickard, 1991, for example, details the difficulties this has given rise to in at least one television company); and existing levels of informal or voluntary flexibility which employers already have access to (see above) and which may be judged to be preferable to more formalized arrangements.

A more restricted version of annual hours contracts is the seasonal hours arrangements which have been introduced in a number of companies in the domestic appliance sector, particularly Japanese companies such as Toshiba, Hitachi and Panasonic. This represents a management response to a fluctuating pattern of demand, with sales concentrated predominantly in the months up to Christmas. At the Hitachi plant in South Wales, for example, this busy period was previously met by higher levels of overtime working and increased numbers of temporary workers. Since 1991, however, the standard (39 hour) working week has been modified to reflect the demand pattern. Employees now work a 42-hour week between August and December, and a 37-hour week at other times; pay, however remains standardized at the 39 hour rate throughout the year. Given the potential savings for management in terms of overtime payments and additional employment, it is possible that seasonal hours arrangements will spread in coming years to other sectors where demand shows a regular, predictable and significant fluctuation.

A third example in which employers discussed the need for greater temporal flexibility was in negotiations with the CSEU over the issue of a shorter working week in engineering. In the joint EEF/CSEU working party, the employers' position was that the costs of a reduction would need to be offset by greater flexibility and improved utilization of working time. Included in this was the proposal to allow weekly hours to vary (by up to one and a half hours above or below a 37.5-hour standard) in line with fluctuations in work demand. In seeking greater variability, the British engineering employers were following their German counterparts who had incrementally gained significant levels of temporal flexibility in the 1984, 1987 and 1990 negotiations on working time (Bosch, 1990; Blyton 1992b).

Conclusions

In the event, however, settlements by British engineering companies contained little or nothing on temporal flexibility. Employers have rather focused on offsetting reductions by increased utilization of the working period (see next section) or more general concessions on flexible work practices (Blyton, 1992a). Among the possible reasons for this are that the potential gains from added variability were seen to be more elusive than other concessions which could be secured, or that fluctuations in workload were neither sufficiently predictable or of a suitable magnitude to be pre-planned to fit the one and a half hour variation boundaries. In Germany, on the other hand, where the availability of training provision and simplified union structures, along with several other factors, have allowed employers to secure higher levels of task flexibility, the opportunity to gain increased flexibility via working time changes has been pursued more vigorously (Blyton, 1992b).

Thus in each of these examples – flexible rostering, annual hours and variable hours in engineering – the development of temporal flexibility remains limited. Several possible explanations for this have already been suggested. In addition, in those organizations with a high degree of stability and continuity in operating patterns, there may be little call for securing greater flexibility of working time. Further, given the degree of voluntary flexibility which other observers have identified, it seems reasonable to argue that in an industrial relations system which still places considerable reliance on voluntarism and informality, this method of dealing with working time variation is widely judged to be preferable to more formalized arrangements. Further, while overtime working remains virtually unrestricted by law or collective agreement in Britain, the continued access of employers to overtime (which, of course, depends largely on the continued willingness of employees to work overtime) may have the effect of inhibiting the development of other means to secure working time variability. Yet, while employers have shown only modest interest to date in new contractual ways of increasing the variability of working time, many have shown a keener interest in increasing the productive use of the time employees spend at work. It is to this that we now turn.

The Intensification of Working Time

While engineering employers in the 1989–91 dispute ultimately sidelined the issue of varying weekly hours, this was not the case in relation to seeking more productive use of working time. There are, of course, several factors which influence the extent of non-productive time. These include scheduling and production problems (e.g. employees waiting for work, materials, instructions and repairs to equipment), the taking of breaks, and conventions over the inclusion of changing and/or washing time etc. at the beginning and end of work periods (White, 1987). White (ibid.: 51) estimates that in engineering, the combination of these and other factors can lead to between 20 and 40 per cent of paid time being non-productive.

In recent years it is clear that many managements have taken various action to reduce this level of non-productive time, such as

through the harnessing of computers to create more efficient scheduling, and the adoption of particular techniques of operations management (materials resource planning, *Kanban* and just-in-time
techniques, for example) to improve the smoothness with which
work flows through the organization. Just as Japanese influence is
evident in some of these approaches to production, so too are
Japanese approaches to personnel management evident in developments in working time arrangements. Twenty years ago, for example, Dore (1973) pointed to the different conventions in Japanese
and British engineering factories regarding the beginning of shifts:
while Japanese workers were characterized as arriving at their
workstation prepared for work before the shift commenced and
leaving their workstation after the shift was completed, the British
working pattern included changing and washing time within the shift
period, thus reducing the productive work time at both the beginning and end of shifts. The notion of being ready for work before a
shift commences and leaving the workstation only after the shift time
has ended forms an important component of 'bell-to-bell' working
which emphasizes the productive work period running from the bell
or buzzer which signals the start of a shift to the one which termi-
nates it. Adherence to bell-to-bell working appears to be becoming
increasingly widespread in Britain. In analyses of 50 agreements
following the engineering dispute, for example, ten contained specific reference to the introduction of bell-to-bell working (*Industrial
Relations Review and Report*, 1990). A total of 13 of the agreements
made reference to cuts in, or elimination of, washing time, while 18
made reference to cuts in, or elimination of, breaks. Other changes
referenced in the agreements included the introduction of staggered
meal breaks to maintain production, and the timing of breaks to
minimize interruptions to production cycles. Examples of change
also include the taking of refreshment breaks at the workstation
rather than adjourning to a canteen, and the apparent gradual elimination of 'job and finish' arrangements whereby employees may end
their shift once specific tasks have been completed (see also
Richardson and Rubin, 1992). Much of this change reflects a
managerial aim to intensify the working period by reducing its
'porosity' (i.e. the amount of working time not actually engaged
in production).

This attempt to offset a cut in hours with reductions in breaks is
not unique. Indeed, in the previous hours-cut to 39 hours in the
engineering industry in 1981, reductions in breaks again formed a
significant element in management's response (White, 1982). The

fact that break times were back on the agenda a decade later may indicate that there has been a tendency for breaks to reappear, or their length to increase over time, as employees seek to modify the working time regime within the organization.

In the longer term, the opportunity to subvert 'managerial' time may decline as production systems become more tightly organized through improved scheduling and production planning. Not least, the introduction of just-in-time and other systems designed to reduce stocks and the amount of work-in-progress, potentially undermine employees' scope to build up 'banks' of work which in many situations have traditionally been used to 'buy' easier time towards the end of work periods or to allow an early finish. At the same time, past experience indicates that even under apparently much more formalized time-control systems, it would be wrong for management to assume that work groups are unable to find ways to modify 'rational' time-reckoning systems to make them more acceptable.

Further, in management's concern for increasing the productivity of working time through improvements in production planning and an intensifying of the working period, relatively little consideration appears to be being given to the possible consequences for levels of physical and mental fatigue and worker motivation. It is well established that over long periods of unrelieved work, individual performance tends to decline. In the past, this was one factor explaining why productivity levels did not decline as the average working day was reduced first from 10 to 9 and later to 8 hours (Blyton, 1985). With continued reductions in the working week, coupled with a reduction in the physical toil involved in many areas of work, the issue of working time and fatigue has tended to become less prominent. However, developments such as greater compression through 12-hour shift working (particularly where this entails night-working), coupled with fewer breaks – not to mention the greater physical and mental fatigue potentially associated both with modern (and generally faster) production technologies and the lower manning levels typically associated with those technologies – raise important concerns about levels of performance and fatigue associated with emerging work patterns. The implication is that, pursued too far, management's search for productivity gain via an intensification of the working period and maintenance of operating hours via compression of employees' work weeks, could in the event lead to work patterns characterized by higher levels of fatigue and reduced performance.

Conclusion

In the past, by far the predominant working hours issue between employers and employees has been the length of the working week. More recently, however, reductions in the duration of individual work time have contributed to bringing issues of the arrangement and utilization of working time to the fore. This has manifested itself particularly in increased attention to reducing non-productive time, and to the creation of work schedules which provide improved cover of operating hours and busiest periods of activity. There has also been considerable discussion of working time flexibility, though new developments in this area remain comparatively modest. Partly this may reflect an established reliance on overtime working as a source of flexibility. There are, however, a growing number of examples of companies substituting less costly forms of flexibility. It may be anticipated that arrangements such as seasonal and annual hours will become more common as employers seek to reduce their reliance on premium-rated overtime hours.

For employees, however, such developments may entail not only the loss of significant overtime earnings, but also a greater measure of fixity in their working time patterns: for example, a reduced choice on whether or not to work 'additional' hours (with hours formerly worked as overtime now built into normal work rosters) and increased restrictions on when holidays can be taken. These potential 'costs' to the employee seem to sum up the essence of several of the working time initiatives evidenced in recent years – a tendency to reflect employers' requirements from working time arrangements rather than those of employees. Trade unions too have played a part in this, for in their continued focus on durational rather than other aspects of working time, unions may be seen to have neglected important membership interests concerning the organization, and thus the overall experience, of working time.

With the benefit of hindsight, certain of the developments now taking place – notably the apparent increase in popularity of 12-hour shifts – may be seen as having been short-sighted. For while such arrangements may facilitate longer operating hours overall, they neglect half a century of evidence that long shifts are more likely to be associated with fatigue, higher accident rates and reduced performance. The future of the EC draft Directive on working time remains uncertain. Nevertheless, it is an important reminder not only of the right of individuals to experience a reasonable working time pattern, but also the longer term drawbacks for employers seeking to operate time schedules which take insufficient account of human preferences and capabilities.

Notes

1 In Britain, both 'basic' and 'normal' are used to denote weekly hours worked excluding any overtime. The term generally used to cover the combination of basic hours and overtime is 'actual' weekly hours.
2 Several parallels can be drawn between the 1989–91 hours dispute in British engineering and the earlier campaign in the German engineering industry which established an average 38.5-hour week in 1984/5. In the latter dispute, which led to the largest number of days lost in a dispute in West Germany's history, the engineering union IG Metall utilized a major publicity campaign, a national strike levy and carefully selected strike action to pursue its claim. These features are also present in the later UK dispute (see Blyton, 1992b for further discussion of these parallels and their implications).
3 This need for the CSEU to make separate agreements with individual engineering companies reflects the Engineering Employers' Federation's withdrawal from national bargaining which it announced during the unions' selective strike action (see Pickard, 1990).
4 The CBI survey also collected information from 107 service sector companies. However, while 57 per cent of these operated a system of shift-working for one or more occupational categories, the proportion of the workforce involved was normally small. This was particularly the case in respect of non-manual workers (for details, see CBI, 1989: 23–4).
5 Shift-work is not a precise term, and opinions differ as to whether patterns of work which involve employees working a fixed schedule without alteration after a fixed period of time should be classified as working shifts or not. Many twilight shift patterns represent this fixed working pattern. Alternatively, a commonly used definition of shift-work is 'a situation in which one worker replaces another on the same job within a 24-hour period' (Ingram and Sloane, 1984: 168).

Bibliography

Abbs, C. 1991. 'The Rewards of Annual Hours'. *Management Services*. November, 16–19.
ACAS. 1988. *Labour Flexibility in Britain: The 1987 ACAS Survey*. London:

Advisory, Conciliation and Arbitration Service.

Ahlstrand, B. W. 1990. *The Quest for Productivity: A Case Study of Fawley After Flanders*. Cambridge: Cambridge University Press.

Batstone, E. 1988. 'The Frontier of Control'. In Gallie, D. (ed.) *Employment in Britain*. Oxford: Blackwell, 218–47.

Bienefeld, M. A. 1972. *Working Hours in British Industry: An Economic History*. London: Weidenfeld & Nicolson.

Blyton, P. 1985. *Changes in Working Time: An International Review*. London: Croom Helm.

Blyton, P. 1988. 'The Mandatory Retirement Question in Canada: Older Workers, Jobs and Human Rights'. *British Journal of Canadian Studies*, 3, 1, 1–14.

Blyton, P. 1989. 'Time and Labour Relations'. In Blyton, P., Hassard, J., Hill, S. and Starkey, K. (eds) *Time, Work and Organization*. London: Routledge, 105–31.

Blyton, P. 1992a. 'Flexible Times? Recent Developments in Temporal Flexibility'. *Industrial Relations Journal*, 23, 26–36.

Blyton, P. 1992b. 'Learning from Each Other: The Shorter Working Week Campaigns in the German and UK Engineering Industries'. *Economic and Industrial Democracy*, 13, 417–30.

Bosch, G. 1986. 'The Dispute Over the Reduction of the Working Week in West Germany'. *Cambridge Journal of Economics*, 10, 271–90.

Bosch, G. 1990. 'From 40 to 35: Reduction and Flexibilisation of the Working Week in the Federal Republic of Germany'. *International Labour Review*, 129, 611–27.

Bosworth, D. L. and Dawkins, P. J. 1980. 'Shiftworking and Unsocial Hours'. *Industrial Relations Journal*, 11, 32–40.

Brewster, C. and Connock, S. 1985. *Industrial Relations: Cost Effective Strategies*. London: Hutchinson.

CBI. 1989. *Hours of Work in British Business: A CBI Survey*. London: Confederation of British Industry.

Daniel, W. W. and Millward, N. 1983. *Workplace Industrial Relations in Britain*. London: Heinemann.

Department of Employment. 1984. 'Recent Changes in Hours and Holiday Entitlements'. *Employment Gazette*, 92, 173–4.

Desmons, G. and Vidal Hall, T. 1987. *Annual Hours*. London: Industrial Society.

Dore, R. P. 1973. *British Factory, Japanese Factory*. London: Allen & Unwin.

Ferner, A. 1985. 'Political Constraints and Management Strategies: The Case of Working Practices in British Rail'. *British Journal of Industrial Relations*, 23, 47–70.

Ferner, A. 1988. *Governments, Managers and Industrial Relations: Public Enterprises and Their Political Environment*. Oxford: Blackwell.

Flanders, A. 1964. *The Fawley Productivity Agreements*. London: Faber &

Faber.

Hepple, B. A. 1988. 'United Kingdom'. In Blanpain, R. and Kohler, E. (eds) *Legal and Contractual Limitations to Working Time in the European Community Member States*. Deventer: Kluwer.

Hill, S. 1989. 'Time and Work: An Economic Analysis'. In Blyton, P., Hassard, J., Hill, S. and Starkey, K. *Time, Work and Organization*. London: Routledge, 57–78.

Horrell, S. and Rubery, J. 1991. *Employers' Working-Time Policies and Women's Employment*. London: HMSO.

Incomes Data Services. 1990. *European Report*. No. 345. September. London: IDS.

Incomes Data Services. 1991. *Annual Hours*. Study No. 486, London: IDS.

Incomes Data Services. 1993. *Report*. No. 634. February.

Industrial Relations Review and Report. 1990. *Report*. Nos 461, 464, 466. London: IRRR.

Ingram, A. H. and Sloane, P. J. 1984. 'The growth of shiftwork in the British food, drink and tobacco industries'. *Managerial and Decision Economics*, 5, 3, 168–76.

Labour Research Department. 1990. *Wage Rates, Hours and Holidays*. London: LRD.

Lynch, P. 1985. 'Annual Hours: An Idea Whose Time Has Come'. *Personnel Management*, November, 46–50.

McEwan Young, W. 1982. 'Flexitime for Production Workers in Britain and Germany'. In Nollen, S. D. (ed.) *New Work Schedules in Practice*. New York: Van Nostrand, 33–53.

McKinlay, A. and McNulty, D. 1991. 'Open Secrets and Hidden Agendas'. In Blyton, P. and Morris, J. (eds) *A Flexible Future? Prospects for Employment and Organization*. Berlin: De Gruyter, 295–310.

Marsh, C. 1991. *Hours of Work of Women and Men in Britain*. London: HMSO.

Meisel, H. 1984. 'The pioneers: STC in the Federal Republic of Germany'. In MaCoy, R. and Morand, M. (eds) *Short-Time Compensation: A Formula for Worksharing*. New York: Pergamon Press, 53–60.

Millward, N., Stevens, M., Smart, D., and Hawes, W. R. 1992. *Workplace Industrial Relations in Transition*. Aldershot: Dartmouth.

National Board for Prices and Incomes, 1970. *Hours of Work, Overtime and Shiftworking*. Report No. 161, Cmnd 4554. London: HMSO.

New Earnings Survey. 1992. *Part D: Analyses by Occupation* London: Department of Employment.

Nyland, C. 1989. *Reduced Worktime and the Management of Production*. Cambridge: Cambridge University Press.

Pendleton, A. 1991. 'The Barriers to Flexibility: Flexible Rostering on the Railways'. *Work, Employment and Society*, 5, 241–57.

Pickard, J. 1990. 'Engineering tools up for local bargaining'. *Personnel Management*, March, 40–3, 55.

Pickard, J. 1991. 'Annual Hours: A Year of Living Dangerously'. *Personnel Management*, August.

Pollard, S. 1963. 'Factory discipline and the industrial revolution'. *Economic History Review*, 16, 254–71.

Rathkey, P. 1990. *Time Innovations and the Deployment of Manpower*. Aldershot: Avebury.

Reid, D. 1976. 'The Decline of Saint Monday 1766–1876'. *Past and Present*, 71, 76–101.

Richardson, R. and Rubin, M. 1992. *The Shorter Working Week in Engineering: Surrender Without Sacrifice?* Working Paper No. 270, Centre for Economic Performance, London School of Economics.

Roy, D. F. 1960. 'Banana time: job satisfaction and informal interaction'. In Salaman, G. and Thompson, K. (eds) *People and Organizations*. London: Longman.

Symons, A. 1978. 'Varied working hours – here to stay?' *Work and People*, 4, 5–12.

Szyszczak, E. M. 1990. *Partial Unemployment: The Regulation of Short-Time Working in Britain*. London: Mansell.

Thompson, E. P. 1967. 'Time, Work-discipline and Industrial Capitalism'. *Past and Present*, 38, 56–97.

Wareing, A. 1992. 'Working arrangements and patterns of working hours in Britain'. *Employment Gazette*, March, 88–100.

Watson, G. 1992. 'Hours of work in Great Britain and Europe', *Employment Gazette*, November, 539–57.

Whipp, R. 1987. ' "A time to every purpose": an essay on time and work'. In Joyce, P. (ed.) *The Historical Meanings of Work*. Cambridge: Cambridge University Press, 210–36.

White, M. 1980. *Shorter Working Time*. Report No. 589. London: Policy Studies Institute.

White, M. 1982. *Shorter Working Hours Through National Agreements*. London: HMSO.

White, M. 1987. *Working Hours: Assessing the Potential for Reduction*. Geneva: International Labour Organization.

16

Change and Continuity in the Status Divide

Liz Price and Robert Price

Introduction

The 'deep foundations of conservatism' referred to in chapter 13, reinforced by powerful sentiments of 'fairness', have not only affected pay structures but have also been at the root of the profound differences in terms and conditions of employment that have traditionally separated manual from non-manual or 'white-collar' workers. Throughout the world, non-manual work has carried with it an assumption of higher status and better terms and conditions of employment, providing, in particular, long-term job security and stability. Britain has been no exception. Indeed, the status divide in Britain has proved to be more durable than in many other countries. While some sections of the white-collar labour force might not, for some periods, earn as much as some manual workers, their pay has been supplemented by better provisions for sick pay, longer holidays, a shorter working week and, often of greatest significance, a pension on retirement. Incremental pay scales, promotion prospects and a 'clean' working environment have also been traditional elements of non-manual employees' work experience which divided them from manual workers. Although there is evidence of some limited progress in recent years towards narrowing the status divide, this has been concentrated in large companies and in new, high-technology industries. Traditional attitudes, combined with Britain's changing industrial structure and certain government policies, have worked against the business and social arguments for closing the status divide.

This chapter begins by exploring the nature and extent of the status divide and goes on to discuss its origins and durability. Some of the important pressures towards narrowing the divide are then discussed and some examples are given of companies where harmonized conditions have been introduced. Finally, the forces which are working against single status arrangements in current circumstances are considered.

The Nature and Extent of the Status Divide

The status divide is concerned with the differences between manual and non-manual workers in the *basis* of their treatment in pay, fringe benefits and other conditions of employment (ACAS, 1982: 1). It is generally concerned with the comparison between manual and non-manual workers below the senior management levels.

Table 16.1 summarizes the results of a postal enquiry carried out at the end of the 1960s into the terms and conditions of employment of manual and non-manual employees in manufacturing industry. The results show very clearly the much less favourable conditions offered to manual workers at that time. They also point to the important divisions *within* the non-manual category, particularly between managerial grades and the other groups. Commenting on these results, Wedderburn and Craig (1974: 145) argue:

> There is overall a greater similarity of treatment between the grades in respect of the more purely economic aspects of the terms of employment, such as sick pay and pension schemes, than in aspects controlling working hours and behaviour such as holidays, attendance recording and certain disciplinary penalties.

This view was reinforced by the results of case studies undertaken to complement the postal enquiry, which revealed that 'manual workers were in every case more closely bound by discipline than were staff' (ibid.: 146). For manual workers, rules were found to be stricter, penalties more frequent and severe, disciplinary procedures more frequently involved, and less discretion was allowed to supervisors. Such differential treatment is symptomatic of the behavioural assumptions which underlie the status divide: manual workers are expected to be less reliable than their 'staff' counterparts because they are assumed to identify less strongly with the company or organization. They have to be placed under relatively stringent management controls because they cannot be relied on to behave in a manner that accords with the interests of the company.

Table 16.1 Terms and conditions of employment (percentage of establishments where the condition applies)

Selected conditions of employment	Operatives	Foremen	Clerical workers	Technicians	Management Middle	Management Senior
Formal sick pay scheme available	46	65	63	65	63	63
Sick pay provided for more than three months	49	58	55	57	65	67
Coverage by formal pension scheme	67	94	90	94	96	95
Pension calculated as fixed amount per year of service	48	18	16	14	13	12
Holidays, excluding public holidays, of 15 days or more a year	38	71	74	77	84	88
Choice of time at which holidays taken	35	54	76	76	84	88
Time off with pay for domestic reasons	29	84	84	86	92	93
Period of notice of dismissal in excess of statutory requirements	13	29	26	29	53	61
Clocking on to record attendance	92	33	24	29	2	4
Pay deduction as penalty for lateness	90	20	8	11	1	—
Warning followed by dismissal for frequent absence without leave	94	86	94	92	74	67

Source: Craig (1969)

Despite the greater similarity noted in the economic aspects of the terms of employment, the evidence presented by Wedderburn and Craig for 1968–70 showed clearly that manual workers had a longer working week and shorter holidays than non-manual workers. In 1970, 60 per cent of non-manual employees worked less than 38 hours per week, while 65 per cent of manual workers worked more than 40 hours. Only half as many manual as non-manual workers had over three weeks' holiday a year. Manual workers were also far more likely to suffer deductions from pay if they arrived late for work, and for taking time off in domestic emergencies. They also experienced greater irregularity of earnings associated with overtime, piece-rate payments and shift-working. Earnings data also showed that, while non-manual employees could typically expect increased earnings capacity over much of their working lives, manual workers' earnings tended to peak relatively early in their working life and then to level off and decline from age 40 onwards. The effect of incremental salary scales, merit increases and career progression for non-manual workers was to link non-manual pay more strongly to age, while the earnings capacity of manual workers was more closely linked to physical capacities. Very few manual workers were found to have the opportunity to cross the divide between manual and non-manual employment. A final area of economic inequality referred to by Wedderburn and Craig, and documented more fully in other contemporary research, was the insecurity caused by the much greater likelihood of redundancy for manual workers, and their greater job mobility, motivated at least in part by a desire to improve their earnings capacity (Parker et al., 1971).

The survey also showed that a majority of establishments had segregated canteen facilities, and that even where such facilities were nominally the same for all grades, 'in many firms it was customary for different occupational groups to use different facilities' (Wedderburn and Craig, 1974: 146). This type of segregation was also common in the provision of car-parking, toilet facilities and changing and rest facilities. Differential treatment in these symbolic areas of basic human functions is perhaps the clearest simple indication of the attitudinal assumptions underpinning the divide between manual and non-manual workers: it was widely considered as normal for manual workers to be treated as less worthy of humane and comfortable conditions.

How far has the situation altered in the past two decades? Progress has been patchy and variable, but survey evidence (ACAS, 1982;

ACAS, 1988; Industrial Relations Services, 1989a) indicates that there has been a clear trend towards a narrowing or elimination of differences in treatment – that is to say, towards 'harmonization'. Most progress has been made in the harmonization of various forms of leave arrangements (holidays, sick leave, 'special' leave), occupational pensions and certain fringe benefits, while less progress has been made towards harmonizing hours of work, payment systems and grading structures. Each of these areas is explored in more detail below, but it must be noted that the available survey evidence tends to be biased towards the shrinking manufacturing sector, and is not necessarily representative of the labour force as a whole.

Holiday entitlements have been one of the most important areas of harmonization, with very considerable changes taking place during the 1970s. By April 1981, 87 per cent of manual men and 90 per cent of non-manual men had a basic entitlement of 20 days or more (Department of Employment, 1981); a survey by the Policy Studies Institute in 1979 found that manual and non-manual entitlements were usually the same (Policy Studies Institute, 1980). The 1979 engineering industry agreement provided for a move to a 25-day minimum holiday entitlement for manual workers by 1982, and the evidence shows that this resulted in a common basic entitlement for all employees (*Industrial Relations Review and Report*, 1986). An Industrial Relations Services (IRS) survey of 83 companies in 1989 found that the majority (around 90 per cent) had harmonized their holiday entitlements. This survey also demonstrated that in the provision of special leave, such as bereavement leave, 'single status is all but universal' (Industrial Relations Services, 1989a: 10).

Occupational sick pay arrangements for manual workers have traditionally been less widespread and have tended to provide less favourable benefits (Labour Research Department, 1980). In its 1982 Report, ACAS showed that although the proportion of employees covered by occupational sick pay schemes had risen to nearly 88 per cent of all full-time employees by 1974, there were still differences in the coverage of manual and non-manual workers – 90 per cent of full-time non-manual men and women were covered, as opposed to 74 per cent full-time manual men and 55 per cent of full-time manual women. The progress that has been made towards harmonizing sickness schemes may be due to the stimulus which the introduction of statutory sick pay gave to companies to review their sickness arrangements. The ACAS survey of 1988 found that some 40 per cent of companies in the sample (of 584) had already harmonized sick pay provisions or were intending to do so. The IRS survey found a larger proportion in its sample (70 per cent) where sick pay and leave had been harmonized.

On *pensions*, less than half of manual employees were covered by an occupational scheme in the early 1980s, while nearly two-thirds of non-manual employees were so covered. It was still normal for the two groups to be covered by separate schemes within individual firms and for the entitlements to be better for non-manual staff (National Association of Pensions Funds, 1981). Nevertheless, nearly one-third of firms in the 1988 ACAS sample had harmonized pensions within the previous three years and another 13 per cent were planning to harmonize them (ACAS, 1988: 26). The IRS survey of 1989 again produced higher figures for the movement towards harmonization, with eight out of ten companies saying that their occupational pension schemes had been harmonized.

There appears to have been a strong movement towards harmonizing *fringe benefits* (see chapter 13), particularly in larger and more successful companies. The 1988 ACAS survey found that nearly half of its sample already provided or were planning to provide common canteen/restaurant facilities: one year later 90 per cent of the IRS sample said common facilities were already provided. One motivation for change in this area may be the squeeze on company overheads and consequent pressure to provide cheaper, more efficient catering services – whether the service is contracted out or run in-house, one standardized service will be cheaper to run than several outlets. Other fringe benefits commonly found to be harmonized in the IRS survey were product discounts, car parking and loans.

Another area where differences are beginning to break down is in the *method of recording attendance*. Traditionally, manual workers have been expected to 'clock on' whereas white-collar workers were trusted to arrive and leave work without mechanical 'policing'. The ACAS survey found that only 14 per cent of companies had abolished clocking or were planning to do so. However, the IRS survey found that 50 per cent of its sample had harmonized methods of recording attendance and a further 8 per cent planned to do so. Many of these companies introduced common systems of mechanical or computerized time-keeping for all employees, with the introduction of flexitime arrangements requiring the extension of clocking systems to non-manual employees.

There has been some limited narrowing of differences in the length of the basic *working week*, as discussed in chapter 15, but this is one area where progress has slowed. Reductions in the length of the basic working week occurred across the board from mid-1979 to 1983, but have subsequently tended to remain stable. These reductions still leave a gap at the aggregate level between manual and non-manual hours. Table 16.2 shows the extent of the hours gap in 1991. Over half of non-manual males still work 37 or less hours each week (as against 13 per cent of manual males), and 69 per cent of manual males work over 38 hours each week (as against 25 per cent of non-manual males). A further significant difference is in the greater incidence of overtime working for manual workers. Although Table 16.2 shows that male manual overtime significantly reduced between 1990 and 1991 as the recession deepened, it still represented 11.9 per cent of all work, compared with 3.6 per cent for non-manual males.

The areas which appear to be most resistant to harmonization, *payment systems* and *grading structures*, lie at the very heart of the reward package. Non-manual employees still benefit very widely from pay increases through incremental progression and promotion as well as from general annual reviews, while manual workers' pay increases are still largely limited to the annual pay round. Very few organizations (around 5 per cent) in the ACAS study had introduced integrated payment systems or integrated job evaluation schemes, though around 10 per cent declared that they planned to do so in the future (1988: 24). Similarly, only one-third of the IRS sample had harmonized payment systems and grading structures. One aspect of pay which companies are moving to harmonize is the mechanics of payment through the introduction of cashless pay. Nearly 70 per cent of the IRS sample had already introduced, or planned to introduce, a single method of cashless pay.

A final area worth mentioning is the different impact of reductions in demand for a product or service on manual and non-manual staff. *Short-time working* and *lay-offs* at reduced pay almost exclusively affect manual workers and, in respect of *redundancy*, a Labour Research Department survey in 1981 showed that non-manual workers were far more likely to be paid above the statutory minimum entitlement than manual workers. In 175 agreements studied, manual workers were often entitled to less notice, less favourable compensation, less income protection if alternative work was offered, and less favourable minor enhancements (Labour Research Department, 1981).

This review of recent survey data suggests that there has been a movement towards single status since the late 1960s. However, the evidence needs to be treated with caution. The IRS survey in par-

Table 16.2 Hours of work

Average hours for full-time adults – April 1991

	Manual workers		Non-manual workers	
	Male	*Female*	*Male*	*Female*
Average total weekly hours	44.4	39.7	38.7	36.8
Change since April 1990 (hours)	−1.0	−0.3	−0.2	−0.1
Average weekly overtime hours	5.3	1.6	1.4	0.6
Change since April 1990 (hours)	−0.9	−0.3	−0.2	−0.1

Normal basic hours in April 1991: percentage distribution for full-time adults

Percentage with normal basic hours in the range	Manual workers		Non-manual workers	
	Male	*Female*	*Male*	*Female*
below 30 hours	—	—	2.7	4.4
30–34	0.6	6.6	1.9	6.0
34–36	3.2	9.5	21.8	29.7
36–37	9.2	6.8	27.1	24.1
37–38	17.8	18.4	21.4	23.4
38–39	40.8	38.9	9.4	6.5
39–40	21.5	16.8	10.6	4.7
40–44	3.5	3.0	2.7	1.2
over 44	3.6		2.4	

Sources: Employment Gazette, November 1991 (table 1, p. 604); New Earnings Survey, 1991, tables 149 and 150

ticular reflects the position in companies which have something positive to say about progress towards harmonization; it presents a picture of practice at the 'leading edge' and cannot be taken as representative of all industry. Furthermore, there is little available survey evidence which explores the progression towards single status in private service sector industries, particularly in the small companies which dominate industries such as hotel and catering, distribution, construction and miscellaneous services. This is a serious omission as it is clear from both the 1988 ACAS survey and the

IDS survey that organizations which have made the most progress towards single status employ 500 or more people.

Nevertheless the evidence presented above, together with case study evidence from a range of industries and firms (some of which will be discussed later), does indicate that there have been substantial developments towards single status in some companies. It also shows how durable the status divide is proving to be in the economically important areas of payment systems and grading structures. Harmonization has received little attention in the personnel management literature in recent years, suggesting that in the struggle for survival in a severe economic recession, many companies have pushed status issues on to a back burner. One notable exception to this is the Rover car company where the introduction of single status was seen as an integral part of a strategy for survival (*Personnel Management Plus*, 1992, Vol. 3, No. 4: 5).

The Origins of the Status Divide

Before proceeding to look at the pressures for and against change, it will be helpful to reflect briefly on the origins of the distinction, and the operational and attitudinal assumptions which lie behind it. The emergence of 'non-productive' labour to assist employers with the book-keeping, design, merchandizing and supervisory functions of the growing industrial sector during the nineteenth century has been reviewed by many writers (Lockwood, 1958; Braverman, 1974). The growth in scale of the typical industrial enterprise made it impossible for the single entrepreneur to carry out all the functions associated with the control and management of the enterprise. The devolution of some or all of these functions to employees brought into being complex bureaucratic hierarchies, modelled frequently, as in the Weberian ideal type, on military structures.

Two characteristic features of industrial and commercial bureaucracies as they emerged in the early periods of industrialization should be noted. First, the hierarchy of control, through which posts at successive levels were held responsible for the activities of the employees below them, was associated with non-manual status. These employees were the NCOs and junior officers of capital, and were expected to commit themselves to the success of the enterprise as defined by the owner-proprietor. Their privileged status was a natural consequence of their association with the control functions of the enterprise. Second, the creation of a number of tiers of bureaucracy was associated with the notion of 'career', through which loyal and competent performance at a lower level would be rewarded by preferment to the higher levels of the organization. A prerequisite of promotion would inevitably be the demonstration of an appropriate degree of commitment to the goals of the organization as defined by the principal power-holders – either the owner or the senior executive managers.

Non-manual staff have thus traditionally been expected to be motivated by something more than short-term economic rewards; commitment and loyalty to the organization, whether public or private, were expected to be equally if not more important. Non-manual employees could be expected to exercise discretion and decision-making responsibilities in their work in ways which would be in accordance with the organization's objectives. The importance of that discretion being exercised in the interests of the enterprise was clearly greater at the higher levels of the hierarchy, and hence greater proximity to the functions of the employer brought with it higher social status and greater privileges in conditions of employment.

In the public sector bureaucracies such as the civil service and local government, parallel distinctions emerged, although the greater proportionate size of the non-manual workforce, the absence of a 'production' environment, and the strong influence of the public service ethos tended to stimulate a rather closer relationship between the conditions of employment of the two groups of workers. For example, manual worker pensions, sick pay arrangements and holidays have traditionally been relatively generous in the public sector.

While the origins and the nature of the employment differentiation between manual and non-manual workers have been very similar in all industrial societies, the law has played a varying role in reinforcing the distinction. In Britain, the law's role has been very limited. As Bain and Price (1972) have shown, while the distinction between manual and non-manual workers was held to be significant in the provision of social insurance benefits and in the application of the Truck Acts (which prohibited payment in kind) in the early part of the century, legal distinctions ceased to have very much relevance during the inter-war period. In the countries of northern and central Europe, however, tight legal boundaries were drawn around white-collar work, and a privileged social and legal status conferred on these employees. The German categories of *Angestellte* (private sector white-collar employees) and *Beamte* (public sector employees) can be found in similar forms in many countries in Scandinavia and the old Austrian Empire. In a slightly different form they also appear in the southern European countries – France, Italy, Spain and Portugal, for instance. Special social insurance, taxation and legal regimes covering terms and conditions of employment were established for these groups of employees and, as a broad generalization, they can be said to have displayed a closer identification with their employers, and a stronger sense of distance from manual workers, than was the case in Britain (Lockwood, 1958; Bain and Price, 1972; Speier, 1934). The legal entrenchment of these status differences has been of declining significance in the past 40 years and it is something of an irony that, while many European countries continue to have separate white-collar and manual worker union confederations, and separate seats on works councils and company boards for the two groups, the overall extent of the status divide has probably declined faster there than in Britain.

Despite these profound differences of status and treatment between non-manual and manual workforces, it should not be assumed that the non-manual group has been internally homogeneous and undifferentiated, even in an era when it was much smaller than it is today. In particular, a deep schism between male and female clerical workers emerged at a very early point. When women workers began to be taken on in large numbers in clerical and related functions, they were frequently employed on lower pay and with inferior conditions to their male counterparts. There was fierce opposition to the employment of women from male clerical workers precisely because it was seen as a way of undercutting male pay rates and reducing male job opportunities. As Walby (1986: 154) shows, employers often responded to these fears by segregating female clerks in special grades with lower wages, fewer promotion opportunities, less job security and lower status. More generally, the rapid growth of the clerical labour force in the early decades of the century resulted in a decline in the promotion prospects available to the average clerk, creating a greater sense of distance between many clerks and their managerial superiors (Lockwood, 1958). As the non-manual labour-force expanded further after the Second World War, its internal heterogeneity was increasingly marked. With the growth of higher education and the associated development of 'credentialism' in determining access to many upper-level non-manual jobs, notions of an internal community of interest and accessible ladders of promotion were steadily undermined.

It is a tribute to the power of custom and tradition that distinctions rooted in the later part of the nineteenth century between 'white-collar' (itself a term redolent of the nineteenth-century counting house) and manual jobs, which derive essentially from the proximity of the former groups to the employer and which rest on an assumed close identification of interest between them and their employer, should have persisted into the last decade of the twentieth century. For some considerable time, the majority of white-collar workers have been female (not typically wearers of collars) and, whether male or female, most of them work in environments which do very little either to reflect or encourage a close identification with employers' interests – any more, that is, than might be found among their manual counterparts.

The Durability of the Status Divide

So why has the status divide proved to be so durable? Alan Fox in his influential contribution to the sociology of work has argued that the typical relationship between employers and workers in Britain has involved a 'low-trust' and 'contractualized' set of mutual expectations (1985: 92). As far as manual workers are concerned, British employers have typically sought to elicit acceptable levels of performance by what can loosely be described as 'Taylorist' methods of work organization: pay linked to output through piecework systems to provide a direct economic incentive for productivity, close supervision, and the use of disciplinary procedures to enforce sanctions. With a relatively small group of well-known firms as exceptions, little weight has traditionally been attached to the development of a 'moral' involvement by employees with the enterprise. Senior managements have been distant and uninvolved with the shop-floor, and employment conditions have been standardized and depersonalized. In Fox's words (1985: 49–50):

> The . . . low-discretion work circumstances of most wage and lower salary earners cause them to feel excluded from more significant and responsible participation and therefore not really trusted. Their inferior rewards . . . confirm their sense of being low-status 'hands' who are not seen as full members of the higher corporate effort. The old terminology of 'hands' and 'staff' embodied this crucial distinction.

Fox here includes lower level non-manual employees within the area of low discretion work, implying that the historical conditions of manual employment have at some point also begun to apply equally to the lower levels of the white-collar hierarchy. This underlines vividly the ambiguity of the position of these groups. While they continued to enjoy generally better conditions of employment than manual workers, they were increasingly subjected to similar types of routinized and closely supervised work organization, with tight limits placed on the amount of personal discretion either expected or permitted. This relationship does not square with the attitudinal assumptions that were argued earlier to underpin the status divide. The rapid expansion of the non-manual labour force to the point where it is now larger than the manual workforce – 52 per cent against 48 per cent at the 1981 Census (Price and Bain, 1983) – bringing with it a massively increased internal heterogeneity and a sharp increase in the proportion of non-manual workers occupying routine jobs without significant career prospects, inevitably calls into question the continued relevance of sharp differentiation between manual and white-collar workers. However, while the assumptions built into the original distinction have been of questionable relevance for large sections of the non-manual labour force for many decades, there has been little movement to bring together the terms and conditions of employment of the two groups until relatively recently.

The durability of the divide can be accounted for in a variety of ways, but the central element in any explanation must be the value to employers of a structure of control for some groups of employees based on a 'higher-trust' relationship, underpinned by a relatively privileged status within the enterprise. For non-production employees, few of whose contributions to the operation of the enterprise can be easily measured in profit-and-loss terms, and many of whom are still relatively closely related to senior management functions, a strategy of control based on what Friedman (1977: 78–9) has called 'responsible autonomy' can clearly be both effective and rational. By binding non-manual workers closer to the enterprise through privileged conditions, career perspectives (even if somewhat limited), and a degree of autonomy within the workplace, employers can expect to achieve a degree of both legitimacy and commitment.

The durability of the status divide can also be linked to the self-identification of non-manual employees as a distinctive group, as reflected in the structure of collective representation. With a few exceptions, such as the tally clerks in the London docks, non-manual workers in the early years of trade unions established separate organizations from those representing manual workers in the same industry (Lockwood, 1958). Since the early 1970s some of the large general unions have been successful in developing or expanding 'white-collar' sections, but it remains the case that over 90 per cent of unionized white-collar employees are within non-manual organizations. As an early post-war American commentator summed it up:

> The white-collar worker wants to and manages to maintain his [sic] separate identity. This is a persisting situation; and union leaders will have to recognize it as such. (Strauss, 1954: 81)

The majority of non-manual workers have, of course, not joined unions at all. At the three high points in British union membership, in 1920, 1948 and 1979, non-manual density reached 29, 33 and 44 per cent respectively. As Bain (1970) has indicated, employers were generally reluctant to recognize unions for non-manual workers up to the time when he was writing. A relatively brief period ensued in the 1970s when white-collar union bargaining was more readily accepted by employers, but the recession and social and political conditions of the 1980s and early 1990s have stimulated a return to the more negative approach of the earlier decades. The 1990 Workplace Industrial Relations Survey found that 23 per cent of private manufacturing establishments recognized unions for non-manual employees, as against 44 per cent recognizing manual unions; and in the private services, the proportions were 26 per cent against 31 per cent (Millward et al., 1992: 71).

Employers' traditional reluctance to embrace collective representation on behalf of non-manual employees is closely associated with the beliefs that have sustained the manual/non-manual divide. Non-manual staff were expected to be committed to the organization and to identify with its owners and managers. Since they were considered to form part of the managerial function of the organization, it was inappropriate for them to combine against that function. In many instances, as Bain (1970) documents, employers have gone out of their way to reinforce the notional 'high-trust' relationship by making special concessions in the face of a potential threat of unionization by non-manual staff.

The establishment of separate unions or staff associations catering for white-collar workers has served to entrench further the divisions between the two groups over the long term. Where unions have bargained successfully on behalf of non-manual staff, they have fought to preserve a degree of separate identity and special status. The preservation of relative privilege over manual workers in the shape of pensions or sick pay, or a more relaxed regime for time-keeping, have been an important part of their *raison d'être*. Many white-collar workers have joined unions mainly in reaction to declining pay or status differentials, and in the hope that collective representation would halt or reverse that decline (Hyman and Price, 1983: 175–7). On the other hand, employers' desire to keep unions for non-manual staff out of their organizations has encouraged them to strengthen the status divide in order to 'buy' loyalty.

While the durability of the status divide as an important factor in the consciousness of employers and employees alike cannot be doubted, it is clear that the cumulative effect of a number of different processes that have taken place over the past two decades in particular has been to reduce substantially the utility and acceptability of the distinction between white-collar and blue-collar, and staff or works groups.

On the one hand, lower level clerical, secretarial, sales and technical functions have become increasingly routinized and often machine dominated; entry requirements have been low; and labour supply has generally been good since the basic education system has provided most of the necessary training. Such routinization of non-manual work has tended to be associated with reduced career prospects: indeed, routinization has gone hand-in-hand with feminization, in such a way that employers have been able to rely on an implicit secondary labour market role for women to reduce potential pressure for careers from a very large section of the non-manual labour force. Meanwhile, the higher levels of non-manual employment have expanded dramatically in scale and complexity. In practice, entry to these positions is very often through the possession of graduate or professional qualifications and they are thus not open, even in theory, to employees on the lowest rungs of the ladder. In the final decade of the twentieth century, the traditional use of the non-manual label to describe a relatively small and homogeneous group, united in its close relationship to the seat of managerial or employer power, is dead. While some elements of the non-manual labour-force still do retain the traditional closeness to the locus of authority within the enterprise, the majority do not, and it is hardly surprising that this has led to a questioning of the relevance of traditional divisions and privileges.

On the other hand, new forms of work have emerged at the margins of the manual labour force that serve to blur even further the traditional distinctions. In many traditional 'craft' areas, the application of microelectronic technologies has produced a range of jobs that are manual in their day-to-day physical requirements, but demand non-manual levels of technical training and expertise. The day of the 'craftician' has dawned in some industries, and, more generally, craft functions are becoming closely aligned with technical functions. Even jobs that require relatively little technical training are being transformed by microprocessor applications into semi-technical, 'white-coat', process control jobs (Boddy and Buchanan, 1986). The transition in printing from Linotype machines to visual display units and computer-controlled printing, and in retail distribution from shop assistants to checkout staff using electronic point of sale systems, graphically illustrate the blurring of old divisions.

It is important, however, to keep these changes in perspective. Despite its reduced share of the labour force, manual work still consists overwhelmingly of jobs in cleaning, assembling, building, driving, processing and providing food and drink. Their manual content is as high as it has ever been, and the occupants of these jobs face the same limitations on personal discretion and on career progression that their predecessors did. Similarly, there is still a considerable group of professional and managerial jobs for which the traditional notions of status and privileged relationships with the employer continue to be relevant. Nevertheless there are a number of powerful pressures outside the occupational changes discussed above which are working in favour of reducing the status divide, particularly between the manual and 'intermediate' white-collar strata. There are also a number of significant forces that are holding back progress. These are examined in more detail below.

Pressures for Change

New technologies

The widespread emergence of microprocessor-based technologies at the end of the 1970s led many employers to seek to modify traditional 'low-trust' relationships with manual workers, and to achieve with them a relationship of integration and commitment very similar to that historically associated with non-manual employees. Major changes to products and production systems were set in motion by the application of the microchip (Gill, 1985; Francis, 1986). This radical restructuring of the labour process, coinciding with a further 'oil shock' and a world recession, stimulated employers to reduce the size of their labour forces and to drive up the productivity of those remaining. Status differentials and job demarcations were increasingly viewed as obstacles to the efficient utilization of labour and the capacity of an enterprise to react flexibly to product market and technological changes. Harmonization has frequently been introduced as part of a package of measures to improve working practices and change payment systems, in order to derive optimal utilization of new capital equipment. New technologies, with an attendant emphasis on employees' willingness to show flexibility, discretion and initiative in the interests of the enterprise, have frequently led employers to seek ways of winning workers' wholehearted commitment to the objectives of the enterprise.

Japanization

The steady growth in the penetration of European markets by manufactured goods from Japan and other nations in the Far East, and the more recent arrival in Britain of a number of major Japanese manufacturers such as Nissan, Toshiba, Hitachi, Komatsu and Isuzu have stimulated enormous – some would say obsessive – interest from British employers in Japanese personnel practice and production systems (Ackroyd et al., 1988). The apparent success of these companies in avoiding industrial relations conflict and achieving high levels of worker commitment to quality and consistency of output has had a major impact on British companies' thinking. The influential book by Pascale and Athos (1981) on the 'art' of Japanese management has been followed by a series of well-publicized success stories in the restructuring of traditional industrial relations systems (e.g. Pegge, 1986; Trevor, 1988; Wickens, 1987).

While there is no comprehensive evidence on the degree to which specifically Japanese practices have been adopted by British companies, there is no doubt that the Japanese example has reinforced some of the most important themes already affecting domestic management thinking. The single-union 'no-strike' deals at firms like Nissan, Toshiba and Hitachi have received wide media attention, but in practice the more influential changes have probably been those abolishing status distinctions such as separate canteens, car parks, and different types of clothing, and the introduction of quality circles and other group-based methods of involving workers in the quality of production. In its 1981 document, *The Will to Win*, the CBI was already contrasting the perceived unity of purpose of the typical Japanese enterprise with the 'unnecessarily divisive' distinctions typical of British companies which could not be 'functionally justified'. 'British industry still suffers from too many social divisions, ranging from canteen facilities to pension provision, which bear no relation to work done.'

The central impact of Japanese practice has been to underline the apparent links between greater status equality, labour flexibility and a sense of personal commitment to the quality of the finished product. The continuing influence of Japan reinforces the declining acceptability of the status divide.

Single table bargaining

There is evidence (Marginson and Sisson, 1990; Industrial Relations Services, 1990) that small but increasing numbers of companies are embracing 'single table bargaining' in which all recognized unions bargain jointly with management. Marginson and Sisson argue that one of the main reasons for introducing this form of bargaining is a management commitment to harmonized conditions. This may come from a strong management philosophy about equality of treatment or it may form part of a wider programme of change in which single status is used as a quid pro quo for more flexible working practices.

Many of the arguments in favour of single table bargaining are similar to those used to support single status: reducing a source of conflict between groups of workers/unions, removing old occupational demarcations, providing unified salary/grading structures which may reduce the potential threat of equal value claims, and saving management time by avoiding duplication of effort and streamlining administrative arrangements. Strong arguments can also be deployed against single table bargaining and harmonization: for example, employers may see continuing advantage in 'divide and rule' or may wish to preserve their ability to reward particular groups in a focused way, perhaps in response to changes in the labour market. For their part, trade unions may find it difficult to set aside old differences, especially where there has been a history of inter-union rivalry. Nevertheless, the research described by Marginson and Sisson, which is generally supportive of single table bargaining, was commissioned by the TUC's Special Review Body, and the IRS survey of 1990 found evidence of trade unions taking the initiative in seeking single table bargaining. The trend towards trade union amalgamations, such as the formation of UNISON and the Amalgamated Engineering and Electrical Union, is likely to stimulate the development of single table bargaining and single status throughout public and private sectors.

Human resource management

The debate about the precise meaning of human resource management (HRM) and the extent to which HRM approaches have been adopted in practice have been discussed in earlier chapters. There is little dispute, however, that a distinctive feature of the HRM model is the integration of corporate strategy and personnel policies reinforced by a strong company culture, and that the model has exercised a pervasive influence on contemporary British personnel management. HRM stresses the need for a harmonious and mutually supportive system of human relations integrating all employees. In Fowler's view (1987: 3) this amounts to a 'dominant emphasis on the common interests of the employer and the employee in the success of the business . . . [to] release a massive potential of initiative and commitment within the workforce'. Such a framework of policy points strongly towards the elimination of status divisions to give weight to the philosophy of common interests and commitment. In this way, too, contemporary management thinking is seeking to establish a new legitimacy through unitary or integrative personnel strategies based on the extension of 'non-manual' conditions to 'manual' employees.

It would be a mistake, however, to see this as a return to the simple 'unitary' notions of traditional managements as described by Fox (1966; 1985). The traditional unitary approach is closely analogous to the authority structures of the military, in which commands flow from the top down and subordinates are required to show obedience to those set in authority. In sharp contrast, the message of human resource management is to establish looser, more flexible structures, which give wide scope for individual initiative. Traditional status divisions clearly do not fit easily with this style of management.

While the evidence indicates that the full HRM model has not been widely embraced in British industry (Storey and Sisson, 1990; Storey, 1992), many companies are operating a dual system of employee relations in which an ongoing commitment to pluralism and all that is associated with it runs hand-in-hand with 'extensive engagement with large parts of the HRM recipe'. One part of the HRM recipe that is conspicuously lacking is the adoption of full harmonization. Storey's research shows harmonization, described as one of the key HRM 'levers', as having the lowest take-up of all the HRM features explored. Piecemeal adaptation to HRM has apparently been accompanied by only a partial movement towards single status in many British firms.

Flexibility

'Flexibility' is an important theme running through the sets of influences on management identified above. The introduction of new technologies and the associated changes in work organization, together with the need to cut labour costs in the face of international competitive pressures, have put a premium on securing maximum value from the labour force. This has led to a greater use of part-time and temporary workers, and to more subcontracting (ACAS, 1988; National Economic Development Office/Institute of Manpower Studies, 1986). For the 'core' workforce of full-time employees, the search for flexibility has led to reduced demarcation between jobs, and increased use of individual merit payments and performance-related pay.

In the 1988 ACAS survey, between 45 and 51 per cent of firms had either relaxed demarcations to enable production workers to do routine maintenance tasks and to enable craftsmen to do work usually performed by other craftsmen, or had ended divisions between manual, technical and clerical staff (ACAS, 1988: 15). This type of functional flexibility between members of the full-time workforce, while increasing the use of part-time and temporary staff to achieve more numerical flexibility, has been a common approach in manufacturing and service sectors alike. It adds further weight to the case for dismantling the status divide in order to achieve maximum functional flexibility with the core workforce but it also underlines the trend towards the development of a new status divide between employment conditions in the core and periphery.

Europe

The move towards single status in other European countries has been more rapid than in Britain. Two features of European industrial relations help to explain the differences. One is the role of the state in employment affairs. Whereas in Britain the debate about state involvement has been over the most basic elements of employment protection, in many European countries, notably France and Germany, there has been considerable pressure from governments to introduce and develop single status arrangements. In France and Sweden there has been legislation to underpin the principle of single status, and, in Germany, the state has consistently sought to harmonize key employment conditions, such as pay systems, holiday and sick pay entitlement. The second feature is the structure of collective bargaining. In France, Italy and West Germany, the structure of national and multi-employer bargaining has provided an effective forum in which the broad principles informing comparative conditions of employment could be examined. In France, in particular, negotiations involving the equivalent of the Confederation of British Industry and the various union confederations have provided a framework for the introduction of single status arrangements covering entire industries or sectors.

Britain's membership of the European Community has already had a significant impact on basic employment rights in the UK and the influence of European employment practices is likely to grow over the next decade. As the EC integrates further under the umbrella of the Social Charter, moves towards a harmonization of basic terms and conditions across Europe can be expected and this is likely to include encouragement of single status arrangements. Although the UK has resisted the introduction of the Social Charter provisions and rejected the protocol on social policy agreed by the other eleven at Maastricht in December 1991, it will be difficult for UK companies to buck wider European trends. British multinationals with subsidiaries in other European countries will come under considerable pressure to adopt European standards in their domestic plants.

Examples of Change

It was argued earlier that the origins of the status divide can be found in the creation of an elite body of employees performing specific 'employer functions'; in a real sense, they were 'employers' substitutes' (Wedderburn and Craig, 1974). It was expected that the special status granted to these employees would be reciprocated by a high degree of commitment to, and co-operation with, the employer. These elite members were distinguished by their style of dress and the locale of their work, as well as by their more favourable terms and conditions of employment. The functional basis of the distinction was thus linked to important normative and behavioural differences. Over time, the functional basis of the distinction has been substantially eroded, but employers have continued to operate as if the normative and behavioural differences were still relevant to their relationship with the two parts of the labour force, and have widely continued to treat them differently.

The pressures for change towards single status discussed in the previous section have nevertheless influenced some managements to put manual workers on the same footing as non-manual workers, and to establish similar normative and behavioural patterns for both groups. The functional differences which remain are considered to be largely irrelevant to the task of creating a committed and co-operative workforce or, as in the case of integrated pay structures, to pose major short-run technical problems involving job evaluation (Incomes Data Services, 1988). An analysis of those employers who have pursued single status arrangements shows that they can be divided broadly into two categories: those who have used single status as a tool for *changing* existing working practices, and those who have used it as part of a comprehensive package of policies when *setting up* a 'greenfield' site.

Early examples of single status deals used to *change* traditional working practices were the ICI Weekly Staff Agreement and the Electricity Council's Status Agreement in the 1960s (Roeber, 1975; Wedderburn, 1966; Edwards, 1967). Both deals affected highly capital-intensive and technologically dynamic industries. They sought to link the abolition of status distinctions to greater flexibility in the use of labour, increased productivity and the creation of 'non-manual attitudes from manual workers' (Wedderburn, 1966). The aim of transforming manual worker attitudes to the employer and the workplace is even more strongly evident in more recent examples (Incomes Data Services, 1988). At Tioxide UK, for example, a single status deal in 1987 formed part of a radical restructuring of employee relations, involving the withdrawal of recognition of the TGWU, a totally new payments system including a profit-related element, and complete flexibility with no demarcation between jobs. As Kennedy (1988: 51) put it:

> traditional collective bargaining methods had begun to lose their relevance and no longer provided a satisfactory means of dialogue

between the company and its employees. The need to foster attitudes of commitment, accountability and flexibility was clearly recognised, and means other than traditional collective bargaining were needed to bring this about.

At Johnson and Johnson, harmonization had been conceived as an expression of the 'corporate credo' which stressed the need to respect the dignity of all employees and to recognize their merit. Equally significant was the company's belief that their ability to meet the challenge of the market-place would increasingly depend on the flexibility of the workforce:

> That seems most likely to come from a salaried workforce unencumbered by payments-by-results systems and able to switch effort from one product area to another on demand. (Mullins, 1986: 38)

At Hitachi in Hirwaun, the failure of the joint venture with GEC was linked to poor management and poor operator performance. The new management installed after the Hitachi buy-out saw its main task as turning round a demoralized workforce. Two key principles were complete job flexibility and single status conditions to 'facilitate the job flexibility change and to remove the general frustrations and distractions created by blue-collar/white-collar differentials' (Pegge, 1986: 43). At Ind Coope's Burton Brewery, the declining market, changes in customer tastes requiring flexibility and innovation, and intensified competition led management to set up a 'greenfield assessment' of existing operations. This was designed to integrate the capital investment programme with major changes in personnel policy. The key findings of the assessment (*Industrial Relations Review and Report*, 1987a: 3) highlighted the need for:

- team-working, seen as fundamental to the key goal of flexibility;
- harmonized terms and conditions to remove barriers to flexibility and change;
- a new industrial relations style based on co-operation and involvement;
- an end to demarcation and separate negotiations; and
- retraining and redeployment, supported by payments systems that helped, not hindered, change.

The *setting up* of new factories on greenfield sites in the UK over recent years is largely a result of inward investment by foreign-owned companies. When we examine the industrial relations style typically associated with these companies, familiar themes emerge:

Sole bargaining rights for one union; complete labour flexibility; a
highly developed system of employee involvement and participation;
single status terms and conditions; a peace clause and unilateral
reference to binding pendulum arbitration; and an emphasis on high
product quality. (Industrial Relations Services, 1991b)

Komatsu, a Japanese-owned construction equipment manufacturer,
which opened its greenfield site in Gateshead in 1986, is a typical
example of this approach. Terms and conditions have largely been
harmonized and the company argues that harmonized terms will
play a key role in retaining staff in a tightening job market, especially
for skilled manual staff (Industrial Relations Services, 1989b). Another example is Bosch's high-technology factory in Wales which
began production in 1991 on a greenfield site. The company based
its personnel strategies on those of the more 'progressive' companies
operating in Britain – in particular, Sony, Nissan, Inmos, Sanyo and
Pirelli – together with some features from the German parent company. Single status and 'complete flexibility in the use of labour at
all levels and across job grades are key components of the classic
industrial relations style of inward investors' (Industrial Relations
Services, 1991b).

There are also examples of UK companies adopting a similar
approach when setting up a greenfield site. At BICC Optical Cables,
Whiston, a greenfield spin-off from an existing cable plant in Manchester, gave management the opportunity to establish a seven-grade
integrated pay structure, common pay and performance review
structures, incorporating individual merit payments, and harmonized conditions of employment. The new pay package was seen as
establishing a fresh framework for employee relations, outside the
industry agreement, and incorporating single union and binding
arbitration clauses (*Industrial Relations Review and Report*, 1987b:
13–15).

Similarly, when GKN Sankey and Jaguar set up Venture
Pressings, a car body panel manufacturing plant, working practices
quite different to those in a traditional factory were established.
These included a single union deal, a single status workforce, full
flexibility, innovative recruitment procedures, a substantial commitment to training and a no-strike ethos (Industrial Relations Services,
1991a).

Companies adopting the industrial relations features associated
with greenfield sites acknowledge that there is a cost in providing

single status, but argue that the costs are more than outweighed by improved employee commitment and productivity savings.

> Komatsu's estimate is that harmonization of terms and conditions has meant 'massive savings' for the company. There is a cost in supplying better, more pleasant conditions, but the company says, this is heavily outweighed by the value of the employees' greater motivation and commitment. (Industrial Relations Services, 1989b)

And in the words of the Bosch agreement:

> Full flexibility and mobility of all employees is required so as to make the best use of capital equipment and people. (Industrial Relations Services, 1991b)

It has often been argued that this approach to industrial relations is more easily introduced on greenfield sites where there is no baggage of established relationships and employment practices to overcome. However, the earlier examples in this section have shown that the extension of non-manual conditions to manual workers can be used to facilitate the introduction of flexible working practices and an integrated workforce. A key question which arises in such situations is the response from the non-manual employees, namely, are the benefits in motivation and commitment from manual workers lost in reduced morale among their non-manual counterparts? In particular, where non-manual staff are unionized, a levelling up of benefits might be expected to provoke demands for compensation. Perhaps surprisingly, the cases that have been documented reveal very few reactions of this type. The examples of Tioxide and Johnson and Johnson suggest why this may be. At Tioxide, management was acutely aware of the potential backlash from non-manual employees when they saw a decline in their former differentials. To avoid this, new integrated pay-scales were introduced in advance of the move to staff status, with performance-related merit increases to give 'headroom' for relatively well-paid groups. In addition, an across-the-board profit-sharing scheme was introduced, replacing the production bonuses that had gone only to manual workers. Non-manual staff were able to look towards potential benefits in pay, linked to both personal and company performance: they were not being required to stand still while others caught up. Harmonization in a generally dynamic environment is likely to reduce significantly non-manual concern at the loss of their privileged position.

At Johnson and Johnson, piecemeal harmonization of selected elements of pay and conditions over the period 1974–82 had led to common pensions, sick pay, redundancy and holidays. Pay structures and job evaluation arrangements were still separate, but the significance of the manual/non-manual divide had been eroded over the years and was thus much less an issue of principle. Johnson and Johnson's proposals also involved the replacement of individual incentive schemes for manual workers with group incentives and profit-sharing schemes on an across-the-board basis. As at Tioxide, non-manual staff were not being required to stand still, but could look forward to some improvement in their position. A further element in harmonization at Johnson and Johnson was the allocation of new responsibilities to supervisory staff and retraining of these employees to meet the new requirements (Mullins, 1986: 41). As far as non-manual workers are concerned, it would seem that the preceding gradual narrowing of differences reduced the perceived significance of the status divide. It also seems that if harmonization is introduced as part of a much wider package of measures to change the personnel 'culture' of the organization, there is typically some scope for providing additional benefits that are attractive to non-manual employees.

This may also explain why the trend towards harmonization has been relatively muted in recent years: recession and economic difficulties have reduced the scope for 'buying out' traditional relationships. If single status or harmonization of conditions is introduced as part of a wider package it provides scope for productivity gains to offset some, or all, of the additional costs incurred. In the manner of the more genuine productivity deals of the 1960s (Donovan, 1968), the linking of flexibility elements to improvements in conditions can reduce labour costs per unit of output, and, over the longer run, can reduce the need to employ additional labour as output expands. In the Johnson and Johnson case, an initial estimate of a 5 per cent increase in pay-bill costs over three years came down to 3 per cent through productivity gains; and, as in many similar cases, there were sizeable savings through the introduction of cashless pay. Wider experience seems to indicate that the potential productivity gains can only be secured if management organization is modified to ensure effective control of, for example, sickness absence and time-keeping. This reinforces the logic of setting harmonization/single status in the context of more thoroughgoing organizational change, including the development of new managerial control systems.

The End of the Status Divide?

In the first edition of this book, this chapter concluded confidently that 'the decline of the status divide seems destined to be terminal'. The insistent product market pressures and rapid technological changes which characterized the 1980s placed a powerful premium on low-cost, high-productivity production systems, with considerable flexibility in organization. Management's re-evaluation of work organization in these conditions was leading to a reassessment of the relationship between workers, managers and the enterprise, in which single status or harmonized conditions were often an important element. Moves to create 'higher trust' relationships, which would secure employee 'commitment' and establish a new basis of trust and legitimacy for the employment relationship, were seen as key elements in the search for maximum productive efficiency to meet the challenges of the product market. As Mullins (1986: 41) argued:

> Future success will be with companies which are highly focused by technology and market expertise, which are able to adapt rapidly to changes in markets and technology. Such companies will have an overwhelming emphasis on cohesion and the fullest identification of their people with the overall business purpose . . . There will be no room for differences and divisions which consume energies and are unrelated to the work that has to be done.

Subsequent developments in the British economy have demonstrated clearly the limitations of this perspective. There are still some powerful factors working against the development of ever higher levels of harmonized conditions across industries. The first is the changing structure of British industry; the second is the development of core and peripheral workforces and the contracting out of ancillary services in the public sector; a third factor is the stance of Conservative governments since 1979. While the state has not proposed any specific policy objectives in relation to single status, many of the wider employment policies pursued by the Conservatives have worked against progress in this field.

Changing industrial structure

There have been two significant changes in the structure of British industry over the past two decades which have probably worked against harmonization: the decline of the manufacturing sector in favour of the service sector, and the increasing number of small firms. These developments have worked against harmonization due to the personnel practices found in large parts of the service sector and in small firms. As was shown earlier in this chapter, least progress has been made towards harmonization in small firms (ACAS, 1988; Industrial Relations Services, 1989a).

Between 1971 and 1990 the number of people employed in manufacturing fell by one-third while there was a corresponding increase in employment in service industries. By June 1990 employment in manufacturing stood at 23 per cent of all employees and employment in service industries was 69 per cent of all employees (*Social Trends* 22, 1992: 74). This trend looks set to continue, with the University of Warwick's Institute of Employment Research (1989: 9) projecting a modest decline in employment in manufacturing industries between 1987 and 1995 and growth in business services, miscellaneous services, construction, distribution and hotels and catering. While the impact of the recession will be significant, the long-term structural shift is likely to continue. On the whole, private services are not industries where sophisticated human resource management practices, including harmonization, are likely to be found to any great extent. One of the features of these growing parts of the service sector is that they include a large number of small firms. Overall, firms employing less than 20 people accounted for an estimated 35 per cent of all those employed outside central and local government in 1989, compared with 27 per cent in 1979 (Department of Employment, 1992: 12).

Rainnie (1989) has shown that small firms tend not to be in the vanguard of enlightened personnel practice. Rather, they are characterized by low pay, poor working conditions, restricted benefits, bad safety records, direct forms of supervision and insecurity of employment (see also Millward et al., 1992). In general, small firms are either dependent on larger firms for business in that they supply them or take on subcontracted work from them, or they have to compete with large firms and find themselves forced into specialized markets (Rainnie, 1989: 83). In either case there is considerable pressure to keep labour costs low and to see employees as commodities to be bought and dispensed with rather than as valued assets. It may well be that all employees, manual and non-manual, experience a similar level of disadvantage in many small firms. However, where there is a distinction in treatment, movement towards single status would be too expensive for many small firms. Other trends within the large corporations which still dominate both manufacturing and service sectors may have had similar effects. Purcell (1991: 68) argues that the trend within large conglomerates towards decentralization and devolution driven by financial controls has worked against the realization of the ideals of HRM. This may go some way towards explaining the slow progress towards harmonization in the cases discussed by Storey (1992).

Contracting out of ancillary services

In recent years there has been a considerable increase, notably in the public sector, in the contracting out of ancillary services. Firms who choose to contract out such services do so for a variety of reasons: it may be because they believe a contractor can provide the service more cheaply or more effectively; or because they wish to concentrate resources and protect 'core' staff in uncertain market conditions. Public sector bodies, on the other hand, have no choice about embarking on the competitive tendering process. Under the terms of the Local Government Act 1988 all Direct Service Organizations (cleaning, refuse collection, catering, vehicle maintenance and grounds maintenance) must compete to provide services alongside commercial companies and similar requirements apply in the National Health Service (Mailly, 1986). To date, only 25 per cent of local government contracts have been won by outside contractors (*Local Government Management*, spring 1992: 8), though the figure may increase in the future as companies hit by the recession in their traditional markets bid more vigorously for public sector contracts. It is probable that the government will continue to change the rules on competitive tendering to facilitate the success of outside companies – for example, by modifying the right to include redundancy costs in tender comparisons and by changing the rules on contract packaging to reduce the scope of contracts.

The impact of subcontracting on moves towards single status is likely to be strongly negative. There is no survey evidence available to make comparisons, but since many organizations contract out to cut costs, the conditions of manual workers employed by contractors are usually worse than those of the former direct employees. For example, manual workers employed by a local authority or hospital would have enjoyed harmonized conditions over a broad range of benefits such as pensions, sick pay arrangements and holidays prior to contracting out. These are precisely the areas which are threatened by the competitive contracting process. Even where staff are re-employed by large contractors with good employment practices, they may find single status for a range of employment conditions, but at a much lower level (e.g. for sickness benefits, holidays and pensions) than in their former contracts of employment.

Overall, the subcontracting process has been working against the development of harmonized working conditions between certain groups of manual and non-manual workers, and is almost certainly reinforcing the emergence of a new status divide between core and peripheral workers, with the latter being subject to employment conditions characterized by greater instability, marginality and insecurity.

Government policy

Conservative governments since 1979 have not enunciated any specific policy objectives in relation to single status, but in practice many of their employment policies have worked against progress in this field. Throughout this period there has been a gradually widening gap between the pay of the better paid and the lower paid (Kessler and Bayliss, 1992: 195). Table 16.3 shows that since 1979 non-manual earnings have increased substantially more than manual earnings and this trend towards widening inequality is also reflected in other conditions of employment.

One of the main explanations for the widening gap in basic conditions is the government's policy of deregulation of the labour market. In an employment 'free for all', the strong tend to get stronger while the vulnerable, particularly the low-paid and non-unionized workers, fare less well. The situation has been exacerbated by the gradual reduction of the legal protective framework provided by the Wages Councils and some weakening of the basic framework of employment rights, which in the 1970s had been a motor for encouraging better and more equitable employment practices, as well as providing a form of protection in its own right. This situation has been accentuated by the changing industrial structure discussed earlier. Many of the growth industries such as hotel and catering, tourism and distribution characteristically draw their manual workers from the secondary labour market in which small firm size and relatively poor employment conditions are common features.

Table 16.3 Average gross weekly earnings in the UK 1979–90

	Male						Female						RPI
	Manual		Non-manual		All		Manual		Non-manual		All		
April	£		£		£		£		£		£		
1979	93.0	100	113.0	100	101.4	100	55.2	100	66.0	100	63.0	100	100
1980	111.7	120	141.3	125	125.4	124	68.0	123	82.7	125	78.9	125	121.8
1981	121.9	131	163.1	144	140.5	139	74.5	135	96.7	147	91.4	145	136.4
1982	133.8	144	178.9	158	154.5	152	80.1	145	104.9	159	99.0	157	149.3
1983	143.6	154	194.9	172	167.5	165	87.9	159	115.1	174	108.8	173	155.2
1984	152.7	164	209.0	185	178.8	176	93.5	169	124.3	188	117.2	186	163.3
1985	163.6	176	225.0	199	192.4	190	101.3	184	133.8	203	126.4	201	174.6
1986	174.4	188	244.9	217	207.5	205	107.5	195	145.7	221	137.2	218	179.9
1987	185.5	199	265.9	235	224.0	221	115.3	209	157.2	238	148.1	235	187.5
1988	200.6	216	294.1	260	245.8	242	123.6	224	175.5	266	164.2	261	194.9
1989	217.8	234	323.6	286	269.5	266	134.9	244	195.0	295	182.3	289	210.5
1990	237.2	255	354.9	314	295.6	292	148.0	268	215.5	327	201.5	320	230.0
% increase in real earnings, 1979–90		+11		+37		+27		+17		+42		+39	

Source: Kessler and Bayliss, 1992, table 10.1

Conclusion

While some parts of the manufacturing sector, notably the larger and more high-technology companies, have continued to evolve towards single status arrangements, others, particularly small companies, have been so hard-pressed by recessionary conditions that there has been no scope for providing better conditions for manual workers. The manufacturing sector itself has been a declining part of the economy, thus reducing the impact of some of the influences described in the case studies above. Rising unemployment has reduced labour market pressures to adapt the employment relationship, while the gradual weakening of individual employment rights has led to a deterioration in the working conditions of many manual workers. The steady increase in service sector employment has brought an increased proportion of workers into industries in which status divisions are still very much in evidence, and the distinction between 'core' and 'peripheral' jobs across the economy has introduced a further element of status division which has been fuelled by the trend towards 'contracting out'. From the perspective of the early 1990s, the status divide in UK employment can be seen to have taken on a subtly different character from the traditional white-collar/manual distinction, but there can be no doubt that it continues to be a pervasive feature of the workplace for many British employees.

Bibliography

ACAS. 1982. *Developments in Harmonisation*. Discussion Paper No. 1, March. London: Advisory, Conciliation and Arbitration Service.

ACAS. 1988. *Labour Flexibility in Britain*. Occasional Paper No. 41. London: Advisory, Conciliation and Arbitration Service.

Ackroyd, S., Burrell, G., Hughes, M. and Whitaker, A. 1988. 'The Japanisation of British Industry?'. *Industrial Relations Journal*, 19, Spring.

Bain, G. S. 1970. *The Growth of White-Collar Unionism*. Oxford: Clarendon Press.

Bain, G. S. and Price, R. 1972. 'Who is a White-Collar Employee?'. *British Journal of Industrial Relations*, 10, November.

Boddy, D. and Buchanan, D. A. 1986. *Managing New Technology*. Oxford: Blackwell.

Braverman, H. 1974. *Labor and Monopoly Capital*. New York: Monthly Review Press.

Craig, C. 1969. 'Men in Manufacturing Industry'. Cambridge: Department of Applied Economics, University of Cambridge (mimeo).

Department of Employment. 1981. 'Pattern of Holiday Entitlement'. *Employment Gazette*, 89, December.

Department of Employment. 1992. *Labour Market Quarterly Report*, May.

Donovan. 1968. 'Royal Commission on Trade Unions and Employers' Associations', 1965–1968. *Report*. Cmnd 3623. London: HMSO.

Edwards, Sir Ronald Stanley. 1967. *An Experiment in Industrial Relations: The Electricity Supply Industry's Status Agreement for Industrial Staff*. London: Electricity Council.

Fowler, A. 1987. 'When Chief Executives Discover HRM'. *Personnel Management*, January.

Fox, A. 1966. *Industrial Sociology and Industrial Relations*. Research Paper 3, Royal Commission on Trade Unions and Employers' Associations. London: HMSO.

Fox, A. 1985. *Man Mismanagement*, 2nd edn. London: Hutchinson.

Francis, A. 1986. *New Technology at Work*. Oxford: Oxford University Press.

Friedman, A. 1977. *Industry and Labour: Class Struggle at Work and Monopoly Capitalism*. London: Macmillan.

Gill, C. 1985. *Work, Unemployment and New Technology*. Cambridge: Polity.

Hyman, R. and Price, R. (eds) 1983. *The New Working Class? White Collar Workers and Their Organisations*. London: Macmillan.

Incomes Data Services. 1988. *Integrated Pay*. Study No. 411. London: IDS.

Industrial Relations Review and Report. 1986. 'Holidays – 1986 Annual Survey'. 376, September, 2–10.

Industrial Relations Review and Report. 1987a. 'A Greenfield Strategy for Ind Coope's Burton Brewery'. 394, June 2–8.

Industrial Relations Review and Report. 1987b. 'BICC Optical Cables Unit Goes "Into 2000"'. 398, August, 12–17.

Institute for Employment Research. 1989. *Review of the Economy and Employment*. Coventry: IER, University of Warwick.

Industrial Relations Services. 1989a. 'Harmonization: A Single Status Surge?' *IRS Employment Trends*, 445, 8 August.

Industrial Relations Services. 1989b. 'Komatsu Two Years On'. *IRS Employment Trends*, 453, 5 December.

Industrial Relations Services. 1990. 'Single-Table Bargaining – A Survey'. *IRS Employment Trends*, 463, 9 May.

Industrial Relations Services. 1991a. 'Full Flexibility at Venture Pressings'. *IRS Employment Trends*, 496, 20 September.

Industrial Relations Services. 1991b. 'Bosch: An Industrial Relations Strategy for a New Start Up'. *IRS Employment Trends*, 501, 6 December.

Kennedy, G. 1988. 'Single Status as the Key to Flexibility'. *Personnel Management*, February.

Kessler, S. and Bayliss, F. 1992. *Contemporary British Industrial Relations.* London. Macmillan.

Labour Research Department. 1980. *Sick Pay: A Negotiator's Guide.* London: LRD.

Labour Research Department. 1981. *Bargaining Report 14,* May/June. London: LRD.

Local Government Management. 1992. 'CCT Success for Councils': Vol. 1. Issue 1. Spring.

Lockwood, D. 1958. *The Blackcoated Worker: A Study in Class Consciousness.* London: Allen & Unwin.

Mailly, R. 1986. 'The Impact of Contracting Out in the NHS'. *Employee Relations*, 8, 1.

Marginson, P. 1991. 'The Employment Structure of Large Companies'. In Pollert, A. (ed.) *Farewell to Flexibility?* Oxford: Blackwell.

Marginson, P. and Sisson, K. 1990. 'Single Table Talk'. *Personnel Management*, May, 46–9.

Millward, N. and Stevens, M. 1986. *British Workplace Industrial Relations 1980–1984: The DE/ESRC/PSI/ACAS Surveys.* Aldershot: Gower.

Millward, N., Stevens, M., Smart, D. and Hawes, W. R. 1992. *Workplace Industrial Relations in Transition: The ED/ESRC/PSI/ACAS Surveys.* Aldershot: Gower.

Mullins, T. 1986. 'Harmonisation: The Benefits and the Lessons'. *Personnel Management*, March.

National Association of Pension Funds. 1981. *Survey of Occupational Pension Schemes.* 1980. London: NAPF.

National Economic Development Office/Institute of Manpower Studies. 1986. *Changing Working Patterns: How Companies Achieve Flexibility to Meet New Needs.* London: NEDO.

Parker, P. A. L., Hawes, W. R. and Lumb, A. L. 1971. *The Reform of Collective Bargaining at Plant and Company Level.* Department of Employment Manpower Papers 5. London: HMSO.

Pascale, R. T. and Athos, A. G. 1981. *The Art of Japanese Management.* New York: Simon & Schuster.

Pegge, T. 1986. 'Hitachi Two Years On'. *Personnel Management*, October.

Policy Studies Institute. 1980. *Shorter Working Time.* London: PSI.

Price, R. and Bain, G. S. 1983. 'Union Growth in Britain: Retrospect and Prospect'. *British Journal of Industrial Relations*, 21, March.

Price, R. and Steininger, S. 1987. 'Trade Unions and New Technology in West Germany'. *New Technology, Work and Employment*, 2, Autumn.

Purcell, J. 1991. 'The Impact of Corporate Strategy on Human Resource Management'. In Storey, J. (ed.) *New Perspectives on Human Resource Management.* London: Routledge.

Rainnie, A. 1989. *Industrial Relations in Small Firms: Small Isn't Beautiful.* London: Routledge.

Roeber, J. 1975. *Social Change at Work: The ICI Weekly Staff Agreement.* London: Duckworth.

Speier, H. 1934. 'The Salaried Employee in Modern Society'. *Social Research*, February.

Storey, J. 1992. 'HRM in Action: The Truth is Out at Last'. *Personnel Management*, April.

Storey, J. and Sisson, K. 1990. 'Limits to Transformation: Human Resource Management in the British Context'. *Industrial Relations Journal*, Vol. 21, No. 1. Spring.

Strauss, G. 1954. 'White-Collar Unions are Different'. *Harvard Business Review*. September–October.

Trevor, M. 1988. *Toshiba's New British Company: Competitiveness Through Innovation in Industry.* London: Policy Studies Institute.

Walby, S. 1986. *Patriarchy at Work.* Cambridge: Polity.

Wedderburn, D. 1966. 'Staff Status: Its Meaning and Problems'. *IPM Digest 19.* November.

Wedderburn, D. and Craig, C. 1974. 'Relative Deprivation in Work'. In Wedderburn, D. (ed.) *Poverty, Inequality and Class Structure.* Cambridge: Cambridge University Press.

Wickens, P. 1987. *The Road to Nissan: Flexibility, Quality, Teamwork.* London: Macmillan.

17

Discipline and the Creation of Order

Paul Edwards

Discipline is not only the removal of disorder, but if any visible shape can be given to divine things, the very visible shape and image of virtue
(*John Milton, quoted by Corrigan and Sayer, 1991: 14*)

At first sight, discipline is part of the 'old' world of collective management–union relations, with its emphasis on formalism and procedures, as against the new order of team-work and commitment. The term certainly covers topics such as punishment and formal rules of behaviour, but, as in concepts such as the discipline of a profession, it also has connotations of the rigorous pursuit of goals without externally imposed sanctions. This is what the new order of self-discipline is supposed to be about. As one text puts it, 'the best discipline is self-discipline, the normal human tendency to do one's share and to live up to the rules of the game' (Strauss and Sayles, 1980: 218). This point may seem to be axiomatic but it in fact raises large issues of organizational functioning. Who decides what a reasonable share is, what the rules are, and in what ways breaches of the rules are to be penalized? This chapter tries to analyse discipline in the light of such questions. It will help to begin by considering their neglect in many treatments.

Disciplinary action has been defined as 'the corrective action which is taken when the organizational discipline is found to have been significantly breached by one or more workers' (Sokolik, 1970: 381). Yet, as Ashdown and Baker (1973: 1) note, this definition is too broad: it would even include any form of collective industrial action. Their own solution is to distinguish group behaviour, with its widespread rejection of an existing practice, from 'individual indiscipline' which 'indicates merely a personal deviation from standards generally accepted by others'. Beach (1975: 599) likewise says that workers 'must reasonably conform to the code of conduct established by the leadership of the organization'. Torrington and Hall (1991: 538–44) go somewhat further by identifying three elements of discipline: *managerial*, where everything depends on one leader; *team*, involving mutual dependency; and *self*, with solo performance depending on expertise and self-control. Managers are engaged in discipline when they are engendering team spirit and self-discipline as much as when they are penalizing wrong-doers. This at least broadens the definition, but there is then no discussion of the contested nature of the disciplinary process or the possibility that self-discipline may involve demands and pressures imposed on those allegedly practising it. Nor is there any consideration of the extensive literature discussing how discipline actually works.

Such studies assume that there is a clear dividing line between group and individual conduct. Yet the distinction is often unclear. For example, a worker found leaving before the official finishing time may apparently be engaged in an individual breach of the rules, but if the practice is at all common it involves more than the isolated individual. This example offers a second theme, the nature of rules. How people expect to behave depends as much on day-to-day understandings as on formal rules. Workplaces may have identical rule-books, but in one it may be accepted practice to leave early near holidays; in another, on Fridays; in a third, when a relatively lenient supervisor is in charge; and so on. What the rule is cannot be discovered from the rule-book. Moreover, there may well be a clear difference between 'generally accepted standards' and the expectations of 'the leadership'. Day-to-day experience will create standards which may differ sharply from official rules. It is not even the case that formal rules inscribe managerial expectations while informal standards represent workers' understandings. In some workplaces supervisors have been found to encourage breaches of rules on leaving times (Ditton, 1979a). The making of rules is a process in which different levels of management may have different priorities.

Discipline has three faces. The first is the application of punishment for breaches of the rules. Second, there is the formulation of the rules themselves, together with the procedures to be followed in their application. Third is the creation in practice of the expectations and understandings that govern behaviour. Much of the existing literature offers advice on the first two. The third is addressed in new works on human resource management. As Peter Wickens (1987: 100), personnel director of Nissan, says, 'if the Supervisor and his staff have the right relationship and everyone is properly motivated, good time-keeping does not depend on a mechanistic form of time recording but on the *self-generated discipline* within the group' (emphasis added). These texts are, however, prone to draw a sharp line between the old and the new. Along with some other contributions to this volume, the present chapter argues that the new is in important ways similar to the old. Moreover, to understand the present it is important to know how discipline evolved in the past. The chapter therefore begins with the past, examining the first two faces of discipline and then considering the third face of discipline in action. It then assesses how far self-discipline has altered the expression on this face.

No recommendations are offered as to 'best practice', for several reasons. First, purely technical advice on the design of procedures is available in the standard texts. Second, the relevance of this advice depends on the context: as will be seen, there are several ways of exercising discipline, and in some contexts a conventional recommendation for formal procedures may be inoperable or even conflict with other aspects of an organization's functioning. This is the irony of many conventional texts. Though allegedly 'relevant', they were part of the world of proceduralism and had little means of grasping the challenge of self-discipline as expressed by Wickens and others. An account based on the actualities of discipline can understand the nature of practice in the past, including the extent of self-discipline, and can thereby place newer forms of self-discipline in their proper context. Third, once the differing interests between workers and managers, and indeed within the two groups, are acknowledged, there may be no best practice on which all can agree. Discipline is part of a continual negotiation of order, not simply a technical activity.

An absence of recommendations does not mean a lack of practical relevance. On the contrary, exploring the actual construction of rules throws more light on the nature of discipline than does an exposition of procedures alone. This perspective can also be carried through to the study of 'new' modes of discipline, in particular by assessing how self-discipline attempts to alter the terms of the negotiation of order.

Disciplinary Rules and Procedures

The origins of discipline

Employers have always needed to ensure the adequate performance of work tasks by their employees. Formal rules became necessary when organizations became large and bureaucratic, with the result that the employer could not oversee operations personally. Pollard (1965: 181–9) has described the disciplinary problems of the early industrial employers: the new factories demanded regular attendance and the carrying out of tasks in the prescribed fashion.

Writers who adopt what Henry (1983: 71) calls a consensus approach have seen such developments as characteristic of an authoritarian approach to discipline. Ashdown and Baker (1973: 5–7), for example, argue that managers saw their own authority as absolute, and imposed discipline in a harsh and arbitrary manner. Since the Second World War, the authors continue, managements have become aware that punitive discipline has adverse effects on morale and efficiency. They have also faced pressure from trade unions, legal restrictions on their powers, and difficulties of recruitment in tight labour markets. As a result, the aim of disciplinary action has become correction instead of coercion, and the administration of policy has been based less on the absolute authority of the employer and more on a democratic approach. Such an interpretation is not limited to 'consensus' theorists. An explicitly radical account of changes in work organization in America sees nineteenth-century work discipline as being based on 'arbitrary command' in which motivation was based on the dictum: 'perform your task correctly or be docked in pay, fired, or, on occasion, beaten'. Under bureaucratic systems of control that have developed since 1945, by contrast, punishment flows 'from the established organizational rules and procedures' and is no longer coercive in purpose or arbitrary in application (Edwards, R., 1979: 33, 142).

Such interpretations need to be treated with caution. First, they sit uneasily with evidence that in large parts of industry – notably, cotton and steel and some areas of coal-mining – employers subcontracted sets of operations to skilled workers who were responsible for recruitment, payment, and discipline (Littler, 1982). Employers here exercised their authority at one remove. Second, it is hard to conceive of all workers being subjected to an identical form of discipline: skilled craftsmen were proud of their skills and independence, and would not have reacted meekly to harsh discipline. Third, standards of regular attendance were enforced slowly and unevenly. Industrialization was a lengthy process in which earlier forms of discipline and control could survive for considerable periods. In Birmingham, for example, it was not until the 1860s that employers were successful in eroding the tradition of taking Monday as a holiday (Reid, 1976). Finally, many early employers adopted a paternalistic, and not an overtly authoritarian, approach. Though paternalism involved power relationships as well as a fatherly concern for employees' welfare, it was a means of establishing discipline which relied on many mechanisms other than force (Newby, 1977; Prude, 1983).

Neither should the shift to a corrective approach be exaggerated. One of the assumptions underlying the shift is that, as firms have grown increasingly bureaucratic, old and informal modes of discipline have become unworkable. But bureaucracy is not a product of the period since 1945. Rules emerged in many organizations before then. The railways (Hudson, 1970; Bagwell, 1963: 20–8) and the Post Office (Clinton, 1984: 45–59) are good examples of organizations which had formal and detailed rules specifying workers' duties long before then.

A second assumption is that rates of disciplinary sanction will fall, as firms cease to wield the big stick in an arbitrary fashion. Data on the actual use of sanctions, as compared with the fearsome-sounding penalties in rule-books, are rare. However, studies of the American textile industry (Gersuny, 1976) and the British railways (Edwards, P. K., 1992) point to remarkably similar rates of discipline during the nineteenth and twentieth centuries. The latter study also found that the use of discipline, in both periods, correlated with times of financial exigency. The actual use of penalties thus reflected pressures on managers, and not any automatic progression towards a corrective approach.

All this evidence suggests it is dangerous to make sharp distinctions between punitive and corrective approaches. Any organization is likely to use a mixture of both: even the most 'punitive' management may well remind employees of their obligations, for co-operation cannot be secured by force alone. This suggests an important lesson when current shifts towards 'self-discipline' are considered: the evidence from the past suggests that continuity can be as important as change. It is true, however, that there have been significant changes in procedures for handling discipline.

The formalization of procedures

As against the view that there was a gradual drift towards a corrective approach, the shift to formal procedures was sudden. Surveys in the 1960s suggested that as many as 90 per cent of establishments had no formal disciplinary procedures (Anderman, 1972: 22–4). In 1978, the Institute of Personnel Management (IPM) (1979: 7) surveyed 273 organizations and found a major change: 98 per cent had written disciplinary procedures for blue-collar workers. Since these tended to be large firms, this figure may exaggerate the growth of procedures. But the Workplace Industrial Relations Survey (WIRS), which covers all manufacturing and service establishments with at least 25 employees, confirms the general picture. Between 1980 and 1990 the proportion of establishments with procedures for discipline and dismissal rose from 81 per cent to 90 per cent. Procedures have also been widely adopted by non-union firms: 83 per cent of those with no recognized union have a procedure (Millward et al., 1992: 187, 191). Small firms falling below the survey threshold remain, however, relatively informal: only one-third of those with fewer than 20 employees studied by Evans et al. (1985: 30) had a written disciplinary procedure.

A small survey of 70 large organizations in 1991 confirmed the growth of formalization (Industrial Relations Services, 1991a; 1991b). Not only did they all have a procedure, but the systems operated in similar ways, reflecting the good practice consolidated in ACAS handbooks. All but one of the procedures allowed for up to one formal oral warning and two written warnings before dismissal or other penalties were applied. And all had an appeals mechanism.

Explanations of this growth focus above all on the intervention of the law (IPM, 1979: 7). The Industrial Relations Act 1971 introduced provisions relating to unfair dismissal, and this legislation has been widely seen as stimulating companies to reform their procedures. Employers interviewed in 1977 felt that the effect of employment protection laws had been to tighten up on recruitment and dismissal arrangements. Although they claimed that management's power in discipline had been eroded, they also stressed that there had been an increase in the use of proper procedures and a decline in arbitrariness (Daniel and Stilgoe, 1978: 37). The Industrial Relations Services (IRS) survey found that seven in ten of the organizations covered had changed their procedures between 1987 and 1991: this was often in response to legal developments.

The law was plainly not the only influence. As Henry (1983: 102) has argued, legal changes were part of a broader policy of intervention by the state which reflected a belief that formalized and standardized procedures would reduce the number of shop-floor grievances and strikes, thereby contributing to a more general process of industrial relations reform. The influence may not have been all one way. Authors of official and quasi-official reports looked to the practice of progressive firms in drawing up their recommendations. A manager interviewed by Henry (ibid.: 104) argued that official bodies consulted widely in industry, and that they brought together existing practices by saying 'this appears to be what industry does and finds acceptable and therefore this is what we will recommend'. It is unlikely that firms would have responded so rapidly had not legal provisions and advice on what constituted good practice been broadly congruent with ways in which they were already moving.

It should not be inferred that possession of a written document necessarily altered actual practice in a dramatic fashion. Writing at the time of growing formality, a practising personnel manager castigated British managers' unthinking approach and their resistance to formalization, noting that arguments about a lack of flexibility were used as excuses to be inconsistent and capricious (Welch, 1978). This suggests that formalization may have been embraced with less enthusiasm than is sometimes suggested. As argued below, there is a greater variability in disciplinary practice than the widespread existence of procedures suggests, and even in firms whose practice is generally in line with the policy stated in the procedure, the actual conduct of discipline is more complex than it appears at first sight.

The content and operation of procedures

For discipline to be applied effectively, the rules must be clear. Accordingly, most procedures specify the type of conduct which is likely to trigger disciplinary action. It is not, however, possible to be comprehensive: there will always be contingencies that cannot be predicted. Procedures typically do no more than indicate the type of action which is liable to be punished. Such actions fall into two types: very serious misconduct, such as theft and violence, which may lead to instant dismissal; and less serious offences, such as excessive absenteeism or poor time-keeping, which will be dealt with initially through warnings and, if performance does not improve, through increasingly severe sanctions.

The main types of action that lead to the operation of discipline seem to be common among small and large firms. Plumridge (1966: 139) found in a survey of 50 organizations that absenteeism was the most common reason, followed by 'incompetence and unsuitability'. Respondents to the IPM (1979: 28–31) survey listed time-keeping, unauthorized absence and poor work standards as the main issues. The mainly small firms studied by Evans et al. (1985: 27) gave time-keeping and absence together as the most common reason, followed by 'incompetence or incapacity in work performance'.

The operation of a procedure involves many levels of management. Most formal procedures start with action by the immediate supervisor, with higher levels being involved as more severe sanctions are applied. In only 2 per cent of companies surveyed by the IPM (1979: 41) did final authority to dismiss rest with the supervisor; in 32 per cent, it rested with the personnel manager; and in 39 per cent it was the responsibility of the factory manager. Underlying these figures is the well-known tendency in the 1970s for authority in the area of discipline to be removed from the supervisor and placed in the hands of the personnel specialist.

Current trends towards the decentralization of responsibility to line managers may suggest a shift in the opposite direction. The IRS (1991b: 14) survey noted that 'formally, discipline is very much a line management responsibility' and quoted some cases in which first line supervision was given considerable authority. A study of the handling of absenteeism in 25 organizations found that personnel specialists were increasingly seeing their role as to provide expert advice and support to line managers (Edwards and Whitston, 1989a). Such trends do not, however, represent a return to the days of the foreman's empire on the shop-floor. Arbitrary authority is constrained from outside the firm by laws on unfair dismissal, while within the organization personnel departments continue to establish overall policies. But within those policies, as discussed below, line managers may be less prone to seeing discipline as something to be passed on to 'personnel' and more likely to take responsibility for tackling the issue.

Decentralization highlights the role of the first line supervisor. They were at one time portrayed as 'men in the middle', caught between workers and management proper, and hence willing to bend or ignore rules. A more realistic view is that supervisors generally espouse broad managerial goals and that they do not differ fundamentally from other managers in seeing the need for discipline (see, especially, Armstrong, 1983; also Child and Partridge, 1982). They may be less prone to subvert rulings from above than to complain that they are not given sufficient support when they act to assert managerial rights (Edwards and Scullion, 1982a: 327–31). During the 1970s it was probably quite common for supervisors to feel that the authority to discipline was being taken away from them. At the same time, of course, they were having to negotiate the day-to-day application of the rules and in doing so may have promoted custom and practice that interpreted the silences of the formal rules or even supplanted them (Brown, 1973). During the 1980s, a reduction in trade union bargaining power on the shop-floor, together with managerial decentralization, meant that supervisors were probably less likely to perceive a loss of authority over discipline. Case studies in four organizations suggested that there was little problem with a loss of influence (Edwards and Whitston, 1993).

Another major influence on the operation of procedures is that of trade unions. Unions' formal involvement appears to be considerable. The WIRS results point to two roles: the representation of individual members (reported by managers in 71 per cent of establishments with procedures); and discussion of the form of procedures, with procedures being agreed in 90 per cent of plants with recognized unions (Millward et al., 1992: 194). Agreement does not, however, necessarily mean substantive negotiation. The IPM (1979: 17) survey for example reported that only 38 per cent of respondents negotiated with unions representing blue-collar workers, and only 25 per cent agreed the rules with the unions. Procedures are likely to be agreed with unions, but in most cases this is likely to involve notification and acceptance of a procedure whose shape is set by management and not negotiated from scratch.

One view of union shop stewards' behaviour is that they will always attempt to challenge the application of discipline. This appears to be incorrect. First, it implies too narrow a role for the steward. A survey of 1400 stewards carried out in 1966 reported, 'when asked whether they considered their management reasonably fair in dealing with workers who break rules and disobey orders, 93 per cent of stewards said "yes"' (McCarthy and Parker, 1968: 48). As a detailed study of ten workplaces showed, stewards communicate managerial concern about breaches of rules to their members, give warnings about plans to tighten up, talk to members privately and warn them about their behaviour, and provide 'information as to the extent of breaches of rules' (McCarthy, 1966: 12). Second, stewards will not take up cases that they consider to be unreasonable: they may try to persuade members that they are in the wrong, or they may go through the motions of defending them while making it clear to management that they do not agree with the members' claim (Batstone et al., 1977: 108–9). Third, as noted above, they are likely to accept the general need for discipline, challenging management only if they feel that the rules have been applied unfairly.

Finally, the role of outside agencies in procedures needs comment. The WIRS data found that reference to bodies outside the individual establishment occurred in about two-thirds of cases. Over the 1980s, two different trends were evident: a growth in reference to management above establishment level (suggesting, note the WIRS authors, concern about public scrutiny of an approach to dismissals and hence a need to check with higher management); and a decline in the use of third parties, with ACAS involvement falling from 29 per cent to 15 per cent of establishments with any reference outside (Millward et al., 1992: 194–6). As Upton (1987) notes, there is in Britain – in contrast to the USA – a reluctance to codify the final stages of a procedure by specifying independent adjudication as the final stage.

There is dispute as to the relative merits of North American arbitration and British industrial tribunals (Collins, 1982a; 1982b; Glasbeek, 1984). But it is clear that the latter are less able to alter managerial decisions: they are required to accept any managerial decision that a 'reasonable' employer might reasonably have taken (Dickens et al., 1985), whereas arbitrators have more freedom to make their own judgements on the merits of a case. A comparative study found that arbitration can improve managerial organization: when a case goes against management, they review the implications and try to ensure that the same mistake is not made again, whereas in the less formalized British system much more is left uncodified (Haiven, 1988). As the author concludes, if a case reaches the stage of dismissal North American workers are better protected by arbitration than are British workers by industrial tribunals. But at the day-to-day level disciplinary procedures backed by arbitration and ultimately the law regulate the North American workplace in clear ways, whereas in Britain the employer's authority is less codified: it is often greater though, in certain circumstances it can, as shown below, be challenged on the shop-floor.

Formalization may thus have gone less far than it would seem. Even with the developments of the 1970s, management remains the leading party: procedures operate 'without an independent element and without union agreement or involvement, other than in a representative capacity . . . the definitions of indiscipline remain managerially determined' (Dickens et al., 1985: 242). Weakening union power made this even more true during the 1980s. Procedures are more formal but the practice of discipline still leaves a great deal of discretion to management in deciding what is acceptable conduct and how it is to be enforced.

The Extent and Pattern of Dismissal

The use of discipline short of dismissal is hard to measure: how serious does a conversation between a manager and a worker have to be before it constitutes discipline? Two recent surveys (Industrial Relations Services, 1991a: 7; Millward et al., 1992: 200) do, however, give some indication of the use of sanctions: just over 3 per cent of workers are likely to receive some disciplinary sanction each year.

The frequency of dismissal has received more attention. Writing at the end of the 1970s, Daniel and Stilgoe (1978: 59) detected a decline in the use of dismissal over the decade. Most plants continued to have some dismissals, but fewer had very high rates. The WIRS data for the 1980s point to decline followed by an increase: the rate of dismissal per thousand workers fell from 14 in 1980 to 9 in 1984, but reached 15 in 1990 (Millward et al., 1992: 201). There is thus little evidence of any secular decline in the rate of dismissal, despite more formalized procedures. The data on the 1980s are consistent with a growing use of discipline by managements seeking tighter control of labour. The WIRS data thus showed a clear tendency for establishments operating below capacity to dismiss more than those working at full capacity.

Deaton (1984), analysing the 1977–8 Warwick Survey of manufacturing plants, found that there were five main influences on the dismissal rate. The risk was lowest in large plants, where wages were high, and where there was a high proportion of skilled workers, a high proportion of white-collar employees, and a high level of union density. The WIRS data confirm the result for the size of plants, and also show that plants with a high proportion of atypical workers and workers from ethnic minorities had high rates of dismissal.

Some firms are thus far more prone to dismissals than others: this reflects not inherent differences between workers but the policies of the firms themselves. In the more progressive companies, dismissal is a relatively rare sanction, employed only when other means have failed. In others, dismissal or the threat of it remains an important form of control.

Popular attention has focused not on disciplinary practices, but on the operation of the unfair dismissals legislation, with worries frequently being expressed that it is difficult or impossible to sack anyone. Most dismissals do not, however, even enter the unfair dismissal system. Daniel and Stilgoe (1978: 62) found that only 26 per cent of their plants had been subject to formal unfair dismissal complaints, and they estimated that only one dismissal in 14 led to a complaint. Detailed research on those cases that enter the industrial tribunal system suggests that employers' fears about the impossibility of sacking workers have been exaggerated. Less than one-quarter of applicants who go to a hearing win their cases, and the typical redress for this minority is a relatively small amount of money. The criteria for judging fairness are, moreover, restricted, being based on a judgement of what a reasonable employer would have done in the given circumstances (Dickens et al., 1985). It has been held in cases of alleged theft, for example, that an employer does not have to prove beyond reasonable doubt that someone sacked for theft had in fact committed the offence, a reasonable belief being all that is necessary.

As well as encouraging procedural reform, the law has been seen as one factor in the reduction in rates of dismissal. But the effect may not be direct. Citing Daniel and Stilgoe's evidence, together with the results of a survey of 301 establishments, each with fewer than 50 employees (Clifton and Tatton-Brown, 1979), Dickens et al. (1985: 257) conclude that managers generally attribute 'little effect to the unfair dismissal provisions in terms of inhibiting dismissal'. One indirect effect may be an improvement of disciplinary procedures, such that managements feel less need to rely on the ultimate sanction of the sack.

When considering the issue of labour control more generally, the distinction between dismissal for disciplinary reasons and 'normal' labour turnover breaks down. People who quit 'voluntarily' during the first few months of service with a firm may do so as much for reasons connected with the work that they are expected to do and the form of discipline to which they are subject as for reasons associated with their personal characteristics. A study of seven factories showed that at least one-third of leavers had been employed by their present firm for less than a year (Edwards and Scullion, 1982b: 63–73). More revealing, however, are variations between plants. In two clothing factories, over 40 per cent of leavers had been employed for less than six months. This was associated with very close managerial control of the work process, with disciplinary warnings for poor work performance being commonplace and with very strict control maintained of starting and finishing times. Not only was dismissal an ever-present possibility, but 'voluntary' quitting was also influenced by the control regime: a worker given a couple of warnings, or who found the work pace intolerable, might find leaving the only option. Such quitting helped to reinforce managerial authority because those who might question it did not stay long. This illustrates the point that the conduct of discipline cannot be separated from overall patterns of workplace relations, and that the niceties of corrective discipline and proceduralism are not necessarily followed on the shop-floor. The following section elaborates on this argument.

Discipline in Action

Types of rules

Prescriptive treatments of discipline start from the assumption that all organizational rules have the same status. There are in fact different sorts of rules, which have different origins and are treated differently by people in organizations, and which need not stem from shared interests or perspectives. In his classic study of a gypsum mine and factory, Gouldner (1954) identified three types of bureaucratic rule. 'Mock' bureaucracy covers rules that are ignored by all: Gouldner's example is a no-smoking rule that management generally made no attempt to enforce. 'Representative' bureaucracy was exemplified by safety rules, to which management devoted considerable attention and against which workers expended few energies, the result being that safety matters were highly bureaucratized and rules were enforced. 'Punishment-centred' bureaucracy involves rules that are enforced by one party against another, with sanctions being imposed for disobedience, an example being the rule against absenteeism, which managers wished to enforce rigidly and which workers resented. Breaches of different rules will be treated very differently in practice. Mock rules are ignored. Representative rules are important to all, so that a worker disobeying a safety rule is likely to be seen, by workmates as well as management, as careless and as requiring some sanction. Punishment-centred rules are imposed, and the group on whom they are imposed may well feel that they are unfair, and may react by trying to evade them, supporting those who are punished, and questioning their relevance.

Rules are not, then, all alike. Gouldner stresses (1954: 205) that his types are not fixed: in another organization a safety rule might have a punishment-centred and not a representative character. He also makes an important but implicit qualification about representative bureaucracy. Safety rules can be used to control workers. For example, management introduced a rule preventing movement between parts of the factory that was justified on safety grounds and therefore hard for workers to resist, but its real purpose was to strengthen managerial control over what workers were doing. In addition, management neglected safety interests where these conflicted with the demands of production, a point which has also been made by other writers (e.g. Nichols, 1975). Even 'representative' rules may not serve everyone's interests, and they can be used as a cloak for other things.

Rules, together with the sanctions that go with their breach, are part of wider relations of conflict and control within workplaces. Mellish and Collis-Squires (1976) develop this point in their critique of the 'consensus approach' as represented by the work of Anderman (1972) and Ashdown and Baker (1973). The approach tends to concentrate on procedures and not on the substantive rules that the procedures are intended to enforce. The stress on formalization, moreover, ignores evidence from factory case studies (Brown, 1973; Terry, 1977) that informal rules may supplant formal ones. Managers may grant concessions to workers in order to meet production demands, but concessions can rapidly grow into precedents and then into relatively well-established custom and practice rules. These rules will reflect the reality of bargaining power on the shop-floor, and attempts to codify and formalize procedures are unlikely to have much effect on behaviour.

A further criticism is the inadequate view of management that is adopted. It is assumed that management has the will and the freedom of action to institute reform. But in cases where union organization is weak, there may be little felt need among managements to reform, while, where unions are strong, managers may be unable to institute reform that effectively alters behaviour. In addition, the concentration on management leads to the neglect of discipline that can be imposed by unions and work groups. In situations where workers are organized collectively, discipline ceases to be an individual matter but involves bargaining. And the distinction between the two may lie not in the intrinsic nature of an issue but in the approach taken by the parties in respect of any issue. That is, an apparently individual act such as theft may, in fact, stem from collective norms and understandings.

Mellish and Collis-Squires (1976) outline an alternative view based on their research on the docks. They found that formal rules on time-keeping were ignored, with gangs of workers deciding when to start work and how many workers would be working at any one time. In addition, systematic overtime was worked on a 'task and finish' basis, so that, although workers were supposed to be present for all the overtime period, in practice they went home when the job was finished. Such practices would involve breaches of formal rules such as leaving work without permission and associated clocking offences. The actual rules governing attendance and work conduct were very different from those inscribed in formal rule-books and procedures.

Some of these points require elaboration and qualification. One important elaboration concerns the activities of production managers and supervisors. Mellish and Collis-Squires see workers and shop stewards as the main authors of rule-bending. But the demands of the productive system itself must be given attention. Armstrong et al. (1981) studied three small firms. They found that managers had to juggle a large number of competing demands: orders from customers, the supply of raw materials, and the flow of goods through the production process all created conflicting pressures. Nichols and Beynon (1977: 33) studied the apparently more ordered world of a chemicals factory: they also found that managers faced unremitting pressures of scheduling production so as to try to meet cost and delivery targets. In trying to balance different objectives, managers are unlikely to pay close attention to formal rules about workers' behaviour. It is easy to see how they can permit practices such as task and finish to emerge: managers need workers' co-operation to attain production requirements, and may be willing to buy this co-operation with concessions.

But how universal is this tendency? Mellish and Collis-Squires (1976) imply that all work groups tend to develop collective norms that undermine managerial rules and, while admitting that the docks are in many ways exceptional, they treat their research material as illustrative of a more general phenomenon. But as the authors themselves note in criticizing the corrective approach, there are also circumstances in which workers' shop-floor organization is weak and in which firms have little incentive to bring their disciplinary arrangements in line with the corrective model. Informal practices do not necessarily emerge to challenge formal rules. And, even where such practices exist, they need not pose a direct threat to managerial rules. That is, they may form part of a set of shop-floor understandings about appropriate forms of workplace behaviour, but they may not be so strong as to replace the formal rules – instead formal and informal practices may have an uneasy co-existence.

Varieties of shop-floor relations

The different meanings of discipline may be pursued by considering a range of cases. The aim is to illustrate two points: first, how the construction of discipline depends on a day-to-day negotiation of order; and, second, how the form of this order varies significantly even though the formal rules may be the same. The cases may be roughly ordered according to the degree to which managerial rules were openly challenged by workers (for details of this classification, see Edwards, P. K., 1986: 224–81).

We will begin with cases used by Mellish and Collis-Squires to argue that shopfloor rules effectively supplant the rule-book. As Mars (1974) shows in his study of dockers, there are strong work group standards of behaviour, and members of the group display a high degree of commitment to these standards. The norms have both a positive and a negative aspect: positive in that certain behaviour is prescribed, and negative in that there are powerful sanctions for non-conformity. A member of a dockers' gang who told management about illicit practices would find himself severely penalized. Among the main practices involved are what is known in some ports as 'welting' (i.e. the practice of organizing work such that half of the crew works while the other half rests, sometimes away from the workplace) and the systematic pilferage of cargo. There are strict rules on the latter concerning what types of goods should be pilfered and how much should be taken. Attempts to enforce the formal rules are likely to be met with a collective response. Gangs of workers are self-governing and self-regulating. Just how typical such arrangements are, even within the docks themselves, is of course an open question. It is likely that containerization and the growth of small independent ports have altered the dockworkers' tradition in important respects, but the example remains important as an extreme case of the strength of social norms.

A second pattern exists where work group control is weaker. Workers are unable to enforce their informal rules against the formal ones, but they enjoy some collective control over their own efforts. Leading examples are of piece-workers in engineering factories (in Britain, Lupton, 1963; Brown, 1973: in the US, Roy, 1954; Burawoy, 1979). Workers often develop 'fiddles' which allow them to control the variability of earnings and to attain 'loose' times for their work. Practices include running machines faster than work study standards allow and starting one job when still booked in on another. There are collective norms about behaviour, notably about not producing too much output for fear of 'damaging the rate'. But these norms are enforced through the relatively informal means of work group pressures, whereas in more strongly organized plants shop stewards can police a factory-wide earnings ceiling and have the power to fine rate-busters. Though the studies do not describe how disciplinary procedures worked, it is likely that management had more discretion than in the case of strong work groups. Issues such as absenteeism, for example, could probably be handled without the risk of organized reaction. Managements needed, however, to view the workplace regime as a whole. Thus Lupton stresses that in his case toleration of fiddles may have meant that more costly and unpredictable behaviour, like absence and quitting, was constrained. Though fiddles broke or bent some rules, they contributed to the maintenance of a shop-floor order.

These cases illustrate particularly clearly two themes of general applicability. First, it is not possible to break behaviour down into the normal, which falls within the rules, and the abnormal breaches of rules. Running a machine outside established tolerances, for example, may conflict with a formal rule, but if it increases output without endangering quality standards – as often seemed to be the case – everyone gains. Second, and relatedly, understandings on the shop-floor may help to achieve management's substantive goals, even when the formal rules are breached. Burawoy (1979: 171–6), for example, notes a common cycle: senior management, worried that costs are out of control, imposes a crack-down; the rules are followed absolutely; the result is chaos; and shop-level management allows a return to normality. As Roy tartly notes, the image of an economically rational management faced with recalcitrant workers is often an inversion of the truth, for workers often strive to meet production goals despite the rules to which they are subject, and managers can impose rules that actually interfere with production.

In a third pattern, fiddles are still prevalent but management has more power and shop-floor organization is weak or non-existent. The retail and hotel and catering industries (Mars, 1973; 1982: 66–75) are examples. In Ditton's (1979b) study of a bakery, illicit practices were rife. They included short-changing customers and pilfering the company's goods. Such practices are endemic in sectors where money changes hands and where it is hard to check the quantity and quality of goods. They were encouraged by management either directly, supervisors often coaching workers in appropriate ways to fiddle, or indirectly, because basic wages were kept low and workers were provided with plenty of opportunities to fiddle (Ditton, 1977). Managers were well aware of the practices, and occasionally cracked down with dismissals – unlike more strongly organized groups, workers lacked the power to resist. Yet such action had only a temporary effect, for identical practices would soon reappear: 'sacking one workforce and then replacing it with another is merely expensive in recruitment and training' (Ditton, 1979b: 101).

In cases of this kind, formal discipline and day-to-day conduct are disconnected. Management can hardly be seen as the custodian of rules that are in the interests of all. Fiddling is endemic, and it is not a matter of applying rules to deal with the minority who step beyond acceptable standards. The rules themselves are applied as the chance of a fiddle's coming to attention dictates. Rules cannot be operated even-handedly between different offences and offenders. And managerial omission and commission encourage the practices which are then penalized.

A fourth type of case occurs where managerial power is considerable and where the opportunities for fiddles are less available than they are in sectors such as hotels. In three plants studied by Armstrong et al. (1981) there were a few informal practices, but management could clamp down on them with confidence. However, it was not a matter of the simple application of the rule-book: managers would bend their own rules when it suited them. For example, fork-lift trucks should have been driven only by qualified drivers, but management successfully argued that workers without qualifications should continue at the job because this was the established custom. Similarly, despite a national agreement that required notice to be given of short-time working, managers were able to evade this by persuading workers to accept lay-offs, because the benefits (having time off, albeit unpaid, and keeping in with managers) outweighed the returns through insisting on their rights. Managers can thus impose their own interpretations of rules, which are not necessarily a statement of the rights of the industrial citizen but are instead a set of political resources.

A similar picture emerges from the clothing plants in the Edwards and Scullion study discussed above. Discipline there was highly visible, with workers frequently being admonished for poor work standards. Yet three features temper the image of autocracy. First, the rules were applied in very different ways to different groups of workers. Male machine-tenders were supervised in a relatively relaxed way, and a few breaks to go outside for a smoke were tolerated. Female workers, by contrast, were the direct producers, and managers saw any non-productive time as lost. Even among these workers, however, there were differences: longer serving employees with valued skills were allowed to bargain over effort standards in ways which would have led to the threat of discipline had they been attempted by less strategically placed groups. Second, there were some escape routes. Thus absence rates were high but managers did not crack down on them, largely because absence imposed few direct costs on them. Third, there were genuine efforts to sustain a paternalist atmosphere, so that, for example, workers who became ill might be driven home by managers. There was also an implicit bargain there, with managers being careful to maintain certain standards of fairness, notably ensuring an even distribution of 'good' and 'bad' work. Discipline was a long way from the corrective model, but it was also not based on straight autocracy.

Before leaving the case of strict managerial control, it should be stressed that 'authoritarian' methods are not limited to small and medium-size firms. Cavendish (1982: 84) reports an incident that happened while she was working on the assembly-line in a firm employing 20,000 people. A young woman was doing a particularly difficult job and expressing her dissatisfaction by working slowly. She was taken to the supervisor's office and told to work properly or hand in her resignation: she did the latter, and was thus recorded as having left voluntarily. The niceties of disciplinary procedures are a long way from a reality in which workers are weak and uncertain of their formal rights. Pollert (1981) describes very similar experiences of women working in one of the subsidiaries of the Imperial Group.

The plants described above each employed several hundred workers. But what of smaller firms? One image is one of harmony, with discipline being achieved through consent. Rainnie (1989) has tried to overturn this view by using evidence from clothing firms to paint a picture of unrelieved managerial domination. As Ram (1991) points out, however, the detailed research evidence to support this picture is lacking. In his own study, Ram considered very small Asian-owned firms. One might expect autocracy to be particularly severe here, as the firms faced intense market competition and as the managers could use family loyalties to regulate their female workers. In fact, there was tacit negotiation. Managers could not be too assertive for fear of losing workers and then being unable to meet peaks of demand; and piece rates were set according to informal understandings and not managerial diktat. Workers were also able to use gender as a resource, for the Asian culture made it hard for male managers to control female workers directly. This certainly did not mean that there was anything like harmony, for there were clear differences of interest between employers and workers, but these differences were handled through what Ram calls a negotiated paternalism.

Other studies of small firms also point to considerable informality, though its nature can vary. Swaffin-Smith (1982) studied 36 firms each with fewer than 200 workers. Discipline was handled informally, and an employer might give a worker a 'last chance' instead of sticking to the letter of the procedure. Evans et al. (1985) likewise found that employees did not want a proceduralized system, for fear that flexible working relationships would be damaged. Goffee and Scase (1982) have identified a distinct variant of this view. In small building firms, there was not paternalism but 'fraternalism': boss and employee worked alongside each other, the employer had often worked at the trade before running his own firm, and relations were brotherly rather than hierarchical.

Such studies indicate the various ways in which discipline is negotiated in practice. Managements would need to be alive to the politics of the situation before deploying the rule-book: in the strongly organized cases, it might be met with resistance; in workplaces where fiddles flourish, a crack-down might upset existing expectations about the bargain between manager and worker and could well be counter-productive; and so on. The meaning of discipline on the shopfloor turns on the wider form of order which is negotiated, not the rule-book.

Rules and power

The cases described above do not cover every eventuality. What, in particular, of firms with sophisticated human resource policies: can they not create a more integrated approach to discipline? This point is taken up with direct reference to the present in the following section but, in doing so, the weight of evidence from the past needs to be taken into account. The studies surveyed above point to the negotiability of order, even in cases where employment policy was well-developed. Nichols and Beynon's (1977) study, which found a great deal of 'muddling through', was conducted in a large chemicals firm which is often seen as at the forefront of advanced employment policy. A subsequent study disagreed with much of the interpretation but also stressed managers' reliance on workers to interpret instructions intelligently, rather than stick to the letter of an order, and the need of supervisors to make deals in order to cajole workers into working effectively (Harris, 1987). Even 'modern' and 'sophisticated' firms rely on negotiation to establish what the rules actually mean. A major element of this negotiation involves workers in reading the intent of managerial instructions. Not for nothing is one of the more effective forms of industrial action called 'working to rule': withdrawing a willingness to bend and interpret the rules can lead to chaos.

It follows that the operations of disciplinary procedures by personnel managers is not just a technical matter. It will depend on the broader objectives of management and the situation in which it finds itself. Consider, for example, the discussion by Strauss and Sayles (1980: 225) of a case in which a disciplinary suspension was withheld because there was a rush of jobs and management needed the worker in question. The authors criticize the decision, arguing that there should be consistency and that the employees learnt that the relevant rule would not be enforced. Similar practices have been reported by Henry (1983: 114) and by Cunnison (1966: 94), and appear to be quite common. They may be necessary in particular circumstances, and a personnel manager who insisted on procedural correctness in all circumstances would not be popular with other managers trying to meet delivery dates. The application of rules must reflect organizational necessities and the demands and interests of different groups within management, as well as the reactions of workers on the shop-floor. A disciplinary policy which tries to ride roughshod over these realities will be resisted or ignored.

Discipline thus turns on the politics of the management of labour. But this is not to follow the usual 'radical' approach of stressing power and inequality: the approach offers a stark vision of the enterprise in which managers control workers, who either knuckle under or resist, and in which any disciplinary reform is seen as a means to assert better control. This approach has an image of management as unduly unified and rational, a view which it shares, ironically, with the prescriptive texts' assumption that it is possible to produce rules that are in the interests of all. It also sees workers as simply recalcitrant, whereas the prescriptive view assumes that they are obedient. The approach adopted here stems from a view of management as an uncertain and continuous process and of workers as having interests which can conflict with those of managers while also having elements in common (Edwards, P. K., 1986; Hyman, 1987).

W(h)ither Discipline?

It is widely assumed that there has been a shift away from a 'them and us' atmosphere, with discipline being accordingly more consensual. As noted above, self-discipline is a popular theme. From a conventional standpoint, Torrington and Chapman (1979: 245) detect a shift in managerial thinking away from penalties and towards an internalized sense of duty. From a more radical viewpoint, Henry (1982) discerns a move towards peer-group discipline based on notions of participation and responsibility. Such claims are part of a wider analysis which identifies a breakdown of collectivism and the growth of a sense of common purpose. In a celebrated article, Walton (1985) spoke of a shift from control to commitment. Some of these wider themes are taken up in other chapters in this volume. The present discussion focuses on how the disciplinary rules are changing. It is not a matter of the disappearance of control but of its operating in different ways: control through formal procedures may be being replaced by control through commitment.

Any shift towards self-discipline is probably less dramatic than it might seem. The above discussion has stressed the ways in which workers have always used their creativity: the traditional craft worker is a prime example of a self-disciplined individual. Since any worker will have some idea of the responsibilities of the task, how can we distinguish an allegedly new self-discipline from anything else? Proponents of the idea would probably link it with broader trends in human resource management such as the development of a long-term strategic perspective and an integrated approach to the management of people (Guest, 1987). As indicated at the start of the chapter, Nissan would be one example of a firm claiming to have created a qualitatively new style of employee relations.

Before looking at some trends in discipline, the context needs to be understood. It is a commonplace that competitive pressures are making all kinds of organization more conscious of the demands of efficiency. There is a hard edge to ideas of self-discipline. A good example is the increasing attention being given to absenteeism. A survey of 25 organizations found that half of them were regulating absence more closely than in the past, and a review of the literature found several studies noting in passing the same tendency (Edwards and Whitston, 1989a; 1989b). Reports in the specialist press cite growing interest in absence control in organizations such as the police and local authorities as well as private sector firms (Industrial Relations Services, 1990). This interest does not generally stem from any rise in rates of absence, which have remained constant over the past few years. It seems to reflect a problem of labour costs: as pressures for efficiency increase, and as any slack through generous staffing levels is eliminated, firms begin to look at ways to utilize their labour forces more fully. The implication for discipline is that attendance standards will be identified more carefully and that absences which in the past might provoke no comment will now involve some kind of managerial action.

Case studies in four organizations (a food manufacturer, a hospital, an area of British Rail and a financial services organization) illustrate the possibilities (Edwards and Whiston, 1993). In all four, managers were giving more attention to absence control. In the first three, about two-thirds of workers in a questionnaire sample said that they were aware of managerial pressures to attend work and of changes in the approach, towards a tighter regulation of attendance. These demands were not necessarily resented, and managers did not act arbitrarily. None the less, it was striking that the reasons for tighter control were not explained to workers or unions: managers simply decided on a new policy and put it into effect. Standards of acceptable behaviour were thus managerially defined. One strand running through many sorts of firm is likely to be such a systematization of demands on workers.

Within this overall picture, several different strands can be identified in current practice. First, there is the traditional small firm sector, where relationships are likely to continue to depend on informality. Second, some larger firms retain an essentially Taylorist form of work organization. For example, Gabriel (1988) studied a fast-food chain. He found that workers were required to follow operating procedures laid down in very precise detail. Though such firms often use the language of 'teams' and 'crews' there were no teams in the sense of autonomous working groups, and workers were well aware that a departure from required procedures would lead to a warning and possibly dismissal.

A third trend involves firms where there has been an effort to overturn the collectivism of the past. It is, for example, widely argued that in the public sector pressures for efficiency are replacing consensus management with a more commercial logic. The implication is that discipline is operated in a harsher manner than in the past, with some suggestions being made that managers now have the power to act as they wish. There have been few studies investigating this directly. The case studies mentioned above threw some light on the question. In the two public sector cases, BR and the hospital, there was deep distrust of management, reflecting changed working practices and a dislike of a commercial ethos. But there had not been a total shift to a new regime. In the case of BR, there was a clear increase in the use of disciplinary penalties, notably a willingness of managers to dismiss more readily than in the past. But the practice was too complex to be described simply as autocratic. For example, absence was being regulated more closely but it was only a minority of poor attenders who were identified for close attention. And the day-to-day operation of the workplace continued to depend on a negotiation of consent. Workers were, for example, still able to slip out of the workplace during working hours: supervisors tolerated this because it did not directly reduce efficiency and because to attack the practice would sour relationships and make it more difficult to persuade workers to co-operate, for example by working overtime at short notice. In the hospital, workers remained committed to the idea of the public service, and there was little evidence of stricter discipline. As against the image of a unified, commercially driven management there were important differences between managers in labour policy, and this was a major factor in the continuation of former practices at workplace level. Both cases, moreover, illustrate that workers can be committed to their work and to the ideal of service to the client while being distinctly distrustful of management.

If we turn to firms claiming to have made a break with the past, we can begin with Nissan. As noted at the start of the chapter, Wickens sees self-discipline as replacing mechanistic controls, one concrete result being an absence rate of 3 per cent as against the motor industry average of 10 per cent. The independent observer will, however, ask whether the former causes the latter. As Wickens (1987: 107) notes, 'the workforce is young and all have undergone a stringent medical examination': some potential sources of absence have been organized out of the system. There is, moreover, no direct evidence that workers displayed high levels of loyalty to the company. Some stories have appeared suggesting that, on the contrary, there was a strict regime and an unremitting pace of work (Briggs, 1988). Garrahan and Stewart (1991) claim to explore the realities of the 'Nissan way'. Much of their account is descriptive, and the basis of their argument is not always clear. But running through it is a sense that team-working imposes new pressures on workers, as in the view that the success of the system 'depends upon a high level of subordination of individual needs to those of the company' (ibid.: 58). Self-discipline creates pressures, and taking responsibility means demands as well as independence. But this is arguably not a case of workers' needs and the company's wishes being simply opposed. It is, rather, one in which the company has created a new structure in which workers' interests are organized in new ways. Some of these interests – for example in clean working conditions and job security – may be advanced further than they are in more traditional firms, even though there are also new demands.

John Geary's chapter in this volume uses this and other examples to show how new systems of work organization restructure the relationship between managers and workers. They mean neither the generation of harmony nor a return to simple autocracy but the establishment of a new balance of responsibilities. Externally imposed controls have not disappeared but they have become less overt as managers speak the language of self-discipline.

For present purposes, three studies are instructive. Wall et al. (1986) found that dismissal for disciplinary reasons was actually higher where autonomous working groups had been established than they were in other parts of the same firm. Managers were conscious of applying a tougher approach, which they attributed to pressures to meet production targets in a greenfield operation and to the way in which the groups worked: under conventional systems, supervisors would act at once to warn an employee who was stepping out of line, but the groups were reluctant to apply their own disciplines and managers were left relying on formal penalties because problems were not identified early enough. This study offers some rare hard evidence on the links between self-discipline and actual practice. If at all representative, it suggests that the coercive edge of new forms of work organization may be in some ways more evident than under conventional bureaucratic methods. Similarly, Sewell and Wilkinson (1992) studied a plant using just-in-time systems and found that the demands of the technology were substantial, with electronic monitoring identifying workers' errors and with warnings for poor performance being regularly applied. Finally, an American study of a participative system noted that workers generally found the rules not more relaxed, but tougher: the new code of conduct was 'pleasingly philosophic, yet disturbingly imprecise', and it left management with a 'much more unrestricted hand in meting out penalties' (Zipp and Lane, 1987: 75).

Demands on workers do seem to have increased. The meaning of 'discipline' may thus have changed. In the past, especially when capitalized, the term meant the first two faces of formal rules and their enforcement. The third face, of day-to-day conduct, was part of a shop-floor reality that was often separate from rules and procedures. As managements have aimed to regulate this reality, they have become more interested in the third face. Self-discipline can be more demanding than a bureaucratic system because it is more difficult for the worker to hide behind the argument that his or her responsibility stops at a specified point. 'New' forms of self-discipline may thus differ from the 'old', not because there is now active commitment when in the past there was none, but because firms have been able to take the world of disciplinary practice and shape it in ways which are more amenable to their own goals. The third face of discipline, which used to exist in a shadowy world of customs and informality, is now more subject to deliberate managerial policy.

As John Geary's chapter shows, self-discipline remains a minority practice. Like any other means to regulate labour, it needs active management. Since the tensions may be more hidden than they would have been in the past – no lightning strikes to warn of trouble – sensitivity to potential workers' discontents is required. For the majority of firms, even more caution may be needed. It is easy to believe that new initiatives can promote commitment, but it may also be the case that managements are imposing stricter disciplinary regimes. This was certainly the implication of some studies discussed above, the result being that the message of discipline impinges far more forcibly on the shop-floor than that of commitment, and indeed undermines it. As ever, discipline can conflict with other corporate goals. It needs to be understood as one element in continuing efforts to regulate the balance of conflict and consent in the workplace.

Bibliography

Anderman, S. D. 1972. *Voluntary Dismissals Procedure and the Industrial Relations Act*. London: Political and Economic Planning.

Armstrong, P. 1983. 'Class Relationships at the Point of Production: A Case Study'. *Sociology*, 17, 3, 339–58.

Armstrong, P., Goodman, J. F. B. and Hyman, J. D. 1981. *Ideology and Shop Floor Industrial Relations*. London: Croom Helm.

Ashdown, R. T. and Baker, K. H. 1973. *In Working Order: A Study of Industrial Discipline*. Department of Employment Manpower Papers 6. London: HMSO.

Bagwell, P. S. 1963. *The Railwaymen: The History of the National Union of Railwaymen*. London: Allen & Unwin.

Batstone, E. 1986. 'Labour and Productivity'. *Oxford Review of Economic Policy*, 2, 3, 32–42.

Batstone, E., Boraston, I. and Frenkel, S. 1977. *Shop Stewards in Action: The Organization of Workplace Conflict and Accommodation*. Oxford: Blackwell.

Beach, D. S. 1975. *Personnel: The Management of People at Work*, 3rd edn. New York: Macmillan.

Briggs, S. 1988. 'The End of the Nissan Honeymoon'. *New Statesman and Society*, 15 July, 25–6.

Brown, W. 1973. *Piecework Bargaining*. London: Heinemann.

Burawoy, M. 1979. *Manufacturing Consent: Changes in the Labor Process under Monopoly Capitalism*. Chicago: University of Chicago Press.

Cameron, D. 1984. 'The When, Why and How of Discipline'. *Personnel Journal*, July, 37–9.

Cavendish, R. 1982. *Women on the Line*. London: Routledge & Kegan Paul.

Child, J. and Partridge, B. 1982. *Lost Managers: Supervisors in Industry and Society*. Cambridge: Cambridge University Press.

Clifton, R. and Tatton-Brown, C. 1979. *Impact of Employment Legislation on Small Firms*. Department of Employment Research Paper 6. London: HMSO.

Clinton, A. 1984. *Post Office Workers: A Trade Union and Social History*. London: Allen & Unwin.

Collins, H. 1982a. 'Capitalist Discipline and Corporatist Law'. *Industrial Law Journal*, 11, 1, 78–93.

Collins, H. 1982b. 'Capitalist Discipline and Corporatist Law'. *Industrial Law Journal*, 11, 3, 170–7.

Corrigan, P. and Sayer, D. 1991. *The Great Arch: English State Formation as Cultural Revolution*, rev. edn. Oxford: Blackwell.

Cunnison, S. 1966. *Wages and Work Allocation: A Study of Social Relations in a Garment Workshop*. London: Tavistock.

Daniel, W. W. and Stilgoe, E. 1978. *The Impact of Employment Protection Laws*. London: Policy Studies Institute.

Dawson, P. and Webb, J. 1989. 'New Production Arrangements: The Totally Flexible Cage?' *Work, Employment and Society*, 3, 2, 221–38.

Deaton, D. 1984. 'The Incidence of Dismissals in British Manufacturing Industry'. *Industrial Relations Journal*, 15, 2, 61–5.

Dickens, L., Jones, M., Weekes, B. and Hart, M. 1985. *Dismissed: A Study of Unfair Dismissal and the Industrial Tribunal System*. Oxford: Blackwell.

Ditton, J. 1977. *Part-Time Crime: An Ethnography of Fiddling and Pilferage*. London: Macmillan.

Ditton, J. 1979a. 'Baking Time'. *Sociological Review*, 27, 1, 157–67.

Ditton, J. 1979b. *Controlology: Beyond the New Criminology*. London: Macmillan.

Edwards, P. K. 1986. *Conflict at Work: A Materialist Analysis of Workplace Relations*. Oxford: Blackwell.

Edwards, P. K. 1992. 'Disciplinary Practice: A Case Study of the Railways, 1860–1988'. Paper presented to Tenth Annual Conference on the Organization and Control of the Labour Process, Aston University, April.

Edwards, P. K. and Scullion, H. 1982a. 'Deviancy Theory and Industrial Praxis: A Study of Discipline and Social Control in an Industrial Setting'. *Sociology*, 16, 3, 322–40.

Edwards, P. K. and Scullion, H. 1982b. *The Social Organization of Industrial Conflict: Control and Resistance in the Workplace*. Oxford: Blackwell.

Edwards, P. K. and Whitston, C. 1989a. *The Control of Absenteeism: An Interim Report*. Warwick Papers in Industrial Relations 23, January. Coventry: Industrial Relations Research Unit.

Edwards, P. K. and Whitston, C. 1989b. 'Industrial Discipline, the Control of Attendance and the Subordination of Labour'. *Work, Employment and Society*, 3, 1, 1–28.

Edwards, P. K. and Whitston, C. 1993. *Attending to Work: The Management of Attendance and Shopfloor Order*. Oxford: Blackwell.

Edwards, R. 1979. *Contested Terrain: The Transformation of the Workplace in the Twentieth Century*. London: Heinemann.

Elger, T. 1990. 'Technical Innovation and Work Reorganization in British Manufacturing in the 1980s: Continuity, Intensification or Transformation?' *Work, Employment and Society*, Additional Special Issue, May, 67–102.

Evans, S., Goodman, J. F. B. and Hargreaves, L. 1985. *Unfair Dismissal Law and Employment Practice in the 1980s*. Department of Employment Research Paper 53. London: HMSO.

Gabriel, Y. 1988. *Working Lives in Catering*. London: Routledge & Kegan Paul.

Garrahan, P. and Stewart, P. 1991. 'Work Organisation in Transition: The Human Resource Management Implications Of The "Nissan Way"'. *Human Resource Management Journal*, 2, 2, 46–62.

Gersuny, C. 1976. '"A Devil in Petticoats" and Just Cause: Patterns of Punishment in Two New England Factories'. *Business History Review*, 50, 2, 131–52.

Glasbeek, H. J. 1984. 'The Utility of Model Building: Collins' Capitalist Discipline and Corporatist Law'. *Industrial Law Journal*, 13, 3, 133–52.

Goffee, R. and Scase, R. 1982. '"Fraternalism" and "Paternalism" as Employer Strategies in Small Firms'. In Day, G. et al. (eds) *Diversity and Decomposition in the Labour Market*. Aldershot: Gower, 107–24.

Gouldner, A. W. 1954. *Patterns of Industrial Bureaucracy: A Case Study of Modern Factory Administration*. New York: Free Press.

Guest, D. E. 1987. 'Human Resource Management and Industrial Relations'. *Journal of Management Studies*, 24, 5, 503–22.

Haiven, L. 1988. 'The Political Apparatuses of Production: Generation and Resolution of Industrial Conflict in Canada and Britain'. Ph.D. thesis, University of Warwick.

Harris, R. 1987. *Power and Powerlessness in Industry: An Analysis of the Social Relations of Production*. London: Tavistock.

Henry, S. 1982. 'Factory Law: The Changing Disciplinary Technology of Industrial Social Control'. *International Journal of the Sociology of Law*, 10, 4, 365–83.

Henry, S. 1983. *Private Justice: Towards Integrated Theorising in the Sociology of Law*. London: Routledge & Kegan Paul.

Hudson, K. 1970. *Working to Rule. Railway Workshop Rules: A Study of Industrial Discipline*. Bath: Adams & Dart.

Hyman, R. 1987. 'Strategy or Structure: Capital, Labour and Control'. *Work, Employment and Society*, 1, 1, 25–56.

Industrial Relations Services. 1990. 'Attending to Absence'. *Industrial Relations Review and Report*, 461, April, 5–9.

Industrial Relations Services. 1991a. 'Discipline at Work 1: The Practice'. *IRS Employment Trends*, 493, August, 6–14.

Industrial Relations Services. 1991b. 'Discipline at Work 2: Procedures'. *IRS Employment Trends*, 494, August, 5–15.

IPM. 1979. *Disciplinary Procedures and Practice*. London: Institute of Personnel Management.

Kelly, J. and Kelly, C. 1991. '"Them and Us": Social Psychology and the

"New Industrial Relations"'. *British Journal of Industrial Relations*, 29, 1, 25–48.

Littler, C. R. 1982. *The Development of the Labour Process in Capitalist Societies*. London: Heinemann.

Lupton, T. 1963. *On the Shop Floor: Two Studies of Workshop Organization and Output*. Oxford: Pergamon.

McCarthy, W. E. J. 1966. *The Role of Shop Stewards in British Industrial Relations*. Research Paper 1, Royal Commission on Trade Unions and Employers' Associations. London: HMSO.

McCarthy, W. E. J. and Parker, S. R. (1968). *Shop Stewards and Workshop Relations*. Research Paper 10, Royal Commission on Trade Unions and Employers' Associations. London: HMSO.

Mars, G. 1973. 'Chance, Punters and the Fiddle: Institutionalized Pilferage in a Hotel Dining Room'. In Warner, M. (ed.) *The Sociology of the Workplace: An Interdisciplinary Approach*. London: Allen & Unwin, 200–10.

Mars, G. 1974. 'Dock Pilferage'. In Rock, P. and McIntosh, M. (eds) *Deviance and Social Control*. London: Tavistock, 209–28.

Mars, G. 1982. *Cheats at Work: An Anthropology of Workplace Crime*. London: Counterpoint.

Mellish, M. and Collis-Squires, N. 1976. 'Legal and Social Norms in Discipline and Dismissal'. *Industrial Law Journal*, 5, 3, 164–77.

Millward, N., Stevens, M., Smart, D. and Hawes, W. R. 1992. *Workplace Industrial Relations in Transition*. Aldershot: Dartmouth.

Newby, H. 1977. 'Paternalism and Capitalism'. In Scase, R. (ed.) *Industrial Society: Class, Cleavage and Control*. London: Allen & Unwin, 59–73.

Nichols, T. 1975. 'The Sociology of Accidents and the Social Production of Industrial Injury'. In Esland, G., Salaman, G. and Speakman, M.-A. (eds) *People and Work*. Edinburgh: Holmes McDougal, 217–29.

Nichols T. and Beynon, H. 1977. *Living with Capitalism: Class Relations and the Modern Factory*. London: Routledge & Kegan Paul.

Plumridge, M. D. 1966. 'Disciplinary Practice'. *Personnel Management*, September, 138–41.

Pollard, S. 1965. *The Genesis of Modern Management: A Study of the Industrial Revolution in Great Britain*. London: Arnold.

Pollert, A. 1981. *Girls, Wives, Factory Lives*. London: Macmillan.

Prude, J. 1983. 'The Social System of Early New England Textile Mills: A Case Study, 1812–40'. In Frisch, M. H. and Walkowitz, D. J. (eds) *Working-Class America*. Urbana, IL: University of Illinois Press, 1–36.

Purcell, J. 1987. 'Mapping Management Styles in Employee Relations', *Journal of Management Studies*, 24, 5, 533–48.

Rainnie, A. 1989. *Industrial Relations in Small Firms: Small Isn't Beautiful*. London: Routledge & Kegan Paul.

Ram, M. 1991. 'Control and Autonomy in Small Firms: The Case of the West Midlands Clothing Industry'. *Work, Employment and Society*, 5, 4,

601–20.

Reid, D. A. 1976. 'The Decline of Saint Monday, 1766–1876'. *Past and Present*, 71, 76–101.

Roy, D. 1954. 'Efficiency and "The Fix": Informal Intergroup Relations in a Piecework Machine Shop'. *American Journal of Sociology*, 60, 2, 255–66.

Sewell, G. and Wilkinson, B. 1992. '"Someone to Watch over Me": Surveillance, Discipline and the Just-in-Time Labour Process'. *Sociology*, 26, 2, 271–90.

Sokolik, S. L. 1970. *The Personnel Process: Line and Staff Dimensions in Managing People at Work*. Scranton, PA: International Textbook.

Strauss, G. and Sayles, L. R. 1980. *Personnel: The Human Problem of Management*, 4th edn. Englewood Cliffs, NJ: Prentice Hall.

Swaffin-Smith, C. 1982. 'Small Businessmen and Disciplinary Issues'. *Employee Relations*, 4, 1, 27–31.

Terry, M. 1977. 'The Inevitable Growth of Informality'. *British Journal of Industrial Relations*, 15, 1, 76–90.

Thomason, G. F. 1988. *A Textbook of Human Resource Management*. London: Institute of Personnel Management.

Torrington, D. and Chapman, J. 1979. *Personnel Management*. Englewood Cliffs, NJ: Prentice Hall.

Torrington, D. and Hall, L. 1991. *Personnel Management: A New Approach*, 2nd edn. New York: Prentice Hall.

Trevor, M. 1988. *Toshiba's New British Company: Competitiveness through Innovation in Industry*. London: Policy Studies Institute.

Upton, R. 1987. 'What Makes a Disciplinary Procedure Appealing?' *Personnel Management*, December, 46–9.

Wall, T. D., Kemp, N. J. and Jackson, P. R. 1986. 'Outcomes of Autonomous Work Groups: A Long-term Field Experiment'. *Academy of Management Journal*, Vol. 21, No. 2, 280–304.

Walton, R. E. 1985. 'From Control to Commitment in the Workplace'. *Harvard Business Review*, 53, 2, 77–84.

Welch, B. 1978. 'Keeping the Discipliners in Line'. *Personnel Management*, August, 21–4.

Wickens, P. 1987. *The Road to Nissan: Flexibility, Quality, Teamwork*. London: Macmillan.

Wood, S. 1986. 'The Cooperative Labour Strategy in the US Auto Industry'. *Economic and Industrial Democracy*, 7, 4, 415–47.

Zipp, J. F. and Lane, K. E. 1987. 'Plant Closings and Control over the Workplace'. *Work and Occupations*, 14, 1, 62–87.

PART VI

Participation and Involvement

18

Communicating with Employees

Barbara Townley

It is generally true to say that British management has not placed a strong emphasis on employee communication programmes. Communications is an area which has been neglected, ignored, taken for granted or left to others, despite many prescriptive statements that communication is of central importance for the effective functioning of an organization. Within general management and personnel literature, communication programmes have often been prescribed as a universal panacea for a variety of ailments: low employee morale, high absenteeism and turnover rates, low productivity, resistance to change and, perhaps most frequently, labour conflict. Where recognized, the communication 'gap' is seen as bridgeable. The 'content and techniques' approaches to communication programmes have exhorted management to 'identify your audience', 'know your objective', and discuss the relative merits of the various methods available to communicate what employees 'ought to know'. The aim of this chapter is to locate corporate communication systems in a broader context. In doing so, it considers the extent to which companies have taken prescripts concerning the need for effective communication to heart, and examines the rationale for, and the implications of, their introduction. Although recognizing the importance of communication at all levels in the organization, the emphasis here will be on direct communication between management and individual employees.

Communications in Practice

A survey conducted in the mid-1970s found that 80 per cent of employees did not feel that their company kept them informed of corporate developments (CBI, 1976: 32). Reasons advanced for this apparent neglect include the limited demand for information from employees and a lack of employee interest in the company. There is evidence, however, that British management is beginning to take the area of employee communication more seriously, with a growing awareness of the role that formal programmes can play within the organization. A survey by the Institute of Personnel Management (IPM, 1981a) indicated an increasing financial commitment to such programmes, from an average expenditure of £8 per employee in 1977 to an estimated £15 in 1983, although one-third of the organizations did not undertake systematic costings of their programmes. This is paralleled by an increase (to 42 per cent) in the number of companies which had appointed individuals with sole responsibility for employee communication at senior management level, and an increase (to 40 per cent) in those with written policy statements (ibid.: 6). Significantly, the number with written policy statements is more than twice the earlier estimates of 13 per cent (Knight, 1979) and 21 per cent (Reeves and Chambers, 1978).

Later surveys also indicate an increased commitment to employee communication programmes. A survey by the Institute of Directors (IOD) and Communications and Employee Relations Training, of organizations which in total employed over 400,000 workers, reported both a major increase in companies' commitment to communicating with employees and a wider range of communication techniques in use. Eighty per cent of large companies (i.e. with over 1000 employees) had some form of regular communication system (Thomson and McAdam, 1988). Small firms employing less than 100 and medium-size companies (100–1000 employees) improved employee communication in response to business growth, or where they were affected by a merger or takeover. The Third Workplace Industrial Relations Survey (WIRS 3) indicates that there has been an increase in communication programmes in the late 1980s, in terms of the new initiatives which have been introduced. Forty-five per cent of establishments reported newly introduced initiatives in the 1990 survey, as compared to 35 per cent in 1984, these being more prevalent in the public and service sectors. Over 90 per cent of establishments used one or more methods of communicating with employees, with numerous methods being used in conjunction more than before (Millward et al., 1992).

Downward communication – from employer to employee

Management communication systems are likely to use a number of different methods, although with a preference for oral rather than written presentations (see table 18.1). The most common form of communication with employees across all employment sectors is the systematic use of the 'management chain', with 60 per cent of employers reporting its use (Millward et al., 1992). This is supported by the use of annual meetings between senior management and all sections of the workforce (41 per cent). These are increasingly being supplemented by in-house newspapers, magazines and special reports. The latter, however, tend to be the prerogative of larger multi-establishment enterprises. Forty-one per cent of managers reported the distribution of regular employee newsletters (Millward et al., 1992: 166), a figure reflected in the CBI survey (46 per cent), although slightly lower than the 53 per cent reported by ACAS (1991). These three most popular forms of communication – management chain, meetings with all employees and newsletters – reflect the reported rankings of the earlier Second Workplace Industrial Relations Survey (WIRS 2). Face-to-face communication and staff meetings were the most usual form of communication reported by small and medium-size companies (Thomson and McAdam, 1988). The most common combination of communi-

Table 18.1 Methods of communication – percentage of organizations using them

	WIRS 1984	Higher Level 1985	WIRS 3 1990	ACAS 1990	CBI 1990
Regular meetings (senior management)	34	45	41	N/A	N/A
Regular meetings (junior management)	36	54	48	55	36
Management chain	62	74	60	N/A	N/A
Newsletters	34	61	41	53	46
Videos	N/A	37	N/A	N/A	29
Suggestion schemes	25	36	28	36	35
Surveys and ballots	12	27	17	31	19

cation methods is the use of the management chain allied with newsletters (Marginson et al., 1988: 105). However, traditional written presentation of information (e.g. employee notice boards) are still used in 98 per cent of companies according to one survey (ACAS, 1991).

Conferences and seminars are also becoming more popular, supplementing the more traditional method of direct communication via line management (IPM, 1981a: 28). Audio-visual methods, such as videos and closed-circuit television (CCTV), are used by a minority of companies, largely reflecting cost considerations, although their use is increasing. For example, 63 per cent of the large companies responding to the Institute of Directors survey reported the use of videos compared to 18 per cent in 1983 (Thomson and McAdam, 1988). Where they are used, they tend to be integral to training programmes and the introduction of new working arrangements. A number of larger companies (e.g. IBM, Dunlop, Ford, Shell and ICI) have introduced videos in this context (Maude, 1977: 118). The Warwick Company Level Industrial Relations Survey (CLIRS) showed that 37 per cent of respondents used videos at establishment level. Although the decision to communicate to employees is largely an operational matter, taken at establishment level, the decision to use videos and newsletters is usually taken by division or corporate level staff (Marginson et al., 1988).

The material and channel of communication depends largely on the objectives of communication, corporate culture and the importance of the message to be delivered. Rather than indicating the superiority of one particular method over another, there is a reliance of a series of interlocking channels as the basis of a communication system or network (Marchington et al., 1992). Some methods, for example face-to-face communication, are considered to have greater impact, especially where this is a component of organized line management communication. Employee newspapers, reports, conferences and seminars have a more supportive role: 'useful but not vital' (IPM, 1981a: 34). Research into the extent to which the various methods are appreciated by employees (or the degree to which) they would be missed if not used) indicates that communication through line management is the most popular method of receiving information (IPM, 1981a; Marchington et al., 1992).

Two methods in particular have gained in prominence: employee reports and team briefings. Employee reports, which are the equivalent of shareholder reports, are 'statements produced at least annually, in written form, especially for all employees, which provide information relating to the financial period of the undertaking' (Hussey, 1979: 9). Some of the larger companies have issued these for several years. A survey of the *Financial Times* 30 Share Index found that 27 of the companies prepared them (Holmes, 1977). There are indications of an increase in the number of companies issuing them. Although a relatively low level (22 per cent) was reported by the BIM (1975), a later survey by Hussey and Marsh (1983) reported that 41 per cent of companies were issuing such a report, sometimes on a quarterly or monthly basis. In the IPM (1981a) survey this figure had risen to 62 per cent, with a 21 per cent growth in the years 1977–80, although much of this was in 1979. Companies producing such reports tend to be larger, multi-establishment, public companies with 500 or more employees. Single establishment private companies, employing fewer that 500, make less use of them, although there are some indications that this could change in the future. Marsh and Hussey (1979: 10) conclude that 'the practice of employee reporting is now well established and unlikely to recede'. In some cases employee reports have been supplemented by employee annual meetings, paralleling shareholder meetings, where the company elaborates on the state of the company and future plans.

Of all the communication methods in use, team briefing is perhaps the most systematic in the provision of 'top-down' information to employees. Information is disseminated or 'cascades' through various managerial tiers, being conveyed by the immediate superior to a small group of employees, the optimum number being between four and 20. In this way, too, employee queries are answered. This takes place throughout all levels in the organization, the information eventually being conveyed by supervisors to shop-floor employees. On each occasion the information received is supplemented by 'local' news of a more immediate relevance to those being 'briefed', usually in the ratio of 70 per cent local information to 30 per cent detail from senior management levels. Actively promoted by the Industrial Society, which estimates that is has helped introduce such arrangements in 400–500 organizations, these groups have the advantage of face-to-face communication, increased contact with immediate supervision and involvement of all layers of management, for whom communication becomes a 'normal part of the job' (Garnett, 1980; 1981). The Second Workplace Industrial Relations Survey found that 36 per cent of organizations made use of communication systems which relied on the team briefing principle (Millward and Stevens, 1986: 153), a figure which increased to 48 per cent in the 1990 survey. CLIRS showed that 54 per cent of companies used regular junior management/employee meetings at establishment level (Marginson et al., 1988). The ACAS (1991) and the CBI (1990) surveys reported 55 per cent and 36 per cent respectively. The variation in response is likely to reflect the diversity of methods used which may or may not be officially designated 'team briefing'.

/ New technology has increased the role for interactive communication as part of corporate communication networks. For example, electronic mail networks are now used by some organizations to communicate to their employees. Digital Equipment (UK), for example, uses E-mail as part of its communications programme. Digital also uses videotext which is seen as the main medium of communication for the 1990s. A service called 'Live Wire' carries information, updated daily, on company issues, stories concerning the computing industry, and headlines from daily newspapers. In addition, the programme carries information about personnel matters, job advertisements, details of training courses, and information about employee stock purchase plans (Smith, 1989). This technology also facilitates 'personalized' or 'customized' communications to a greater degree/It is likely that public access terminals or screens which employees can scroll through are going to play an increasingly important part in companies' attempts to keep employees informed. Video-conferencing is also gaining ground in some organizations as costs are lowered. Desktop publishing has also allowed organizations to increase their communication networks considerably.

Organizations with 5000 or more employees are more likely to have formal communication systems, although this is more associated with the structural complexity of the organization rather than size *per se*. They are also more common where there is a specialist personnel function, the latter usually providing the impetus toward the introduction of such schemes (IPM, 1981a: 8). Foreign ownership is another factor correlated with the existence of such schemes (Purcell et al., 1987; Millward et al., 1992; ACAS, 1991).

The nature of information disclosure to employees is difficult to ascertain, with the tendency for employer estimates to give a more favourable impression than employee or trade union estimates. Generally, issues relating to pay and conditions (wages, salaries, fringe benefits, payment systems and pension schemes) are the subject of more communication to the workforce than manpower requirements (issues affecting job security and maintenance of employment), although personnel data (number of employees, labour turnover, absenteeism and redeployment) are usually divulged. Information communicated on production issues (productivity, work scheduling, unit costs, etc.) varies widely. Equally, future plans and prospects (expansion, closure, merger, investments, etc.) are also disclosed to varying degrees. In the IPM (1981a: 43) survey, 40 per cent of companies supplied all employees with production and employment prospects for the following six months. Financial information (details of company finance before and after tax, turnover, etc.) was the subject of least communication, although there is some indication of a slight move away from the traditional pattern of management jealously guarding this type of information (Moore, 1980). The Third Workplace Industrial Relations Survey (Millward et al., 1992) confirms the patterns of disclosure reported in the earlier surveys.

Terms and conditions of employment and major changes in working methods or work organization were the two areas which were more frequently communicated to employees, with 62 and 68 per cent of managers respectively reporting disclosure on these topics. Staffing or manpower plans were the next most common topic for disclosure, however at a much lower level of communication, with only 33 per cent of managers reporting this. This is down from the 40 per cent reported in WIRS 2, with the decline in disclosing this type of information particularly marked in large establishments and where there was recognition of unions. The financial position of the establishment and the organization as a whole, together with investment plans, were the least likely subjects for communication, at 28 and 19 per cent respectively (Millward et al., 1992: 169). CLIRS reported a high percentage (approximately 75 per cent) of companies with a stated policy of communicating information on financial matters and performance to employees. However, on closer inspection less than one-quarter gave employees 'a lot of information' about the financial position of the division, usually the key level of decision making. Fewer than 40 per cent gave a lot of information about investment plans, with nearly one half of respondents claiming they gave no information about investment plans. Generally it was the case that those organizations disclosing a lot of information about financial plans also disclosed information on investment plans (Marginson et al., 1988). When it does occur, disclosure of information on financial issues relies on the use of briefing groups and employee reports.

Not all information is disclosed to every employee. Status within the organizational hierarchy usually determines the amount of information received. Management also draws a distinction between the type of information disclosed and the forum for its disclosure. There is a preference for consultation committees as the medium for disclosure of general performance indicators, on the grounds that this forum was seen as being inherently less conflictual and membership was not just restricted to unionized employees. Information disclosed in this forum is then circulated to other employees usually via written minutes for non-manual employees or notice boards for manual employees, or informal oral communication (Daniel and Millward, 1983: 138). Expansion plans are also released in joint consultation forums, whereas closures and information on income are usually restricted to union channels.

The Third Workplace Industrial Relations Survey found a greater disclosure of information by larger enterprises and foreign-owned companies (Millward et al., 1992: 173) while CLIRS (Marginson et al., 1988) found that companies concentrated in a single sector, those that were profit centres and those in the service sector were more likely to disclose information. Companies holding joint consultation meetings were also more likely to disseminate more information, as were companies where there was a personnel or industrial relations specialist represented on the board (Millward et al., 1992). An early survey (BIM, 1975) showed that those companies recognizing a number of trade unions were more likely to disclose information, a finding reflected in WIRS 3, which found that collection and dissemination of information was related to union recognition and union density. Also, new initiatives in employee communication were more likely to be found in unionized than non-unionized workplaces – 48 per cent as compared to 36 per cent. CLIRS, however, found greater disclosure in those companies which were less likely to recognize trade unions or, where they did, negotiated with them at higher organizational levels. Companies reporting stability or growth in employment tended to disclose more information, including financial information. Companies experiencing employment decline, although reporting that they communicated financial and investment details, were less likely to monitor its implementation (Marginson et al., 1988).

One of the reasons given for limited disclosure of information, especially financial information, is the difficulty it is assumed employees will have in understanding it. Training in information handling, however, was provided by only 35 per cent of companies and even then was usually restricted to managerial and supervisory employees (BIM, 1975). Limited training was also confirmed in the IOD survey (1981): however, case study material reveals that some companies see training as a serious adjunct of a communications system (IPM, 1981b).

Two-way communication

Having given details of the communication methods used to convey information from management to employees, the methods used to ascertain the views of employees will now be examined. Obviously, not all the schemes outlined above are purely 'one-way'. They are, however, primarily designed as a means of imparting information from management to employees and are limited in the extent to which they provide the opportunity for employee feedback, particularly when it comes to opinions on issues not directly related to a predetermined agenda. In an attempt to address this, companies have devised a number of 'two-way' communication systems. WIRS 2 shows that of the initiatives introduced in the 1980–4 period, two-way communication is the most frequently cited (Millward and Stevens, 1986: 165). Twelve per cent of the sampled establishments operated such schemes by 1984, as opposed to 5 per cent in 1980. However, by 1990 there had only been a small further increase in the proportion of companies operating two-way communication schemes, the figure reaching just 13 per cent. The growth of schemes in the public sector (up from 11 to 19 per cent in 1984) was countered by the decrease in the private sector (from 15 to 7 per cent) (Millward et al., 1992: 180).

The most common forms of two-way communication are 'speak out' programmes, suggestion schemes, attitude surveys, and employee appraisals. In 'speak out' or 'speak up' schemes, employees are able to contact a counsellor or ombudsman with a grievance or query. Assured of the strictest confidence, grievances are passed on, anonymously, to whomever has responsibility for the issue concerned, and the individual is usually guaranteed a response within a set time. Where the point is thought to be of general relevance, replies may be printed in company newspapers. In the USA, such schemes have for some time been a feature of communication programmes of large, mainly non-union, corporations – such as Caterpillar, Xerox, Polaroid and Raytheon – where they usually function as useful 'warning devices' in potential litigation cases, for example, sexual harassment cases (Berenbeim, 1980; Foulkes, 1980). In the UK, the IBM 'speak up' system, which is supplemented by an 'open door' programme allowing an employee to appeal against a manager's decision, handles approximately 1000 cases a year covering a range of issues (Incomes Data Services, 1984). Although in theory it is possible for an employee to take an issue to the UK Chairman's office, most are resolved at middle or senior management level (Bassett, 1986: 168–70).

Employee suggestion schemes are also a prominent feature of North American communication programmes. Beneficial in terms of improved employee participation and 'identification', there is also the advantage of increased efficiency and financial savings which can be gained for such schemes. In the UK, a suggestion scheme introduced in Jaguar Cars was estimated to have made savings of 20 per cent in its first year and to have given 'rewards' to employees ranging from £5 to £1250 (*Industrial Relations Review and Report*, 1982). IBM recorded savings of approximately £0.5 million in 1984 (Bassett, 1986: 168). Evidence of cost savings, estimated to be over £8 million in a recent survey of 125 companies, has resulted in the increased adoption of suggestion schemes in the UK (Industrial Society, 1986). WIRS 3 showed 28 per cent of establishments had such schemes, an increase from 25 per cent in WIRS 2 (Millward et al., 1992). CLIRS showed 36 per cent of respon-dents had suggestion schemes at establishment level (Marginson et al., 1988: 106). A survey by ACAS reported that 36 per cent of establishments operated suggestion schemes, a figure affirmed in the CBI (1990) survey (which gives the proportion as 35 per cent). In the ACAS survey, this figure is broken down further to show that such schemes are run in 31 per cent of firms with under 300 employees, compared to 46 per cent of larger firms.

A more systematic means of obtaining feedback is the attitude survey. Dating back to the 1930s, when the National Institute of Industrial Psychology started experimenting with such surveys in the studies on labour turnover, their use has since been expanded to include surveys of attitudes to supervision, remuneration and working conditions, as well as specific aspects of personnel policies, such as pensions or incentive schemes (IPM, 1981b). Some companies place great value on surveys. IBM, for example, started using attitude surveys in 1962 and so has access to information on a long-term basis. In biennial surveys, which usually receive a high response rate

(99 per cent), employees are asked over 100 questions covering aspects of job satisfaction including evaluations of managers (Bassett, 1986: 168). The surveys have played a key role in the development of personnel policies and have enabled the company to gauge how change has been received (IPM, 1981a; Incomes Data Services, 1984). WIRS 2 shows that only a small percentage of companies (12 per cent) make use of surveys (Millward and Stevens, 1986: 153). Although CLIRS (Marginson et al., 1988) reported surveys to be the least common method of two-way communication, it revealed that 27 per cent of companies used surveys or ballots at establishment level. WIRS 3, too, indicated that surveys or ballots were the least frequently mentioned method of communication but it also showed that there had been an increase from the earlier survey to 17 per cent. Around one-fifth of respon-dents in the CBI survey reported the use of employee attitude or opinion surveys, although ACAS (1991) reported a higher percentage (31 per cent) in its survey. Companies using surveys were most likely to have been large and foreign-owned establishments.

Although surveys are a valid method of achieving a systematic measure of employee attitudes (Keohane, 1971a; 1971b; Cross, 1973), their agenda is circumscribed to particular areas of manage-ment interest, and as instruments of communication they remain very passive. One way in which they have been used to enhance the element of participation is in conjunction with project teams or task forces. Areas highlighted by surveys as being of concern to employees are given as 'problems' to project teams comprising a small number of employees and supervisors who attempt to de-vise 'solutions'. Usually confined to job-related tasks, employees are released from work to follow up particular issues and make recommendations.

Another potential source of feedback is the employee appraisal system – discussed in chapter 7. Its value in a communication programme is very much dependent on the perceived function of appraisals within the organization and the success with which the often conflicting objectives of appraisals are managed. Its use as a communication channel requires the assessment and overt control function of appraisal to be highly modified to a more open develop-mental approach, with discussion of achievements, aspirations, val-ues and, in addition, grievances (IPM, 1982). The IPM appraisal survey (Long, 1986) reveals that there has been an increase in the use of trait rating methods for non-managerial employees, which is not in itself conducive to a more open appraisal style. Other factors which might indicate that appraisal was being taken seriously as the basis of a two-way communication system were not positive. Individual self-rating or review was rarely used, training of employees to be able to participate more fully in appraisals was rare, and follow up action of appraisal reviews was limited, suggesting that the use of the appraisal review as a fully integrated component of a communication system remains underdeveloped. Subordinate appraisal of management was not commented on, although developments in US companies indicate that this is an increasing component of an upwards communication system.

Two-way communication in practice is associated with organizations which have established employee involvement programmes (e.g. quality circles and formal consultative arrangements), where there are profit-sharing schemes and in organizations which do not recognize trade unions. It is also more likely to be used by foreign-owned organizations. Employee communications programmes are often very elaborate in large US organizations, and are frequently the responsibility of public relations departments. Such programmes can include employee publications, video magazines, face-to-face meetings between employees and senior management. Feedback on programmes involves communications audits, video surveys, information tracking data and quality culture surveys (McKeand, 1990). AT&T, for example, carries a daily newsletter on its network. This is in addition to a monthly magazine mailed to all employees, and a 'Newsline' audio news service which has a menu of options for callers who wish to hear reports on specific subjects (*Public Relations Journal*, 1990). US companies are also more likely to monitor the effectiveness of employee communication programmes, especially through the use of employee surveys (Troy, 1989).

The Impetus to Increased Communication

The 1970s and 1980s saw a great emphasis being placed on various forms of employee involvement and participation, requiring provisions for the disclosure of information and greater sophistication in channels of communication. The IPM survey (1981a: 6) showed that the trend to the formalization of employee communication policies, which began in the 1970s, doubled in the years 1976–9. The WIRS surveys also indicate increased initiatives in the early and late 1980s. What follows is a consideration of some of the changing political and economic factors which prompted the gradual move away from the 'management by concealment' practice that had earlier characterized British management (Moore, 1980).

The legislative imperative

Several statutes were enacted in the 1970s and 1980s for the purposes of, both implicitly and explicitly, increasing the dissemination of information to employees, either individually or through recognized trade unions. Two different underlying rationales prompted their enactment. The first, the 'democratic imperative', placed an emphasis on access to information as right and as an essential prerequisite to greater participation in decision making. The second stressed the 'educative' function of disclosure which, it was hoped, would have beneficial effects, particularly in the 'reform' of industrial relations and modified wage demands, by making employees more aware of the financial circumstances of companies.

Statutory disclosure of information was first proposed in the unsuccessful 1969 Industrial Relations Bill by a Labour government, although it was not an area in which unions were actively seeking assistance, nor was it recommended by the Donovan Commission. This provision was subsequently taken up by the incoming Conservative government's Industrial Relations Act 1971, influenced partly by the desire to reform industrial relations but also with a view to Britain's entry to the European Community. Although this section had not come into effect by the time of the Act's repeal in 1974, attention was focused on the importance of the provision of financial information to employees and trade union representatives for the purposes of collective bargaining.

The 1974 Labour government took a number of legislative steps to increase the flow of information. The 1974 Health and Safety at Work Act placed an obligation on employers to publish a written safety policy and provide employees with information on health, safety and welfare arrangements. This information also had to be included in company annual reports. The disclosure provisions of the 1975 Employment Protection Act, which came into effect in 1977, placed a duty on employers to disclose information, albeit unspecified, to trade unions for the purposes of collective bargaining. Reference was restricted to information without which bargaining would be impeded to a 'material extent'. ACAS (1977) produced a Code of Practice listing areas of relevant information but, in keeping with the voluntarist tradition, the subjects disclosed were to be determined through collective bargaining.

Further developments taking place during the final years of the Labour administration came with the establishment in 1975 of the Bullock Committee of Inquiry on Industrial Democracy which led to the government's White Paper on Industrial Democracy issued in 1978. Although considerably diluting the majority of Bullock's proposals, the recommendation of worker involvement on a participatory company board required detailed consideration of policies on disclosure and channels of communication (Elliot, 1978). A further White Paper on the Future of Company Reports recommended that companies with workforces of more than 500 should issue employees with annual reports and accounts, giving a detailed breakdown of company activities (Hussey and Marsh, 1983). The controversy surrounding the industrial democracy proposals, divisions within trade union ranks and pressure from other events resulted in both legislative initiatives being shelved. Three years of continuous debate and the prospect of imminent legislation, however, did much to focus attention on the whole area of disclosure of information and communication.

The legislative concerns of subsequent Conservative governments have not placed a high priority on information disclosure. However, a Liberal amendment to the 1982 Employment Act obliged employers of both public and private companies with more than 250 employees to include in the company's annual report a statement indicating action taken to 'introduce, maintain or develop' arrangements aimed, amongst other things, at 'providing employees systematically with information about matters of concern to them'; 'consulting employees or their representatives on a regular basis' to ascertain their opinions; and 'achieving a common awareness on the part of all employees of the financial and economic factors affecting performance of the company' (Rochester, 1982; Wates, 1983). With no legal obligation to consult or communicate, only to report, the only tenuous sanctions which apply are enforceable through the Companies Act.

Legislative initiatives have not been confined to Britain. A number of EC proposals, principally the Fifth Directive on Harmonization of Company Law and the Directive on Procedures for Informing and Consulting Employees (the Vredeling-Davignon proposals), are designed to increase access to information. The former proposes having employee directors on a company supervisory board, while the latter obliges multinationals to consult on closures, mergers and major company changes. As a result of political manoeuverings, both directives have already undergone a number of changes, and the final outcome is difficult to predict, except to say that any enactment will have serious implications for communication channels and access to information (*Industrial Relations Review and Report*, 1984b and 1984c; *European Industrial Relations Review*, 1985).

Although the increased incidence of communication policies and programmes coincides with the legislation of the 1970s, this is not often cited by management as a reason for the introduction of such schemes in the surveys of this period (see table 18.2). This may be because the impact of the law is diffuse, being absorbed via seminars and employer association reports into management thinking, or due to a reluctance by management to admit to a reactive stance. The strongest evidence of the impact of legislation is in the rapid rise in the publication of employee reports. Although a few companies (4 per cent) issued reports prior to 1971, a rapid growth took place in the period 1975–7 (Marsh and Hussey, 1979). Faced with the threat of imminent legislation it seems that companies were anxious to introduce their own schemes before being obliged to do so by law, a conclusion which is in part substantiated by the sharp fall in companies issuing reports in 1978 when legislation appeared less likely. The direct impact of the other statutes is difficult to assess, and where evidence is available it is ambiguous (see Townley, 1989).

The increased emphasis given to communication systems has not been solely as a response to legislation, although it undoubtedly provides a backcloth against which to view company policies, especially in the 1970s. However, to account for the reason why communication is still considered important even though legislative underpinning and formal proposals for increased participation have been removed we need to consider some of the more significant changes which have been taking place in approaches to personnel management. As was argued earlier, two rationales underlay the early legislative initiatives: the right to greater participation in decision making and the 'educative' function of increased disclosure. Despite lip-service being paid to democratic principles, the former was not readily espoused by management. The second rationale, especially in relation to the reform of industrial relations, has had a more direct relevance.

Table 18.2   Reasons given for the introduction of
communication schemes (%)

	IOD 1981[a]	*Hussey and Marsh 1983*[b]	*IPM 1981*[a]
Participation and involvement			
Involve employees in company affairs – participation and involvement	18	84	—
Motivate employees/improve morale	6	—	66
Production benefits			
Motivate employees toward higher productivity	—	14	51
Make the organization work better	—	—	78
Gain acceptance of change	—	—	66
Increase work flexibility	—	—	16
Educative purposes			
Encourage sense of responsibility	—	46	—
Improve employees' understanding of company policy and business generally	64	23	—
'Industrial relations purposes'			
Moderate wage demands/influence negotiations	3	4	20
Reduce work disruption	3	—	31
Minimize trade union influence	4	—	—
Make managers manage	—	—	42
External pressures			
Employee pressure	—	4	10
Trade union pressure	—	2	14
Legal requirements	—	4	18
Pre-empt expected legislation	—	—	13
Broader 'political' considerations			
General social trend	—	—	21
Discharge responsibilities of company/'right to know'	—	42	60
	n. 115	n. 317	n. 145

[a] First reason taken
[b] Relates to publication of employee reports only

Communication as a process of education

The basis of this approach can be seen in the CBI (1976) report *Priorities for In-Company Communications*. Critical of British management for failing to explain the economic context in which companies operate, it identified several 'objectives for education' aimed at making employees more aware of economic 'reality'. Widespread ignorance of levels of company profitability and the tendency of employees to overestimate this were identified as leading to unrealistic expectations, contributing to the 'rampant inflation and breakdown of free collective bargaining' occuring in the 1970s (ibid.: 19). The report states, 'if communications are to be relevant they must be designed in such a way that employees' action in response to particular situations is better informed . . . not merely that employees should understand the theory of how the market economy works . . . but also that they should be aware of how it is working in practice at that particular time in their own workplace' (ibid.: 6). Communication which makes employees more aware of their contribution to the creation of wealth through increased productivity and to its distribution through wage bargaining was seen as contributing to more 'informed' and 'realistic' bargaining. Also stressed was the importance of investment and the return to shareholders in dividends, the role of entrepreneurs in wealth and job creation, and the importance of the managerial role (ibid.: 36).

Communication in this sense bears a close resemblance to the role ascribed to it by Drucker (1970), namely that of propaganda. With its emphasis on the workings of the free market system, it is aimed at producing a greater degree of consensus on macroeconomic and political issues, giving the logic of managerial decision making a greater legitimacy. The argument was made that management had been unable to counter alternative sources of information concerning the economic performance of the company because it had abdicated the task of communicating to the workforce to the trade unions. Not only had management lost a major source of influence, it had also contributed to its own loss of credibility and status. The CBI survey found that employees had little understanding of managers' contribution to the organization or the complexity of the issues they had to deal with. Thus, a complementary function of the 'educative' approach was to reassert the role of management, particularly line management, and emphasize the importance of leadership. The communication programme introduced at Austin Rover (then BL) was indicative of this type of approach, representing in Edwardes' (1983: 164) terms 'taking over the driving seat for the first time in twenty years'. Case studies of approaches in the 1970s and early 1980s (Incomes Data Services, 1984; *Industrial Relations Review and Report*, 1981b; 1982; 1984a; 1984d; 1986) reveal that in general the introduction of communication schemes was in response to a major crisis, usually serious financial circumstances, or an unenviable industrial relations record – lifeboat democracy in the words of Cressey et al. (1985). In this respect support is given to Legge's (1978: 93) view that only in times of crisis are aspects of personnel policy seriously considered.

Given that the economic circumstances of the companies in themselves would have been sufficient to secure the changes required, the question arises as to why communication and involvement programmes should have been introduced. The 'cycle of control' thesis presumes that such programmes only gain prominence when economic conditions render employee compliance difficult (Ramsay, 1977). The prevalence of 'bad news', however, may reduce the element of risk involved in information disclosure, and function as an implicit threat which reinforces compliance. There is some evidence to support this interpretation with the tendency of information disclosed to emphasize 'bad news' (Daniel and Millward, 1983: 159), and for companies with below average performance to disclose more information than average performers (Millward and Stevens, 1986: 159). Reliance on communication programmes to convey 'bad news' items, however, may prove counter-productive. The IPM survey (1981a: 16) found that high levels of unemployment and the recession increased feelings of insecurity and with this a resistance to organizational change – feelings which would only be reinforced by negative disclosures. The survey identified an acknowledged need to improve employee morale.

The 1980s saw an extension of the educative function with the introduction of the 'enterprise culture'. The instruction of individuals in business and market 'realities' informed government initiatives in both the public and private sectors, prompting privatization, increased share ownership, and the extension of profit-related pay schemes. All had the intention of minimizing the 'us' and 'them' distinction, and discouraging the view that there is a separation of interest between shareholders, management and the workforce. The rationale behind such schemes was that employees would have an increased personal interest in the organizations' operating results, which would lead to increased feelings of company loyalty. Designed to support a unitarist view of the workplace, there was also an expectation that increased exposure to the demands of market discipline would lead to more 'realistic' wage demands, and that an awareness of the financial health of the enterprise would result in modified bargaining claims.

There seems to be some indication that organizations which have employee share ownership schemes or have been privatized engage in more employee communication. A 1990 joint Stock Exchange-Treasury survey of 443 UK quoted companies listed in *The Times* Top 1000 indicates that companies with all employee share schemes made greater use of traditional and other methods of communicating financial information to employees and greater use of consultation-participation procedures than companies which did not. The survey also indicated that privatized companies engaged in even more employee reporting-consultation practices (Peel et al., 1991). In terms of the expected benefit of such schemes, a problem arises in that employees may not understand the nature of the share ownership schemes in which they participate, and may be only vaguely aware of how such schemes operate. A lack of technical expertise may lead to a greater willingness of employees to accept managements' presentation of financial information (Knights and Collinson, 1987). Despite this, there is evidence to suggest that there is resistance on the part of management to the disclosure of financial information, even where this is for 'educative' purposes. Ogden (1992: 229) concludes that 'employers are reluctant to pursue such a strategy of involvement because of the risk of stimulating employees to demand greater influence in how the enterprise is managed'. Indeed, he concludes that reluctance to engage in profit-related pay systems results from the resistance to disclose the information these systems would entail, for fear that this would lead to business decisions being called into question, demands for increased involvement in decision making, and an extension of the area of collective bargaining.

One of the themes of the educative rationale is the need to improve overall organizational effectiveness in highly competitive market situations. The recognition that employee compliance is no longer sufficient and that there is the necessity to secure commitment to organizational change has been the main factor behind a third rationale prompting the introduction of communication schemes, a *commitment* strategy. The need to retain a competitive advantage has stimulated approaches which stress increased involvement and identification, prompting some companies to review their personnel policies and develop those with a 'human resource' ethos.

Communication as a strategy of commitment

Premised on a theory of motivation which holds that employees have an interest in work beyond the mechanics of the task in hand, the emphasis of this approach is on securing normative compliance by paying attention to these wider needs. Lack of a formal communication programme, especially in circumstances which encourage rumours of mergers, rationalizations and redundancies, is seen as fostering low morale, low trust and the pursuit of disparate goals – all detrimental to organizational effectiveness and not conducive to the acceptance of change. With the satisfaction of individual needs projected as a prerequisite of achieving organizational objectives, a communication programme is seen as fulfilling the role of both increasing the individual's identification with the company and furthering the acceptance of organizational goals. The advantages are held to be more favourable employee attitudes, informed involvement and increased productivity. In this respect a developed communication system is usually seen as an integral part of a range of personnel policies which may include profit sharing, greater job discretion, harmonization and single status, and merit pay schemes, all of which are designed to reinforce the overriding strategy of individual identification with and commitment to the organization.

The importance of increased motivation through employee communication is reinforced by international comparisons, particularly with the role model of the 1980s' Japan. The latter's impressive productivity record, it is frequently held, results from the greater identification employees have with their company. Although many factors contribute to this, the 'Monday morning assembly' of employees and senior management, daily section meetings with foremen, quality circles and briefing groups have, in particular, been identified as prominent features in this (*Industrial Relations Review and Report*, 1981a; 1981c; Incomes Data Services, 1984). The USA also provides examples of companies which attribute their success to personnel policies which emphasize well-developed employee communication and identification programmes (Peters and Waterman, 1982; Foulkes, 1980).

The role of communication as a 'motivator' or 'hygiene factor', increasing organizational commitment, has featured in managerial orthodoxy since the popularization of the human relations school (Rose, 1975). Increased international competition and the changing nature of production systems, however, have given this strategy of commitment, and the role of communication in this, a more immediate relevance (Walton, 1985). Communication which concerns itself only with the narrowly defined task at hand is no longer considered adequate for competitive strategies which rely on increased product quality, or where workforce reductions or the introduction of new technology requires greater task flexibility. The move away from Taylorist concepts of work organization and towards increased functional flexibility necessarily requires that previous divisions between conception and execution are bridged, and that employees are provided with a greater understanding of the results of their work and the goals of the organization.

An added imperative for this commitment strategy lies in the increasing adoption of 'total quality management' (TQM), 'continuous quality improvement' (CQI) and customer service programmes. The vocabulary of the new ethos is that of communications and empowerment. These approaches stress that only by 'empowering' employees will organizations ensure that customer needs will be satisfied. First-line employees, as contact points for the organization, need to understand its products and objectives to be in a better position to communicate these to customers. An employee who is not informed and committed may cause the organization to lose customers long before such problems are recognized and rectified. Communication is seen as essential to sustaining the total quality initiative, with the recognition that employees at all levels have crucial information about the operation of the business. Such policies have led to pronouncements that nothing short of a new approach to employee communications will be called for in the 1990s, involving regular surveys of employees, personalized communication, and innovation in communication techniques. As the literature espousing this approach remarks, 'the commitment to quality cannot be achieved simply by passive information provision or exhortation' (National Economic Development Committee, 1986: 27).

Whereas previous communication practices have been criticized for being propagandist, raising expectations which cannot be fulfilled, or compromising wage negotiation, communication under commitment schemes is viewed in much more strategic terms than the mere dissemination of information. 'Many firms have concluded that a significant step forward lies in developing systems of communication and consultation which enable employees to participate to the greatest measure of their skills, experience and responsibilities in decisions about the work they do' (ibid.: 4). It is no longer sufficient that employees receive random bits of unrelated information from in-house newsletters and staff meetings. Rather, communication is specifically targeted at encouraging employees to know their organizations and to enlighten them about their contribution to the organization (their value added). It involves telling employees about future plans and the implications for the organization and the workforce. It is a project which places strong reliance on top-down communication involving, for example, monthly departmental meetings, employee news articles, etc., the efficacy of which is to be monitored through employee surveys. Communication programmes are often introduced in conjunction with other employee involvement programmes aimed at increasing employee identification with the organization, and these also require increased attention to internal communications programmes.

Allied to these projects is a change of vocabulary. Communication is seen in terms of giving 'ownership' to employees: employees are one group of 'stakeholders' in the organization, alongside customers, shareholders, competitors, prospective recruits and, possibly, society at large. In some cases the customer satisfaction regime has been extended to include the 'internal customer', namely the employee. Although the sentiments are expressed in terms of disclosure of information to 'equal parties', communication is still given on a 'need to know' basis, as the following recommendation illustrates: 'Managers should pass along everything their employees need to know in order for them to succeed. While employees do not need to know everything about their companies, they do need to know all about the things that will have an impact on their areas of involvement. They also need to know about plans and changes that will affect their performance' (Blanchard, 1987). The emphasis of such programmes is geared towards priority business issues.

One key component of this 'commitment communications strategy' is the mission statement – written documents or key concepts stating the organization's statement of purpose or general philosophy which is communicated to all employees (Campbell, 1991). Although more commonplace in the US, UK organizations are increasingly adopting them. Creating a sense of mission is designed to provide a focus as well as contribute to better decision making and generally clearer communication. More detailed mission statements identify the company's basic products and services, primary markets and principal methods and technologies. They may also involve the identification of actions and behaviour which are important to achieving organizational objectives (Lidstone, 1989). A survey carried out in 1989 and reported by Klemm et al. (1991) of UK companies' mission statements identified that their main purpose was internal, being designed to provide staff motivation, although other purposes included their role in trying to get managers to agree on common objectives and the reconciliation of potentially conflicting interests through a hierarchy of objectives. Concern for employees was one of the nine key components of the formal mission statements (David, 1989).

In many respects communication as an element in a commitment strategy can be seen as developing from the 'educative' approach outlined earlier. The individual is taken to be the unit of response in each case. The underlying objective, that of safeguarding or improving economic performance, remains the same. Both are premised on the view that management and labour are mutually dependent. Neither perceive communication to be the simple transmission of data but are, in Walton and McKersie's (1965) terms, an exercise in 'attitudinal restructuring'. Communication in this instance is 'the process by which an idea is transferred from a source to a receiver with the intention of changing his or her behaviour. Such behaviour may encompass a change in knowledge or attitude as well as in overt behaviour' (Rogers and Rogers, 1976: 9).

Although the underlying objectives remain the same, there is a distinction between the 'educative' and 'commitment' rationales in terms of their emphasis or tone. They differ in their views of motivation, the means of achieving compliance and the concepts of managerial prerogative. The 'educative' view can be seen as more reactive in its approach, stemming from the attempt to fill a perceived vacuum left by the retreat of trade union power; nor is it as integrated into a comprehensive package of personnel policies designed to achieve organizational objectives. The 'commitment' or 'human resource' approach eschews the more overt reference to the nature of the power relationship between management and workforce, and functions more as an integrative mechanism aimed at influencing prevailing perceptions of the organization and stressing a commonality of experience. It displays a greater commitment to the view that management can only manage effectively with the active co-operation of its workforce and is more conducive to an integrative problem-solving approach. The degree to which each is emphasized will vary according to economic circumstances and the variety of factors which influence management's approach to the handling of labour relations. The two approaches may also be in evidence in the same organization, with divisions within management reflecting different views of the communication system. Supervisors, for example, tend to see communication as a means of getting the job done more efficiently and quickly, accepting management's logic or 'business realities', while among senior management there is a tendency to view communication as a means of instilling confidence and motivation, or even giving workers a say in decisions affecting them (Reeves, 1980; Edwards, 1987).

Responses to Communication Schemes

It is difficult to estimate the impact of a communication programme, not least because of the problem of isolating its effects from other aspects of both personnel and organizational policies which may accompany its introduction. Perhaps because of this, systematic data are limited. Certainly very few of the companies undertake an evaluation of their communication system's effectiveness. Although 61 per cent of respondents in the IPM survey carried out some assessment, this relied heavily on informal feedback and other factors generally taken to be indicators of organizational health. Only 22 per cent of respondents used attitude surveys as a source of evaluation, with only 10 per cent using them on an annual or more frequent basis (IPM, 1981a: 50). Thirty-nine per cent of companies using employee reports conducted assessments of employee responses (Marsh and Hussey, 1979: 50). Table 18.3 gives management's views of responses to the introduction of communication programmes. These positive results also find support in case studies. Reports of unsuccessful cases are difficult to find.

Employee responses to communication schemes tend to be mixed. The move toward increased information is generally treated with suspicion when communication has been neglected in the past. The assumption is usually that the news is bound to be 'bad news'. After initial scepticism, however, communication systems are often received favourably (CBI, 1976: 31). This is more likely to be in

Table 18.3 Results reported from the
introduction of communication systems (%)

Increased productivity	65
Fewer industrial disputes	68
Less time lost through absenteeism	41
Reduced employee turnover	46
Improved morale/loyalty	80
Better customer relations	47
No improvements	3
Difficult to evaluate	8
	n. 115

Source: Institute of Directors, 1981

response to the fact that the company has 'taken the trouble', with the move toward increased communication being taken as indicative of a change in attitude toward the workforce. It is the expressive nature of the communication rather than the factual content *per se* which is valued. As Marsh and Hussey (1979: 35) conclude, 'it may be that these external messages are sometime more important than the actual contents.' While employee responses to increased communication may be more positive than negative, employees are critical of the substantive issues communicated. Some forms of communication have been recognized as increasing the amount of information, such as team briefings, while others, for example employee publications, are seen as needing improvement in the range of material covered. Criticisms were still made that employees did not have enough information about what was 'going on' in the company, and nor had these avenues of communication necessarily either improved employees' understanding of management decisions or increased commitment or encouraged employees to work harder (Marchington et al., 1992).

This is not to deny, however, the importance of the factual information given. Employees appear to show a preference for 'local' information dealing with prospects for the plant or that part of the organization with which they have daily contact, reflecting the most immediate concerns with security of income and employment. This includes reference to staffing policies and job prospects, departmental performance and future plans (Hussey and Marsh, 1983: 115–22). In other areas – finance, profit and loss, new investments, exports, mergers and takeovers – employees do not report the desire for more information, largely because this is not perceived to be of direct relevance to their immediate concerns. Satisfaction of demands for 'basic' information (for example, decisions about salaries, holidays and hours of work, and changes affecting working conditions), however, leads to a greater demand for disclosure on how these issues are arrived at.

On the whole, employees give a favourable rating to the credibility of information disclosed, although this is heavily influenced by job status, with manual workers showing a much greater distrust of company information than managers. This is particularly true of financial information, especially profits, with a strong belief that figures had been 'fiddled' (CBI, 1976: 32). Scepticism tended to be highest amongst young, male skilled manual employees in the private sector (Opinion Research Communications, 1978: 62). There is also a discrepancy between the two groups in terms of access to information, particularly employee reports, with managerial grades having the most access (Hussey and Marsh, 1983: 115–22). The issue of credibility highlights the tension inherent in communication systems between the desire to influence behaviour and the need to provide 'objective' information. Where the 'educative' element becomes too prominent, or is seen as controversial or inappropriate, it detracts from the credibility of the other information (Marsh and Hussey, 1979: 37). Even where there is a degree of consensus on the exigencies of market requirements, this does not necessarily lead to unquestioning acceptance of some managerial decisions. 'Acceptance of the system does not necessarily constitute an unconditional mandate for companies to redeploy capital and pursue growth targets as they please', as the CBI recognizes (1976: 21).

Although the most frequently cited response to a communication system is that of improved employee morale, concrete evidence on this is ambiguous. The 1976 CBI survey reported a high correlation between those employees regarding themselves as well-informed and generally accepting as credible the information disclosed by the company, and those reporting a high degree of job satisfaction. Those considering themselves to be ill-informed and disbelieving of company information reported greater dissatisfaction with their job. The Second Workplace Industrial Relations Survey found that the industrial relations climate, both with trade unions and the workforce as a whole, was more favourably assessed when a lot of information was given to employees (Millward and Stevens, 1986: 159). There are several difficulties is assessing the significance of these claims, however. The causal relationship between the benefits of a communication system and its impact on well-established pre-dispositions, the industrial relations 'climate' and the amount of information disclosed, are difficult to distinguish. As to responses to increased communication, the CBI (1976: 36) report concluded, 'we found no conclusive evidence that behaviour at work has actually changed and team-work functions of individuals improved.'

Although 'directed' toward employees, a formal communication programme has major implications for management, especially concepts of managerial prerogative, styles and the respective roles of personnel and line management. Under such programmes communication constitutes an important dimension of management, with all levels being responsible for acting as 'conduits'. The emphasis is on managing through influence rather than control, with the manager as 'facilitator'. This has implications for the nature of managerial job definitions – no longer narrowly task-oriented but with an emphasis on interpersonal skills – and for roles, particularly the supervisory role. At its most practical level, the criteria used in managerial selection, appraisal and recommendations for promotion, as well as management training and development requirements, have to be seriously reviewed. It is no coincidence, for example, that three-quarters of IBM's annual training programme for managers, for example, concentrates on 'people management' (Bassett, 1986: 167). Research commissioned by the National Economic Development Office, citing companies such as ICI Paints, British Airways and H. J. Heinz Co., illustrates how communications programmes and the development of a more 'open' style of management have been an integral part of introducing change into key areas of the organization.

There is, however, resistance to such programmes, especially from middle management and supervisors (Marchington et al., 1992). The implications of a move towards improved communication, not least in terms of resources, may make management wary of steps in this direction. Resistance centres around a number of issues: lack of senior management understanding and support; organizational politics; and fear. Managers report that they are not clear about what their communications system is designed to deliver, complaining that communication often resembles little more than a confusing collection of random information (Drennan, 1989). There is also resistance because of the amount of time and effort such programmes require, especially where this aspect of managerial responsibility is not adequately supported through training and other personnel policies. Often, information is viewed as a commodity. 'Giving away' information becomes tantamount to 'giving away' power and prompts fears of managing in a 'goldfish bowl' and a concomitant dilution of managerial authority. Resistance also reflected a lack of ease with the new definitions of managerial roles, these often contradicting firmly established beliefs as to what shop-floor workers responded to (Marchington et al., 1992).

Communication programmes also have implications for established management–trade union relationships. For management, communicating directly to employees, rather than through established trade union channels, has the obvious advantage of promoting a commonality of interests between employee and organization. For the trade union representative, there is sometimes the advantage of not having to convey to the workforce the company's position on a particular issue, thus avoiding a possible loss of credibility and workforce acceptance that this dual role may bring. In these circumstances the trade union channel functions as the principal means of reporting back employees' feelings. However, the development of a separate channel of communication deprives unions of an important source of power, that of the control over information, and it is perhaps in the implications for established trade union representation that communication programmes have their greatest impact. The development of a channel for management's views paralleled with that of trade union views works to promote the idea of a third constituency, the workforce, the 'electorate' forced into choosing between differing interpretations – a perspective which has informed government industrial relations initiatives in the 1980s. In a context where this view is fully developed, trade unions are no longer the natural voice of the work group, but become increasingly distanced: another constituency in a pluralist association of interests or, in more extreme cases, an outside influence disturbing a harmony of interests.

The potential for communication systems to be used as a means of undermining trade union representation has aroused considerable distrust and, not unnaturally, provoked some resistance from trade unions, particularly in those sectors where union presence has been strong, for example printing and engineering. In other areas there has been limited or no resistance from trade unions (Institute of Directors, 1981: 36). From initial 'veto' responses of attempting to implement boycotts, there has been an increasing tendency for trade unions to respond in the like manner by improving communications to their members. In general, trade union response has been highly contingent on the nature of the existing relationship with the employer, the extent to which they have been involved in the new systems, and on the attitudes of key individuals such as convenors (Incomes Data Services, 1984; Marchington et al., 1992).

There is no direct evidence from the surveys to indicate that communication programmes are being introduced as a tactic in a strategy of 'union substitution', that is, in reducing employees' perceived needs for a union. Early surveys indicated that non-unionized firms did not communicate more regularly or systematically to individuals than unionized firms, nor were they more likely to have a formal communication policy (IPM, 1981a; BIM, 1975). CLIRS, however, indicates greater communication where there was no trade union recognition (Marginson et al., 1988). 'Industrial relations' criteria – minimizing trade union influence, reducing work disruptions, assisting in wage negotiations – are not reported as primary objectives of such policies except in a small minority of companies (Institute of Directors, 1981: 20). Rather than being a weapon in an armoury of managerial attacks on established trade union representation, communication systems function more as a means of bypassing union influence rather than explicitly confronting it (Batstone, 1984: 235). Management is still willing to talk *to* unions, though not *through* them (Edwards, 1985). However, this is not to deny that in specific instances, especially where shop steward resistance has combined with severe economic problems, communication and involvement policies have been aimed at reducing the trade union role (Batstone, 1984). Equally, elaborate communication programmes often feature as an important component of personnel policies designed to minimize the need for union organ-ization, usually associated with some large, non-union, American companies (Foulkes, 1980).

The impact of communication programmes on collective bargaining is difficult to gauge. There has been an effect on the *conduct* of bargaining. Whereas previously management abstained from communicating directly with employees, because this was seen as undermining the authority of trade union negotiators, management communication in the form of fact sheets distributed through all stages in negotiation is increasingly an integral part of their strategy. Information, however, is used to counter trade union claims, rather than as a means of persuasion to management's point of view. The impact of increased dissemination of information on bargaining *outcomes* is ambiguous. While increased access to information may lead to a more 'realistic' bargaining stance, possibly based on a more integrative, problem-solving approach, as the 'educative' approach holds, it may also significantly alter the balance of power in favour of unions as information concerning one sector is used as a bargaining counter in another. Trade union representatives reported that the information disclosed, particularly financial information via employee reports, was of limited value (Moore, 1980; Gill, 1979). Where bargaining takes place at plant level, information required includes operating accounts, costing information, stock levels, transfer prices, and orders. However, information disclosed through any of the communication channels is rarely this specific. Financial information, when disclosed, tends to refer to the group level, with the IPM survey (1981a: 43) showing that only 26 per cent of companies provided information specific to the operating unit. Ogden (1992) reports that management is reluctant to disclose information where there is a likelihood that this will be used in collective bargaining by trade unions, even for the purpose of engaging in integrative bargaining. Fear that disclosure of information would lead to a contesting of decisions seems to be the principal reason for the reluctance.

The effect of increased information has to be seen in the context in which bargaining takes place and the nature of existing bargaining relationships. Supporting the results of earlier research (Mellinger, 1956) that increased information only aids the accuracy of opinions held if it takes place within a trust relationship, evidence from the WIRS 1 indicates that it is the pre-existing relationship which is the determinant both of the amount and value of the information disclosed (Daniel and Millward, 1983: 152). Certainly a move to increased disclosure only when a firm is in trouble, or to prove a particular pay claim cannot be met meets with suspicion. A sudden increase in communication in an organization where there is a history of distrust generally only serves to fuel scepticism, if not cynicism. In such circumstances it is all too readily dismissed as propaganda. As Knights and Collinson (1987: 461) say of one such unsuccessful attempt, 'managerial assumptions of worker naivety – that they could actually believe what was written in the magazine – merely added insult to the injury of manipulation and deceit.'

The view that information will automatically be translated into 'rational' decision making in bargaining is, however, based on several dubious assumptions. The ability to pay, although becoming influential, has never been the only or, indeed, the major factor in determining pay levels (Sisson, 1984). Other such factors such as the cost of living and comparability feature strongly (Daniel, 1976). In some respects the role ascribed to information denies the very nature and process of bargaining (Hussey and Marsh, 1983: 124). While information may lead to more sophisticated bargaining, as claims and counterclaims are more fully prepared and substantiated, by itself it cannot invalidate the division of interest which necessarily accompanies the bargaining process. 'If we look at the central problem in industrial relations – the struggle between labour and capital for higher returns for their respective inputs – there is no communications problem at all . . . no amount of paper, no quantity of briefing sessions will counter the basic disparity of interest' (Gill, 1979: 8).

Concluding Remarks

Communication programmes cannot be viewed from a simple systems framework, as is often the case in the literature recommending their use, as 'inputs' to bring about reduced levels of conflict or higher levels of trust. To view communication as a universal panacea for organizational ills leads both to unwarranted expectations in its introduction and qualified failure in its implementation (e.g. Thomson, 1983; Hyman, 1982). Increased communication remains ineffective when there is resentment towards new management: the introduction of employee reports is no compensation for dissatisfaction with other aspects of personnel policies. Equally, communication cannot be viewed merely as a reflection of a pre-existing relationship – the often held view that 'good' communication is the logical outcome of 'good' industrial relations. Rather than being viewed in isolation, communication programmes have to be evaluated in relation to the overall strategy of management towards its workforce. IBM practices cannot be divorced from other elements of a policy which have stressed a high degree of job security, harmonization of terms and conditions, and an emphasis on the individual, etc. (IPM, 1981b). Nor can the Japanese system be adequately assessed apart from the whole panoply of policies which emphasize product quality.

This obviously renders any generalized statements on the significance or likely future developments of communication programmes difficult to make. One factor which may be isolated, however, is the extent to which such programmes have been integrated into corporate personnel policies. Any comment on the significance of such schemes must distinguish between those which have been introduced as the result of a well-considered philosophy or policy, and those which are an *ad hoc* pragmatic response to a number of different stimuli, reflecting little of a conscious, strategic analysis – the distinction between those companies, such as IBM, where communication programmes have been a long-established component of corporate personnel policies and those more recently established as part of a crisis management approach.

Generally four 'types' of companies may be identified: the *proactive* – those companies where communication is a well-established practice; *preactive* – where schemes are 'voluntarily' introduced but usually in response to perceived threats, usually legislation; *reactive* – where their introduction corresponds with an organizational crisis; and those companies where communication systems are not developed and control is much more overt. Where programmes are a component of a fully integrated 'human resource' policy, a well-developed communications programme is likely to be considered an essential feature of future personnel policies designed to secure employee commitment. Communication programmes in such companies are seen as both allied to competitive advantage and an integral component of facilitating organizational change. The communication systems of reactive companies, however, are much more volatile, with the possibility that they may fall into disuse once the 'crisis' – labour unrest, poor organizational performance, industrial relations problems – has passed. One cannot be certain that the management of these companies will have recognized some of the implications of a comprehensive communications policy, or have introduced the support mechanisms necessary to sustain it.

The evidence points to a dramatic rise in the number of companies introducing formal communication programmes, but it is difficult to tell whether these are in response to the exigencies of the continuing recession or herald a significant change in the handling of labour–management relations. One indication of the seriousness of management's approaches will be seen in its response in different economic conditions. Management may well be more cautious if an upturn in economic conditions renders news more palatable. Evidence from present practice is not a good indication of future response, and, in all probability, management itself is unsure of its approach in such a context. One thing that may be predicted, however, is the continuation and increasing claims made for communication programmes.

Why are such claims perpetuated and why do most initiatives fall short of the claims made for them? Implicit within the claims made for communication programmes are a number of assumptions. Principally the communication of information is viewed in a very constrained way. There is the assumption that information is 'neutral', reflective of an external reality, which can be depicted, more or less accurately, and which is common to all. Hence the concern that information provided conforms to that aspect of reality it is supposed to reflect; debates as to which account is a more accurate representation of reality; and what information is required to give the 'full picture'. There is also a view of communication as a commodity – information as an enclosed and bounded entity – to be 'conveyed' or 'transmitted'. The problem with these views is that they fail to recognize the relational nature of communication, both to the context in which it occurs, and the individual who is asked to interpret it. There is the assumption that the substance of information can be dissociated from the social context of its utterance. This, however, fails to recognize the importance of 'lived reality' – the day-to-day experience which constitutes the individual's understanding of the world. Where information contradicts this, it loses credibility. It is this lived reality, part of which is the physical and symbolic distance between management and workforce, which is part of the explanation for the failure of communication.

Equally the significance of that which is communicated is gained not only from the substance of what is said, but also from that which it lies in relation to. Meaning derives from context. There is not an easily dissociated 'essence'. Just as information cannot be divorced from the context of its dissemination, neither can it be easily compartmentalized in terms of its significance. Almost inevitably in language there is a transitive meaning, 'an excess of meaning over and above the particular operational referent' (Cooper, 1986: 325) – not only a denotative but a connotative meaning. The disjuncture between the sayer and the said results in language having the power to generate meanings irrespective of the wishes of those who authored them. There can be no concept of mastery: 'texts generate meanings with terrible liberality' (Sturrock, 1986: 149). Control through language can never be secured: as Clegg (1989: 193) notes, 'relations of meaning are as resistant to control as are relations of production'.

Perhaps the most serious criticism which may be levelled at these pronouncements is that they neglect power. They depict communication as an ideal speech act (Habermas, 1984). There is the assumption that all the pertinent evidence available is brought into play; that with logical and reasoned argument, consensus will ensue; that there are no external constraints on participants; and that there is an equal and open chance of entering into discussion. Communication is undisturbed by structures of dominance, whether this reflects organizational positioning within a hierarchy, class or gender. It is unrelated to power. Structures of dominance, part of people's 'lived experience', however, have implications for the way communications are perceived, and also what constitutes 'communication' in the first place. As Knights and Collinson (1987: 471) recognize in their case study of an unsuccessful communications programme 'the shop-floor continually complained about the lack of communication. What was at issue was the relevance of the communication. Workers were uninterested in the kinds of public relations issues which dominated management's preoccupation. For the shop-floor, the important matters were the immediately practical ones of daily production since this was what affected their bonus.'

Repeatedly peddled beliefs that information is a neutral commodity whose meaning is apparent irrespective of the power relations of its context necessarily deny the inherent ambiguity involved in the process of communications. Although largely conceived of in terms of a process by which management wishes to direct or dominate the behaviour of the workforce, communication, by definition, also implies dialogue – the reciprocal exchange of ideas with a view to influencing opinion or bringing about change. Engagement in dialogue is not a controlled activity. Although inequality in power renders communication as a process of equal exchange invalid, there is the implicit invitation to respond. The latter may be heavily circumscribed but cannot be totally constrained. Communicating the factors which led to a particular decision being taken necessarily introduces the possibility that the wisdom of that line of reasoning, and the final decision, might be questioned. Expectations are created, and a communications programme, to maintain its credibility, must bring about a degree of change. It is perhaps in the expectations to which communications, and involvement schemes in general, give rise, particularly in the desire to question and perhaps to influence decision making, that management's main difficulty lies. Any systematic move toward increased communication inevitably raises the issue of the increased accountability of management and may require a redefinition of the basis of managerial authority. It is the ambiguity involved in communication programmes which has led the CBI (1976: 7) to counsel management to identify 'the maximum price to be paid for successful communications'.

Note

In addition to the WIRS 2 and 3 and Higher Level Survey, reference is also made to a survey by ACAS (1991) based on 573 private sector manufacturing and services, excluding those with fewer than 50 employees. A CBI survey (1990) was a postal survey of a cross-section of CBI members. Findings are based on 943 organizations employing approximately 900,000 employees.

Bibliography

ACAS. 1977. *Disclosure of Information for Collective Bargaining Purposes.* Code of Practice 2. London: HMSO.

ACAS. 1991. *Consultation and Communication.* Occasional Paper 49. Victor James Press.

Bassett, P. 1986. *Strike Free.* London: Macmillan.

Batstone, E. 1984. *Working Order: Workplace Industrial Relations Over Two Decades.* Oxford: Blackwell.

Berenbeim, R. 1980. *Non-Union Complaint Systems: A Corporate Appraisal.* Report No. 770. New York: The Conference Board.

BIM. 1975. *Keeping Employees Informed: Current UK Practice on Disclosure.* Management Survey Report No. 31. London: British Institute of Management (Prepared by R. Smith).

Blanchard, K. 1987. 'Employees Need the Complete Facts'. *Bottom Line,* Vol. 4, No. 12, 69.

Campbell, A. 1991. 'A Mission to Succeed'. *Director,* Vol. 44, No. 7, 66–8.

CBI. 1976. *Priorities for In-Company Communications.* London: Confederation of British Industry (Prepared by M. Brandon and M. Arnott).

CBI. 1990. *Employee Involvement – Shaping the Future for Business.* London: Confederation of British Industry.

Clegg, S. 1989. *Frameworks of Power.* London: Sage.

Cooper, R. 1986. 'Organization/Disorganization'. *Social Science Information,* Vol. 25, No. 2, 299–335.

Cressey, P., Eldridge, J. and MacInnes, J. 1985. *Just Managing*. Milton Keynes: Open University Press.

Cross, D. 1973. 'The Worker Opinion Survey: A Measure of Shop Floor Satisfaction'. *Occupational Psychology*, Vol. 47, No. 3, 193–208.

Daniel, W. 1976. *Wage Determination in Industry*. London: Political and Economic Planning.

Daniel, W. and Millward, N. 1983. *Workplace Industrial Relations in Britain*. London: Heinemann.

David, F. R. 1989. 'How Companies Define Their Mission'. *Long Range Planning*, Vol. 22, No. 1, 90–7.

Drennan, D. 1989. 'Are You Getting Through?' *Management Today*, August, 70–2.

Drucker, L. 1970. 'What Communication Means'. *Management Today*, March.

Edwardes, M. 1983. *Back from the Brink*. London: Collins.

Edwards, P. K. 1985. 'The Myth of the Macho Manager' *Personnel Management*, April, 32–5.

Edwards, P. K. 1987. *Managing the Factory: A Survey of General Managers*. Oxford: Basil Blackwell.

Elliot, J. 1978. *Conflict or Co-operation? The Growth of Industrial Democracy*. London: Kogan Page.

European Industrial Relations Review. 1985. 'EEC: A New Approach on Vredling'. No. 133. February.

Foulkes, F. 1980. *Personnel Policies in Large Non-Union Companies*. Englewood Cliffs, NJ: Prentice Hall.

Garnett, J. 1980. *The Manager's Responsibility for Communications*. London: Industrial Society.

Garnett, J. 1981. 'Team Briefing'. *Industrial Society*, 63, September, 29–30.

Gill, K. 1979. 'Employee Reports under Attack'. *Industrial Society*, Vol. 61, May/June, 8–9.

Habermas, J. 1984. *The Theory of Communicative Action: Volume 1*. Translated by McCarthy, T. Boston: Beacon Press.

Holmes, G. 1977. 'How UK Companies Report to Their Employees'. *Accountancy*, November, 64–8.

Hussey, R. 1979. *Who Reads Employee Reports?* London: Touche Ross.

Hussey, R. and Marsh, A. 1983. *Disclosure of Information and Employee Reporting*. Aldershot: Gower.

Hyman, J. 1982. 'Where Communication Schemes Fall Short of Intention'. *Personnel Management*, March, 30–3.

Incomes Data Services. 1984. *Employee Communications*. Study No. 318. London: IDS.

Industrial Relations Review and Report. 1981a. 'The Japanese Approach to Employee Communication'. 241, February.

Industrial Relations Review and Report. 1981b. 'Employee Involvement and Disclosure at Greenall Whitley'. 246, April.

Industrial Relations Review and Report. 1981c. 'Toshiba Consumer Products (UK) Ltd – New Start, New Industrial Relations'. 243, August.

Industrial Relations Review and Report. 1982. 'Quality Circles at Jaguar Cars'. 277, August.

Industrial Relations Review and Report. 1984a. 'Involving Employees at Vaux Breweries'. 312, January.

Industrial Relations Review and Report. 1984b. 'EEC Proposals on Employee Involvement. Part 1'. 318, April.

Industrial Relations Review and Report. 1984c. 'EEC Proposals on Employee Involvement. Part 2'. 320: May.

Industrial Relations Review and Report. 1984d. 'Cadbury Somerdale – The Management of Change'. 328, September.

Industrial Relations Review and Report. 1986. 'Babcock Power – Long Term Survival Plan'. 367, May.

Industrial Society. 1986. *Successful Suggestion Schemes*. London: Industrial Society.

Institute of Directors. 1981. *Communications at Work: The Challenge and the Response. A Survey of Communication within Britain's Medium-sized and Larger Companies*. London: IOD and Bolton Dickinson Associates.

IPM. 1981a. *Employee Communication in the 1980s: A Survey Covering 145 Organisations Conducted for the IPM 1980 Conference*. London: Charles Barker Lyons. (Prepared by M. Arnott, C. Minton and M. Wilders.)

IPM. 1981b. *Practical Participation and Involvement 1: Communications in Practice*. London: Institute of Personnel Management.

IPM. 1982. *Practical Participation and Involvement 3: The Individual and the Job*. London: Institute of Personnel Management.

Keohane, J. 1971a. 'Methods for Surveying Employee Attitudes'. *Occupational Psychology*, Vol. 45, No. 3.

Keohane, J. 1971b. 'Methods for Surveying Employee Attitudes'. *Occupational Psychology*, Vol. 45, No. 4.

Klemm, M., Sanderson, S. and Luffman, G. 1991. 'Mission Statements: Selling Corporate Values to Employees'. *Long Range Planning*, Vol. 24, No. 3, 73–8.

Knight, I. B. 1979. *Company Organisation and Worker Participation: The Results of a Survey*. London: HMSO.

Knights, D. and Collinson, D. 1987. 'Disciplining the Shop Floor: A Comparison of the Disciplinary Effects of Managerial Psychology and Financial Accounting'. *Accounting, Organizations and Society*, Vol. 12, No. 5, 457–77.

Legge, K. 1978. *Power, Innovation and Problem Solving in Personnel Management*. Maidenhead: McGraw-Hill.

Lidstone, J. 1989. 'Projected Image: Making Corporate Identity Work'. *Director*, Vol. 42, No. 11, 88–93.

Long, P. 1986. *Performance Appraisal Revisited: Third IPM Survey*. London: Institute of Personnel Management.

McKeand, P. J. 1990. 'GM Division Builds a Classic System to Share Internal Information'. *Public Relations Journal*, Vol. 46, No. 11, 24–6, 41.

Marchington, M., Goodman, J., Wilkinson, A. and Ackers, P. 1992. *New Developments in Employee Involvement*. Department of Employment, Research Series No. 2.

Marginson, P., Edwards, P. K., Martin, R., Purcell, J. and Sisson, K. 1988. *Beyond the Workplace: Managing Industrial Relations in the Multi-Establishment Enterprise*. Oxford: Blackwell.

Marsh, A. and Hussey, R. 1979. *Survey of Company Reports*. Croydon: Company Secretary's Review.

Maude, B. 1977. *Communications at Work*. London: Business Books.

Mellinger, G. C. 1956. 'Interpersonal Trust as a Factor in Communications'. *Journal of Abnormal and Social Psychology*, Vol. 52, 304–9.

Millward, N. and Stevens, M. 1986. *The Second Workplace Industrial Relations Survey 1980–1984*. Aldershot: Gower.

Millward, N., Stevens, M., Smart, D. and Hawes, W. R. 1992. *Workplace Industrial Relations in Transition: The ED/ESRC/PSI/ACAS Surveys*. Aldershot: Dartmouth.

Moore, R. 1980. 'Information to Unions: Use or Abuse?' *Personnel Management*, May, 34–8.

National Economic Development Committee. 1986. *Communicating for Change*. London: NEDC.

Ogden, S. 1992. 'The Limits to Employee Involvement: Profit Sharing and Disclosure of Information'. *Journal of Management Studies*, Vol. 29, No. 2, 229–48.

Opinion Research and Communications. 1978. *A Survey of Employee Attitudes to Special Employee Reports and to Other Management Communication Techniques*. London: ORC.

Peel, M., Pendlebury, M. and Groves, R. 1991. 'Wider Share Ownership and Employee Reporting'. *Management Accounting*, Vol. 69, No. 5, 38–40.

Peters, T. J. and Waterman, R. H. 1982. *In Search of Excellence*. New York: Harper & Row.

Public Relations Journal. 1990. 'AT&T Revamps Employee Communications to Emphasize "New Direction" for '90s'. Vol. 46, No. 11, 26.

Purcell, J., Marginson, P., Edwards, P. and Sisson, K. 1987. 'The Industrial Relations Practices of Multi-Plant Foreign Owned Firms'. *Industrial Relations Journal*, Vol. 18, Summer, 130–7.

Ramsay, H. 1977. 'Guides to Control: Worker Participation in Sociological and Historical Perspective'. *Sociology*, Vol. 11, No. 3, 481–506.

Reeves, T. K. 1980. *Information Disclosure in Employee Relations*. Bradford: MCB Publications.

Reeves, T. K. and Chambers, B. P. 1978. *Employee Communications – An Act of Faith? A Report on the Use of Mass Media Techniques to Communicate with Employees*. London: Business Decisions Ltd.

Rochester, Lord. 1982. 'The 1982 Employment Act'. *Industrial Society*, 64, December, 8–9, 14.

Rogers, E. M. and Rogers, R. 1976. *Communication to Organizations*. New York: Free Press.

Rose, M. 1975. *Industrial Behaviour: Theoretical Development since Taylor*. Harmondsworth: Penguin.

Sisson, K. 1984. 'Changing Strategy in Industrial Relations'. *Personnel Management*, May, 24–7.

Smith, A. 1989. 'I Read It on the Grapevine'. *Industrial Society*, June, 30–1.

Sturrock, J. 1986. *Structuralism*. London: Paladin Grafton.

Thomson, F. 1983. 'The Seven Deadly Sins of Briefing Groups'. *Personnel Management*, February, 32–5.

Thomson, F. and McAdam, S. 1988. 'Communicating When it Really Matters'. *Director*, Vol. 42, No. 2, 139–40.

Townley, B. 1989. 'Employee Communication Programmes'. In Sisson, K. (ed.) *Personnel Management in Britain*. Oxford: Basil Blackwell, 329–55.

Troy, K. 1989. 'Internal Communication Restructures for the '90s'. *Communication World*, Vol. 6. No. 2, 28–31.

Walton, R. 1985. 'From Control to Commitment in the Workplace'. *Harvard Business Review*, Vol. 63, March–April, 74–84.

Walton, R. and McKersie, R. 1965. *A Behavioural Theory of Labor Negotiations*. New York: McGraw-Hill.

Wates, J. 1983. 'Reporting on Employee Involvement'. *Personnel Management*, March, 32–5.

19

Task Participation:
Employees' Participation
Enabled or Constrained?

John F. Geary

Introduction

There has been much discussion in recent years as to the extent, properties, and variation of management's efforts to introduce new working practices in Britain (Batstone, 1989; Bradley and Hill, 1987; Collard and Dale, 1989; Elger, 1990; Hill, 1991a and 1991b; Pollert, 1991; Wilkinson et al., 1992). The debate has ranged over a number of issues: the reasons why management might be seeking to make changes in long-standing working arrangements; the nature and extent of these changes; whether these changes have led to significant alterations in authority relations, people's working lives, or in employees' attitudes towards their employers; and to what extent have British managements been able to move towards the more participative style of management which is being increasingly recommended in the prescriptive literature.

This chapter focuses on the implementation of task participation in Britain. It begins by briefly considering how employers' interest in task participation has changed in recent years. The second section proposes a definition of task participation as well as identifying its two main forms and the third discusses the nature and extent of task participation in Britain. The fourth section, which comprises the main body of the chapter, looks at task participation in practice by examining its impact on the shop-floor, the role of trade unions in its introduction and the manner in which it affects employees' and managers' working lives. The fifth and final section looks at the prospects for a wider adoption of task participation in Britain and identifies some of the main factors which may impede its diffusion.

Changing Contexts: Changing Approaches

At various points in time, management has adopted a variety of task participation initiatives to resolve problems encountered in indus-trial relations and personnel management. In the 1970s, for in-stance, autonomous work groups were hailed as a key innovation, in the 1980s it was quality circles, and more recently, it has been total quality management, team-working and continuous improvement. As chapter 3 has pointed out, other techniques like job rotation, job enlargement and job enrichment have also been used to varying degrees. Many of the earlier task participation devices were designed primarily to improve the quality of peoples' working lives. Often the initiative came from trade union and employee demands. In some instances it came from managers themselves who feared the alienat-ing and de-humanizing effects of fragmented assembly line work.

This concern to improve the quality of working life was more pronounced elsewhere in Europe than in Britain. Lupton et al. (1979) claimed that their case study companies in Britain had shown less concern to redesign jobs than their counterparts in other Euro-pean countries: 'manufacturing industry', they asserted, 'has done very little to develop new work structures.' Furthermore, they re-ported that there had only been a few recorded cases of work restructuring in the UK where more than a few score of employees had been involved. The introduction of autonomous work groups at Volvo's Kalmar plant was probably the most acclaimed attempt to restructure work in Europe. Similar experiments were conducted at Philips in Holland and at Alfa Romeo and Olivetti in Italy. Govern-ments, too, took an interest. In the 1970s, work reorganization programmes had the active support of the Social Democratic gov-ernment in Germany and, in 1982, the French government intro-duced legislation which provided for rights for groups of workers to express their views. By contrast, in the 1960s and 1970s, at least, it was more typical for British employers to redesign work according to specific efficiency criteria and any movement towards new participative forms of work organization was almost accidental and was rarely informed by theories of the virtues of worker involvement (Batstone, 1989). Those experiments which did take place were more concerned to tinker with individual jobs than to institute a fundamental reorganization of the structure of work or of employees' responsibilities.

In more recent years, however, there has been a significant increase in employers' interest in the reorganization of work. As other chapters have pointed out, terms such as lean production, total quality management, just-in-time, employee involvement, direct participation and team-working abound. Commentators speak of the need for, or indeed the existence of, a new managerial strategy which no longer relies on merely securing employees' compliance but seeks instead to win over their consent and commitment. It has become common for management to claim that the old adversarial style of industrial relations has been replaced by a strategy which seeks to win over the hearts and minds of employees by developing an individualized relationship between them and their employers.

The lack of stable markets and the erosion of firms' competitive position, together with the introduction of new technologies, have compelled employers to look again at the technical and social organization of work in their enterprises. These new competitive pressures have forced companies to reduce costs, raise productivity, improve quality, de-layer management and achieve greater flexibility in the deployment of labour. This is true both of British and other European employers. The telling lesson comes from Japan, where an important reason for Japanese competitive advantage, it is claimed, lies in the organization of production, a vital constituent of which is the greater involvement of employees in their work. They are often organized into production teams which overcome many of the inefficiencies associated with traditional forms of work organization.

Thus, while the main motivation for management in altering the organization of work in the past was labour turnover, absenteeism, recruitment and retention, the principal stimuli now include improved quality, flexibility, productivity and the optimal use of technology and manpower. It was found in the most recent Workplace Industrial Relations Survey (WIRS 3) – which interviewed managers and trade union representatives in over 2000 establishments, each with a minimum of 25 employees – for instance, that only 1 per cent of establishments had introduced a quality of working life initiative. A crucial implication of many of these newer initiatives is that they are directed primarily at the manner in which management (ought to) behave. Thus, as is the case with 'total quality management' (TQM) in particular, it is not that employee participation is unimportant, but rather that this is seen as an outcome dependent on prior changes in the attitudes and behaviour of management (Hill, 1991b). Implicit in this recognition of the central role of management is an acknowledgment that many of the problems within an organization are not always the fault of the workforce, but rather may result from managerial error or inattention and it is their responsibility to see them corrected. Thus, some forms of task participation (like TQM) endeavour to unite everyday management of the enterprise and managing for innovation in one set of organizational arrangements and practices (Hill, 1991b). In other words, the managers who are responsible for implementing change on the shop-floor are also responsible for dealing with its outcomes as part of their daily managerial duties. There is an argument, then, that management's approach to involving employees has altered and that managers are more eager to adopt task participation practices than they may have been in the past. Whether actual practice has changed, and, if so, in what manner or by how much, remains to be explored, however.

Defining Task Participation

There is an obvious danger in equating task participation with labels such as job rotation, job enlargement, quality circles, team-working, problem-solving groups and TQM, in particular, when some are referred to as *old* forms of task participation and others as *new*. It is better that task participation is looked on as a set of processes. It is also the case, of course, that the specific practices are rarely applied as they appear in the textbooks, and there are numerous different definitions for team-work and TQM in the literature. It is for this reason that the term 'task participation' is used and a broad definition offered.

Task participation is defined as opportunities which management provides at workplace level for consultation with and/or delegation of responsibilities and authority for decision making to its subordinates either as individuals or as groups of employees relating to the immediate work task and/or working conditions. With this conceptualization, task participation is rendered timeless. What may be new now is that management is increasingly adopting new work organization strategies, with greater urgency than heretofore, and defining the terms of its implementation and operation. So, having rejected many similar techniques in the past, employers are beginning to discuss the advantages of task participation with renewed interest.

While this definition of task participation lays stress on the role of managers – that they are increasingly defining the terms of task participation – it must be understood that its ultimate shape, as it manifests itself on the shop-floor or in the office, will have evolved through continuous negotiation and definition: it does not have an automatic effect once implemented. Existing institutions, formal and informal rules of behaviour, modes of understanding and ways of managing will all have a bearing on the shape assumed by task participation. It is not a question of managers having a free hand to design task participation as they please: it is an ongoing process, evolving within a given arena of opportunities and constraints.

With task participation, then, employees are granted more control over their immediate work situation and are invited to participate in decisions which relate to the organization of work at the point of production. Thus, workers may influence the manner in which work is allocated, the scheduling of work and when to take breaks. They are also actively encouraged to seek solutions to problems and to make suggestions which will improve the organization's efficiency. This, of course, means that workers are expected to adopt the ends of the enterprise as their own: workers' interests and those of their employer are to be inextricably linked. Task participation is used thus as a means of generating employee commitment, motivation and co-operation. It is an effort on management's part to gain employees' active consent and to persuade them to work hard and diligently.

It is useful to think of task participation as having two key forms, one *consultative*, the other *delegative*. With consultative participation, employees are encouraged, and enabled, to make their views known. Management, however, retains the right to accept or reject employees' opinions as well as reserving the right to take action. An example of this form of participation might be quality circles, where employees, typically in small groups, meet on a regular basis to discuss solutions to work-related problems. Employees are not normally empowered to implement, however, only to recommend.

With delegative participation, responsibility for what has traditionally been an area of management decision making is placed largely in employees' hands: participation is designed into peoples' jobs. Examples here may include semi-autonomous work groups and team-working. In its most developed or purest sense, this form of participation refers to the granting of autonomy to workers by management so that they may become self-managing. The distinctive feature of this form of task participation is that participation extends into new forms of work organization: employees are entrusted to plan, conceive and execute the daily organization of work.

The Nature and Extent of Task Participation

Consultative participation

Two-way communication   There is some debate in the literature as to whether two-way communication constitutes participation. Some commentators have argued that it is not, while others suggest that it is a necessary ingredient and accompaniment to the successful implementation of task participation. In the 1990 WIRS 3 study it was reported that 45 per cent of establishments had taken initiatives to increase employees' involvement in the operation of the establishment in recent years. This represented a significant increase from the 1984 figure of 35 per cent. This growth was particularly marked in both private services and the public sector. By far the most significant mechanism adopted was two-way communication. Its increase was particularly marked in the public sector (from 11 per cent to 19 per cent), although it declined in private manufacturing from 15 per cent to 7 per cent. It is also significant that, despite this increase in two-way communication, there was only a very small increase in the number reporting an increase in the amount of information being communicated to employees (from 4 per cent to 5 per cent). Thus, management may have been more concerned to use these initiatives to tap the knowledge which employees possess of the production process than to extend their decision-making powers.

Quality circles   Quality circles (QCs) have been one of the most popular forms of consultative participation initiatives adopted by British employers in recent years (Collard and Dale, 1989). While there is no standard format for the operation of QCs, they typically involve a small group of employees, usually between six and eight people, in discussions seeking to resolve problems which are work related, generally under the guidance of their supervisor. Circles normally meet on a regular basis, perhaps once a month or fortnightly, for an hour or so. Its members select the issues or problems they wish to address; collect the necessary data and information; and use a variety of statistical techniques to resolve the problems and suggest to management ways of overcoming them. Management, however, retains the right to accept or reject employees' proposals and may request employees to desist from taking any further action. Employees' involvement in quality circles, it is argued, leads to the procurement of new skills and teaches them to work in teams. It is an attempt on management's part to encourage people not only to identify with the quality of their own work but also with the managerial objectives of better quality and increased efficiency throughout the organization.

At the end of the 1970s, the companies in Britain operating QCs were few and far between. By the mid-1980s, however, management interest would seem to have increased dramatically, as the number had grown to about 400 (Incomes Data Services, 1985). Similarly, while Batstone (1984) found that only three of his 130 large manufacturing plants had operated QCs before 1978, by 1983 the proportion had increased to 19 per cent. This significant growth, however, has been matched only by their equally impressive decline. A CBI survey (1990) revealed that the number of QCs decreased by more than half over the last decade. Other commentators, too, have spoken of their demise (Hill, 1991b; Marginson et al., 1988; Oliver and Wilkinson, 1989). But even if we take the period when QCs were at the peak of their popularity their number remained very small. In manufacturing alone, only about 5 per cent of organizations had adopted them (Sisson, 1989). The recent WIRS 3 study found, surprisingly perhaps, that quality circles increased from a low of less than 0.5 per cent in 1984 to 5 per cent of manufacturing firms in 1990 (Millward et al., 1992). Nonetheless, they remain confined to only 2 per cent of all enterprises overall.

Delegative participation

Semi-autonomous work groups   Semi-autonomous work groups (SAWGs) represent a more significant form of task participation than quality circles. With SAWGs, responsibility for the organization of work is placed largely in employees' hands: participation is designed into peoples' jobs. They are a delegative form of task participation, sometimes referred to as self-managing multi-skilled teams.

Batstone (1984) found that a significant minority of firms (20 per cent) had operated SAWGs in 1983, although he admits in a later publication (Batstone, 1989) that this finding exaggerated their popularity. In the 1984 study, half of the SAWGs had been introduced prior to 1978, and the other half had been adopted nearer to the research date. They were found to be slightly more common in foreign-owned plants and their use was unrelated to the size of the establishment. Another survey by Batstone and Gourlay (1986) – this time of shop stewards in a wide range of industries – found that, of a range of employee involvement techniques, SAWGs were the least widely used and showed the smallest increase over a five-year period. Perhaps the most reliable figures come from WIRS 3, where it was found that only 2 per cent of workplaces had AWGs in 1990, a similar proportion to that reported in the 1984 study. There was some increase, however, in private manufacturing from fewer than 0.5 per cent to 1 per cent, but they declined in private services from 2 per cent to 0.5 per cent. The proportion of public sector workplaces using this form of task participation remained at 4 per cent.

Team-working In more recent years there has been much talk of the prospects for greater employee participation with the introduction of team-working and cellular manufacturing. Because of the newness of these initiatives, evidence of their nature and extent is sparse and of varied quality. The term 'team-working' has come to be used in a variety of ways and contexts. It is espoused by some in the form of a rousing cry to summon all team members to the cause of promoting the company's interests. The interests of employees and the organization are seen to be one and the same: hence, the necessity, and not just the requirement, that everyone works as a team. In other instances, team-working refers to a team *at work*, where people from a variety of functions and departments may come together to produce a particular product or service. Team-working may also be accompanied by new working practices or may at least aid in their introduction.

Team working is thought to lie at the heart of many organizations' responses to competitive pressures. In its most developed or purest sense, team-working refers to the granting of autonomy to workers by management to design and prepare work schedules, to monitor and control their own work tasks and methods, to be more or less self-managing. There may also be considerable flexibility between different skill categories, such that skilled employees do unskilled tasks when required and formerly unskilled employees would receive additional training to permit them to assume responsibility for more skilled tasks. At the other end of the pole, management may merely wish employees of comparable skill to rotate between different tasks on a production line or in a cell; or the integration of maintenance trades people into cells may simply mean that they become responsible for maintaining a particular group of machines. It may not result in production operators assuming tasks which were formerly the preserve of craft's people or vica versa. Thus, flexibility may be confined within comparable skill groupings. In between there is likely to be a diversity of practice.

In its more sophisticated form, team-working would seem to be largely confined to a small number of well-publicized companies, many of which were originally established on greenfield sites, like Rothmans, Trebor, Whitbread and Fisher Body (Incomes Data Services, 1984; 1988b). In such instances, companies' efforts are aided by negotiating single union agreements, recruiting a young, green workforce and by adopting exhaustive recruitment procedures. Atkinson and Meagher (1986) found that team-working was limited to only 'several' manufacturing companies in their study. Japanese companies in the UK like Nissan, Komatsu, Hitachi and Matsushita are also associated with team-working (Incomes Data Services, 1988b). Indeed, these incoming Japanese companies have often inspired indigenous firms to experiment with team-working. On other, brownfield sites, change has of necessity been more gradual. Recent examples of trade union agreements to introduce team-working include Ford, IBC, BP Chemicals (Incomes Data Services, 1988a), Rover, Vauxhall, and Rolls Royce (Incomes Data Services, 1992). Team-working has also been introduced at Cadbury Schweppes', Wandsworth Health Authority (Incomes Data Services, 1988b), JCB, Pirelli and Hoover. Of course, it is another matter whether these agreements have culminated in team-working on the shop-floor, or will in the future.

As chapter 3 has already noted, team-working has also been associated with the introduction of cellular manufacturing. It has been adopted by a number of companies in Britain, including BICC, Cummins Engines, Jaguar, Lucas Automotive and Lucas Aerospace. One of the main reasons for implementing this form of group technology is that it can lend organizations increased productivity as batch sizes become smaller. Within these so-called 'cells', employees are encouraged to work as a team and identify with the production of a particular product or family of products. To identify with a particular craft is, therefore, thought to be no longer necessary. With this reduction in the range of products, employees become familiar with a particular stage of the process quite quickly and the opportunity to rotate between work tasks increases. They, therefore, have the opportunity to participate in the production of an entire product, rather than working at only one stage in the production process. Formerly they would have been more likely to work exclusively within their trade, but they would have had the opportunity to work with a greater variety of products.

Total quality management   TQM places considerable emphasis on enlarging employees' responsibilities, reorganizing work and increasing employees' involvement in problem-solving activities. The search for continuous improvement is placed centre stage. The manufacture of quality products, the provision of a quality service and the quest for continuous improvement is the responsibility of all employees, managed and manager alike, and all functions. TQM requires quality to be 'built in' to the product and not 'inspected in' by a separate quality department. Where employees are not in direct contact with the organization's customers they are encouraged to see their colleagues at successive stages of the production process as internal customers. Thus, a central tenet of TQM is the internalization of the rigours of the market-place within the enterprise.

The second feature of TQM follows on from the first. As each employee and department is a customer to the other, the resolution of problems requires the development of new organizational structures which will facilitate inter-department and inter-functional co-operation. Thus, 'cross-functional management' is an essential feature of TQM (Hill, 1991b). A concomitant of this strategy is that problems are best solved by those people most immediate to them. People are therefore to be encouraged and given the resources to solve problems for themselves. This empowerment of employees at all levels in the organization inevitably involves a certain decentralization of decision-making procedures and a willingness on management's part to relinquish certain traditional powers. It is assumed that employees will welcome this job enlargement and will actively pursue activities which lead to an improvement in the organization's efficiency.

While there has been very little research into TQM in Britain, we can reasonably assume that the level of its practice is uneven and sparse (Incomes Data Services, 1990). Of the companies which claim to have adopted TQM, the majority would appear to be foreign-owned and many would seem to have only just begun to introduce it. Examples include Texas Instruments, Dow Chemicals, Iveco Ford, Jaguar Cars, Rank Xerox, British Airways Engineering, ICL, Johnson Matthey, ICI, Hewlett Packard, G-P Inveresk and British Telecom.

In summary, then, while we can say that it is undoubtedly significant that management has begun to take greater interest in task participation in recent years, it is very clear that initiatives which extend *into* delegative forms of participation remain remarkably rare.

Task Participation in Practice

Having considered the extent of task participation in Britain, this chapter goes on to examine its impact on the shop-floor. A number of issues will be addressed. First, how is task participation introduced? Is it imposed on trade unions and employees? Does this form of participation seek to erode or strengthen existing institutional forms of employee participation and representation? Are trade unions being marginalized? Second, what impact does task participation have on people's working lives? Are employees experiencing greater autonomy? Are they 'contributing' more? How have authority relations changed? Are employees working harder? Finally, what has been the response of managers? Do first-line and middle managers feel threatened by the introduction of task participation and why?

How is task participation introduced?

If, as is so often claimed, the provision of a quality service or the manufacture of a cost-competitive and reliable product is critically dependent on the introduction of task participation, then one might reasonably expect that employees and their representatives would be intimately involved in its introduction. If, on other hand, these techniques are being used to marginalize trade unions, then we may expect to find very little trade union involvement in their implementation. Since there has been little research on this subject, it is difficult to offer precise conclusions. We do know, however, that with the frontier of control shifting increasingly towards employers and away from trade unions throughout the 1980s, that the former have at least been afforded the opportunity to make a choice between involving or marginalizing trade unions in the introduction of change.

As chapter 21 points out, despite this increase in managerial power, there is little evidence to suggest that most employers have sought to, or wished to, remove trade unions completely from their enterprises. When introducing change it has been more typical of employers to try to bring their workforce and its representatives along with them. 'Involvement' and 'participation' have become the key terms. In assuming the right for themselves to adopt a particular course of action, like introducing task participation, employers have often willingly communicated the reasons for such action to trade unions and their members. The idea of negotiating the principle of whether these changes are worthy or desirable seldom becomes an issue (cf. Marsden and Thompson, 1990). However, employees have rarely had a say in the decision to adopt these new initiatives (Daniel, 1987; Kelly and Kelly, 1991; Millward et al., 1992). This has also been the case for a number of sites currently being studied by the present author. Management is more concerned to convince employees of the need for, and the desirability of, change. Trade unions, for their part, have been realistic enough to know the folly of over-using their diminishing power resources and have generally resigned themselves to accepting changes in work organization: to resist would endanger peoples' employment and the survival of the enterprise (Colling and Geary, 1992).

Once the principle of change has been established, however, management has often conceded to shop stewards the opportunity to bargain at the margins on how the changes may be implemented. The extent to which this has been permitted has obviously varied from firm to firm, but management has been acutely aware that the success of initiatives of this type depend on enlisting trade union support and winning over employees' co-operation from the outset. One of the best ways of gaining such support is when management seeks trade union agreement, for once accepted it is easier for management to justify the changes to the shop-floor. In a number of case study sites currently being examined by this author it was found that management relied heavily on shop stewards to convince the rank and file of the necessity of implementing task participation. Indeed, management claimed that the success of the programme was dependent on extensive trade union involvement.

There is considerable evidence also that even in instances where management has been forceful in introducing change, it has still relied on trade union co-operation and assistance. The recent case of organizational change at Cadbury's illustrates how changes to the organization of work, although intimately bound up with a new management assertion in industrial relations practice, were not divorced from some form of union co-operation (Smith et al., 1990). 'Cadburyism', a formerly benign, consensual philosophy of labour management was seen in the late 1970s as a constraint on management's efforts to transform the company's fortunes. Established institutions like the Works Council were dissolved and the privileges and authority once accorded to shop stewards were resolutely withdrawn. However, in parallel with management's efforts to suppress certain shop stewards' influence, other more moderate stewards' authority was being actively sponsored. Thus, it was not simply a matter of coercion replacing consent: the battle to gain employees' and their representatives' commitment continued but within a different political arena.

In Lucas, too, management's approach to introducing cellular manufacturing and team-working was characterized by an aggressive, forceful style, where occasional threats of dismissal signalled a new toughness and where trade unions were only dealt with in a selective manner (Elger and Fairbrother, 1992). Evidence from the public sector would also suggest that management has been prepared to introduce change if necessary in the face of trade union and workforce opposition (Ferner, 1989). But even here (see, for example, Pendleton, 1991, on British Rail) it was found that in spite of senior management's preference and efforts to reduce trade union influence over working practices, local management, which lacked the necessary expertise to reconstruct work organization, needed to call on trade union representatives to design and implement the changes. As a consequence, the scope for workplace bargaining was considerably enhanced and the influence of shop stewards retained.

Important though it is to recognize the limits and extent of trade union co-operation, it should not be overlooked that many of these agreements are designed to permit management the discretion to manage the organization of work as it sees fit. Thus, the paradox of these trade union *agreements* is that they often contain clauses which prohibit further negotiations over subsequent changes in working practices. The significance of these changes must not be passed over lightly, for it would seem that one of the most distinctive features of

British industrial relations – where the deployment and organization of the labour force was subject to collective bargaining – has been superseded by the need to accept managerial views on what forms of working practices are required (Edwards et al., 1992). By contrast, although unions in other European countries may face similar difficulties, the significance of the perceived 'threat' is often qualified by a set of institutional structures which supports unions' or works councils' rights to consultation and/or negotiation over the introduction of changes to work organization. In Britain, however, there has been a shift away from collective bargaining to consultation.

Together with this repudiation of the traditional role of collective bargaining, the ideology which accompanies task participation (which speaks of team-work, shared interests and the dismantling of separate divisional loyalties and collectivities) challenges, be it implicitly or explicitly, the legitimacy of trade unions' independent role in the workplace. For many trade unionists, this managerial approach which deliberately couches task participation in a language which requests that employees and their representatives submit to a reasoned and harmonious discussion of the needs of the enterprise and accept the need for constant revision and change in working practices is very difficult to discredit. There can be little doubt, therefore, that the introduction of task participation has presented management and trade unions with fresh challenges. And while management has been successful in using the threat of imminent job losses and the reality of intensified competition to remould the ideological domain of collective bargaining (Terry, 1989), it has also been aware that these same pressures have afforded managers the opportunity, where their and shop stewards' priorities, efforts and power may be reoriented along similar lines, to ensure the successful implementation of task participation practices (Terry, 1986).

Impact on employees

What happens when employees participate in task participation initiatives? Are they permitted increased autonomy? Have their working lives been enriched? Studies of task participation in practice, particularly the rare studies of delegative participation, show that it often accompanies other changes in the organization of production, like a move to just-in-time production (JIT), modular and cellular manufacturing, or total quality control. Increased employee discretion is often thought necessary to ensure the success of these production changes. It is clear, however, that management places discrete and definite limits to the autonomy given to employees, and that managerial expectations are clearly defined and monitored closely. Bratton (1991), for instance, found that although operators were given increased discretion in scheduling work and job assignments within cellular manufacturing, the parameters for such freedom were set by the companies' computer. The computer, in turn, provided management with the necessary information on the flow of production and employees' performance. These new advanced technologies, therefore, offered management an unobtrusive form of surveillance and control. Thus, it was not a case of management relinquishing control to the shop-floor, but rather that the discretion granted to employees was a closely circumscribed one. Hence the paradox: as workers were given more autonomy they were increasingly coming under tighter managerial control.

It has also been found, in a research project being undertaken by the present author, that as one moves from a single cell module to a module containing two or more cells (i.e. where each cell is responsible for a discrete part of the products' manufacture), the level of overall co-ordination and task interdependence increases and employees' discretion over the pace and methods of work is restrained.

The introduction of JIT, too, has ambiguous effects on employees' autonomy. Unlike traditional methods of production which permit the insertion of buffer inventories between successive stages of the production process and allow for variability in the time and pace of production, JIT seeks to reduce slack and variability by establishing a high degree of standardization throughout the production process. As a mechanism of process control JIT, however, impinges on group and individual autonomy (Klein, 1991; Tailby and Whitston, 1989; Turnbull, 1989). In a study of three organizations in the US which had introduced team-working and JIT, Klein found that the new process controls fundamentally altered the manner in which tasks and team activities were coupled. In one organization, where employees had already grown accustomed to high levels of autonomy, JIT's introduction was seen to restrict their freedom. Previously, the slack and buffers which were built into the production process had provided employees with substantial discretion in determining the pace of work and choice of work methods. As inventory levels were reduced, and as the right amount of product had to be produced at just the right time, so too did employees have to synchronize their team meetings, breaks, starting and finishing times: JIT forced the withdrawal of their former freedom of choice. The pace and time of production was now outside of employees' control. Klein did find, however, that the introduction of JIT in her other two sites did increase employees' autonomy compared to the previous system where hierarchical centralized decision making was predominant. This autonomy was confined though to task design (consultative participation) and did not extend to task execution (delegative participation): employees could discuss and suggest improvements, but the principles of standardization imposed strict limits on their freedom in executing their work tasks.

It has also been found that where management has introduced new participative forms of work organization managers do not rely on them alone to persuade workers to work hard. In a study of autonomous work groups in a US electronics plant in Ireland, for example, Geary (1991) found that the self-control permitted to employees in the organization of their work was located within a larger structure of control which clearly delineated what type of work behaviour was expected. Close, over-the-shoulder type of supervision may have been absent, but management's expectations of employees were clearly defined in job descriptions and enforced at appraisal time.

There is also a considerable amount of evidence which would suggest that management continues to use other, more traditional forms of control. At Toshiba in Plymouth, Trevor (1988) found that although workers were granted substantial discretion and flexibility in their work, they were very much aware of management's close policing of time-keeping and attendance. The significance of this finding is that work behaviour rules continue to be enforced by non-team members. The disciplinary system does not reside within the work groups but remains separate and is enforced from without. Nissan, a company which it is claimed has transformed the social relations of production by introducing team-working, *inter alia* (Wickens, 1987), continues to maintain close forms of supervision – a ratio of 20:1 (Incomes Data Services, 1988b). This would suggest that conventional forms of authority relations persist even where one might most have expected task participation to have ordained the reverse. Thus, while some employers emphasize team-working and employee participation, alongside them exists a regime that is overtly based on an assertion of managerial control (Edwards and Whitston, 1989). Evidence from another study, using a national sample, also found that supervisors continue to wield substantial power and authority in the workplace and that the allocation of tasks and control over work effort remains largely in their hands (Rose et al., 1987). The authors conclude with the bold claim that: 'independent, direct, and authoritative supervision is still a significant element in the apparatus of social control at the point of production' (ibid.: 20). It is significant, then, that although management may grant employees considerable freedom to be self-managing, it is a practice which has not diluted managerial control over the labour process: it has rather been redefined and exercised in a different form. It would seem that management has at once become enabling and restraining.

Task participation and effort intensification

There is substantial agreement that, while changes to production technologies have offered employees some benefits in the form of new skills and responsibilities, they have also been accompanied by certain undesirable effects. JIT, for instance, has been associated with increased anxiety and stress in the workplace (Turnbull, 1988). As employees are expected to dispense with traditional notions of what constitutes 'hard work', they are required to engage in other activities which might lead to improvements in the production process. This departure from conventional working can, however, as Dawson and Webb (1989) suggest, lead to increased pressures. With JIT, therefore, traditional workplace disciplines are remoulded to suit new production arrangements. The pressures associated with these changes represent an intensification of effort levels, not as commonly understood by the term, but perceived by employees to be sufficient to detract from, or outweigh, the other benefits associated with task participation. These new pressures have not been confined to shop-floor employees alone. Managers and indirect staff, too, have suffered from stress in introducing and in trying to adapt to and maintain these new forms of work organization (Elger and Fairbrother, 1992; Wall et al., 1986).

Of course, job intensification can and does arise from other aspects of job restructuring, apart from JIT. Some commentators have argued that management's primary objective in enlarging jobs and in increasing labour's flexibility has been to increase work loads and reduce the amount of spare or free time available to employees: 'Multi-skilling has rarely been a priority. The major concern of many managements has been to reduce the porosity of the working day, to increase the intensity of labour as much by cutting down pauses and waiting time as by increasing effort more directly . . . the dominant feature of work organization is the mobilization of productivity through stress, for the moment underpinned by a compelling ethos of competitive team-working' (Elger, 1990: 82, 90). In Japanese firms, too, these ambiguous effects of team-working have been recognized (Oliver and Wilkinson, 1989; Williamson, 1989). Similarly, in the service sector, O'Connell Davidson (1990) found that the introduction of multi-skilling and team-working into office work in a privatized public utility was also accompanied by a managerial attempt to intensify the pace of work.

Some word of caution is necessary here, however. While management may wish to improve productivity through the introduction of new production methodologies and task participation, it is not inevitable that employees will necessarily perceive this to be undesirable or unacceptable. First, it would seem that, as their introduction is often accompanied by the removal of piece rates, and as the production flow becomes more balanced, the pressure on unskilled and semi-skilled employees in particular will have been reduced. In addition, if the reorganization of production leads to a more systematic and better planned manufacturing process and to a reduction in overtime working, it is conceivable that employees would also look on this as a decrease in effort levels.

It should also be noted that increased effort levels may arise from additional voluntary effort expended by employees. It may be that, with the introduction of task participation, employees would be infused with a new willingness to work harder and be happier to work more diligently. The comments here remain speculative as there has been little, if any, research on this. Plainly, much remains to be done. There is some evidence, however, that team-working has successfully inculcated norms of behaviour among employees which are congruent with managerial goals. In two of Bratton's (1991) sites, for instance, work groups had developed a shared understanding of what constituted a reasonable amount of effort and many employees felt obliged to 'put a full day in'. Thus, while there is some evidence of an increase in employees' effort levels, it is by no means clear that it is a universal accompaniment of task participation, or, on the other hand, that employees inevitably feel aggrieved or dissatisfied.

A transformation in employees' attitudes?

There is considerable agreement that, in spite of managements' efforts to change the structure of work, employees' trust has not increased significantly: the 'them and us' syndrome remains stubbornly persistent (Kelly and Kelly, 1991). In a number of detailed case study examinations of a variety of task participation techniques it has been found that the difference in attitudes between those employees who do participate and those who do not is not significant. One recent study, for example, in a company considered by Hill (1991b) to be a 'leading light in the British quality circle movement', found no significant differences in the attitudes of members and non-members towards job satisfaction, long-term commitment to working for the company and perceptions of the company as a fair employer. Also, there had been no apparent progress in overcoming 'us and them' attitudes. Similar findings have been reported by Bradley and Hill (1983; 1987).

Another study, this time a longitudinal survey of employees' attitudes in the US, revealed that the benefits which accrued to management and employees through the introduction of quality circles were short-lived (Griffin, 1988). Members' job satisfaction and involvement scores increased through the early period of the quality circle programme, but they steadily declined and eventually returned to their original level after a period of three years.

It has also been found that, if task participation initiatives are introduced without changes to other aspects of a company's personnel management policy, then it is unlikely that they will be viewed favourably by employees. For instance, in a study of one of Lucas' plants in Birmingham, Elger and Fairbrother (1992) found that, while employees welcomed team-working, the lack of resources allocated to training prevented them from acquiring a wider repetoire of skills to rotate between work tasks within the manufacturing cell. The flattening of job hierarchies, which is often associated with task participation, has also been found to induce discontent among employees by removing promotion opportunities. Thus, there is an inherent tension between the need to reduce the number of job descriptions, so as to promote flexibility, and the need to retain these job hierarchies in order to enlist employees' ideological and normative commitment (Ahlstrand, 1990).

A similar rigidity in employees' views of managements and their objectives has been found in another so-called leading-edge company. Garrahan and Stewart's (1991; 1992) study of Nissan, argues that employees displayed a significant degree of ambiguity about the desirability of the 'Nissan Way'. Labour turnover was high at between 15 per cent and 20 per cent. The co-operation achieved by management was not due to any sense of shared interests or mutual benefit but, rather, it derived from a subordination of individual needs to those of the company. Traditional methods of gaining compliance were also important, such as locating the plant in an economically depressed area, recruiting a young, green workforce, paying high wages and according a very limited role to the trade union. And despite the claim of having introduced team-working, work remained repetitive, its pace dictated by the speed of the assembly-line.

Another longitudinal study which looked at the implementation and operation of SAWGs over a period of 30 months on a greenfield site in a large, non-union British company found that, although employees enjoyed the new working practices and the attendant responsibilities, employees' commitment to the organization did not improve (Wall et al., 1986). Moreover, the productivity benefits were not due to an enhancement in employees' motivation and effort, but rather arose from the delegation of responsibility to the shop-floor and the elimination of supervisory positions. Geary (1993a) also found that one unanticipated consequence of SAWGs was that employees' commitment and loyalty was directed inwards towards the immediate work team and co-operation between work groups was prevented as a result. There is substantial agreement, then, that employees' favourable response to task participation has not been generalized to affect their wider relationship with management. The employment relationship continues to be characterized by mistrust.

Reaction of managers

It has been widely recognized that management commitment and support is essential for the success of task participation (Bradley and Hill, 1983; Buchanan and Preston, 1992; Collard and Dale, 1989; Geary, 1993a; Hill, 1991b). Quality circles' sudden demise, for example, has been explained by a lack of managerial understanding of the necessity for a *total* system of quality and business improvement and the failure to give adequate attention to adapting organizational structures and personnel policies (Collard and Dale, 1989;

Hill, 1991b). Circles were adopted as island solutions. They were also seen to disrupt managers' lives for sparse returns and to create an organizational complexity that confused existing structures (Hill, 1991b). Senior managements, too, were seen to lack the necessary resolve and commitment to make them work (Bradley and Hill, 1987). Thus, in a situation where senior management fails to make the necessary organizational changes and is equivocal in its support, one might expect middle management to think it rational not to support the changes. Moreover, the belief that change could be propelled up through the organization from below was naive.

Even in instances where senior management has been committed to introducing task participation, middle and line management indifference and resistance has shown itself to be a significant impediment. While task participation may be said to offer certain advantages to line management – by enabling them to resolve problems at source on the shop-floor, leaving them free to turn their attention to issues of strategic concern, and enhancing their leadership skills by permitting them to develop their problem-solving and man-management skills – it would seem that the empowerment of their subordinates represents a threat sufficient to outweigh and detract from any benefits. Line management's fear that greater involvement of employees in decision-making procedures would threaten their traditional right to manage has been a prominent factor in explaining the failure of quality circles (Bradley and Hill, 1983). Moreover, employees' suggestions for improving the manner in which work is organized may not only be seen as a criticism of managers' performance, but also, if employees continue to identify problems and implement solutions, supervisors, in particular, may fear for their future employment prospects.

In other situations, too, an extension in employees' participation may be prevented by managerial recalcitrance. Middle manager's suspicion of TQM and team-working, for example, has usually centred on a fear that, although these new participative structures give them increased involvement in decision-making procedures, both with their superiors and with other managers from other departments, it allows their counterparts from other areas to interfere in what had hitherto been the preserve of their discretion. So, while TQM may be appreciated by some managers as a way of extending their influence and encouraging more co-operation and team-work, for others it may seem like an unwelcome encroachment which is as likely to give rise to new problems as to resolve old ones (Geary, 1993b).

Important though these considerations are, it would seem that management has often been concerned more with conforming to fashion when adopting task participation initiatives than acting from conviction (Collard and Dale, 1989). Furthermore, there is also the urgency among management in general, and within personnel management in particular, to be seen to be doing something effective and relevant: the fact that the change is less dramatic than may have been expected is often less important than the symbolic meaning attached to managerial action (Ahlstrand, 1990; Edwards and Whitston, 1993). Storey (1992), for instance, suggests that the significance of QCs may not reside so much in whether they deliver or not, but that employees can be persuaded to participate in activities which extend beyond the narrow confines of a labour contract.

At a more fundamental level, the evidence would also suggest that British management, in contrast to that in other European countries, has rarely fashioned a debate which portrays the possibility of delegative task participation on the one hand, and centralized management control on the other, as representing credible alternatives. It is more the case that management chose the latter as a matter of course rather than as a preference following deliberate and considered debate of the merits of other possible approaches (Daniel, 1987; Jones, 1988; McLoughlin, 1990; McLoughlin and Clark, 1988).

Task Participation in Britain: A Look Ahead

This chapter has focused on the difficulties, disadvantages and the tensions which task participation holds for managers, employees and trade unions. It has pointed to the more exploitative and dysfunctional features of task participation and emphasized the manner in which it conspires to provide the conditions favourable for the preservation of managerial prerogative. This focus has been deliberate, aiming to temper the sometimes naive optimism which one sees in the more prescriptive literature.

Looking to the future, the argument suggests that Britain is not well placed to adopt, or see a wider diffusion of, task participation, particularly in its delegative form. The evidence from the preceding discussion reveals that management has not greatly changed its approach to work organization. Some of the relevant reasons have already been recounted. Chapter 1 has pointed to the severe constraints Britain's financial system imposes on management and to the lack of investment made in management and employee training. But task participation is likely to be applied in an *ad hoc* and inconsistent manner for other reasons. Employers' strategy in large sections of manufacturing, public and private services – particularly with subcontract work and compulsory competitive tendering – depends to a large extent on the availability of a cheap and dispensable workforce, employment conditions which are antithetical to increasing employees' discretion and skills. Such an approach has little space for a broader and fuller utilization of workers' competences. Moreover, this is a management strategy which is most likely to induce a low trust relationship (Fox, 1974).

Comparisons with other European countries are particularly instructive here. To a British audience the suggestion that institutional constraints on managerial freedom may in fact promote the implementation of task participation may, at first sight at least, appear counter-intuitive. But the companies most likely to adopt task participation are those which operate in countries, like Germany and Sweden, where union representation and negotiation rights are ensured by legislation. Unable to pursue the low-wage, low value-added route for their advantage, these companies are forced to innovate in other ways to overcome the handicap of strong shop-floor organization (Streeck, 1985; Turner, 1991). The introduction of new production techniques and working methods are therefore necessary to sustain a high-wage economy. It has also been found that the presence of legal guarantees for trade union organization in Italy has helped to foster a more positive approach to restructuring and the introduction of new technology (Terry, 1993). As paradoxical as it may seem, British unions have been too weak to close off a cheap labour avenue for management, although they have not been helped by recent government legislation which has been aimed at deregulating the labour market.

For those employers who do wish, and have the resources, to invest in task participation the lessons from this analysis are clear. First, it will require a considerable investment in training, both for employees on the shop-floor and for management, which will need to be sustained over a long period. Second, middle management and supervisors must be intimately involved in its introduction: they must not feel that task participation is designed to enlarge employees' responsibilities to an extent where they will be rendered redundant. The same goes for employees and their representatives: for task participation not to be a contradiction in its own terms, it must involve their active participation from the outset. It is difficult to see how the hearts and minds of employees may be won over if management deliberately seeks to marginalize their representatives' influence. Thirdly, if workers are to be convinced to relinquish old job classifications and territories in exchange for new work structures with increased participation, then managers in turn must be trained to facilitate their involvement: any hesitancy to move away from old, authoritarian styles of supervision may shatter employees' expectations. Thus, line management's role in developing task participation among its subordinates must be closely monitored and, where appropriate, rewarded. Finally, other aspects of management's personnel policy must complement and support moves to involve employees. If management persists, for example, with recruiting a cheap disposable workforce, it is unlikely that personnel strategy will convey a unified purpose to its employees. Security of employment should also be a consideration: the 'New Deal' at Rover, for example, was arguably made successful by management's ability to convince employees and shop stewards that the introduction of team-working and other new working practices would not lead to wide-scale job losses. And when task participation gives rise to productivity improvements, as it is designed to, then the challenge for management is not to be tempted to use the new efficiencies merely to reduce head count but to work towards acquiring new markets for the company's products.

Bibliography

Ahlstrand, B. W. 1990. *The Quest for Productivity: a Case Study of Fawley after Flanders*. Cambridge: Cambridge University Press.

Atkinson, J. and Meagher, N. 1986. 'Is Flexibility just a Flash in the Pan?'. *Personnel Management*, September.

Batstone, E. 1984. *Working Order*. Oxford: Basil Blackwell.

Batstone, E. 1989. 'New Forms of Work Organization in Britain'. In Grootings, P., Gustavsen, B. and Hethy, L. (eds) *New Forms of Work Organization in Europe*. New Brunswick: Transaction Publishers.

Batstone, E. and Gourlay, S. 1986. *Unions, Unemployment and Innovation*. Oxford: Basil Blackwell.

Bradley, K. and Hill, S. 1983. 'After Japan: the Quality Circle Transplant and Productive Efficiency'. *British Journal of Industrial Relations*, 21, 291–311.

Bradley, K. and Hill, S. 1987. 'Quality Circles and Managerial Interests'. *Industrial Relations*, 26, 68–82.

Bratton, J. 1991. 'Japanization at Work: The Case of Engineering Plants in Leeds'. *Work, Employment and Society*, 5, 377–95.

Buchanan, D. and Preston, D. 1992. 'Life in the Cell: Supervision and Teamwork in a "Manufacturing Systems Engineering" Environment'. *Human Resource Management Journal*, 2, 55–76.

CBI. 1990. *Employment Involvement – Shaping the Future for Business*. London: Confederation of British Industry.

Collard, R. and Dale, B. 1989. 'Quality circles'. In Sisson, K. (ed.) *Personnel Management in Britain*. Oxford: Blackwell.

Colling, T. and Geary, J. F. 1992. 'Trade Unions and the Management of Change in the Workplace'. Paper presented at the IREC Network Conference, Changing Systems of Workplace Representation in Europe, Dublin, 5–6 November, 1992.

Daniel, W. W. 1987. *Workplace Industrial Relations and Technical Change*. London: Pinter.

Dawson, P. and Webb, J. 1989. 'New Production Arrangements: the Total Flexible Cage?' *Work, Employment and Society*, 3, 221–38.

Edwards, P. K. et al. 1992. 'Great Britain – Still Muddling Through?'. In Ferner, A. and Hyman, R. (eds) *Industrial Relations in the New Europe*. Oxford : Blackwell.

Edwards, P. K. and Whitston, C. 1989. 'Industrial Discipline, the Control of Attendance, and the Subordination of Labour: Towards an Integrated Analysis'. *Work, Employment and Society*, 3, 1–28.

Edwards, P. K. and Whitston, C. 1993. *Attending to Work: The Management of Attendance and Shopfloor Order*. Oxford: Blackwell.

Elger, T. 1990. 'Technical Innovation and Work Reorganization in British Manufacturing in the 1980s: Continuity, Intensification or Transformation?' *Work, Employment and Society*, Special Issue, May, 67–101.

Elger, T. and Fairbrother, P. 1992. 'Inflexible Flexibility: A Case Study of Modularization'. In Gilbert, N., Burrows, R. and Pollert, A. (eds) *Fordism and Flexibility: Divisions and Change*. London: Macmillan.

Ferner A. 1989. *Ten Years of Thatcherism: Changing Industrial Relations in British Public Enterprises*. Warwick Papers in Industrial Relations No. 27. Coventry: University of Warwick, Industrial Relations Research Unit.

Fox, A. 1974. *Beyond Contract: Work, Power and Trust Relations*. London: Faber and Faber.

Garrahan, P. and Stewart, P. 1991. 'Work Organization in Transition: The Human Resource Management Implications of the "Nissan Way"'. *Human Resource Management Journal*, 2, 2, 46–62.

Garrahan, P. and Stewart, P. 1992. 'Management Control and a New

Regime of Subordination'. In Gilbert, N., Burrows, R. and Pollert, A. (eds) *Fordism and Flexibility: Divisions and Change.* London: Macmillan.

Geary, J. F. 1991. 'Human Resource Management in Practice: Labour Management in Irish Electronics Plants'. D.Phil. thesis, University of Oxford.

Geary, J. F. 1993a. 'New Forms of Work Organization: The Case of Two American Electronics Plants: Plural, Mixed and Protean'. *Economic and Industrial Democracy,* 14, 4, 511–34.

Geary, J. F. 1993b. 'Total Quality Management: A New Form of Labour Management in Britain?'. In Ambrosini, M. and Saba, L. (eds) *Participation and Involvement in Great Britain.* Milan: Franco Anglei.

Griffin, R. 1988. 'Consequences of Quality Circles in an Industrial Setting'. *Academy of Management Journal,* 31, 338–58.

Hill, S. 1991a. 'How do you Manage a Flexible Firm? The Total Quality Model'. *Work, Employment and Society,* 5, 3, 397–416.

Hill, S. 1991b. 'Why Quality Circles Failed but Total Quality Management Might Succeed'. *British Journal of Industrial Relations,* 29, 541–68.

Incomes Data Services. 1984. *Group Working and Greenfield Sites.* IDS Study 314. London: IDS.

Incomes Data Services. 1985. *Ever Increasing Circles.* IDS Study 352. London: IDS.

Incomes Data Services. 1988a. *Flexible Working.* IDS Study 407. London: IDS.

Incomes Data Services. 1988b. *Teamworking.* IDS Study 419. London: IDS.

Incomes Data Services. 1990. *Total Quality Management.* IDS Study 457. London: IDS.

Incomes Data Services. 1992. *Teamworking.* IDS Study 516. London: IDS.

Jones, B. 1988. Work and Flexible Automation in Britain: A Review of Developments and Possibilities'. *Work, Employment and Society* 2, 4, 451–86.

Kelly, J. and Kelly, C. 1991. ' "Them and Us": Social Psychology and The New Industrial Relations'. *British Journal of Industrial Relations,* 29, 25–48.

Klein, J. A. 1991. 'A Reexamination of Autonomy in Light of New Manufacturing Practices'. *Human Relations,* 44, 1, 21–38.

Lupton, T., Tanner, I. and Schnelle, T. 1979. 'Manufacturing System Design in Europe'. In Cooper, C. and Mumford, E. (eds) *The Quality of Working Life in Western and Eastern Europe.* London: Associated Business Press.

McLoughlin, I. 1990. 'Management, Work Organization and CAD – Towards Flexible Automation?' *Work, Employment and Society,* 4, 2, 217–37.

McLoughlin, I. and Clark, J. 1988. *Technological Change at Work.* Milton Keynes: Open University Press.

Marginson, P. M., Edwards, P. K., Martin, R., Purcell, J. and Sisson, K. 1988. *Beyond the Workplace: Managing Industrial Relations in the Multi-Establishment Enterprise*. Oxford: Blackwell.

Marsden, D. and Thompson, M. 1990. 'Flexibility Agreements and their Significance in the Increase in Productivity in British Manufacturing since 1980'. *Work, Employment and Society*, 4, 83–104.

Millward, N., Stevens, M., Smart, D. and Hawes, W. 1992. *Workplace Industrial Relations in Transition – The ED/ESRC/PSI/ACAS Surveys*. Aldershot: Dartmouth.

O'Connell Davidson, J. 1990. 'The Road to Functional Flexibility: White Collar Work and Employment Relations in a Privatized Public Utility'. *The Sociological Review*, 38, 4, 689–711.

Oliver, N. and Wilkinson, B. 1989. 'Japanese Manufacturing Techniques and Personnel and Industrial Relations Practice in Britain: Evidence and Implications'. *British Journal of Industrial Relations*, 27, 1, 73–91.

Pendleton, A. 1991. 'The Barriers to Flexibility: Flexible Rostering on the Railways'. *Work, Employment and Society*, 5, 2, 241–57.

Pollert, A. (ed.) 1991. *Farewell to Flexibility*. Oxford: Blackwell.

Rose, D., Marshall, G., Newby, H. and Vogler, C. 1987. 'Goodbye to Supervisors?'. *Work, Employment and Society*, 1, 1, 7–24.

Sisson, K. 1989. 'Personnel Management in Transition'. In Sisson, K. (ed.) *Personnel Management in Britain*. Oxford: Blackwell.

Smith, C., Child, J. and Rowlinson, M. 1990. *Reshaping Work: The Cadbury Experience*. Cambridge: Cambridge University Press.

Storey, J. 1992. *Devleopments in the Management of Human Resources*. Oxford: Blackwell.

Streeck, W. 1985. 'Industrial Relations and Industrial Adjustment in the Motor Industry'. Public Lecture, Industrial Relations Reasearch Unit, University of Warwick.

Tailby, S. and Whitston, C. 1989. 'Industrial Relations and Restructuring'. In Tailby, S. and Whitston, C. (eds) *Manufacturing Change: Industrial Relations and Restructuring*. Oxford: Basil Blackwell.

Terry, M. 1986. 'How do we Know if Shop Stewards are Getting Weaker?'. *British Journal of Industrial Relations*, 24, 169–80.

Terry, M. 1989. Recontextualizing Shopfloor Industrial Relations: Some Case Study Evidence'. In Tailby, S. and Whitston, C. (eds) *Manufacturing Change: Industrial Relations and Restructuring*. Oxford: Basil Blackwell.

Terry, M. 1993. 'Workplace Unions and Workplace Industrial Relations: Some Lessons from the Italian Experience'. *Industrial Relations Journal*, 24, 2, 138–50.

Trevor, M. 1988. *Toshiba's New British Company*. London: Policy Studies Institute.

Turnbull, P. J. 1988. 'The Limits to Japanization: Just-in-Time, Labour Relations and the UK Automotive industry'. *New Technology, Work and Employment*, 3, 1.

Turnbull, P. J. 1989. 'Industrial Restructuring and Labour Relations in the Automotive Components Industry: "Just-in-Time" or "Just-too-Late"?'. In Tailby, S. and Whitston, C. (eds) *Manufacturing Change: Industrial Relations and Restructuring*. Oxford: Basil Blackwell.

Turner, L. 1991. *Democracy at Work: Changing World Markets and the Future of Labor Unions*. Ithaca, NY: Cornell University Press.

Wall, T. D., Kemp, N. J. and Jackson, P. R. 1986. 'Outcomes of Autonomous Work Groups: A Long-Term Field Experiment'. *Academy of Management Journal*, 29, 2, 280–304.

Wickens, P. 1987. *The Road to Nissan: Flexibility, Quality and Teamwork*. London: Macmillan.

Wilkinson, A., Marchington, M., Goodman, J. and Ackers, P. 1992. 'Total Quality Management and Employee Involvement'. *Human Resource Management Journal*, Vol. 2, No. 4, 1–20.

Williamson, H. 1989. 'Back to the Melting Pot? Re-thinking Trade Union Perspectives on Japanese Motor Industry Investment in Britain and "Japanese-style" Industrial Relations'. Paper presented to the Socialist Economists Conference, Sheffield.

20

The Dynamics of Joint Consultation

Mick Marchington

Introduction

After being written off in the 1960s and early 1970s, interest in joint consultation has been revitalized over the course of the past 15 years. There are several reasons for this, each of which is discussed in more detail below. First, contrary to 'received wisdom', the number of organizations which had some form of joint consultative committee (JCC) grew during the post-Donovan years of the 1970s, and remained at a significant level throughout the early part of the 1980s. Second, despite the growth in importance of direct communications and task participation, for many employers joint consultation has remained a key part of the 'employee involvement mix' (Marchington et al., 1992): it is one of a range of forms of participation and involvement which many organizations, especially those which employ large numbers of people, are likely to operate. Thirdly, moves within the European Community to strengthen employee involvement and industrial democracy point to a continued role for JCCs, particularly if European 'works councils' (or some equivalent) become more widespread.

In addition, the subject of joint consultation also occupies an interesting theoretical position within analyses of personnel management and industrial relations. On the one hand, JCCs are one of a set of managerially initiated employee involvement schemes designed (among other things) to increase employee commitment to and compliance with employer objectives. As such, consultation is often castigated because it fails to challenge the status quo and indeed helps to strengthen existing patterns of power and authority. It is sometimes seen to act as a sort of Trojan Horse with which managements are able to weaken trade union opposition to their policies via representative participation other than through collective bargaining. On the other hand, some employers are concerned that JCCs provide a channel via which employees may be able to extend their collective influence. In the case of non-unionized firms, employees may start to demand rights to consultation and involvement rather than having this offered on management's terms. In unionized organizations, conversely, shop stewards may – through consultation and negotiation – be able to limit the degree to which managers are able to communicate directly with individual employees.

This brief introduction sets the scene for the rest of the chapter, which is organized as follows. In the next two sections, there is a brief history of joint consultation, followed by a short analysis of the competing theories of growth and decline, as well as an identification of the key components of consultation. It is argued that JCCs can take a number of different forms in organizations, and four ideal types (supported by examples) are presented to extend our understanding of how consultation operates in practice. These are each analysed in relation to collective bargaining, that is, as an alternative, as marginal, as a competitor, and as an adjunct. Finally, we examine the dynamics of consultation to assess the ways in which organizations may shift from one ideal type to another and to evaluate JCCs against the emerging European initiatives.

History and Development

Joint consultation has a long and somewhat chequered history in Britain, starting with so-called 'common interest' committees in a small number of organizations in the nineteenth century. This idea received a boost towards the end of the First World War through the proposals of the Whitley Committee of Inquiry, which prompted a growth in the use of JCCs during the early part of the 1920s. According to Brannen (1983: 41–2), there were over 1000 local joint industrial committees by 1922, although it should be noted that none was formed in coal-mining or engineering where trade unionism was well developed. Indeed, one of the best-known consultative structures of the present day (that at ICI) was first set up during this period, although at that time the system was not based on union channels. JCCs became less popular in the 1930s but increased in numbers again during the 1940s via the institution of JPACs (joint production and advisory committees) which had governmental support. By the end of the 1940s, a postal survey of management carried out by the National Institute of Industrial Psychology found that 73 per cent of respondents claimed to have some form of formal consultation machinery in their establishments (Brannen, 1983: 46). During the 1950s and 1960s, the conventional wisdom holds that consultation went into decline again. Marsh and Coker (1963: 183–4), for example, estimated, on the basis of shop steward responses, that the number of JCCs in engineering declined by one-third between 1955 and 1961. This is supported by other surveys reported by Brannen (1983: 46). The decline in formal joint consultation was largely due, it was argued, to the development of shop steward organization at workplace level. The proponent of this thesis, McCarthy (1966: 33–4), suggested that shop stewards preferred negotiation to consultation, and would either boycott committees or, conversely, change their character so as to make them indistinguishable from negotiating bodies. It was felt that consultation would only retain a primary place in workplace relations where union organization was weak or non-existent. A generation of scholars thereafter accepted that joint consultation was in a state of terminal decline, especially in well-organized workplaces (Guest and Knight, 1979).

The 1970s and 1980s produced a quite different outcome, however, and this reawakened interest in joint consultation. For example, a survey by Brown (1981: 76) showed that over 40 per cent of manufacturing establishments with 500 or more employees had JCCs, and he estimated that 60 per cent of these had been introduced between 1973 and 1978. And Daniel and Millward (1983: 129–33) found that 37 per cent of establishments with 25 or more employees had committees in 1980, 20 per cent of which had been established in the previous two years and 40 per cent in the previous five. Almost half of the JCCs were in workplaces in which there was no union representation, suggesting that consultation has a wide coverage and serves a variety of purposes. Most commentators were in agreement that there had been an increase in the extent of formal consultation over the 1970s, although MacInnes (1985: 106) dissents from this position, arguing instead that 'the high birth rate and apparent renaissance of consultation is paralleled by an equally high but less visible death rate'. He argues, with some justification, that managers are more likely to remember the births of new schemes than the deaths, especially if they have played a part in the inception of a JCC at the workplace. At the same time, because the death of a JCC is rarely a dramatic affair, it is less easily recalled, a tendency which is exacerbated by the high degree of turnover among managers. Nonetheless, Daniel and Millward's (1983: 132) finding of an introduction to abandonment ratio of 9:1 between 1975 and 1980 seems to point to some expansion, even allowing for some fairly severe lapses of memory.

There was no great change in the extensiveness of consultation during the early part of the 1980s. According to Millward and Stevens' (1986: 139) survey, the proportion of workplaces with JCCs remained at 34 per cent between 1980 and 1984. However, this did mask a decline in the extensiveness of formal consultation within manufacturing from 36 per cent to 30 per cent over the same period. A large proportion of these JCCs included both manual and non-manual workers on the same committee, and a substantial minority had JCCs based on non-union channels (ibid.: 143–5): that is, unions did not nominate any of the representatives for these committees, although this does not mean that these individuals were not union members. The decline in the number of manufacturing workplaces with JCCs was due largely, the authors argue, to reductions in the size of the typical workplace rather than any tendency for establishments with committees to abandon them (ibid.: 183). Marginson et al. (1988: 114–15) support this view, and provided further evidence about the extent of multi-establishment JCCs, especially in large organizations which operate in a single sector. Batstone (1984: 254) and Edwards (1987: 117) also indicated that the existence of formal JCCs was much more likely at large establishments than small workplaces.

Two more recent surveys also demonstrate that JCCs remain an important aspect of employee involvement in Britain. The 1989 CBI study indicated that consultation is still well established, with over 40 per cent of respondents stating that their organization operated some form of consultative committee (CBI, 1990: 27–8). Once again, the key findings were that JCCs are more likely to exist in large establishments/organizations, and that nearly half the sample reckoned that nominations/elections for the JCC were not based on union channels, though of course the participants were often union members. The 1990 ACAS study showed that 40 per cent of the establishments surveyed by its advisory staff used JCCs. Formal consultation was found to be more widespread in manufacturing than services, and once again it was more extensive in larger workplaces (ACAS, 1991: 10). Interestingly, the JCCs in foreign-owned companies engaged in discussion covering a wider range of issues than their UK counterparts (ibid.: 19).

The most up-to-date and comprehensive assessment of the extent of consultation in Britain can be gathered from the data contained in the WIRS 3 survey (Millward et al., 1992). This shows (ibid.: 153) that the overall proportion of workplaces with 25 or more employees which have JCCs declined in the latter part of the 1980s from 34 per cent to 29 per cent. The decline over the course of the 1980s was most marked in the manufacturing sector (36 per cent to 23 per cent), whereas there had been little or no change either in private services or the public sector. According to Millward et al. (1992: 154), the changing composition of workplaces was 'the major influence on the fall in workplace-level consultative committees' over this period. There was also less trade union involvement in JCCs in 1990 than there had been earlier, but once again this owed a lot to the changing composition of workplaces – where union organization continued to be strong, they remained just as involved as before (ibid.: 157).

Competing Interpretations of Consultation

Theories of growth and decline

There are at least three alternative explanations of how and why the practice and extensiveness of consultation (and, for that matter, participation) has varied over time. First is the view that, no matter what happened in previous periods, the era since 1970 has seen an initial growth and then sustenance of JCCs in Britain. This 'evolutionary' approach suggests that participation is likely to grow both in extensiveness and richness as employees (through their representatives) expect to be provided with mechanisms which allow them to become more involved in the business, and managers believe that it is only right and proper to consult with staff during the decision-making process. As Brannen (1983: 47) suggests, 'whilst there are ebbs and flows, the general process is more akin to a ratchet effect; the fall-back after the surge always stops at a higher level.' This argument rests on the notion that employees are more educated than in previous times, that there has been an erosion of deferential attitudes, and that managers are more prepared to treat their staff as 'resourceful humans'. A formal consultative committee can therefore act not only as an effective forum for disseminating information, but also as a conduit through which employee representatives can contribute to the decision-making process within a consensual framework, as opposed to an adversarial negotiating environment. Moreover, influences from abroad – especially Japan and the rest of the EC – are putting greater direct and indirect pressure on employers to modify traditional approaches to the management of employees. From this perspective, therefore, participation and consultation is likely to become more extensive and realistic throughout the remainder of the century.

The second view, which uses a 'cycles' metaphor, is that consultation waxes and wanes over time, both in terms of its extensiveness and its nature. The initial proponent of this view was Ramsay (1976; 1977) and he has returned to this on a number of occasions since (1983; 1990). Broadly, he argues that management is only attracted to the notion of participation and consultation when its legitimacy is under threat from below (that is, from workers), and that this 'represents an attempt to regain control by making a show of appearing to share it' (Ramsay, 1976: 137). The idea is that participation and consultation is not introduced in order to extend employee influence (which is the implication of the evolutionary model), but rather to nullify pressures from labour and so maintain the status quo through incorporation (Ramsay, 1983: 204). Just as the growth of involvement could be attributed to growing pressures on management from organized labour, so too could its demise be related to the removal of these pressures. Accordingly, once the threat to management control has passed, employers resort to more 'traditional' techniques and either allow schemes to fade into more trivial forms or vanish altogether. As he notes (Ramsay, 1977: 493) about the passing of the JPAC phase in the late 1940s, 'worker participation once more faded from the agenda both of unions and employers. The pressure was off management as industry was able for the time being to deliver the goods, quite literally affluence.' Other authors (e.g. Child, 1969: 48; Poole, 1975: 37) offer support for the cycles of control thesis as an explanation for changes at the macro-level and Friedman (1977) also uses a similar idea when examining shifts in management strategies between direct control and responsible autonomy.

Although the 'cycles' of control argument relates relatively well to the growth of consultation during the 1970s, it has rather more difficulty in explaining why consultative committees remained at a relatively stable level during the 1980s when trade union power was severely weakened. It is not totally at a loss, however, and it could be argued that the JCCs which continued throughout the decade changed in character to become increasingly dominated by management: JCCs, in other words, either became marginal to the organization, surviving on a diet of trivia, or, if they were upgraded, it was to undermine rather than consolidate the position of employee representatives.

The final view is one which interprets the dynamics of consultation in terms of a less deterministic and more fluid metaphor. Schuller (1985: 44) uses the idea of a 'rhythm' because this is less bound by conceptions of similarity than that of cycles. He argues that 'the cyclical model muffles the diverse rhythms of change . . . and suggests only two directions, up and down, instead of the swirling plurality which more closely resembles reality.' Accordingly, rhythms may coincide with or contradict one another, and they may have an element of repetition but no symmetry. The present author (Marchington et al., 1992) adopts a similar line to Schuller in attempting to explain patterns of employee involvement (and, within that, joint consultation) at workplace level, although making use of a 'waves' metaphor. Unlike 'cycles', 'waves' come in different shapes and sizes, and last for varying lengths of time in different organizations, depending on the forces which impel and constrain them, as well as govern their progress. Some may endure for long periods, whereas others fail to gain momentum or break soon after formation. Moreover, although waves may appear to be losing strength, they may increase in intensity again due to an extra push from the parties involved. Furthermore, the waves metaphor also allows for the fact that internal tensions within management may lead to conflicting perspectives at the same time: that is, some managers or functions may be keen on developing a particular vision of consultation, whereas others – by accident or design – may be pursuing goals which directly undermine this orientation. In short, a lack of omniscience, omnipotence and cohesiveness within management may lead to competing rationales and practices both between functions and different levels in the hierarchy. Thus, as we shall see in the next section, depending on the motives and actions of the parties, the industry in which they operate, and the time at which the JCC is introduced, the objectives for, and operation of, consultation may vary considerably between workplaces as well as over time.

Definitions and components

There has been a number of attempts to define exactly what is meant by the term 'joint consultation', and it is from these that we can isolate its primary components. For the Whitley Committee in 1917, joint consultation was seen as a means of improving the utilization and practical knowledge and experience of work people: it was particularly concerned with improvements to decision making, especially at a time of change, and with ways to increase employee commitment to agreed courses of action. Clegg and Chester (1954: 342–3) refer to a 1947 Ministry of Labour pamphlet in which the function of joint consultation was 'the regular exchange of views between employers and workers on production matters'. They also raise questions about the role of unions on JCCs and the overlap between consultation and collective bargaining (ibid.: 323–6). The Ministry of Labour in its evidence to the Donovan Commission was clear about the 'generally understood' meaning: 'discussion between management and workers in an establishment of matters of joint concern which are not the subject of negotiation with trade unions'. Thus, there is reference to 'processes' (discussion), 'parties' (management and workers), 'subject matter' (those of joint concern) and limitations on responsibilities and scope of interaction, although there is no mention of objectives or anticipated outcomes. The idea of common interests or joint concern, or ideas of an integrative nature, has been central to most other definitions of joint consultation (e.g. Armstrong, 1977: 311), and has also been the focus of criticisms about its likely achievements (e.g. McCarthy, 1966: 36; MacInnes, 1985: 101–6).

Putting these definitions together, there are at least five primary components which may vary between different schemes and from one time period to another. The *objectives* for joint consultation may be clear from the constitution of a JCC, or they may be hidden and/ or implicit in the processes which take place. Published objectives tend to refer to the benefits in terms of improved output, greater efficiency, and enhanced employee commitment to organizational decisions. Quite clearly, these are employer objectives, although there may well be incidental (and sometimes quite substantial) benefits for employees if these are realized. Equally, however, greater efficiency may also mean tighter work controls, and that is less likely to be seen as an advantage by employees. Nonetheless, some constitutions actually go so far as to highlight mutual benefits to employees and company, and to stress this as one of the underlying philosophical aspects of the scheme. At the other end of the spectrum, there are also instances in which consultation may be developed and extended in order to prevent union intervention and recognition, but it is hardly likely that such objectives as these will be committed to paper and disclosed to employees.

While most definitions tend to agree that consultation is about issues of common interest, the *subject matter* of JCCs is also likely to vary. Some concern themselves with parochial matters of relatively minor importance – such as social and welfare activities, the quality of the canteen tea or reports on personnel – while others consider issues relating to production and order statistics, commercial matters or business and investment decisions. Again, the range of subject matter depends to some extent on the intentions and stances of the parties, and the extent to which each wishes to operate in an open manner.

Thirdly, the *processes* which accompany consultation can also vary quite considerably, and the flow of information can be perceived as either predominantly upward or downward, or both. The upward flow idea focuses on the contribution of employees to improvements in the quality of decisions by tapping in to shop-floor experience, such that consultation is a process 'which enables the views of employees to be expressed, discussed and taken into account before management makes a final decision on a proposal' (Dowling et al., 1981: 186). Others assume the flow to be mainly downward and to have the aim, as per Section 1 of the 1982 Employment Act, of encouraging a common awareness of economic and financial factors which can affect company performance. In this view, therefore, consultation has an educative role, one which may help to achieve employee commitment to management decisions, and one in which managers' primary training needs are those of improved selling techniques. For many consultative committees, however, two-way communication is more usual, and each side may use the machinery to feed information to the other in an attempt to structure their expectations prior to bargaining, or to prevent bargaining altogether (Marchington and Armstrong, 1981: 13–14).

The *powers* of a consultative mechanism may be stated quite explicitly in constitutions, or may be left rather loose and ill-defined. If they are stated explicitly, there is usually some reference to what may *not* be discussed, and the places to which such issues should be referred for resolution. The clarification of this distinction between consultative and negotiable items may be desired equally by both parties, and both may act as custodians of collective agreements within the consultative machinery. Consultation does not generally involve decision making although, if unions are well organized and strongly represented on the committees, this is not necessarily a source of weakness. On the contrary, it may actually be viewed as advantageous, and an arrangement which allows both parties to explore ideas and test out the water before entering the more competitive collective bargaining arena. Conversely, machinery with no explicit clarification of powers may produce a vagueness within constitutions which can either reflect, or result in, a greater *inequality* of power between management and employee representatives. It is this fluidity which probably most worries the opponents of consultation since this arena can be used by managements to impose their views on employees in situations where employees are not independently represented.

Finally, the *parties* to consultation may vary. The employer may be represented and led by line or personnel management. The 'employee' side could consist of manual or staff workers alone, a combination of the two groups, and even some relatively senior managers. Of these, the former is probably still the most common. Representation of employees can be based on union channels alone or by department irrespective of union membership. The character of consultation may be quite radically different, depending on the presence of unions within the workplace and the degree to which contentious items can be channelled through separate negotiating committees.

Overall, therefore, it can be seen that joint consultation can take a variety of forms and serve a number of interests, depending on the context in which it operates. If it has been introduced specifically for the purpose of preventing the development of trade unionism, it is likely to function somewhat differently from the context in which both parties use consultation as a valuable adjunct to, or preliminary process for, collective bargaining. Similarly, if managements see an advantage in making consultation work, consultation is likely to be very different from that in a situation where both sides feel unwilling to expose their thinking to the other, and where it is marginal to the management process. Consequently, the search for a universal definition of joint consultation is ill-founded. Researchers who write of a renaissance of interest and activity through high-level bodies are right in certain circumstances, though not all. Those who regard consultation as a marginal exercise which is used to confirm management's powers are also quite correct in certain circumstances, though not all. So too are those who believe consultation to be an adjunct to collective bargaining, not its competitor. The point is that the character of joint consultation may vary, depending on a variety of influences, and each view may be accurate in certain situations.

Contrasts in Joint Consultation

We have come a long way from the days when consultation was conceived as some sort of monolithic entity, taking a similar form in all types of employing organization. It should be clear by now to readers that its form and character can vary quite significantly between workplaces, as well as over time, depending on a number of factors. The most important of these are management objectives and actions, union organization and strategies, the level of trust between the parties at work, and the environmental context within which personnel management is located. We shall return to these in the next section. In this section, however, four different ideal type models of joint consultation are outlined which reiterate and extend those which appeared in the first edition of this book and elsewhere (e.g. Marchington, 1987; 1988). Despite Ramsay's criticisms of these models (1990: 43–7), it is felt that they still offer a convenient way in which to characterize joint consultation in practice. Admittedly, each of the models is a simplification of reality, and it is possible that aspects of each may be apparent within the same workplace. Equally, although these variants may be regarded as static, it is also perfectly feasible to see movements between models over time within the same workplace.

The four ideal types are discussed in relation to collective bargaining. In non-union workplaces, the prevention of collective bargaining may be a major reason for the implementation of JCCs, while in unionized companies collective bargaining and joint consultation are typically intertwined given that both are capable of being used by management for the same sorts of issues. For each ideal type, a short example is provided as an illustration.

An alternative to collective bargaining?

In the first variant, employers initiate and develop consultation in order to resist collective bargaining. This rests on the assumption that a JCC has the potential to allow the simultaneous representation of employee views and transmission of information from management to the workforce. That this approach has been successful in the past is well documented by Clegg and Chester (1954: 329–30) and Hawkins (1979: 40–1). Judging by their reactions to proposals for the introduction of Works Councils (e.g. Goodhart, 1991), it still appears to strike fear in the hearts of unions. Certain sectors of the economy – such as private services or small firms – are more likely to be prone to this usage of consultation than others.

The stance adopted by employers in this model is essentially unitarist both in philosophy and practice, but it is of the sophisticated paternalist variety whereby management feels it has a duty to persuade employees of the benefits of its policies. The organization would be likely to devote considerable time and energy to the process of consultation, the central objectives of the system being to promote industrial harmony and the willing acceptance of management decisions. The process will be one-way and fundamentally educative, although the system will also have value in highlighting areas of employee concern since this provides senior management with the facility to monitor the effectiveness of their communications. Thus, apprehension or dissent will be seen, in a typically unitarist fashion, as evidence of inadequate communications or influencing skills on the part of managers, and is likely to be met with a search for better ways in which to present data to employees. It is not the message which is seen to be wrong, but the medium.

Because employees lack independent representation, and may well be dubious about its benefits in any event, there is unlikely to be any overt challenge to managerial prerogatives. The desire for more information is either met or refused on the basis of confidentiality, complexity or inappropriateness. Meeting with senior managers on a regular basis, and perhaps spending time discussing issues in an informal social atmosphere before or after the JCC meeting, may reinforce the belief that these individuals do have the employees' interests at heart. Perhaps representatives are also likely to be impressed by these senior managers, and either share their beliefs or values about current affairs or defer to them due to their status and assumed expertise.

At the same time, however, experience of sitting on the JCC may make representatives more aware of the ambiguities, limitations and contradictions in the system, and eventually lead to its downfall. Participants may begin to realize that they are powerless in relation to managers. This can lead to increasing criticism of the system and its proponents, and may ultimately lead to demands for independent union representation. The fragility of consultation may become apparent as managers become more authoritarian in response to employee demands (Cressey et al., 1985). Equally, attempts to prevent unionization by a mixture of threats and inducements can lead to the evaporation of interest in both the idea of unionization and the role of consultation (Marchington and Armstrong, 1985: 23).

This kind of JCC is most likely to be found in the private service sector or among groups of white-collar or professional workers who may be members of a staff association. A good example can be drawn from the leisure industry (see Marchington, 1992) in which a company had set up a system of JCCs which operated at each hotel within the group. The company negotiated a procedure agreement with the General, Municipal and Boilermakers' Union (GMB) which allowed for representation in the event of grievance and disciplinary matters, but not collective bargaining. There is also provision in the agreement for a national twice-yearly JCC, but only if union membership exceeds 25 per cent in at least half the hotels in the group – as membership is just 6 per cent, this committee has never met and it is unlikely to do so given the lack of union tradition in the whole industry. However, there is also an arrangement whereby JCCs are required at each hotel, and these committees are quite separate from the national machinery. This system was introduced in the mid-1980s as part of an attempt to improve communications within the company and resolve grievances before these escalated into a formal complaint via the union. Restricting the role of the union was therefore a key element in management's decision to introduce JCCs at local level. Meetings are held at least every three months and most of the larger units meet on a monthly basis. The whole climate which surrounds the JCC is informal, not only in terms of membership and organization but also in relation to the style of writing up the minutes. Some of the material which is dealt with at the JCC is related to the broader aspects of the business but most of it is concerned with items of a local nature such as health and safety, working methods, and sports and social issues. In short, the JCCs appear to double-up as a safety valve for staff grievances and a forum for educating employees about the business, especially in terms of the current and projected performance of their own hotel. Although there is no formal link between these JCCs and any higher level body, the personnel and training manager receives all minutes and answers queries as appropriate. It also enables him to maintain up-to-date intelligence on issues which are of concern to employees around the group, information which is important, among other things, for determining the pay award to be made each year.

Marginal to collective bargaining and employee relations?

This describes the situation in which joint consultation achieves little or nothing for the parties, is marginal to any activity in the workplace, and is in the process of stagnation, leading perhaps to the eventual collapse of the system. It is the type of joint consultation which is usually described by critics as typical of machinery in general, but it certainly does not provide a total picture. This type is more likely to operate in organizations where there is little trust and where management or union use opportunistic tactics to undermine each other. Depending on the relative power imbalance, managements may not consider it to be worth the time or effort to go through the motions of the consultative process, and either starve the committees of information or key personnel. Unions may lack the strength or the motivation to object. It is the kind of situation in which the fluidity, flexibility or vagueness which may surround consultation is its primary source of weakness.

This is the ideal type JCC which leads MacInnes (1985) to argue that consultation is fundamentally contradictory because it cannot possibly meet the conflicting objectives sought by managements and stewards. It is beset by internal tensions and, in addition to being marginal to any regulatory processes, it is also unstable. He feels that consultation is best described in terms of a circular pattern, in which the initial enthusiasm is enough to overcome the looseness of its definition. As time goes by, it achieves less and less for the parties until one day it eventually peters out, only to be resurrected by a new manager at some future date. The death of consultation is described vividly in the following way:

> Eventually either one of the parties decides the effort is not worth while and the attempt is abandoned, or consultation becomes a very marginal activity, going through the motions on a diet of trivial issues. There is rarely a dramatic end. Usually committees become progressively less regular and meaningful as members fail to turn up or have more pressing priorities. Eventually someone not only forgets to organise a meeting, others forget that they have even forgotten. (MacInnes, 1985: 104)

The subjects dealt with at this kind of JCC tend to be mostly 'soft' and parochial in nature, issues which appear on the agenda precisely because they have always been discussed at these meetings, including social or welfare matters, or those concerned with highly specific production problems. Occasionally, more business-oriented items do appear on the agenda, but usually only for the purpose of passing information to the representatives. Meetings will probably be chaired by a relatively junior manager, often from personnel, who lacks authority within the organization. This means that the meetings can be quite informal and friendly in character, but that the JCC system lacks any influence within the decision-making structures of the firm. A good deal of time is taken up with issues which have rearisen over the course of several meetings, and with any other business raised at the meeting itself. Given the chair's lack of status in the organization, it is rare for issues to be resolved at the JCC because they have to be referred elsewhere for further consideration. Membership of the JCC can be a mix of union-nominated and other employees, but what is apparent is the lack of cohesiveness of the representative body and its inability to force management to take action. It is also unlikely that this type of JCC will operate at more than one level within the organization, thus further confirming the marginality of consultation. Indeed, the symbolic importance of consultation means that it is a process which needs to be managed by employers in a sensitive and low-key manner if they are keen on maintaining it within the workplace. Its substantive importance, conversely, is minimal to the effectiveness of the organization.

It should also be recognized that employers are unlikely to set up a JCC with marginality as their initial objective: if they anticipate at the outset that consultation will be a marginal activity, there is little point in introducing it in the first place. A more typical process would be for the JCC to become increasingly irrelevant to the management of employees but, for symbolic reasons, employers are reluctant to dismantle the consultative structure. Accordingly, a marginal JCC may continue in operation for quite some time.

The case study which illustrates the marginality of consultation machinery is drawn from manufacturing, at a site which is part of a much larger European-owned organization. The parent company allows each operating subsidiary a good deal of freedom in choosing its own employee relations arrangements, and the site in question has had a plant-wide JCC system since the mid-1940s. The committee was implemented at that time 'to provide a regular method of communication between management and workforce on matters of mutual interest, and to secure maximum co-operation in settling differences of opinion'. There is a complete set of minutes going back to the 1940s, and the JCC is a source of much pride and affection at the works. The committee comprises members drawn from all across the site, who are elected on a departmental basis, and the works convenor. At the time of my research at the site, only one other person was a shop steward. The JCC is chaired by the industrial relations manager, the secretary is the public relations manager, and the convenor acts as vice-chair. The meetings are held monthly, in line with a pre-arranged and adhered-to time schedule, and usually last about an hour. At one level of analysis, therefore, the JCC is to be applauded because of its smooth-running nature and its long history at the site. On the other hand, its activity has become increasingly marginal to affairs at the site, and the issues with which it deals are of a parochial nature – for example, production issues which would be better examined in the departments concerned. In addition, any major issues which come before the committee tend to have been discussed previously at monthly meetings between the shop stewards and management, or have been the subject of one-off communications exercises to all employees. Most members of the JCC feel that it is now a waste of time, and serves little purpose other than being an hour off work spent in a relatively congenial atmosphere. The role of the JCC seems primarily to be symbolic, although suggestions that it should be disbanded are treated with horror both by managers and staff at the establishment. Accordingly, it continues to meet on a monthly basis while contributing little to the effectiveness of the organization or of relevance to its employees.

Competing with collective bargaining?

Within this perspective, joint consultation is seen as being in direct competition with collective bargaining, although in this instance the objective of management is to upgrade consultation such that negotiations become less necessary or meaningful. This is the view of the renaissance theorists, and it is founded on the continuing, albeit changed, role of union representation in workplace arrangements. As Terry (1983: 56) indicates:

> Part of the strategy is an intention to involve stewards more closely in an understanding of the problems and issues confronting the com-

pany and hence of the logic and inescapability of the conclusions and policies proposed by management. But it is important to note that the logic of this strategy rests upon the maintenance of the representative structure of the workforce, and of its authority and legitimacy, rather than upon their destruction.

The subject matter of consultation has, therefore, to be of substance rather than trivia, and put across in the essentially co-operative climate of consultation rather than the competitive environment of negotiations. According to Terry (ibid.: 56) the agenda items of these 'new' JCCs are, 'investment plans, new product development, competitiveness, amalgamation, takeover and rationalization'. Previously, these may or may not have been dealt with during negotiations, but now they come before the consultative committee for discussion (Chadwick, 1983: 6).

Upgraded consultation is likely to be just one aspect of employee involvement, all of which is designed to convince employees of the reasons for managerial actions, and also perhaps to apply a brake on steward activity. Some of these have been well publicized: quality circles, total quality management, briefing groups, company videos, management walkabouts and employee reports. But, it should be noted that there does not appear to have been an explicit attack on steward organization *per se* in these companies. Nonetheless, there can be little doubt that this may be fostered in order to weaken unionism by the back door. All of this relies on the expenditure of a good deal of time and effort on the part of management, which is presumably regarded as necessary in order to encourage co-operative relations at work. Employees and their representatives need to be persuaded, not bludgeoned, into compliance with managerial plans.

There is certainly anecdotal evidence to support the notion of revitalized consultation and the development of more direct forms of employee involvement. Joint consultative arrangements are likely to have more strategic items on their agendas in such organizations, but it is difficult to assess whether the process of consultation is actually more meaningful than it was previously, or whether the powers of the JCC have in any way been extended. Business plans may be unveiled, but they are not open to change. Decisions about rationalization may be communicated to the employee representatives after they have been taken, but they may still be contested in the negotiating arena. The success of managements who aim to use upgraded consultation in order to undermine collective bargaining depends on their ability to shift the focus of the debate away from the negotiating arena. If they are successful, bargaining arrangements are likely to continue with rather less substance than before.

Working through established networks of employee representation is, of course, one way in which to seek an upgrading of consultation in order to displace collective bargaining. Another is to operate the two systems – consultation and negotiation – side by side but independent of each other. Bargaining can be conducted by union representatives while representation on consultative committees will be on the basis of expertise, function or department *irrespective* of union membership. Upgrading the significance of consultation can therefore have the effect of divorcing the union from its members, particularly if successes in the negotiating arena are few and far between. The union can come to be seen as less 'real' in the eyes of its members, only raising anxieties about the future or complaining about lack of influence or information.

The competitive model of consultation is illustrated by another example from manufacturing, and indeed this is the sector in which it has probably been most noticeable over the last decade. At this organization, the JCC became less central to employee relations during the 1970s as stewards preferred to deal with issues through the bargaining arena. Consequently, the consultation machinery came under assault and, as in the previous example, it was 'going through the motions, surviving on a diet of trivia', although, on occasions there were outbursts about its lack of influence. However, in the early 1980s, faced with a much more competitive market environment, management reduced numbers employed by more than one-third across the site. Although this process was managed by voluntary severance, it still came as a severe shock to most employees. As part of the 'reconstruction' package, management agreed to increase communications about business issues to all employees. The package included not only the introduction of team briefing, employee reports and management walkabouts, but also a re-evaluation of the JCC. Rather than being allowed to decline, it was felt by management that the JCC should assume a more prominent place within the framework of representative participation at the site – there is no provision for meetings above the level of the plant. The bimonthly plant meetings are now chaired by a senior line manager and attendance includes all the senior shop stewards as well as a number of managers from different functions whose purpose is to provide information and answer queries about high-level issues. In addition, other employees are invited to attend the JCC so as to find out more about the company and its products/performance. There seems to be little doubt that the extension of direct employee involvement and the upgrading of the JCC has had an impact on employee relations more generally. As one of the managers suggested, 'we communicate now when we used to consult, and we consult when we used to negotiate'. Employees and shop stewards have become more aware of the company's fortunes in the marketplace, and negotiations have been conducted with a greater realization of competitive circumstances.

An adjunct to collective bargaining?

The previous models assumed that joint consultation and collective bargaining are competing processes of regulation in the workplace and, depending on the climate, one or the other will provide the primary focus in employee relations. Within this model, the two can be seen as operating in conjunction with each other, and the two processes are kept strictly separate, although the representatives on each committee will be the same people. Collective bargaining is used for matters concerning wages, working conditions and aspects of a distributive nature, whereas joint consultation fills in the gaps by focusing on issues of an integrative character and helping to oil the wheels of industry. If asked to choose between them, shop stewards would have no doubt in going for collective bargaining. But the two are not necessarily viewed as competitors, and both can provide benefits for employees and the organization for which they work. Contrary to the stance taken by McCarthy and his adherents, there has been increasing support for the efficacy of this model, especially in well-organized workplaces (Marchington and Armstrong, 1981: 15; Daniel and Millward, 1983: 134–5; Callus et al., 1991: 157).

Significantly, some major trade union leaders have recognized that a new institution would be needed if there was to be joint discussion of the kind of issues set out in the *New Agenda* which they wish to promote (Edmonds and Tuffin, 1990; Edmonds, 1991). In the words of the joint statement of intent, *Towards Industrial Partnership*, subsequently signed by a number of leading management and trade union representatives, this includes a range of subjects which have not featured prominently in collective bargaining in the UK in the past, i.e. quality through improvement, training, education, investment, communication, equal opportunity, corporate values, company success, environment, and health and safety (Stevens, 1992). It was largely as a result of this kind of thinking that the 1991 Trades Union Congress carried a resolution calling for an examination of 'how features of the Franco-German approach to industrial relations – such as works councils and greater rights to information and consultation – might be adapted to British circumstances and traditions'.

Indeed, strong workplace organization may be regarded as a necessary prerequisite for this model, since stewards will be keen to occupy the places in both consultative and negotiating machinery, and will have the potential power to prevent any attempts to undermine the role of the latter by upgrading the former. Stewards argue that by sitting on both types of body, their centrality to regulatory processes is protected, and not only do they receive information relevant for bargaining purposes but they can also use the consultative forum as a way in which to convey their attitudes to management. In this way, stewards may be able to influence managerial actions before decisions are made. Of course, managements may similarly use the consultative machinery to test employee reaction, and influence the thinking of employee representatives. Unlike the previous two models, therefore, this conception is not predicated on the inability of shop stewards to resist management preferences and actions. Experienced stewards are unlikely to be hoodwinked by elaborate management tactics designed to indoctrinate or confuse them, and are likely to resent any attempt by management to use consultation for this purpose.

In any event, managements in these kinds or organizations are unlikely to try and use consultation to undermine trade union organization, and indeed see great value in operating the two systems alongside one another. Some companies, such as ICI, pride themselves on their consultative approach to employee relations and, it could be argued, such systems have become synonymous with the overall approach of the employer to personnel issues. Therefore, managements who wish to use consultation alongside collective bargaining will do all they can to protect the unions role as a bargaining agency, provided the latter was well organized and was in tune with the wishes of its members.

In multi-plant organizations, there is likely to be a hierarchy of committees between the employment units and the corporate headquarters. Shop stewards are just as likely as managers, perhaps more so, to sit on higher level committees beyond the immediate establishment, and to have access to a good deal of information and a wide range of contacts within the organization. There may even be subcommittees which are set up to investigate more complex or detailed issues, and these will usually be jointly staffed by management and employees. The actual practices which accompany consultation will probably differ from one company to another, but could include: joint control over the agenda and minutes; a chair which rotates between management and unions; an action list to identify the appropriate person to investigate issues; a date for reporting back; pre-meetings for stewards; statistics packs providing information on business and production matters; and other practices which are illustrative of an open and co-operative approach to managing. If possible, information will be provided in advance, although companies may be anxious about committing confidential information to paper. In addition to all of this, there are likely to be regular reviews of progress, and monitoring of activities which may involve the use of outside independent consultants (Guest and Knight, 1979: 267–86; Marchington, 1992).

The final case study – again from manufacturing – describes the case in which consultation and collective bargaining operate in tandem with one another. Here, the JCC machinery was introduced in the early 1970s following a joint union–management conference, with the objective of dealing with matters affecting the well-being and progress of the company. The committee structure has three tiers – departmental, plant, and divisional – and meetings are held on a monthly basis for the first two of these: the divisional JCCs meet when required. At the plant committees, the chair rotates between the works manager and the senior steward, and the minutes – which are written up by the personnel officer – have to be cleared with the stewards prior to being posted around the site. The major focus of attention at the plant JCCs is on business issues, the information for which is contained in a statistics pack updated each month. As well as running smoothly in processual terms, the JCC is also felt both by managers and stewards to be playing a key role in workplace employee relations. The stewards believed management to be sincere in their commitment to the consultative process and, while there were occasions when problems arose, this did not appear to detract from their trust in the other party. This was substantiated by other signs, both of a formal nature (e.g. support for the position of the trade unions via check off and time off for training) and more informally through close and relatively open relationships. For its part, management believed the stewards to be reasonable in their approach and equally committed to the future of the organization. The fact that matters could be progressed up and down the hierarchy of consultative committees was also valued by the stewards, who in any event kept in touch with their colleagues from other sites within the division. Whether or not these stewards or managers achieved more through this co-operative approach than they would have done through a less open relationship is of course an open question. However, both sides had taken the view, mistakenly or not, that working together would enable them to satisfy their own objectives better than trying to destabilize and undermine the other.

Consultation in Context

The dynamics of joint consultation

The four ideal types analysed in the previous section demonstrate that JCCs can take a variety of forms in different workplaces, and that to conceive of consultation as a unified concept is both misguided and simplistic. The differences between a low-level JCC which discusses parochial matters on an irregular basis and a high-level, jointly chaired, multi-tiered formal structure which focuses on business-related information are immense, and show the value of attempts to present a more textured analysis. Although each of the ideal types was drawn – with a little artistic licence – from examples which have been observed by the author over the last decade, this is not to suggest that every single JCC in Britain fits neatly and exclusively into just one of the four ideal types. It is in the nature of typologizing that certain nuances and intricacies are played down, and that each attempt to create ideal types deals in approximations to reality. On the other hand, to be effective and useful, the ideal types which are constructed must be sufficiently comprehensive in coverage and distinctive in comparison with one another.

Clearly there is a danger with any form of typologizing that it will present a static image of the subject which is being analysed by drawing permanent and insurmountable boundaries between different ideal types. While there are always likely to be cases where there is little movement between categories, this is by no means universal. Indeed, it is possible for there to be shifts between each of the ideal types analysed in the previous section. For example, the non-union variant – in which JCCs are introduced as an alternative to collective bargaining and as part of an attempt to stem or prevent the development of trade union organization – may work well to help management attain its objectives. However, if trade unionism develops, there is no reason why JCCs should not be transformed into a competitive model, or even – though less likely – an adjunct to collective bargaining. For the latter to take effect, it would undoubtedly require a change in management values and probably among senior managers as well. More likely perhaps is the shift from the non-union type, in which high-level information is provided to JCC members as part of their 'education' about the activities of the organization, to the marginal role. In this situation, if union membership in the company remains low, the JCC will be marginal to all aspects of employee relations, and is likely to wither before eventually being quietly allowed to die. A further example would be the shift between the adjunct and competitive ideal types, and this could occur in either direction, depending on local circumstances and personnel. Clearly, a change in senior management philosophy might lead to a more or less hostile approach to the future of unions at the site (or organization) in question, and a committee which worked on the principle of co-operation could then adjust to one of competition, or vice versa. Given that most analysts (e.g. Purcell, 1981) reckon that it takes rather longer to build trust than it does to destroy it, a shift from the adjunct to the competitive model is probably the more likely transformation. Finally, each of the ideal types could degenerate into marginality, as demonstrated in the example used to illustrate that particular category. There, the JCC had at one time been a valuable adjunct to the collective bargaining machinery, but over time it had become less central to all major aspects of employee relations at the plant. In recent years, not only had the subject matter become more marginal, but so too had the representation – employee nominees were less integrated with the shop steward network, and the chair of the JCC was taken by a manager with low status.

Sometimes these shifts are easy to observe, especially if the committee is disbanded before being reformulated with a different constitution, agenda and membership. On other occasions, the shift may be less dramatic, but be part of a restructuring of the existing arrangements – for example, when meetings of the JCC become less frequent (say, quarterly as opposed to monthly), when the agenda items are changed, or when in a multi-tiered JCC structure the corporate-wide meetings are abandoned or reduced in significance. In other circumstances, of course, the adjustments are likely to be more gradual and difficult to detect at the time either by independent observers or the participants themselves.

Analysing variations in consultation

Although it is helpful to provide descriptions of consultation in practice, as well as examine its dynamics over time, it is also necessary to analyse the reasons why JCCs may take a variety of different forms. There are a number of important influences on the nature of consultation, some of which are specific to individual organizations whereas others are felt throughout the economy as a whole.

First, there is management's approach towards consultation as well as employee relations more generally. Central to textbook prescriptions for success is the notion that managements must be committed to consultation and willing to invest time and energy in improving the process. Of course, this is predicated on the assumption that managements actually *want* consultation to be successful, and that they will be open and participative in their approach to involving employees. In some instances, this is plainly not true, and it is particularly the case in relation to the models in which consultation is marginalized or trivialized in its operation. Conversely, under the adjunct model, it is anticipated that working with the unions in strongly organized workplaces will produce the fruits of co-operation rather than confrontation. Indeed, some companies ascribe the maintenance of industrial peace to their underlying co-operative philosophy as evidenced through their desire to make consultation work. But there may also be a hidden motive – to weaken the hold of the unions by undermining collective bargaining – which places the model more firmly in the adversarial camp, and can lead to the view that joint consultation is a 'joint con!' (Dowling et al., 1981: 19). In consequence, therefore, management philosophy exerts a crucial influence over the nature of joint consultation in practice, particularly since most schemes are initiated by managements.

Secondly, the attitudes and organization of employees is an important influence on the character of consultation. If consultation is being used to undermine union organization, the ability of managements to exclude union representatives from the consultative pro-

cess, or to channel issues through consultation rather than the negotiating arena, is dependent on a lack of union strength to prevent this
happening. If the union's strength has been built on its sectional
ability to exploit product market demands, its lack of centralized
resources could then act as a restraint on its powers. This can be
contrasted with the situation in which consultation is seen, by both
parties, as an adjunct to bargaining. Here, union representatives
are likely to have joint ownership of a number of aspects of the
constitution and, like management, the right to refer matters to
the negotiating committee should that be deemed appropriate. The
separation of the two committees may be rather easier to maintain if
unions are well organized and able to combat managerial actions
centrally. As Marchington and Armstrong (1983: 31) note, 'where
stewards were well organized they seemed to value joint consultation, albeit with limited powers, and where they were poorly organized they were generally negative or neutral about it.' The
explanation for events in the 'marginal' schemes is somewhat more
complex, depending on which party expresses least interest in consultative affairs. If unions are relatively powerless, they may not be
able to challenge managerial attempts to marginalize activity either
in the consultative or in the negotiating area. If unions are relatively
powerful, they may withdraw from consultation if they feel that
management is not taking it seriously.

The relationship between the parties at work is the third influence
on the character of consultation. Of prime importance is the degree
of trust between them. One major advantage of consultation cited by
stewards and managers is the way in which it can lead to better
relations between the two parties, which can then spill over into the
bargaining area (see Walton and McKersie, 1965). Although those
subscribing to the competition and prevention models outlined
above believe that this leads to a structuring of the attitudes of
representatives *alone*, there is enough evidence of stewards in well-
organized workplaces using consultation meetings to try and influence management opinion. Both parties use the JCC to 'test the
water' about future issues, and feel they can use consultation to trade
information. Each has sufficient trust in the intentions of the other to
want to do this rather than spring a surprise on the other when that
party may be off guard. This is perhaps to be expected, as too is the
absence of trust at the sites where consultation achieved little for
either party. At these, the blame for delays in the consultative machinery is immediately put at management's door and is sympto-

matic of low trust. At a poorly organized site, management's use of the JCC to structure the expectations of the representatives can be seen as an underhand use of this machinery and leads to a lack of trust of anything which management says.

Finally, we need to evaluate the impact of political influences on the character and extensiveness of consultation. Throughout the 1980s and 1990s, the British Conservative government has advocated a voluntarist line in relation to participation and consultation, although there have been exhortations to develop employee involvement in whatever form managements deem to be relevant and appropriate to their own circumstances. In particular, there have been publications of so-called 'good practice' (Department of Employment, 1989), but these are of a relatively insubstantial nature, and there is great emphasis on informality and the sanctity of managerial choice. Although joint consultation has not been celebrated in the way that direct communications with individual employees has, it has not been castigated like collective bargaining. If managements see fit to engage in formal joint consultation with employee representatives, then that is their business, or so the argument goes.

Future Prospects

Looking to the future, the major imponderable is whether developments in Europe, which are beyond the UK government's immediate control, will have a significant impact on the practice of joint consultation. A key technical point concerns the Directive dealing with collective redundancies and business transfers. The European Commission has already questioned whether the current British system is adequate for applying the existing arrangements. Infringement proceedings, if successful, could result in the European Court of Justice requiring the UK to make provision, in the absence of recognized unions, for the designation of employee representatives who would be consulted under the Directive (for further details, see Hall, 1992: 560–1).

Then, there are the European Commission's proposals for new legislative initiatives in the area of participation and involvement. The Commission has three such initiatives in play. One is the 'fifth' Company Law Directive which includes provision for employee involvement in the decision making of limited public companies. The second is the European Company Statute, which would require

'European' Companies to adopt one of three models, including a JCC, for enabling employee representatives to 'participate in the supervision and strategic development of the company'. The third is the Directive which would require the setting up of a European Works Council in large international companies (i.e. those with 1000 or more employees throughout the EC and at least 100 employees in each of at least two member states).

Of these initiatives, the European Works Council Directive is potentially the most important, even though the UK opted out of the Social Chapter of the new Treaty on European Union proposed at Maastricht in December 1991. This is because the structure of capital in the UK is the most international of the 12 EC member states. The UK is not only the home of the largest number of international companies which satisfy the European Works Council Directive's thresholds (332 out of a total of 880, according to Sisson et al., 1992: 16), it is also host to an equivalent number of companies satisfying these thresholds which (a) have their headquarters in other EC member states and (b) have their headquarters outside the UK (e.g. Ford, General Motors, IBM). Moreover, a significant number of the international companies in these three groups also satisfy these thresholds in respect of their employees in the 11 member states which have agreed to implement the EC's Social Charter in the form of the special social policy protocol entered into at Maastricht. The eleven may decide not to go ahead with the European Works Council Directive. If they do, however, or if the European Trade Union Confederation and Union of Industries of the European Community introduce its key provisions in a 'joint opinion', it is difficult to imagine that the companies involved will not include their UK employees in any works councils set up.

Even in the absence of Directives and agreements, some international companies may decide of their own volition to set up European Works Councils, so as to keep up with 'good' European practice and be seen as model employers (Ramsay, 1991). At least 16 in the EC already have done so (Gold and Hall, 1992) and there are more in the Nordic countries (Agotnes, 1992; Myrvang, 1990). The number of companies with such bodies is expected to grow as the Single European Market develops (see the arguments in Carly, 1993; Marginson, 1992).

Despite the well-orchestrated and entirely negative response from many employers as well as the Conservative government to these proposals, organizations may have less to fear than they think. For example, those which have well-developed and multi-tier systems for consultation across the company as a whole should have little difficulty in coping with some of these proposals. The subject matter dealt with at these committees tends to include business and financial matters, various sets of statistics relating to employment and production, as well as (on occasion) longer term plans and policies. In other multi-establishment organizations, where there is no provision for consultation beyond the workplace, there would be rather more of a problem, not so much with the type of information which is disclosed but with the opportunity to meet with senior managers at the European head office. Those employment units with marginal JCCs would need to revamp their entire committee structure and character.

Concluding Comments

The principal purpose of this chapter has been to expose the inadequacies of any attempt to analyse joint consultation with reference to one all-embracing theory. The institution, like most in the sphere of industrial relations and personnel management, is extremely complex. The motives of the parties and their philosophical approach to employee relations are mixed: managements may wish to use consultation to prevent or compete with unionism, or they may wish to use it as another plank in their essentially co-operative approach to managing people; employee representatives may be suspicious of collaboration or powerless to make consultation work, or they may trust management sufficiently – and have the muscle to sustain their position – to use consultation as an adjunct to bargaining.

Of course, this raises wider questions of power and control which are beyond the scope of this chapter, but at the same time contribute to the debate about joint consultation. If shop stewards feel that they gain greater benefits from partaking in collaborative activities, is this sufficient to suggest that labour can gain from JCCs, especially if the people making these assessments are themselves experienced in the labour movement? Alternatively, is their satisfaction with JCC arrangements merely a measure of how effectively worker representatives have been incorporated into management thinking, and of their lack of willingness to challenge the status quo? As ever, answers to questions such as these depend to a large extent on the judgement of the individual observer.

Bibliography

ACAS. 1991. *Consultation and Communication*. London: Advisory, Conciliation and Arbitration Service.

Agotnes, H. 1992. Quoted in Hall, M., Marginson, P. and Sisson, K. *The European Works Council: Setting the Research Agenda*. Warwick Papers in Industrial Relations. No. 41. Coventry: Industrial Relations Research Unit.

Armstrong, M. 1977. *A Handbook of Personnel Management Practice*. London: Kogan Page.

Batstone, E. 1984. *Working Order*. Oxford: Blackwell.

Brannen, P. 1983. *Authority and Participation in Industry*. London: Batsford.

Brown, W. (ed.) 1981. *The Changing Contours of British Industrial Relations*. Oxford: Blackwell.

Callus, R., Morehead, A., Cully, M. and Buchanan, J. 1991. *Industrial Relations at Work*. Canberra: AGPS.

Carly, M. 1993. 'Voluntary Initiatives – An Update'. *European Participation Monitor*. Issue No. 6, 14–21.

CBI. 1990. *Employee Involvement – Shaping the Future for Business*. London: Confederation of British Industry.

Chadwick, M. 1983. 'The Recession and Industrial Relations: A Factory Approach'. *Employee Relations*, 5, 5, 5–12.

Child, J. 1969. *British Management Thought*. London: George Allen and Unwin.

Clarke, R., Fatchett, D. and Roberts, B. 1972. Workers' *Participation in Management in Britain*. London: Heinemann.

Clegg, H. and Chester, T. 1954. 'Joint Consultation'. In Flanders, A. and Clegg, H. (eds) *The System of Industrial Relations in Great Britain*. Oxford: Blackwell, 323–64.

Cressey, P., Eldridge, J., MacInnes, J. and Norris, G. 1981. 'Participation Prospects: Same Scottish Evidence'. *Employment Gazette*, March.

Cressey, P. and MacInnes, J. 1984. 'The Recession and Industrial Relations'. Paper presented to an ESRC Conference, University of Warwick, March.

Cressey, P., Eldridge, J. and MacInnes, J. 1985. *Just Managing*. Milton Keynes: Open University Press.

Cuthbert, N. and Whitaker, A. 1977. 'The Rehabilitation of Joint Consultation: A Recent Trend in the Participation Debate'. *Personnel Review*, 6, 2, 31–6.

Daniel, W. and Millward, N. 1983. *Workplace Industrial Relations in Britain*. London: Heinemann.

Department of Employment. 1989. *People and Companies: Employee Involvement in Britain*. London: HMSO.

Dowling, M., Goodman, J., Gotting, D. and Hyman, J. 1981. 'Employee

Participation: Survey Evidence from the North West'. *Employment Gazette*, April.

Edmonds, J. 1991. '1992 and the Social Partnership'. Speech at Trades Union Congress, Blackpool.

Edmonds, J. and Tuffin, A. 1990. *A New Agenda*. London: General, Municipal and Boilermakers' Union/UCW.

Edwards, P. 1987. *Managing the Factory*. Oxford: Blackwell.

Friedman, A. 1977. *Industry and Labour*. London: Macmillan.

Gold, M. and Hall, M. 1992. *Report on European-Level Information and Consultation in Multinational Companies – an Evaluation of Practice*. Dublin: European Foundation for the Improvement of Living and Working Conditions.

Goodhart, D. 1991. 'Unions Consider Continental Model of Industrial Relations'. *Financial Times*, 3 September.

Guest, D. and Knight, K. 1979. *Putting Participation into Practice*. Farnborough: Gower.

Hall, M. 1992. 'Behind the European Works Council Directive: The European Commission's Legislative Strategy'. *British Journal of Industrial Relations*, Vol. 30, No. 4, 547–66.

Hawes, W. and Brookes, C. 1980. 'Change and Renew: Joint Consultation in British Industry'. *Employment Gazette*, April.

Hawkins, K. 1979. *A Handbook of Industrial Relations Management*. London: Kogan Page.

McCarthy, W. E. J. 1966. *The Role of Shop Stewards in British Industrial Relations*. Royal Commission on Trade Unions and Employers' Associations, Paper No. 1. London: HMSO.

McCarthy, W. E. J. 1988. *The Future of Industrial Democracy*. Fabian Tract 526. London: Fabian Society.

MacInnes, J. 1985. 'Conjuring up Consultation: The Role and Extent of Joint Consultation in Post-War Private Manufacturing Industry'. *British Journal of Industrial Relations*, Vol. 23, March, 93–113.

Marchington, M. 1987. 'A Review and Critique of Recent Research into Joint Consultation'. *British Journal of Industrial Relations*, Vol. 25, No. 3, 339–52.

Marchington, M. 1988. 'The Four Faces of Employee Consultation'. *Personnel Management*, May.

Marchington, M. 1992. *Managing the Team: A Guide to Successful Employee Involvement*. Oxford: Blackwell.

Marchington, M. and Armstrong, R. 1981. 'A Case for Consultation'. *Employee Relations*, 3, 1, 10–16.

Marchington, M. and Armstrong R. 1983. 'Shop Steward Organization and Joint Consultation'. *Personnel Review*, 12, 1, 24–31.

Marchington, M. and Armstrong, R. 1985. *Joint Consultation Revisited*. Glasgow: Centre for Research in Participation and Industrial Democracy, University of Glasgow.

Marchington, M., Goodman, J., Wilkinson, A. and Ackers, P. 1992. *New Developments in Employee Involvement.* Employment Department Research Series No. 2. London: HMSO.

Marginson, P. 1992. 'European Integration and Transnational Management–Union Relations in the Enterprise'. *British Journal of Industrial Relations,* Vol. 30, No. 4, 529–46.

Marginson, P., Edwards, P. K., Martin, R., Purcell, J. and Sisson, K. 1988. *Beyond the Workplace: Managing Industrial Relations in the Multi-Establishment.* Oxford: Blackwell.

Marsh, A. and Coker, E. 1963. 'Shop Steward Organization in the Engineering Industry'. *British Journal of Industrial Relations,* Vol. 1, June, 170–90.

Millward, N. and Stevens, M. 1986. *British Workplace Industrial Relations 1980–1984.* Farnborough: Gower.

Millward, N., Stevens, M., Smart, D. and Hawes, W. R. 1992. *Workplace Industrial Relations in Transition. The DE/PSI/ESRC Survey.* Gower: Aldershot.

Myrvang, G. 1990. *Information and Consultation Rights in Transnational Companies: The Nordic Experience.* Dublin: European Foundation for the Improvement of Living and Working Conditions.

Nicholson, N. 1978. 'Can Consultation Work?' *Personnel Management,* November.

Poole, M. 1975. *Workers' Participation in Industry.* London: Routledge & Kegan Paul.

Purcell, J. 1981. *Good Industrial Relations: Theory and Practice.* London: Macmillan.

Ramsay, H. 1976. 'Participation: The Shop Floor View'. *British Journal of Industrial Relations,* Vol. 14, No. 2, 128–41.

Ramsay, H. 1977. 'Cycles of Control'. *Sociology,* Vol. II, 481–506.

Ramsay, H. 1983. 'Evolution or Cycle? Worker Participation in the 1970s and 1980s'. In Crouch, C. and Heller, F. (eds) *Organisational Democracy and Political Processes.* London: Wiley, 203–25.

Ramsay, H. 1990. *The Joint Consultation Debate: Soft Soap and Hard Cases.* CRIDP Working Paper, No. 17. Glasgow: Centre for Research in Participation and Industrial Democracy, University of Glasgow.

Ramsay, H. 1991. 'The Community, The Multinational, The Workers and Their Charter: A Modern Tale of Industrial Democracy?'. *Work, Employment and Society,* Vol. 5, No. 3, 541–66.

Roeber, J. 1975. Social Change at Work. London: Duckworth.

Schuller, T. 1985. *Democracy at Work.* Oxford: Oxford University Press.

Sisson, K., Waddington, J. and Whitston, C. 1992. *The Structure of Capital in the European Community: The Size of Companies and the Implications for Industrial Relations.* Warwick Papers in Industrial Relations, No. 38. Coventry: Industrial Relations Research Unit.

Stevens, B. 1992. 'IPA Launches Towards Industrial Partnership'. *Involve-*

ment and Participation, No. 615, November, 20–3.

Terry, M. 1983. 'Shop Stewards through Expansion and Recession'. *Industrial Relations*, 14, 3, 49–58.

Walton, R. and McKersie, R. 1965. *A Behavioural Theory of Labour Negotiations*. New York: McGraw-Hill.

21

Management and Trade Unions

Jon Clark and David Winchester

Introduction

This chapter analyses some of the more significant recent changes in the relationship between management and trade unions in Britain. It explores the extent to which dramatic changes in the political and economic environment of industrial relations have altered the approach of personnel specialists and corporate management towards unions, and influenced the objectives, content and style of company policies and practices. Within this broad overview, some important sectoral variations in management–union relations are identified, and developments in other countries are noted where the comparison highlights distinctive features of British experience.

The chapter is divided into five parts. The first explains how a strong, reformist version of the 'pluralist perspective' implicit in public policy in the 1960s and 1970s strengthened the legitimacy of trade unions, established the strategic importance of industrial relations, encouraged the growth of specialist personnel management, and specified the main components of the reform of collective bargaining. The second section offers an overview of the main changes in management approaches towards trade unions since 1979. It reviews the survey evidence on the extent to which the industrial relations 'orthodoxy' of the 1970s survived during the dramatic political and economic changes of the early 1980s, and considers the impact of the more recent developments in human resource management on management–union relations, focusing particularly on the implications of employee involvement initiatives.

The third section examines management recognition and de-recognition policies. In particular, it explores the relationship between union membership decline, de-recognition, and reduced participation in national, multi-employer collective bargaining. The fourth section discusses management policies towards occupational unionism and inter-union relations by considering moves towards 'single-union agreements' and 'single-table' bargaining. It uses a case study to analyse the significance of single-union agreements, examining the origins and content of the 'greenfield site' agreement between Pirelli Cables and the General, Municipal and Boilermakers' Union to illuminate the wider debate on 'new style' agreements. The concluding section draws together the main arguments of the chapter and identifies some of the key features of management–union relations in the UK in the 1990s.

Management Perspectives and Industrial Relations Reform

Personnel management students and practitioners have long been familiar with the comparison of pluralist and unitary perspectives on the business enterprise or work organization. Whether described as perspectives, frames of reference, or theories, they embody contrasting views on the nature of organizational interests and authority, the source of conflict and the preferred methods for containing it, and the legitimacy and influence of trade unions – the main concern of this chapter.

As Fox (1985: 26) has argued, the pluralist perspective conceptualizes work organizations as 'a coalition of interest groups presided over by a top management which serves the long-term needs of the "organization as a whole" by paying due concern to all the interests affected'. As the interests of employees sometimes diverge from those of shareholders or customers, their ability to express their claims depends on a sufficient degree of collective organization to negotiate acceptable compromises with management. Trade unions are, therefore, viewed as legitimate representatives of employees' collective interests and collective bargaining procedures welcomed as appropriate methods for resolving claims and grievances that might otherwise lead to disruptive action.

In contrast, the unitary perspective asserts that top management presides over a unified authority and loyalty structure based on the common interests and values shared by all members of the organization. There is thus no rational basis for conflict between management and employees, and trade union organization is viewed as unnecessary or illegitimate. It follows that conflictual industrial relations can be explained only by past or present management failings, such as poor communications, or by the actions of irrational or subversive trade unions in exploiting them. In the latter circumstances, the reassertion of management prerogative would be justified through the imposition of economic or legal sanctions on unions.

This schematic outline of the core assumptions of unitary and pluralist perspectives offers only a limited insight into management perceptions of trade unions and the ways in which they shape policies and practice. It is necessary to specify the distinctive features of the values and policies, and to identify the contextual factors that explain variations in their meaning over time and between different work organizations. Two important sources of variation can be identified here.

First, management perceptions of the role of unions in work organizations are derived partly from wider political and social values, and may be modified in line with broader movements in political ideology. In general terms, it can be argued that pluralist values on the role of trade unions have been embedded in British public policy for the last century. Indeed, the granting of union immunities and the evolution of 'voluntary' collective bargaining differentiates the history of industrial relations in Britain from that of most other countries. These pluralist values, however, have been periodically challenged and at times substantially undermined. As we shall see, the shift in public policy after the end of the 1970s changed dramatically the political and legal environment in which managers' perceptions of unions are formed.

Second, at any one time, the perspective through which managers view trade unions will be shaped by their prior expectations of the attitudes and behaviour of different groups of employees, and their calculation of the ways in which these may be modified by different forms of collective organization. For example, if managers expect little more than grudging compliance from unskilled or semi-skilled workers, they may be willing to recognize trade unions as participants in a relatively 'low-trust' or adversarial bargaining relationship. In contrast, if managers expect a more positive degree of employee commitment from technically qualified staff, they may resist union recognition claims, or if forced to concede, may actively try to shape the character of union representation. More generally, as the literature on union recognition indicates (see below), management values and policies are influenced significantly by the number of workers employed in the workplace or enterprise and by the occupational composition of the workforce.

The origins of the widespread discussion of pluralist and unitary perspectives in Britain can be located specifically in the debate on industrial relations reform in the late 1960s. The analysis and recommendations of the 1968 Donovan Report can be viewed as the most comprehensive pluralist defence of the role of trade unions and a benchmark against which subsequent changes in management policies and collective bargaining can be assessed. The Report did not blame unions for the 'disorder in factory and workshop relations' and did not recommend the imposition of legal sanctions to restore management authority. It thus disappointed the politicians and the representatives of employers and managers whose evidence had been imbued with unitarist values.

The recommendations of the Report were informed by clear research findings that managers had often encouraged informal workplace bargaining and the growth of a more extensive shop steward involvement in the resolution of workplace disputes (McCarthy, 1966; McCarthy and Parker, 1967). Managers reported that they were broadly satisfied with the results, and shop stewards were more likely to be viewed as 'lubricants' than 'irritants'. The Report's detailed prescription for the reform of collective bargaining was directed primarily at management, challenging boards of directors and senior managers to develop more explicit industrial relations policies and to join with unions in the reconstruction of more extensive and formal bargaining procedures.

The recommendations thus accepted that trade unions and collective bargaining serve a number of 'managerial functions'. In the terms used by the Harvard economists, Freeman and Medoff (1984), trade unions perform an agency function by 'voicing' the grievances of employees, thereby relieving management of the time-consuming and costly process of dealing with employees individually and separately. Moreover, the 'due process' embodied in collective bargaining may increase the legitimacy of the substantive and procedural rules needed to manage the employment relationship: in dealing with claims and grievances in an agreed and orderly manner, trade union representatives become 'managers of discontent', in the graphic phrase of Wright Mills (1948: 224–5).

In the 1970s, the industrial and political conflicts generated by a series of largely unsuccessful incomes policies and legislative initiatives strengthened this pluralist agenda in distinctive ways. In many large organizations, 'enlightened managerialism' was associated with the concession of greater union legitimacy: trade union recognition was extended to more non-manual employees, including quite senior grades of staff; the organizational security of unions was enhanced through tacit or formal support for the closed shop; and shop stewards were provided with extensive facilities and time off for union work. Personnel managers were able to argue that an increase in union legitimacy was the prerequisite for wide-ranging bargaining reforms that would strengthen overall management control by securing more stability and predictability in industrial relations (Purcell, 1979; Fox, 1974). Radical critics of pluralism indirectly accepted the logic of this strategy in their analysis of the 'bureaucratization of the rank and file' (Hyman, 1979) and in the argument that many shop stewards had become 'unpaid personnel managers' (Lane, 1974).

While the strong, reformist variant of the pluralist perspective was directed primarily at the reconstruction of fragmented and multi-union bargaining structures in large-scale manufacturing, its influence was much wider. Managers elsewhere could see that rapid trade union growth had been encouraged by positive employment legislation and other government policies that had increased the visibility, political status and apparent power of trade union leaders. The steady increase in the size of enterprises, the reorganization of the health service and local government, and the high and fluctuating levels of inflation also offered a more positive organizing environment for unions (Bain and Price, 1983). All of these factors also contributed to the substantial increase in the number of personnel managers over the next decade (Brown, 1981), especially the 'contracts managers', whose status was derived from their ability to resolve day-to-day problems through their intimate knowledge of procedures and their personal relations with senior stewards and union officials (Tyson and Fell, 1986: 12).

It should not be assumed, however, that most managers' individual beliefs coincided with the pluralist values of industrial relations reformism in the 1970s. As Purcell and Sisson (1983: 113) have argued, 'many industrial relations specialists may be pluralist in their views, but the vast bulk of managers are more likely to incline to the unitary position.' The values of individual managers are most likely to influence the policy and style of industrial relations in smaller organizations and family-owned firms, or in larger organizations where a strategic view of employment policies was established by key personalities early in the organization's history. These kind of organizations provide many illustrations of the continuing influence of unitarist values, whether in the forceful opposition to trade unions by 'traditionalists', or in the elaborate, usually non-union, personnel strategies of 'sophisticated paternalists', such as Marks and Spencer (Purcell and Sisson, 1983).

More generally, the essentially pragmatic or opportunistic approach to industrial relations found in many organizations in the 1970s probably reflected a range of conflicting or ambiguous management perceptions of the role of unions. Nonetheless, the reformist perspective of the period influenced the theory and practice of personnel management and encouraged line managers to accept the broad outlines of the reform agenda.

Changes in Policies and Practices in the 1980s

The economic, political and legal context of industrial relations changed dramatically with the election of the Conservative government in 1979. In assessing the impact of the new environment on management approaches towards trade unions, the discussion is organized into three main parts. The first examines the findings of a series of large-scale surveys of industrial relations, trade unions, and personnel management conducted during the first half of the decade, using the interpretative framework of Legge (1988). The second part focuses on arguments and evidence from the more recent debate on the implications of human resource management (HRM) for the role of trade unions. It notes the apparent unitarist and individualist values of HRM and examines the evidence on changes in management practice in the company case studies of Storey (1992). The third part focuses on one important component of the HRM agenda – the growth of employee involvement initiatives – outlining the findings of the survey conducted by Milner and Richards (1991) which explores their impact on union organization and practice.

A 'new industrial relations' in the early 1980s?

The economic consequences of government policies in the 1980s, as well as the ideological exhortation which accompanied their implementation, offered a stark contrast to the public policy priorities of the previous decade and, indeed, to the broader 'post-war compromise' in British industrial relations. The general election campaign of 1979 was dominated by the issue of trade union power. The Conservative government entered office with an explicit commitment to reduce the influence of unions in the workplace, and to exclude it from national political representation. This commitment was vigorously pursued through the step-by-step creation of a more restrictive legal regulation of trade union activities. It was supported by monetarist macro-economic policies, public expenditure controls and privatization policies, and other measures designed to restructure the British economy. The ideological core of most government policies was provided by a constant appeal to the principle of 'market freedom' and the values of 'individualism' in the creation of an 'enterprise culture'.

Deep recession in the early 1980s, and the concentration of job losses in strongly unionized manufacturing and nationalized industries, led to a loss of over two and a half million trade union members by 1985. Other expressions of union weakness could be seen in a number of highly publicized defeats in disputes over pay, working practices and closures, and in the intense ideological divisions between union leaders in the debate over 'new realism' that followed the re-election of the Conservative government in 1983 and the year-long miners' strike (Winchester, 1988). Anecdotal evidence and intuitive reasoning thus suggested that the power of labour had been substantially undermined and the conditions had been created for a very different pattern of management policies, practices and attitudes towards trade unions.

In discussing the implications of these developments for personnel managers, Legge (1988) argued that academics and practitioners developed four contrasting interpretations of changes in the first half of the decade. The first, characterized as *The Fall of Personnel Management*, suggested that 'industrial relations has ceased to be a major uncertainty facing organizations and no longer counts as a "strategic contingency" on which personnel specialists can base their power' (ibid.: 13). The demand for even the more routine functions of personnel specialists – such as shop-floor problem solving, recruitment, training and pay administration – was in decline. The activities were either less important, passed on to line managers, or subcontracted to outside specialists in the attempt to reduce overhead costs. This interpretation fitted closely with a second, widely held view, namely *The Rise of Macho Management*. It was argued that line managers were able to reassert their management prerogative by imposing new working practices and a harsher work discipline, thereby undermining the rights that trade unions had established and sustained during the years of appeasement. A third interpretation, as its characterization *Business as Before* indicates, rejected the first two views, arguing that workplace union organization and the importance of personnel management remained relatively unchanged from the 1970s. The final interpretation, characterized as *Flexible Management for Flexible Firms*, raised different questions from the other three. Instead of estimating how the relative weakness of unions affected management roles, it explored the relationship between organizational strategy and structure, market conditions, the organization of personnel departments, and the choice of industrial relations style (ibid.: 16).

Legge tested the four interpretations in a comparative analysis of the findings of eight major industrial relations surveys conducted in the late 1970s and the first half of the 1980s (Brown, 1981; Daniel and Millward, 1983; Batstone, 1984; Millward and Stevens, 1986; Edwards, 1987; Mackay and Torrington, 1986; Batstone and Gourlay, 1986; and Marginson et al., 1988). Her conclusion was that there was no substantial and general empirical support for the first two interpretations, while data on establishment level union membership, density and recognition, on the institutional arrangements covering closed shops, shop stewards' organization, consultation and negotiation machinery, and on the status and style of personnel management, provided broad support for the *Business as Before* interpretation.

The data showed no general and significant decline in union influence at the workplace, and thus did not support the argument that management had been willing to retain the existing institutional procedures merely because they had become 'empty shells'. There was evidence that many managers had attempted to co-opt senior stewards, but their initiatives were often unsuccessful and, in any event, they did not signify a distinctive change from the common practices of the 1970s. The minority of cases where management had directly attacked union organization and rights tended to be found in 'poorly performing plants of highly unionized, diversified companies', or in the public sector. More generally, expressions of 'macho' management were motivated primarily by the desire to impose changes in working practices rather than the intention to undermine union organization directly (Legge, 1988: 55, 61).

Although it has not been possible to explore fully Legge's detailed review – or the vast amount of data and analysis in the surveys on which it was based – the overall findings were clear enough and, at first sight, somewhat surprising. In the first half of the 1980s, trade unions had been defeated in a number of high-profile disputes in which the government had been the architect or cheer-leader – for example, in British Leyland, steel, coal-mining and newspapers. Why did these widely publicized examples of 'macho' management not exert more influence on the attitudes and policies of managers elsewhere, and encourage more general attempts to confront, marginalize or bypass unions?

Part of the answer is provided by Legge in her concluding arguments: namely, the high levels of unemployment caused by the recession in the early 1980s did not undermine the bargaining power of employees and unions to the extent that many commentators had assumed. First, the costs of substituting recruits from the unemployed for existing employees with skills and job-related experience would be high in many organizations. Second, the assumption that employers are better able to resist union claims and threats during a recession is contingent upon the state of their company's order books and competitive position. Moreover, given the scale of job losses in manufacturing and nationalized industries in the early 1980s, employers were willing to maintain or increase the real pay of the 'slimmed down' workforces, especially if skilled workers indicated their willingness to accept new working practices as part of the pay deal. Most employers, therefore, considered that 'strategies of co-operation are more effective than those of confrontation' (Legge, 1988: 65).

To what extent does this *Business as Before* interpretation of management–union relations in the first half of the 1980s require amendment in the light of subsequent developments? The results of the third Workplace Industrial Relations Survey (WIRS 3) conducted in 1990 offer the most comprehensive and authoritative answer to the question (Millward et al., 1992). The overarching conclusion of the study was that 'in workplaces where trade union representation and collective bargaining persisted, surprisingly little altered', but that major structural change in the economy had led to a marked decline in the number of such workplaces. This resulted in the 'decline in the representation of workers by trade unions and the decline in the coverage of collective bargaining, particularly in the private sector. Indeed, so great were the changes that it is not unreasonable to conclude that the traditional, distinctive "system" of British industrial relations no longer characterized the economy as a whole' (ibid.: 350). More specific and detailed reference to other findings of WIRS 3 will be made in the rest of this chapter.

Human resource management and trade unions

The philosophy and practice of human resource management (HRM) provides the second focus for our discussion of changes in management policies towards unions. The intense academic interest in HRM in Britain drew some of its inspiration from the publication of *The Transformation of American Industrial Relations* (Kochan et al., 1986). The book raised numerous points of comparative interest: it explored the continuing decline of union membership in manufacturing industry; employers' successes in 'concession bargaining'; and, more important for our purpose here, the argument that between 1960 and 1980 the growth and diffusion of a non-union HRM system took place 'across a broad enough array of industries and firms to cause major changes to be introduced in unionized relationships during the 1980s' (ibid.: 47).

The debate about the meaning and extent of HRM is interesting also because it has spanned a period of time in which extreme fluctuations in the performance of the British economy have taken place. As chapter 1 has pointed out, some of the earlier expositions of the promise of HRM were shaped by a concern with the anticipated shortages of skilled and qualified labour resulting from the mid-1980s 'economic miracle' and the 'demographic timebomb'. Later contributions had to consider the limits and possibilities of HRM during the longest recession since the inter-war years. Throughout the debate, however, analysis has often focused on the potential incompatibility of the values and practice of HRM, and conventional pluralist approaches to industrial relations.

Guest has argued that HRM values are unitarist 'to the extent that they assume no underlying and inevitable differences of interest between management and workers'. They are also 'essentially individualistic in that they emphasize the individual–organization linkage in preference to operating through group and representative systems' (Guest, 1989: 43). He suggests that three of the four central components of HRM – strategic integration, quality and flexibility – may generate some negotiating problems for unions, but are not intrinsically incompatible with union activity. In his view, the pursuit of the fourth component, employee commitment, was likely to present the greatest challenge to unions, and this issue will be explored later.

The analysis of HRM practice, rather than its normative values, has been limited until recently by the paucity of empirical research. John Storey's study, *Developments in the Management of Human Resources*, based on 350 interviews with line managers from 15 large, unionized, multi-site organizations, provides a valuable data set and some interesting arguments on the ways in which 'managers in those organizations which were seeking to bring about a new approach to people management had acted with regard to trade unions and industrial relations' (Storey, 1992: 242). He suggests that the organizational tension between the old 'collectivist' management of industrial relations and the new 'individualist' human resource initiatives could, potentially, be accommodated in four different ways: managers could attack unions and the joint procedures directly; they could ignore them; they could run the established and the new approaches in parallel; or they could try to integrate them. While elements of all four responses were found in some of the cases, most of the organizations chose the third option – that is, they operated dual arrangements.

In comparison with the early 1980s survey data discussed above, Storey's case study interviews in the late 1980s with line managers at all levels in the organizations found 'a generally more aggressive stance' towards the unions. For example, Massey Ferguson managers set out explicitly to reduce the number of shop stewards, and managers at Lucas and Jaguar made little attempt to rectify the generally conflictual relations with trade unions, instead seeking to wrest areas of control from the stewards' committee. In a number of companies, management policy moved from periods of aggression against unions to ones that stressed product quality and the need to elicit co-operation, but this scarcely increased union legitimacy: the earlier 'adversarial stance towards the union was replaced by an approach which essentially trivialized the unions' contribution, and trade unions were thereby pushed to the margins of concern' (ibid.: 248).

In a few of the case study organizations, the Ford Motor Company for one, management involved trade union representatives in 'bargaining for change' and 'invested time in building and maintaining constructive relations with the unions' (ibid.: 252). In most cases, however, neither national nor workplace union leaders were involved in the managerial initiatives. This was partly because specialist personnel managers – especially the 'contracts managers' whose authority depended on trade unions – were 'often marginal to the change process . . . and frequently ambivalent about the new initiatives' (ibid.: 251). In cases where personnel managers were involved in new human resource initiatives, they had less time to devote to trade unions: they expected suspicion or hostility from union representatives and on occasions provoked it (ibid.: 256).

As Storey indicates, the mixture of traditional and experimental managerial approaches to trade unions and industrial relations in his case studies revealed many of 'the dilemmas and uncertainties surrounding the whole enterprise of human resource management in the British context' (ibid.: 258). There were significant differences in the policies and practices of the case study companies, only some of which could be explained by sectoral, ownership and organizational factors. Despite this variety of approaches, Storey concludes that 'there was hardly an instance where anything approaching a "strategic" stance towards unions and industrial relations could be readily discerned . . . [this] studied neglect . . . carried a symbolic message: managers are in the driving seat, unions and industrial relations have to be demonstrated as relatively secondary and incidental to meeting market priorities, and secondary also to the newly discovered alternative ways of managing the labour [human] resource' (ibid.: 259, 260).

Employee involvement

The recent growth in employee involvement (EI) initiatives offers a potential challenge to traditional forms of management–union relations. The first two chapters in this final section of the book have reviewed a number of trends in EI which encompass a multitude of different forms of direct workforce participation. These range from employee attitude surveys, team briefings and job enrichment programmes through to quality improvement teams and the creation of autonomous work groups. Employee involvement initiatives also include various forms of indirect workforce participation, such as joint consultative committees and works councils, discussed in the previous chapter. Data from WIRS 3 showed that managers in nearly half of the establishments surveyed had introduced changes in the previous three years 'with the aim of increasing employees' involvement in the operation of the establishment', with new initiatives reported more frequently in the public and private service sectors (Millward et al., 1992: 175). Our aim here is to assess how far such initiatives reflect a growing management hostility to trade unions and collective bargaining, or whether they are neutral or even compatible with a more positive relationship between management and unions.

The research conducted by Milner and Richards (1991) sheds some light on this question. In 1989 they conducted a TUC-sponsored postal survey of employee involvement in more than 200 workplaces in the London docklands, mainly small workplaces in non-engineering manufacturing, distribution and banking and finance. Just under one-quarter of the companies recognized unions or staff associations for collective bargaining purposes. In the survey employee involvement was measured by cumulative counting of four separate EI initiatives: quality circles, joint consultative committees, suggestion schemes, and regular internal newsletters. The authors admit that treating these four methods equally for statistical purposes fails to recognize that some, for example quality circles, are richer and fuller expressions of EI than others, such as suggestion schemes. The relatively crude measure, however, does allow the development of some broad findings that offer some insight into the question under review and the broader themes of this chapter.

First, the data suggest that the probability of union recognition increased significantly with a greater use of EI schemes, confirming the findings of the much wider WIRS 3 survey. As the authors recognize, this finding contradicts the 'incompatibility thesis' and lends support to the view of Kochan et al. (1986) that unions can play a major role in the introduction and operation of EI systems. Second, there was also a positive correlation between the employment of a specialist personnel manager and the use of EI schemes. Third, EI schemes were less prevalent in single-plant companies, suggesting that initiatives tend to be taken at management levels beyond the immediate workplace, that is, at company or corporate levels. Finally, all of the findings were strongly related to the well-known 'positive workplace size effect'. Overall, the study demonstrated a set of strong interconnections between workplace size, union recognition, the existence of specialist personnel management and the use of EI techniques.

The findings of Milner and Richards, and the data from the 1990 ACAS Survey on Consultation, which showed that increases in consultation tended to augment existing collective bargaining arrangements (Scott, 1991: 509), suggest that the British evidence offers no support for the proposition that EI initiatives are incompatible with unions and collective bargaining. It might be argued, however, that survey data offer only a limited insight into the texture of management–union relations. More qualitative case study evidence may provide a more convincing means of exploring whether managers can use EI initiatives to marginalize unions and reduce the substantive importance of collective bargaining. The earlier discussion of Storey's case studies on broader HRM developments, for example, suggests that union representatives should not be complacent in their view of the potential impact of employee involvement initiatives. More generally, the future development of EI schemes will depend on changes in establishment and company characteristics, such as size, ownership, union recognition and density, and the status of specialist personnel management. Managers in recently established workplaces, particularly on greenfield sites, may be more likely to introduce EI techniques, alongside other employee relations initiatives, as we shall see in a later section.

Changes in Collective Bargaining

Union recognition and de-recognition

In their study of the transformation of American industrial relations, Kochan et al. (1986) viewed the trend towards the de-certification – or de-recognition – of trade unions as an extreme example of a growing anti-union attitude among US employers. This in turn is identified as one of the major causes of the declining membership and activity of American trade unions since the 1950s: membership density peaked at 35 per cent in 1954, declined to 24 per cent in 1978 and fell to just 17 per cent in 1991. In this section, the British evidence is reviewed in considering whether there has been a shift in management attitudes and behaviour towards union recognition, and in exploring some of the reasons for both continuity and change over the past decade.

Union recognition and membership are two of the most important indicators of union 'presence'. Indeed, the relationship between recognition, membership growth and participation in collective bargaining was described by Bain and Price (1983: 18) in the early 1980s as a 'virtuous circle of cause and effect in which the more that unions obtain recognition and succeed in participating in job regulation, the more likely they are to increase their recognition and deepen their participation in job regulation'. The following discussion assesses the extent to which in more recent years there has been a 'negative circle' of membership decline, de-recognition and reduced participation in collective bargaining, and how far this indicates a growing management hostility towards unions.

Aggregate trade union membership in Britain peaked at nearly 13 million in 1979 and declined continuously to around 9 million in the early 1990s. Trade union density, defined as the proportion of employees (or potential union membership) in unions, also declined from around 55 per cent to 40 per cent over the same period of time. Estimates of aggregate membership and density vary depending on whether the unemployed are included or excluded from 'potential union membership'. Union density figures disaggregated by sector, industry or occupational status are very difficult to calculate because of the inability or unwillingness of general or conglomerate unions to publish disaggregated membership returns (see Waddington, 1992).

The data in table 21.1 serve three useful purposes: they show some of the connections between union presence, union density, and collective bargaining coverage; they facilitate comparison between sectors and occupational status; and they indicate the degree of change between 1984 and 1990. As the Workplace Industrial Relations Survey, from which the data have been extracted, excluded establishments with fewer than 25 employees, the figures on union presence, density and bargaining coverage overstate the strength of trade unions.

First, the WIRS data on union presence show a significant decline in the number of workplaces with trade union members in the 1980s: indeed, by 1990, 36 per cent of the establishments surveyed had no union members at all. Second, overall union density declined from 58 per cent in 1984 to 48 per cent in 1990. The decline was greater for manual than non-manual employees, and in manufacturing and the public sector than in private services: that is, the decline was greatest in areas of traditional union strength. Third, the decline in the aggregate coverage of collective bargaining from 71 per cent in 1984 to 54 per cent in 1990 is, in the words of Millward et al. (1992: 93), 'one of the most dramatic changes in the character of British industrial relations that our survey series has measured'.

Data on union membership and density offer an important indication of the strength of trade unions and their organizational capacity to represent the workforce in dealings with management, but they do

Table 21.1   Union presence, membership density and collective bargaining coverage in 1984 and 1990

Percentages	1984	1990
% of establishments with union members among:		
All employees	73	64
manual employees	68	58
non-manual employees	58	51
Union membership density		
All industries		
all employees	58	48
manual employees	66	53
non-manual employees	51	43
Private manufacturing		
all employees	56	48
manual employees	70	60
non-manual employees	32	22
Private services		
all employees	30	27
manual employees	40	32
non-manual employees	23	24
Public sector		
all employees	80	72
manual employees	82	72
non-manual employees	79	72
% of employees covered by collective bargaining		
All establishments	71	54
Private manufacturing	64	51
Private services	41	33
Public sector	95	78

Source: Millward et al., 1992: 58–9, 94

not guarantee it. Management recognition of trade unions for the negotiation of pay and conditions of employment is, of course, the key determinant of presence, density and bargaining coverage. It is, therefore, important to identify the extent to which union recognition has declined and also to assess whether the decline can be explained mainly by changes in the structure of the economy affecting the composition of employment or by shifts in management attitudes and policies.

At first glance, evidence on employers' attitudes to union recognition appears to show more continuity than change since 1979. This is clearly demonstrated in table 21.2 taken from a 1990 National Institute survey of more than 500 UK companies. The vast majority of employers reported no change in their recognition arrangements during the 1980s, and only a tiny minority reported complete de-recognition. This latter finding was broadly replicated in WIRS 3 and in the specific research on de-recognition conducted by Claydon (1989) to which we now turn.

Claydon identified 50 successful, and four unsuccessful, cases of de-recognition between 1980 and 1988 and interviewed managers and union representatives in 36 of the companies to try to find out the reasons for the outcomes in particular cases. He found that the most common form (in 23 of the 36 cases) was not de-recognition of all unions in a company or plant, but 'grade-specific' de-recognition of non-manual employees, especially senior and middle managers and professionals. In half of the cases, union recognition for collective bargaining purposes was withdrawn, with unions retaining some form of representation rights in individual disciplinary and grievance hearings, and in the other half complete de-recognition occurred.

In order to assess the generalizability of his findings, Claydon explored the context of de-recognition and the apparent reasons for success or failure. He found a number of common external pressures on the companies – for example, increased product market compe-

Table 21.2 Changes in recognition in UK companies 1980–1990

	1980–1984		1985–1990	
	No.	*%*	*No.*	*%*
Unions newly recognized	5	0.9	3	0.5
Some establishments with newly recognized unions	5	0.9	14	2.5
No change but unions present	250	44.8	236	42.3
Some establishments de-recognizing unions, others not	8	1.4	32	5.7
Complete de-recognition	5	0.9	8	1.4
Unions never recognized	163	29.2	185	33.1
Recognition changes not reported	125	22.4	80	14.3

Source: Gregg and Yates (1991: 364)

tition, technical change, weak labour market conditions, and government legislation – but noted that most unionized companies in Britain did not respond to similar pressures by de-recognizing unions. Instead they took advantage of the more favourable 'balance of power' to negotiate or impose change through the existing bargaining machinery. Claydon therefore sought other explanations for his data on de-recognition and explored three main variables.

First, the ownership, management and organization of the company seemed important. Of the 36 companies investigated, 15 had undergone a recent change in ownership or senior management: in seven cases, ownership had passed to companies with a non-union history and outlook (for example, P&O had taken over Townsend Thoresen), and in three cases ownership had been transferred from the public to the private sector (for example, British Telecom). In another 16 cases, including several book publishers and regional newspaper houses, there had been major company reorganizations or relocation. In all the cases, changes in ownership and company reorganization had led to a reconsideration of the role of unions and collective bargaining.

Second, Claydon found that specific changes in company industrial relations objectives and policies lay at the heart of the de-recognition process. The withdrawal of collective bargaining rights from managerial and professional staff facilitated the introduction of individual contracts and performance-related pay. The de-recognition of manual workers' and technicians' unions was associated with the desire to change staffing levels and working practices. All the managers reported that they wanted to achieve greater employee involvement and commitment and to move away from adversarial industrial relations. These views and objectives were, of course, also widespread in the British companies that did not seek union de-recognition in the 1980s. Claydon therefore analysed a third explanatory variable, union organization and industrial relations history, in the survey companies.

Here the profile of the companies showed clear common characteristics. In a few of the companies, de-recognition had followed bitter industrial disputes in the recent past, but this was exceptional. Indeed, many managers described their relations with unions as 'good'. The common factor in most cases was the relative weakness of the unions. The union density in most cases was below 50 per cent and, in one case, it was only 1 per cent. In other cases (for example, journalists in provincial newspapers), union density was less important than a lack of willingness among union members to act collectively, and the weak links between workplace organization and the wider trade union. In some cases, the management of de-recognition was important, with package deals (including staff status) being offered to specific occupational groups in return for the surrender of negotiating rights. In short, the crucial factor was the 'quality of membership support and the degree of attachment to the wider union which enables organizational resources to be mobilized in defence of collective bargaining' (Claydon, 1989: 221).

In summary, while there was a small number of cases where employers expressed strong anti-union and anti-bargaining attitudes, most cases of de-recognition in the 1980s related to managerial and professional staff and were part of a move towards individual contracts and performance-related pay. In nearly all cases the trade union and its members lacked organizational strength. Thus, although it is possible to identify a significant 'principled' trend towards the de-recognition of managerial staff unions, British employers do not appear to be generally anti-union and they continue to tolerate union recognition and bargaining for non-managerial employees, even against the background of weakened trade unionism in the 1980s. (Indeed, British Institute of Management surveys have documented the changing perceptions of union power – in 1980, 82 per cent of managers thought that trade unions had too much power, whereas only 32 per cent thought so in 1990.) This is reflected in the conclusions to Claydon's study which suggest that, in Britain, de-recognition is an extreme expression of a wider shift, not away from collective bargaining (as in the USA), but in the frontier of control within it.

The demise of national bargaining

Within this broadly pragmatic approach, there is one major trend in employers' policy over the last 20 years which represents a form of de-recognition and confronts trade unions with an important challenge in the mid-1990s. This is the termination by many employers of national and industry-wide bargaining arrangements (Brown and Walsh, 1991). The demise of multi-employer bargaining amounts to a *de facto* de-recognition of unions as industry-wide bargaining agents. This general trend has been expressed in several different forms.

In the public sector, two important developments have taken place. First, the national pay bargaining machinery covering 500,000 nurses, midwives and allied professions and 400,000 school teachers, has been terminated by government and replaced by independent review bodies (in 1983 and 1991 respectively). It is not yet clear whether the 'quasi-bargaining' involved in the pay review process represents a significant diminution of trade union influence or merely an alternative institutional forum for its expression – after all, government intervention in nurses' and teachers' pay determination has been pervasive for the last 30 years.

Second, many large public sector organizations have been privatized or reorganized in ways that have led either to the termination or fragmentation of national agreements, or to the removal from the organization of the obligation to abide by the terms of the national agreements that survive. Privatized utilities, such as the regional water and electricity distribution companies, self-governing hospital trusts, civil service 'agencies', locally managed schools and private contractors providing publicly funded services under competitive tendering face differing legal and financial constraints on their pay determination policies. In all cases, however, the legitimacy that unions previously gained through recognition for national bargaining has been threatened or undermined.

Third, industry-wide bargaining arrangements in the private sector, regarded until the late 1960s as the backbone of the British industrial relations system, have been terminated in many industries. This culminated in the decision of the Engineering Employers' Federation (EEF) to give notice of its intention to end national collective bargaining for around a million manual workers in federated companies in 1990. This decision has usually been interpreted as an important example of the 'decentralization' of collective bargaining. It can be argued, however, that it amounts effectively to the de-recognition of unions as national bargaining agents, undermining their rationale as the representatives of all employees in the industry. Henceforth, as the *Future Strategy* document of the EEF noted, companies 'should be able to choose whether or not they wish to be party to national agreements' (Engineering Employers' Federation, 1991:1).

In the past a local union officer or representative could approach a local employer for recognition strengthened by the fact that the union was recognized by the national employers' organization for bargaining purposes. Now, with the end of national industry-wide bargaining in many sectors, this organizing rationale has been undermined. In the absence of any legally guaranteed role for collective bargaining, recognition of trade unions is increasingly dependent on their direct appeal to employees (or, in some cases, to employers, as we shall see below) at establishment or company level. This contrasts strongly with the position in most other European countries. In Germany, for example, industrial unions enjoy a legal right to bargain with employers' associations, and the collectively agreed basic terms and conditions of employment are invariably legally 'extended' to cover employees throughout the industry. For this reason, nearly 90 per cent of employees in Germany are covered by the terms of collective agreements compared with fewer than 50 per cent in Britain, even though union density is still higher in Britain.

The main argument of this section can be summarized briefly. Most survey and case study evidence suggests that there was no trend towards a general and 'systematic rejection of trade unions by management in UK firms' (Gregg and Yates, 1991: 373). Much of the decline in union presence, density and recognition can be explained by the compositional effects of structural change in the economy rather than significant shifts in management attitudes and policies. And, although 'wholesale de-recognition of trade unions rose from extreme rarity in the early 1980s to a more substantial phenomenon in the private sector' (Millward et al., 1992: 362) at the end of the decade, it occurred usually when support for union representation was already weak. Changes in the structure of collective bargaining, however, appear to be encouraging the growth of company or establishment unionism, under which continued recognition and membership density will depend much more on local union strength and relevance than on national recognition and national union resources and leadership. The implications of this management-inspired trend towards 'enterprise' or 'business unionism' will be discussed further in the conclusion.

Single-Union Agreements and Single-Table Bargaining

The degree of multi-unionism and the complexity of bargaining arrangements have been distinguishing characteristics of British industrial relations since the nineteenth century. The virtual abstention of the law from the regulation of union recognition has discouraged the practice of 'exclusive jurisdiction', which became almost universal in establishments where unions were able to win certification elections in the US. Moreover, although mergers have drastically reduced the number of British unions, the survival of ex-craft unions alongside numerically dominant general unions prevented the development of industrial unionism and the principle of 'one union, one establishment', which was achieved in the post-war reconstruction of the German labour movement. Employers in Britain and, to a lesser extent, trade unions have therefore sought various ways of 'managing' multi-unionism to limit its disadvantages.

In the 1980s, a great deal of publicity was focused on the negotiation of 'new style' single-union agreements, particularly on greenfield sites in manufacturing. These agreements attracted enormous interest, despite their relative rarity, because each was seen as a kind of laboratory experiment in which managers had a comparative *carte blanche* to establish the kind of industrial relations and employment practices they wanted. As such the agreements provide an important insight into management thought and practice. The following pages explore the single-union agreement made in 1987 between Pirelli Cables and the GMB at the company's new automated factory in South Wales (Yeandle and Clark, 1989a; 1989b). The analysis highlights both the unique features and other more typical aspects of the Pirelli agreement.

Two aspects of the process by which Pirelli concluded the agreement are of particular interest. First, the company, like others faced with a similar situation, had to make the initial decision whether to recognize the union at all. The decision in favour of union recognition was made for a mixture of pragmatic reasons: the non-management workforce would be recruited in South Wales, an area with very high levels of trade unionism, and failure to recognize a union might lead to major industrial relations problems in the early years of operation, either in South Wales or in the company's highly unionized factories in South Hampshire. Thereafter the company might still be forced into union recognition.

Management then had to decide whether to seek a single-union agreement or to recognize several unions, as in the Hampshire factories. The eventual decision to opt for a single-union agreement was strongly influenced by the overall personnel philosophy for the new plant. As this was centred on team working and maximum flexibility, it was believed that the recognition of more than one union might emphasize divisions within the workforce rather than co-operation and commonality. Moreover, a single-union agreement would allow the company to select the union that they believed would be most appropriate to their objectives. In short, the decision to go for union recognition was made on pragmatic grounds, but the preference for a single-union agreement was more 'principled'. This mixture of motives had a clear parallel with the similar decisions made by Nissan for their new factory in the north-east of England. As the personnel director stated: 'We considered the alternatives of no trade unions and a multiplicity of trade unions . . . We rejected the first because it would lead to several years of counter-productive antagonism, and the latter because sooner or later it would lead to an erosion of our flexibility and single status objectives' (quoted in Bassett, 1987: 151).

The procedure adopted by Pirelli to select the 'appropriate' union to represent all non-management staff was also typical of other single-union agreements. As a first step, the company prepared a detailed statement of its philosophy for the plant. This outlined a range of personnel policies which, both in scope and substantive terms, went way beyond most collective agreements on brownfield sites. This statement was sent to five unions – selected after taking advice from the Wales TUC – which were asked if they were interested in applying for recognition. All five unions – the AEU, EETPU, GMB, MSF and TGWU – were then invited to make presentations to company representatives prior to the opening of the site, and the company then decided which union to choose. This procedure has become known as the 'beauty contest' and has been used, in one form or another, by nearly all companies seeking single-union agreements on greenfield sites.

It is this aspect of single-union agreements, plus the inclusion of 'no strike' clauses and compulsory arbitration in most cases, which has incurred the greatest opposition of trade unions, culminating in the 1991 TUC Conference decision to condemn such procedures as 'alien' to the tradition of British trade unionism. The gap between rhetoric and reality, however, was apparent, as the motion was proposed and seconded by representatives of the MSF and TGWU, both of whom were at that time bidding to become the single recognized union in a 'beauty contest' for Toyota's new car factory in Derbyshire (recognition was subsequently awarded to the AEU). As Bassett (1987: 150–1) wrote, prophetically, in connection with the Nissan 'beauty contest' in 1985: 'reluctant or not, it is a contest most unions would go through again if they felt they had to.'

The main features of the Pirelli/GMB agreement were as follows.

- *Philosophy*: explicit statement of company philosophy, management style and operational requirements.
- *Coverage*: all non-management employees, with no recognition for trade unionism among managers or professional specialists.
- *Work requirements*: detailed outline of work structuring arrangements, including the requirement for full functional flexibiliy across production, maintenance and administration.
- *Single status*: all employees have the right to six months off work for certified sickness on full pay.
- *Integrated salary structure*: only two grades for non-management staff, otherwise skill-based increments.
- *Training*: commitment to continuous training required of all employees, tied to payment for acquisition of new skills.
- *Single union*: only one union recognized for representation and bargaining purposes.
- *Pay determination*: to be decided at establishment level by management and union representatives.
- *Collective disputes*: a no-strike clause with binding arbitration in the case of a failure to agree.
- *Consultation*: direct consultation with the workforce through monthly business review meetings and three-monthly general meetings.
- *Grievance and disciplinary procedures*: mix of union and non-union representation; arbitration or final unilateral management decision in the event of a failure to agree.

The importance of 'new style' single-union agreements arises because on some greenfield sites they offer unions the only available route to recognition and, crucially, one which is tied to the prior acceptance of a management-determined package of employment relations practices. Thus, such agreements should be differentiated from the more general pattern of union recognition in Britain. As WIRS 3 showed, separate unions for manual and non-manual employees remained the dominant form of representation; multi-unionism was more widespread in the public sector; and throughout the 1980s, there was relatively little change in the proportion of unionized establishments with only one recognized union (e.g. 66 per cent for manual workers) compared with those that had three or more (e.g. 15 per cent for manual workers) (Millward et al., 1992: 77–81).

The extent of 'new style' single-union agreements on greenfield sites cannot be estimated with any precision. A survey of the employment policies of 41 overseas companies that had invested in Wales in the 1980s, however, found that only ten had single-union agreements, and around half had no form of union recognition at all (*Industrial Relations Review and Report*, 1991). Another survey of new high-technology companies located in the south-east of England, conducted at the same time, found that 80 per cent of the organizations had no union recognition (McLoughlin and Gourlay, 1991). This comparison, and the previous discussion of management policies at Pirelli, suggest that the degree of union recognition in local labour markets exerts a significant influence on the overall approach of employers to union recognition.

Managers in brownfield locations face much greater difficulties in trying to change patterns of union representation as part of a wider reform of employment practices. One interesting innovation in the late 1980s was the development of 'single-table' bargaining in a number of companies. Again this reflected a pragmatic management response to the perceived disadvantages of multi-unionism: it assumed the continued presence of multi-unionism; demonstrated a reluctance to de-recognize existing unions; and attempted instead to rationalize bargaining structures in what the CBI Employment Affairs Director called 'a half-way house' between existing arrangements and single-union deals (Gilbert, 1992: 81). It became clear that major employers in both the public and private sector were attempting to reduce the number of bargaining units, although the ACAS Annual Report (1991) noted that successful attempts had been relatively rare.

Research by Marginson and Sisson (1990) found three main reasons for the adoption of single-table bargaining strategies by employers in the late 1980s: multi-union bargaining arrangements were costly, time-consuming and a potential source of conflict; single-table bargaining facilitated changes in working practices that increased functional flexibility, which required the joint agreement of all occupational groups; and it encouraged moves towards 'single status', or the harmonization of conditions of employment between manual and non-manual employees.

Single-table bargaining is clearly no panacea for management. In some circumstances it may create problems: management may find it more difficult to deal flexibly, quickly and independently with the problems of particular groups of workers. According to Marginson and Sisson, however, a number of structural economic and employment trends appear to be encouraging employment flexibility and the breakdown of traditional status differences. These include legislative pressures to harmonize non-pay benefits, such as pensions; technical change which blurs occupational boundaries; the emphasis of HRM on employee involvement, commitment, and team-working; and trade union mergers.

Conclusions

Management approaches to trade unions in the mid-1990s will be influenced in important ways by a range of factors outside the direct influence of either party. It is almost certain that the changes in the structure of the economy and the composition of the workforce that contributed to the decline in union density and the coverage of collective bargaining in the 1980s are 'enduring and mostly irreversible' (Millward et al., 1992: 356). Competitive pressures on companies, arising from the increasing internationalization of economic activity and the uncertain emergence of the British economy from the longest post-war recession of the early 1990s, will have a variable impact on union–management relations in different sectors. The British government is likely to continue with its policies of labour market de-regulation: the latest restrictions on lawful industrial action, the threat to check-off arrangements, the abolition of Wages Councils, the symbolically important removal of the duty of ACAS 'to encourage the extension, development and reform of collective bargaining' contained in the 1993 Trade Union Reform and Employment Rights Act, and the possibility of de-recognition of white-collar unions in the civil service in the run-up to the privatization of many of its current activities, seem more potent than the prospect of the regulation of labour market competition through the European Community's 'social dimension'.

Within these contextual constraints, employers and managers will still have considerable freedom in choosing whether to involve trade unions in the management of key aspects of the employment relationship. Their decisions will, in turn, be influenced by the manner in which trade unions develop their policies and practices in response to management and union members' preferences. It is certain that management approaches to unions will continue to exhibit a considerable unevenness – between different sectors and industries, and according to the ownership, size, values, and 'newness' of particular companies and workplaces. Three broad trends, however, are discernible.

First, managers are likely to extend further the recent development of direct interaction with their employees through various forms of employee involvement. These initiatives will be targeted on groups of employees with skills, experience, or qualifications that are important to the organization and which may be in short supply in the external labour market. Second, the trend towards the rationalization of representation and bargaining arrangements will almost certainly continue. It is likely that the pace of change will increase, especially in the public sector, where both multi-unionism and structural reorganization are currently most pervasive. Generally, there are likely to be more successful attempts at single-table bargaining, a reduction in the number of unions recognized for bargaining purposes and in the number of cases of de-recognition and, on greenfield sites, a clear choice between a single-union agreement or no unions at all. Third, the importance of national and industry-level relations between management and unions is likely to decline further, with an increased emphasis on specific approaches to the management of the employment relationship at company and establishment level. Significant shifts towards greater 'enterprise autonomy' in industrial relations have, of course, been apparent for 20 years or more in parts of the private manufacturing sector: over the next decade the 'providers' of public services may be pushed, willingly or otherwise, into more enterprise-specific policies in order to retain their place in the new 'internal markets'.

It is not clear whether these pressures will lead to an increasing individualization of employment relations, the consolidation of enterprise unionism, or new forms of (non-union) collective employee representation in the enterprise, such as directly elected works councils. Apart from the relatively few cases where management attempt to de-recognize unions, however, few of the above developments are likely to result from explicit and coherent management strategies to marginalize trade unions. The evidence of the recent past suggests that the attitudes and behaviour of UK managers towards trade unions are likely to continue to be pragmatic and contingent rather than principled and strategic. If employers can achieve their objectives by gaining union agreement to their proposals on pay, conditions, work organization and labour utilization, or, in some cases, achieve their employees' acquiescence or support by simply bypassing existing agreements, then they are unlikely to seek more drastic solutions, such as the dismantling of representation and bargaining arrangements.

Bibliography

ACAS. 1991. *Annual Report*. London: Advisory, Conciliation and Arbitration Service.

Bain, G. S. and Price, R. 1983. 'Union Growth: Dimensions, Determinants, and Destiny'. In Bain, G. S. (ed.) *Industrial Relations in Britain*. Oxford: Blackwell.

Bassett, P. 1987. *Strike Free: New Industrial Relations in Britain*. London: Macmillan.

Batstone, E. 1984. *Working Order*. Oxford: Blackwell.

Batstone, E. and Gourlay, S. 1986. *Unions, Unemployment and Innovation*. Oxford: Blackwell.

Brown, W. A. 1981. *The Changing Contours of British Industrial Relations*. Oxford: Blackwell.

Brown, W. and Walsh, J. 1991. 'Pay Determination in Britain in the 1980s: the Anatomy of Decentralisation'. *Oxford Review of Economic Policy*, Vol. 7, No. 1, 44–59.

Claydon, T. 1989. 'Union Derecognition in Britain in the 1980s'. *British Journal of Industrial Relations*, Vol. 27, No. 2, 214–24.

Daniel, W. W. and Millward, N. 1983. *Workplace Industrial Relations in Britain*. London: Heinemann.

Edwards, P. K. 1987. *Managing the Factory*. Oxford: Blackwell.

Engineering Employers' Federation. 1991. *Future Strategy for the EEF*. London: EEF.

Fox, A. 1974. *Beyond Contract: Work, Power and Trust Relations*. London: Faber.

Fox, A. 1985. *Man Mismanagement*. London: Hutchinson.

Freeman, R. and Medoff, J. 1984. *What Do Unions Do?* New York: Basic Books.

Gilbert, R. 1992. 'Is There a "New Industrial Relations"?' (Interview with Ian Beardwell). *Human Resource Management Journal*, Vol. 2, No. 2, 74–82.

Gregg, P. and Yates, A. 1991. 'Changes in Wage-setting Arrangements and Trade Union Presence in the 1980s'. *British Journal of Industrial Relations*, Vol. 29, No. 3, 362–76.

Guest, D. 1989. 'Human Resource Management: Its Implications for Industrial Relations and Trade Unions'. In Storey, J. (ed.) *New Perspectives on Human Resource Management*. London: Routledge.

Hyman, R. 1979. 'The Politics of Workplace Trade Unionism'. *Capital and*

Class, VIII, 54–67.

Industrial Relations Review and Report. 1991. 'The Employment Policies of Overseas Inward Investors in Wales?' No. 482, 6–14.

Kochan, T. A., Katz, H. C. and McKersie, R. B. 1986. *The Transformation of American Industrial Relations*. New York: Basic Books.

Lane, T. 1974. *The Union Makes us Strong*. London: Arrow Books.

Legge, K. 1988. 'Personnel Management in Recession and Recovery'. *Personnel Review*, Vol. 17, 3–69.

McCarthy, W. E. J. 1966. *The Role of Shop Stewards in British Industrial* . *Relations*. Royal Commission on Trade Unions and Employers' Associations, Paper No. 1. London: HMSO.

McCarthy, W. E. J. and Parker, S. R. 1967. *Shop Stewards and Workshop Relations*. Royal Commission on Trade Unions and Employers' Associations, Paper No. 10. London: HMSO.

Mackay, L. and Torrington, D. 1986. *The Changing Nature of Personnel Management*. London: Institute of Personnal Management.

McLoughlin, I. and Gourlay, S. 1991. 'Transformed Industrial Relations? Employee Attitudes in Non-Union Firms'. *Human Resource Management Journal*, Vol. 2, No. 2, 8–28.

Marginson, P., Edwards, P. K., Martin, R., Purcell, J. and Sisson, K. 1988. *Beyond the Workplace: Managing Industrial Relations in the Multi-Establishment Enterprise*. Oxford: Blackwell.

Marginson, P. and Sisson, K. 1990. 'Single Table Talk'. *Personnel Management*, May, 46–9.

Millward, N. and Stevens, M. 1986. *British Workplace Industrial Relations, 1980–84*. Aldershot: Gower.

Millward, N., Stevens, M., Smart, D. and Hawes, W. 1992. *Workplace Industrial Relations in Transition*. Aldershot: Dartmouth.

Milner, S. and Richards, E. 1991. 'Determinants of Union Recognition and Employee Involvement: Evidence from London Docklands'. *British Journal of Industrial Relations*, Vol. 29, No. 3, 377–90.

Purcell, J. 1979. 'A Strategy for Management Control in Industrial Relations'. In Purcell, J. and Smith, R. (eds) *The Control of Work*. London: Macmillan.

Purcell, J. and Sisson, K. 1983. 'Strategies and Practice in the Management of Industrial Relations'. In Bain, G. S. (ed.) *Industrial Relations in Britain*. Oxford: Blackwell.

Scott, A. 1991. 'Consultation and Communication'. *Employment Gazette*, September, 507–11.

Storey, J. 1992. *Developments in the Management of Human Resources*. Oxford: Blackwell.

Tyson, S. and Fell, A. 1986. *Evaluating the Personnel Function*. London: Hutchinson.

Waddington, J. 1992. 'Trade Union Membership in Britain, 1980–87: Unemployment and Restructuring'. *British Journal of Industrial Relations*,

Vol. 30, No. 2, 287–324.

Winchester, D. 1988. 'Sectoral Change and Trade Union Organization'. In Gallie, D. (ed.) *Employment in Britain*. Oxford: Blackwell.

Wright Mills, C. 1948. *The New Men of Power*. New York: Harcourt Brace.

Yeandle, D. and Clark, J. 1989a. 'A Personnel Strategy for an Automated Plant'. *Personnel Management*, June, 51–5.

Yeandle, D. and Clark, J. 1989b. 'Growing a Compatible IR Set-up'. *Personnel Management*, July, 36–9.

Index